The Cool Stuff in Premiere Pro

Learn advanced editing techniques to dramatically speed up your workflow

Second Edition

Jarle Leirpoll

Dylan Osborn

Paul Murphy

Andy Edwards

Apress®

The Cool Stuff in Premiere Pro

Jarle Leirpoll
Elverum, Norway

Paul Murphy
Sydney, Australia

Dylan Osborn
New York, USA

Andy Edwards
New York, USA

ISBN-13 (pbk): 978-1-4842-2889-0
DOI 10.1007/978-1-4842-2890-6

ISBN-13 (electronic): 978-1-4842-2890-6

Library of Congress Control Number: 2017954372

Managing Director: Welmoed Spahr
Editorial Director: Todd Green
Acquisitions Editor: Natalie Pao
Development Editor: James Markham
Technical Reviewer: Colin Brougham
Coordinating Editor: Jessica Vakili
Copy Editor: April Rondeau
Compositor: SPi Global
Indexer: SPi Global
Artist: SPi Global

Distributed to the book trade worldwide by Springer Science+Business Media New York, 233 Spring Street, 6th Floor, New York, NY 10013. Phone 1-800-SPRINGER, fax (201) 348-4505, e-mail orders-ny@springer-sbm.com, or visit www.springeronline.com. Apress Media, LLC is a California LLC and the sole member (owner) is Springer Science + Business Media Finance Inc (SSBM Finance Inc). SSBM Finance Inc is a **Delaware** corporation.

For information on translations, please e-mail rights@apress.com, or visit www.apress.com.

Apress and friends of ED books may be purchased in bulk for academic, corporate, or promotional use. eBook versions and licenses are also available for most titles. For more information, reference our Special Bulk Sales–eBook Licensing web page at www.apress.com/bulk-sales.

Any source code or other supplementary materials referenced by the author in this text are available to readers at www.apress.com. For detailed information about how to locate your book's source code, go to www.apress.com/source-code/. Readers can also access source code at SpringerLink in the Supplementary Material section for each chapter.

Printed on acid-free paper

Contents at a Glance

Contents

About the Author

Jarle Leirpoll

Photo by Polina Sudokova

Jarle Leirpoll is a Premiere Pro Master Instructor Trainer and runs PremierePro.net, where he shares free Premiere Pro tutorials, templates, presets, and projects. He worked at the Norwegian Broadcasting Corporation (NRK) for 14 years before starting his own company in 1996, which makes corporate movies and documentaries. He's also writing books, doing Premiere and After Effects training for companies worldwide, and teaching media production at Norwegian universities.

Jarle has trained people at Disney, Warner Bros., BBC, NRK, DR, Monster, Valve Media OY, Nordic Film & TV, and countless other broadcasters and media production companies. He has even trained Adobe's own employees in Premiere Pro! He is also an official Test Pilot for Premiere Pro.

Training info: premierepro.net/training
Blog: PremierePro.net

Thanks

This book could not have been updated without the help of co-writers Dylan Osborn, Paul Murphy, and Andy Edwards. They put in countless hours despite their busy schedules to make the book as good as possible. I am proud to have worked with them and forever thankful that they let me tap into their huge knowledge about Premiere.

Thank you to my partner in life, Grete Nordhagen, who will finally get her partner back from several months in the "book bubble." I owe her and my bonus daughters, Tove and Ida, a lot for their patience.

A big thank you to my students who have called me when they got stuck in the editing process. All those emergency calls have given me a good understanding of what people struggle with when they're on their own in Premiere. Many of my students have also given me permission to use their footage in the book, and I'm grateful for that.

My helpers on this project are too many to list, but some of them I just must mention. Max Hagelstam, Adobe Sweden, who knows all the techy details and is always willing to share. Steve Hoeg, Sr. Engineering Manager for Premiere Pro, who is a walking encyclopedia when it comes to Premiere Pro code. Dennis Weinmann, Sr. Quality Engineer at Adobe, who answered all my color- and Lumetri-related questions. Chris Bobotis, Director Immersive at Adobe, who explained the Mettle VR tools for me. Tim Kurkoski and Victoria Nece from the After Effects team, who asked me to be part of the development of Motion Graphics Templates. Colin Brougham, Quality Engineer on the Premiere Pro team, who did the tech editing and corrected all the bad info. Thank you all for helping me in the writing process.

About the Contributors

Dylan Osborn

Emmy-winning editor and Certified Premiere Pro Instructor **Dylan Osborn** shows broadcasters and professional editors how to maximize their Adobe software in post-production. He has built workflows and conducted on-site training at CNN, CBS, A+E Networks, Spectrum SportsNet, and the EPiX channel and has been producing and editing broadcast television, short films, and documentaries in Los Angeles and New York City for over ten years.

dylanosborn.com

Thanks

It's an honor to be contributing to this revised edition of Jarle's incredibly useful book. Thank you to Van Bedient and Mitch Wood at Adobe for starting my journey back into Premiere Pro; Dennis Radeke and Sue Salek for continuing that journey in NYC; and Vashi Nedomansky and Maxim Jago for inspiring me to share my knowledge. Biggest thanks to my wife, Lelah, and sons, Truman and Holden, for their support during the writing process.

Paul Murphy

Paul Murphy is an in-demand editor and trainer based in Brooklyn, New York.

With over 13 years' experience, he was an early adopter of Premiere Pro in feature film editing. In 2012, he used it to edit *Red Obsession*, which won the Australian Academy of Cinema and Television Arts award for Best Feature Documentary.

As a trainer, he has taught classes large and small, from beginners to industry veterans, for such clients as Bloomberg, CBS, HBO, Viacom, and Vice.

thepremierepro.com
paul-murphy.net

Thanks

Thanks to my endlessly supportive wife, Jessica, my son, Orson, my mum and dad, Kerry and Steve, my brother, Anthony, and my cat/editor's assistant, Guffman. Thanks also to Jon Barrie at Adobe for all his encouragement and advice over the years. For a lifetime of inspiration, thanks to Welles, Spielberg, Kubrick, Coppola, and, of course, Walter Murch.

Andy Edwards

Andy Edwards is an Emmy Award–winning cameraman with over 27 years of television production and post-production experience. His editing experience has included broadcast television shows, documentaries, Inc. 500 corporate clients, and government clients. Andy has delivered hundreds of weekly TV episodes to air at HDNet and AXS TV in Denver. Andy's current position is Post-Production Engineer for AXS TV's three locations in Denver, Dallas, and LA.

Thanks

My sincere thanks to Jarle Leirpoll for bringing me onboard for this project. Your profound knowledge of Premiere is amazing. Thank you for your friendship and pushing me into some deep dives with Premiere.

To my wife, Andrea, and my son, Walker, thank you for all your support and patience during all the late nights and weekends working on the book.

Big thanks to the entire Adobe Premiere Pro team. You all have been an amazing resource, and I look forward to where you take Premiere in the future. Thanks also to Van Bedient and Karl Lee Soule at Adobe for always taking the time to dig into my Premiere questions.

About the Technical Reviewer

Colin Brougham worked as a video producer and editor for more than 15 years in commercial and promotional video, broadcast documentary and independent film. In 2015, he joined Adobe as a Software Quality Specialist for Adobe Premiere Pro. When not helping make software better, he enjoys biking, gardening and homebrewing. He lives with his family in Minneapolis, Minnesota.

Foreword

By **Patrick Palmer**, Program Manager for Adobe Premiere Pro

Adobe Premiere Pro is 25 this year. Looking back at earlier versions, you can see not only how much the product has changed, but also how the industry itself has evolved. Today, Premiere Pro is used by video professionals around the globe. The application includes a deep toolset, meeting the needs of a wide range of different post-production workflows, from broadcast to online content; from event videography to documentary and feature film editing–and pretty much everything in-between.

Choosing the right workflow in Premiere Pro can make all the difference in meeting your deadlines and delivering high production quality. This is where this book offers great value. It covers what you need to know about getting organized before you start editing, how to make the most out of the various tools that allow you to automate parts of your workflow, and lots of great editing tips and tricks, too. The writers share the many hidden gems in the application, features and functions that can make all the difference for you in increasing your productivity or unleashing your creativity.

Each chapter is written by an industry expert with years of experience using the application and offers a wealth of practical insight, whether you need to go deep in some of the core areas of editing with Premiere Pro or learn more about recently introduced workflows for color and light, audio, and motion graphics. There's almost no limit to what you can do with video in Premiere Pro, and this book provides an excellent guide to getting the most out of your tools so that you can truly deliver your best work.

Introduction

It's been bothering me for a few years that there were no really advanced books on editing in Premiere Pro. Other books tend to start from scratch and take the reader to a certain level. That leaves no room for the really advanced stuff.

A few years back, I read Mark Christiansen's excellent book on compositing in After Effects. It was very hands-on and practical, and at the same time it had the technical info that visual effects professionals need in order to work efficiently in the high-end VFX industry.

I wanted to write a book on Premiere Pro for video and film editors with the same level of practical and hands-on info for professional editors, as well as for those who want to become professional editors. Based on hundreds of positive reviews, comments, and messages from customers, I must have done something right. And the good news is, this version is even better!

May your renders be quick and your bugs infrequent. Happy editing!

CHAPTER 1

▪ ▪▪ ▪

Accelerated Workflow

By Jarle Leirpoll and Andy Edwards

There are many ways to edit in Premiere, and there is no right or wrong way—but there are slow and quick ways! Accelerated workflow is about working faster and getting better results. A cliché, I know, but you do want to work smarter, not harder. With the intense daily deadlines, especially in news broadcasting and sports, editors must be extremely efficient. Every keystroke counts.

If you find yourself doing a task repeatedly, find a way to automate or accelerate that task. Ideally, you should be able to work as fast as you can think. We're not quite there yet, but we're getting closer with every release of Premiere. Accelerate and automate as much of your editing workflow as possible, and you'll be home in time for dinner more often.

In this chapter, we'll focus on streamlining the different steps of the workflow, shown in Figure 1-1, as much as possible, and look at ways to automate them whenever we can.

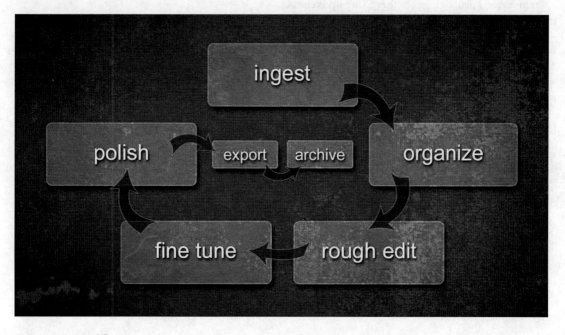

Figure 1-1. Workflow steps

© Jarle Leirpoll 2017
J. Leirpoll et al., *The Cool Stuff in Premiere Pro*, DOI 10.1007/978-1-4842-2890-6_1

Get Rid of Bad Habits

Before you begin any project, make sure you employ good work habits. Your workflow is entirely up to you, of course, but sadly a lot of video editors work slowly and with less than stellar results at the cost of creative time. They do this out of bad habit or because they don't have the knowledge, but most of all because they never stop to think "how can I do this quicker?" We'll take a look at common tasks for an editor and see if we can get more done in less time.

What follows is a collection of timesaving techniques I use when approaching a documentary or corporate film project. Most of the techniques will be very useful even when editing news stories, reality shows, feature films, and episodic TV.

Yeah, I know all this workflow stuff sounds boring, but actually doing this (not just reading about it) will save you a lot of time. Compared to starting every task from scratch, you'll save hours on short projects and several days on long-form projects. OK, enough bragging about the greatness of a smooth workflow—let's get our hands dirty and use these principles in a project.

Lucky Me—No Client over Shoulder

You should know this when reading about my methods: I usually don't have clients watching over my shoulder. I'm lucky, I know! If you work with a client watching you or in a facility where several people work on the same project, some of these methods may need a little tweaking.

Use Prelude If You Want

You may want to use Adobe Prelude for Logging and Ingest. I just find that I can do the same things in Premiere, so I usually don't bother to fire up Prelude.

Your editing workflow starts before you copy the files from your camera's memory card to the computer.

Before You Start Editing

You need a logical folder structure on your drive, but you don't want to create all the folders each time you start a new project. Instead, copy the folders from a project folder template so you know where to put all the material, and then add subfolders when needed.

Copy Folder Template

You can make your own structure with more (or less) folders than me if the structure makes logical sense. Notice in Figure 1-2 that my project folder template is to the left and the folders in a project in progress are to the right.

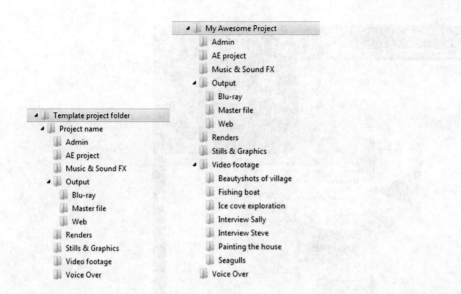

Figure 1-2. *Even though you start with a folder template, you will add several subfolders when you add material to the project*

The structure needs to be logical not just to you, but also to your clients, your team colleagues, or the guy you hire to finish your project while you recover from a skiing accident or go on a well-deserved holiday.

■ **Note** For compatibility across OS platforms and media servers, avoid using "special" non-alphanumeric characters, such as : ; ® ™ ¢ $ € / \ , ( ) [ ] { } < > ! ? | " ' * in file and folder names.

Copy the Media Files

OK, so you've created your project folder. Now, copy the media from the camera's memory card to your new folders. Copy everything from the card, including the folders, subfolders, metadata files, and so on, as shown in Figure 1-3. This way, Premiere's media browser can recognize the format and display only the media files.

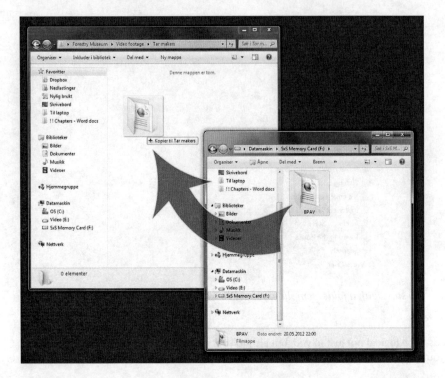

Figure 1-3. *Copy all your media to your project folder*

Take XDCAM-EX as an example; every video clip lives in its own folder with the same name as the clip. These clip folders live inside a CLPR folder, and that folder lives inside a BPAV folder. See Figure 1-4. What a mess! You absolutely do not want to wade through all these subfolders to see each clip, so make sure you copy everything from the camera card to your drive.

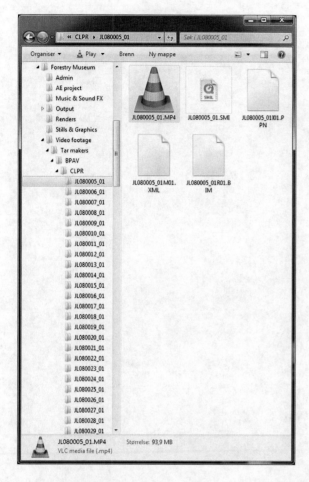

Figure 1-4. *Memory card folders from a Sony XDCAM-EX SxS card*

Figure 1-5 shows a snapshot of the folders in one of my projects. The project had about 1,500 video files, and I ended up creating 39 folders for the footage I shot myself and some extra for additional footage. I copied each camera card into folders with names that described the content.

5

Navn	Dato endret
EEV Arkivmateriale	20.07.2011 18:14
EEV Branntomt	30.10.2009 08:13
EEV Einunna	05.08.2009 11:36
EEV Elsikkerhet Norge	16.10.2009 00:25
EEV Fjernvarme	05.08.2009 10:18
EEV Fjernvarme rør montering	11.09.2009 11:55
EEV Fjernvarme sveising	07.07.2009 13:01
EEV Fugler på linja	07.07.2009 13:02
EEV Gutta i slo-mo	20.10.2009 09:01
EEV Gutterommet	07.07.2009 13:04
EEV Helikopterbilder	13.07.2009 03:41
EEV Jubileumsfest	07.07.2009 13:28
EEV Jubileumsfest LYD	20.07.2011 16:33
EEV Kabelpåvisning	02.11.2009 23:19
EEV Klasserom	07.07.2009 13:59
EEV Kontorbygg	26.12.2009 11:16
EEV Kraftlinje Bjølseth	07.07.2009 14:02
EEV kranbilder	08.10.2009 16:53
EEV Linjerydding	21.10.2009 16:00
EEV LYS	07.07.2009 14:09
EEV Museumsspel	07.07.2009 14:10
EEV Nils og Vippe	07.07.2009 14:16
EEV Nils og Vippe i grøfta	11.09.2009 11:54
EEV Pressekonferanse	07.07.2009 14:31
EEV Riving av linje	28.08.2009 14:48
EEV Scooter i traseen	07.07.2009 14:37
EEV Skifter pære	30.10.2009 08:14
EEV Skjefstadfoss gamle, interiør	26.12.2009 11:21
EEV Skjefstadfossen høst	20.10.2009 08:58
EEV Skjefstadfossen i flom	07.07.2009 14:39
EEV Skjefstadfossen tåke	07.07.2009 14:46
EEV Skjefstadfossen vinter	07.07.2009 14:47
EEV Sommer 2008	07.07.2009 14:58
EEV Stolpe på gamlemåten	20.10.2009 08:54
EEV Stolpereising	07.07.2009 15:00
EEV Trefelling	21.10.2009 10:33
EEV Vinterbilder	07.07.2009 15:04
EEV Vippe får kyss	16.10.2009 00:26
EEV Øksna	05.08.2009 10:21

Figure 1-5. The folder structure from one of my projects

Keeping the files in properly named folders also helps when doing incremental backups manually. You only need to copy the new folders and the newest version of your project file, and your data is safe.

Why Not Strip Out the Bad Material?

With the rapidly falling prices on storage, I have become increasingly less concerned about the size of my projects. So, I copy everything relevant from the dailies and other sources (archive material, stock footage, and so on) to my media drives sorted in logical folders, and I don't bother to sort out the bad material.

Yes, copying everything does make my projects larger than necessary, but I save a lot of time not having to sort the material. It's simple math; if you spend two hours sorting out unnecessary material, and save 100 GB, you lose money. The storage cost is nowhere near what your time is worth.

Transcoding? I Don't Usually Do It

If you're coming from older NLEs, you may be used to transcoding the video files into easier-to-edit formats. In Premiere, you usually don't have to. Unless your system is too slow or you're working in an environment where you share the material with people working in other software, don't bother to transcode. Start editing instead.

OK, so we're ready to fire up Premiere and start our new project.

Create a New Premiere Project

Always make sure that the file name of the actual project contains the actual name of the project, as I've done in Figure 1-6. This is critical! A search for *Aliens Attack* will not give you any hits if the project was called *Finished movie 02* or *New version – rev 1*. *Untitled Project* is a bad name for just about any film.

Figure 1-6. *Give your projects and folders descriptive names*

Save your project file in the project folder you made before copying your media files. Some editors will disagree here, wanting media files and the project file to be on separate drives. That's OK, of course, but I like to have everything in one single folder, as it makes backup and project management very easy. Buy faster RAIDs if you're concerned about read/write speeds.

Project Setting for Labels and Clip Names

There is a little checkbox in the Project Settings dialog that has the long and informative name *Display the project item name and label color for all instances*. See Figure 1-7.

Figure 1-7. The arrow points to the checkbox for syncing label colors and clip names

Checking this makes sure that whenever you change the label color or name of a clip in the timeline, it will also get changed in the Project panel and bins—and the other way around.

You may wonder why we have a choice to turn this off, and it's because some workflows depend on the clip names and labels in the bins' being the same throughout the editing process, and editors still want to change the label color and name in the timeline. When unchecked, changes in either place will not affect the other. Clips that are changed in the bin before you put them in the timeline will of course get the new name and color.

Import Template Project

Next, you want to create folders and import commonly used graphics. We will not do this from scratch, but rather will use a template project. A template project is just a normal project that you don't intend to use as is, but rather will import into your working project when needed or open it and then do a Save As. The file can be write-protected to prevent accidental changes to the template file.

Starting with a template project with your standard bins, graphics, intros, vignettes, and an empty sequence with your settings will save several minutes of your time in every project.

This also makes sure you use the same layout on every project, so you know where to find stuff in complex timelines. Template project files can be created with no media; in other words, just metadata display, empty sequences, and search bins.

Figure 1-8 shows the content of my Project panel after starting from a template project. Notice in Figure 1-9, where bins are twirled open, that some graphic templates are already in place, like logo, rolling credit, lower third, and so on.

Figure 1-8. *A template saves you from a lot of steps later*

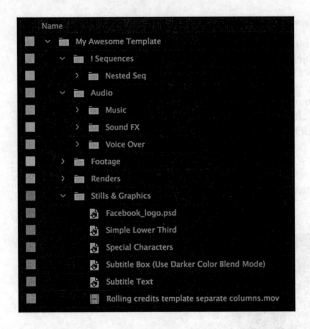

Figure 1-9. *Add logos, adjustment layers, and other often-used stuff to your template*

If this were a series of TV shows or web-distributed reportages, I'd make a template with music, openers, and other shared material.

Import All the Media via the Media Browser

Finally, it's time to get your footage inside the project! As just seen, the folder structure of new video formats can get quite convoluted, but the media browser lets us view the media files without even seeing the irrelevant files, and takes care of spanned clips and metadata, making it far superior to the old **File ➤ Import** route.

The media browser shows thumbnails of the footage, and you can hover scrub to quickly get an idea of the content of each clip. It might be tempting to import small batches of clips to different bins in your project, but it's far too risky, in my opinion. There is a chance that you'd forget to import some clips, and the time spent searching for them in the project later can break the creative flow and even prevent you from finishing before deadline.

Create Bin from Media Browser

I recommend dragging all the clips in the folder on your drive from the media browser to a temporary bin in your project, then moving the clips from this bin to bins where they belong. Here's how. Navigate to the chosen folder in the media browser, hit **Ctrl+A** (**Cmd+A** on Mac) to select all the clips, then grab the clip closest to the Project panel's New Bin icon, drag it over the icon, and let go, as seen in Figure 1-10.

Figure 1-10. *Drag all the clips from the media browser to the New Bin icon in the Project panel to automatically create a new bin*

The files are imported, and then you're asked to give the new bin a proper name. Let's call this one *Temp*. The name field for the new bin is automatically highlighted, so just start typing to give it a name (Figure 1-11).

Figure 1-11. *Give the bin a good name*

Sorting the Clips into Bins

What's a clip? In Premiere, we use the term *clip* for just about everything we can put on the timeline, be it a still image, an audio file, or even a nested sequence. Note that the media files themselves remain on the disk and are not embedded into the project file. The clips in Premiere are just links to the media on disk.

Now, create new logical bins when required by hitting **Ctrl+B** (Cmd+B), and drag related clips from the Temp bin to the new bins. See Figure 1-12. Notice that I've docked the Temp bin to the right showing icon view, and the Project panel to the left showing list view. This makes the sorting and drag-n-dropping easy.

Figure 1-12. *Drag groups of clips to New Bin icon*

Don't bother to scroll up and down the Temp bin—just grab the clips you see in the panel at any given time. When the Temp bin is empty, delete it. Figure 1-13 shows the bins I ended up creating for a three-and-a-half-minute short I made on making tar.

Figure 1-13. *The bins from my short on making tar*

If you have more material from more camera cards, repeat this procedure until all the material is imported. Make sure you use a proper workspace for this. You don't have to see anything else—just the Project panel and its bins. You can have several bins open at the same time and drag-n-drop or cut/paste quickly between them.

A Logical Bin Structure in Your Project Panel

Just like you need a logical structure on your hard drive, you also need a good structure inside Premiere. A bit boring, but very important! To edit efficiently, you need to find everything fast. You don't have the time to search for every clip. I'm a big fan of organizing the projects, but I also take great care not to overdo it.

A simple two-minute news story doesn't need a lot of organization, and you could have everything in one large "assets" bin. But making well-organized projects a habit will help you immensely on bigger projects. When editing a documentary or a reality show, editing without a good structure that has everything labeled and sorted will be a nightmare. In a large, tightly scripted production, everything needs to be properly labeled.

Anyway—whatever kind of production you do, you need a logical structure. What if you need to walk away from the project for three weeks? Will you still know your way around it? What if you get hit by a car, and someone else needs to take the project to finish? Will they be able to find everything and work effectively?

Set Poster Frames When Needed

A clip will often start before a person comes into the frame or before something happens. That "empty" frame doesn't tell you who's in the scene or what's happening. If the thumbnail you see in the icon view doesn't tell you what's in the clip, hover scrub to a frame that's more representative of the content, then right-click and choose **Set Poster Frame**, or just hit **Shift+P**.

Time for Backup

I travel a lot when I make corporate movies and documentaries. Each day after shooting, I copy the dailies to my laptop, import the material and sort it into bins, and then run a backup to an external drive. I do the backup after importing. This way, the backup even contains the helper files that Premiere Pro needs, so they don't have to be recreated if I should ever need to do a recovery.

On the road, I don't use any special software for this. I just drag the whole project folder onto an external drive. Subsequent backups can be done by just copying the new folders and the new project file.

What About Helper Files?

To make it easier to work across different systems, you can tell Premiere Pro to keep the helper files (audio conform files, index files, peak files, and so forth—aka media cache files) next to the source files. When you move the project from a laptop to a workstation, you can just start editing without any delay. Figure 1-14 shows this setting in the Preferences panel.

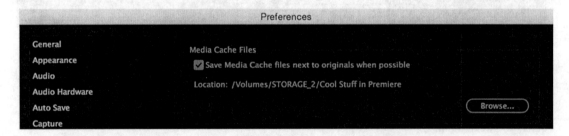

Figure 1-14. *Save helper files next to the source files if you move projects between systems*

Some editors hate that these files live in the same folders as their media files, but I don't really care. Recreating these helper files when a project is moved to another system is time consuming and boring, and they can easily be deleted with a Search & Destroy command in the OS anyway. As long as they're immediately available wherever I edit, I'm happy.

If you're editing on shared storage, having the media cache files on the server may slow things down, so I recommend that you keep them on a fast, local SSD if possible.

Make Your Material Searchable

In a big project, you need quick access to your clips. Premiere has powerful search features, but searching doesn't work if the clips have strange names and no extra info. If you enter metadata, add markers, and rename clips, you will be able to find everything with a few keystrokes.

Renaming Clips

Renaming clips inside of Premiere does not alter the name of the actual media file on the hard drive. It's only changing the internal name of the clip in Premiere. In large projects and when cutting fiction films with a script, everything will need proper naming, but usually in smaller projects, I only need to rename the clips for interviews and other scenes for which several thumbnails may look identical, as in Figure 1-15. Other scenes will be recognized by their thumbnails.

Figure 1-15. *Rename clips when necessary so you can easily find them later*

If I have a bin named *Snowmobile* that contains 15 shots of a snowmobile driving along a power line, and a sequence named *Snowmobile*, I can quickly find them in the project panel without searching. Even if the clip names are strange, like A003_B007_071106_001.R3D, I can find a relevant clip in a few seconds by opening the Snowmobile bin. Renaming the clips and adding metadata to them will take more time than the quick manual search. In this case, the extra organizing is a waste of time. But when you need it, renaming is easy. Select the clip and hit **Enter**, then write the new name and hit **Enter** again. This takes you to the next clip, and you can rename that one, and so on until you hit **Escape** and *Deselect All* (I've mapped that to **F2**) to exit renaming mode.

Make Subclips When Needed

If I have long interviews, they'll be chopped into subclips, making it easier to find the right portion. I usually don't do long takes when shooting, but sometimes we can't stop the camera because we need continuous audio or because we risk losing a great line or a wonderful reaction. Such long material is also a good candidate for subclipping, where we strip out small pieces of golden material from the long take.

To make a subclip, open the clip in the source monitor by double-clicking it in the bin. Then set in and out points and hit the keyboard shortcut for Make Subclip. It's **Ctrl+U** on Windows and **Cmd+U** on MacOS. Give your subclips proper names, as shown in Figures 1-16 and 1-17. If you prefer to work in the Project panel, you can mark in and out on a clip in icon view and create a subclip with the keyboard shortcut. If you've set in and out points in the timeline, you can **Ctrl-drag** (Cmd-drag) the clip to the Project panel to create a subclip.

Figure 1-16. *Make Subclip dialog*

Figure 1-17. *Give your subclips proper names*

Premiere will ask you to name the subclip, so enter a clever one. You can make several subclips from each file, and the subclips' in and out points can be edited later via the *Edit Subclip* feature available in the context menu—or you can make your own shortcut.

When going through interviews, it's time consuming to play them in real time. Try playing them back a little quicker. **Shift+L** will play the clip quicker for each time you hit the keyboard combo. Hit **Shift+J** to slow down if you need to listen carefully to a specific sentence. This gives you finer control than just **J** and **L**.

To make it easier to find clips, subclips, and sequences in large projects, it's good practice to add metadata to make them searchable.

Add Metadata

Metadata is data about your data, just like your passport is metadata about you; DVD covers (do you even remember those in this age of streaming?) have metadata (info) about the film content; and your photo album has metadata (notes) about who we see in the photo and where it was taken.

The Metadata panel in Premiere is very powerful. You can make custom fields if you want to, but I find that adding some keywords in the existing Description, Comment, and Log Note fields usually does the trick for me. Use a suitable metalogging workspace when adding metadata. I've made my own. I find that the bins and the Metadata panel are too far apart in the default one. I like them to be close to each other so the mouse and my eyes don't have to travel that far.

You can add metadata for several clips in one go. See Figure 1-18. Note that I only show the metadata I need in order to avoid clutter and scrolling. In large projects, I'll select all the clips in a bin first to enter basic stuff like topic, client, and so on. Then, I'll select all clips with related content, like all the clips featuring a snowmobile in the image, and enter *Snowmobile* in the Clip Name field.

Figure 1-18. You can add metadata for several clips in one go

Then, I'll select them one by one and enter unique names, like adding *jumping, turning, long shot, 1, 2,* etc. after the shared name.

If I work for a client, I'll make sure every file is tagged with their name. All the files in a project for the Norwegian Army would of course be tagged *Norwegian Army* in the Client field.

You decide what metadata to display by checking the ones you want in the Metadata Display panel. You find it in the fly-out menu in the Metadata panel (Figure 1-19). There are many you will never need (Figure 1-20), so make sure you uncheck them.

Figure 1-19. Metadata panel menu

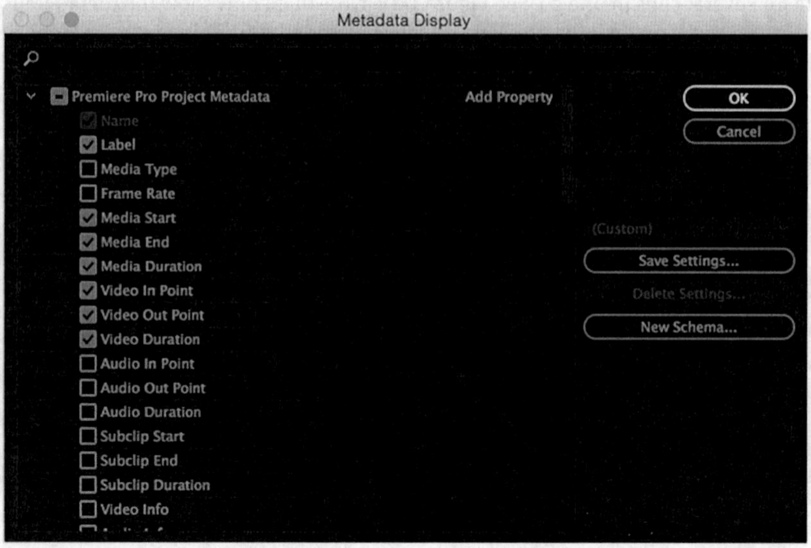

Figure 1-20. *Decide what metadata fields you want to see*

Shot List, RIP

In my workflow, I don't have any use for a shot list anymore. The metadata panel can store everything I'd have in a shot list and much, much more, and it's searchable and integrated right inside my project. As an added benefit, all the metadata you add in Premiere is also available to Bridge, After Effects, and other Adobe applications.

It's possible to make your own "metadata schemas," and even to customize the creation and exchange of metadata, using the XMP Software Development Kit available from Adobe. But that's beyond the scope of this chapter.

Decide What Metadata to See in the Project

OK, so we've sorted the clips, added some metadata and markers, and renamed some clips. How does this help us? Well, all the markers for a chosen clip in a bin will show up in the Markers panel. And all the bins and the metadata can be seen in the Project panel. Very few users of Premiere bother to make their custom metadata display in their Project panel. Some don't even know it's possible. We'll set you apart from the crowd.

Choose *Metadata Display* in the panel menu in the Project panel (Figure 1-21). Here, you can select what metadata fields to display, just like from the Metadata panel. Codec and fields info might be useful, as well as notes usage and custom fields.

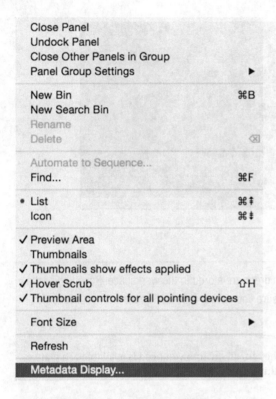

Close Panel
Undock Panel
Close Other Panels in Group
Panel Group Settings   ▶

New Bin   ⌘B
New Search Bin
Rename
Delete   ⌫

Automate to Sequence...
Find...   ⌘F

• List   ⌘⇞
  Icon   ⌘⇟

✓ Preview Area
  Thumbnails
✓ Thumbnails show effects applied
✓ Hover Scrub   ⇧H
✓ Thumbnail controls for all pointing devices

Font Size   ▶

Refresh

Metadata Display...

Figure 1-21. *Panel menu in Project panel*

After deciding what data to show, close the Metadata Display panel and maximize the Project panel. If you've selected a lot of data for display, you may need to scroll horizontally to see all the columns, but I usually don't want that much data on display. The columns can be reordered simply by dragging the column headers right or left (Figure 1-22). Want *Media Duration* to be to the left of *Description*? Drag it there. You can add and edit metadata in the bins and Project panel too (Figure 1-23), but only for one clip at a time.

Figure 1-22. *Drag the column headers to shift the order*

Figure 1-23. *Edit metadata in bins and project panel*

▓ **Note** The Metadata Display choices and the column order are stored in the workspace. Resetting to the default workspace will mess up your columns, so make sure you save a new workspace with your favorite columns in view.

Once you've customized the metadata display in the bin, all the info you need is available at a glance. This will make it much easier to find stuff during the editing process.

Locating Assets in the Project

Hitting **Shift+F** takes you to the search field in the active panel, and typing a few characters is usually enough to take you to the right clip. The search works best in list view, since all subfolders will be twirled down and search matches inside them will be displayed. The search works OK in icon view with single bins. All matching clips in that particular bin will show, but no matches from other bins will pop up.

Also note that the search will not work for bins, just for clips and metadata. So, if you want to use the search, then you'll need to rename the clips or add some metadata. Naming a bin does not make the clips in it show up in a search.

Find Clips from the Timeline

To find a clip in the Project panel while browsing through an existing timeline, just context-click the clip in the timeline and choose *Reveal in Project*.

This opens its bin with the clip highlighted. Now you can rename the clip, open it in the viewer, move it, make subclips, add metadata, or whatever you want.

If you want to open it in the source monitor, there's a quick keyboard shortcut for that: **F**. This is the shortcut for *Match Frame*, which opens the clip under the playhead (actually the clip from the highest targeted track) in the source monitor at the frame where you're parked.

Why not just double-click the clip to open it in the source monitor? Setting in and out points after double-clicking it from the timeline will cause the clip instance in the timeline to be altered and can cause timeline gaps and other unpredictable results. You want to avoid this at any cost!

Advanced Search and Search Bins

If your clips are buried in a lot of bins, you can use the regular search field in every bin, or hit the shortcut for Find, **Ctrl+F** (Cmd+F), to invoke a more advanced search. See Figure 1-24.

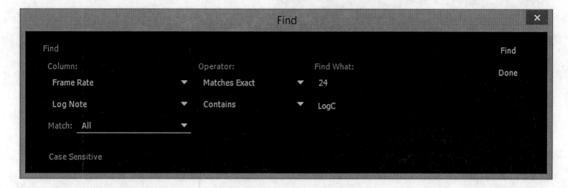

Figure 1-24. *You can do advanced searches by hitting Ctrl+F (Cmd+F)*

If you need a more permanent search, create a Search bin to collect all the clips that match your chosen criteria. You'll find the Create New Search Bin icon to the right of the Search field in every bin. You can specify two different criteria to filter by (Figures 1-25 and 1-26).

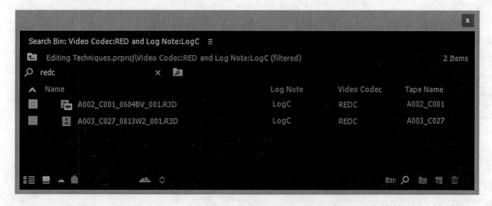

Figure 1-25. *This search bin collects all LogC clips shot on a RED camera*

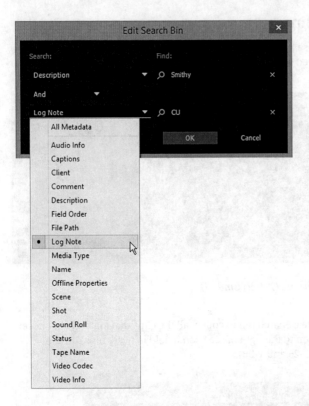

Figure 1-26. *Filter by two different criteria*

Metadata Origins

The number of available metadata fields feels overwhelming, and it can be difficult to understand what the different choices are. Mostly, the choices are divided into standards. *Standard* just means a few people agreed about a description and hoped that other people would use it. Knowing a thing or two about the standards can't hurt, so here's info on a couple to get you started.

XMP (Extensible Metadata Platform) is a specific form of XML used for metadata for photos and video. It was developed by Adobe, and is now an ISO standard. More info here: en.wikipedia.org/wiki/Extensible_Metadata_Platform.

EXIF (Exchangeable Image File Format) is commonly associated with still images, but sometimes also used for video shot on DSLRs, smartphones, and other devices. Link: en.wikipedia.org/wiki/Exchangeable_image_file_format.

Info on IPTC (International Press Telecommunications Council) can be found here: iptc.org/std/photometadata/specification/IPTC-PhotoMetadata.

Info on Dublin Core metadata can be found here: en.wikipedia.org/wiki/Dublin_Core.

Sidecar File or Embedded Metadata?

Premiere can add metadata to the original media files, and will do this if the file format supports metadata in the header and the read/write privileges are enabled on the file. Common file formats like MOV typically support metadata in the file header, but there are some exceptions.

As an example, some flavors of MPEG-2 do not support extra metadata in the header. In such cases, Premiere will create an XML file (with the .XMP extension) in the same location as the original clip and store the file metadata there.

Understanding Clip Metadata and File Metadata

Some metadata is project specific, like notes, descriptions, and comments related to the project. This kind of metadata should be added in the *Clip metadata* and will not be available for other editors when they import the same media files.

Other metadata belong in the raw clips, so all editors can take advantage of the information added, like location, people in the shot, and so on. This kind of metadata should be added in the *File metadata*.

Link Clip Metadata to File Metadata

Some properties have a link box next to them. See Figure 1-27. When this is ticked, Premiere automatically copies the information you enter into the *Clip* field into a corresponding *File* field, and vice versa, provided this is enabled in **Preferences ➤ Media** (Figure 1-28).

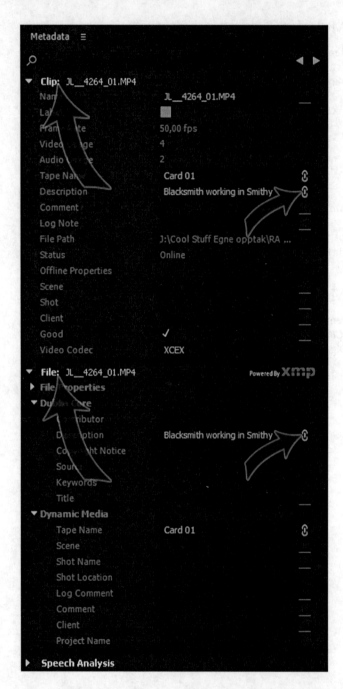

Figure 1-27. *The Metadata panel shows both Clip metadata and File metadata, and they can be linked*

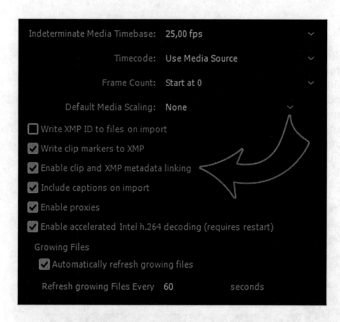

Figure 1-28. *Enable Clip and File metadata Linking*

Once a property is linked in the Metadata panel, it doesn't matter where you enter the metadata—for example, if Description is linked, you could enter it directly in the Project bin, and you'd see it show up under both Clip metadata and (since it's linked) in the File metadata.

■ **Note**   Activating this link doesn't magically auto-sync existing metadata. But when you modify the existing text or add new text, it will appear in both properties. This feature will not overwrite existing metadata unless you enter something.

■ **Note**   If you use subclips or multiple instances of clips that reference the same media file, you probably don't want to automatically change all File metadata properties, since changing the name or description of one instance will effectively change all the other instances–probably not what you want.

Deciding on Your Keywords

Every bit of metadata you add will help you sort and find your clips later. I usually add keywords in one of the standard text fields, like the Comment or Log Note fields. There are some general keywords that would fit most productions, like *B-Roll*, *Interview*, and *Beauty Shot*. I like to start by adding these to a lot of similar clips, and then do another pass where I input more clip-specific keywords like names and locations, *CU*, *MS* or *Pan Left*.

If you work with some Log and some non-Log footage, you may want to tag the Log footage on ingest or when sorting them before spreading them into different bins so you can easily add a LUT to them all in one go. You can write *Log* in the Log Note field (no pun intended) or create a custom metadata field for easy access.

If you like to add metadata before sorting clips into bins, that's OK. Go ahead and enter keywords, then do a quick search and move the found clips to a new bin. You will come up with other keywords that make sense in your productions.

Use Older Versions for Speech Recognition

Although speech recognition is no longer a feature in Premiere, it still exists in older versions, like CS6. The Creative Cloud subscription lets you download and install older versions of Premiere, so you can import a clip into that version, do the speech recognition, and save the project. Then, you can import the project in the current version and keep all the analyzed dialog.

The accuracy of speech recognition can be vastly improved by adding a reference script. This doesn't have to be a script per se. It can be just a bunch of words (Figure 1-29). In a documentary about magicians, for example, you may want to add some magician talk: *misdirection, palming, force, culling, Hofzinser*, and so on. Just create a text file (.TXT) and write those words, then link to that file in the **Analyze ➤ Speech Recognition** section of the Metadata panel.

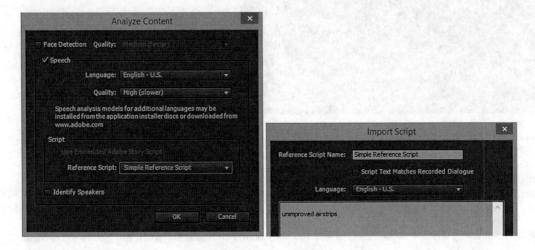

Figure 1-29. *Speech analysis reference script. Screen grabs from CS6*

Figure 1-30 shows the analysis before attaching a reference script, and Figure 1-31 shows the result after adding the text file.

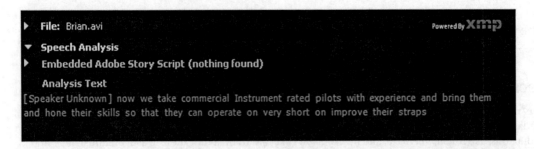

Figure 1-30. *Speech analysis before attaching a script*

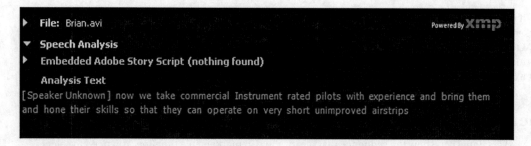

Figure 1-31. Speech analysis after attaching a text file

Order Transcripts Online

If the speech recognition in Premiere doesn't cut it, you can have your dialog transcribed by companies like 3playmedia.com, productiontranscripts.com, iprobesolutions.com, and so on.

As we've seen, metadata helps us find our material quicker. Another feature that helps us find our clips faster and get a better overview of the content is markers.

Add Markers

By adding markers, you make it easier to navigate in the clip later. If you see something interesting while browsing the footage—like where a person pops into the frame—put in a clip marker by hitting **M** when the clip is loaded in the source monitor. The marker is placed where the playhead is parked.

You can make notes about what happens or is being said in the clip. If there's a notable zoom in, pan, focus shift, and so forth, make a note of that in a marker. See Figure 1-32.

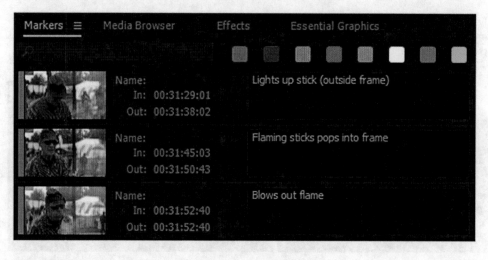

Figure 1-32. Markers make it easier to navigate in the clip later

You don't need to double-click a marker to edit it. To work efficiently with markers, I believe strongly in using keyboard shortcuts. Hit **M** to create a sequence marker, hit **M** again to open the Marker dialog, and hit **Tab** to move to the Comment field, then write your comment and hit **Enter** on the numeric pad to close the dialog. If you have the Markers panel open, you can just hit **M** once and start typing in the panel. If your playhead is over an existing marker, **M** opens the Edit dialog for that marker.

If you're in the timeline and want to add a clip marker, place the playhead where you want to add a marker and select the clip you want a marker on—preferably by using the *Select Clip at Playhead* shortcut, **D**. Hit **M** to make a clip marker. If you don't select a clip before hitting **M**, you get a sequence marker instead.

Alt-click (Opt-click) on a marker to split it and drag out a duration. If you're in the timeline and want to split a clip marker, hit **F** to match frame it to the source monitor and split and name the marker there.

The Markers Panel

The Markers panel can show the sequence markers or the clip markers in a timeline. You need to select *Sequence Timecode* in the panel menu to be able to jump to the markers by clicking on them in the Markers panel. See Figure 1-33.

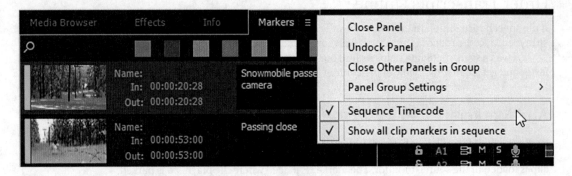

Figure 1-33. *Activate Show all clip markers and Sequence Timecode*

I usually don't give my markers a name. I just write a comment, since those are much easier to read in the Markers panel (Figure 1-34). They stand out a lot better in a separate column. You can use different-colored markers and filter out the ones you don't need to see (Figure 1-35).

Figure 1-34. *Clip markers versus sequence markers*

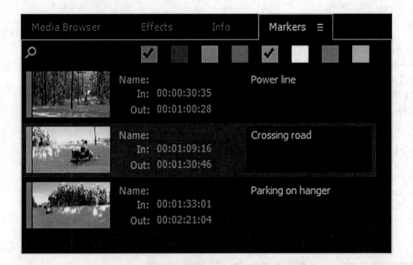

Figure 1-35. *Markers filtered by color*

■ **Note**   You cannot change the color of the marker with keyboard shortcuts in a timeline ganged to the source monitor when the Marker dialog is open. It's kind of counterintuitive, but just hit the shortcut after you have closed the panel, and the color will change.

Change Marker Colors with Shortcuts

You can assign keyboard shortcuts to the eight available marker colors to quickly change the color of your markers. Search for *Set Marker Color* in the Keyboard Shortcuts dialog (Figure 1-36). You can develop your own color system, where markers of different colors have different meaning or mark different types of content.

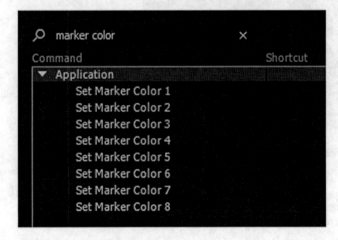

Figure 1-36. *Set marker color*

Search for Markers

You can search for markers in the Project panel Search field. The clip with matching marker text will be highlighted, as will every clip with other matching metadata. You can't search for markers only from here.

If you hit **Ctrl+F** (Cmd+F) in the timeline to invoke the *Find in Timeline* dialog, you can specify a search for markers only. The playhead will jump to the first marker that matches the search. Add a keyboard shortcut for *Find Next* to quickly jump to more matching markers.

Use Labels to Quickly Find Stuff in Timelines and Bins

You can change the label color of selected clips in a bin. This can be used to make them stand out in the timeline and/or bin. It can be useful to see where interviews, beauty shots, or hand-held shots are at a glance. If you make your own color-coding system, you'll get a better understanding of what's in your timeline. You have eight colors to choose from (see Figure 1-37).

Figure 1-37. *There are eight label groups and colors to choose from*

You can change the colors to your liking and set the label names to something more meaningful (for you) in the Preferences (Figure 1-38)—Red for specials, Blue for interviews, Yellow for B-roll, and Green for dialog scenes. Using label colors is a powerful way to organize clips and get visual feedback of what's in your project and in the timeline (Figure 1-39).

Figure 1-38. *You can change the label names*

Figure 1-39. *Use label colors to make important clips more visible*

Label groups and label colors can also be useful when organizing clips in your bins. You can sort clips in the bin by label color, and choosing **Label ➤ Select Label Group** in the context menu in an open bin will select all the clips in a bin that are colored the same as the clip you're context-clicking on (Figure 1-40). Doing so in the Project panel will mark every clip in your project with that label color. Now you can move them, add metadata, drag to the timeline, or whatever you need to do to the whole group.

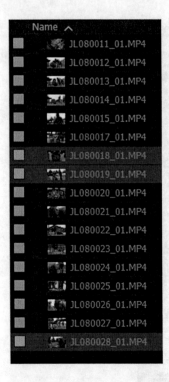

Figure 1-40. Right-click a clip and choose Label ➤ Select Label

Once you've imported and organized your footage and added metadata and markers, you could start editing. But if your audio settings are wrong, you will need to fix this later, and that means extra work. It's much smarter to deal with the audio settings before you start editing.

Decide What to Do with Your Audio

If all the clips in a bin are of the same kind, you might want to decide now what audio tracks to use. If it's a bin with interviews, you may want to use just track 1 with the good sound. If the material was recorded with the built-in camera microphone on one track and a shotgun microphone on another, you'll want to use the shotgun track. If your camera records four tracks, and you only had one microphone attached, you'll want to kill the three empty tracks. So, let's go to **Clip ➤ Modify ➤ Audio Channels** so we don't have to deal with that in the timeline later (Figure 1-41).

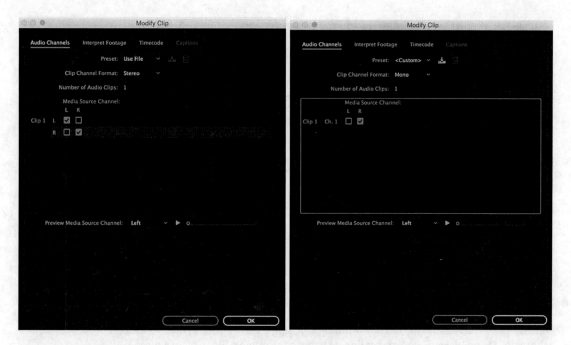

Figure 1-41. *In the Modify Clip dialog, you can decide what audio source channels should be used and what kind of tracks they are*

If you use the same recording system often, you should save the new settings as a preset so you don't have to fiddle with these settings in the future. I use one for interviews and other recordings with external mikes, and one for clips where just the camera mike is used, plus a whole host of others. You'll find more on this in Chapter 3, "Audio in Premiere Pro," and Chapter 10, "Customizing Premiere Pro."

If the clips are already used in a sequence, Premiere tells you very clearly that these changes will not affect clip instances already in the sequence, just new ones you add after the change is done (Figure 1-42).

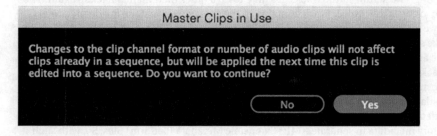

Figure 1-42. *Modify audio warning*

■ **Note**   If you come from Final Cut Pro or for other reasons would like stereo pairs to be treated as dual mono, set this in preferences. ***Preferences ➤ Audio ➤ Default Audio Tracks ➤ Stereo Media*** set to *mono* makes Premiere work very much like FCP. See Figure 1-43.

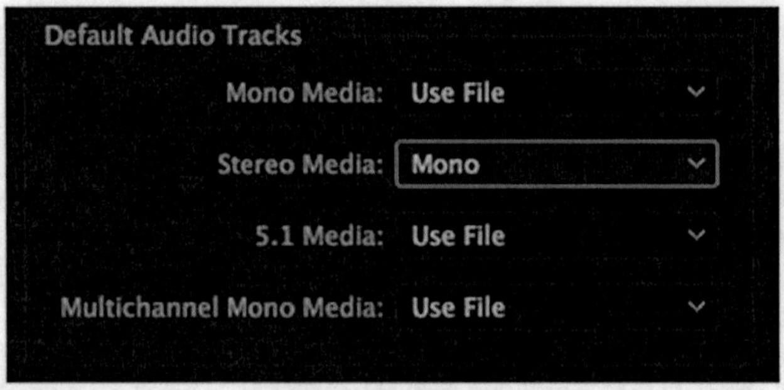

Default Audio Tracks	
Mono Media:	**Use File** ⌄
Stereo Media:	**Mono** ⌄
5.1 Media:	**Use File** ⌄
Multichannel Mono Media:	**Use File** ⌄

Figure 1-43. *A good audio choice for former FCP editors*

Merge Clips? I Don't Think So!

DSLR video has become very popular, but since the audio quality is quite bad, most DSLR shooters will record good-quality audio on a separate audio recorder. This has been done with high-end professional cameras and film for many years, and is called *dual-system audio*. You'll need to connect the separately recorded audio to your video clips, and they can be synced using audio, time code, in/out points, or markers.

Premiere has great built-in syncing tools. The most commonly used one, *merge clips*, is actually my least favorite one, as it requires me to know what clips belong together, is slow, messes with the way my favorite shortcuts, **Q** and **W**, work, and makes linking back to the original files a bit of a mess.

By using multi-camera auto-syncing instead, I don't need to know what clips belong together, it's much faster, I can still use **Q** and **W** as I normally do, and I can get the original files back with a right-click. Automatic, fast, and easy—why would I ever want to do it the slow and cumbersome merge clips way?

Watch a video tutorial on the huge advantages of using multi-camera source sequences instead of merged clips at premierepro.net/editing/audio-syncing/.

Backup Again

With file-based workflows, backup is essential. Have two of everything—always. So, now that we're finished organizing, sorting, tagging, and setting audio tracks, it's time to do a quick incremental backup again. The most important file to back up is the Project file. It contains all the changes we've done inside the project.

But the metadata we've added will sometimes, depending on the video file format, be stored inside the video file itself. So, make sure you back up all the changed files. The easiest way to achieve this is by using proper backup software and doing an incremental backup, automatically copying all the files that have been altered since the last backup.

Premiere will store metadata differently depending on the video file format. For instance, MOV and AVI files can store metadata inside, so with these files Premiere will do that. If you don't back up the video files after adding metadata, your backup will not contain the metadata. With other formats, like MPEG-2, Premiere will have to store metadata in separate XMP (Extensible Metadata Platform) files. So, with such formats, these files need to be backed up as well.

Do It!

I know that many readers will think that all this organizing and data input is way over the top, and for small projects like a news story, it is. But if you had seen all the students (and even pro editors) that I have seen wading through their material looking for untitled files in bins and timelines with no name, searching in folders and on drives, you'd not be so sure anymore. Add to that the fact that this kind of searching tends to come at the end of a project, close to deadline, when you need that special clip that you absolutely know is there somewhere but can't find for the life of you.

All these steps are designed to avoid those stressful situations close to deadline. I'd say that every project with more than half an hour of source material will greatly benefit from better organizing. Even though it takes a lot of words and images to explain, the process itself is actually really quick.

When we've organized the footage into logical folders and the metadata is in place, it's time to get those clips onto a timeline! Yay!

The Rough Cut

You might prefer the terms *selects* or *string-out sequence*, but whatever you call it, it's just a first assembly. Watch every single piece of source material and grab everything that might be good. Don't worry about story, structure, or length for now. You'll need to cut away most of the material later anyway.

You don't know yet what shots will make it to the finished film, so spending 20 minutes polishing a cut just might turn out to be a waste of time.

To illustrate this, the first rough cut of one of my documentaries was 70 minutes, and it had to be cut down to 29 minutes before airing on national TV. A lot of babies had to be killed before that film was finished!

We work faster when we work with a limited amount of material. If your sorting has been smart, clips that belong together will share the same bin, so working with one bin at a time is a good strategy. However, don't automatically start throwing clips on the timeline. You can do some of the rough cutting in the bin by storyboarding, and sometimes it's faster that way.

To Hover Scrub, or Not to Hover Scrub

You can set in and out points while hover scrubbing in the bin. Hit **Shift+H** to enable/disable hover scrubbing temporarily. Hover scrubbing is a great way to quickly see the contents of a clip. If you select a clip, you get the tiny timeline that shows the in and out points (Figure 1-44).

Figure 1-44. *Set in and out points*

After you've gone through all the clips that make up a sequence, drag them all to the New Item icon in the bin (Figure 1-45), and Premiere creates a new sequence. *If you have special needs for your sequences, use your custom settings instead.*

Figure 1-45. *Drag clips to the New item icon*

Storyboarding

With storyboarding, we're by-passing the source panel, going directly from the Project panel to the timeline. I love this way to edit! I choose icon view in the bin and then shuffle clips around to the desired order and make a new timeline from them.

This storyboarding technique is incredibly fast and easy, and with the flexible workspaces in Premiere, I can make the bins as big as needed, so I have enough room for these shuffling acrobatics. Who needs the program monitor while storyboarding? Dock the bin with the Project panel to make it "maximize-able." Floating bins cannot be maximized. Hit the *Maximize Frame* key (or use the panel menu) and use the whole screen as your storyboard! See Figure 1-46.

Figure 1-46. *Here's a maximized bin showing 70 clips*

Maximize Frame is the ` (accent key) by default on English keyboards and varies in different languages. You can also make your own custom shortcut, of course.

On a 24-inch monitor you can easily see 70 clips simultaneously with the smallest icon size, 48 with the size two clicks larger. I never have as many as 48 clips in one bin, so I tend to use the largest thumbnails possible, making hover scrubbing - the act of mousing over the clip to browse through the content - a lot more accurate.

Now, hover scrub or use the **JKL** keys to find out what each clip contains. Then, drag the clip to its logical place in the order (Figure 1-47). Continue with the rest of the clips. When you've storyboarded the ones you'll use, the bad ones will be gathered at the bottom, and you can just **Shift-Select** the ones you want and drag them to the New Item icon (Figure 1-48).

Figure 1-47. *Before storyboarding. Drag-n-drop clips to change the order*

Figure 1-48. *After storyboarding, the best clips are at the top. Drag the selected clips to the New Item icon to create a sequence.*

The new sequence will match the video size and frame rate of the clips and will be created inside of the bin. Immediately change its name, as the name is taken from the first clip, and that won't make much sense in four weeks when you need to edit this sequence again. So, make sure you give it a proper name. I don't like to have sequences living in my source bins, so I'd move it to the bin named *! Sequences* immediately. Having that bin docked with the Project panel and the active bin facilitates this, as a quick drag-n-drop is all it takes.

Some Tips for Storyboarding

There is normally no need to choose *Automate to Timeline.* Just shift-selecting or lassoing around the whole thing and dragging to the New Item icon is faster, as you'll not be interrupted by a dialog box.

Don't throw the bad bits away—you might need them later for cutaways or for stealing a few seconds of audio or that quick eyeline shift or evil smile.

■ **Note**   With some material, the clips just appear to find the right order themselves without our interfering. This is especially true for sequences where we follow a development or a process. Imagine you've shot a sequence where a man cuts down a tree. There is only one logical order of clips in that sequence. Starting with the falling tree and then showing the man starting the chain saw wouldn't make much sense. Every process normally starts with the first clip you shot and ends with the last one.

In these cases, you can skip the storyboarding and go straight to Top & Tail editing. You can even drag the whole bin to the New Item icon without even opening it.

Top & Tail Editing

Top & Tail is by far the quickest way to do your rough cut on documentaries, news stories, corporate movies, and just about every other genre. I'm proud to be personally responsible for this feature being added to Premiere Pro! I talked to several members of the Premiere team, constantly explaining how this way of editing would save me from thousands of keyboard hits on every project. Literally! They finally "got it" and added the feature.

The Top & Tail editing features in Premiere have strange, but descriptive names: *Ripple Trim Next Edit to Playhead* is **W** and *Ripple Trim Previous Edit to Playhead* is **Q**.

Now, what does Top & Tail do? They're essentially macros that do the following operation with one single finger touch on the keyboard: take away all the stuff from the playhead to the previous or next edit point and remove the gap that this creates. So, with a single key stroke we can trim off the top or tail of a clip, leaving just the good part of the clip.

Top & Tail in Action

Here's how easy it is to edit with this feature.

1. When playing back, find the frame where you want to start the clip and hit **Q**. Premiere removes the top of the clip and parks the playhead at the new edit point.

2. Start playback again until you reach the frame where you want the out point. Hit **W**, and Premiere removes the tail of the clip.

3. Rinse and repeat.

You can play the timeline at increased speed while setting the points if you still feel you can make good edit point decisions.

When you encounter a situation where you need to use more than one part of a clip, use **Ctrl+K** (Cmd+K on Mac) to cut the clip in two when setting the out point instead of hitting **W**, then proceed as usual. I've changed this keyboard shortcut (Add Edit) to **R** because it's closer to **Q** and **W**.

Figures 1-49 to 1-56 show the progress of my rough cut.

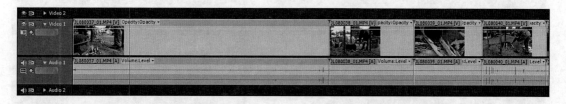

Figure 1-49. *Park the playhead where you want the clip to have its in point*

Figure 1-50. *Hit Q, and Premiere ripple trims the top of the clip away*

Figure 1-51. *Play to where you want to have the out point. If you want to use more of the clip instead of ripple trimming off the tail of it, hit Ctrl+K to split it.*

Figure 1-52. *Play to where you want a new in point, then hit Q*

Figure 1-53. *Play to where you want a new out point, then hit W*

Figure 1-54. *Play to where you need an in point and hit Q*

Figure 1-55. *Play to where you want the out point, and hit W, and so on*

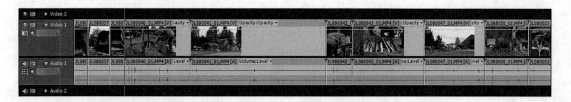

Figure 1-56. Notice that the first three clips have now been trimmed shorter

This combination of the **JKL** playback commands (or dragging the playhead), trimming the top or tail, and cutting clips in two works great, and is by far my favorite way of rough-cut editing! When playing back in slo-mo and with frame-by-frame playback, it can even be used for fine-tuning.

■ **Note**   When doing your rough cut, I can't think of any faster way to edit than the combination of storyboarding and Top & Tail. Making a rough cut means deciding on the order in which the clips are placed and what part(s) of each clip to use. Using the storyboarding technique, you decide the order amazingly fast, and with Top & Tail you trim away the unwanted stuff with single keystrokes.

This is simply the ultimate editing technique for quick assemblies! It's just amazing how quickly you can do your rough cut in this way. People who see this for the first time often can't believe what they just saw. And if you've edited in the "old-fashioned way" until now, you'll be surprised too. By old-fashioned, I mean double-clicking to open the clip in the source monitor, setting in and out points, and then putting it on the timeline.

It works, of course, but it's too many freaking clicks!

I don't think we can expect to be able to edit any quicker, not even in the future. We will always have to decide on in and out points, and we will always have to tell the computer where these points are. I don't think we'll ever be able to tell the computer this faster than by hitting one single key. OK, maybe if we could talk to Premiere instead of using the mouse and keyboard. . .

Top & Tail Editing Works Best in Simple Timelines

Note that Top & Tail editing is best suited to single-track timelines and rough cuts. When you've got more than one track of video it can get a bit nasty because it works on all video tracks simultaneously regardless of Target and Sync Lock settings on the tracks. So, it's great for rough cuts, but not so much for multi-track situations.

Quick Navigation in the Timeline

For Top & Tail editing to work the best, you need to use the keyboard to navigate the timeline. Most users know that J, K, and L can be used to play forward or backward and pause playback. They even know that the timeline plays faster for each time they press J, and so on. But very few are familiar with the more hidden features of JKL. Here's a list of the most useful ones.

Shift+L increases playback speed in smaller increments than repeatedly hitting **L**.

Shift+J decreases playback speed in smaller increments than repeatedly hitting **J**.

Holding down **K** while pressing **L** moves one frame forward.

Holding down **K** while pressing **J** moves one frame backward.

Holding down **K** and **L** means forward slo-mo.

Holding down **K** and **J** means backward slo-mo.

Keep Notes Inside of Premiere

When you're assembling a rough cut, you'll encounter lots of things that need your attention. But your first cut is not your final cut, so don't become focused on trivial details now—save the fine-tuning for later and take notes. Concentrate on cutting away everything that's not needed and developing structure. Work on the story now and worry about details later.

You can import TXT documents into Premiere Pro even though they're not among the "Supported Media" displayed in the Import dialog box. But no one can stop you from dragging it from a folder on your drive into Premiere's Project panel or bins! So, do that.

Now you can double-click the file in the bin to open it in Notepad (Figure 1-57). Close the file when you've typed in the notes so you don't accidentally get more than one instance of the file opened at the same time.

Figure 1-57. Keep editing notes in a TXT file in your bin

Work with PDF Files Inside of Premiere

With the product from Primal Cuts called PDF Viewer (Figure 1-58), you can import and work with PDF files right inside Premiere. The same product also allows you to work with PDF files inside of After Effects and Audition.

Figure 1-58. PDF Viewer

Visit the website at `primalcuts.com/site/` for new special bundle pricing.

Post Notes Panel

A company called PostNotes.io has a CEP Panel (Figure 1-59) that plugs right into Premiere for making to-do lists and keeping notes while you edit. Once you install the custom panel onto your computer, you have the ability to type notes and create to-do lists tied to specific sequences.

Figure 1-59. Post Notes

Visit the website at `postnotes.io/`.
When the rough cut feels right, you can go back and massage it until it shines. Time for trimming.

Trimming and Fine-Tuning

Try to feel what's missing or if some shots are redundant. Try holding that shot a little bit longer. Try cutting in that other angle. Undo if the changes don't make things work better. Have fun and experiment! It's amazing how nudging a clip a few frames left or right or swapping clips in the sequence can alter the whole piece and make the story take an interesting turn. Details are important—a few frames can make a huge difference.

Don't be afraid to play around. Cut, snip, and chop until it feels right, or completely wrong, but make a copy of the sequence before you make all these changes so you can easily get back to where you were.

Trim Mode

The Trim mode in Premiere is the best I've ever used. It's very powerful and at the same time very quick and easy to use. Use the Trim mode whenever you can.

I've seen so many, both newbies and seasoned editors, fickle with small adjustments in the timeline when the same adjustments could have been accomplished much quicker and easier in Trim mode.

There's nothing that you can do in Trim mode that cannot be accomplished with other tools in the timeline, but it's generally much quicker to use the dedicated Trim mode.

Hit **Shift+T** when positioned near a cut in the timeline (or double-click the cut point), and you're about to discover the greatness of the Trim Mode.

In Trim mode, Premiere shows a two-up display in the program monitor. See Figure 1-60. Depending on where you hold your mouse over the images while in Trim mode, you'll get a Ripple Out, Ripple In, or Roll edit when you click and drag. It feels so intuitive to use the mouse in Trim mode it's almost too easy. Because of the large area you have available for dragging the edit points, you can be much more exact than if you did the same thing in the timeline. It's kind of strange that I use the mouse so much in Trim mode, because I'm actually a dedicated shortcuts user.

Figure 1-60. *You can Ripple Trim left or right by dragging in the image, or do a Rolling edit by dragging between the images. Or use the keyboard.*

When in Trim mode, the Spacebar no longer plays the timeline like it normally does. Instead, it performs a Play Around, playing a couple of seconds before and after the edit point and continuing to loop playback.

Keyboard Shortcuts for Trimming

You can find most keyboard shortcuts in menu commands and tool tips. Additional shortcuts can be found by typing "trim" in the Keyboard Shortcuts dialog box (Figure 1-61). Use **Up Arrow** to go to the previous cut and **Down Arrow** to go to the next cut. Hit **Ctrl+Shift+T** (Ctrl+T) to change between the five modes of trimming.

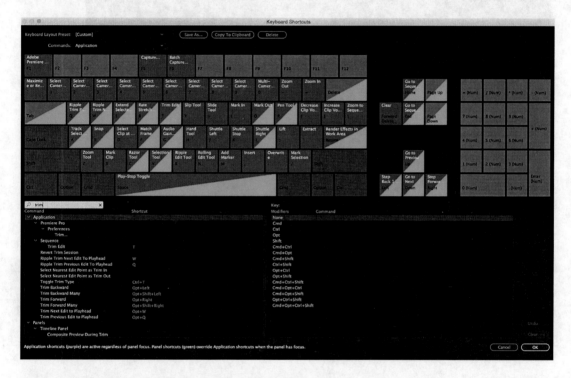

Figure 1-61. *Search for "trim" in the Keyboard Shortcuts dialog*

Using these shortcuts, you can easily adjust in and out points very precisely. If you need to go frame by frame, use the keyboard shortcuts (**Ctrl+Left Arrow** (Option+Left Arrow) and **Ctrl+Right Arrow** (Option+Right Arrow)), or click the +1 or -1 buttons. Jump longer by adding the **Shift** key. In the program monitor, you'll get all the info you need about incoming and outgoing clips, time code, amount of trimming, and so on. The pre- and postroll times, and the amount of frames to jump when **Shift** is added, can be set in preferences: **Edit ➤ Preferences ➤ Trim**.

Play Around and Tweak

When you hit Spacebar, you get to see the cut with a pre- and postroll (Figure 1-62). This is called Play Around, and will not stop when you use shortcuts to fine-tune the edit point, so keep tweaking while the playback loop continues. Each time it starts the preroll, the changes since last time will show. This is very nice when you're tweaking a difficult cut and want to try different edit points. Just keep on tweaking while looping until the cut sounds and looks good.

Figure 1-62. *Trim mode Play Around*

■ **Note**   Thanks to Walter Murch, who asked for this feature, we can also use **I** and **O** during the looping playback to move the edit point to the playhead at that point in time, and then reset the preroll and start playing again. It's hard to explain this feature in a book, but if you try it you'll see how quick and powerful this is.

Dynamic Trimming

The greatness of the Trim mode doesn't stop here. In addition to the expected frame-by-frame trimming, we've got dynamic trimming. Hit **J** or **L** while in Trim mode, and you're performing a Dynamic trim. When you stop the playback, that's where the new edit point will be. See Figures 1-63 and 1-64 for a before-and-after comparison. I selected the edit point and hit **L** to play, then stopped where I wanted the new edit point. This is about as easy as it gets!

This is fantastic for trimming dialog and for cuts that need to have the right rhythm! It's impossible to feel the rhythm of a cut without playing it in real time. Dynamic trimming lets you do that, and because the new cut point is already set when you hit **Spacebar** or **K**, it's also very fast.

You can use all the great slo-mo, fast play, and frame-by-frame playback **JKL** modes while doing a Dynamic trim, so you can work incredibly accurately. If you've never tried Dynamic trim, I urge you to do it ASAP.

Figure 1-63. *Dynamic trim before*

Figure 1-64. *Dynamic trim after a Dynamic Roll edit*

Trim Mode Makes You a Better Editor

To be a good editor, you still need to know your craft. Solid knowledge about cutting on movement, eye tracking, screen direction, cut-aways, 180° and 30° rules, and so on will help smooth your cuts to achieve the ultimate level of continuity editing: invisible cuts. When you know what you want to achieve and why, dynamic trimming and careful fine-tuning in Trim mode will help you get there faster.

If you have lots of material, the main timeline gets long and complex, and you must take extra care to keep audio and video in sync. Small adjustments can affect things way behind the clips you're editing on. Nesting makes complex timelines more manageable.

Avoid Complex Timelines—use Nesting

Nesting means putting a sequence into another sequence (Figure 1-65) and is one of the main pillars of my workflow. I use nesting to organize my material and to quickly and easily get an overview of the flow of the film in the main timeline. Nesting keeps my timelines tidy and the performance snappy, and enables me to do much quicker changes to the order of scenes.

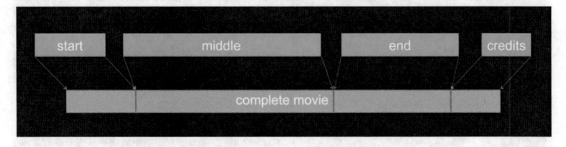

Figure 1-65. *Nesting is when we put one or more sequences into another*

For me, nesting is a must for effective editing. I can split the film into manageable pieces, easily create different lengths and versions, quickly change the order of scenes, and put effects on a whole scene in one go. To top it all off, it makes the system more stable and responsive. What's not to like? Well, there are a few gotchas that we'll get back to. But first, let's look at the advantages.

Short Sequences—More Done, Quicker

Updating the timeline will get slower when your timelines get very long. If you have five hundred clips in a timeline and do a change at the beginning, Premiere needs to update all the changes. With extremely long timelines and/or slow drives, you can even see the thumbnails in the sequence update along the timeline the first time you open it. You don't want to wait for this, so use nesting to avoid it. Editing shorter segments of the film separately will dramatically increase your productivity and flexibility. Here's how I use nesting.

Each Nested Sequence Is a Mini-Story

I start by editing all the separate situations in the film in their own sequences, treating my sequences as mini-stories. As a general rule, the clips from each bin in my project panel will make up one mini-story. Each logical sequence has a very short timeline, as in Figure 1-66—typically around 30 seconds to a minute long, but sometimes two or more minutes. It depends on the material. Anyone can keep track of changes in such a short timeline! Put those finished sequences in their parent sequence, and you've done your nesting.

Figure 1-66. *Each logical mini-story is one sequence*

How Many Sequences?

There is no such thing as a "normal" number of sequences or "standard" length of a nested sequence. But here's one example: a half-hour documentary film I made had 59 nested sequences in the main timeline (Figure 1-67) and a total of 78 sequences, including "helper" sequences used for effects work, different exports, and short versions.

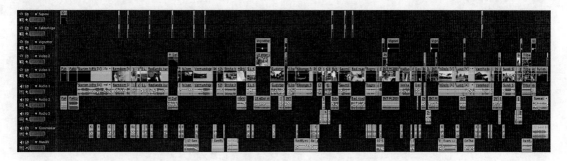

Figure 1-67. *The main timeline from a documentary. The green clips are nested sequences*

Yes, I'm a heavy user of nesting, and I can't imagine ever editing a long-form film without it. It really simplifies a lot of things.

Another Real-world Nesting Case

When I made 12 films for the Norwegian Directorate for Cultural Heritage riksantikvaren.no/Tema/ Verdiskaping/Filmar, we visited 12 areas in Norway that had 63 individual restoration projects going on. I kept these in separate folders on my drive (Figure 1-68), so my logical choice was to dump the recordings from each project into separate bins in my Premiere project (Figure 1-69).

Figure 1-68. Project folders

Figure 1-69. *Material from one bin will be placed in its own sequence and edited separately*

I ended up having more than 200 bins in the Project panel when music, voiceover, beauty shots, interviews, and other stuff also got their own bins.

Then, each restoration project got its own sequence, as did other mini-stories like the local photographer club's visit to an abandoned factory for a shoot or a band's jam session in one of the old factory buildings (Figure 1-70). A woman reading out loud from a book about life in the factory also became a separate sequence.

Figure 1-70. *Each sequence is a mini-story*

Figures 1-71 to 1-83 show all the sequences from one of the 12 six-minute films, the one about Odda—a small town in Norway. Notice how tidy and simple each sequence is. Anyone can wrap their brain around every simple sequence.

Figure 1-71. *Odda Sequence 1*

Figure 1-72. *Odda Sequence 2*

Figure 1-73. *Odda Sequence 3*

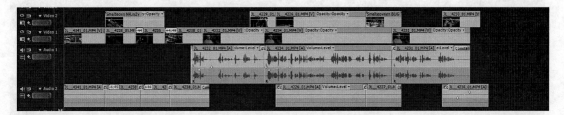

Figure 1-74. *Odda Sequence 4*

Figure 1-75. *Odda Sequence 5*

Figure 1-76. *Odda Sequence 6*

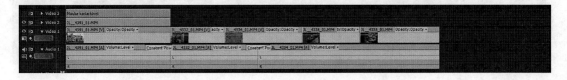

Figure 1-77. *Odda Sequence 7*

Figure 1-78. *Odda Sequence 8*

Figure 1-79. *Odda Sequence 9*

Figure 1-80. *Odda Sequence 10*

Figure 1-81. *Odda Sequence 11*

Figure 1-82. *Odda Sequence 12*

Figure 1-83. *Odda Sequence 13. This last sequence only had some graphics and rolling credits*

Then, all these mini-stories were weaved together in the main sequence, where transitions between the stories, music, and voiceover were added. Notice how tidy and clean the main Odda sequence is (Figure 1-84)? That's just one of the benefits of nesting.

Figure 1-84. *The main sequence for a six-minute film is tidy and simple*

Figure 1-85 shows the main sequence for the whole 72-minute film made from the 12 shorter ones. Even this long one is very simple, as a result of nesting.

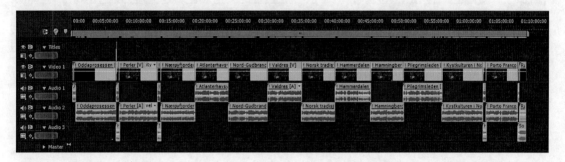

Figure 1-85. *Twelve of these six-minute shorts were combined into a seventy-two-minute film in another sequence*

Nesting and Restructuring

Want to change the order of scenes? No problem! If you've used nesting, each scene will be in its own nested sequence. Swapping two scenes is just a matter of holding down **Ctrl** (Cmd) and **Alt** while dragging a nested sequence to where you want it. Figures 1-86 to 1-88 shows the timeline before, during, and after swapping two nested sequences.

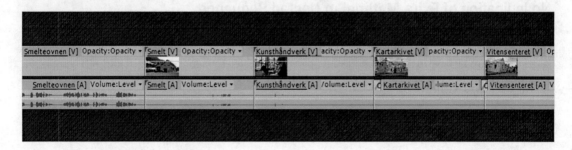

Figure 1-86. *Nesting before swap*

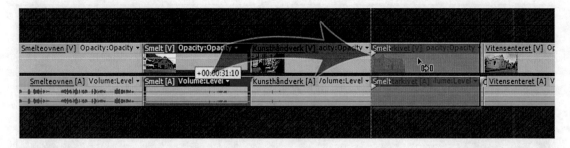

Figure 1-87. *Nesting during swap*

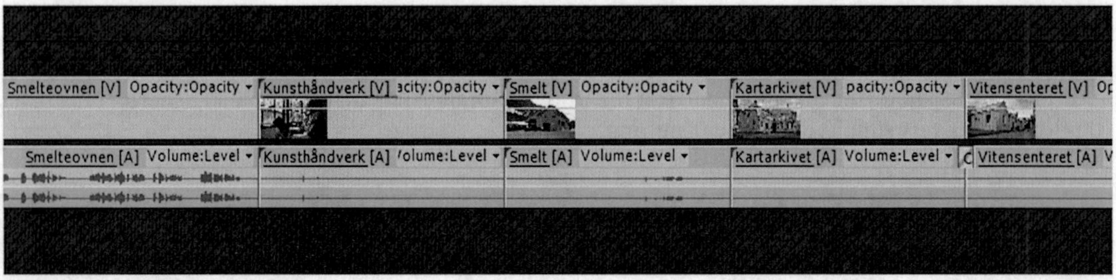

Figure 1-88. *Nesting after swap*

Imagine doing this without nesting. The director wants you to swap two scenes. Now you have to zoom into the timeline to find out exactly where in the timeline the scene starts and where it ends. Next, you need to select all the clips between those two points, then you need to find out where the other scene starts and, finally, do a cut-n-paste or ripple-drag action. There's a good chance you'll miss some stray clips, like cut-ins, voiceovers, or extra lines that live on different audio and video tracks.

Compare this to the incredibly easy **Ctrl/Cmd-Alt-dragging** a clip from here to there. 'Nuff said.

Nesting Gotchas

Premiere has a "do no harm" philosophy when it comes to timelines. It will not move stuff in the timeline unless you specifically tell it to. So, when you make changes in a nested timeline, it will show up in the main timeline, but the length of the nested sequence in the main timeline will not change even if you add or delete stuff in the nested timeline.

No Indication of Extra Material in Nested Sequence

If your nested sequence is originally 35 seconds long, and you add some material, making the nested sequence five seconds longer, the last five seconds of the nested sequence will not show in the main timeline (Figure 1-89). You'll have to ripple trim the out point of the nested sequence, making it longer (Figure 1-90). When you reach the end of the sequence and continue dragging the out point, you'll get a message saying "Trim media limit reached."

Figure 1-89. *If you make the nested sequence longer, there is no indication in the main timeline*

Figure 1-90. Ripple trimming reveals the extra material

Danger Stripes in the Main Timeline

If you delete five seconds from a nested sequence, the main timeline will have five seconds of black in it, but the nested sequence will still be the same length. You need to ripple trim the out point of the nested sequence in the main timeline to get rid of the empty frames indicated by the warning stripes (Figure 1-91).

Figure 1-91. *Making the nested sequence shorter will result in "danger stripes" in the main sequence. Drag the out point beyond the danger stripes, then let go.*

Unfortunately, Premiere will not snap to the end of the nested sequence when trimming from outside the out point, so you need to go beyond that point, then let go of the mouse, and finally trim it back until it snaps and you get the "Trim media limit reached" message. See Figure 1-92. This is one extra step that wouldn't be necessary if it snapped to the out point when trimming the out point to the left.

Figure 1-92. *Then trim back again. When you reach the end of the nested sequence, Premiere will throw a message telling you this.*

Colin Brougham has a clever workaround for this: put a sequence marker at the end of the nested sequence and keep *Ripple Sequence Markers* enabled. When you're inserting or ripple-deleting clips, it always represents the end of the content in the main/nesting sequence, and even if clip markers are hidden, the trim cursor will always snap to it. See Figure 1-93.

Figure 1-93. *The marker at the end of the nested sequence enables snapping to its end*

No Audio Waveforms Until You Render

Audio waveforms don't show for even simple nested sequences (Figure 1-94) until you render the audio (Figure 1-95) by clicking **Sequence ➤ Render Audio** (or assign a keyboard shortcut). Audio rendering is quick, so it's not a big problem, but sometimes it's annoying. If the nested timeline is very long, Premiere will render audio for the whole sequence, even if you've just used a small part of it. So, don't leave a lot of garbage at the end of your nested timelines. Yes, audio handling in nested sequences could be more streamlined. But, all in all, these small speed bumps in the workflow don't keep me from often using nesting.

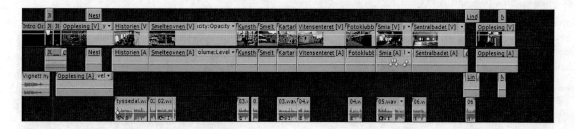

Figure 1-94. *No waveform for nested sequences*

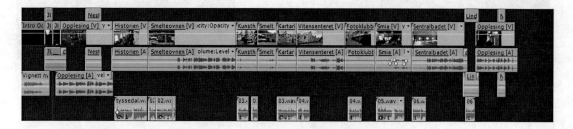

Figure 1-95. *Render the sequence audio to show waveforms*

Third-party Software May Need a Flattened Sequence

When you're outputting an EDL, OMF, AAF, or XML for color grading, audio mix, or VFX in third-party software, nested sequences will not always work. Some software can only take very simple timelines, so you'll need to flatten the film into one sequence. Don't use nesting if this is your workflow. Multicam sequences can be flattened in Premiere Pro CC.

■ **Note** You can still edit in short, manageable sequences before you bring the content over to the main editing sequence. Just make sure the *nest-or-not* button (aka "Insert and overwrite sequences as nests or individual clips") in your main timeline is not blue, so you don't get nested sequences.

Use Grouping When Nesting Is Not an Option

Grouping can be an alternative. It will at least keep clips that logically belong together in one single bunch, and you can move, copy, delete, and otherwise manipulate them as one single item in the timeline. See Figures 1-96 and 1-97.

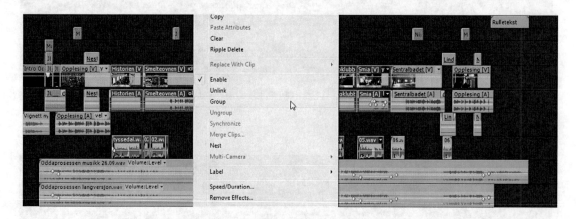

Figure 1-96. *Grouping clips*

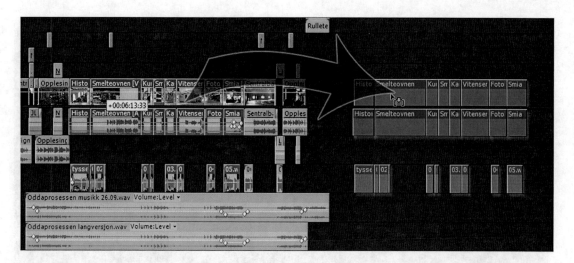

Figure 1-97. *If nesting doesn't suit your workflow, you can use grouping instead and move groups of clips as one unit*

OK, so the rough cut is done—with or without nesting—and you can concentrate on making every clip look its best.

Make It Shine

After the rough edit and fine-tuning, it's time for color correction, audio sweetening, compositing, titles, graphics, and so on. This whole polishing and tweaking thing can be the most labor-intensive part of the editing process, but these topics will be dealt with in depth throughout the book, so I will not waste time discussing them in detail here.

You can spend as much time as you like in this phase until it's an awesome little film or you run out of time.

Color Grading

There is a lot of information on color grading in Chapter 6. Suffice it to say that I do all my color grading inside of Premiere, that I've made a lot of custom effects presets, and that I use the scopes a lot. Figures 1-98 and 1-99 show a clip before and after applying a grading preset (look).

Figure 1-98. *Before grading*

Figure 1-99. *Grading is very quick in Premiere when we use presets*

Effects and Compositing with Template Projects

Need a reflection, a swish pan, picture-in-picture, a slideshow projector, or some skin smoothing? I've made template projects for all these effects and more, and when I need an effect like this I'll import the template project and do it in seconds. I only need to swap the footage in the template for the footage in my current project, and it's done. Complex effects can be added in seconds, not hours. Figure 1-100 shows a Light Wrap template project in use.

Figure 1-100. *Make presets and template projects for compositing tasks you do often. Green-screen footage by Geir Rossebø.*

Chapter 8, "Compositing," goes into great detail on chroma keying, blending modes, and the track matte key effect, as well as how to build and use template projects.

You can download some free compositing presets from premierepro.net to get you going quickly.

Motion Graphics with Template Projects

You don't want to spend a lot of time creating motion graphics from scratch. Most likely, you'll have an old project where you've done something similar. Whenever you create motion graphics you think might come in handy later, make a habit out of building template projects, like the reflection template shown in Figure 1-101. I literally takes just 20-30 seconds to create this effect when you import a template project. Make templates for everything!

Figure 1-101. *Make presets and templates for motion graphics effects that you use often*

If you have ready-made template projects for subtitles, scan lines, image animated in 3D, cool text animations, lower thirds, and other stuff, you can just import that template project into your current project, swap out the source material, write new text if necessary, and you're good to go. Template projects will shave hours off your motion graphics work.

Chapter 7, "Motion Graphics," explains how to build and use template projects and covers the nitty gritty details on every aspect of motion graphics work in Premiere. You can download some template motion graphics projects from premierepro.net to get a kickstart.

Sound Mix

A lot of the audio handling can be automated. Use normalizing and make presets for the audio effects that you use often. In Chapter 3, we'll have a thorough look at audio mixing, equalizing, normalizing, compression, and other useful audio stuff. Let's review a few steps that you need to understand to be a good sound editor.

Choose which tracks to use from the source material, normalize interviews and speech, apply compression (Figure 1-102), add audio cross fades, split audio and video cut points, mix using audio-level keyframes, use equalizing when called for, change audio channel output mapping (Figure 1-103), and do your final audio mix.

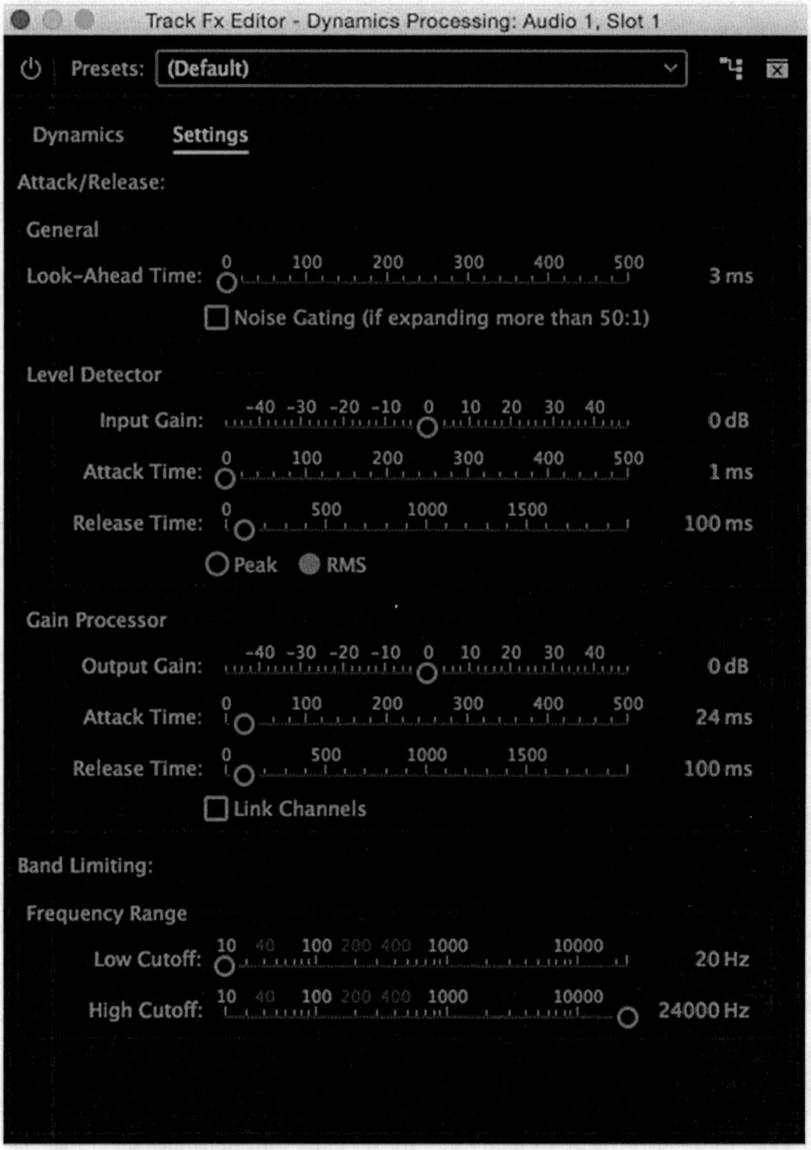

Figure 1-102. *Audio compressor*

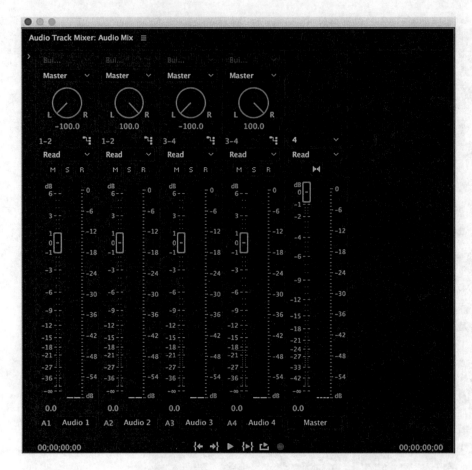

Figure 1-103. *Audio Track Mixer*

Get a Second Opinion

When you think you're finished, get a second opinion. And get it from someone you trust. I've been saved by calling in another editor more times than I can count. He or she would say, "*Why don't you just. . .*" and it would be crystal clear to me what needed to be done. If you want to get good advice from others, you'll also have to be willing to give it. I've saved the bacon of my fellow editors the same way many times.

If you're working for a client, his or her opinion will count too. A great way to get feedback from anyone, including clients, is to post private, password-protected videos with burnt-in time code on Vimeo, DropBox, or YouTube. Then, ask for feedback with timecode references.

If you can't get another person to watch your edit, then at least step away from the project for a while. Come back the next day, and your eyes will be more objective.

When you're sure your film is finished, or the deadline is so close that you must deliver your film no matter what, it's time for export.

Output

You guessed it; we'll deal with this in a lot more detail in Chapter 3, "Exporting." These days, your finished film will probably not be exported as a DVD or to tape, but as a file. You'll want to have several versions of your masterpiece for different uses. A master file for long-term storage, a Blu-ray disc and an H.264 file with great quality for playback on your computer, then another H.264 version for the web.

All these can easily be output from Premiere, and the good thing is that it's easy and can be done as a background process while you're editing the teaser trailer for your film.

When exporting long-form material, check your computer sleep settings so your computer doesn't go into energy-saver mode after a couple of hours of "inactivity."

Organized Timeline Helps Export

Even when exporting, it pays to be organized. If you keep music on one track, voice on another, and so on, you can easily export versions with and without music, voiceover, and titles. These so-called i-versions are great for the archives. A clean sequence is needed when you want to reuse that particular sequence from that five-year-old film, but don't want it littered with graphics, music, and voiceover.

Creating a Master File

So, you think this might be a good time to render the timeline? Not really. Only render it if you feel very strongly about it, or if you're allergic to red lines in the timeline. You don't really have to. Rendering the timeline is only necessary if you need to archive the project back to tape or play it directly out on air. But you should, of course, export your film.

One thing I do on almost every project is to make a master file of the entire film. When exporting a master file, I want to keep as much of the quality as possible. On short projects, I don't care how big the file will be, so I make a lossless file, either with no compression or with a lossless codec like UltraPix JPEG 2000.

On longer projects, where the massive lossless files would be prohibitively big, I'll make a lossy master file with a high bit rate and a high-quality codec like DNxHD or GoPro Cineform. Mac users can also use ProRes with high-quality settings.

Actually, I make two master files of most of my projects. One with everything, and one where music and narration tracks are muted and the graphics tracks are switched off.

Depending on the complexity of the project, I will either go directly from my export timeline to Adobe Media Encoder (AME), or make a new timeline with just the master file. All the effects, color corrections, custom transitions, titles, and graphics will need to be rendered internally by Premiere when exporting, so if there's a lot of this, I'll use the master file. This saves time, and, courtesy of the lossless master file, I'll keep good quality all the way. Life is good.

For the Web, and for Playback on Mac and PC

The YouTube export settings in Premiere and AME are quite good. They will also work beautifully for both Vimeo and local playback on Mac and PC.

New and powerful systems will be able to play back higher quality files than old and tired systems. There is no guarantee that a file that plays flawlessly on your editing workstation will play smoothly on Auntie Bertha's old laptop.

Putting It on the Shelf

We're not done yet! You don't want to have this project on your main computer forever. But you might want to come back to it later and do some more—make a short version or put in a new sequence. So, keep the whole thing on two external hard discs. Yes, two; one extra for backup. We don't trust drives, do we? Even RAIDs do fail.

So, archive the project folder—and a copy. My backup drive is not stored anywhere near my editing bay. I use a safety deposit box in my bank, but I guess my friend's house would work too. As long as the two houses don't burn down at the same time, I'm covered. I also keep the master file and image files for Blu-rays and DVDs so I can easily make copies if needed.

The following section is a collection of workflow tips that will speed up your editing. Not all the methods will be suitable for all projects, but if you know these techniques, you can choose the best one for every job.

More Workflow Tips

Make Sequence and Project Dupes

Some editors make duplicates of their sequences and number them in increments. The highest number is the most recent. If you duplicate the sequence you can go crazy and not worry about destroying anything, because the original is always there. If you screw up, just delete it and duplicate again.

Duplicating sequences can cause problems on large projects because the sequences add to the project file size. To avoid this bloating, you can create a copy of the project and then delete all the sequences you are not going to use.

Don't worry about losing anything. With the media browser, you can access all your old sequences from the previous versions of the project file and open them within the current project. You reduce the complexity and size of your current project, and you still have access to everything you've done.

I know some editors who end each day by duplicating the project file. This makes them sleep well at night, not worrying about messing up their projects.

Offline (Proxy) Editing

Traditionally, throughout the era of computer-based editing, feature films were edited in pretty much this fashion: **Negative film ➤ scanned to Digital high-res files ➤ Digital low-res proxies made from these ➤ Offline Editing ➤ Reconforming ➤ Color Grading ➤ Export.** *Offline* refers to the fact that the files that we edit actually will be never included in the final movie. *Reconforming* means we're linking back to the original high-res files.

Today, it's possible to skip many of these steps, so we get this workflow: **Digital high-res recordings ➤ Online Editing ➤ Color Grading ➤ Export.** All the post-production steps can be done inside of Premiere. This requires a beefy system, though, so a lot of editors decide to go with offline editing of lower-quality files, often called *proxy editing*.

Read about proxies in Chapter 2, "Proxy Editing."

Render & Replace

If your system isn't working well with heavily compressed material like H.264, you can use timeline search to locate the files with that file type and then *render and replace* those as editing-friendly codecs like Cineform, ProRes, or DNxHD. You get access to Render and Replace via a simple right-click on the clips.

To get the originals back, just right-click again, and choose *Restore Unrendered.*

Help! All My Media Is Gone!

No, it isn't! Take a look at the Search box in the Project panel. Is the magnifying glass blue, as in Figure 1-104? Then you're definitely searching for something—and it isn't there, so nothing shows up. Click the little x to clear the search and make the magnifying glass icon a neutral gray again.

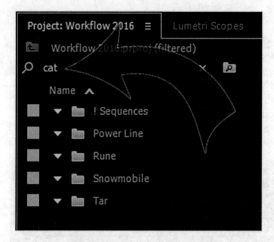

Figure 1-104. *Media gone–NOT*

String-outs

When you do string-outs with the good stuff on V2 and the riff raff on V1, just duplicate the sequence and select everything on V1 and hit **Shift+Delete**. Boom—condensed gaps at the push of a button, no click and drag.

Pancake Tips

There are many ways to use the Pancake layout for faster editing. When going through dailies in a string-out sequence, you can use **Q** and **W** to trim top and tail, and just remove bad takes. But if you want to keep all the material in your sequence, you can nudge the selected clip up to a new track using the keyboard shortcut **Alt + Up Arrow** and then copy it to a new sequence. You may want to map this to a one-key shortcut if you use this method.

I prefer to turn off the *Linked Selection* button in the timeline and turn on *Selection Follows Playhead* when moving selects up one or more tracks (Figure 1-105), so I can just play the timeline until I see a clip I like, and then stop (you have to stop for the automatic clip selection to kick in) and hit the *Nudge Clip Selection Up* shortcut. See Figure 1-106.

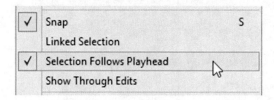

Figure 1-105. *Selection follows playhead; linked selection off*

Figure 1-106. *Selections are moved to track 2*

Whatever way you use to choose your selects, now open the selects sequence in the source monitor by dragging it from the bin to the source monitor, or right-click it and choose *Open in source monitor*. Or use the shortcut **Shift+O**. Then, you want to open it in a timeline. You can move the cursor over to the source monitor, click on the wrench, and choose *Open Sequence in Timeline*, but I much prefer to create a shortcut for this.

This will open the Selects timeline ganged to the source monitor, as indicated by the (source monitor) suffix in the timeline (Figure 1-107). So, now you can set markers and add comments to clips or groups of clips by hitting **M** twice and creating a spanned marker (a marker with a duration).

Figure 1-107. *Selects sequence*

You can also set in and out points and edit with Insert and Overwrite shortcuts as usual, or you can drag and drop clips from the selects sequence to the main editing sequence (Figure 1-108).

Make sure that under **Preferences ➤ General**, the *Set focus on the Timeline when performing Insert/ Overwrite edits* choice is not checked.

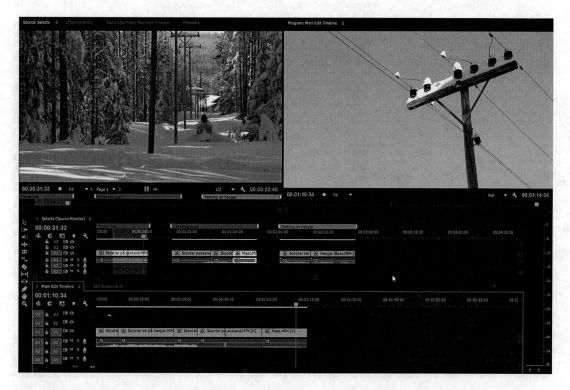

Figure 1-108. *Pulling selects from a string-out sequence*

If you want to delete the gaps between selects, feel free to do so, but make sure that *Ripple Sequence Markers* is turned on (Figure 1-109), so you don't mess up the timing of your markers. If you don't want to use markers, you can use text graphics on a higher track.

Figure 1-109. *Ripple Sequence Markers*

Note that I've turned the *Insert and overwrite sequences as nests or individual clips* button off, so I get the actual clips, not a nested sequence. I've also chosen to show markers as an overlay in my source monitor so I don't have to look away from the monitor to know what part of the Selects timeline I'm in.

You can have as many open selects sequences as you want (Figure 1-110). If you have two monitors, you can fill an entire screen with Source timeline panels. Depending on your screen resolution, you may handle a grid that's at least six panels high and two panels wide, giving you immediate access to 12 selects sequences to grab from! Figure 1-111 shows eight timeline panels on a standard 1920 × 1080 monitor.

Figure 1-110. *Multiple selects sequences*

■ **Note** To quickly switch between your string-out sequences, use the source monitor keyboard shortcut (**Shift+2**) to tab through them. Both the source monitor and the timeline will switch simultaneously.

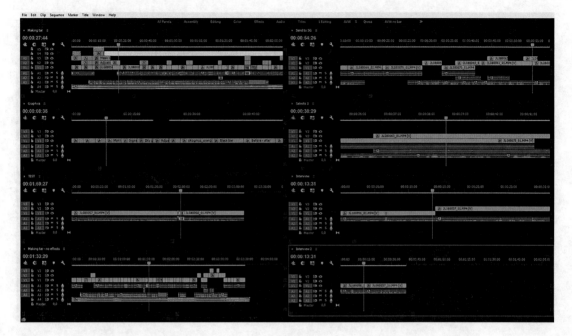

Figure 1-111. *Eight Selects sequences*

■ **Note** Dylan Fallen Osborn has a great tutorial on the Pancake Timeline techniques at `vimeo.com/179981501`.

Importing DPX Image Sequences

Having problems importing DPX shots into Premiere? Use After Effects as the intermediate importer. Import your DPX files into After Effects (Figure 1-112). Copy the DPX file After Effects creates and paste it into Premiere's Project bin (Figure 1-113).

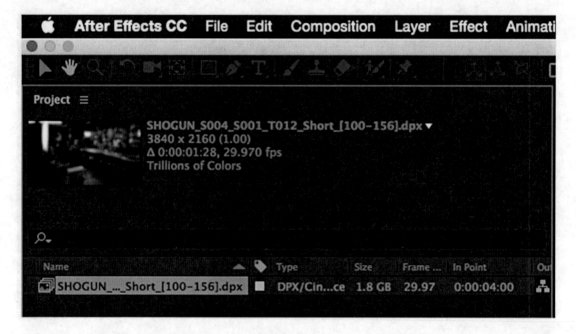

Figure 1-112. *DPX from After Effects*

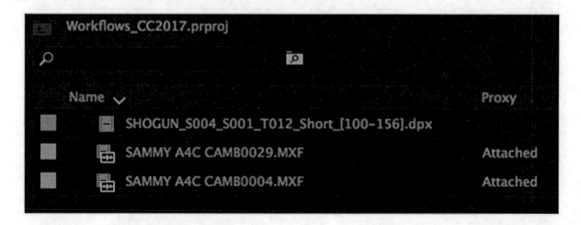

Figure 1-113. *Paste DPX Iinto Premiere project*

New Sequence from Clip—Why Is the Arri Preset Chosen for My DSLR Footage?

The New Sequence from Clip feature matches the first sequence preset (in alphabetical order) that matches the settings of your clip. So, often, you'll see your sequence settings be listed as Arri Cinema or AVC because they are the first ones to match the frame size, frame rate, and so on.

Variable Frame Rate Footage

Footage from smartphones, screen-recording software, and tablets may have **variable frame rate**, which Premiere Pro doesn't like—and your video and audio will get out of sync. Convert with Handbrake, handbrake.fr, or other third-party software to **constant frame rate** before importing. Edit as usual.

Create a Subsequence from a Segment of the Sequence

This feature in Premiere allows you to select a portion of a sequence in the source monitor or in a sequence with an in/out range and create a new sequence that just contains the in/out range with all original media content and track layout. You can also select clips in the sequence and hit the keyboard shortcut for *Make Subsequence*, **Shift + U** (Figure 1-114). Subsequences get a Sub_01, Sub_02, etc. extension added to their sequence name.

Figure 1-114. *Make Subsequence option*

■ **Note** If you make a subsequence out of a Multicam Source Sequence open in the timeline, Premiere will not make a new multicam sequence, just a regular sequence.

Warning When Making a Subsequence

Make sure you target all the video tracks you want to include in your subsequence, or when you click *Make Subsequence*, Premiere will not include video elements in non-targeted tracks.

In Figure 1-115, I did not include V2-V4 targets even though clips are on those tracks. Premiere created the subsequence with only V1 targeted (Figure 1-116).

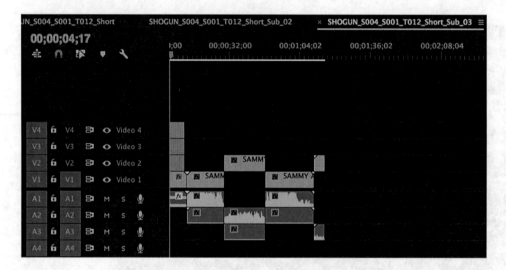

Figure 1-115. Only Track V1 is targeted

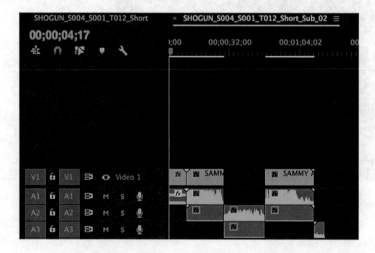

Figure 1-116. Subsequence created with clips on V1 only

In Figure 1-117, V1–V4 were selected, and Premiere created a subsequence with all the tracks intact.

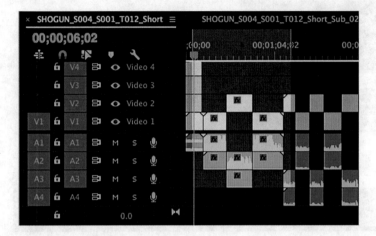

Figure 1-117. *Subsequence with video tracks 1–4 targeted*

Hide What You Don't Need to See

A *Hide* checkbox has been added to the Project panel, and a *View Hidden* option to the contextual menu in the Project panel (Figure 1-118), so that editors can have items in sequences that are not visible in the Project panel by default.

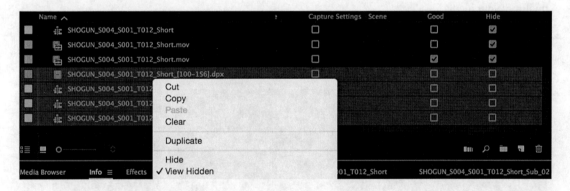

Figure 1-118. *Hide checkbox and View Hidden feature in bin*

Search bins have an option to show hidden clips, even when the Project panel display setting is set not set to View Hidden. The Shogun clip in the preceding figure has *Good* metadata and also a checkbox for *Hide*. A search bin with only "Good" in the Search criteria will not show the clip if View Hidden is set to *off*. Adding *Hidden=True* will reveal the hidden clip, regardless of the View Hidden setting. See Figures 1-119 and 1-120.

Figure 1-119. Search Hidden

Figure 1-120. Search Hidden Good

New Media-Scaling Preferences

There is a new *Default Media Scaling* preference (Figure 1-121) where you can select how you scale your media. These choices now optimize the quality scaling when dealing with differences between your source media frame size and the sequence frame size. When your media is a larger frame size (4K, 6K, 8K) and your sequences are an HD frame size, *Set to Frame Size* is the choice you should make to keep the maximum quality of your media.

If your computer system is not very powerful, you could set this menu to *Scale to Frame Size* while editing. Just remember to change this setting to *Set to Frame Size* before zooming in on the media.

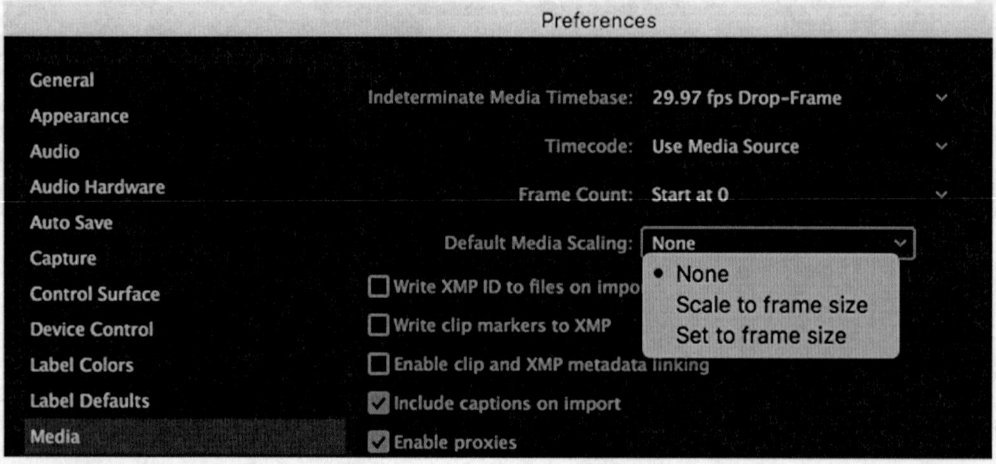

Figure 1-121. Media-scaling preferences

When you're working in a team, most workflow steps are the same as if you were working alone, but there are some extra things you need to keep in mind. Adobe recently introduced Team Projects and Project Locking to make such multi-user workflows easier.

Project Locking

Project locking is a new feature in the CC2017 version of Premiere. You can lock your project from being used by other editors by going into **Preferences ➤ Project Locking** and checking the box for *Enable project locking* (Figure 1-122). The project will be assigned to your user name and should not be useable by other editors until you disable the project-locking feature.

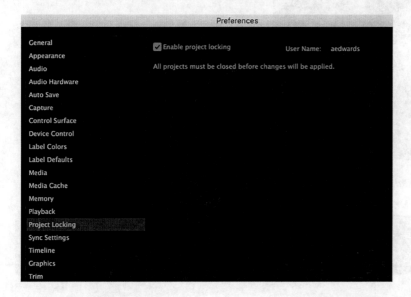

Figure 1-122. *Project locking*

If you go into the folder where you keep your projects, Premiere will add a file next to your project with a new file extension called `.prlock` (Figure 1-123).

Figure 1-123. *Project-locking file*

If you are in a SAN environment or network environment where you share projects, this feature can help keep other editors from accessing your project. If the feature is enabled, the other editor should see a grayed-out icon for your project and not be able to open it.

You can check for locked projects through the media browser by turning on an additional column in your view. Click on the wing menu of the media browser and select *Edit Columns*. Scroll down to the category called *Bin Locked* and check the box (Figure 1-124). Under the *Bin Locked* column you can now see the name of the user who locked the project (Figure 1-125).

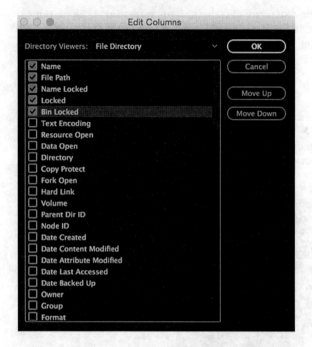

Figure 1-124. *Media browse Edit Columns dialog*

Figure 1-125. *Bin Locked name*

Recovering a Locked Project

There are two main ways to recover a locked project.

1. Open the Premiere project on the same machine with the same user who
    originally locked the project. Then, have the original user unlock the project in
    the preferences and save it again without the lock applied.

2. Follow path to the project file on your storage and delete the lock file next to the
    Premiere project file.

As the project lock feature is new to Premiere, ways of handling locked projects and recovery options
might change. Contact Adobe Support for any additional ways to recover your project if you run into
problems opening the file.

Team Projects (Beta)

With the release of the 2017 version of Premiere, Adobe introduced Team Projects (Beta) so users can collaborate on projects through the Cloud. It includes version control and conflict resolution right inside Premiere so editors can take control of what they share and accept in a project with other editors. The main current requirement to use this feature is for editors to have a Creative Cloud Teams license or an Enterprise License for their Creative Cloud applications. A team account is a bit more expensive, but you also get more storage in Creative Cloud and 24/7 tech support.

Team Projects (Beta) is currently supported in Adobe Premiere Pro, Adobe After Effects, and Adobe Prelude. See Figures 1-126 and 1-127.

Figure 1-126. Team Projects in Premiere and After Effects

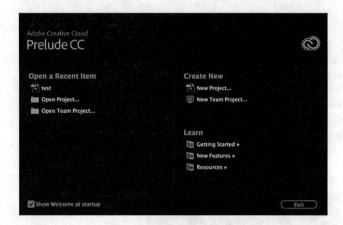

Figure 1-127. *Team Project in Prelude*

If this is your first time creating a team project, you will become the owner of the project and will need to invite other editors to collaborate on the project. Click on the *New Team Project* button, name your project, give it a description, and add collaborators to the project. You use the email address of a fellow Team License or Enterprise Creative Cloud user to send them the invitation (Figure 1-128).

Figure 1-128. *Team Project Invite dialog*

Once the invite has been sent out, other users will get a notification in their Creative Cloud desktop application. Each user must accept the invite to allow them to collaborate on the project. See Figure 1-129.

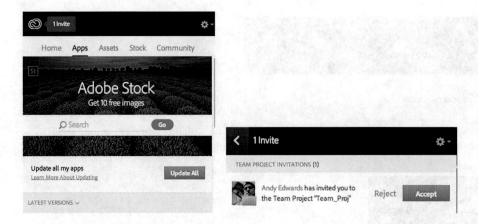

Figure 1-129. *The Creative Cloud app shows you have an invite*

Import your media and start your first edit, which you will share with other editors (Figure 1-130).

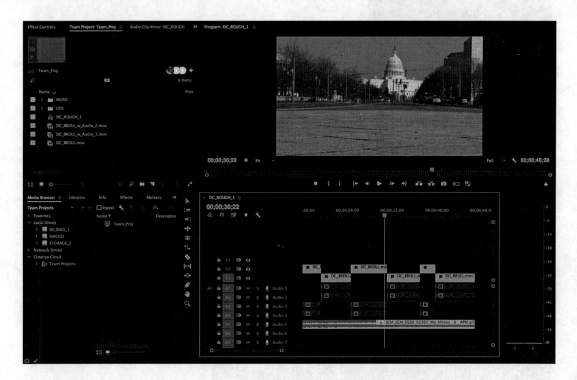

Figure 1-130. *Edit your team project as usual*

Once you are ready to share your first draft with other editors, click on the *Share My Changes* button (Figure 1-131). This button is located at the bottom of the Project panel. This will upload your project changes to the Cloud for the other editors to see.

Figure 1-131. *Upload changes*

When the other editor first opens the team project, the project bin will be empty. The editor needs to click on the *Get Latest Changes* button at the bottom of the Team Projects panel (Figure 1-132).

Figure 1-132. *The other editor must click the button to get the changes*

A Cloud Syncing menu will open (Figure 1-133) and start syncing the project so that the new editor can see the first cut.

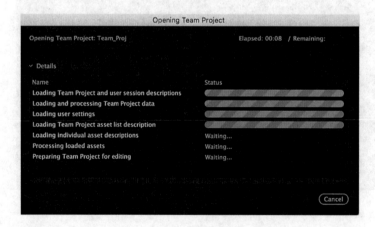

Figure 1-133. *Team Project Cloud Syncing*

The empty Project panel will now populate with all the media, sequences, and folders from the first editor (Figure 1-134).

Figure 1-134. *Team Project bin updates*

After each editor has made changes, you use the same process of uploading and downloading the project through the *Share My Changes* button and the *Get Latest Changes* button. The Comment field (Figures 1-135 and 1-136) allows each editor to communicate the changes made in their cut.

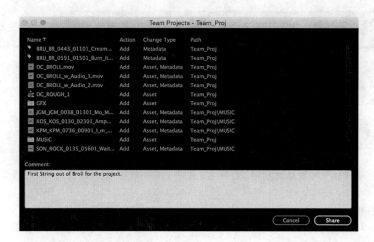

Figure 1-135. *Team Project sharing notes*

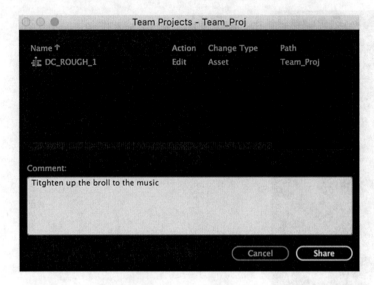

Figure 1-136. *Team Project sharing notes*

History Slider

When you use a team project, the media browser introduces a new slider bar on the right-hand side of the panel (Figure 1-137). You can use this slider to view all the changes and shared versions of the project.

Figure 1-137. *In a team project, the media browser gets a History slider, with comments*

In the media browser, you can right-click on the project name and reveal other options you can choose, including *Browse Latest Version, Browse Previous Versions,* and *Select the Team Project History* (Figure 1-138).

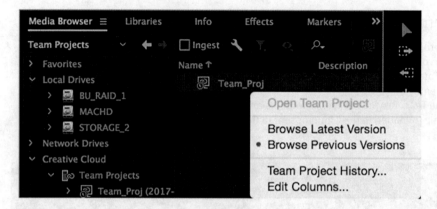

Figure 1-138. *Media browser offers new options in team projects*

Saving a Team Project

One thing you will not see while using a team project is the *Save* option in the File menu (Figure 1-139). All changes are recorded in the Cloud instantaneously.

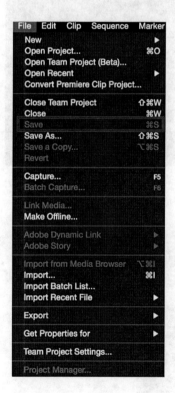

Figure 1-139. *In a team project, there is no Save option*

Media Management

When starting a team project, all media used by the editors will need to be accessible on an SAN, NAS, or Cloud storage that everyone can see. A remote editor can work on a team project on their own external storage away from the internal SAN or NAS; the duplicate media will have to be relinked locally through the Media Management menu.

In Figure 1-140, the Team Project Graphics folder is missing when one of the team editors opens the project. Have the graphic uploaded to the Cloud or sent to the editor so it can be relinked locally.

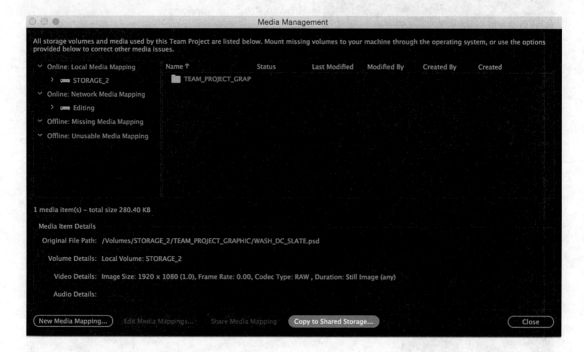

Figure 1-140. *Team Project Media Management*

Resolve Conflicts

When one editor makes a change to the project that conflicts with changes from another editor, select *Resolve Conflicts* (Figure 1-141).

Figure 1-141. *Team Project Resolve Conflicts*

There are three options to address the conflict:

1. Keep your version.

2. Accept the shared version.

3. Copy and rename your version, then accept the shared version.

Converting Your Team Project

Premiere enables you to convert the team project to a local regular project file (Figure 1-142). Click **Edit ➤ Team Project ➤ Convert Team Project to Project**.

Figure 1-142. *A team project can be converted to a standard project*

Archiving a Team Project

When you are done with your team project, you can choose to archive your project by selecting **File ➤ Open Team Project (Beta)** and choosing the *Archive* option (Figure 1-143).

Figure 1-143. Team Project Archive option

Archive Warning

You will receive a warning when you choose to archive a team project (Figure 1-144). All editors and team members accessing the project will no longer get access. This also includes all local copies of the specific team project. If you want to continue to have local access, remember to convert your team project to a regular Premiere project prior to archiving.

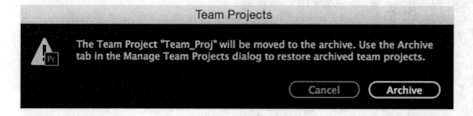

Figure 1-144. Team project archive warning

Restore an Archive

You can restore an archived team project by selecting **File ➤ Open Team Project (Beta)**. Click on the Archive tab, then your team project, then click *Restore* (Figure 1-145). You can delete your team project from this menu as well. You will receive a warning that deleting your team project is a permanent change and cannot be undone.

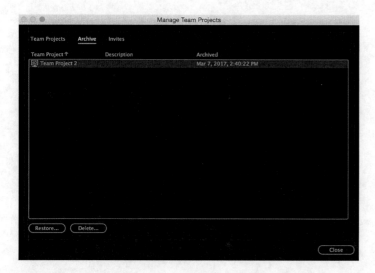

Figure 1-145. *Team project archive restore*

Summary

If you use the techniques you've learned in this chapter, you will have more time for creative decisions and fine-tuning. You will not use all these techniques, but you must make sure all your workflow steps are as effective as possible. Hopefully, I've managed to raise your awareness of workflows, and I hope you've learned something that makes you change the way you work, so you can edit faster.

You may wonder why I never mentioned backups again after we started on the rough cut. That's because you already had all the media files in the project by then, so the only file you need a backup of from there on is your Premiere Pro project file (.prproj). If you set your Project Auto Save destination to a Cloud service like your DropBox folder, OneDrive folder, or Google Drive, you'll have a backup in the Cloud. You set this under Scratch Disks in Project Settings.

You'll find clever workflow tips in Chapter 4, "Editing Tips and Techniques," where you can read more in-depth tips about multi-sequence workflows.

CHAPTER 2

■ ■ ■

Proxy Workflow

By Jarle Leirpoll and Andy Edwards

4K, 6K, or even 8K footage is becoming commonplace in all forms of video editing. These large file sizes can bring your video hardware to its knees if you don't have massive hard-drive raids or very fast network throughput to play back the large files. By using a proxy workflow, an editor can take advantage of the smaller file sizes to build out a project before switching the footage to full resolution for final output.

Premiere now has support for native formats, including 6K and 8K files from the Red Weapon camera. Even if you want to work with a laptop, when you ingest your footage you can now generate proxies that automatically match up with the full-resolution media. Figure 2-1 highlights some important user interface (UI) elements in the proxy workflow.

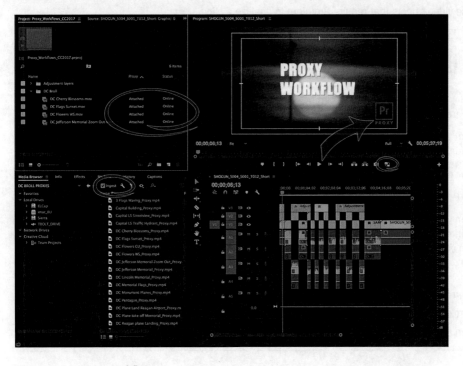

Figure 2-1. *Proxy workflow*

© Jarle Leirpoll 2017
J. Leirpoll et al., *The Cool Stuff in Premiere Pro*, DOI 10.1007/978-1-4842-2890-6_2

Why Proxies?

When you choose to ingest, you can also create proxies. Proxies are lower-quality and easier-to-decode copies of your media that are easier for the system to process. Your system may struggle if you ask it to play back three camera angles of 6K RAW or 4K H.264, while it will play seven streams of DNxHD 35 or ProRes LT at 1080p without breaking a sweat. Proxies are also much more responsive when you're scrubbing and shuttling the timeline, and overall you get a much nicer experience while editing.

If you find the performance of your system to be less than stellar when you edit, you will probably want to use proxies during the creative process. Then, after the edit is done, you can switch back to the full-quality original media before color grading and finishing. This can be done with a click of a button—the *Toggle Proxies* button (Figure 2-2). You can add your own proxy presets if you don't like the default formats, codecs, or settings.

Figure 2-2. *Switch between proxies and original files with the Toggle Proxies button*

■ **Note** If the original clips are not offline, Premiere will always use them when you render previews, export your media, or use video effects that require Premiere to analyze a clip.

The Main Ways to Get Your Proxies

There are several ways to create proxies. It can be done automatically or manually, in Premiere or by third-party software or hardware.

- When you import high-res media, you can auto-create proxies on ingest, or do it manually from a bin later for more control.

- Some recording formats create in-camera proxies.

- Third-party software or hardware transcoders can create proxies.

- When you work remotely with another editor, you may get only the proxy files and no original media. The switch to original media files before export will be done by the main editor, who is the only one who has them.

■ **Note** If the proxy files are created outside of Premiere, make sure they have _Proxy added to their file names. The proxy file for Dog.ari should be named Dog_Proxy.mov. This will ensure that the one-click switching between originals and proxies works as expected.

Ingest

Earlier versions of Premiere Pro offered no help with file management on ingest. You had to manually copy all your files using Finder (MacOS) or Explorer (Win) and then import the media into Premiere. With the summer 2016 release, we got a new Ingest tab in the Project Settings panel, as shown in Figure 2-3.

Figure 2-3. *Ingest setting*

Edit During Ingest

You can use the files immediately while the complete import of media finishes in the background. An example: If you choose to copy and transcode from a camera card, you can start editing as soon as you've imported the media, and Premiere will use the files on the camera card. Whenever a file has been copied to your hard drive, Premiere will automatically switch to using that file instead.

Then, when a proxy file has finished transcoding, Premiere will switch to that file. It all happens seamlessly in the background in Media Encoder, and your system will get more responsive as more files are copied and transcoded.

You can easily switch between original and proxy files when editing, even on multiple systems. It's just one click.

Ingest Warnings

If you move to another edit system and launch Premiere with a copy of your project, Premiere will warn you that the ingest settings are not enabled on your new edit system (Figure 2-4). Click on the *Settings* button to adjust your Proxy settings, or if you want to ignore the Ingest settings, click on the *Disable* button.

Figure 2-4. *Ingest warning*

■ **Beware**   Check your Ingest settings before you import your media. Once started, it's not always easy to stop the process, and if you didn't want Premiere to copy and transcode files it's a hassle to undo, delete, and remove stuff.

Ingest Settings and Media Browser

Premiere's Media Browser panel allows you to ingest media automatically in the background (Figure 2-5). You can begin editing while the proxies are created.

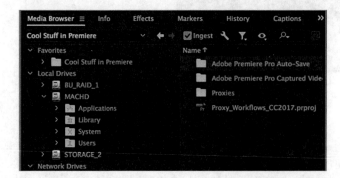

Figure 2-5. *Check the Ingest box in the Media Browser panel to toggle the Ingest option on or off*

The wrench icon opens the Project Settings dialog, where you can choose your Ingest settings (Figure 2-6). This might look similar to the *Ingest* checkbox in the Project Settings dialog you would see when starting a new project. It is actually the same interface, and both are kept in sync with the Media Browser panel's settings.

Figure 2-6. *Project's Ingest settings*

Ingest Settings: A Deeper Look

When Ingest is enabled, you can choose one of the four available settings you want to start automatically when files are imported into the project. Whatever method you choose for adding new media into the project, it will automatically start the chosen ingest process. Let's look at the options.

> **Copy** - Copies media to the Primary Destination folder you've chosen. Once copied, the clips in the project point to these copies of the files on disk. The bonus with this choice is that the copy is made with MD5 Checksum verification (Figures 2-7 and 2-8). Some productions require this verification for insurance reasons. After this task is complete, the clips in the project will point to the copies of the files.

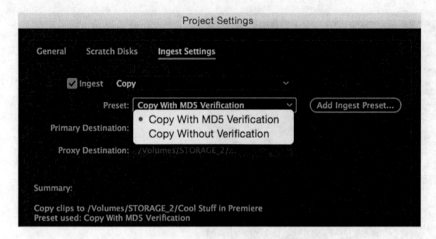

Figure 2-7. *Copy ingest MD5 checksum*

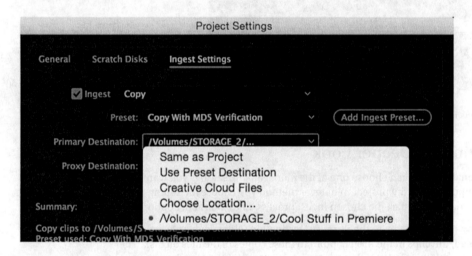

Figure 2-8. *Copy ingest location*

Transcode - Transcodes the media to a new format in the Primary Destination folder you've chosen. The format is of course specified by the chosen preset (Figure 2-9). Once transcoded, the clips in the project point to these transcoded copies of the files on disk.

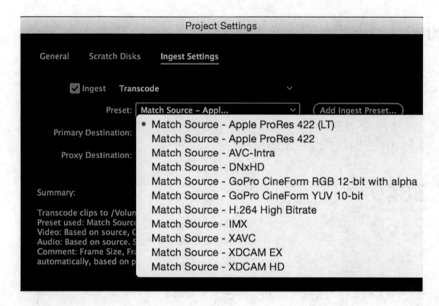

Figure 2-9. *Transcode preset options*

As shown in Figure 2-10, you have multiple options for choosing your primary destination.

Figure 2-10. *Transcode primary destination*

Create Proxy - Creates proxies in the Proxy Destination folder you've chosen and attaches them to the media. The format is again specified by the chosen preset. After proxies are generated, they are automatically attached to the clips in the project.

Copy and Create Proxies - This is a combo operation doing both operations as just specified. You can choose a custom location for proxies, or even the *Creative Cloud Files* folder, which would sync the files automatically to the cloud.

Creating Proxies

Premiere comes with nine basic proxy presets that are based on certain frame sizes. If you need additional frame sizes, you will have to create your own ingest preset that has evenly divisible frame dimensions. Divide your source frame size aspect ratio (width by height, as shown in Figure 2-11).

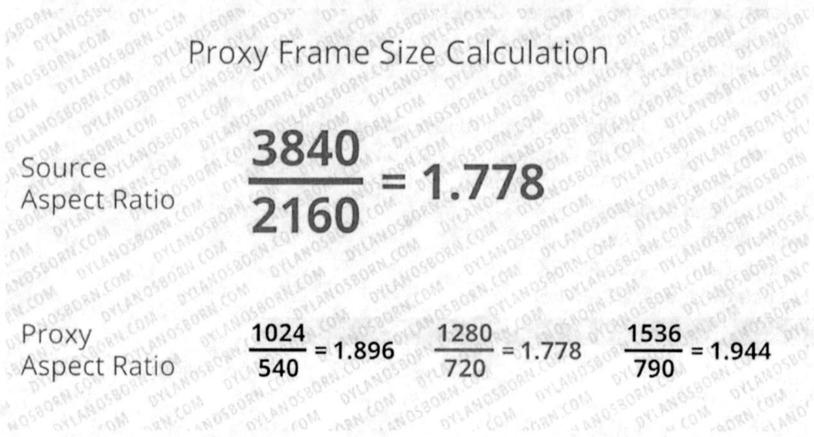

Proxy Frame Size Calculation

Source
Aspect Ratio

$$\frac{3840}{2160} = 1.778$$

Proxy
Aspect Ratio

$$\frac{1024}{540} = 1.896 \qquad \frac{1280}{720} = 1.778 \qquad \frac{1536}{790} = 1.944$$

Figure 2-11. *Proxy frame size calculation. Image courtesy of Dylan Osborn.*

Dylan Osborn, one of the co-authors of this book, has graciously provided a worksheet that has all the frame sizes broken out for you to choose from. You can find the proxy frame size conversion chart (Figure 2-12) on Dylan's website: dylanosborn.com/training/done-with-dylan/.

Proxy Frame Size Conversion Chart

Find your source media frame size. Then use one of the smaller, matching aspect ratio frame sizes for your proxies. Green indicates one of the default Premiere Pro ingest preset frame sizes.

Source Media Frame Size	Proxy Frame Size	Small Proxy Frame Size	Aspect Ratio
8192 x 4320	1024 x 540	512 x 270	1.896
6560 x 3100	1640 x 775	328 x 155	2.116
6144 x 3160	1536 x 790	768 x 395	1.944
5120 x 2880	1280 x 720	640 x 360	1.778
5120 x 2700	1024 x 540	512 x 270	1.896
4608 x 2592	1280 x 720	640 x 360	1.778
4608 x 1920	1536 x 640	768 x 320	2.400
4512 x 2376	1504 x 792	752 x 396	1.899
4320 x 2880	1440 x 960	720 x 480	1.500
4096 x 2636	1024 x 659	512 x 330	1.554
4096 x 2304	1280 x 720	640 x 360	1.778
4096 x 2160	1024 x 540	512 x 270	1.896
4096 x 1716	1024 x 429	512 x 215	2.387
4000 x 2160	1000 x 540	500 x 270	1.852
3840 x 2160	1280 x 720	640 x 360	1.778
3424 x 2202	1712 x 1101	856 x 551	1.555
3424 x 1926	1280 x 720	640 x 360	1.778
3414 x 2198	1707 x 1099	596 x 384	1.553
3200 x 1800	1280 x 720	640 x 360	1.778
3168 x 2160	1056 x 720	528 x 360	1.467
3168 x 1782	1280 x 720	640 x 360	1.778
3168 x 1778	1584 x 889	528 x 296	1.782
3168 x 1772	1584 x 886	528 x 295	1.788
3154 x 1764	1584 x 886	528 x 295	1.788
3072 x 2560	1296 x 1080	648 x 540	1.200
3072 x 1620	1024 x 540	512 x 270	1.896
2880 x 2160	1280 x 960	640 x 480	1.333
2880 x 1620	1280 x 720	640 x 360	1.778
2868 x 1612	1281 x 720	641 x 360	1.779
2704 x 2028	1280 x 960	640 x 480	1.333
2704 x 1520	1281 x 720	641 x 360	1.779
2592 x 2160	1296 x 1080	648 x 540	1.200
2578 x 2160	1289 x 1080	645 x 540	1.194
2560 x 2145	1280 x 1073	644 x 540	1.193
2432 x 1366	1280 x 719	641 x 360	1.780
2400 x 1350	1280 x 720	640 x 360	1.778
2048 x 1920	1280 x 1200	640 x 600	1.067
2048 x 1536	1280 x 960	640 x 480	1.333
2048 x 1152	1280 x 720	640 x 360	1.778
2048 x 1080	1024 x 540	512 x 270	1.896
2048 x 858	1024 x 429	512 x 215	2.387
1920 x 1440	1280 x 960	640 x 480	1.333
1920 x 1080	1280 x 720	640 x 360	1.778
1280 x 720	640 x 360	320 x 180	1.778

This chart incorporates frame sizes from these camera manufacturers:

AJA VIDEO SYSTEMS   ARRI

Blackmagicdesign   Canon

DJI   GoPro Be a HERO

Panasonic   SONY

© 2016 Dylan Osborn / Adobe Premiere Pro Training / dylanosborn.com

Figure 2-12. *Dylan Osborn's proxy frame size chart*

Creating Proxies after importing

If you choose to import your media into Premiere and not run the ingest workflow, you can create your proxies after you have imported all your media in the Project bin. Highlight your media, right-click, and choose **Proxy ➤ Create Proxies** as shown in Figure 2-13.

Figure 2-13. *Create proxy from bin*

Choose your format (Figure 2-14) and preset, either H.264 for the smallest file size or QuickTime ProRes (Mac only) for double the proxy file size but better quality. Or, lastly, choose GoPro Cineform, which is six times the size (Figure 2-15). Also, choose your destination.

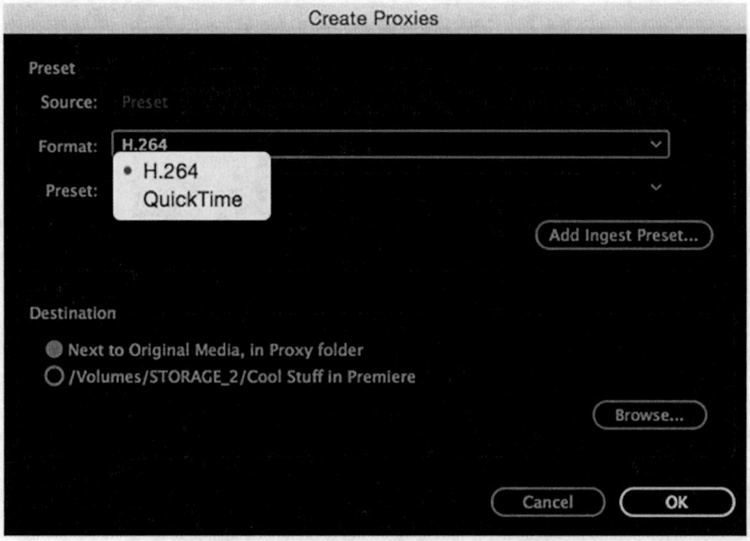

Figure 2-14. *Proxy format choices*

Figure 2-15. *Proxy format QuickTime options*

Adobe Media Encoder/Progress Panel

Once you have imported your media, done the math, chosen your proxy preset, chosen your destination, and clicked *OK*, Adobe Media Encoder will launch in the background and start creating your proxies (Figure 2-16).

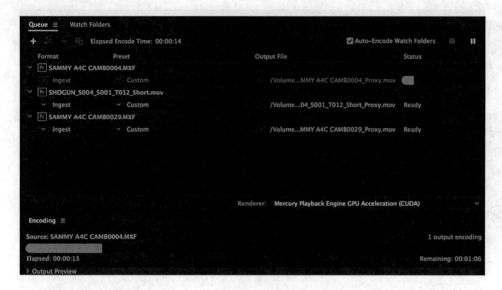

Figure 2-16. Adobe Media Encoder creating proxies

If you want to monitor proxy creation inside of Premiere rather than in Adobe Media Encoder, Premiere provides a Progress window you can open up. Choose **Window ➤ Progress** (Figures 2-17 and 2-18).

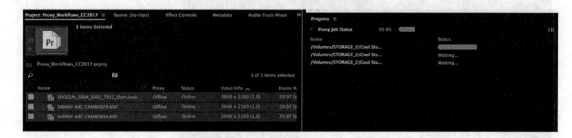

Figure 2-17. Proxy Progress window

Figure 2-18. Proxy progress complete

Once complete, you will see the word *Attached* now listed under the Proxy Metadata column.

Metadata Column for Proxies

If your Project bin is not set up to display metadata proxy information, right-click on the column header to bring up the Metadata Display menu (Figure 2-19).

Figure 2-19. *Right-click Metadata column to get the Metadata Display choice*

In the search box, type the word *Proxy*, then check the *Proxy* box to display the column header (Figure 2-20). Also, remember to add the *Status* metadata column as well. Type the word *Status* in the search box and check the box (Figure 2-21).

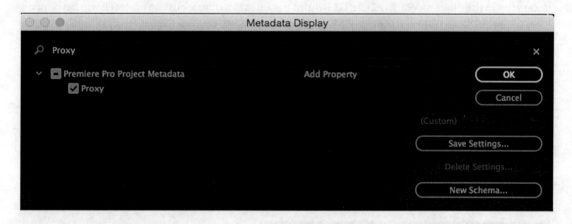

Figure 2-20. *Proxy checkbox*

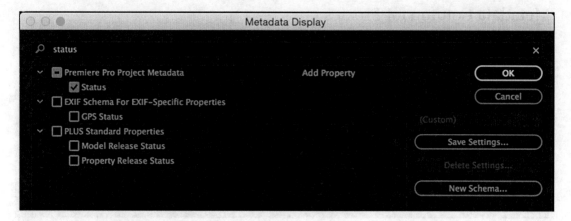

Figure 2-21. *Status checkbox*

Create Your Own Proxy Presets

The default proxy presets are OK for basic use, but if you use proxies a lot, you will probably want to add your own customized presets. This is necessary if you use footage with aspect ratios other than the defaults, and if you want to use other codecs, like DNxHD. It's also a good idea to create custom presets if you have special needs for audio-track types and if you want to watermark the proxies.

Watermarking Your Proxies

To avoid confusion while editing with proxy media, it is highly recommended to use a text watermark or graphic overlay on your proxies. This allows you to visually see if you are using full-resolution media or the proxy-file media while editing your project. To accomplish this task, follow this two-step process.

Step 1 – Create an Encoding Preset

Open Adobe Media Encoder and click **Preset ➤ Create Encoding Preset** or go to the Preset Browser and push the + button ➤ **Create Encoding Preset**. See Figure 2-22.

Figure 2-22. *Adobe Media Encoder Preset Browser*

In the Export Settings, choose H.264 for your proxy format. Then, adjust the bit rate to a lower setting (1 for Target Bitrate and 2 for Maximum Bitrate, as shown in Figure 2-23). Hit the *Match Source* button to keep the remaining settings the same from your source media. Then, uncheck the *Width & Height* box and input the proxy frame size you have already determined to match your source footage (Figure 2-24).

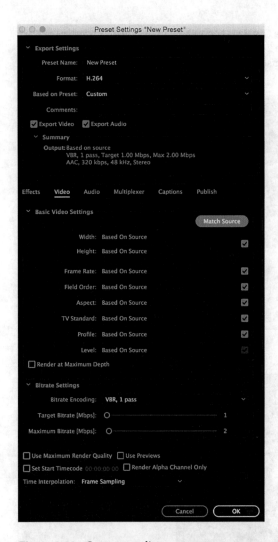

Figure 2-23. *Create encoding preset*

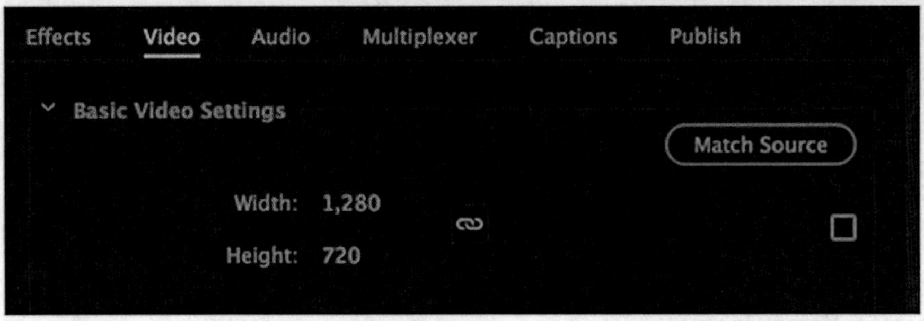

Figure 2-24. *Preset width and height adjustment*

Click on the Effects menu, scroll down to the Name Overlay section, and check the box. Under the Format menu, choose *Prefix and Suffix Only* (see Figure 2-25). Type in the word *PROXY* in the Suffix box. Choose the position of where you want the text and adjust opacity (Figure 2-26).

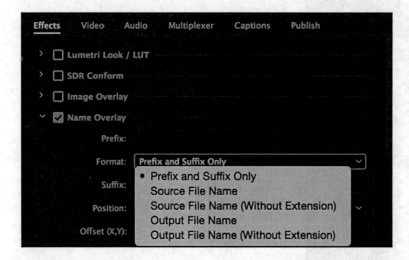

Figure 2-25. *Preset name overlay*

Figure 2-26. *Preset Name Overlay Suffix*

Apply a Graphic to Your Proxy

If you want to use a premade graphic for your proxies, in the Effects window check the *Image Overlay* box. In the Applied drop-down, find the path to the folder on your hard drive that contains the graphic overlay and select it. Then, choose the position and adjust opacity. See Figure 2-27 for details.

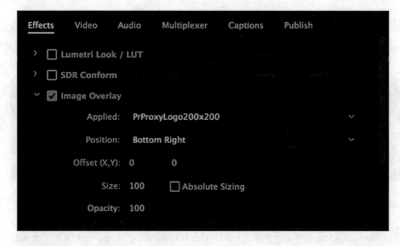

Figure 2-27. *Preset image overlay*

You can download the premade proxy images from Dylan Osborn here: dylanosborn.com/training/ done-with-dylan/.

Save your custom encoding preset so you can later import into Premiere to create your proxies with a watermark or graphic overlay.

Naming Your Encoding Preset

Name your proxy encoding preset carefully, as the .epr files are saved in the same folder as your regular Media Encoder presets (Figure 2-28).

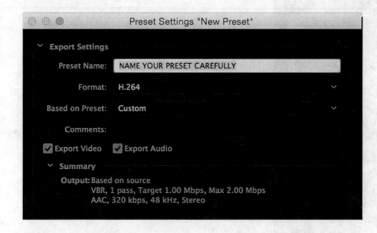

Figure 2-28. *Give the encoding preset a good name*

Step 2 – Create an Ingest Preset

Go to the Preset Browser in Media Encoder and choose *Create Ingest Preset* (Figure 2-29).

Figure 2-29. *Create ingest preset*

Choose *Transcode files to Destination* (yes, making proxies includes transcoding) and select a folder for your proxies, then choose format and the encoding preset you just created (Figure 2-30).

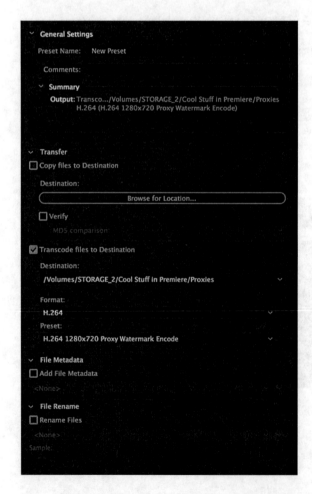

Figure 2-30. *Choose transcode destination, format, and preset*

Creating a Rename Preset

If you want Premiere to auto-connect to your proxy files, you need to make sure the output files get _Proxy added to their file name. To do this, we'll create a Rename preset (Figure 2-31).

Figure 2-31. *Create file Rename preset*

The first field is the file name (Figure 2-32).

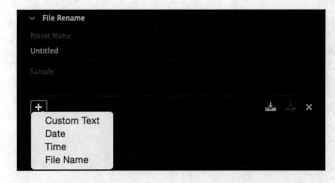

Figure 2-32. *File name*

The second is the suffix. Type in *_Proxy* (Figure 2-33).

Figure 2-33. *File name plus suffix*

113

Save the renaming preset for future use (Figure 2-34).

Figure 2-34. *Save the Rename preset*

Save your Ingest preset and be careful to not name this preset the same as your other proxy presets (Figure 2-35).

Figure 2-35. *Final Ingest preset settings*

Add the Ingest Preset to the Proxy Presets List

Now, when back inside Premiere, you can add your Ingest preset to create proxies from the list. Right-click and choose **Proxy ➤ Create Proxies**, and then click the *Add Ingest Preset* button (Figure 2-36).

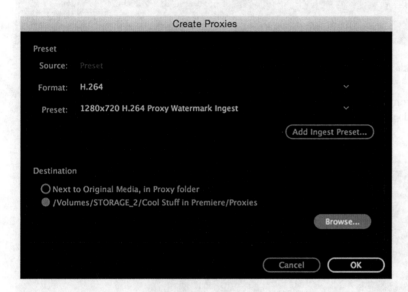

Figure 2-36. *Add Ingest preset in Premiere*

Work Offline with Proxies

If you have a beefy system at home but need to take the project on the road on a not-so-beefy laptop, it makes sense to edit with proxies only. You don't want to fill your laptop drive with large original media files, but you have enough drive space for the smaller proxy files.

To use this workflow, create proxies as usual on your main system and then add metadata if you want. Save the project and exit Premiere. Copy the project file and the *Proxies* folder to the laptop.

On the laptop, when you get the missing media warning for the high-res originals (Figure 2-37), choose *Offline All* and edit with proxies only. The *Toggle Proxy* button now does nothing (another reason to add watermarks to proxies). All project metadata is still present and searchable (Figure 2-38).

Clip Name	File Name
Cenote Ojos Indigenas.mp4	Cenote Ojos Indigenas.mp4
Punta_Cana_01.mp4	Punta_Cana_01.mp4
Punta_Cana_03.mp4	Punta_Cana_03.mp4
Punta_Cana_11.mp4	Punta_Cana_11.mp4

Figure 2-37. *Offline the missing full-res media files*

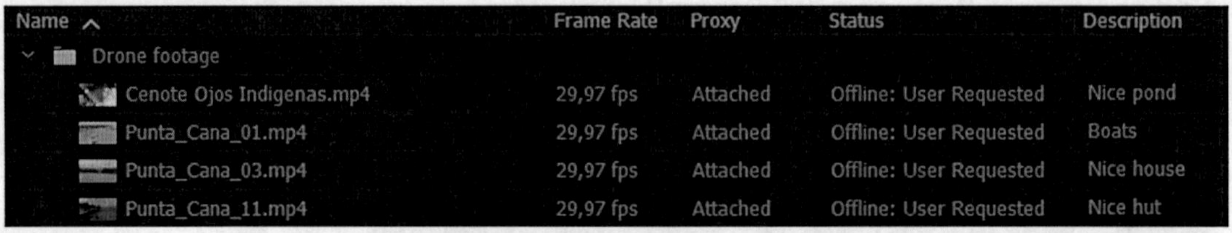

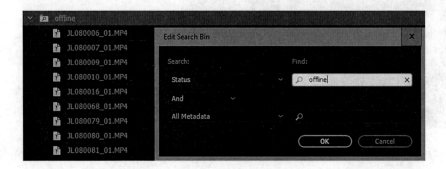

Name
Frame Rate
Proxy
Status
Description
Drone footage
Cenote Ojos Indigenas.mp4
29,97 fps
Attached
Offline: User Requested
Nice pond
Punta_Cana_01.mp4
29,97 fps
Attached
Offline: User Requested
Boats
Punta_Cana_03.mp4
29,97 fps
Attached
Offline: User Requested
Nice house
Punta_Cana_11.mp4
29,97 fps
Attached
Offline: User Requested
Nice hut

Figure 2-38. *Proxies are attached, and the metadata is intact*

When you come home, copy the project file from the laptop to the main system and open it. Create a Search bin that looks for media with the status "offline" (Figure 2-39). I keep one in my template project for convenience.

offline
JL080006_01.MP4
JL080007_01.MP4
JL080009_01.MP4
JL080010_01.MP4
JL080016_01.MP4
JL080068_01.MP4
JL080079_01.MP4
JL080080_01.MP4
JL080081_01.MP4
Edit Search Bin
Search:
Find:
Status
offline
And
All Metadata
OK
Cancel

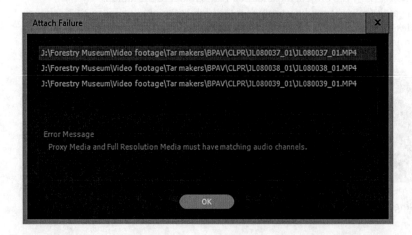

Figure 2-39. *Create a Search bin for offline files*

Select the clips in the Offline bin, right-click, and choose **Proxy ➤ Reconnect Full Resolution Media**. Locate the first file that Premiere asks for and attach it. The rest will be found automatically. If you get an error about audio channels' not matching (known bug in 2017.1.2 version, see Figure 2-40), use the *Link Media* option for each clip instead.

Attach Failure
J:\Forestry Museum\Video footage\Tar makers\BPAV\CLPR\JL080037_01\JL080037_01.MP4
J:\Forestry Museum\Video footage\Tar makers\BPAV\CLPR\JL080038_01\JL080038_01.MP4
J:\Forestry Museum\Video footage\Tar makers\BPAV\CLPR\JL080039_01\JL080039_01.MP4
Error Message
Proxy Media and Full Resolution Media must have matching audio channels.
OK

Figure 2-40. *If you get a matching audio channels error, use Link Media instead*

■ **Note**   If you want to save the steps of copying files back and forth, save the project and proxies in your DropBox, Google Drive, or OneDrive folder—or use the Creative Cloud folder if you have enough space.

Proxy Workflow Tips

Before you tie up your edit system making proxies, see if you can offload the proxy-creation process to another machine. If you have access to a Telestream Vantage Server (Figure 2-41), you can create a workflow to process the original media and then reattach the proxy files inside Premiere.

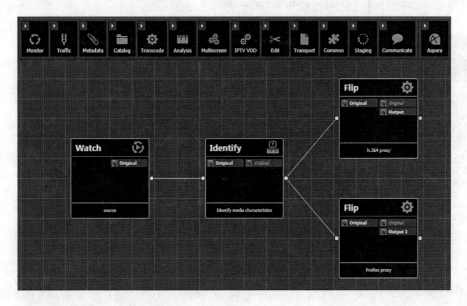

Figure 2-41. *Telestream workflows*

If you are using a single machine to create proxies while you edit, remember that, by default, all ingest operations are paused during playback of files inside Premiere. You can change this if you go to **Preferences ➤ Playback** and uncheck *Pause Media Encoder queue during playback*. Only do this if you have a beefy system or if you can live with stuttering playback.

Camera Cards

Create a uniquely named parent folder when using source camera folder structures. Place your camera folder structure inside this folder when copying the sources using an ingest setting. To prevent data loss of your camera folder structure, make sure you name your destination folder properly, as this may result in name conflicts with multiple camera cards and lead to ingest failures or overwriting of your files.

Partial Proxies

There is no support for partial proxies yet. You always get a proxy file the same length as the original file. As a workaround, you can create a subclip and make proxies of only the subclipped portion of the original file.

Proxy Information

If you want to view information on your proxy clips, you can right-click on your source media and choose *Properties* to view information (Figure 2-42). Or, select your source media in your Project bin and click on the Info tab inside Premiere. The properties of a source clip with a proxy attached contains information of the full-res source in the top, and below that shows information for the proxy file.

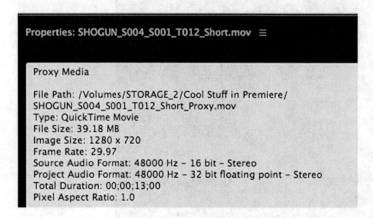

Figure 2-42. *Proxy properties*

Rendering and Exporting

When you render previews, export your sequences, or use certain effects (Warp Stabilizer, Rolling Shutter Repair, Morph Cut), Premiere will always use and display full-res, even if you toggle on/off the *Proxies* button. If your full-res source material is offline and the proxy file is the only file available, then the proxy will be used.

Camera Card Naming Confusion

Most editors who have been dealing with camera card media instead of tape-based media have by now dealt with the common naming structure for files. How many times have you received multiple camera cards that have the same C0001.mxf file? If you plan on running the proxy workflow for similarly named files, be aware that this can cause confusion with the Attach and Link Media menus if you choose to *Relink others automatically*. If you are not careful, you can attach the wrong clip. To avoid this problem, uncheck the *Relink others automatically* box and attach similarly named clips manually one by one.

No Full Support for Proxies Yet

As of the 2017 spring release, the proxy workflow still had a few limitations. Expect at least some of these to go away in future updates.

Project Manager, Render and Replace, AAF, FCP XML, EDL, OMF, Modify Audio Channels, and Interpret Footage are not supported with a proxy workflow. Red R3D Full Res to H.264 Proxy is supported, but Red R3D Full Res to DPX Proxy is not supported.

Proxy Attaching Scenarios

What happens when you quit a Premiere project and AME is still in the middle of building your proxies?

1. All proxy clips that finished encoding while your Premiere project was still open should now be attached when you reopen your project.

2. All proxy clips that finished encoding in AME while your Premiere project was closed should now be attached when you reopen your project.

3. All proxy clips that are still processing in AME, or have not started encoding, will have offline proxies when you open up your Premiere project.

If your proxy clips are still being processed in AME and you close and open Premiere again, you might not see your proxies attached. If you quit and do not save the project, then reopen the project, the proxies should now be attached to your media.

If your proxies finish encoding in AME while Premiere is closed and you do not see the files attached when you reopen the project, you can manually reattach them in the Project bin. Right-click on your media files and choose **Proxy ➤ Attach Proxies**. See Figure 2-43.

Figure 2-43. *Attach proxies*

Multi-Camera Proxy

If you run into a problem where your proxy files will not attach to your multi-camera media, try the following steps:

1. Check if the *Metadata Display* column for proxy (in list view in your bin) is reporting "Attached" or "Offline."

2. If proxies are "Attached," save your project, restart Premiere, and reset your preferences (more later on this).

3. With Premiere closed, move your proxy file folder to a new location, open Premiere where the proxies show "Offline," and reattach the proxies manually.

To reset the preferences, press **Alt** (Opt) while launching Premiere Pro. You can release the key when the splash screen appears.

Proxy Workflow Gotchas

Proxy generation in Premiere will do its best to match the original clip's audio settings. If the Preset/Format does not support the audio channels, then it will fail to create proxies, and you'll get a warning in the Events panel.

▪ **Note**   The H.264 proxy presets only support two audio channels. QuickTime has the largest audio channel support, so the QuickTime wrapper would be your best bet.

Audio Issues in the 2017.1.2 Version

Just like proxy generation ignores the frame rate interpretation in the Modify Clip dialog, the settings in the **Modify ➤ Audio Channels** dialog are also ignored—even by the built-in proxy presets. Since your Default Audio Tracks settings in Audio Preferences are just a way to make Premiere use the chosen settings for Modify Clip, that preference is also ignored. So, if the camera has tagged a clip as stereo audio, and you have the Default Audio Tracks settings set to interpret stereo media as dual mono, you might be in trouble.

The proxy generation will work fine in that case, and you should be fine. But if you ever try to do the **Proxy ➤ Reconnect Full Resolution Media** thing after offline editing, you will get an error message (see Figure 2-40 a few pages ago). If you choose *Use File* in the **Modify ➤ Audio Channels** dialog before you create proxies (Figure 2-44), you will not get this error.

Figure 2-44. *Set Use File in Modify Audio Channels dialog as a workaround in the 2017.1.2 version*

Knowing this, a workaround would be to select all the clips, hit **Shift+G** to get the dialog, and choose *Use File*. Then, create proxies, and when the job has been sent to Adobe Media Encoder you can safely hit **Shift+G** again and choose the Mono preset, or whatever other preset you had before. Let's hope that Adobe can fix this in future releases.

Interpreted Footage and Proxies

The **Modify ➤ Interpret Footage ➤ Frame Rate** setting in Premiere does not currently (summer 2017) carry over to proxies. So, if you interpret 50 fps footage to 25 fps for slo-mo, the proxy file will still be 50 fps, and the footage will not be slo-mo when you show proxies—but it will when showing original media! This can be very confusing. Let's look at a workaround.

Select the clips in the bin, right-click, and choose **Proxy ➤ Create Proxies** as usual. Immediately stop the queue in Adobe Media Encoder—before the first clip is finished—and choose to not finish the current file. Now, select all the jobs, right-click, and use the *Interpret Footage* option in Adobe Media Encoder.

You will get a warning sign on the first job line in Adobe Media Encoder since you stopped the encoding. Duplicate it via the right-click menu or by hitting **Ctrl+D** (Cmd+D). Then, delete the original line and the partially finished proxy file. You may have to exit Premiere to be allowed to delete it.

When the proxies are ready, attach them manually in Premiere: right-click and choose **Proxy ➤ Attach Proxies**.

Match Your Audio Tracks

For the reasons explained earlier, it's good practice to make the proxies' presets match the exact number of audio tracks in your video files. For example, if you create an Encode preset in Media Encoder that has two-channel stereo and your media actually has eight channels of audio, you will get a warning when trying to set up your proxy media ingest (Figure 2-45).

Figure 2-45. *Audio Channels mismatch error*

Use an application like MediaInfo (`sourceforge.net/projects/mediainfo/`) to analyze your media prior to making your encode and ingest presets. MediaInfo will give you the exact number of audio channels you have in your video files so you can match the needed number of audio channels and avoid errors while ingesting and attaching proxies to your files (Figure 2-46).

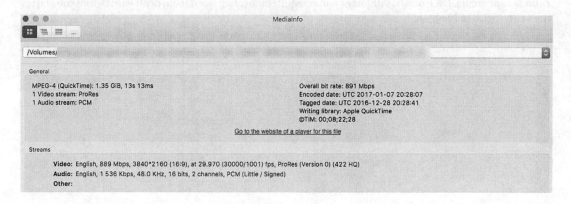

Figure 2-46. *MediInfo shows existing audio channels*

If you create proxy files outside of your Premiere project on another computer, you can attach them manually (Figure 2-47). If your audio channels from your encode and ingest presets do not match the source media, Premiere will give you an Attach Failure warning that the channels are incorrect (Figure 2-48).

Figure 2-47. *Attach proxies manually*

Figure 2-48. *Audio channel mismatch error*

Create Custom Encode and Ingest Presets for Each Camera

When you deal with a lot of different cameras on a production shoot, you need to make sure all your Media Encoder presets match the audio channels properly. In Figure 2-49, you will see many folders for different camera card media. Each one has different audio requirements that need to be dealt with before you start the proxy ingest in Premiere.

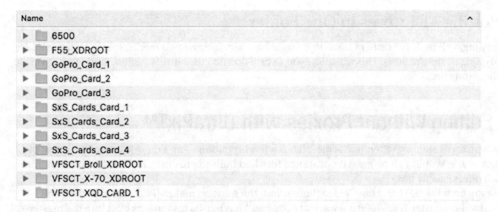

Figure 2-49. *Camera card media can have two channels, four channels, or even eight channels of audio. Build your presets properly to avoid problems in Premiere.*

Create custom Media Encoder presets for each of the camera cards shown in Figure 2-49. When you label your presets during the creation process, make sure to include the number of audio channels so you don't run into any warnings when creating proxies or attaching proxies (Figure 2-50).

⊒ 6500_XAVC_2CH_1280X720_Prores_Ingest.epr
⊒ 6500_XAVC_2CH_1280X720_Prores_WM.epr
⊒ F55_MXF_4CHM_1280X720_ProResProxy_Ingest.epr
⊒ F55_MXF_4CHM_1280X720_ProResProxy_WM.epr
⊒ GOPRO 2CH 1280X720 Proxy_WM.epr
⊒ GOPRO_2CH_Proxy_Ingest.epr
⊒ MXF_8CH_ProRes_Proxy_Ingest.epr
⊒ MXF_8CHM_1280X720_ProResProxy_WM.epr
⊒ X-70_MXF_4CH_Prores_Ingest.epr.epr
⊒ X-70_MXF_4CH_Prores_WM.epr
⊒ XQD_MXF_8CH_1280X720_PrResProxy_Ingest.epr
⊒ XQD_MXF_8CH_1280X720_PrResProxy_WM.epr

Figure 2-50. *Custom Proxy Presets*

Duplicate Camera Card Media

Pay attention to camera card source media names. On multiple-camera productions, cameras can record the same file name; for example, C001.MXF. If you create proxies of the source media, Premiere is smart enough to truncate the files with a _1 of the same name file. A problem could arise when you go to attach proxies to your full-res files. You might attach the wrong proxy to the wrong source media from the camera card. If you manually attach the proxy files incorrectly because of a duplicate file name, you can check for this mismatch by toggling the *Proxy* button in the PGM monitor. If the original high-res media doesn't match the proxy, check for duplicate file names in your source folders.

Once you find the media that is incorrectly attached, the quickest way to fix this issue is to detach the proxy from your source media by moving the proxy file to a new folder. This will cause Premiere to show the proxy as offline and give you a chance to swap the proxy to the proper file.

Avoid Putting All Proxies in One Folder

If you are dealing with multiple camera cards that might have similarly named media, create separate folders for your proxy ingest destinations. This will allow you to drill down to the correct camera card folder to avoid attaching the wrong proxy file.

Proxy Editing Without Proxies with UltraPix™

Although the proxy workflow in Premiere is nice, it has a few limitations—and they do come at the cost of time and disk space. Wouldn't it be great if our source files had built-in proxies? The UltraPix solution from Comprimato offers exactly this.

By utilizing both the GPU and the CPU to their fullest, the solution makes JPEG2000 encoding and decoding many times faster. JPEG2000 is a wavelet codec and has partial resolutions built into the master file. This is great when you're dealing with 4K, 8K, and 360° VR footage:

comprimato.com/products/ultrapix/

Additional Proxy Workflow Resources

From Adobe

For a deep dive into this feature, check out this Adobe web page:

helpx.adobe.com/premiere-pro/kb/ingest-proxy-workflow-premiere-pro-cc-2015.html

Proxy Tutorials by Dylan Osborn

dylanosborn.com/2016/09/21/proxy-workflow-part-1/

dylanosborn.com/2016/10/05/proxy-workflow-part-2/

Proxy and Ingest Tutorial by Chinfat

youtube.com/watch?v=fUU8AptSvts

3 Ways to Work with Proxies in Premiere Pro by Sofi Marshall

blog.frame.io/2017/03/20/premiere-pro-proxies/

Summary

As we're moving toward higher resolutions and still want to edit on laptops, the proxy workflows are very useful. Using proxies in Premiere can be super-simple—just click the button to switch between full-res and proxy footage.

The proxy workflow is down-right fantastic when it works and invaluable when you're on a slow system, but the potential stumbling blocks we've covered in this chapter make it much harder to use than necessary. I think Adobe will improve these features a lot in future versions, making the proxy workflow a lot more streamlined.

CHAPTER 3

■ ■ ■

Audio in Premiere Pro

By Jarle Leirpoll

In this chapter, you'll get a thorough understanding of the audio signal chain in Premiere and how to best work with audio editing, restoration, and mixing. To treat an audio clip in the best way you need to identify what kind of audio it is, so we start with an overview of the different types of sound you'll encounter.

You'll get familiar with the different audio track types and the two mixers available in Premiere, then learn how to work with audio in the source monitor, the bin, and the timeline. Figure 3-1 shows some of the panels you'll use for audio treatment. For more-advanced workflows, we'll have a look at multi-channel audio routing and the syncing of separate audio recordings.

We'll also cover the final audio sweetening and mixing, including how to use the new Essential Sound panel and how to send the files, or the whole project, to Audition for advanced audio treatment. Figure 3-1 shows a few of the audio-related panels in Premiere.

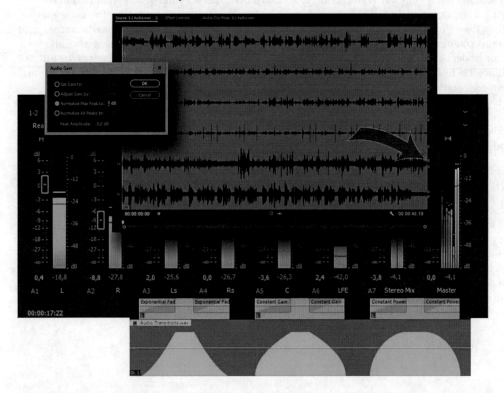

Figure 3-1. *Audio editing*

© Jarle Leirpoll 2017
J. Leirpoll et al., *The Cool Stuff in Premiere Pro*, DOI 10.1007/978-1-4842-2890-6_3

Oh, What a Difference a Sound Makes

Try animating a text or other motion-graphics element slowly. Then, add a deep, oscillating bass tone and see how the movement gains emphasis. Animate an element with a quick movement that suddenly stops. Then, add a whoosh and an impact sound, and the animation instantly gains some punch. Sound really makes your images look much, much better!

Audio Adds to the Continuity

A continuous ambience can help keep the feeling of continuity in a scene. We constantly cut between different angles and shots, creating discontinuity. If the audio is cut simultaneously, we will feel each cut. If the ambient sound is continuous, without cuts, we will feel that the scene is more real, and we will not think about the editing. Continuity is restored. Music can have the same effect.

Why does this work? Because this is how we experience life in general. We're constantly looking at different things in different directions, and we pay attention to small details or see the whole situation—all this by just moving our eyes and focusing on different things in different places. While all this is happening to our visual perception, the ambient sound is not changing. The noise from the air conditioner, the music from the radio, the cars in the street—all these sounds are continuous, not constantly cut.

So, that's why we can cut the video freely, but need to smooth out the audio transitions to make them unnoticeable. We're just mimicking the way we perceive life.

Audio Quality Matters

What differentiates many indie films from major Hollywood blockbusters? Sound quality! They may have great lighting, framing, acting, and VFX, but somehow they often forget about audio quality. The same goes for student films. Even after three years of film school, the audio quality is almost never as good as the image quality.

The most common reason for a film's being rejected from film festivals is—you guessed it—audio quality. Low-budget TV shows have the same problem. The most common viewer complaint at the BBC is that it's difficult to hear dialogue. Sound sweetening can help clarify and emphasize the dialog and will make the audience subconsciously experience the film as being more professional.

The basis for good audio quality is of course that the sound recorded on location is the best it can be. In most cases, that means getting the microphone close enough. And close enough is much, much closer than most people think. We can add reverb and simulate room tone if the dialog is too dry, but we cannot remove reverb and room tone without degrading the dialog.

Always Record Sound

Never record video only; always record audio too. Even if you need to remove the recorded audio and recreate it in the editing suite, you'll at least know how it sounded originally. I've seen a lot of student films where they didn't record audio. "We were going to add music to this anyway." But even when we use music, it's very common to have some natural sound as well.

If you have nat sound, you can choose to use it as is, lower it, or cut it away. If you don't have it, you have no option. You're stuck with the silent version. It's always good to have options in post-production so you can try out different solutions and see what works best.

■ **Note**   Absence of sound is a technical error. There needs to be sound: music, ambience, or sound effects—or whatever. There should always be sound, period. There. I said it. Now, don't you ever forget it! If you do, I will hunt you down and bully you until you fix it.

Some kind of sound should always be present. If you decide to start your film with fifteen seconds of total silence after equally silent opening titles, the viewers will not watch the screen. They will be busy grabbing their remote control to see what's wrong; if in a theater, they'll turn and look toward the machine room. Their brains are busy finding out what's wrong, so you'll lose them.

Temporal Relations of Sound

The sound will most often be synchronous with the video and the story. We hear the sounds from the scene. But even a voiceover and the internal thoughts of a character will be perceived as sync sound.

Sound can be taken from earlier in the story, and it will get a different meaning in the new context. An audio flashback is pretty common and will not create as big a break in the story as a full flashback using both video and audio would.

We can also make sound flash-forwards. We hear sound that we don't fully understand until later in the story, when the source, reason, or meaning of the sound is revealed.

Sound bridges are the most-used method for creating forward movement in a scene. Introduce the audio from the next clip a second or two before you cut the video, and the scene automagically becomes more fluid and feels like it's moving at a faster pace. We love sound bridges!

Please don't underestimate sound in your storytelling!

Types of Audio

Audio comes in many different shapes. Here are some of the audio flavors you might stumble upon.

SOT

SOT is an acronym for Sound On Tape and is used even though we don't really use tape anymore. It usually refers to the audio recorded along with the video, as opposed to audio recorded later.

MOS

MOS means a video recording with no sync audio. It's supposed to be an acronym for Motor Only Sync or Motor Only Shot, but I like the Mit Out Sound legend better. Google it. Anyway, it's video without sound.

Dialogue

Dialogue is people talking to each other. One person talking might technically be a monologue, but it will still be referred to as dialogue. If the dialogue is muffled, add some EQ and raise frequencies at 2000 Hz up to about 3000 Hz to make it more intelligible.

Ambience, Nat Sound, Atmos, Presence

This is the silence recorded at a location while no one speaks or moves. Sound recordists will always record a minute or more of natural sound from the shooting location. This is very useful when editing dialogue and interviews. We can smooth out transitions and bridge cuts between takes, make pauses where there were none, and so forth. If we're doing ADR, we absolutely need *ambience*.

It might be quite low in the final mix, but it makes a huge difference. When there's no ambience, the audience will feel that there's something lacking, even though they may not be able to tell you what it is. We love ambience!

Room Tone

Room tone is the sound of a room, or how the room sounds without people in it. So, think of it as ambience in a room.

Wild Sound

Wild sound is sound that doesn't have to be sync, but will add to the realism or mood of a scene, like dogs barking in the distance, trains passing by, children playing on a playground, and so on. Background sounds will help create a richer and fuller soundscape. Wild sound is often overlooked by newbie editors.

Silence

Again, total silence is a technical error. There is always some sort of ambience—everywhere. You'll have to decide what "silence" should sound like in the room, the woods, or the street where the scene is taking place.

The terms *ambience, ambient sound, natural sound, atmosphere, presence, room tone,* and *wild sound* are used differently in different production ecosystems, so you might find other definitions than the ones here.

Foley

Named after Jack Foley, a sound effects pioneer who developed many sound effects techniques, this is sound recorded later in a sound studio and synced to events in the image. This can be footsteps (on gravel, carpets, or hardwood flooring), doors opening or closing, stirring a cup of tea, opening a wine bottle, and so on.

Why do we need Foley? Because when we're shooting, getting good-quality dialogue is the main goal, so other sounds are given lower priority. Also, if we're doing ADR, the whole soundscape needs to be built from scratch, and Foley becomes even more important.

Adding a few footsteps can be done manually by syncing steps to video one by one. But if you have several hundred steps, it's much more efficient to record the steps in a studio in sync with the video playback.

Sound Motif

A *sound motif* is a sound effect or music, or a combination of these, that is used every time a certain character, situation, or place appears in the movie.

Sound FX

These are the sounds that we add for dramatic effect, sounds that aren't necessarily there in real life—explosions, gun fire, strange computer sounds, screeching tires, hits and punches, whooshes, and so on.

Some editors use sound libraries, but on most feature films the audio people will record their own collection of sounds. Why? Because the sound libraries you can buy, others can buy too, and your film ends up sounding just like all the others. Also, searching for and listening to a lot of sounds in a sound library is very time consuming.

While searching, you might think you've found just the right sound for the Harley Davidson bike, but when you listen to it you can hear that it was recorded in a city where the sound is reflected from buildings, and that it accelerates more aggressively than the one in your scene that was shot by a cabin in the wood. And the tire screeches will not fit so well on that dirt road either.

For some destruction scenes in *Man of Steel*, they recorded concrete blocks being dropped from a high crane and dragged them through gravel, over concrete, and on asphalt to get a library of destruction sounds.

On *Titanic*, they recorded hours and hours of water sounds—splashing, rippling, pouring, dripping, and flowing water—in many different rooms and places, including ships, water tanks, oceans, and swimming pools. They got the Oscar for best sound. They did not rely much on existing sound libraries. Just thought I'd mention it.

Make Your Own Sound Effects

You can record your own sound effects. Hit watermelons to make punches, twist celery to simulate an arm breaking, fry some bacon to imitate a rain sound, and so on. The Great Interweb will reveal a lot of recipes for cool sound effects.

When you've recorded the sounds, tweak them in Premiere Pro. A real gunshot may sound thin and wimpy. Duplicate it a couple of times and use it at varying speeds on the different tracks. Normal speed on one track, half speed on one, and even slower on another one. Adjust levels and add EQ. This will give you both oomph and attack.

You can have lots of fun with EQ, speed changes, reverse sounds, reverbs, and delays. Try adding the Flange and Chorus effects to make a robotic voice. Have you ever tried reversing a sound, then adding delay and re-reversing it? That makes for a very scary sound. You might need to nest your audio clip to achieve this.

Walla

This is the sound of people in the background, a crowd. If your scene with a happy couple is shot by a table in a restaurant, there should be some sound from all those other people in the room. But during the shoot they can't talk, as that would prevent the recording of clean dialogue.

So, when you see lots of people talking in the background, they're probably not really talking, they just pretend to. We record that sound separately and add it later, and that's *walla*. We generally do not want to hear distinct words or sentences when recording or editing walla; we just want to hear indistinguishable voices talking.

It's common practice to add EQ with high- and mid-frequency dampening to walla so it doesn't interfere with the dialogue sound. Wonder why it's called walla? Historically, to create an indistinct sound of group chatter, a group of people would be told to constantly repeat the sound "walla".

ADR, Dubbing, Looping

When you're recording dialogue on location, noise from airplanes, wind machines, shouting directors, trains, barking dogs, and ambulances can all destroy an otherwise good recording. That's when we do ADR.

ADR is an acronym for Automatic (or Automated) Dialogue Replacement or Additional Dialogue Recording, depending on who you ask. It also goes by other names, like Looping. Typically, the actor watches a short part of a scene with the production sound a few times (hence the term looping) to feel the rhythm and mood, and then delivers the line, trying to keep it in sync. The voice recording from the studio will be very dry and "perfect" and will need some treatment before it sounds like it was recorded on location.

A better way, in my opinion, is to do the ADR at the location where the scene was shot, and get the correct sound for free. If this is done immediately after the scene was shot, the actors will also remember the mood and rhythm, and will possibly even perform better. Since we're working on very short lines, there's a good chance you'll be able to get an even ambience noise during each take. If the ambulance passes by, take a short break.

Bring a laptop with Premiere or Audition and the project, headphones for the actor, an audio recorder, and the same microphone you used for the original recording. First, let the actor watch the whole scene to get into the mood of the scene.

When you're ready to do the actual recording, set In and Out points around the line you want to record and click the *Loop* button. Now, play the line three or four times on the actor's headphones, then stop the playback and cue the actor to deliver the line. Start your portable audio recorder during the last loop playback, and stop it a few seconds after the actor finishes the line. Do this for every line.

Voiceover (Narration)

This is scripted words, read over a scene or a sequence, often in a studio or insulated sound booth. Sometimes the term is also used to mean the voice of an interviewee when it's laid over a sequence illustrating what the interviewee is talking about.

Voiceover goes by many names, among which are Narration, Speak, and Commentary.

Music

Music is, well, music. It can be the music score—music we add to the mix to create a mood or to trigger certain thoughts in the viewer's head based on the lyrics. But it can also be diegetic sound—music that seems to come from a source in the scene, like a radio, TV set, or computer. Music adds drama—good and bad.

Now that you have an understanding of the purposes of different audio types, let's look at the way Premiere handles audio.

The Audio Chain in Premiere

When working with audio in Premiere, it can be useful to know what's going on under the hood. Figure 3-2 and the following sections provide an overview of the way audio flows through the chain in Premiere.

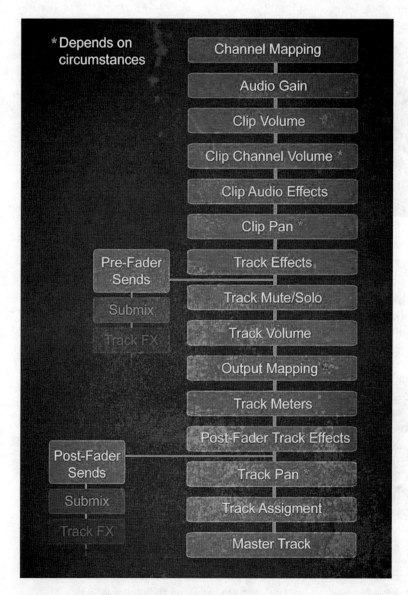

* Depends on
circumstances

Channel Mapping

Audio Gain

Clip Volume

Clip Channel Volume *

Clip Audio Effects

Clip Pan *

Pre-Fader
Sends

Track Effects

Submix

Track Mute/Solo

Track FX

Track Volume

Output Mapping *

Track Meters

Post-Fader Track Effects

Post-Fader
Sends

Track Pan *

Submix

Track Assigment

Track FX

Master Track

Figure 3-2. *The audio chain in Premiere, a bit simplified*

Channel Mapping

This is where you decide what audio channels to use in a clip and how to use them. Go to **Clip ➤ Modify ➤ Audio Channels** or press **Shift+G.** Figure 3-3 shows how to use only the right channel of a stereo clip, using it as a mono source.

131

Figure 3-3. *Modify audio: You're the boss, so you decide what audio channels to use from the source*

Audio Gain

Audio gain can be applied to master clips in the Project panel or bins, or to clips in the timeline. Adjusting audio gain in the Project panel or bin will affect all clip instances that you place in timelines after the adjustment. It will not affect clip instances already in the timeline. Audio gain goes from minus infinity (silent) to +96 dB. In Figure 3-4, I've adjusted audio gain by 6 dB.

Figure 3-4. *Audio gain*

■ **Note** Gain or normalize a whole bin! Select a bin, hit G, and adjust gain on all the clips within it.

Clip Volume

Clip volume goes from minus infinity to +6 dB. Clip volume can be adjusted by the timeline's rubber bands or with the Audio Clip Mixer, as shown in Figure 3-5.

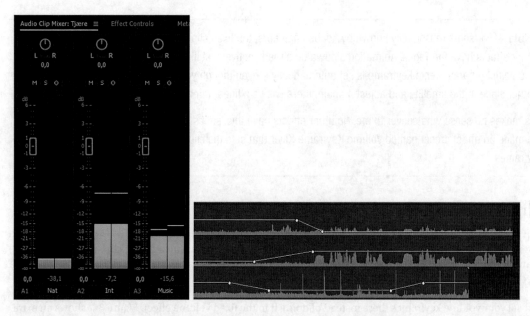

Figure 3-5. *Audio Clip Mixer volume, rubber bands: Clip volume can be adjusted in the Audio Clip Mixer or in the timeline using rubber banding or keyboard shortcuts*

Clip Channel Volume

Channel volume is a fixed effect on all non-mono clips, and you can adjust it in the Effect Controls panel or in the Audio Clip Mixer. This is another minus infinity to +6 dB adjustment, with separate controls per channel for multi-channel sources.

This trick is quite well hidden; if you right-click on a fader area in the clip mixer you'll find *Show Channel Volume*. Very handy! Figure 3-6 shows where to find the channel volume in the Audio Clip Mixer, and how it looks in both the Audio Clip Mixer and in the Effect Controls panel.

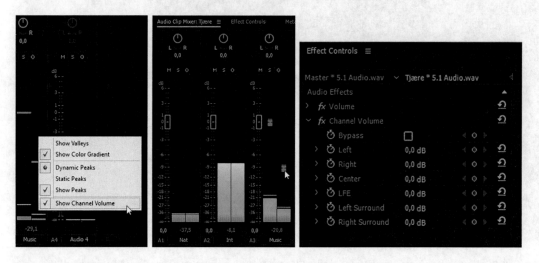

Figure 3-6. *Right-click in the fader area to get access to the clip's channel volume for multi-channel sources in the Audio Clip Mixer*

133

■ **Note**   For some reason only known by Adobe engineers, the fixed clip volume, clip channel volume, and panner effects have the Toggle Animation stopwatch already active, just like Opacity and Time Remapping. So, if you adjust a parameter, a keyframe is set automatically—even though you didn't ask for it. If you move to another place in the timeline and adjust it again, there will be a linear interpolation between the two settings.

This makes no sense whatsoever to me. No other effects have this, so it's a trap you should be aware of. I've made an effect preset named Volume Keyframe Killer that sets the clip volume to 0 dB and removes all keyframes.

Clip Audio Effects

Clip audio effects means any audio effects that you add to clips in the timeline. These are adjusted in the Effect Controls panel, and there's no limit to how many audio effects you can add to a clip. You can also add channel volume (discussed earlier) as an audio effect from the Effects panel, and that will be added to the fixed channel volume and must be adjusted in the Effect Controls panel.

   If you want clip effects to act like they're pre-fader, you can add the volume effect after the clip effect, and set your volume keyframes there instead of doing it in the fixed volume effect. Figure 3-7 shows an extra volume effect in the Effect Controls panel.

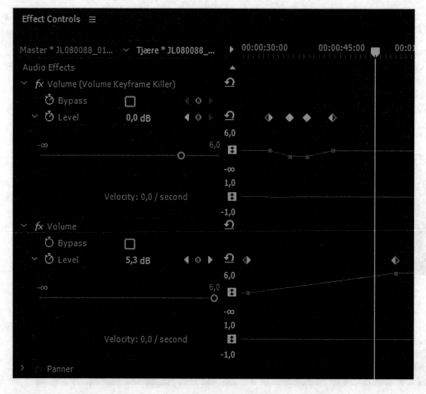

Figure 3-7.   Clip audio effects are adjusted in the Effects Control panel. You can even add an extra clip volume effect.

Clip Pan

On some clip types in certain track types, there is a fixed clip panner effect. This works differently on different clip types. Figure 3-8 shows the Effect Controls panel for one mono clip and one stereo clip.

Figure 3-8. *The panner works differently on mono and stereo clips*

Track Effects

Track effects are added in the Audio Track Mixer. Open the little twirly in the upper-left corner of the mixer to reveal the five available slots for track effects. The default position is Pre-Fader, which puts them—well, yeah—before the fader in the chain. See Figure 3-9.

Figure 3-9. *Twirl down the twirly in the Audio Track Mixer to be able to add track effects. This reveals five available slots for audio track effects.*

Track Volume, Solo, and Mute

This is the fader in the track mixer—another audio-level adjustment that goes from minus infinity to +6 dB. If the *Mute* button in the Audio Track Mixer or the timeline headers is active, then track volume is effectively zero. If the *Solo* button is active, tracks that are not soloed are set to zero output. Figure 3-10 shows the fader and the buttons in the Audio Track Mixer.

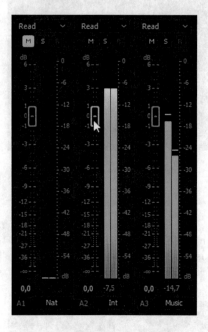

Figure 3-10. *Audio Track Mixer fader, plus Mute and Solo buttons*

Post-Fader Track Effects

You find Post-Fader effects in the same slot as Pre-Fader effects. To switch a track effect to Post-Fader, right-click on its slot in the track mixer as shown in Figure 3-11.

Figure 3-11. *The audio track effects can be applied Pre-Fader or Post-Fader*

Channel Output Mapping

This is only available for adaptive tracks. You'll learn about audio track types in just a few pages. You get to this by clicking the Channel Output Mapping icon in the timeline or in the Audio Track Mixer, as shown in Figure 3-12.

Figure 3-12. *In multi-channel sequences, you can access the Channel Output Mapping*

Track Meters

Any time you see meters for a track—in the track mixer, clip mixer, or timeline—you are seeing the amplitude of the signal at this point. Figure 3-13 shows track meters in the timeline.

137

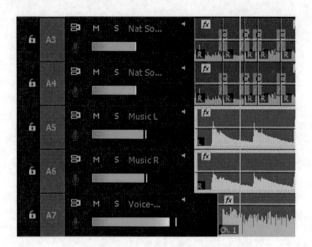

Figure 3-13. *The track meters show the volume at their point in the audio chain*

Track Assignment

This controls where the tracks are routed to in the Audio Track Mixer. By default, the tracks are routed to the master track. You can also route them to submixes. The first six tracks in Figure 3-14 are routed to submixes.

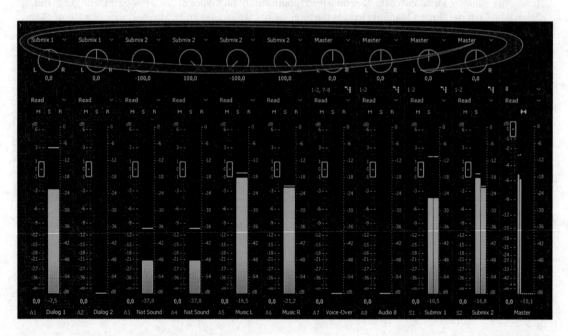

Figure 3-14. *Track assignment (routing)*

Track Pan

This is the panning done in the Audio Track Mixer or the timeline. Not all audio tracks in all kinds of sequences will have a track pan. Figure 3-15 shows tracks with track pan.

Figure 3-15. *Track pan is found in the Audio Track Mixer*

What About Sends?

Both pre-fader and post-fader sends can be thrown into this chain. When a send is done, the audio is sent via a submix, and a submix has its own track effects, track volume, and so on, just like normal tracks. When submixes are sent to other submixes, the signal flow will get quite complex.

Nesting

This whole chain will happen inside every nested sequence in a sequence. When nesting several layers deep, the whole signal flow is repeated many times.

With a good understanding of the whole audio chain, let's have a look at the different kinds of audio track types in Premiere, as they can be somewhat confusing to editors who come from other Non-Linear Editors (NLEs).

Audio Track Types in Premiere

Premiere Pro has four different audio track types for different purposes. Figure 3-16 shows the available track types. Figure 3-17 shows what happens when you try to put a stereo clip on a 5.1 track.

Figure 3-16. *Audio track types can cause some confusion if you're not used to them*

Figure 3-17. *Here, I'm trying to place a stereo clip on a 5.1 track, and that will not work. Premiere creates a new standard track below the existing tracks where the clip is placed.*

Standard Tracks

Standard audio tracks are somewhat format agnostic, letting you place both stereo and mono audio clips on the same single track. This is the kind of track that most users will probably choose. Standard tracks do not have an icon in the Sequence Track Header.

Mono Tracks

Mono tracks are meant for mono audio, of course, but you can also place stereo sources in them. Stereo clips are simply downmixed to mono within the mono track. Mono tracks have a small loudspeaker icon in the Sequence Track Header.

When working with OMF export, your safest bet is to use mono clips referencing mono audio files on mono tracks. Support for other clips and track types is not very good in OMF.

Adaptive Tracks

Adaptive tracks can take any sort of source, except 5.1. The number of channels in an adaptive track always follows the master track. Adaptive tracks have a small patch panel icon in the Sequence Track Header where you can access Channel Output Mapping. Adaptive tracks are easy to use once they are set up, but the initial setup can be a bit complex. You will probably not use adaptive tracks unless you cannot accomplish what you want with standard, mono, or 5.1 tracks.

5.1 Tracks

5.1 tracks will only take 5.1 sources. You cannot put mono, stereo, or multi-channel sources on a 5.1 track, and 5.1 sources can only be placed in a 5.1 track. Also, 5.1 sources cannot be panned.

5.1 tracks have a small icon that says 5.1 in the Sequence Track Header.

Master Track

A master track dictates the audio output from the sequence. A master track can be mono, stereo, 5.1, or multi-channel. A multi-channel master track can have 1 to 32 tracks, and the number can be changed during the edit. Mono master tracks will only have one audio track, stereo master tracks have two, and a 5.1 sequence will of course have six, panned to its respective speaker.

The icons are the same as on other audio tracks, and stereo master tracks have two small loudspeakers as their icon in the Sequence Header—one pointing to the right and one to the left.

Submix Tracks

Submix tracks will show the same icons as master tracks of the same type. A submix is a way to gather the output of several tracks into one common submix track. Instead of sending the audio output from a track directly to the master track, we route it through an additional track.

This way, we can route all related audio tracks to one fader, or put audio effects on the submix track instead of adding them to all the tracks separately. An example could be that we want to route all dialogue tracks and voiceover tracks to one submix and all tracks containing ambience and wild sound to another. This way, we can easily mix the voice levels and the ambience levels with two faders only. We can also add the same compressor setting to everyone who's talking, all in one place.

The Preferences panel lets you choose how Premiere deals with source audio tracks, but there are some other interesting settings too. Let's have a closer look.

Notable Audio Preferences

We can make some audio decisions even before we import our source clips to the project! Let's have a look at some audio preferences.

Preferences for Audio Channel Mapping

You can set a preference for your audio source channel mapping in **Edit (Premiere Pro) ➤ Preferences ➤ Audio ➤ Default Audio Tracks**. As you can see in Figure 3-18, you have the option to set the default track format to Use File, Mono, Stereo, Adaptive, or 5.1—plus any presets you've made.

Figure 3-18. *You can set your preferred default handling of audio tracks in Preferences ➤ Audio*

This means you can decide to import all stereo clips as dual mono or to use only the left or the right channel as mono. Or, you could decide to use only the first two tracks from a camera that records four tracks.

This is nice, but we can't make presets like these here in the Audio Preferences panel. We need to create them in the Project panel or in a bin, and when they're created we can choose them here in our preferences.

Audio Settings for FCP 7 and Avid Users

If you come from FCP7 or Avid, take a look at Figure 3-19. That one setting will make your life a lot easier.

Figure 3-19. *Audio preferences for FCP and Avid users*

■ **Note**　I recommend that FCP 7 and Avid users switching to Premiere Pro adjust their preferences for audio so that stereo audio comes in as mono pairs. Also, I recommend making your own sequence presets with mono tracks only.

This ensures audio behaves exactly like in FCP 7, and everything will work as you expect. Now every stereo clip you import will be imported with two mono tracks instead of one stereo track. Note that this does not change the clips you've already imported. It's a setting for future imports.

Other Audio Preferences

We can also set a preference for how 5.1 audio is mixed down to stereo (see Figure 3-20), turn audio scrubbing on and off, and so on. If you're recording voiceover in the same room as your speakers, you need to check *Mute input during timeline recording*.

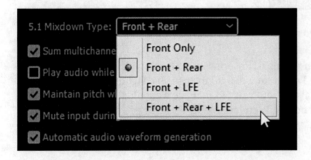

Figure 3-20. *Want to downmix 5.1 in a different way to your stereo speakers? Go ahead!*

Automatic audio waveform generation is great most of the time, but if you're recording a live feed from a satellite or an event, it can be turned off, like I've done in Figure 3-21.

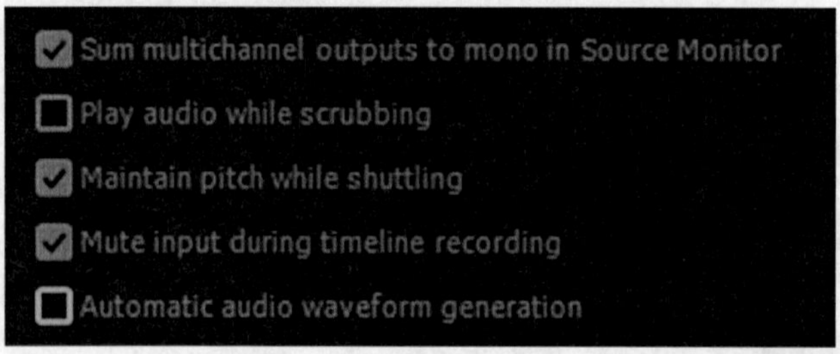

Figure 3-21. *When recording a live feed, deactivate peak file generation*

By default, the Audio Clip Mixer and the Audio Track Mixer create way too many keyframes for my liking. I prefer to set the *Minimum time interval thinning* to a much longer time than the default. In Figure 3-22, I've set it to 100 milliseconds.

Figure 3-22. *I find that the audio mixers write too many keyframes, so I increase the time between them*

Also, I find the default 6 dB increments when raising or lowering audio levels with the Large Volume Adjustment keyboard shortcut to be too large, so I often set it to 3 dB instead. See Figure 3-22.

If you use third-party audio plug-ins, this is also where you can manage what plug-ins to use in Premiere. Figure 3-23 shows all the audio preferences in Premiere.

Figure 3-23. Audio Preferences panel

Audio Hardware Preferences

Under Audio Hardware Preferences, you can control what audio hardware you record audio from and output the sound to and adjust the sample rates, input levels, and so on, if required. Click the *Settings* button to open the OS audio in/out settings. See Figure 3-24.

Figure 3-24. Audio Hardware Preferences: Other device classes may be available if you have an I/O card that taps into Mercury Transmit

If you start Premiere Pro on your system and your audio hardware has changed, you will get a dialog telling you that the previous device is not available. See Figure 3-25. Click the *Yes* button to be taken to the Audio Hardware settings automatically so you can choose one of the existing outputs.

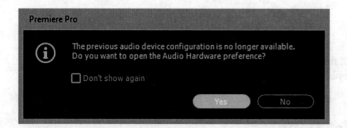

Figure 3-25. *When your previous audio hardware is not available, click Yes in this dialog to fix it*

Your Audio Hardware settings can have a big impact on responsiveness and playback performance, so if you experience stuttering playback of some video formats and high-CPU loads, try changing your Device Class (if available) and Latency (I/O Buffer Size) settings.

Playback Preferences

It's important that audio and video are in sync on your system. If they go through the same output device, you're probably good, but if the video is fed through a GPU to a 4K TV monitor via HDMI and the audio goes directly to your computer speakers, then they're most likely out of sync. The audio goes a faster route, so the image will be delayed.

When you watch full-screen video on a separate monitor via Mercury Transmit, you can compensate for this delay in the Playback Preferences (Figure 3-26). If you set the offset to 100ms, the video will be sent 0.1s before the audio. If you have an audio device other than Adobe Desktop Audio, you will most likely have an Offset setting for the audio device too.

Figure 3-26. *Mercury Playback preferences*

Mercury Playback Test

To check sync, put one-frame bits of Bars & Tone every second and play back. It's quite easy to tell if things are not right when you get short beeps and flashes like this.

The Preferences panel is not the only place where you can make audio-related choices. A lot can be done in the Project panel and in bins before you put files on a timeline.

Audio Stuff in the Project Panel

We can do some work on audio in the Project panel or bins, and in most cases it will be quicker and smarter to do it there than in the timeline later.

Audio Channel Patching in the Project Panel

As mentioned, we can make presets in the Project panel or a bin for what audio channels to use and what kind of source they should be interpreted as. Select one or more clips in a bin and go to **Clip ➤ Modify ➤ Audio Channels**, or use the right-click menu or the keyboard shortcut, **Shift+G**. Here, you can apply a preset, make new presets, or just do a change to existing settings. Figure 3-27 shows how the two channels in a stereo clip can be treated in different ways. Figure 3-28 shows how to save a preset.

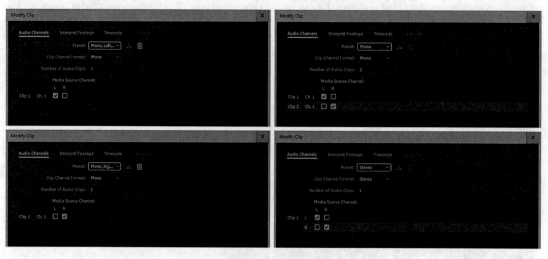

Figure 3-27. *Stereo clip channels treated in four different ways*

Figure 3-28. *Make presets for oft-used track choices*

Say you've decided to import stereo sources as dual mono. This means you'll end up with two separate audio channels on that clip in the timeline when you drag it there. But if this is an interview with the good audio on only the left channel, it makes no sense to put the right channel (probably a camera mic) on the timeline and then delete it. So, you'll use this panel to select the left channel only, giving you no extra audio clips in the sequence.

Figure 3-29 shows the same clip in the timeline with three different settings for audio channels mapping. The stereo one comes in a single track with two audio channels. The dual mono one comes in as two separate audio tracks. The last one was set to use the left channel only and output it as a mono clip.

Figure 3-29. *The same clip three times, with three different audio channels mapping settings*

Get Rid of Audio Channels

A very common thing is for cameras to record four channels of audio, but in a typical situation only one or two channels may actually have microphones wired to them. So, you want to get rid of channels 3 and 4, leaving you with 1 and 2 only.

Select all the clips you want to modify in the Project panel or bin, or choose *Select All* if they're all the same audio type (interview, ambience, and so on). Go to **Clip ➤ Modify ➤ Audio Channels** or hit **Shift+G**. Deselect channels 3 and 4. Now, when you drag these clips to the timeline only channels 1 and 2 will be there.

Changing the audio source channel mapping on clips in the bin does not affect the clips' instances in the timeline. For that reason, it makes most sense to do the mapping right after the initial import. You can of course change the channel mapping for clips that are used in a timeline, but you'd have to put them in the timeline again to see the changes.

You can also fix problems where the mic was accidentally plugged in to the wrong channel by setting which order you want the tracks to appear in when you drag them to the timeline.

A clip with 5.1 audio will have six channels, and you can patch them differently if needed. See Figure 3-30.

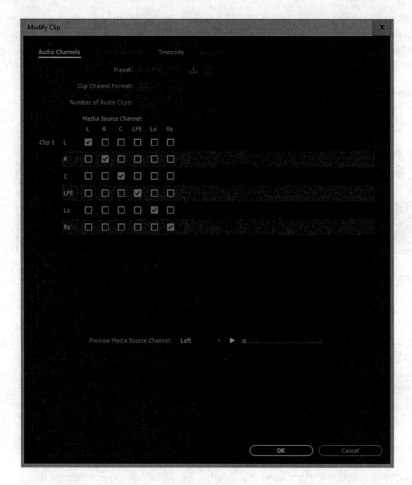

Figure 3-30. *Modify Clip dialog for a 5.1 clip*

If you're not sure what audio channel to keep, select a channel in the Preview Media Source Channel drop-down menu and hit the small *Play* button seen in Figure 3-31 to listen to that channel only.

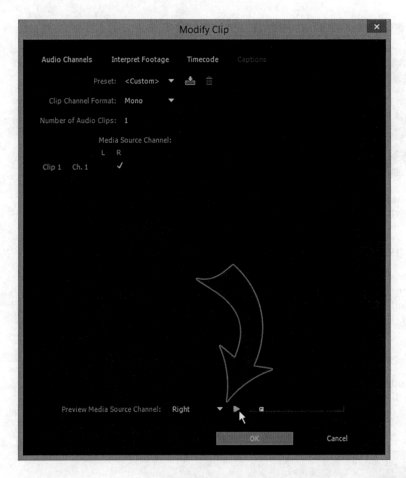

Figure 3-31. *You can preview the different source channels before you decide which ones to keep*

You can also change the channels of clips that have been put in the timeline with the wrong channels. Just select the clips and hit **Shift+G**, and you will change the mapping for only the selected clips. We'll have a closer look at this later.

Modify Audio on Sequences

Modify Audio Channels also works on sequences in the Project panel and bins. It will not change the source sequence at all, just how the audio is handled when you put the sequence into a new sequence. See Figure 3-32.

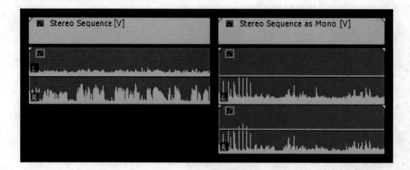

Figure 3-32. *Use the Modify Audio Channels dialog to decide how the sequence behaves when nested. Here, the same clip was added to the timeline twice, with different settings in the dialog.*

Premiere Only Reads the First Audio Stream

If you get an audio file with two or more audio streams (as opposed to audio channels), Premiere only reads the first stream. Some screen-capture software can record several streams. If you can make your screen-recording software record or export the audio as channels, not streams, do that to avoid problems. If not, use this method in the free software VirtualDub to export the audio streams as separate files: youtube.com/watch?v=NJW1BxtgoyI.

Working with Dual-System Sound

The popularity of DSLRs and other cameras with bad or non-existing audio recording has made dual-system audio pretty common (Figure 3-33). When recording audio on a separate device, we end up with two clips that need to be synchronized.

Figure 3-33. *7D & H4n: DSLR and an audio recorder—a common combination these days*

Keeping track of two clips every time we do an edit is too much work, so we merge the clips into one. That's what a *merged clip* is.

To merge an audio and a video clip, select them and go to **Clip ➤ Merge Clips** or use the right-click menu or a shortcut. Figure 3-34 shows the right-click menu, the dialog, and the result of merging two clips. You can also merge clips in a timeline, but you need to synchronize them first (see the "Merging Clips in a Timeline" section later in the chapter).

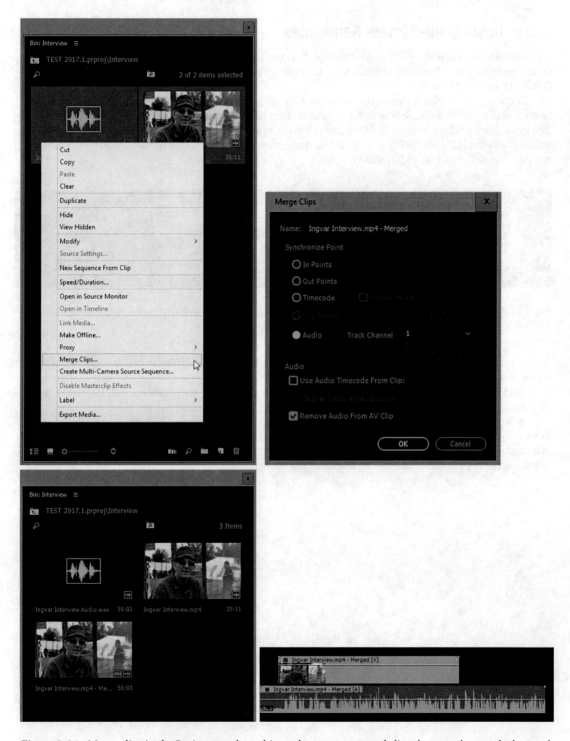

Figure 3-34. *Merge clips in the Project panel or a bin and you get a merged clip where you have only the good audio. When you place this in the timeline, the audio and video will have different start and stop times.*

Merge Using Multi-Camera Sequences

It's way too labor intensive to merge a lot of clips, because you need to do them one by one. Also, merged clips may cause problems if you're sending your project to audio post-production or are color grading via OMF, AAF, or FCP XML.

Plus—and for me this is the biggest problem with merged clips—it creates trouble for Top & Tail editing (which Adobe, for "short," calls *Ripple Trim previous/next edit to Playhead*) with **Q** and **W**. Because the audio and video start at different times, the Q and W shortcuts will leave portions of the audio or video at the start and end, as seen in Figure 3-35. You must delete these manually, and it's a big hassle. Merged clips are not good for Top & Tail editing with Q and W.

Figure 3-35. *Merged clip result after editing with Q and W to the left. To get the desired result on the right, I had to manually delete the two bits of audio.*

For these reasons, some editors prefer to synchronize audio and video files to one or more MultiCam sequences instead. You can create a lot of MultiCam sequences in one go automatically. And after editing with the MultiCam sequences as sources, they can be flattened, solving the problems with OMF, AAF, and FCP XML export.

In Figure 3-36, I've ended up with two MultiCam sequences after syncing four clips—two audio and two video—by audio waveforms. Since no part of the audio for the two interviews was the same, the MultiCam syncing feature decided to make two sequences, which was exactly what I wanted. Read more on MultiCam versus merge clips in the "Multi-Camera" section of Chapter 4.

Figure 3-36. *Using MultiCam sync to merge audio and video lets you flatten the sequence, which increases the compatibility in OMF, AAF, and XML exports. Also, Top & Tail editing with Q and W works as expected with no extra work.*

Unexpected Panning After Syncing

Mono clips in adaptive tracks are now panned left. In older versions of Premiere, they were panned to the middle. This means we can't just drop a multi-camera source sequence on the New Item icon or right-click it and choose *New Sequence from Clip*. If we do this, Premiere will create a new sequence with adaptive tracks, and the Mono audio from the multi-camera source sequence will be panned left.

A workaround is to create a shortcut for *Set Clip Pan to Center* so you can select all the clips and hit the shortcut. But if you want to flatten the clips later, you'll need to do this again for the flattened clips.

So, instead, I recommend that you never create your edit sequence directly from the multi-camera source sequences, but instead create your edit sequence separately. See Figure 3-37.

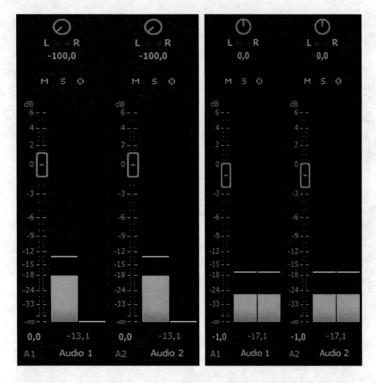

Figure 3-37. *When you create a new sequence based on a multi-camera source sequence, all the clips will be panned left. Create the edit sequence separately to avoid this.*

Gaining and Normalizing in the Project Panel

Audio gain and speed are the two "effects" that can be applied to master clips. This means we can set the audio level before we even open a clip in the source monitor. It can be a good idea to put all music clips in one bin, select them all, and normalize the level to about 6-10 dB lower than you would for speech. Then, normalize interviews and dialogue scenes to a standard level, and your levels will be in the ballpark. Use the Clip menu, the right-click menu, or the keyboard shortcut, **G**.

Break Out to Mono and Extract Audio

Clips with more than one audio channel can be split into mono channels inside of Premiere. Just select the clip you want to split and then go to **Clip ➤ Audio Options ➤ Breakout to Mono**. If done to a stereo clip, this populates the bin with two new audio clips containing the left and the right channels, respectively. This method tends to clutter my bins, so I choose to use the *Modify Audio Channels* method instead if I need mono tracks.

  Clip ➤ Audio Options ➤ Extract Audio does a similar thing, except that new audio files are created on your drive. This is useful when you need a separate audio file for audio post work or you need to send the audio file to someone.

Speech Analysis

Not exactly an audio feature, but, hey, at least it's speech. If you're among the lucky people who live in a country where one of the supported languages is spoken, you can use speech analysis to get a text version of the spoken words.

The feature was removed in the CC2015 version because very few editors used it, so I keep an older version of Premiere around for this feature only.

Select the clips you need to analyze and go to **Clip ➤ Analyze Content** and tell Premiere what language the recording is. See the dialog and the result in Figure 3-38.

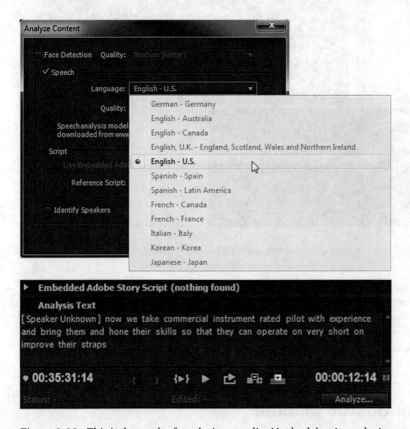

Figure 3-38. *This is the result of analyzing my clip. Not bad, but it can be improved.*

This will fire up Adobe Media Encoder, which will analyze the clips in the background. When ready, the clips will have metadata in the Analysis Text field.

Now you can click on words to jump there and even set in and out points without listening to the spoken words. The better your audio quality is, the better this will work. It's not perfect.

In my example, Brian is really saying, "We take commercial, instrument-rated pilots with experience and bring them in and hone their skills so that they can operate on very short, unimproved airstrips." We can improve the result by creating a TXT file with a few keywords. Figure 3-39 shows my added "script" and the result after re-analyzing the clip with the help of the TXT file.

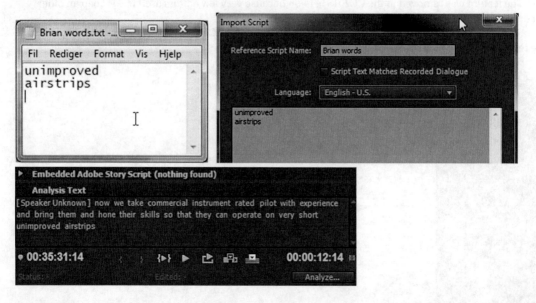

***Figure 3-39.** Attach a reference script to improve accuracy. I added two words, and the result is almost perfect.*

As you can see, the TXT file doesn't have to be a complete list or transcript—a few keywords are enough. This helps a lot in interviews where special technical or scientific terms are used or when uncommon names for people or places are mentioned. If you're working on scripted material from an Adobe Story script, or if you have manual transcripts of the interviews, this analysis will be very close to 100 percent accurate.

Import the project or the analyzed files into your current version of Premiere to use the metadata for editing. Everything still works as in older versions; it's just the analysis itself that has been removed.

Audio Stuff in the Source Monitor

OK, so the Project panel has some nice audio features. What about the Source Monitor panel? The next few sections address this.

Adjust Audio Volume in Source Monitor

Hitting the Audio Gain shortcut while the Source Monitor is active will let you set the audio gain for the clip before adding it to the timeline. This is very convenient for music that's too intense or to normalize audio on an interview before putting it in the timeline if you forgot to do it in the Project panel. Click the mini waveform icon below the image in the Source Monitor as shown in Figure 3-40 to show audio waveforms for the clip.

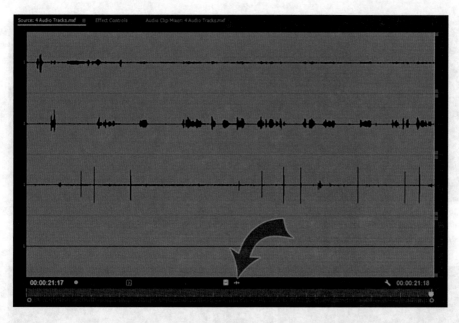

Figure 3-40. Source Monitor showing waveform for four audio tracks after I clicked the waveform button that the arrow points to

Gaining the clip in the Source Monitor is often necessary if the interview is recorded at a very low level, as you might not be able to hear the voice properly. Normalizing it will bring the levels up so you can hear what's being said.

You can choose what audio channel to listen to by soloing tracks in the audio meters or by soloing or muting in the Audio Clip Mixer. Note that this soloing or muting does not affect what tracks you get on the timeline when putting the clip there. It's only for previewing audio. But if you adjust the volume for an audio channel in the Audio Clip Mixer, that level will carry over to the timeline.

Audio Waveform in the Source Monitor

You can also choose *Audio Waveform* from the wrench menu to show the waveform in the Source Monitor. All your tracks will show, and you can zoom both vertically and horizontally to get a better view. Figure 3-41 shows the waveforms before and after zooming vertically. Figure 3-42 shows waveforms before and after zooming horizontally.

159

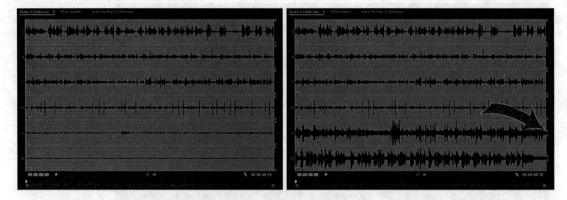

Figure 3-41. *You can zoom vertically to see details. The bars on the right side are zoom bars. Here, I've zoomed in on the surround tracks to get a better view of the waveform.*

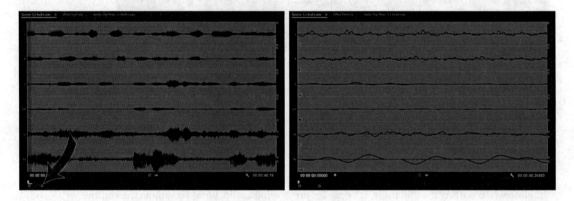

Figure 3-42. *The zoom bar below the monitor lets you zoom horizontally to take a closer look*

You can work more accurately and set perfect audio in and out points if you use the vertical zoom bars in the Source Monitor. Horizontally, you can actually zoom all the way in to individual audio samples if you choose *Show Audio Time Units* in the wrench menu.

Edit Multi-Clips in the Source Monitor

A *multi-clip* is two or more clips that are linked together. To make a multi-clip you select all the clips you want to link in the timeline and click **Clip ➤ Link**, or use the right-click menu or the shortcut **Ctrl+L**.

If one or more clips are already linked—like most video clips have linked audio—they need to be unlinked first. You can use the same shortcut—it's a toggle. Although you can edit multi-clips in the Source Monitor, the functionality is somewhat limited.

You can drag in and out points of any track to change them, and you can set in and out points for audio only (**Marker ➤ Mark Split ➤ Audio In/Out**), but every change you do to one clip in the linked group will be applied to all the tracks.

So, if you change the out point of one clip/track by 1 second, all the other tracks will also be changed by the same amount. If they're different lengths, the length of the shortest clip will be your limit.

I recommend changing in and out points of multi-clips in the timeline, where you have much more control because you can hold down the **Alt** key to edit the tracks individually.

Audio Stuff in the Timeline

Even though you can do lots of audio-related stuff in the Project panel and in the Source Monitor, the timeline is where you'll spend most of your time dealing with audio.

Using a Control Surface

Premiere supports Mackie, Tangent, and EUCON (Extended User Control) control-surface protocols, so you can choose from a variety of control surfaces. With an external control surface, you can control the audio mixer in Premiere in a more tactile way by dragging physical faders instead of icons on a screen.

To configure Premiere for use with a control surface, go to **Preferences ➤ Control Surface** and add your device class and your device. You may have to install some software on your computer to enable the control surface to talk to Premiere. Read the manual for your control surface for details.

After selecting the control device in the Preferences dialog, select *Toggle Control Surface Clip Mixer Mode* from the panel menu in the Audio Clip Mixer. You can also assign a keyboard shortcut to this command. The control surface supports faders, pan/balance, mute, and solo controls. Figure 3-43 shows the dialog boxes for control-surface settings.

Figure 3-43. Set your device type, and you can control faders and other stuff with a control surface

Control surface apps for tablets also work fine. They do not give the same tactile feeling, but using one frees up space in your Premiere workspace. Figure 3-44 shows two screenshots from the free version of the V-Control Pro iPad app from Neyrinck, available at neyrinck.com.

Figure 3-44. *Control surface apps for tablets can also be used to save screen real estate*

Ways to Adjust Audio Level

There are many ways to adjust the audio levels in the timeline. We can use audio gain, use keyframes, drag fades in a mixer, or use keyboard shortcuts. Use the tools that do the job most effectively and intuitively.

Audio Gain and Normalizing

Select a clip and hit **G** to get to the Audio Gain dialog box (Figure 3-45). You can increase or decrease the volume by entering a number in the dB field or by dragging the numbers. You can also normalize the audio. *Normalizing* means adjusting the level of a clip so that the highest peak reaches a certain level.

Figure 3-45. *Normalizing is done in the Audio Gain dialog box*

Normalizing works best when the audio levels are somewhat even. Normalizing an interview to -1 dB will work fine if the interview was shot in a controlled environment. But if there were loud background sounds, even just a short transient like the one in Figure 3-46, that's the peak that will be measured, and the interview will still be too low, as you can see in Figure 3-47. In such cases, you'll have to adjust gain manually. Figure 3-48 shows a clip that's well suited for normalizing.

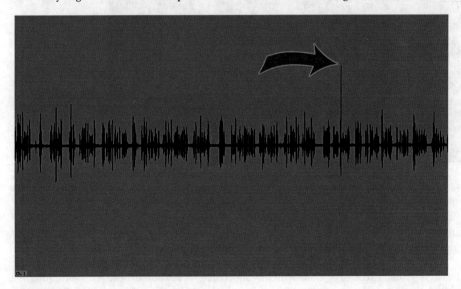

Figure 3-46. *This clip is not very well suited for normalizing because of the short peak that is much louder than the rest of the clip*

Figure 3-47. *The clip is gained until the loud peak reaches the normalize level, but the rest of the clip is still too low*

Figure 3-48. *This clip has more-even peaks, and when the loudest peak is at the normalize level, the rest of the clip is also much louder*

Figure 3-49 shows a good example of how normalizing will help you get your ambience levels in the ballpark, evening out levels nicely. These four clips had widely different ambience levels. Normalizing them all to -15 dB in one go (see Figure 3-51) made the levels very close to even, as shown in Figure 3-50. Adding crossfades to all the cuts—which can also be done with one shortcut—would make these level variations almost imperceptible. Add voiceover or music, and that will cover the audio transitions even further.

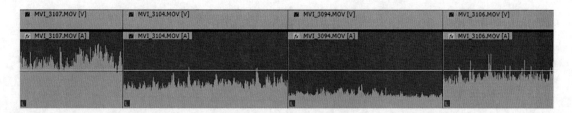

Figure 3-49. *Uneven ambience levels. Even if we add audio crossfades, the level changes will be very apparent, destroying the illusion of continuity.*

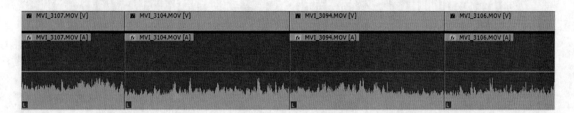

Figure 3-50. *After normalizing, the levels are even. When we add audio crossfades, this will feel like a continuous recording.*

Figure 3-51. *Normalize settings used for the ambience clips*

Keyboard Shortcuts to Raise and Lower Volume

The shortcuts for increasing and decreasing the audio level on selected clips or on the clips under the playhead will vary depending on your keyboard language. On an English keyboard it's the bracket keys, [and].
The bracket keys alone will increase or decrease volume in 1 dB increments. Holding the **Shift** key when hitting [and] will make adjustments in larger increments. You can decide in your audio preferences just how many dBs the Shift key should add.

Since these are not available on some non-English keyboards, they're mapped to some arbitrary keys. I highly recommend that you map them to more meaningful keys, as these are shortcuts you'll use all the time.

These shortcuts will work on any audio clip under the playhead on any targeted track. If you select one or more clips, only these clips will be affected.

Premiere Helps Too Much When Adjusting Volume!

When you use keyboard shortcuts to adjust the audio level you may get some surprises. In the example in Figure 3-52, I've selected the whole clip so I can adjust all the keyframes up and down. The level where I have the mouse cursor is -3 dB. Then, with the playhead parked over that section of the rubber band, I hit the keyboard shortcut to increase my level by 1 dB three times.

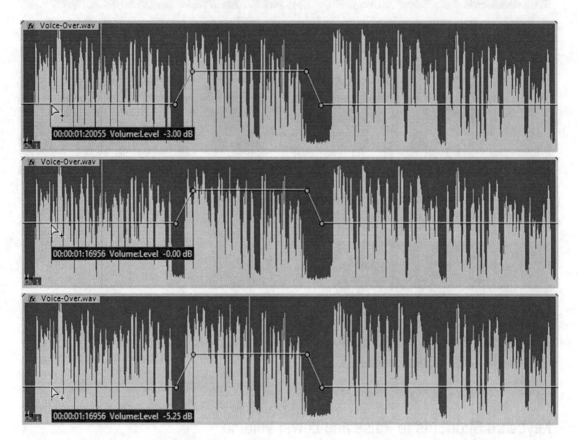

Figure 3-52. *Strange result after adjusting audio level up, then down, with the playhead parked in different places*

As expected, the level is now 0 dB. Now comes the big surprise: I park my playhead over the next section of the rubber band and hit the keyboard shortcut to lower the level by 1 dB three times. The result? The level at the spot is now -5.25 dB! What's going on here?

Since the level in the middle section was 2 dB, it was louder than the one I started on (which was -3 dB). So, when I raised the level, the part I was parked over got a 3 dB raise, but the middle section was only raised by 1.81 dB to 3.81. When I parked over that section and lowered the level by 3 dB, its level ended up at 0.81, while the left part was lowered to -5.25 dB.

None of the levels end up where they were originally after increasing the levels and then lowering the level by the same amount because I moved the playhead between the commands.

This is supposed to help us, but is quite confusing. Here's the logic behind this.

Note   The keyboard commands for Increase/Decrease Audio execute a change to the slider in the Audio Clip Mixer, and the ratios of the keyframes are adjusted on a logarithmic scale to maintain the same perceived volume between them. Since the commands execute on the clip mixer, the position of the playhead determines the starting reference point for the scaling.

Rubber Banding

Keyboard shortcuts are great for overall level adjustments to clips, but if you need to increase or decrease the volume gradually, you need keyframes. **Ctrl+click** (Cmd+click on MacOS) with the Selection tool to add keyframes, or use the Pen tool. Ctrl-clicking again (Cmd+click on MacOS) will give you nice Bezier curves with handles, as seen in Figure 3-53, so you can make custom fades and get really fine control over the audio. You can also do this in the Effect Controls panel, as shown in Figure 3-54.

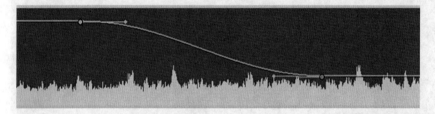

Figure 3-53. *Ctrl-click (Cmd-click) on the audio level line to add keyframes. Ctrl-click (Cmd-click) an existing keyframe to create Bezier handles.*

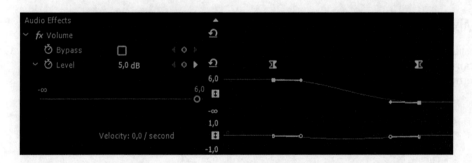

Figure 3-54. *Audio rubberbanding in the Effect Controls panel*

Select Multiple Keyframes

To select multiple audio keyframes, you can **Shift+click** the ones you want to select. You can also marquee-select audio keyframes in the Effect Controls panel. You can also marquee-select audio keyframes in the timeline, but you need to use the Pen tool and press the **Alt/Opt** key. Figure 3-55 shows marquee-selected keyframes.

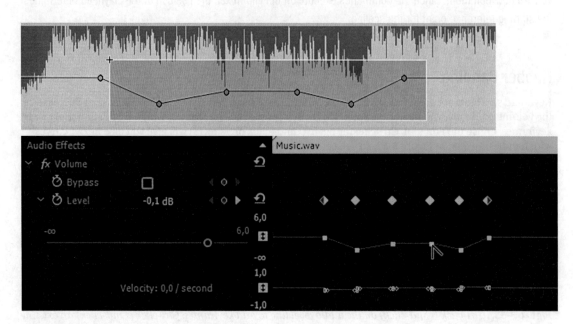

Figure 3-55. *You can marquee-select keyframes and adjust all of them in one go*

Audio Clip Mixer

We can also adjust the audio level in the Audio Clip Mixer. If the Write Keyframes icon is activated, as seen in Figure 3-56, we can play back the timeline and drag the fader to set keyframes "live." The distance between keyframes is determined by the *Minimum time interval* thinning setting in Audio Preferences. See Figure 3-57.

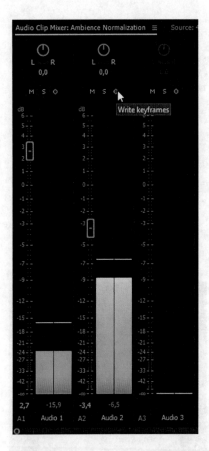

Figure 3-56. *To write keyframes in the Audio Clip Mixer, activate the Keyframes button*

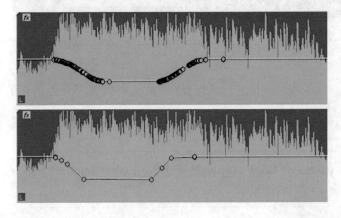

Figure 3-57. *Adjust minimum time interval thinning to get fewer keyframes*

If the Write Keyframes icon is not activated, the volume we set here applies to the whole duration of the clip.

Clip Channel Volume

This sets the levels on the individual channels in a clip. You can adjust clip channel volume for stereo, 5.1, and multi-channel clips in the Effect Controls panel. Twirl open the Channel Volume twirly to get access to them. Personally, I prefer adjusting this in the Audio Clip Mixer. You can make it show channel volume by right-clicking in the fader area, as shown in Figure 3-58.

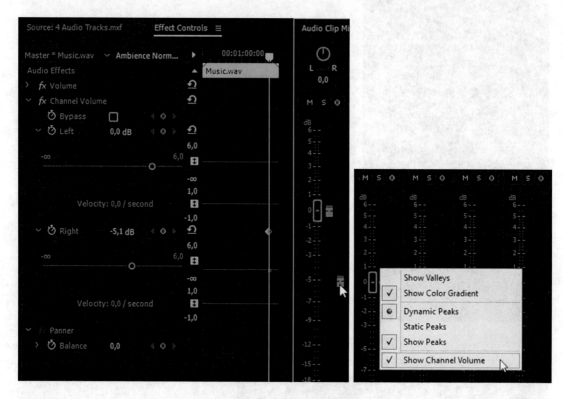

Figure 3-58. *Channel volume gives you access to the individual source channels so they can be adjusted individually*

Clip Volume vs. Track Volume

We have two very different ways of working with volume in Premiere: clip volume and track volume.

■ **Note**   Any adjustments we make to clip volume will follow a clip when we move it. Adjustments to track volume stay on the track. They don't even move with ripple edits.

We can adjust track volume in the Audio Track Mixer, and if we choose to show track keyframes in the timeline (Figure 3-59) we can also do rubber banding there. The default is to show clip keyframes.

Figure 3-59. *Right-click the keyframe icon in the audio track header to toggle between showing clip keyframes and track keyframes*

Track Volume Trouble

Figure 3-60 shows a good example of the track volume smurfing your audio adjustments. These tracks are set to show track keyframes, and the music is lowered a bit before the interview starts. All is well.

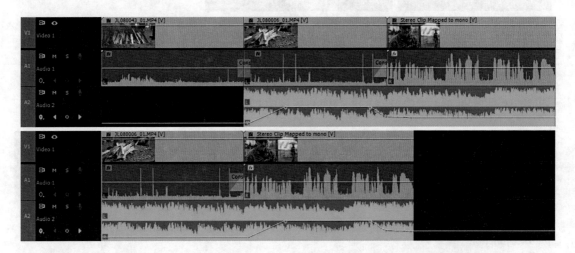

Figure 3-60. *Here, I've faded the music before the interview. Then, I deleted the first clip, and now the fade is in the wrong place, missing the interview. The Audio Track Mixer is only useful for a locked-down edit.*

Then, we decide to cut a few seconds from the start of the sequence, and the fade remains at the same time in the sequence, totally missing the interview. Our audio mix is now messed up.

Had we used clip keyframes, everything would be fine after the edit. Track volume should only be used when your cut is locked. For me, that's never the case, so I almost never use the Audio Track Mixer or the track keyframes to adjust my levels. I use clip volume all the time.

Panning

You can pan your *tracks* in the Audio Track Mixer or in the track header in the timeline. See Figure 3-61. To pan a *clip*, use the Audio Clip Mixer or the panner in the Effect Controls panel. Double-click the dial to reset the pan, and click on the blue L and R to pan all the way to the Left or Right. If you do a lot of panning you can assign keyboard shortcuts to *Clip Pan to Left, Clip Pan to Right*, and *Clip Pan to Center*.

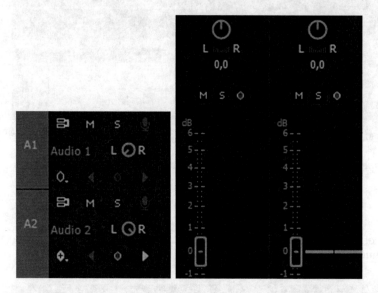

Figure 3-61. *You can pan in the Audio Track Mixer or in the track header*

Pan vs. Balance

For stereo clips, the panner changes from a standard pan operation to a balance operation. See Figure 3-62.

Figure 3-62. *The panner operates differently on stereo clips than on mono clips, changing from a pan to a balance function*

So, panning a mono clip will move it between left and right output channels, and the level remains the same. Panning it all the way to the left will put it in the left channel, and so on.

■ **Note**   A mono clip will pan from left to right as expected. But a stereo clip will adjust the relative volume between the two channels, and the audio will not be panned. Instead, the volume on each channel will change—but they will remain in the same channel. This is called balance.

"Panning" a stereo clip will adjust the balance between the left and the right source channels, leaving them where they were in the stereo field. Panning all the way to the left means we can only hear the left channel. Panning all the way to the right means we can only hear the right channel. Anywhere in between we can hear both, at varying levels.

Fast Forward with Better Audio

When you hit **L** several times, Premiere increases the playback. This is fine if the audio isn't important, as you can still see the video. But the audio quickly gets so distorted you can't hear what people are saying. To hear the audio faster than real-time, play back the timeline, then press the **Shift** key and tap **L**. The more you hit the **Shift+L** combo, the faster it plays–but in much finer increments than if just hitting **L**.

A few taps like this, and the timeline plays back just under 2x speed. The audio is still clear enough for editing decisions. If you want to decrease playback speed, hit **Shift+J**. This works just as well in other places where **JKL** is working, like the Source Monitor, in bins, and even in the Media Browser.

Select Source Audio Channels

What if you have a video clip with good audio from a lavaliere microphone on one channel and just the camera microphone on the other, but you only want the audio from the lavaliere? The best way is probably to adjust Source Channel Mapping in the Project panel before putting the clip on the timeline. But if you haven't done that, there's no reason to contaminate your timeline with extra audio clips that you immediately delete. A lot of editors do that; they drag the clip to the timeline and then delete the unwanted audio clip.

It's not all that obvious how you can do this. Muting the unwanted channel in the Audio Clip Mixer when the clip is in the Source Monitor will seem to do it–you'll hear the good audio only. But when you drag the clip to the timeline, the audio comes back.

The easiest way is to just deselect the track you don't want in the Source Assignment in the timeline. Or, better yet, make a Source Assignment preset for V1 + A1 or A2 only. Hit the shortcut for that preset and then drag the clip to the timeline, and it will take only the chosen audio channel. If you want just the audio, make a Source Assignment preset for no video and A1 or A2 only. Or drag Audio Only from the Source Monitor by dragging the little audio waveform icon at the bottom.

The left set of blue rectangles in the timeline header represent the source channels. The right set of rectangles are the track target buttons. Only the left set matters when you put new clips in the timeline (Figure 3-63).

Figure 3-63. *The source has video and two audio channels*

Since only A2 is blue, A1 will not be put in the timeline when we drag-n-drop or hit the keys for Insert or Overwrite. If we drag, we can decide where to drop it. If we use the keyboard, video from the source will go to Video 2, and Audio 2 from the source will end up on A2 in the timeline.

Changing Source Channel in the Timeline

What if you've used the wrong audio channel from a clip already in the timeline and want to change it? You can re-modify the audio channels. Just select the clip and go to **Clip ➤ Modify ➤ Audio Channels** (or use the right-click menu and choose *Audio Channels*), or hit **Shift+G**, and set it to use the other channel.

Source Assignment Presets

The Source Assignment presets are most useful for audio, as we often have far more audio tracks than video tracks–unless we're editing a music video. Say you're editing a documentary and you constantly switch between adding clips with interviews, voiceover, music, and ambience. You want all the music to be on the same track, the interviews on a dedicated track, and so on. Just make Source Assignment presets that you name Music, VO, Interview, Ambience, and so forth, and you can switch between them with the press of a key.

Here's how to make them, using a three-step process:

1. After you've made the source channel choices like in Figure 3-63, right-click on one of the source patcher rectangles (the ones on the left, remember) and choose *Save Preset*. Give the preset a descriptive name.

2. Then, right-click in the same area again and choose *Manage Presets* to decide on keyboard shortcuts.

3. Then, go to the Keyboard Shortcuts dialog to assign the actual keys to press.

Figure 3-64 shows the dialog boxes and my keyboard shortcuts assignment.

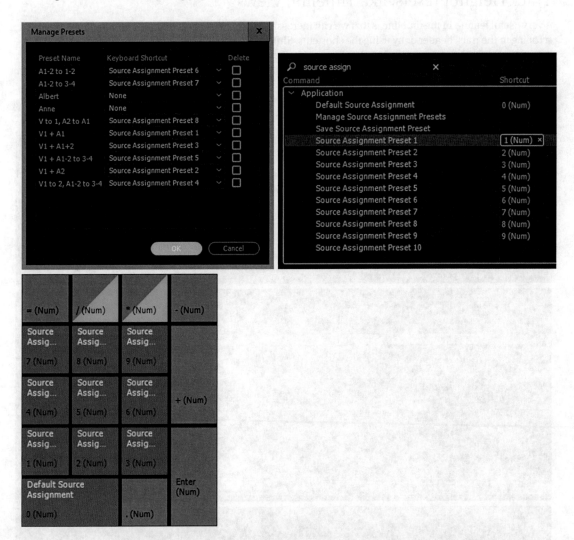

Figure 3-64. *You can create Source Assignment presets and make keyboard shortcuts for them. This way, you can edit multi-channel sources very fast!*

When editing reality-type material, this is also a nice way to work. By having dedicated shortcuts for Source Assignment for every person in a scene, you can easily get all the people laid out on their correct audio tracks.

You can, of course, switch the Source Assignment manually for each clip you drag or add to the timeline, but it means you're doing a lot of unnecessary clicking.

Track Height Presets, aka Timeline Views

A very useful feature in the timeline is that we can increase and decrease the height of individual tracks by scrolling in the track header or by using the shortcuts. **Shift + +/-** expands and minimizes all tracks. **Ctrl/Cmd + +/-** expands and minimizes all video tracks, and **Alt/Opt + +/-** expands and minimizes all audio tracks.

But this feature becomes much more useful if you define your own Track Height presets and assign keyboard shortcuts to them! I like to call them timeline views. Figure 3-65 shows a few different ones. Save timeline views that show nice big waveforms on only the tracks you need—1+2, 3+4, 5+6, etc.—and give them proper names.

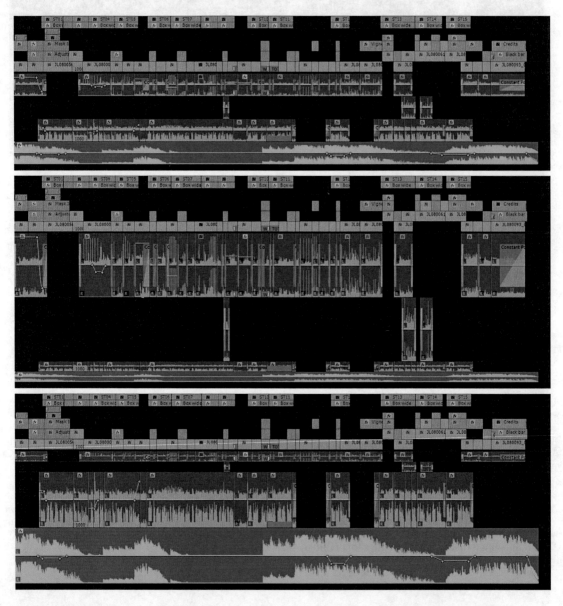

Figure 3-65. *When you create Track Height presets and assign shortcuts to them, you can switch between different timeline views with just a keystroke. Here are four ways to view the same timeline.*

First, make the tracks the height you want them to be in the preset. Actually, we're not saving only the track heights—the presets also remember where the dividing line between audio and video is. That's why I call them timeline views. So, make sure you get the layout exactly as you want it to be. Also, make sure you have enough tracks when making the presets. If you made a preset with all video tracks minimized, and you only had three tracks, tracks 4 and up will not be minimized when you hit that shortcut. When you're finished, click the wrench icon in the timeline and choose *Save Preset*.

Repeat the process with all the timeline views you need. Now, open the Manage Presets dialog box (in the same wrench menu) and assign shortcuts to them all, as shown in Figure 3-66. I recommend using one-key shortcuts for these, as this is something you'll be using all the time. Figure 3-67 shows my settings in the Keyboard Shortcuts panel.

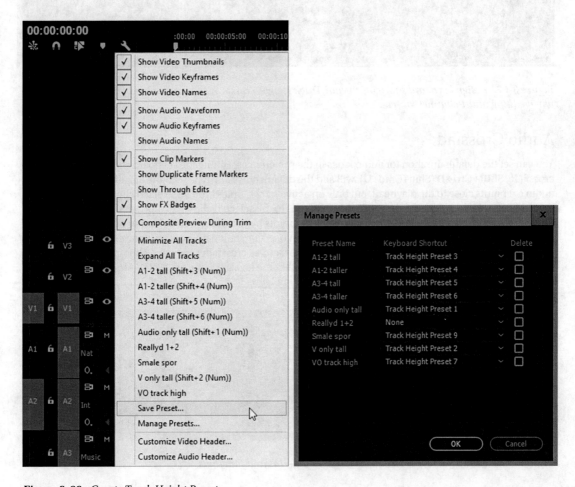

Figure 3-66. *Create Track Height Presets*

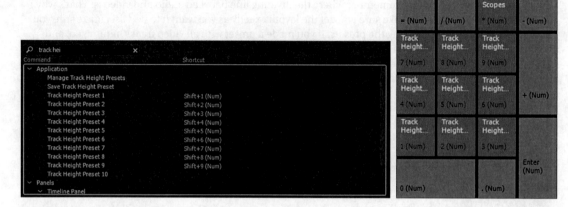

Figure 3-67. *Assign keyboard shortcuts to your Track Height presets. It saves you a ton of time—especially when editing multi-channel sources.*

Audio Crossfades

You can set the default duration for audio fades in the preferences. Hitting the keyboard shortcut for audio crossfade, **Shift+Ctrl+D** (Shift+Cmd+D), will add the default crossfade type with the default duration to the audio cut points close to the playhead, but only on active tracks, unless you've selected clips in the timeline—that will override the track selection and add crossfades to the selected clips. Existing crossfades can be copied and pasted to selected edit points. You can select edit points by **Ctrl-marquee-selecting** them.

There are three different audio crossfades we can use: constant gain, constant power, and exponential fade. I've used the three types of fades as fades on clips and as crossfades between clips in the images here. By using a tone, it's easy to see how the three types affect the levels. I exported a WAV file and imported it so it can sit on the following track, visualizing the result in Figure 3-68.

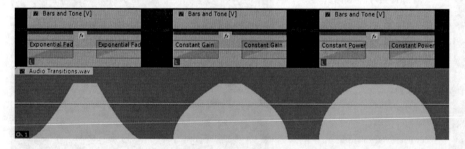

Figure 3-68. *Audio fade types visualized! Here on fade-ins and fade-outs*

As you can see from the images, the fades have different curves, from zero to full gain. Exponential fade increases slowly at the start of a fade in and decreases slowly at the end of a fade out, but speeds up the level change near the top. Constant gain changes quicker in the low values and in a more linear fashion at the top. Constant power is smoother at the top than constant gain. Now that you know the differences, you can choose the right one for any clip. When in doubt, use your ears.

So, what does this mean when you use them as crossfades between clips? It means that if you do crossfades between clips with a more or less constant ambient sound, it's best to use the constant gain flavor. If you're doing crossfades between clips with different sounds, use constant power.

178

I cannot see why you would ever use the exponential fade as a crossfade between clips. It would create a dip in the sound level. See Figure 3-69. That one is meant for smoother fades in and out for single clips.

Figure 3-69. *The same audio crossfades, now fading between clips*

Long Exponential Fade

The exponential fade is pretty smooth, and setting it to a long duration, like 10–15 seconds, will result in a very nice fade out for music and so forth. Sometimes, you need more control, and that's when we use rubber banding in the timeline and use Bezier curves, as shown in Figure 3-70, to get total control over the fade, adjusted to the dynamics in the music.

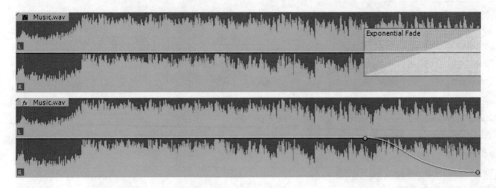

Figure 3-70. *Exponential fade and a manual exponential fade with keyframes. You can make super smooth fades by manually adjusting Bezier handles.*

Sample Accurate Audio Editing

Normally, you can only zoom in to see single frames in the timeline. Activate the *Show Audio Time Units* checkbox in the Timeline panel menu and you can zoom in further, like in Figure 3-71. Now you can adjust your audio in points accurately to avoid clicks and pops, and you can do rubber-band adjustments in very fine areas of the audio, killing that annoying sharp sound.

Figure 3-71. *You can zoom all the way in to see individual audio samples*

Logarithmic Audio Waveforms

Showing logarithmic waveforms and keyframes in the timeline makes it easier to read the low levels. See Figure 3-72. This lets you find cutting points without increasing the track height. You'll find this setting in the Timeline panel menu. You can assign a keyboard shortcut to *Logarithmic Waveform Scaling* so you can toggle between the two views.

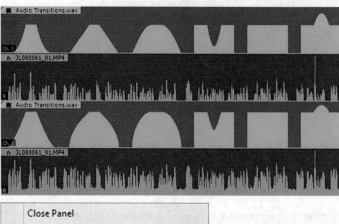

Figure 3-72. *You can set Logarithmic Waveform Scaling and Logarithmic Keyframe Scaling in the Timeline panel menu*

Recording Voiceover

Recording a voiceover is very easy: just park where you want the voiceover to start and click the microphone icon. When the recording starts, you (or your voiceover talent) start speaking. I recommend using a USB microphone. Figure 3-73 shows a Blue Snowflake USB microphone.

Figure 3-73. *USB microphone*

But there are some settings where you can optimize your voiceover recordings, so let's have a look at the details.

Preparation for Voiceover Recording

Make sure you check *Mute input during timeline recording* in the audio preferences (see Figure 3-74) if you, or the voiceover talent, do not like to hear yourself in the headphones—and to avoid any feedback problems. If you're recording another person's voice from a sound booth, you can of course listen to everything while recording.

Figure 3-74. *This preference will avoid feedback and makes sure the VO talent doesn't get her own voice in the headphones (with a delay)*

If you want to watch the levels of the recorded audio, show the Audio Track Mixer and make sure to set it to *Meter Inputs* in the panel menu (Figure 3-75). Unless you do this, the voiceover track in the Audio Track Mixer will not show the level in the track's peak meter. Since it doesn't show in the timeline track meters either, this is the only way to meter the input.

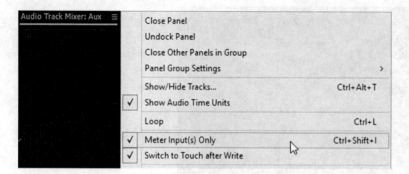

Figure 3-75. *Check Meter Inputs Only if you want to see the VO level while recording*

Show the Voiceover Record Button

You start the recording by clicking the microphone icon, so you need to see it. If you don't see it in the track headers, right-click the track header and choose *Customize* to access the Track Header Button Editor, as shown in Figure 3-76. Drag the microphone icon to where you want it to appear in the track header.

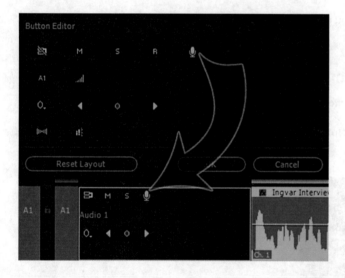

Figure 3-76. *Add the microphone icon to the track header if it's not already showing*

Even though you have the microphone button available, it may be grayed out, as shown in Figure 3-77. To make it active, you need to set the right input in the Voice-Over Record settings.

Figure 3-77. *If the Voiceover Record icons (microphone icons) are grayed out, it means your system doesn't know what microphone to use. You must open the Voice-Over Record settings and choose the input.*

Choose Input

Right-click again in the Audio Track Header in your voiceover track to get to the *Voice-Over Record Settings* dialog shown in Figure 3-78. Choose your microphone or audio mixer as the input and set the audio level using the Levels settings dialog for that microphone in your OS's Input Devices settings—or by adjusting the fader of your mixer if you're lucky enough to have one. Give the clip a new name if you don't want the default one.

Figure 3-78. *Right-click in the track header to find Voice-Over Record Settings. The dialog lets you choose microphone, set pre- and post-roll, check audio levels, set countdown cues, give the clip a name, and so on.*

If you only have a built-in mini-jack mic input on a laptop, the audio quality is not likely to be stellar. I recommend that you use an external USB or Thunderbolt audio card or a USB microphone instead. You can also buy very small XLR-to-USB microphone adapters that convert your analog microphone into a USB microphone. They aren't much bigger than an XLR connector, and just feel like a short extension cord for the microphone.

On a workstation/tower you can have dedicated audio cards that offer great audio quality and sport miscellaneous inputs.

Add a Mono Track

If you use a standard track for the voiceover, you get a stereo voiceover file. This is not what we want. I recommend that you use a mono track for voiceover recording. If you didn't create the sequence from a custom preset with a dedicated VO track, right-click the audio track header and choose *Add Tracks*, as shown in Figure 3-79. Don't choose *Add Track*, as it just adds another standard track. It needs to be Tracks–plural. In the dialog, tell Premiere to add a mono track and choose where you want it to be.

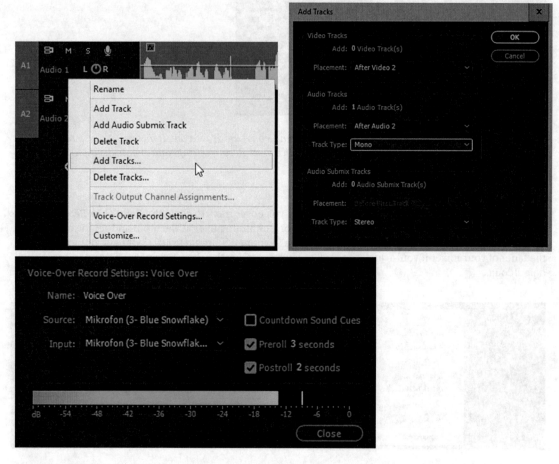

Figure 3-79. *Add a mono track, and you will see that the preview in the Voice-Over Record Settings has changed to mono*

This may seem like a lot of preparation, but it will be second nature in a few tries, and most settings will be kept if you don't change the inputs on your system.

Start the Voiceover Recording

From here on, it's smooth sailing. Activate the bin where you want to keep your voiceover recordings. Then, park the playhead where you want the recording to start in the timeline, as I've done in Figure 3-80. Now, you're ready to record a mono voiceover clip from the right input with the right levels, to the right bin on the right track!

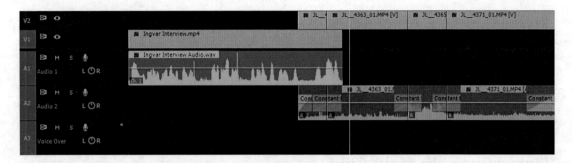

Figure 3-80. *Timeline ready for voiceover recording*

Click the microphone icon in the track header in your voiceover track and watch the preroll and countdown. The track header and the Program Monitor will both inform you in bright red colors that you're recording. See Figure 3-81. When the recording has finished, hit the **Spacebar**. A voiceover audio clip appears in your chosen track, as seen in Figure 3-82, and is saved in the bin you activated before hitting the microphone icon.

Figure 3-81. *The microphone icon turns red, and a banner appears in the Program Monitor. Yep, we're recording—no doubt about that.*

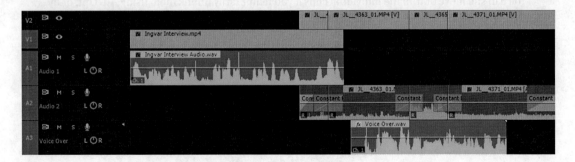

Figure 3-82. *When you stop recording, a voiceover clip appears in the track and in your bin*

Merge Clips in a Timeline

You can merge clips in a timeline if you haven't done it in a bin or the Project panel, but you need to synchronize them first. Place the clips on separate tracks, select them, and go to **Clip ➤ Synchronize**, or use the right-click menu or a shortcut.

Then choose *Merge Clips* from the same menu or use the shortcut. I do not particularly like to merge clips this way. I much prefer to synchronize in a multi-camera source sequence instead, for various reasons. More on that in Chapter 5.

Linked Clips, aka Multi-Clips

You can link several audio clips to one or more video clips, creating a multi-clip. They need to be the same audio type and on different tracks. If any of the clips are already linked, they must be unlinked before you can create a multi-clip. Multi-clips are useful when extra audio clips need to stay synced to the video. Creating a multi-clip will make sure they stay synced until you decide otherwise. To create one, select the clips, right-click, and choose *Link*, or use the keyboard shortcut **Ctrl/Cmd+L**.

A multi-clip will mostly behave like other clips. When you move one of the clips in a multi-clip, the other clips will move with it. The whole multi-clip moves as one unit. If you trim the head or tail of a multi-clip, all the clips in it will be trimmed by the same amount, and you cannot trim past the end of any of the individual clips. Figure 3-83 shows that all clips in the multi-clip are adjusted when the out point of one is selected.

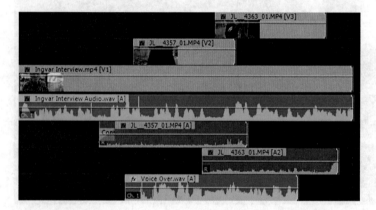

Figure 3-83. *Multi-clips are two or more clips that are linked together*

You can still move or trim the individual clips if you temporarily unlink them using **Alt/Opt**, or by temporarily turning off Linked Selection in the timeline just like you would when making a split edit in a standard video clip with audio.

If you need to change the audio levels for individual tracks in a multi-clip, park the playhead over the clip and use the Audio Clip Mixer, or **Alt-click** on one clip in the timeline and use the keyboard shortcuts to increase or decrease the levels.

If you want to link audio clips that are on the same track, use grouping instead.

Grouping Clips

If you've synced a few audio clips with sound effects to events in the video it might be a good idea to not lose the sync. **Marquee-select** all the clips or **Shift-click** them, and click **Clip ➤ Group**. Again, you can also use the right-click menu or use the shortcut **Ctrl+G**.

You can ungroup them in the same menu, but often you don't have to. You can still adjust in and out points of the individual clips in the group just like with multi-clips. The most obvious differences between multi-clips and a group is that you can group clips on the same track but not link them, and that you can adjust the in and out points on all clips in one go on linked clips, while the in and out points of grouped clips still need to be selected individually.

Time Remapping and Audio

Audio is not affected by time remapping in Premiere, so the audio quickly gets out of sync. You could use speed/duration instead and cut the clip into chunks with different speeds—but there is a much easier and better way! Send the clip to After Effects via Dynamic Link and enable Time Remapping there with **Layer ➤ Time ➤ Enable Time Remapping**. Then, set the frame blending to Pixel Motion: **Layer ➤ Frame Blending ➤ Pixel Motion.** Time remapping in AE works quite differently from the one in Premiere, so you should read about Time Remapping in AE Help.

Generate Audio Waveforms

If you turn off Automatic Audio Waveform Generation in the Audio preferences, you will have no waveforms in the timeline or in the Source Monitor. You can generate audio waveforms when you need them. Select any clip (or multiple clips) and go to **Clip ➤ Generate Audio Waveform**. You can also assign a keyboard shortcut.

Pancake Timeline Audio Track Tips

When you're editing with the Pancake Timeline feature, you'll sometimes get a + in the lowest audio track in the edit sequence, and if you do the edit, you may get an extra audio track in your edit sequence. What's going on here?

If you have too few tracks in your edit sequence, more will be added, and the new audio clip will end up on that new track—*too few* meaning less than the track number in the source you're editing from, as Figure 3-84 shows. So, if you edit from track 4 in the source, you'll need to have four tracks to avoid getting new ones.

Figure 3-84. *When this + sign shows up, it means your source has more tracks than the edit sequence. You may get new audio tracks automatically.*

If you do have enough tracks, no new tracks are added, and the new clip ends up at the right track (chosen by you using your Source Assignment shortcuts). So, the trick is to have enough audio tracks in your edit sequence, like I have in Figure 3-85.

187

Figure 3-85. *If the number of tracks is higher than the highest track number you're grabbing stuff from in your source, everything works as expected*

I very seldom encounter this problem, since I normally use an eight-track custom sequence setup. I already have eight tracks, and my sources almost never have more than eight tracks.

Yes, it's strange that we must create empty tracks for this to work as expected, but it's not a big deal for most workflows. If you feel it's a bit inconvenient to have seven, or even fifteen empty tracks, don't worry. You can delete them very fast with the *Delete Tracks* option in the sequence. See Figure 3-86. Just click the *Delete Audio Tracks* checkbox and press Enter.

Figure 3-86. *You can delete all empty tracks in one go*

■ **Note**   Add a keyboard shortcut to quickly open the Delete Tracks dialog. Now it takes one keystroke, one mouse-click, and pressing Enter to get rid of all the empty tracks when the edit is done.

Using mono or stereo sources and exporting just a stereo mix isn't too hard, but when we add more tracks to the sources or want to export multiple audio tracks or channels, things get complicated. Let's dive in!

Multi-channel Audio: Mono Setup

Please note that this is only one way of setting up a multi-channel sequence. There are many more, and I'm not saying this is the best way. It's just an example. To set up Premiere for multi-channel editing with mono tracks, choose an existing sequence preset. The DSLR one will do.

Go to the Tracks tab and set Master Track to Multi-channel and 8 channels (or whatever number you need), as shown in Figure 3-87. All tracks are now sent to output 1+2. This can be changed in the *Assign* column, but it's actually more intuitive to do it in the Audio Track Mixer later.

Figure 3-87. *Make mono tracks and pan the ones that need panning. Also, give them proper names.*

The tracks are standard tracks, and you might want to use mono tracks only. So, let's delete all the tracks. Then, add eight new tracks and give them names. They will all be mono tracks. Name the new sequence Set-Up. It's just a temporary sequence.

In the Audio Track Mixer, set the proper outputs for each track (1+2, 3+4, and so on) as shown in Figures 3-88 and 3-89. Now the audio tracks get routed to their respective output channels.

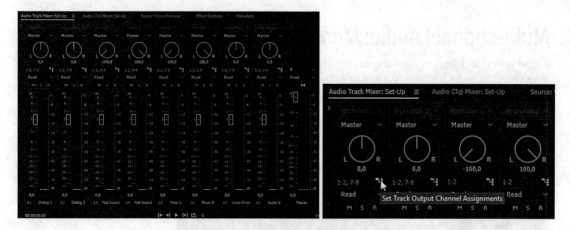

Figure 3-88. *A track can be assigned to one or more pairs of outputs*

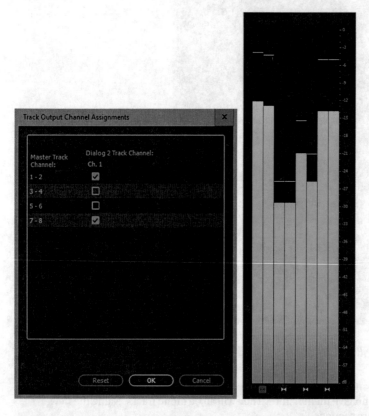

Figure 3-89. *Set the output routing for each track. The audio meter shows all the outputs, but you can decide which stereo pair to listen to by clicking the speaker icon under the pair you want to monitor.*

190

When you're satisfied with your setup, and you've tested it with some real clips, go to the New Sequence dialog again. This time, in the Tracks tab, choose *Load from Sequence* and choose the Setup sequence, as I've done in Figure 3-90. Now all the tracks are routed as they were in that sequence. Save this preset with a proper name and add a description if you want to. See Figure 3-91. Now you can use this preset every time you need a sequence like this. Make sure you sync your setting with the Creative Cloud server so you don't lose your presets.

Figure 3-90. *You can load a track setup from an existing sequence. Choose what sequence to import settings from.*

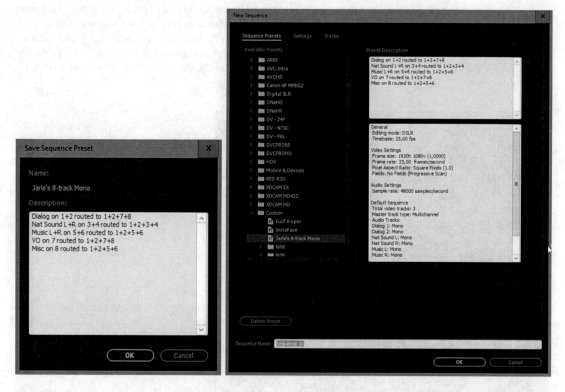

Figure 3-91. *Save the setup as a preset and never do this work again. Adding some descriptive text helps in case memory fails. When you want to make a new sequence in the future, just choose the preset and give the new sequence a name. Done.*

Listen to a Downmix

When you have more than two outputs, the master fader gets an additional button named *Monitor All Channels*, aka the *Downmix* button. See Figure 3-92. It does exactly what it says; it maps all the channels to two mono channels so you can listen to a downmix of all the tracks. This does not affect the output; it's just a setting for how you listen to the tracks. Most setups I've seen don't need this, as they have a Full Mix on tracks 1 and 2 and only listen to those.

Figure 3-92. *Monitor all channels in a multi-channel sequence*

What Did We Just Accomplish?

Broadcast and film editors will often need to output different mixes for different purposes. The Full Mix (aka Original Mix or Final Mix) is what goes on air. M&E is Music and Effects. Filled International Tracks is everything but the dialogue, so dialogue in different languages can be added. The Audio Post-Production Knowledge Base (triggertone.com) has some good explanations for the different kinds of mixes.

With the preceding sequence setup, we're able to edit our show while listening to outputs 1+2 only. All tracks are routed to these, and this will be our finished audio mix. Outputs 3+4 will have only the nat sound and nothing else. This is very useful if you want to use material from the show in other shows later. Outputs 5+6 will have music and miscellaneous sounds only, which is useful if you need to make international versions or get into copyright trouble and need to change the music. Outputs 7+8 will have dialogue and voiceover. But all this can easily be changed in the Audio Track Mixer.

By doing this, we've made a sequence that is suitable for editing and is still very good for archives and master files. When you want to export, choose an output format that supports multiple audio tracks, like ProRes 422 or DNxHD, set the number of channels to 8, and export. More on this follows.

Make sure you interpret all the audio as mono on import when using this approach to multi-channel audio editing.

Multi-channel Adaptive Tracks Setup

If you thought that was complicated, you're in for a treat: use adaptive tracks instead of mono, and you'll potentially add several layers of confusion!

Click on the Output Assignment icon (Figure 3-93) when creating an adaptive track in a multi-channel sequence; you get the Channel Output Mapping dialog. After setting Input 1 to Outputs 1+2, you might be tempted to set output mapping for the rest of the input channels here. The problem is that if you work with mono files, they have only one input—so what you set the rest of the inputs to is irrelevant!

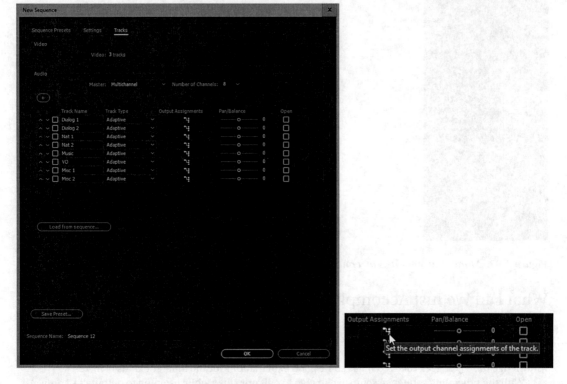

Figure 3-93. Routing adaptive tracks is not as intuitive as routing mono tracks—but it can be done

This dialog counts for one track only. Stereo files will have two inputs, 5.1 files will have six, and so forth. But if you work exclusively with mono files, like a lot of people do for OMF compatibility and other reasons, only Input 1 on each channel is relevant. Read this again if it didn't make sense. It will eventually.

By default, source channel 1 is mapped to track 1, source channel 2 to track 2, and so on, as shown in Figure 3-94. When using mono sources in a sequence with adaptive tracks, only Input 1 (the first column) in each track matters. Figures 3-95 and 3-96 show how VO and music may be routed differently.

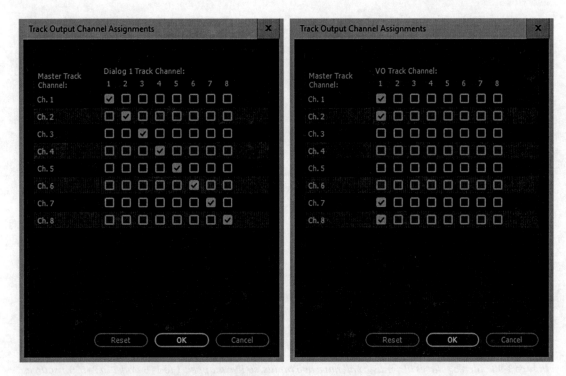

Figure 3-94. *Default settings on the left, my VO track settings on the right. You don't have to deselect all the other tracks, but it gives a clear view of what's going on.*

Figure 3-95. *Here I've mapped the first two channels from the dialogue track to 1+2+7+8. I chose to map both 1 and 2, since some dialog sources may be dual mono or stereo.*

Figure 3-96. *Stereo sources like music will have two inputs, so I've mapped 1 to 1+5 and 2 to 2+6. 5.1 sources will have six inputs*

To avoid confusion with an adaptive track setup, I recommend setting all other inputs to *None* in your presets if you're using mono clips only. Using adaptive tracks has the advantage that you'll see all outputs for all channels in the Audio Track Mixer, so you can easily see where they're routed.

Adaptive tracks show meters for all the channels in every track—even the channels not in use—so the meters can get very narrow, as you can see in Figure 3-97.

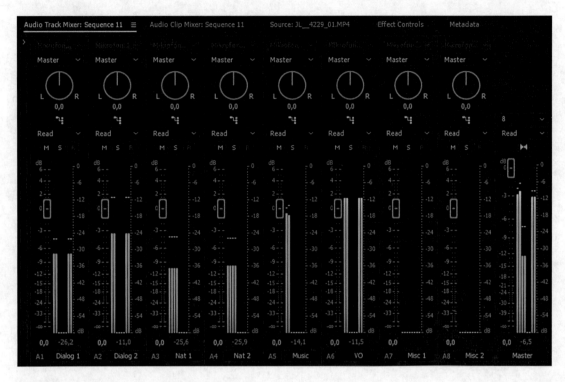

Figure 3-97. *Adaptive tracks can get very narrow meters*

This might seem convoluted, but once you set it up you can save the sequence into a template project and never do it again.

Many Other Set-ups Are Possible

These two examples used solely mono and solely adaptive tracks. You can also have setups with standard tracks for the music, mono tracks for dialogue, and adaptive tracks for others. It quickly becomes complicated to explain in a book, so I'll leave the experimenting to you.

Editors Do It Differently

I've done quite a bit of Premiere Pro coaching for European broadcast companies. I've seen several setups for 8-channel output, and none of them were identical. Even internally within one company, the setup will vary from editor to editor and from project to project. One project could have mono tracks only, mapped with the mapping feature as just shown. Another, also with mono tracks only, would have all the mapping done through submixes and sends in the Audio Track Mixer. Some editors used a mix of adaptive, mono, and 5.1 tracks. The end result is pretty much the same.

So, as you can see, there really is no standard way of doing this. Everyone uses a method that works with the hardware they have, the end delivery format, and their own skills and knowledge.

Who Needs 32 Output Channels?

If you're doing a lot of audio versions of your material, like Disney's localized versions of children's shows all over Europe, you can have a lot of tracks in a sequence. This might be stereo mix on tracks 1-2, 5.1 mix on tracks 3-8, and stereo languages on tracks 9-32, giving you a total of 12 separate languages in one master file. That's actually too few for some companies, but most video formats will only store 32 audio channels, so they need to make more than one master file.

Tweak the Audio Meters

The audio meters have some hidden features for multi-track editing. See Figure 3-98. You can set them to show mono tracks or stereo pairs. You can *Solo Tracks in Place*—meaning they remain in the output channel they're routed to, unrelated to what channels you're listening to. They can show valleys and peaks, static or dynamic, and you can change the magnification or resolution of the scale. Right-click in the audio meter and give it a try.

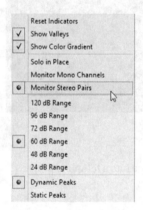

Figure 3-98. *Explore the options in the Audio Meters right-click menu*

Audio Output Mapping Preferences

In the Audio Hardware preferences, you'll find Output Mapping. The left column affects mono and stereo sequences. The middle column affects only 5.1 sequences, and the right column affects only multi-channel sequences.

It doesn't do much good if you only have a stereo system. You can only switch between left and right. But if you have some way of listening to more channels—like a 5.1 system or a third-party output card with eight or more audio channels—then you can decide which channel goes where from the different types of sequences. Figure 3-99 shows the mapping for a BlackMagic card. To change the routing of the channels, drag the icons up or down.

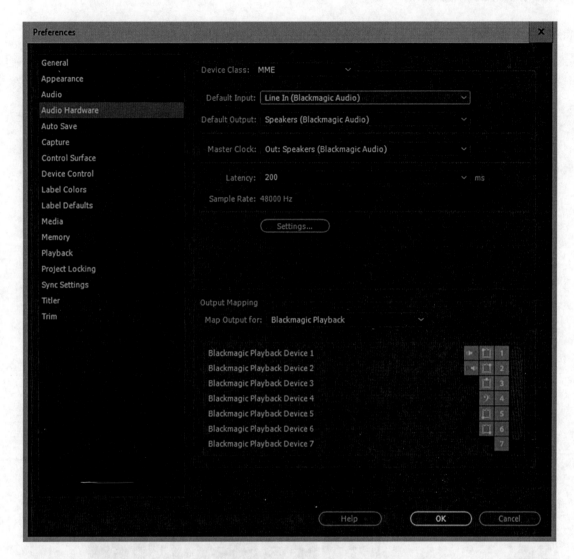

Figure 3-99. *You can route mono, 5.1, and multi-channel outputs to whatever channel you want on your output card. Screen dump courtesy of Bart Walczak.*

When you've edited your multi-channel sequence, of course you need to export multi-channel audio too.

Multi-channel Audio Export

To export multi-channel audio, you need to export from a sequence with a multi-channel master track and export to a format that supports multi-channel audio. Formats like H.264 and MPEG-2 will only support mono, stereo, and 5.1 audio. Formats like QuickTime (including ProRes) with uncompressed audio, DNxHD, MXF OP1a, and Waveform Audio do support multi-channel audio.

When you export to one of these formats, you'll get a drop-down menu (see Figure 3-100) where you can decide how many tracks to include in the export.

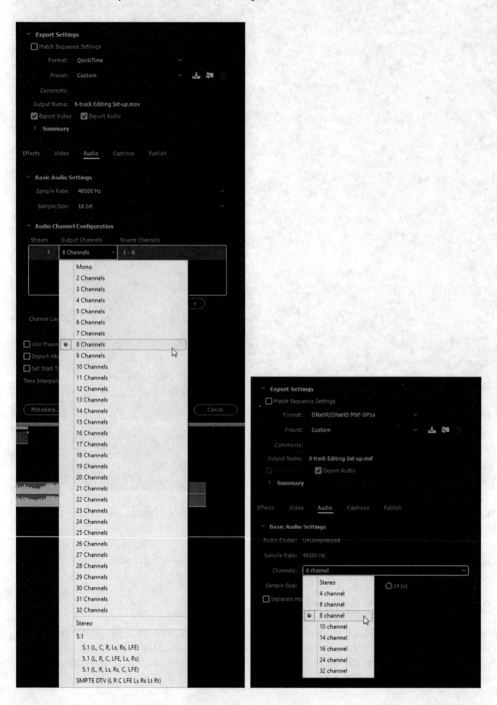

Figure 3-100. *If the export format supports it, and your sequence has a multi-channel master track, you can export up to 32 channels of audio. The left and right images here show the options for two different export formats.*

Export Discrete QuickTime Tracks

Some broadcasters might want you to specify whether the tracks are stereo pairs or discrete mono tracks. You can specify the order and type of tracks in the Audio Channel Configuration section, as shown in Figure 3-101. Hit the + button to add tracks and the - button to remove them.

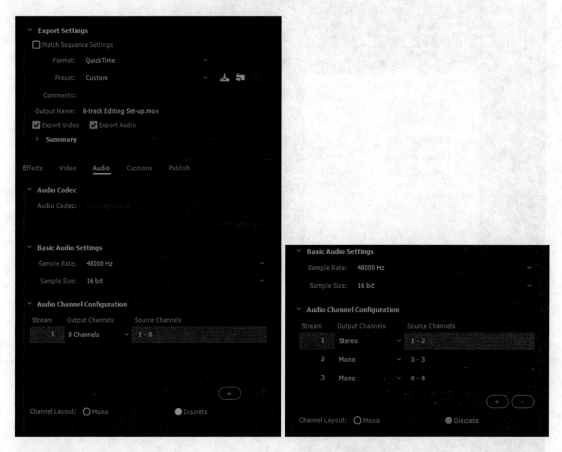

Figure 3-101. *QuickTime export is mostly stereo pairs, mono, or discrete mono tracks, but you can also export 5.1 or multi-channel*

The tracks are called *discrete* because some formats were multi-plexed before, like some Dolby systems, where the surround channels were multiplexed into one track. So, the word *discrete* is just a way of saying it's a clean, separate audio track that is not multi-plexed. It's not different from a mono track in any other way than its nametag.

Some broadcasters use these tags in their playout server systems to automatically route audio, so you need to tag your tracks correctly or your show will be rejected by their quality control system.

5.1 Track Layout for QuickTime

Similarly, you might get different specifications for 5.1 track layouts from different companies. Use the Channel Layout drop-down menu in Figure 3-102 to choose the order of the tracks.

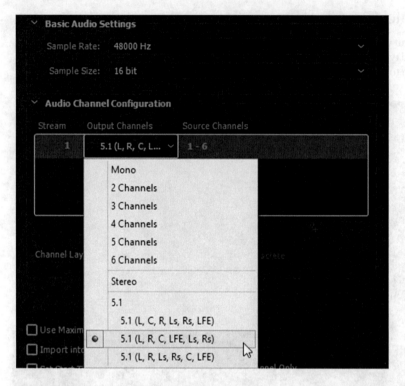

Figure 3-102. *You can specify the 5.1 track layout*

Say you need to export both 5.1 and a stereo mix in the same file. Figure 3-103 shows one possible solution: Ch1 – Left, Ch 2 – Right, Ch 3 – Center, Ch 4 – LFE, Ch 5 – Ls, Ch 6 – Rs, Chs 7&8 - Stereo Mix.

Figure 3-103. *One example of multi-channel 5.1 output layout*

Two Informative Tutorials for Multi-channel Audio in Premiere

Audio Mapping for Lazy People

Paul Murphy has a great tutorial on using submixes for quicker audio mapping and on saving the settings as a preset for future use:

`thepremierepro.com/blog-1/2015/10/17/audio-mapping-for-lazy-people`

Prepping for Audio Post

Michael Kammes has a great video on prepping for audio post-production in his Five Things series:

`5thingsseries.com/prepping-for-post-audio/`

Now that you have an understanding of the whole audio-editing framework, let's go into more detailed descriptions of how to enhance, repair, and mix your audio.

Audio Sweetening and Mastering

Mastering the audio means optimizing audio levels, making sure you've got a good frequency balance, smoothing some transitions, removing noise, possibly adding some decay to certain sounds, and so forth. You're basically cleaning up and enhancing the soundscape. This mastering is where you add some EQ and compression; take away pops, clicks, and noise; add fades; and generally make it sound better. It's also known as *sweetening* the audio.

Mastering also involves making sure the levels are "correct" according to the chosen standards and that the sound levels are equal throughout the show.

Premiere has the Mastering audio effect with some presets you can play with, but I recommend that you learn to control this manually.

Mixing Audio

Your timeline will typically have several audio tracks, maxing out at 99 available tracks. That should be enough for the average filmmaker. But your output will usually have far fewer tracks than this, so the tracks need to be mixed down to a smaller number of tracks.

Your output can be mono, stereo, 5.1, or multi-channel from 2 up to 32 tracks. The average video on Vimeo or YouTube will only need a stereo output. A feature film or documentary can have stereo or 5.1 output, and a film going to the archive—even if produced in stereo—can have 8 tracks or more. For broadcasters dubbing in several languages, 24 or 32 tracks is pretty common.

Miscellaneous Mixing Tips

Make sure to use proper (preferably studio) speakers. Do not do your audio mix with headphones. Mixing on the laptop's speakers can also be fatal because you will not hear the deepest bass sounds, and when played back on a good system you will get some bad surprises.

Sharp EQ filters will severely damage your audio quality. You might get rid of the noise from a bad recording, but you're destroying the quality of speech or other sounds in the same file. Go easy with the EQ. Listen to the voice; don't just listen for the noise.

Some occasional peaking in tracks is okay, but make sure you do not have any peaking in your master track. Apply a soft compressor and a limiter to your master track for final output.

Sometimes you just have to trust your ears. It's great that we have all sorts of audio-level and loudness meters, but if your ears are telling you something needs to be louder or lower, trust them.

We Need Variation

To make the louder (that often means action) parts of your film effective, you need moments with very little sound as a contrast. Quiet followed by powerful. The absence of sound is just as effective as sound itself. Well, not complete silence—just no sounds other than ambience.

If you're adding gun shots, footsteps, and other repetitive sounds, make sure you don't use the same sound with the same level every time. Give the sound some variation through EQ, speed, and levels.

Choose Your Reference Level

Over the years since the dawn of digital audio, many standards for reference levels have been—and are still—used. The North American delivery standard for digital TV audio is -20 dB with peaks no higher than -10 dB. Most European countries use a calibration tone of -18 dB with max peaks at -9 dB.

Why not mix all audio with peaks at 0 dB? Because the levels above that are what the broadcasters use as their headroom. For broadcasters, this is important. They also have live shows, and there's no way they can have full control of every sound, so there will be peaks above their usual max level. Setting the reference level to -18 dB makes sure no peak levels go above 0 and get clipped.

But if you're not mixing for broadcast, you don't need all that headroom. You can have your highest peak at -0.1 dB, and it will all be fine. My approach to this is to do whatever the customer wants me to, but not until the final export. I do my mixing and mastering so that my average peaks are around -6 dB, with the highest peaks almost reaching 0 dB.

Then, if the broadcast network wants the reference level to be -18 dB (with peaks at -9 dB), I will lower the overall level by 9 dB using the Audio Track Mixer's master fader and put a test tone for them at -18 dB. If they want a tone, that is. They're happy, and I'm happy. It takes me just a few seconds.

Loudness Radar

Loudness is not the same as the peak level, sound pressure, or the overall level. It's a way to measure subjective loudness as perceived by the typical human.

European Broadcasting Union (EBU) recommends that the *Programme Loudness Level shall be normalized to a Target Level of -23.0 LUFS*. EBU Recommendation R 128, on loudness and permitted maximum level of audio signals, sets standards for measuring loudness and can be found here: tech.ebu.ch/docs/r/r128.pdf.

In the United States, the CALM ACT (Commercial Advertisement Loudness Mitigation Act) describes the American way to do the same thing: atsc.org/wp-content/uploads/2015/03/Techniques-for-establishing-and-maintaining-audio-loudness.pdf. Australia has the OP-59 standard and Japan uses TR-B32. Beamt TV have a PDF with a list of Broadcast Loudness Standards by Country. Download it here: beam.tv/content/user-guides/beam_international_specifications.pdf. Most standards are based on the same ITU standard.

The Loudness Radar in Premiere (Figure 3-104) can measure loudness based on any of these standards. You'll need to understand some of the acronyms if you need to do your own settings.

Figure 3-104. *Loudness Radar*

LKFS = Loudness, K-weighted, relative to Full Scale

LU = Loudness Units

LUFS = Loudness Units relative to Full Scale

DBFS = Decibel Full Scale

The Loudness Radar effect in Premiere is very good, but it's supposed to operate in real-time, so there's apparently no way you can quickly scan the sequence. A ten-minute film takes ten minutes to check. I've found that playing back at four or eight times real-time speed will produce the same result.

Understanding the Loudness Radar

Add the Loudness Radar to your master track in the Audio Track Mixer by clicking the little Effect Selection triangle in one of the five slots, as shown in Figure 3-105. If you have more effects on the master track, the Loudness Radar should be the last effect in the stack. Double-click the effect to open its UI and choose the settings that match your target, be it European or American broadcast or Digital Cinema.

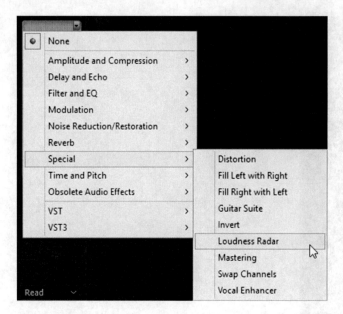

Figure 3-105. *Apply the Loudness Radar effect to the master track*

In these screenshots, I set mine to EBU R128 LUFS since I live in Europe. Remember to set it to measure after the master fader so it measures what you actually output from Premiere, not what you thought you'd output. Do this by right-clicking the effect in its slot and choosing *Post-Fader*, as I've done in Figure 3-106. Now, go to the start of your timeline and hit *Play*. When the whole thing has played through, you'll have a read-out in the Loudness Radar window.

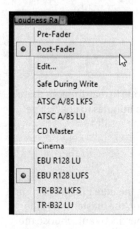

Figure 3-106. *Remember to measure the signal post-fader. You may want to move the master fader to adjust levels.*

The radar just *measures* the levels and gives you the results, so you cannot *adjust* volume in the Loudness Radar. So, what *can* you use this pretty read-out for? Check the Program Loudness numeric value (in the lower-right area of the plug-in) and then adjust your levels manually in the timeline or in the Audio Track Mixer to compensate for the offset.

In my example, the target was -23 and the measured result was -24, so I can raise my master track level by 1 dB. Figure 3-107 shows my measured result after raising the master fader 1 dB. Now it matches the target perfectly.

Figure 3-107. *The yellow number in the lower-right corner is the measured loudness. My first measurement was -24 dB LUFS, which is 1 dBs lower than the EBU standard. So, I raised my master fader by 1 dB and measured again, and landed at exactly -23 dB LUFS.*

The Loudness Radar doesn't have the most intuitive of user interfaces. Take a look at Figure 3-108. What looks like a *Play* button is not a button. It's just an indicator, and turns green when you're playing back the timeline. The *Pause* button will not pause playback—it will just pause the measuring. The *Reset* button wipes out all your measurements so you can start again from the beginning.

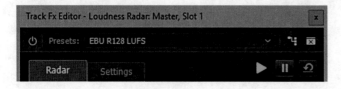

Figure 3-108. *Loudness Radar buttons*

■ **Note**   If you discover after analyzing that you set the wrong standard by mistake, you do not have to analyze again. Just switch the standard in the drop-down menu, and the radar and read-outs will immediately adjust accordingly.

Also, note that muting or soloing some output channels in the audio meters does not affect what tracks are read by the Loudness Radar.

The Loudness Radar can only analyze mono, 5.1, and stereo tracks. If you put it on a multi-channel master track, it will read only tracks 1 and 2. This is great if you're exporting a master file with stereo Full Mix on 1+2 and VO, nat sound, music, and other audio types on the other tracks for archive purposes. Not so great if tracks 1 and 2 are not your full mix . . .

For multi-channel masters, you must route the audio to an appropriate submix track and use the radar there. This way you can measure both a 5.1 Dolby submix and one or more stereo submixes in the same project.

If you are wondering how to send the tracks to a submix, here's how: click on an *Insert Send* slot above the Pan knob and choose the appropriate kind of submix. Then, right-click on it and make sure it's set to *Post-Fader* so it obeys the pan. Mute the submix so it's not sent to the master. It's only used for measurement.

True Peak Level

You will also have to watch out for true peak levels above the allowed levels for the standard. Even though your audio samples do not have too-high levels, the audio waveform that's built from them may be too hot.

Root 6 have a good illustration on their blog that shows this: root6.com/broadcast-engineering/loudness-part-2/.

Loudness Normalization in the Export Settings Panel

If you don't want to care about loudness at all while you're editing, you can add Loudness Normalization as an effect in the Export Settings panel. See Figure 3-109. Unlike the Loudness Radar, this will adjust the audio levels. It will analyze the audio in the sequence and apply the required positive or negative gain to meet the standard you choose.

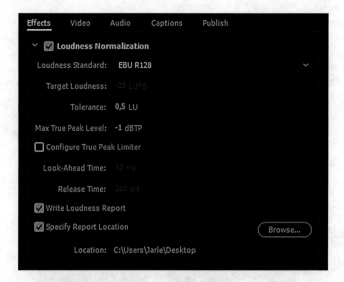

Figure 3-109. *Loudness Normalization in Export settings*

If you create a preset with the required settings for a broadcaster, you can always be sure that your audio passes quality control.

Use Audition for Legalizing

Adobe Audition can batch process files using its Match Volume panel. Drag-and-drop files into the panel and choose the standard you want to match, like the EBU R128–compatible ITU-R BS.1770-2. More on this later in this chapter.

Normalizing

You can normalize an interview so that the highest peak is just below your maximum level, like -1 dB. Music can be normalized to a lower level, around -10 dB. Normalizing your clips before you cut is usually a good idea, at least with interviews and scenes where people talk. You can normalize several clips in one go, and it can be done in the timeline or in the Project panel. Select the clips in the timeline and Hit **G** to access the Audio Gain dialog box, where you can set the Normalize level. Normalization applies the same amount of audio gain to the whole clip, so the dynamic range is preserved.

It can be a good idea to batch normalize all interviews, voiceovers, and dialogue scenes before putting them on the timeline. Select the clips in a bin or in the project panel and hit **G**. Note that any changes you do here do not affect clips already in the timeline! It will just affect new instances you put in the timeline, so you can't use this method from the project panel after the fact. You need to do it from the timeline itself if the clips are already there.

You can even normalize the master track: **Sequence ➤ Normalize Master Track**.

Submixes

Submixes are often used to group some tracks together and treat them equally. One scenario could be that you want to treat all your speech with the same compression. Rather than adding compression to each track, you can send all of them to a submix and add the compression to the submix.

When doing a final mix, it can be convenient to gather all speech tracks on one submix, all ambience and nat sound on another, and sound effects on a third. This way, you get away with only three faders, and you can still adjust the levels of these groups. If you're familiar with submixes in audio mixers, you'll find everything you need in the Audio Track Mixer.

Submix tracks are easily created by right-clicking in the audio track header, where you'll find a menu with *Add Audio Submix Track*. See Figure 3-110. You can also create submix tracks with **Sequence ➤ Add Tracks**.

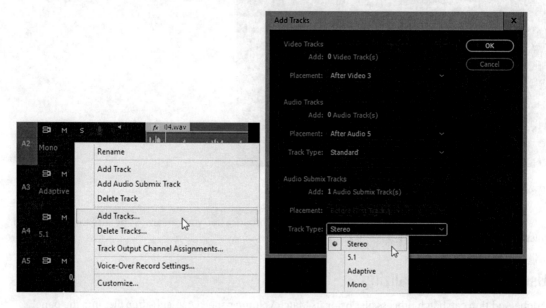

Figure 3-110. You can add submix tracks of any type

Tidy Up Your Audio Track Mixer View

If you have lots of tracks, the Audio Track Mixer gets crowded. To save some screen real estate, you can choose to hide some track types. You'll find this option in the panel menu, as shown in Figure 3-111.

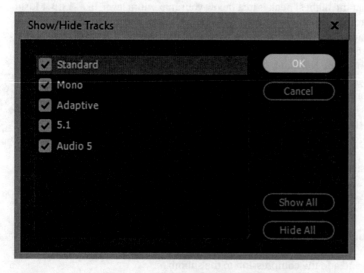

Figure 3-111. You can show or hide the different track types

Listen in a Loop

When adjusting audio parameters, like EQ or compression, you'll need to loop the playback so you can fine-tune the settings. Set in and out points in the timeline and click *Loop* in the Audio Track Mixer, the Program Monitor, or the Effect Controls panel. Or, just hit **Ctrl+L**. Figure 3-112 shows the *Loop* button.

Figure 3-112. *The Loop button*

Noise Reduction

Until recently, we had to go to Audition to get good noise reduction, but now we've got the adaptive noise reduction effect from Audition inside of Premiere—and it's very good. See the UI in Figure 3-113. Sometimes, though, its adaptiveness works against us.

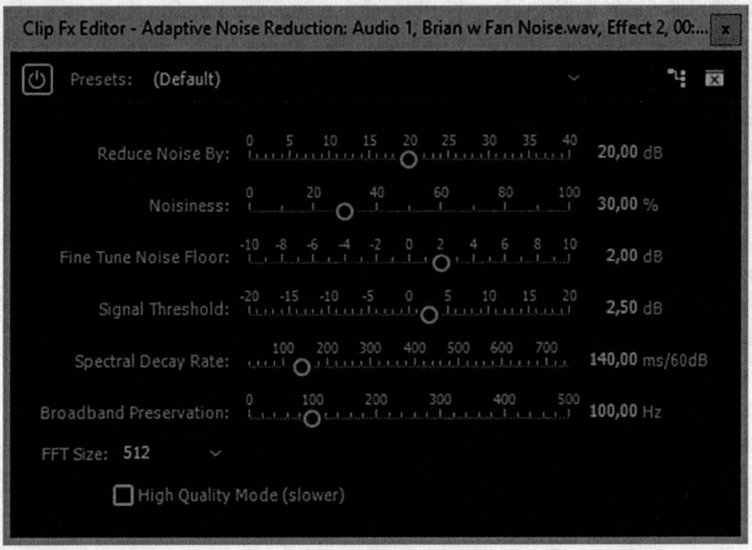

Clip Fx Editor - Adaptive Noise Reduction: Audio 1, Brian w Fan Noise.wav, Effect 2, 00:... x

Presets: (Default)

Reduce Noise By: 0   5   10   15   20   25   30   35   40   20,00 dB

Noisiness: 0   20   40   60   80   100   30,00 %

Fine Tune Noise Floor: -10 -8 -6 -4 -2 0 2 4 6 8 10   2,00 dB

Signal Threshold: -20   -15   -10   -5   0   5   10   15   20   2,50 dB

Spectral Decay Rate: 100   200   300   400   500   600   700   140,00 ms/60dB

Broadband Preservation: 0   100   200   300   400   500   100,00 Hz

FFT Size: 512

☐ High Quality Mode (slower)

Figure 3-113. *The adaptive noise reduction effect*

Guess what happens if you throw this on a clip that starts with some fan noise, and then someone starts talking over the noise? The noise will be gone, but only *after* the first couple of words! If there's more talking before this in the clip, you could fix this problem by nesting the whole audio clip and letting the effect do its magic in the nested sequence. Then you'd have to trim the nested sequence in the main edit sequence, of course.

Another workaround is to leave a two-second handle at the start of the clip in the timeline and set audio-level keyframes on an extra volume effect (from the Effects panel), added *after* the adaptive noise reduction effect, so the clip is silent for two seconds. You could even create an effect preset with both the adaptive noise reduction effect and the volume effect. This makes for untidy timelines, though, so because of this little gotcha, I tend to do the noise reduction in Audition instead.

Equalizing

Why use EQ? To make the sound better! Say you've recorded an interview using a lavaliere mic on the subject. Because the lavaliere is placed in the audio "shadow" below the chin, it will have less high frequencies than what is optimal, and the chest causes resonance around 600-800 Hz. See Figure 3-114.

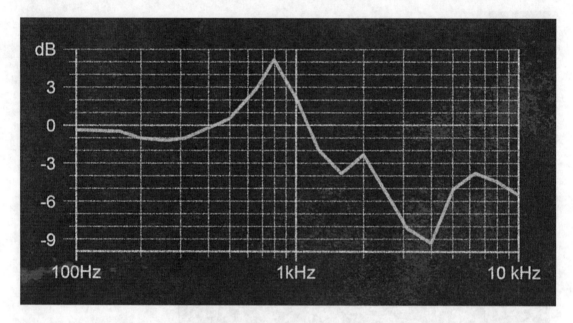

Figure 3-114. *Frequency response from a lavalier microphone placed on the chest, compared to a microphone placed one meter in front of a person. Notice the drop around 4 kHz, which impedes speech intelligibility. Data source: dpamicrophones.com.*

So, lowering the level a bit around 650 Hz and boosting the frequencies around 3–4 kHz can make the voice sound more natural. It will also increase speech intelligibility since the most important frequency range for this is 1-4 kHz. A male voice from the lavaliere might also sound more full if you give it a boost around 200 Hz.

EQ Tips

A quick Google search will give you thousands of tips on EQ settings for different sounds. Warm up a man's voice by adding 3-4 dB at 175-200 Hz, warm up a woman's voice by adding 3-4 dB around 400 Hz, for diction and clarity add 4-5 dB around 3000 Hz for men, and around 4000 for women, and so on.

The problem with most of these tips is that they will not work on all sounds or voices. You will have to tweak every sound individually and use your ears. The EQ presets in Premiere have names like Warm Presence and can be used as a starting point.

Add EQ while the music, ambience, and all other tracks are playing. If you solo the dialogue track and add your EQ you won't hear how it's affecting the rest of the mix.

Be Aware of Conflicting Frequencies

Each sound in a mix will have a range of frequencies. When we mix a voice over a low-frequency base sound we can still hear the voice quite clearly. But if the different sounds start fighting each other at the same frequency range, the mix can sound muddy and untidy. Your goal should be to make each separate audio element sound clear.

If the music is conflicting with a voice, you can try adding EQ to the music and try lowering the level for frequencies where it's conflicting with the voice. Don't overdo this, as the quality of the music will suffer. The Mastering effect has a preset named Make Room for Vocals that has a -6 dB dip at 1.844 Hz with a very soft Q-setting of 0.3. See Figure 3-115. This can be a good starting point for the EQ effect, and you can try moving the dip up and down in the frequency range.

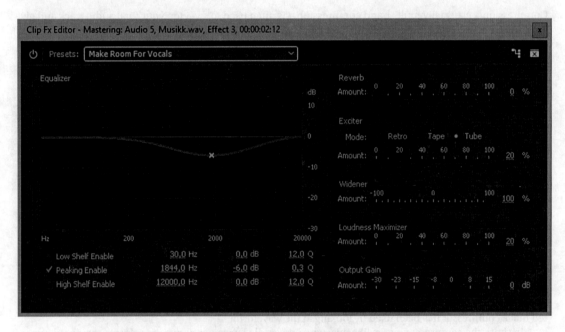

Figure 3-115. *Make room for speech by creating a valley at the frequencies where voices live*

The Targeted Switch

You might have wondered what the *Targeted* switch found in many audio effects does. When you click it, nothing seems to happen, except it turns blue, as you can see in Figure 3-116. What it does is that it toggles between two behaviors; the effects open either in the same floating window or in separate windows. You don't see the difference until you open at least two effects by clicking the *Edit* button in the Effect Controls panel. Mystery solved. You're welcome.

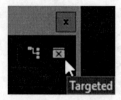 

Figure 3-116. *This is the "Targeted" switch*

Compression

Compression—especially multi-band compression—is often used to sweeten your final audio track and give it more oomph. A compressor will even out the difference between high and low signals (the dynamic range) by heightening the quiet parts and/or lowering the louder parts. Compression is most often used to achieve a louder sound overall, or to control audio peaks by lowering short transients. See Figure 3-117 for a before and after comparison.

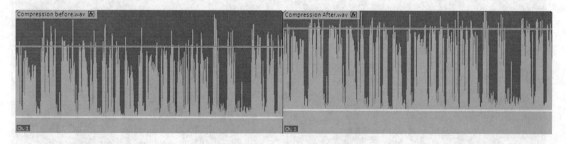

Figure 3-117. *Before (left) and after (right) compression. The average level (indicated by yellow lines—added by me) is higher.*

Good compression is subtle, meaning you shouldn't be able to hear that it's compressed. You can still tell that a compressor has been used by looking at the waveform.

In short, the compressor works like this: when the audio level goes above the selected threshold, the signal is compressed by the selected ratio. This will happen at a selected speed—the attack time—and the compressor will return the signal to its original level after a selected release time. Confused? Read on, while looking at Figure 3-118.

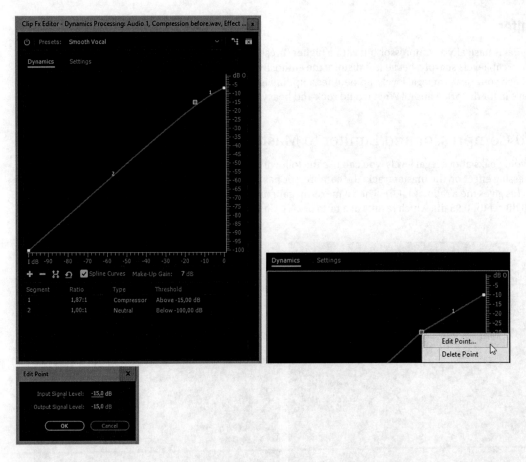

Figure 3-118. *To edit a point in the curve of the Dynamics Processing effect, right-click it*

Threshold: Sets the point where the compressor kicks in. Levels below the threshold are not influenced by the compressor.

Ratio: The ratio between the input and output. A ratio of 3:1 means that for every 3 dB the input increases above the threshold, the output will only be 1 dB higher. A 12 dB increase in input means only 4 dB more at the output. The signal is compressed by the ratio you set here.

These Threshold and Ratio settings are clearly visualized in the Dynamics Processing effect. Here you see the threshold where the compression kicks in, and the flatter curve above the threshold illustrates the compression ratio. The flatter the curve, the harder the signal is compressed.

Attack and Release times: Sets how quickly the compressor should start doing its thing when a higher-than-the-threshold input signal occurs, and how slowly it should "release" the signal when it gets lower. It's difficult to give good advice about these times, as every sound needs different settings. But if it sounds right, it is right. As a general rule, sharp transients will require a shorter attack time.

Output level/Gain/Make-up Gain: When you compress the signal, it gets lower, so you'll need to compensate for this.

215

Limiter

A *limiter* is basically a compressor but with a higher threshold and a much higher ratio. Generally, we don't want to clip levels sharply, because it distorts the audio. But it can be required to tame very loud sounds and keep your peaks at legal levels. Sometimes, clipping is a good thing. Thank whatever god or destiny you believe in for distorted audio! What would rock and heavy metal be without the distorted guitars?

Add Compressor and Limiter to Master Track

To avoid peaks above legal levels, you can use the following settings on two instances of the dynamics processing effect on the master track: the compressor has a knee-point at -10 dB, and 0 dB is lowered to -3 dB. This gives me a ratio of 1.43:1. Then a make-up gain of 2 dB is added. The limiter has a knee point at -1 dB, 0 dB set to -0.95 dB, which results in a ratio of 20:1. See Figure 3-119.

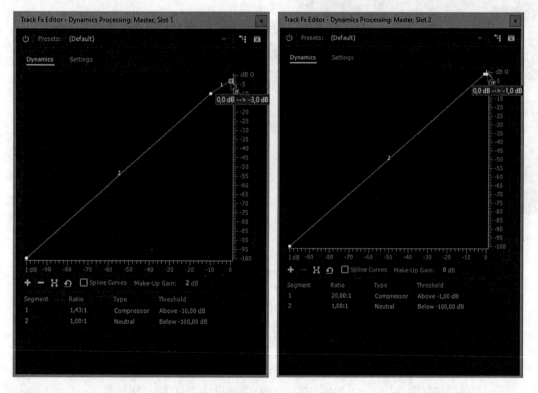

Figure 3-119. *A compressor lowers the highest levels, and a limiter takes care of stray peaks. Note that the actual level for the limiter is -0.95 dB, not -1.0 as shown. The value you get when you're hovering above the point is rounded off.*

These settings are not arbitrary; they're calculated. A peak at 0 dB would end up at -3 + 2 dB = -1 dB, which is safely below 0. An occasional stray peak above 0 dB would be taken care of by the limiter. Don't you just love math?

Adding Compressor to Some Tracks

Rather than compressing the whole mix, compressing a single track or clip to make it stand out more in the mix is often very effective. Compression artifacts in a voiceover track, like a pumping background noise, will often be hidden by the music or other sounds on other tracks, so you can push it further.

When mixing and mastering audio, add a compressor on clips or tracks with speech, such as the VO or interview track, to give them more "punch," especially when they're laid over a loud soundtrack. Merely increasing the volume would not do the trick because the highest levels would be too high, and consequently would be cut off and distorted.

Multi-band Compressor

In a complex mix, there will be a lot of different things going on at different frequencies. A standard compressor will compress all the sounds when one of them is too loud, but there is no reason that the middle frequencies should be compressed if only the high or low frequencies are too loud.

A multi-band compressor (Figure 3-120) will handle the different frequencies separately, and the mix will sound fuller and richer, and also get more oomph because the resulting sound will be louder. If you learn how to use and tweak the multi-band compressor, you can deliver fuller, more professional-sounding audio. This kind of compressor was widely overused in advertising, and that's why there are now regulations on broadcast loudness.

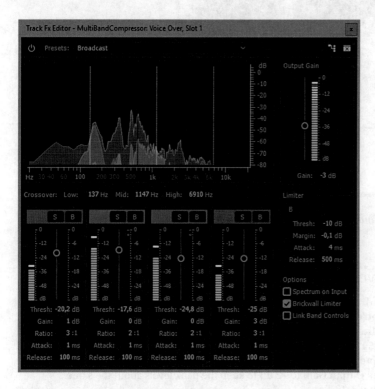

Figure 3-120. The multi-band compressor can compress different frequencies differently

Multi-band Compressor Takes a Lot of Power

It's like having four compressors, EQs, and limiters going on at the same time. Add this to a 5.1 clip—or worse, a clip with eight adaptive tracks—and you have 32 compressors and lots of other algorithms working in parallel on just one clip—and you probably have many clips. Your system will struggle . . . Use the effect on a track or a submix instead.

The multi-band compressor has four frequency bands. You can solo or bypass each band so you can hear what's going on there.

Actually, I like the UI from the old multi-band compressor (Legacy) better than the new one. I think the visual feedback is much more intuitive than the fancy frequency bands in the new one. See Figure 3-121. But the new one from iZotope sounds better, so I guess we better use that one.

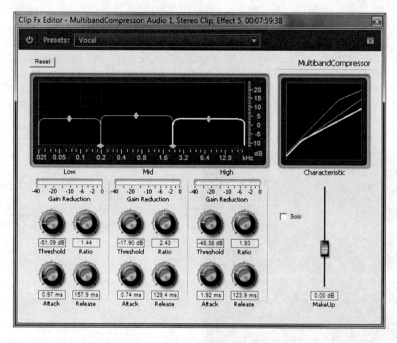

Figure 3-121. *The UI of the legacy multi-band compressor gives a good visual clue as to what's going on with the frequencies*

Create a Richer Voiceover Sound

If you need a richer, bigger VO sound, try the following recipe: normalize the VO to 0 dB. Yeah, I know—it sounds dangerous—but if it's a mono clip it will be lowered to -3 dB when panned to the middle. You're fine!

Then add the parametric equalizer effect and choose the Full Reset preset to get rid of most of the points. Set the L-band to +3.5 dB at 50 Hz, and band 5 to +3 dB at 4 kHz. Set the Q to 0.5. Turn off the H-band.

Now, add the multi-band compressor and choose the Broadcast preset. Compressing the peaks means we can add more gain, so let's set the Output Gain to +2 dB to keep the peak levels about the same. Figure 3-122 shows the settings for both effects.

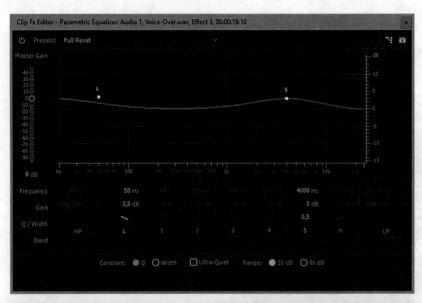

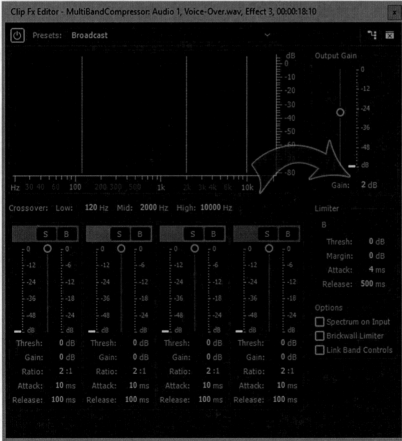

Figure 3-122. *EQ with some tweaking, plus multi-band compressor with the Broadcast preset, is a good starting point for a big voiceover sound*

Reverb and Delays

If the preceding recipe worked OK, try adding a tiny bit of reverb to the VO. It tends to smooth out the voice. Don't add too much reverb. You want to barely notice it's there. I used the studio reverb effect with the Vocal Reverb (small) preset and adjusted the output levels. See Figure 3-123.

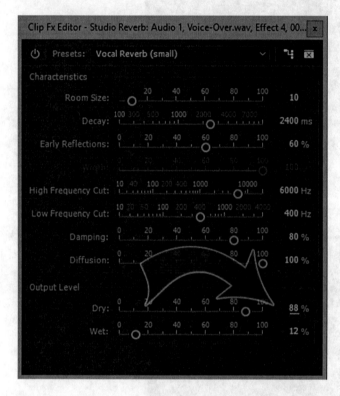

Figure 3-123. *Try adding just a little reverb to the VO to smooth it a bit*

To save as a preset, **Ctrl-click** (Cmd-click) all the effects, right-click one, and choose *Save Preset* as in Figure 3-124. Name it *Rich Voiceover*. Next time you need more oomph in a voiceover, just throw this preset on the clip.

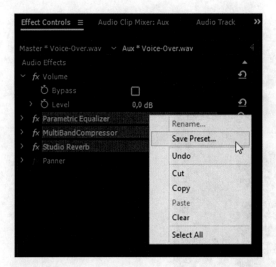

Figure 3-124. *Rich VO save*

Make a Reverb Ring-out

Sometimes we need to cut a clip abruptly because of some unwanted sound right after the cut point. Or maybe we want to end a music clip at a loud drum hit to add a dramatic punch. Most of the time, this will sound awful. Reverb to the rescue!

By quickly fading in some reverb during the last few frames of the audio clip, we can make the sound ring out instead. This is easily done by setting keyframes for the Mix parameter about 5-10 frames apart at the point where the sound ends.

If the clip is long enough, you can just set keyframes for Volume Level to very quickly fade the volume instead of cutting the tail of the clip when the reverb kicks in.

But if the clip isn't long enough for the reverb to ring out completely, you need to add some silence to the tail of it. There is no way to do this directly on an audio clip, but if you nest the clip you can add black video or a color matte after the clip in the nested sequence. Then, add the reverb to the nested sequence, and everything works fine. See Figure 3-125 for my settings, and a before and after waveform comparison.

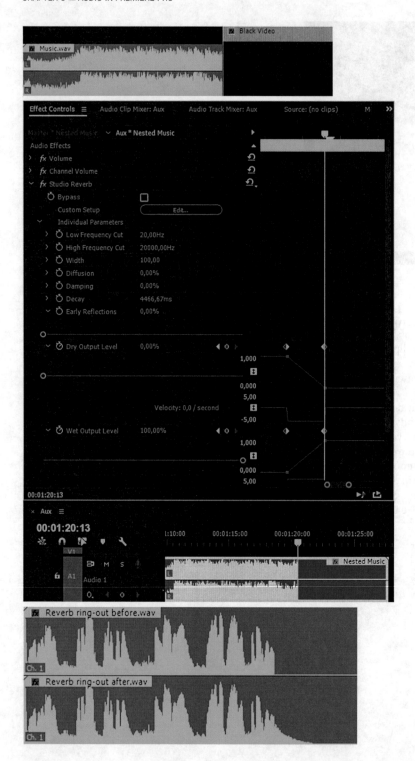

Figure 3-125. *Notice that the clip is nested to make room for the ring-out. Set keyframes on the Dry and Wet levels to introduce reverb just before the clip is over. Compare the waveforms before and after adding the reverb ring-out.*

Using the Essential Sound Panel

As you've seen in this chapter, audio mixing can be a bit challenging if you don't have much experience in audio post-production techniques. To make audio mixing more accessible, Adobe have come up with a panel that simplifies the process. Instead of knowing about technical terms like *compressor threshold*, *Q-value*, and so on, you only need to understand terms like *reduce noise, increase clarity, enhance speech*, and so forth.

The simple controls in the Essential Sound Panel (ESP) are actually adjusting dozens of parameters in the native effects in the Effect Controls panel. It's like having an audio engineer in your back pocket.

Assign an Audio Type and Choose a Preset

To use the ESP, select a group of clips in the timeline that should be treated the same—like all the dialogue or voiceover clips. If your timeline is nice and tidy, like mine in Figure 3-126, it makes this step very easy.

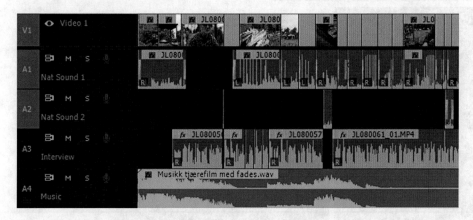

Figure 3-126. *Keeping different audio clip types on separate tracks makes it easy to select them. Here, I have dedicated tracks for music, interviews, and nat sound.*

With the clips selected, click on one of the four audio types in the ESP to assign it to all the clips. This reveals all the choices you have for the audio type you've chosen—dialogue being the most advanced of them. Think of this simple panel as a way to remote control the standard audio effects. You could achieve the same results by adding all those effects individually with the same settings.

You can choose presets to get you quickly to a decent starting point. I chose Balanced Male Voice in this case, as you can see in Figure 3-127.

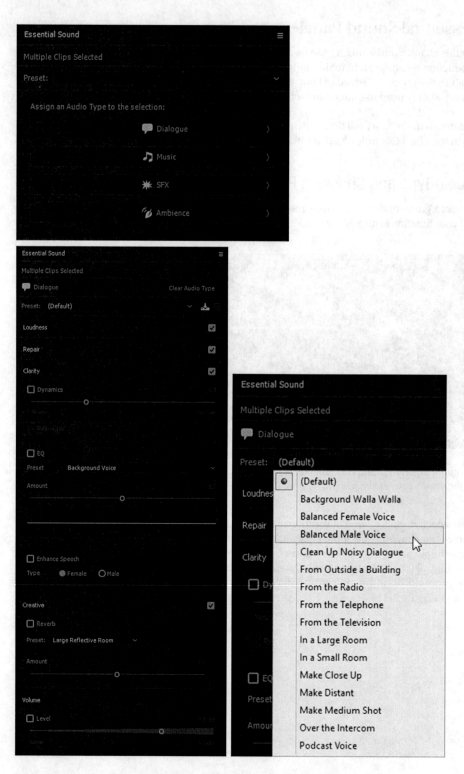

Figure 3-127. *The Essential Sound Panel has presets for different voice treatments*

Figure 3-128 shows the result of choosing the Balanced Male Voice preset. It has set values for loudness so it matches -23 dB LUFS and adds a DeEsser, a compressor/expander, and an EQ boost of around 2-4 kHz for increased clarity.

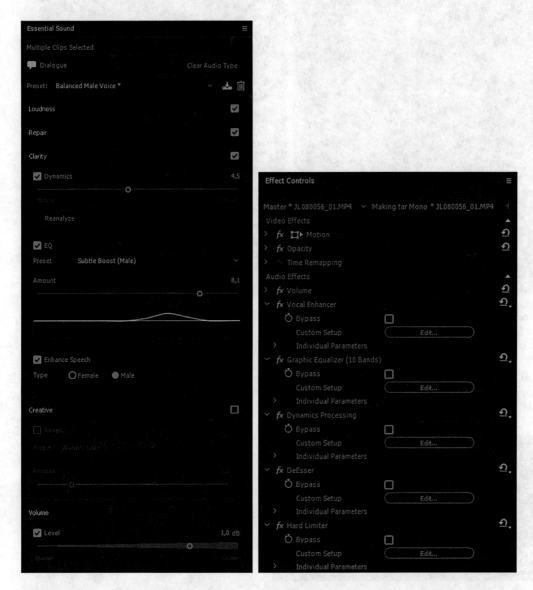

Figure 3-128. *The preset set some values in the ESP. In the Effect Controls panel (ECP), we can see the actual effects that have been added. Any adjustment you do in the ESP will adjust parameters in the ECP.*

■■■ **Note**   This is not the same result you'd get if you made presets for the effects and slapped it on all of them. The clips are analyzed individually, and they will get slightly different settings, as shown in Figure 3-129.

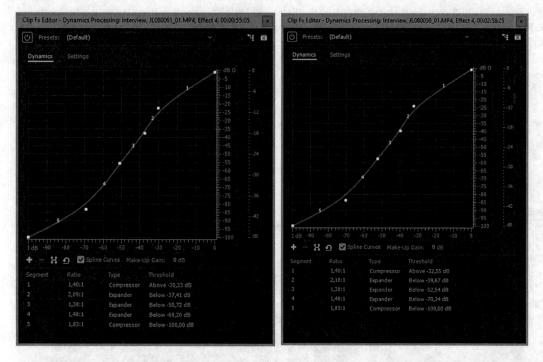

Figure 3-129. *The dynamics processing on each clip is slightly different. Even though these clips are two parts from the same interview, they did not get identical settings. Audio gain will also be set individually for each clip.*

If you want to adjust all the clips of one kind even further, later in the editing process, just deselect all clips in the timeline and click the button for the audio type you want to tweak. Figure 3-130 shows the available types in my sequence.

Figure 3-130. *Click one of the active buttons to select all clips of that audio type in the timeline*

To remove all effects that the ESP has added, just select the clips and click the *Clear Audio Type* button—where the arrow in Figure 3-131 is pointing.

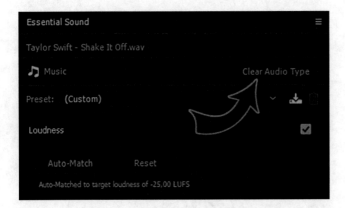

Figure 3-131. You can clear the audio type to remove all the effects from the ESP

■ **Note** Some of the presets for dialogue clips are meant for use on ADR recordings. The Make Close-Up, Make Distant, and Make Medium Shot presets apply reverb and EQ so that a single recording can quickly give the impression of any of those distances from the camera.

So, unfortunately, adding the Make Close-Up preset to a clip with lots of room tone and reflections from walls will not make it sound like a close-up shot.

Be aware that the names of the creative presets for ambience clips can be a bit misleading. They lead you to believe that the presets actually do add ambience. See Figure 3-132. Sorry, but they do *not* add ambience—they add reverb. You'll still need to record ambience in the field. The presets are meant to add more depth and space to your existing ambience clips.

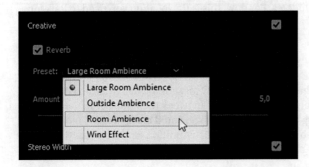

Figure 3-132. The ambience presets add reverb, not ambient sound

Save Presets

You can save your own presets for each audio type. I prefer to start by tweaking one of the built-in ones. The preset name gets an asterisk behind it to tell you that the settings have been changed. Now, hit the *Save Preset* button and give the preset a new name. You can now find your custom preset in the list. See Figure 3-133.

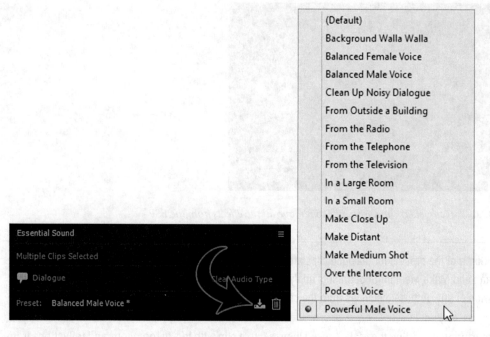

Figure 3-133. Save custom presets for later use

The preset file is saved, rather disappointingly, to the hidden folder **\Users\<username>\
AppData\Roaming\Adobe\PremierePro\11.0\Presets\EssentialSound\Default** on Windows and /
**Users/<username>/Library/Application Support/Adobe/Premiere Pro/11.0/Presets/EssentialSound/
Default** on MacOS. This means the presets are not synced with your Creative Cloud account, which is a
bummer. Let's hope Adobe will fix that in future updates. For now, this is the location you need to look for
when you want to share presets across teams.

Great for Collaboration

While this panel is easy to use, the power lies in the fact you're actually just adding native audio effects to
a clip (in the correct order of operations for typical mixing), and you can tweak them further in the Effect
Controls panel. The project could be passed along to an audio expert who could close the ESP and just work
with the normal effects themselves. You could also send the sequence to Audition, and any work done in the
ESP would transfer over to Audition.

Still Some Shortcomings

Unfortunately, the ESP isn't perfect. There are two big shortcomings at this point—the noise reduction and the music length adjustment. *Reduce Noise* uses the adaptive noise reduction previously described, where the noise reduction kicks in a second or two into the clip. So, for now, I like to use the noise reduction (process) effect in Audition instead of the noise reduction in the ESP.

For music, the *music duration* adjustment (Figure 3-134) is just a speed adjustment. You would think, since this panel comes from Audition, it would use the Remix function like Audition does, which intelligently shortens or lengthens music clips based on an analysis of the music. But for now, it just sets the speed. Adjusting the length of a music clip with speed is just silly, so the only logical explanation I can find for this is that they plan to add remix functionality in the future. I'm really looking forward to that!

Figure 3-134. Music duration in Premiere does not have the Remix option that Audition offers

Since the ESP comes from Audition, you can read more about it in Audition online help: `helpx.adobe.com/audition/kb/editing-using-essential-sound-panel-audition.html`. Most of this will be the same as in Premiere, but we're missing the Remix, at least for now.

5.1 Mixing and Editing

You can choose to mix in 5.1, and it has some great advantages—but do remember that more than 70 percent of the TV audience and close to 100 percent of online viewers will be listening in stereo. Even in 5.1, the primary sound information comes from the front speakers. Mostly, dialogue is in the center channel. Yes, it's mono. Surround is usually for ambience and special effects.

You will of course need a 5.1-capable system to be able to mix properly in 5.1. Fortunately, 5.1 speaker placement is very forgiving, so you don't need to have a perfect environment to do basic 5.1 mixing. But, if you're mixing for a theater release, you better get a good system!

5.1 Sequence Setup in Premiere

To truly mix 5.1 audio we need a 5.1 sequence. In the New Sequence dialog, go to the Tracks tab and change Audio Master to 5.1. In the Tracks tab you can also set the default audio tracks for your sequence, as well as submix tracks.

The 5.1 panner in the Audio Track Mixer (Figure 3-135) lets you pan a mono or standard track (but not a 5.1 track—it's already panned) to one of the four corners, or to the center channel. Use the Center Percentage knob to control what percent of a track goes to the Center channel. To send a track all the way to the LFE, drag the LFE Volume knob to 100 percent and the Center Percentage knob to 0 percent.

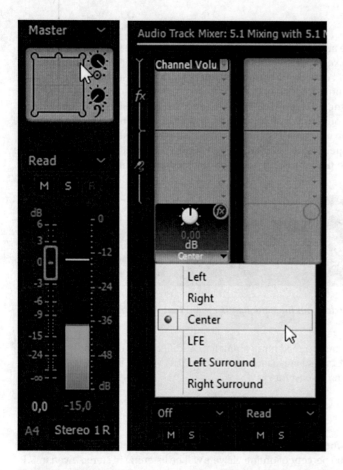

Figure 3-135. *The 5.1 panner is only available on non-5.1 tracks in sequences with a 5.1 master track (or submixes). Use the channel volume track effect to adjust individual channels*

Note that the settings you implement in the 5.1 panner are not saved with a sequence preset, so you'll have to pan every track manually when you create a new sequence. Or, you could save a template project with all the panning in place and import that project when you start a new 5.1 project.

Figure 3-136 shows the full interface while mixing 5.1. If you need to adjust the volume of individual channels in a 5.1 clip, use the channel volume effect in the Audio Track Mixer, or go to the Audio Clip Mixer and drag the individual channel faders, as shown in Figure 3-137. You have to right-click in the fader area and choose *Show Channel Volume* to get to the channel volume sliders in the Audio Clip Mixer.

Figure 3-136. *Mixing two 5.1 tracks and 4 mono tracks. Note that the non-5.1 tracks have the 5.1 panner.*

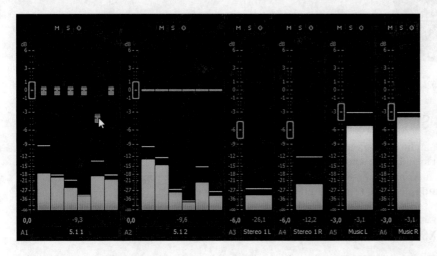

Figure 3-137. *You can adjust volume on individual channels with the faders if Show Channel Volume is activated*

Mix and edit your sequence as usual, and when you're finished, export to a format that supports 5.1 audio, like H.264, or AVI and QuickTime with uncompressed audio.

Using 5.1 Clips in a Multi-channel Sequence

When you put a 5.1 clip in a multi-channel sequence, you can see what channel goes where above the *Track Output Channel Assignment* button, as seen in Figure 3-138. Click the button to change the assignment if necessary. Other than this, everything works as you'd expect. In the Audio Clip Mixer, you can access the individual track levels as usual, and there will be six faders.

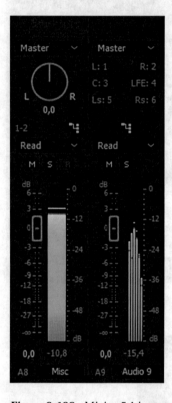

Figure 3-138. *Mixing 5.1 in a multi-channel sequence*

Sending 5.1 and Stereo to Separate Output Channels

Say you need to edit 5.1 audio that's already mixed—maybe you're editing a trailer for a movie and use clips from it. Then, you want to add some whooshes, stereo music, and so on. A very common way to deliver 5.1 masters is to have a 5.1 mix on tracks 1–6 and a stereo downmix on tracks 7–8. You get the sources as eight-track, 5.1, and stereo, and you need to create a multi-channel sequence for this.

5.1 Mixing in Mixed Multi-track Sequence

The easiest way to accomplish this is probably by using both 5.1 and standard tracks. In Figures 3-139 and 3-140 I've used two of each and routed them to their destination output tracks. By soloing the last stereo pair in the audio meters, I'm listening to the stereo output.

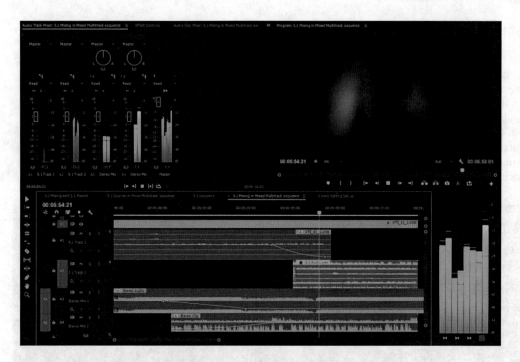

Figure 3-139. *This setup uses a mix of 5.1 and standard tracks*

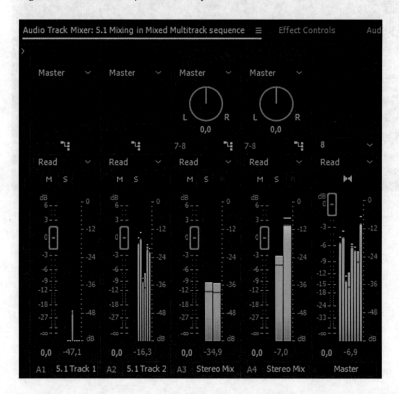

Figure 3-140. *Close-up of the Audio Track Mixer in this setup*

233

5.1 with Mono Tracks

If you're sending the project to software that doesn't understand the concept of 5.1 and stereo (standard) tracks, you need to use mono tracks. First, modify audio channels on 5.1 clips you want to use so they're interpreted as clips with six mono tracks. In an eight-track multi-channel sequence, make a minimum of six mono tracks and one standard track. Pan tracks 1, 3, and 5 to the left and tracks 2, 4, and 6 to the right, and the standard track to the middle. Set the Track Output Channel Assignment to 1+2 for tracks 1+2, to 3+4 for tracks 3+4, 5+6 for tracks 5+6, and 7+8 for track 7 (the standard track).

Put the clips that constitute the 5.1 mix on their respective mono tracks, and the stereo downmix on the standard track, as shown in Figures 3-141 and 3-142, and edit as usual. I highly recommend that you save a sequence preset with these settings so this can be done in seconds.

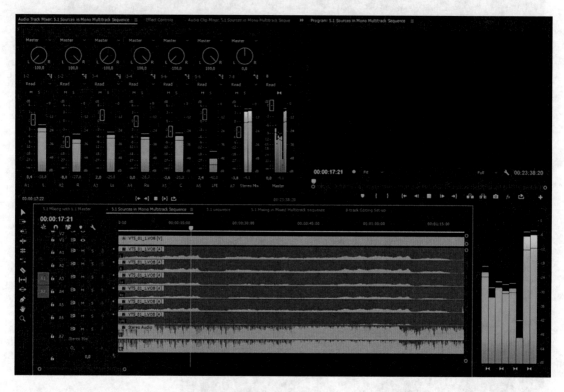

Figure 3-141. 5.1 mixing setup using only mono tracks

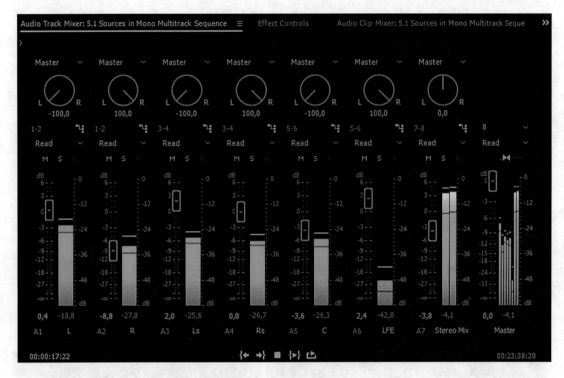

Figure 3-142. *Close-up of the Audio Track Mixer with this setup*

Remember to set your 5.1 QuickTime Channel Layout correctly at export if you're creating a ProRes file. If you want to totally avoid standard tracks, you can of course use two mono tracks for the stereo mix.

5.1 with Adaptive Tracks?

I would avoid this. The meters in the mixers get very small and hard to read, and you'll have to assign a lot of inputs to outputs. But it's doable, and once you've made a setup you can save a template project.

Sound Effects

There are a lot of audio effects in Premiere, like chorus/flanger, DeEsser, delay, etc. These can be used to clean up audio or make out-of-this-world sound effects. Sometimes, we use effects for very different things than they were designed for, like using the pitch shifter on footsteps to create a crowd from one person walking. Let's look at a few examples.

Scary Voice

Let's make a scary voice. We start by nesting the clip and then reversing the speed of the clip in the nested sequence. Next, we add the chorus/flanger effect with the Aggressive Flange preset, and then some studio reverb. We can choose the Vocal Reverb (small) preset in the studio reverb effect. If you want to give the voice a higher or lower pitch, add the pitch shifter effect. I chose the Deathly Ill preset just because of its name. Figure 3-143 shows all the settings.

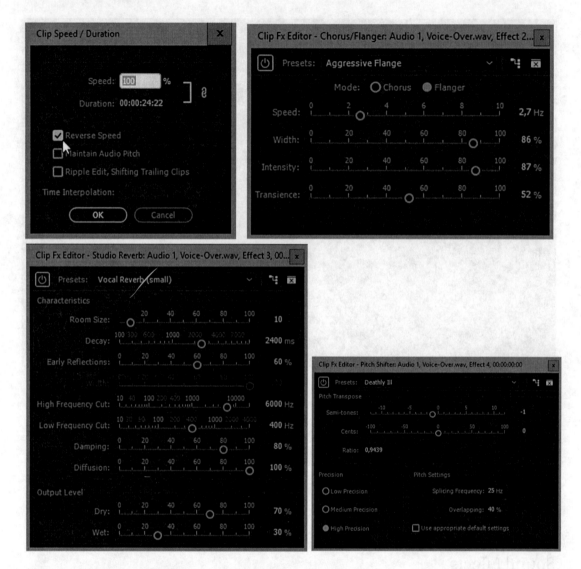

Figure 3-143. *Reverse, add chorus and reverb, then reverse again*

This will sound very strange—and we could keep it like this. But if we want to hear what the person is saying, we'd better re-reverse the sound. We do this in the main timeline, reversing the speed of the nested sequence. If you want to, you can add more Chorus and Reverb here.

Telephone Voice

This one is super easy! Add the multi-band compressor and choose the Walkie Talkie preset, as shown in Figure 3-144. Then, duplicate the effect to double the badness of the sound.

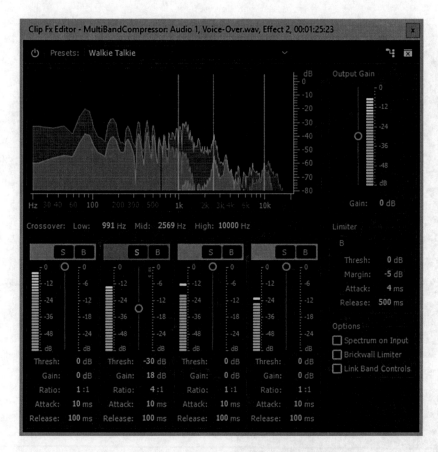

Figure 3-144. *The multi-band compressor has a Walkie Talkie preset*

Distortion

Creating distorted sound might seem easy—just add lots of gain and lower it again. But since Premiere Pro never clips an audio signal internally, that won't always work. So, we'll use the Distortion effect instead.

Say we want to make a voiceover or interview sound like it's coming from a really bad speaker system at an outdoor event. Before we add the distortion we'll use some drastic EQ to remove high and low frequencies. A bit of reverb adds a stadium-like atmosphere. Figures 3-145 and 3-146 show the settings I ended up using.

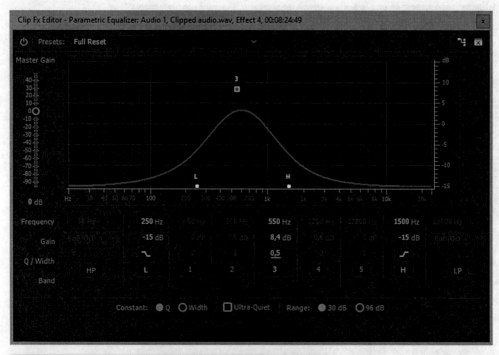

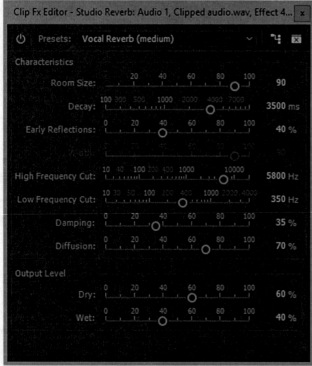

Figure 3-145. *An extreme EQ setting and the Vocal Reverb (medium) preset was a perfect combination for this effect*

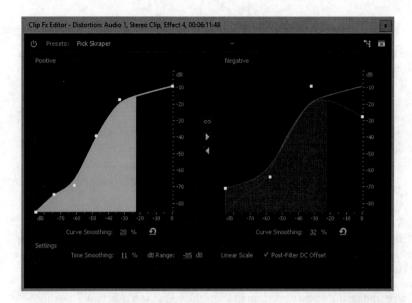

Figure 3-146. The Pick Scraper preset added the right amount of clipping and distortion

Guitar Suite for Distortion

The king of distortion is of course the guitar suite effect! Play with the presets and settings.

Using the Rez Box preset as a starter, I dragged the sliders until the music in my clip sounded like it was coming from a bad old clock radio speaker. See Figure 3-147.

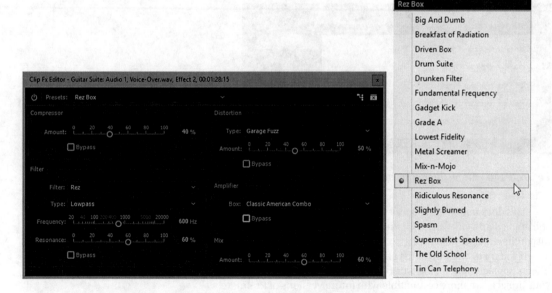

Figure 3-147. Guitar suite for Clock Radio and Guitar Suite presets

DeNoiser Is OK for Analogue Tape Noise

If you have some noise on your audio clips, your first thought could very well be to throw the DeNoiser effect on the clip. That won't necessarily work! It's specifically made for reducing tape noise, and will not always do what you might think it does. It's OK to use it on material from analog audio tape recordings, of course.

■ **From Premiere Pro Help**   The DeNoiser effect automatically detects tape noise and removes it. Use this effect to remove noise from analog recordings, such as magnetic tape recordings.

Fill Left with Right/Fill Right with Left

When editing stereo tracks, you sometimes want to use just one of the recorded channels and put this in both left and right speakers. These effects take care of that, but they only work on stereo clips. Also, the audio waveform on a clip does not change when adding these effects, so you will see two audio waveforms while just hearing one track, which can be confusing.

Generally, I'd recommend that you use the Audio Channels mapping in the Modify Clip dialog (**Shift+G**) instead, as this will also update the audio waveform to show the sound you're actually hearing. You can also reach this dialog via the right-click menu of the clips.

Missing Audio Effects in Old Projects

Premiere has gotten some great new audio effects from Audition in the latest versions, making many of the older audio effects obsolete. When you open or import an old project containing any of these effects, you'll get a warning that the project has obsolete effects (Figure 3-148).

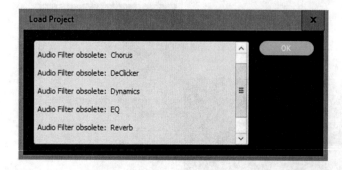

Figure 3-148. *Audio filter obsolete warnings*

This does *not* mean you must redo all your EQ or compression with new effects—the old ones are still applied and still work. But Premiere just wants to make sure you're aware that these effects will be discontinued at some point.

If you try to add one of the effects from the Obsolete Audio Effects folder, you'll be warned via the Audio Effects Replacement dialog (see Figure 3-149). I highly recommend that you avoid the obsolete effects so your projects are more compatible with future versions of Premiere.

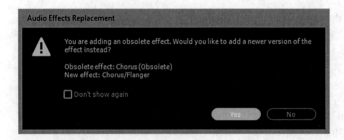

Figure 3-149. *Obsolete effect dialog*

Third-Party Audio Plug-ins

Premiere supports 64-bit Steinberg VST (Virtual Studio Technology), VST2, and AU (Audio Units—MacOS only) plug-ins, so you can buy lots of third-party plug-ins to enhance Premiere's audio capabilities. You'll find the Audio Plug-In Manager in **Preferences ➤ Audio**. Figure 3-150 shows the user interface.

Figure 3-150. *You can manage your VST plug-ins in the Audio Plug-In Manager*

To add a new plug-in, first copy it to a folder where you want to keep your plug-ins. Then, tell Premiere to search for plug-ins in that folder by clicking *Add* under VST Plug-In Folders. Next, hit the *Scan for Plug-Ins* button, and all the compatible plug-ins will show in the list that appears below and will be available under Audio Effects in the Effects panel.

You can enable or disable plug-ins in the same dialog box. This can be useful, especially when using free plug-ins that are not thoroughly tested, as they can cause instability problems in Premiere.

Proximity

In Figure 3-151 I've used the free Proximity plug-in with a setting that enhances the lower frequencies so it feels like the person talking was closer than he really was. By dragging the slider down, the opposite effect is achieved, simulating high-frequency absorption by air.

Figure 3-151. *Proximity Audio plug-in*

This could be a nice way to match recordings made at different distances, or for ADR or Foley work, when sound effects or dialogue is recorded close to the microphone. You'll find Proximity at tokyodawn.net/proximity/.

iZotope Vinyl

Vinyl, shown in Figure 3-152, is a free lo-fi audio plug-in. Want your music to sound like you're spinning down a vinyl record? This plug-in will do it. Want to create old radio sound and generally introduce distortion, narrow frequency bands, noise, drop-outs, and so on? Vinyl's got you covered: izotope.com/en/products/create-and-design/vinyl.html.

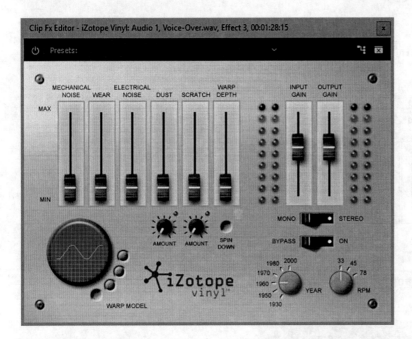

Figure 3-152. *I love the spin-down effect—and to create it just add Vinyl and click the Spin-down button. Easy!*

If you go to their web pages, you'll find recipes for different styles and effects. They do have a sense of humor. Click three of the rivets in the corners in the UI and the "plate" falls down, revealing a circuit board and a note with the names of the team. Figure 3-153 shows some of the Vinyl coolness.

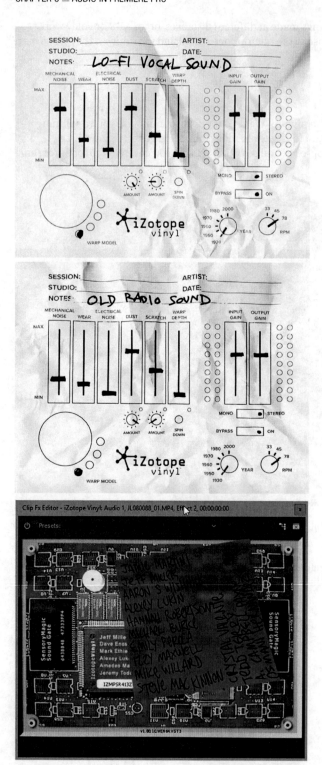

Figure 3-153. *Vinyl lo-fi vocal sound settings, Vinyl old radio sound, and Vinyl Easter egg*

iZotope RX 5 De-reverb

To remove reverb from dialogue, you can try de-reverb (Figure 3-154), which is part of iZotope RX 5 Audio Editor. Expensive, but impressive: izotope.com/en/products/repair-and-edit/rx/comparison.html.

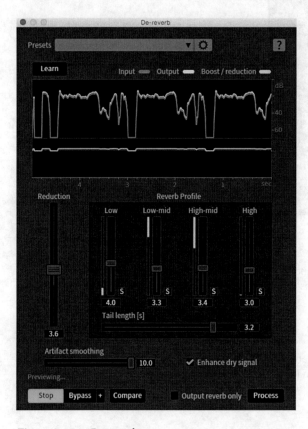

Figure 3-154. De-reverb

iZotope RX 5 Ambience Match

This is perfect if you need to fill a gap between two pieces of dialogue, recreate background ambience for a scene, or match ADR to production dialogue. RX can identify the room tone underneath content and seamlessly replicate it. Figure 3-155 shows the user interface.

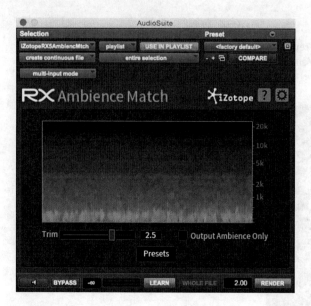

Figure 3-155. *Ambience match*

As you've seen, Premiere has a lot of very good audio tools. But there's another, more advanced, app available for you if you have a Creative Cloud subscription: Adobe Audition.

Using Audition

This is not a book on Audition, so you'll have to look elsewhere to get a thorough understanding of how it works and what it can do. But I want you to get an idea of how powerful this app is and know when it can do a much better job than Premiere.

Edit in Audition

Right-click on one or more clips in the Premiere timeline and choose *Edit Clip in Adobe Audition*, as shown in Figure 3-156, or go to **Edit ➤ Edit in Adobe Audition ➤ Clip**. Extract Audio will make a copy of the audio with *Audio Extracted* added to its name, and it will replace the original sound clip in the timeline with the new file. This will only work on real media clips in the timeline, not on sequences. The original will not be touched, so you can go back to the original later, but since it's a bit cumbersome, I recommend that you make a copy of it in the timeline and disable that copy before you send the original to Audition.

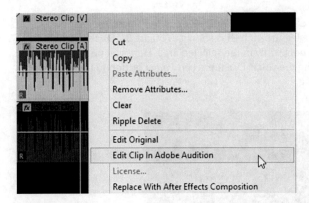

Figure 3-156. *Sending a clip to Audition is super easy. Make a copy before you do this so you can easily get back to the original.*

Now you can do some Audition magic to the audio, and when you hit Save in Audition, the audio is immediately updated in Premiere's timeline. Pretty sleek!

OK, so what can we use Audition for when editing our film? The most obvious feature is Audition's fantastic noise-reduction capabilities, and then there's the DeClipper, the spot-healing brush, and the speech volume leveler—not to mention the superior OMF export.

Noise Reduction

First, select a section of the audio that has only the noise, like a pause in an interview. Go to **Effects ➤ Noise Reduction/Restoration ➤ Capture Noise Print** as shown in Figure 3-157, or hit **Shift+P**.

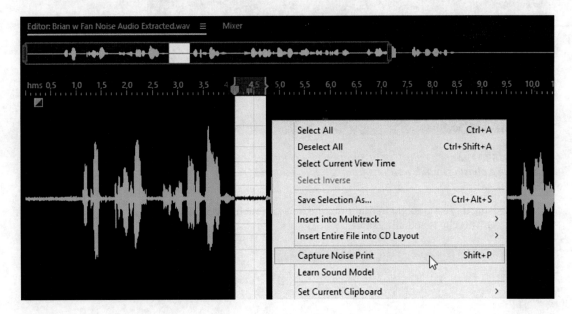

Figure 3-157. *Tell Audition to learn how the noise sounds with Capture Noise Print*

To get to the settings for the noise reduction effect, hit **Ctrl+Shift+P** or go to **Effects ➤ Noise Reduction/Restoration ➤ Noise Reduction**. The feature-rich UI is shown in Figure 3-158. Remember to click the *Select Entire File* button or you'll reduce noise only in the selected area. Here you must find a good balance between lowering the noise and distorting the voice. Use the green *Power* button in the lower left corner to switch the effect on and off while playing.

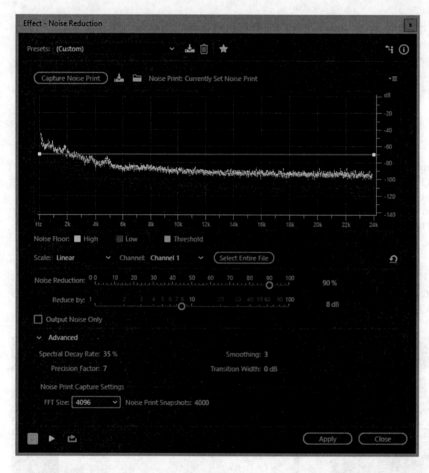

Figure 3-158. *The noise reduction in Audition is very powerful. Use it with care so you don't destroy the audio with strange phasing sounds resulting from extremely sharp EQ curves.*

After using noise reduction in Audition, the noise is much lower than before, as you can see in Figure 3-159. This clip is actually usable.

Figure 3-159. *After noise reduction*

Aggressive settings will introduce a lot of artifacts and make everything sound worse than before, so make sure you don't degrade the audio too much. After all, we're trying to fix problematic sound, not to exchange one problem for a new one. In my example, the file was an interview with fan noise, a very problematic kind of noise because of its broad frequency spectrum. I was able to lower that noise considerably without affecting the voice too much.

Auto-Heal Selection

If you have a problematic or unwanted short sound in your clip, you can try the Auto-Heal effect first. It only works on a short selection—four seconds or less. Select a short portion of the clip around the troublemaker sound and hit **Ctrl+U** or go to **Effects ➤ Auto Heal Selection**. Now, hit Play and listen. If you're lucky, the sound is gone! Hit Undo if you're not satisfied, and move to the spot-healing brush.

Spot-Healing Brush Tool

If the auto-heal doesn't work as well as you hoped it would, use the spot-healing brush. The shortcut is **B**, but you can also just click the icon that looks like a Band-Aid. View the audio in Spectral View and you can easily see what's going on. In Figure 3-160, a lot of beeps from a bird were heard during an interview, and I used the spot healing brush just like we would use a brush in Photoshop, just painting over the problematic beeps. Figure 3-161 shows the beeps are gone, and the quality of the speech is still maintained.

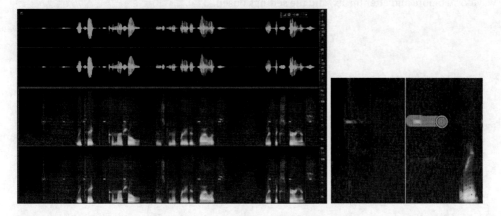

Figure 3-160. *With the spot-healing brush, you can paint out unwanted sounds. Very close to real magic!*

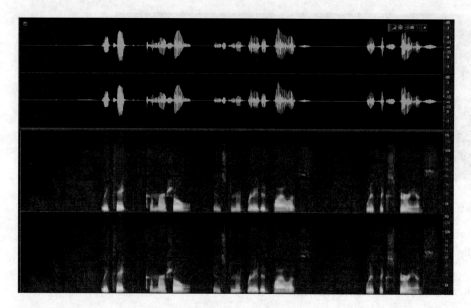

Figure 3-161. *Here's the clip after painting away all the instances of the annoying twitter. The same technique can of course be used to remove low-frequency pops.*

DeClipper

This is a life saver! If you get audio recordings with levels that exceed max level, the peaks will be clipped, and the sound will be distorted. Traditionally, there has been no way to get these clipped levels back. But Audition's DeClipper can analyze the waveform and do a calculated guess as to how the original waveform should look. It actually repairs clipped waveforms by filling in clipped sections with new audio data.

Surprisingly, this works amazingly well! Go to **Effects ➤ Diagnostics ➤ DeClipper** and adjust the settings. I feel that I get the best results when manually tweaking the settings instead of using the presets. Once you've tweaked the settings, hit the *Scan* button and see a list of problems appear. If no problems are found, try tweaking the settings, increasing the tolerance and lowering the gain. Then re-scan, and when the problems are found, click the *Repair All* button and watch Audition generate new waveforms where there were none. Magic! And it actually sounds good even on interviews, VOs, and other speech. Figure 3-162 shows the waveform before and after the fix, and the settings I used.

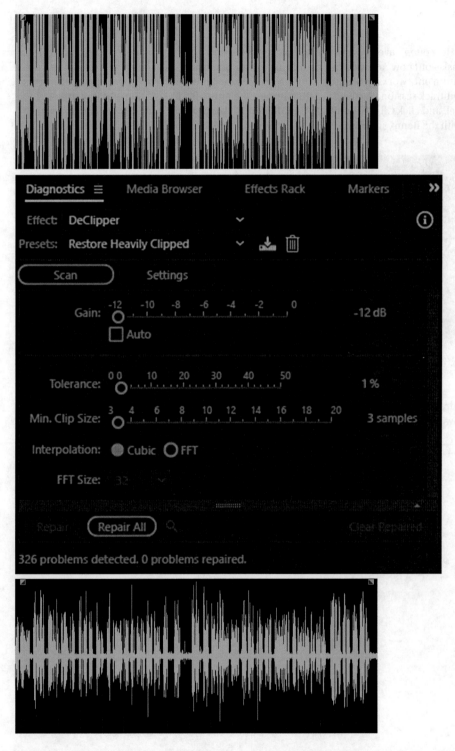

Figure 3-162. *The DeClipper in Audition can magically re-create the missing peaks in the waveform. In this example, using the preset named Restore Heavily Clipped worked great.*

Remix

Another life saver! How often have you had to make a shorter version of a song to make it fit your edit? It's a time-consuming task—but now Audition can do this for you automatically!

The Remix feature only works in Multitrack mode, so click the Multitrack icon in the upper-left corner to create a new Multitrack session. See Figure 3-163. Import the music file in Audition, put it on track 1 in the Multitrack panel, and click **Clip ➤ Remix ➤ Enable Remix**. Audition analyzes the clip and opens the Properties panel with the Remix settings.

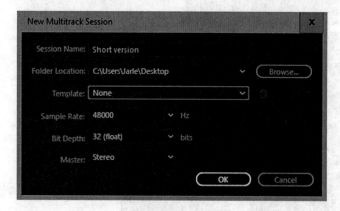

Figure 3-163. *New Multitrack session*

Now you can drag the upper-right corner of the clip to the length you want. In Figure 3-164 I've shortened Taylor Swift's song from 3'47 to 45 seconds. The jagged lines show where Remix has made a transition.

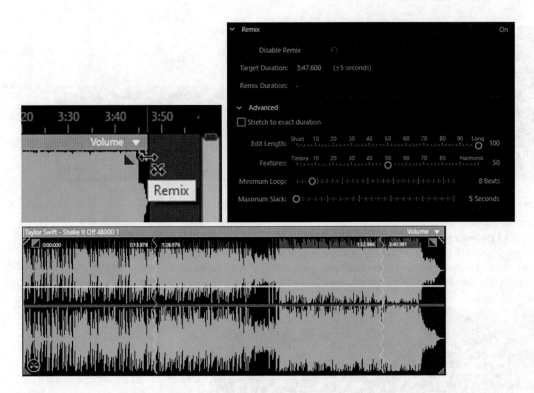

Figure 3-164. *Use Remix to create a shorter or longer version of a music clip*

Play through the song, and if you're not satisfied with the result, try tweaking the parameters. You can also right-click the Remixed clip and choose *Split Remixed Clip into Segments* and manually tweak the edit points and transitions. See Figure 3-165.

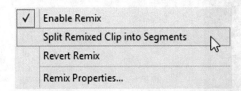

Figure 3-165. *You can split the result of Remix into separate segments*

In Figure 3-166, I just dragged the Edit Length slider and got a completely different result with many more transitions. I liked this version better, so now it's time to send the result to Premiere.

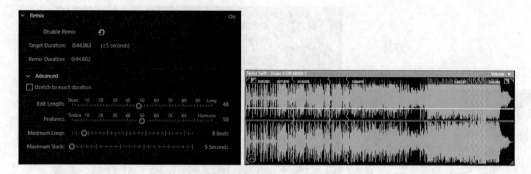

Figure 3-166. *Changing the edit length gave me a completely different result*

Click **File ➤ Export ➤ Export to Adobe Premiere Pro**, and Audition will ask you for a name and location of the XML file and the audio clip. See Figure 3-167. Choose to export session to a stereo file, hit *Export*, and the project panel in Premiere Pro is populated with a new sequence and a new music file. You can delete the sequence, as we don't need it.

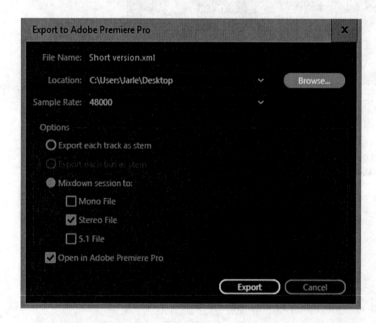

Figure 3-167. *Remix Export settings*

Another way to get the music back to Premiere is to select the music clip in the timeline and go the **Multitrack ➤ Mixdown Session to New File ➤ Selected Clips** route. This just exports the new audio file, and you'll have to import it into Premiere manually.

The Remix feature isn't magic, although it might seem so at first glance. Some music pieces will never sound good, no matter what settings you choose. Remix doesn't understand words, so it can make for some super-nonsense sentences in a song. But most of your music remixes will sound amazingly great.

It's really just made for music, but can actually work well for looping background ambience! If you have too little field sound and want to extend it, it can do a nice job.

Speech Volume Leveler

The speech volume leveler effect will smooth out the levels in human speech so its volume doesn't vary so much—a nice quick fix for voiceovers and interviews that works well if you use less-aggressive settings than the default. The Careful preset shown in Figure 3-168 is quite good.

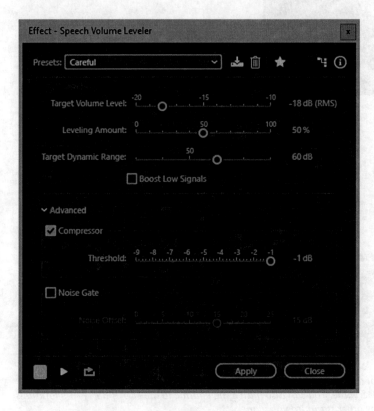

Figure 3-168. *Speech Volume Leveler settings*

You can set the Target Dynamic Range to avoid the amplification of low signals, which would cause pumping in the ambient noise.

Match Loudness

Using this feature, you can batch process files to the level you want, or to an existing file, an average RMS value, a certain peak value—even based on perceived loudness. See Figure 3-169.

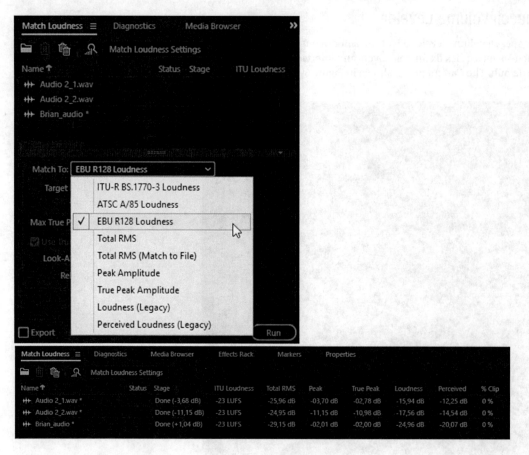

Figure 3-169. *Match Loudness is not an effect; it's a window. You can match clips to the same peak level, to the same loudness, or to the same RMS value. You can also match the volume to the ITU-R BS.1770-3 loudness, which is great for broadcast, or to any other standard you want.*

Match Loudness is found in the Window menu in Audition. **Window ➤ Match Loudness**. Drag files from the Files panel into the Match Loudness panel, or click the folder icon in the panel to add files that aren't already imported. Then, click *Match Loudness Settings* and decide what to match and how. You can click the magnifying glass icon to scan the files, or just hit *Run* and wait. If the magnifying glass icon is pressed, files will be scanned immediately when you drop them into the panel.

Make Your Audio Broadcast Compliant

A very quick way to make your audio ITU legal is to use the Match Loudness panel as just described and set the Match To: field to ITU-R BS.1770-3 Loudness. Be aware that you can't just use this on all your clips and be safe. It's the total mix of all the clips that will decide if your show is approved or rejected by a broadcaster.

So, a nice way to use this in the past was to export your finished audio mix from Premiere, import the file to Audition and make it legal, then save it and import back to Premiere, where you add it to the existing tracks and solo it before export. But since we've now got a Loudness Normalization choice when we export from Premiere, this workflow is obsolete.

ITU-R BS.1770-3 is compliant with the most recent revision of EBU R128 for loudness measurement. If you're in the United States, choose ITU-R BS.1770-3 and then set the Loudness value to -24 LUFS.

Generate Noise and Tones

Audition can generate all kinds of tones, even with sweeps from one frequency to another, so creating cool computer sounds and sci-fi audio effects is easy. Go to **Effects ➤ Generate ➤ Tones**. See Figure 3-170.

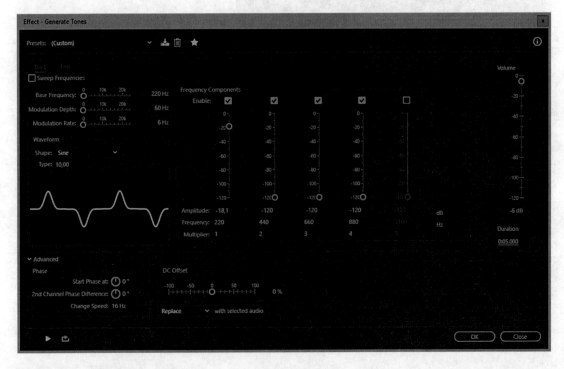

Figure 3-170. *Audition has built-in tone and noise generators*

We can also create White, Pink, Grey, and Brown noise clips. Go to **Effects ➤ Generate ➤ Noise**. For an explanation of the colors of noise, see en.wikipedia.org/wiki/Colors_of_noise.

Film Projector Sound

Noise and tones can be used in strange ways. Generate a Square Wave tone at 12 Hz as shown in Figure 3-171, and then filter out the lower frequencies with some EQ, and you have a sound that could pass for a film projector, at least if it's kept at a low level and mixed with ambience and the sound from the film.

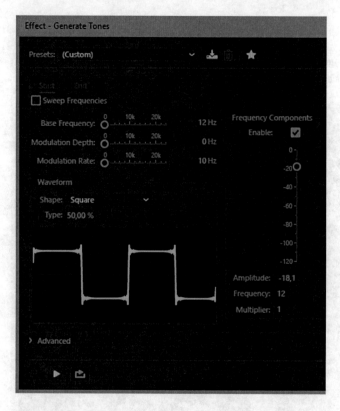

Figure 3-171. *Generate a 12 Hz Square Wave tone and filter out the lower frequencies. This will sound like a film projector.*

Get Audition's Sound FX & Music Library

You can download more than 10,000(!) free sound effects and music files for free from offers.adobe.com/en/na/audition/offers/audition_dlc.html. See Figure 3-172.

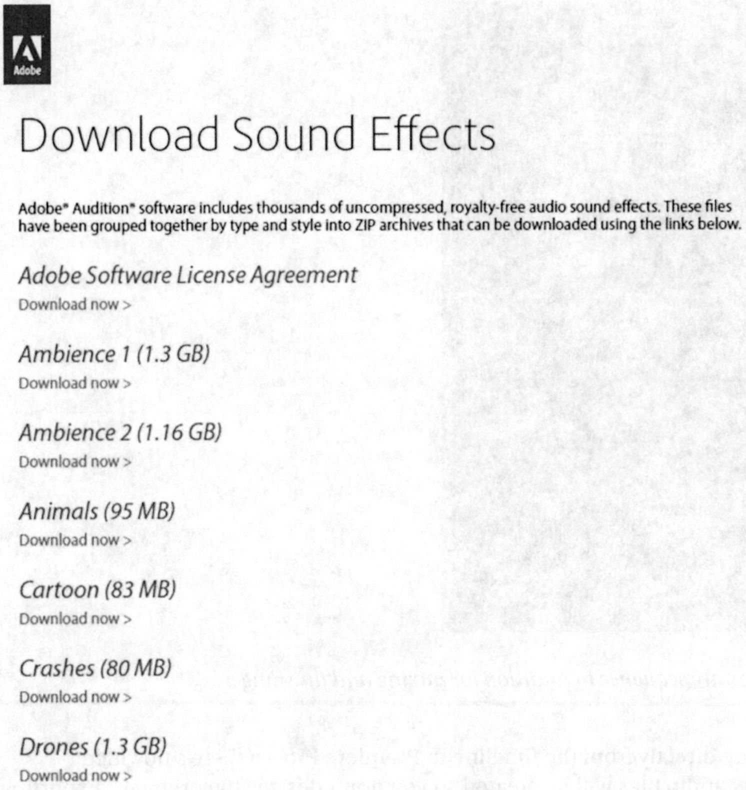

Download Sound Effects

Adobe® Audition® software includes thousands of uncompressed, royalty-free audio sound effects. These files have been grouped together by type and style into ZIP archives that can be downloaded using the links below.

Adobe Software License Agreement
Download now >

Ambience 1 (1.3 GB)
Download now >

Ambience 2 (1.16 GB)
Download now >

Animals (95 MB)
Download now >

Cartoon (83 MB)
Download now >

Crashes (80 MB)
Download now >

Drones (1.3 GB)
Download now >

Figure 3-172. *This is just a small portion of the list of sound effects that you can download for free*

Do Your Final Audio Mix in Audition

If you want to do your final mix in Audition, you can send your sequence there by clicking **Edit ➤ Edit in Adobe Audition ➤ Sequence**. See the dialog box in Figure 3-173.

Figure 3-173. *You can send the entire sequence to Audition for mixing and finishing*

The preview video will come directly from the timeline in Premiere Pro, so there's no video export—unless you want it. New audio files will be created so you don't destroy the originals. Exporting all the audio files will take a while, and when it all opens in Audition, it can look like Figure 3-174.

Figure 3-174. *I've selected all interview clips and marked them as Dialogue in the Essential Sound panel. When I drag sliders and checkboxes in this panel, Audition is adjusting effects in the Effects Rack behind the scenes. I've opened them here just to show what they're doing.*

When you're done mixing in Audition, export a mixdown file that is automatically imported back to Premiere. **File ➤ Export ➤ Export to Premiere Pro**. Add this file to your sequence in Premiere and mute all other tracks.

If you don't need to go back to Premiere you can export directly to Adobe Media Encoder from Audition. **File ➤ Export ➤ Export with Adobe Media Encoder**.

Surround Mixing in Audition

Although it's possible to mix 5.1 surround in Premiere, you're hurting yourself if you don't switch to Audition for this. Look at the big and beautiful Track Panner panel in Audition shown in Figure 3-175, then compare it to the small and clunky 5.1 Panner panel in Premiere. Send the entire sequence to Audition as explained and mix surround sound with ease.

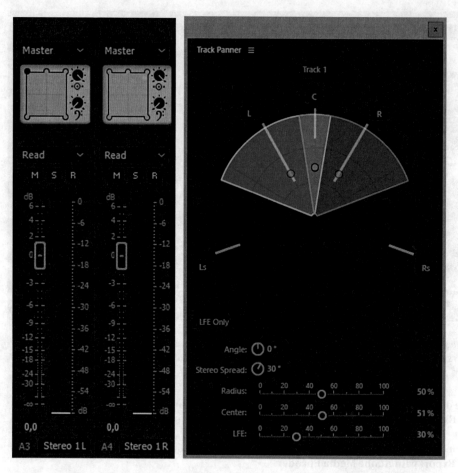

Figure 3-175. *The Track Panner in Audition is more intuitive, and if you dock the panel you can even make it full screen for ultimate panning control*

Export OMF from Audition

Since the OMF support in Audition is better than the one in Premiere, you will most likely get better results by sending your sequence to Audition first and then exporting the OMF from there, rather than exporting the OMF directly from Premiere. Go to **File ➤ Export ➤ OMF**. See Figure 3-176.

Figure 3-176. *OMF export is more robust in Audition than in Premiere. You also get info about which features are not supported by OMF and will be ignored or changed.*

Beware of Back-up and Syncing Software

Some syncing software is known to corrupt WAV files Audition is trying to write on the fly. So, be wary of backup software (that's constantly scanning and taking ownership of files) while working in Audition.

Premiere Pro Sequence Audio Signal Path

As promised, here's a detailed overview of the audio path in Premiere Pro. (By Akil Wemusa, Senior Quality Engineer on the Premiere Pro team at Adobe Systems)

1. Clip ➤ Modify ➤ Audio Channels

2. Audio gain

3. Fixed (intrinsic) clip volume

4. Fixed (intrinsic) clip channel volume

5. Non-fixed (non-intrinsic) clip fx (incl. volume, pan)

6. Fixed (intrinsic) clip pan/balance

7. Track Input Channel (if recording voiceover or metering input)

8. Pre-Fader Track Effects 1–5*

9. Pre-Fader Sends 1–5* ➤ Submix track or Master

10. Track Mute/Solo

11. Track Volume

12. Adaptive Track Open Channel Output Mapping

13. Track Meters

14. Post-Fader Track Effects 1–5*

15. Post-Fader Sends 1–5* ➤ Submix track or Master

16. Track Pan/Balance (mono/standard/adaptive tracks only)

17. Direct Output Assignment (mono/standard/5.1 tracks only)**

18. Track Output Assignment ➤ Submix track or Master

19. Submix track Pre-Fader Track Effects 1–5

20. Submix track Pre-Fader Sends 1–5 ➤ Submix track or Master

21. Submix track Mute/Solo

22. Submix track volume

23. Submix track meters

24. Submix track Post-Fader Track Effects 1–5*

25. Submix track Post-Fader Sends 1–5* ➤ Submix track or Master

26. Submix track Pan/Balance

27. Submix Track Output Assignment ➤ Submix track or Master

28. Master track Pre-Fader Track Effects 1–5

29. Master track volume

30. Master track meters/Audio Meters panel

31. Master track Post-Fader Track Effects 1–5

32. Master track Number of Channels**

33. Render/Export

34. Preferences ➤ Audio Hardware ➤ Output Mapping

---

*Each effect and/or send slot 1–5 can be independently set Pre-/Post-fader, which affects signal path. For example, if effects 1 and 2 are both pre-fader, their audio signal path will match their physical order. However, if effects 1 and 4 are post-fader and effects 2 and 5 are pre-fader, their order would be effects 2-5-1-4 in the audio signal path. Same with sends 1-5.

**Multi-channel sequences only

Summary

The info in this chapter should help you make better audio-editing decisions when working in Premiere Pro. As you've seen, the audio engine in Premiere is quite advanced, and you can get great results editing and mixing your audio just inside of Premiere. And if you learn the basics of Adobe Audition as well, you will have even more powerful tools at your disposal.

CHAPTER 4

Editing Tips and Techniques

By Jarle Leirpoll and Dylan Osborn

Whenever you think you know all the shortcuts and have mastered editing in Premiere, someone will come along and show you a quicker and easier way! In this chapter we'll cover tips for editing quickly and effectively in every situation using the features available in Premiere Pro.

For completeness and ease of reading, you may find some of these techniques mentioned in other chapters as well. But here we'll focus on controlling your clips in the timeline, trimming methods, and speed changes—plus some of the "gotchas" with different frame rates and footage types. So, if you want to harness the editing tools at your fingertips, read on!

Keyboard Shortcuts to Speed Up Your Editing

If you had to, could you do *all* of your editing without touching the mouse? The "no-mouse challenge" is a great way to discover just how many shortcuts there are in Premiere Pro (over 900) and how you can use them (and map them) to work for you. Remember: If yofPancake Timelinesu do the same action several times a day, find a shortcut for it. The time saved will add up fast.

JKL on Steroids

Clicking the *Play* button under the monitors in the transport controls should be prohibited by law. It slows you down. The **Spacebar** is much quicker, but it only plays at normal speed. Professionals use **J, K,** and **L** instead, but don't stop there.

Hide the transport controls under the Source and Program Monitor Settings menus to free up screen real estate, as shown in Figure 4-1.

Figure 4-1. *Transport controls. If you use shortcuts, you don't need these.*

Try **K+J/L** (hold down **K**, and tap **J** or **L**) to advance backward and forward frame by frame. Or, hold down both keys in combination (**K+J** or **K+L**) and you'll get a slow, tape-style jog—useful for finding audio hits you want to edit to.

© Jarle Leirpoll 2017
J. Leirpoll et al., *The Cool Stuff in Premiere Pro*, DOI 10.1007/978-1-4842-2890-6_4

Shift+J/L will go slow or fast, but in small increments. Try this: Hit **L**, then **Shift+L**. It will speed up to be 0.1x faster, and by hitting **Shift+L** again it bumps the speed up 0.1x more. Hit **Shift+J** and it slows down. Combinations of **J**, **K**, **L**, and **Shift** give you excellent Jog and Shuttle control.

Useful Default Keyboard Shortcuts

Insert (**,**) and Extract (**'**) and their non-ripple cousins Overwrite (**.**) and Lift (**;**) are the shortcuts for editing into and out of your sequence with in and out points set.

X will mark the clip under the playhead, but the **/** (forward slash) key will Mark Selection to set ins and outs around all the clips you currently have selected.

Clear in and out points with **Ctrl+Shift+I** (Opt+I), **Ctrl+Shift+O** (Opt+O), and **Ctrl+Shift+X** (Opt+X) for both.

D is the keyboard shortcut for Select Clip at Playhead. It is immensely useful!

To Deselect All clips, effects, or whatever is selected, hit **Shift+Ctrl+A** (Shift+Cmd+A on Mac). I recommend changing this to a one-key shortcut because you're going to use it a lot.

Sure, **Ctrl+C**, **Ctrl+X**, and **Ctrl+V** (Cmd+C, Cmd+X, and Cmd+V on Mac) all work on the selected clips, but **Shift+Ctrl+V** (Shift+Cmd+V) will Paste Insert them at the playhead and ripple other clips down the timeline.

To expand and minimize your timeline tracks, use **Shift+=/ -**. **Ctrl+=/ -** (Cmd+=/ -) handles only video track height, and **Alt+=/ -** (Opt+=/ -) only audio track height.

Hitting **Ctrl+K** (Cmd+K) cuts the clip in two. It's like using the Razor tool, except faster because you don't have to select the Razor tool. This works only on active tracks. Add the **Shift** modifier key, and you cut all clips under the playhead in two. Select a clip or clips before hitting **Ctrl+K**, and only the selected clips will be razored.

Ctrl+D (Cmd+D on Mac) is very useful, as it creates a video dissolve (or any other transition you have set as your default) when parked near a cutting point. It only works on active/targeted tracks. If you select several clips, **Ctrl+D** will add transitions between all the selected clips.

Shift+K is the shortcut for Play Around. It backs the playhead up for a preroll, plays past the place where it was originally parked, and continues for the duration of a postroll. The preroll and postroll durations are set in **Preferences ➤ Playback**. Combine the Play Around feature with Loop if you need to hear or see something repeatedly. **Ctrl+L** (Cmd+L) toggles Loop on and off for the monitor that is currently active (Source or Program).

F is for Match Frame. Park over any clip in the sequence and hit **F** to open the master clip in the Source Monitor at the exact same frame. It opens the clip on the highest targeted/active track underneath the playhead. Selecting a clip before hitting **F** overrides this, so you will always match-frame your selection.

The opposite is the Reverse Match Frame command. When parked on a frame in the Source Monitor, **Shift+R** takes you to the first clip that said frame appears in. Keep hitting **Shift+R**, and you will cycle through all the instances of that frame in the sequence.

Hitting **Ctrl+F** (Cmd+F) when the timeline panel is active opens the Timeline Search (Figure 4-2). This seemingly simple dialog can help you find just about anything you've put in your sequence.

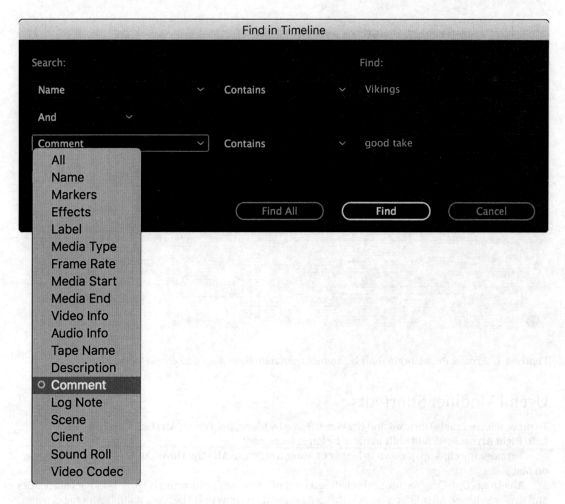

Figure 4-2. *Timeline Search will find your clips instantly*

Shift+F takes you to the search box in the active panel, like a bin, the Project panel, the Metadata panel, or the Media Browser.

To view all of the Premiere Pro default keyboard shortcuts for Mac or PC in a single diagram (Figure 4-3), go to Dylan Osborn's web site and download a printable 11×17 png file: dylanosborn.com/training/keyboard-layouts/.

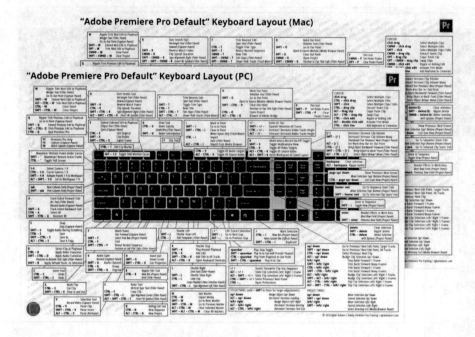

Figure 4-3. *Explore Premiere's default keyboard layout with these diagrams from Dylan Osborn*

Useful Modifier Shortcuts

To move selected clip(s) forward and backward frame by frame, hold down **Alt** (Cmd) and use the **Left/Right Arrow** keys. Add **Shift** to move by larger increments.

To nudge the clips up or down to higher or lower tracks, use **Alt+Up/Down Arrows** (Opt+Up/Down on Mac).

Alt+Drag (Opt+Drag) a clip, and you drag a copy of it to a new destination (Figure 4-4). For legacy titles and dynamic-linked After Effects comps, this is different than copy/paste because it duplicates the clip and creates a new master clip in your Project panel.

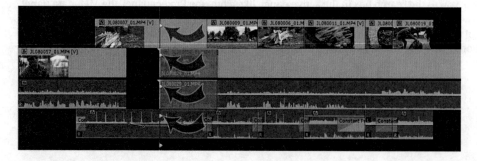

Figure 4-4. *Use Ctrl-drag to do an insert edit. The small triangles show where the clips will be inserted.*

Holding down **Ctrl** (Cmd) when dragging a clip to the timeline makes an insert edit, shifting all the tracks. Use **Ctrl+Alt** (Cmd+Opt) as you drag-insert to shift clips only on the targeted tracks–and on the source tracks if dragging from one spot in the timeline to another (Figure 4-5). This is handy when you want to leave one or more tracks unchanged.

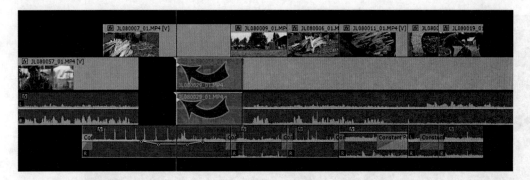

Figure 4-5. *Add Alt to the above to shift clips on only the involved tracks. Again, the triangles indicate what will happen when you release the mouse button.*

Think of **Ctrl** (Cmd) as a way to avoid leaving gaps or overwriting existing clips when you drag and drop clips, as shown in Figure 4-6.

Figure 4-6. *When Linked Selection is enabled (blue), clicking on a clip will select both video and audio. You can also right-click ➤ Group clips and drag clips together. There is no default shortcut to turn this mode on and off, but you can map one for Sequence ➤ Linked Selection.*

If you are editing with Linked Selection mode on, you can quickly select only the audio or video part of a clip by **Alt-Clicking** (Opt+Clicking on Mac). Hit **Delete** to get rid of it, or hold **Alt+Shift** (Opt+Shift) to select multiple different clips. **Alt+Drag** (Opt+Drag) an in or out point to split audio and video to different durations. This also works in the Source Monitor before you cut a clip into the timeline (Figure 4-7).

Figure 4-7. *Split video and audio marks in the Source Monitor*

The shortcut **S** toggles Snap mode on and off. When enabled (blue), your playhead will "snap" to cuts as you move it across them. This is very useful, but you may not want it while scrubbing long sections of clips. Hold down **Shift** to temporarily disable snapping in Snap mode, or enable it when Snap is off (Figure 4-8).

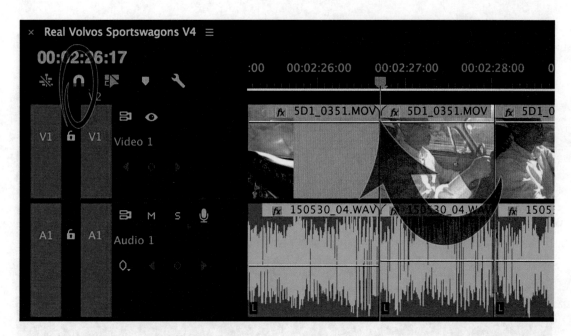

Figure 4-8. Whether snapping is on or off, Shift will give you the opposite behavior. In this example, Snap is off but the playhead snaps to the cut because Shift is held down.

The checkbox **Preferences ➤ General ➤ Snap Playhead in Timeline when Snap is enabled** inverts the way this behavior functions. When unchecked, Snap mode will never give you snapping in the timeline *unless* you hold down **Shift**. Now you know.

If you are working in the default Color workspace, moving the playhead across your clips and stopping will automatically select the clip underneath it (on targeted tracks only). This behavior is controlled by the option **Sequence ➤ Selection Follows Playhead** and is useful for color correcting with the Lumetri Color panel. It won't be enabled in the other default workspaces, so you may want to map a custom keyboard shortcut to toggle it on and off. I prefer **Shift+V**.

Shift-clicking on track target or source patching areas adds or removes all tracks in the video or audio selection. **Alt-Clicking** (Opt+Clicking) on a source patch sets it to "Gap" (note the black outline), which will insert or overwrite empty space for the exact duration you have set in the Source Monitor.

Keyboard Shortcuts Worth Mapping

Learning keyboard shortcuts will make you a faster editor, and so will mapping your own custom shortcuts. **Ctrl+Alt+K** (Cmd+Opt+K) brings up the Keyboard Shortcuts window. In CC 2017 and later, a beautiful visual interface (Figure 4-9) shows where commands are mapped and which keys are still available and enables you to map different application and panel shortcuts to the same key. For an in-depth look at creating custom keyboard layouts, turn to chapter 10 on Customization, and watch this tutorial by Dylan Osborn: dylanosborn.com/2016/11/30/visual-keyboard-shortcuts/.

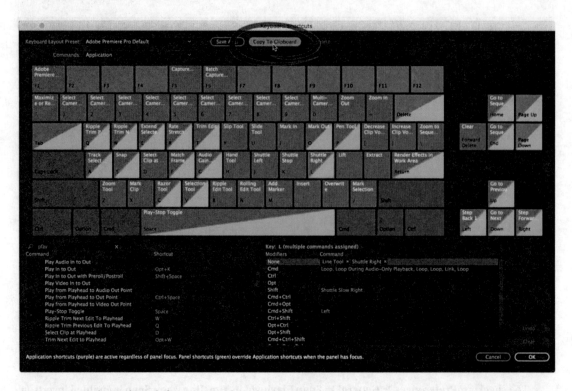

Figure 4-9. *In the Keyboard Shortcuts window, the Copy to Clipboard button enables you to copy/paste a list of all available commands and shortcuts to a text document or spreadsheet for comprehensive study*

For the purposes of this chapter, here is a list of commands that are not mapped to any shortcut by default. Learn them, map them, and see how they can speed up your editing! Keep reading—we cover several of these later in this chapter.

- Add or Remove Audio/Video Keyframe

- Decrease/Increase Audio/Video Keyframe Value

- Move Audio/Video Keyframe 1 Frame Earlier/Later

- Select Next/Previous Keyframe

- Move All Video/Audio Sources Up/Down

- Default Source Assignment

- Generate Audio Waveform

- Join All Through Edits

- Lock/Unlock All Audio/Video Tracks

- Nest

- Remove Effects

- Replace with Clip from Source Monitor

- Replace with Clip from Source Monitor, Match Frame

- Safe Margins

- Scratch Disks

- Sequence Settings

- Select Nearest Edit Point as Trim In/Out

- Select Nearest Edit Point as Ripple In/Out

- Selection Follows Playhead

- Show Audio Time Units

- Zoom to Frame

Switch to Cinema Mode

Ctrl+` is the shortcut for Toggle Full Screen—also known as Cinema mode—where the user interface (UI) is hidden and the video is shown in full screen (Figure 4-10). This keyboard shortcut will be completely different on many non-English keyboards. Search the Keyboard Shortcuts dialog for "full screen" to find out what your shortcut is. Change it if you want.

Figure 4-10. *Cinema mode. Enable Mercury Transmit to get full-screen video on your second monitor or on a broadcast monitor.*

To get full-screen playback on your second monitor, go to **Preferences ➤ Playback** and choose *Enable Mercury Transmit*; select that monitor in the dialog box (Figure 4-11).

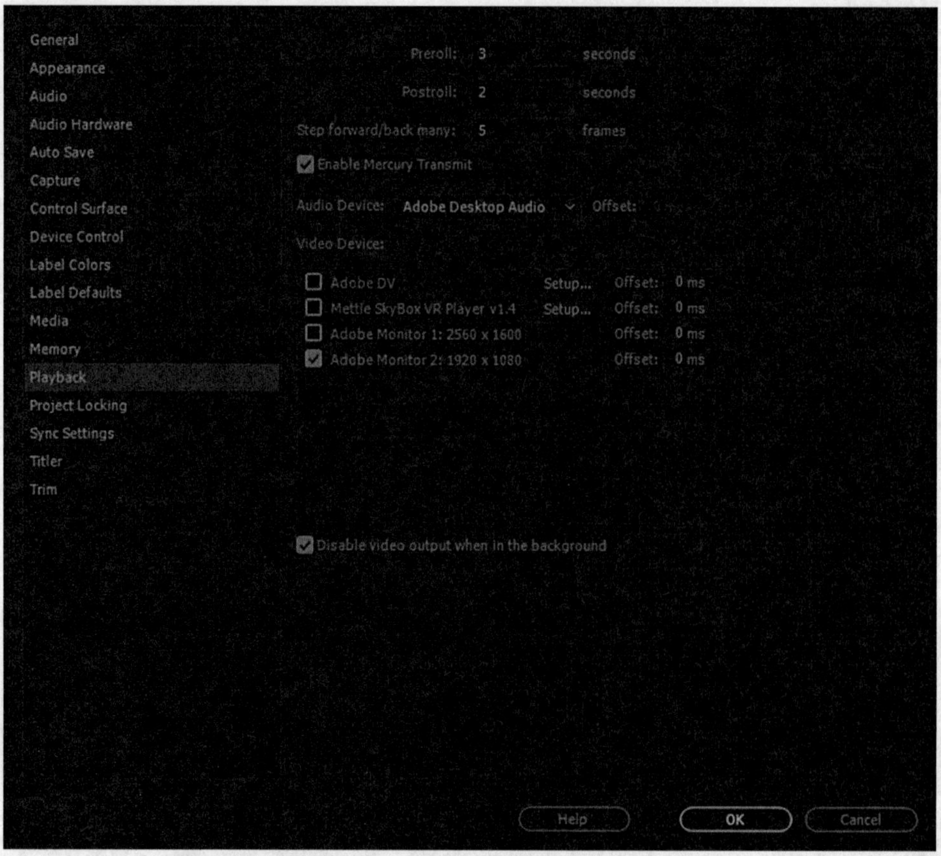

Figure 4-11. *Transmit playback to the second monitor*

Enable (and disable) Transmit can also be found in the Program Monitor Settings menu for quicker access—or you can assign a keyboard shortcut.

Multi-Sequence Workflow Tips

Premiere doesn't warn you if you make long, complex timelines. Maybe it should. Everything gets easier and faster with more, but shorter timelines. One of the best time-saving features in Premiere is that we can use several sequences in different ways to improve editing speed.

The Power of Pancake Timelines

Premiere lets you stack sequences on top of each other, like any other panel within the workspace. This makes it easy to drag or copy and paste clips between them, which is a handy feature that many users call *Pancake Timelines.* You can even do complex edits in a separate sequence and then drag those clips into the main timeline. See Figure 4-12.

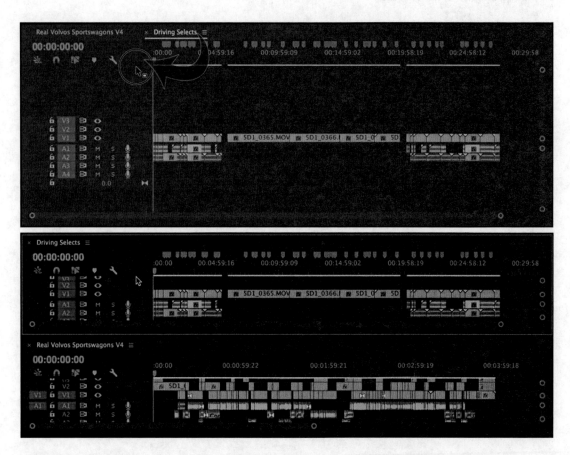

Figure 4-12. *Pancake Timelines. Click and drag a sequence into a new frame above, thus stacking your timelines like metaphorical pancakes (of course, you can place them in any other arrangement that works for you).*

But the real power of Pancake Timelines is not merely stacking sequences; it is using one or more sequences as an actual source—and then insert or overwrite editing the clips from one sequence to another. Here's how it's done:

1. Identify a sequence that you'll edit clips into, such as your main edit sequence. Open this one normally by double-clicking, and you'll see it in the Program Monitor as usual.

2. Identify a sequence you'll edit clips from, such as a selects sequence. Open this one in the Source Monitor by dragging it there, or right-clicking and selecting *Open in Source Monitor.*

3. Click the Source Monitor Settings menu (the wrench icon) and choose *Open Sequence in Timeline.* The red playhead tells you this selected sequence is open in the Source Monitor, while our edit sequence with the blue playhead remains open in the Program Monitor. See Figure 4-13.

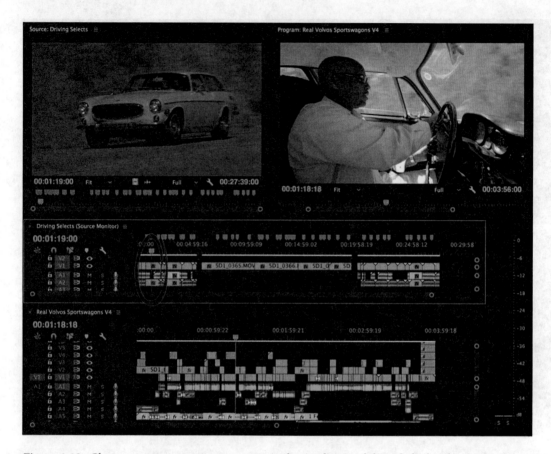

Figure 4-13. *Choose to open your source sequence in the timeline, and the red playhead indicates it is connected to the Source Monitor. Note that you can map Open Sequence in Timeline to your own keyboard shortcut.*

4. You can now stack your timelines in the "pancake" style and perform insert and overwrite edits from one to the other using in and out points and source patching—just like you would with any clip open in the Source Monitor. But there's one more important step . . .

5. Click the oh-so-cleverly-named *Insert and overwrite sequences as nests or individual clips* button (Figure 4-14). I like to call it the "Nest-or-Not" button.

Figure 4-14. *The Nest-or-Not button changes the way sequences are placed in other sequences—as one single nested clip or as all the source clips individually*

Like all Timeline panel buttons, blue is on and gray is off. When you do Insert and Overwrite edits from one sequence to another with this on, you will get a nested sequence (single green clip), even if the in and out range contains multiple clips. If you do the same edit with the Nest-or-Not button off, you will get the actual source clips. In most cases, that is probably what you want, because inserting or overwriting the clips from one sequence to another is a very effective way to edit! Figure 4-15 shows these options.

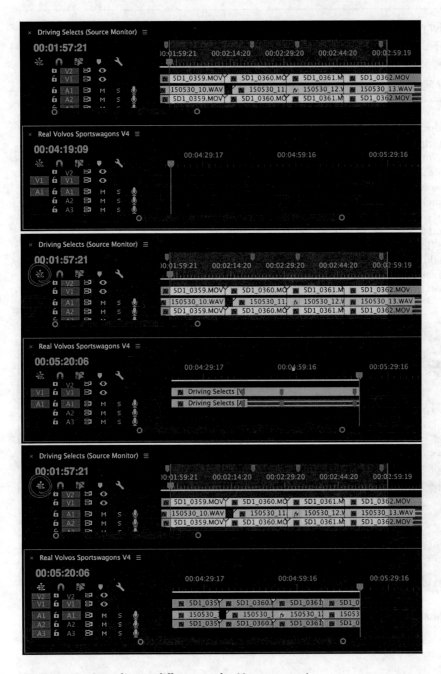

Figure 4-15. *One edit, two different results: Nest . . . or not!*

To see the power of Pancake Timelines in action, watch Dylan Osborn's three-minute tutorial, which demonstrates the preceding steps: dylanosborn.com/2016/08/24/pancake-timelines/.

When you use sequences to gather your b-roll selects or best takes and then open them as a source with Pancake Timelines, it's sometimes called a *virtual KEM-roll*.

■ **Note** *KEM* stands for Keller-Elektro-Mechanik. It was a company that produced one of the most famous flatbed editors: en.wikipedia.org/wiki/Flatbed_editor. A frequently used technique by feature film editors was to put multiple takes of the same scene on the same reel, or KEM-roll, giving the director an easy way to select the best take. Any sequence can be our virtual KEM-roll in Premiere Pro.

Let's look at a few tips for fast KEM-roll editing with Pancake Timelines.

When you have multiple sequences open in the Source Monitor, keep pressing the shortcut **Shift+2** to cycle through them. Notice how the timelines switch together with the Source Monitor. **Shift+3** cycles through all open timelines, Source and Program.

The **Up/Down Arrows** take you to the previous or next edit point in the sequence with the Source Monitor or Timeline panel active. **X** marks the clip your playhead is on. Combine these shortcuts, and you can go between selected sequences, navigate through individual takes, mark the one you want, and insert or overwrite it into your edit sequence—all without touching the mouse!

If you use Pancake Timelines a lot, save a custom workspace with your timelines already stacked. This will save you time adjusting the layout.

To close all but the selected sequence, click the panel menu in that sequence and choose *Close Other Timeline Panels* (Figure 4-16).

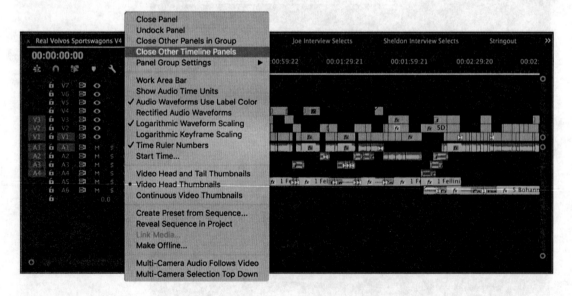

Figure 4-16. *Quickly close all timeline panels other than the selected one*

Navigate Source Sequences with Markers

When using sequences as sources, adding markers can further speed up finding and navigating your footage to edit with it. If you lay out all your b-roll sequentially in a single stringout timeline, you'll know how much you have to choose from (30 minutes? 4 hours? 15 hours?). Set markers for the good shots and use the shortcuts **Shift+M** for Go To Next Marker and **Shift+Ctrl+M** (Shift+Cmd+M) for Go To Previous Marker. All the footage is there to revisit if you need something specific. Figure 4-17 gives an example.

Figure 4-17. *Stringout markers. Adding markers to the "Selects" sequence makes navigating it a breeze. In this example, range markers differentiate shoot days and A versus B cameras, while individual markers indicate good shots, great shots, and nat sound moments.*

Alt+Click (Opt+Click) on a marker to turn it into a duration marker that can be dragged over your clips. **Alt+Ctrl+M** (Opt+M) clears the marker under the playhead, and **Shift+Alt+Ctrl+M** (Opt+Cmd+M) clears all the markers in your sequence.

The **Window ➤ Markers** panel gives you an alternative way to view and sort markers as a list. For more on sequence and clip markers, see the "Customization" chapter.

Nesting

A nested sequence is simply one sequence that is edited into another sequence. That's it. Any sequence can be used as a nest.

I use nesting to simplify my master timeline. Most of the time I'll start editing every scene in a separate sequence, then put those different scenes into the main sequence as nests.

You can also decide to nest clips after the fact. Say you've edited a complex thing in the main timeline, and you want to move those clips to a nested sequence. Just select the clips you want to move to a nested sequence and click **Edit ➤ Nest**, or assign your own shortcut (mine is **Shift+N**). See Figure 4-18.

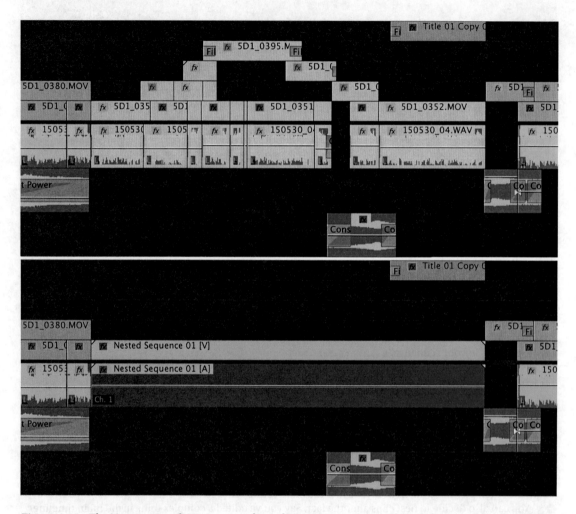

Figure 4-18. *The Nest command creates a nest from clips in your sequence. This works on multiple layers of video clips, but you can only nest a single layer of audio this way.*

Creating a nested sequence from clips in the timeline has its limitations. Video clips from all tracks will work, but Premiere will only nest audio clips on a single track. If you need to get around this limitation, try **Sequence ➤ Make Subsequence** (also found in the right-click menu). This creates a new sequence from your selection, but leaves the selected clips as they are in the timeline. You can then edit the subsequence back into your main timeline as needed. This workaround is good for a complex, multi-layered sound effect that you want to reuse as a nested sequence.

Similarly, nesting is perfect for creating complex, layered lower-third background animations that you want under every name and title. Just nest the whole animation and put that sequence wherever you want to put text in your main timeline. Create the animation once, nest it, and use it as many times as you want. Any changes you do to the animation will be updated in all the instances automatically.

The shortcut for Reveal Nested Sequence is **Ctrl+Shift+F**. It opens the nested sequence in the Timeline panel with the playhead parked at the exact same frame that was showing in the main sequence. This only works when the track with the nested sequence is active or the nested clip is selected.

Un-Nesting

There is no "Un-nest" feature in Premiere. It would quickly become very difficult to make rules for how this should work. What if the original nest has a clip on track 4, and there is already a clip in track 4 in the main timeline? Should the existing clip be overwritten? Should one clip be moved to another track? Which one? What if that clip was used as a track matte for another clip or had a blending mode? What happens to these effects if you put other clips in-between the existing tracks? There are so many variables that I doubt that it's even possible.

A manual, keyboard-driven approach would be to park on the first frame of the nested sequence in the main timeline and hit **F**. This does a Match Frame and loads the nested sequence into the Source Monitor. Set an in point by pressing the **I** key. Then, go back to the main sequence and park at the last frame of the nested sequence. **Down Arrow** followed by **Left Arrow** should do this quickly.

Hit **F** to do another Match Frame to the nested sequence. Now, advance one frame by pressing the **Right Arrow** and set an out point by pressing **O**. Make sure that *Insert and overwrite sequences as nests or individual clips* (i.e., the Nest-or-Not button) is set to individual clips (gray), then edit the marked section back into the parent sequence. Depending on the complexity of your timeline, it shouldn't take too long if you jump from edit to edit, match frame, then overwrite–all the time using shortcuts to navigate and perform the edits.

You may want to check the box **Preferences ➤ General ➤ Set focus on the Timeline when performing Insert/Overwrite edits** while performing this manual un-nest technique repeatedly.

Sometimes, Grouping Is Better

Grouping clips is faster and easier to understand for a client watching the session over your shoulder. Grouped clips remain in the main timeline, and they will also be exported correctly if you plan to export your timeline as an AAF or XML file for someone else to do the final color correction and finishing.

With Linked Selection mode on, select your clips and choose *Group* from the right-click menu. These clips can now be selected and moved together whenever you are in Linked Selection mode. If you want to select only one of them, use the **Alt** (Opt on Mac) modifier key when clicking the clip in the timeline, just like you would when temporarily overriding linked clips. **Alt+Click** (Opt+Click) can also be used when you want to adjust effects on just one clip in the group.

Project Panel and Media Browser Workflow Tips

The Project panel is where we organize our clips into bins for editing. You can also edit directly from the Media Browser panel, taking clips from your drives or even inside other projects and editing them directly into your sequence. There are lots of ways to speed up your workflow by leveraging these two panels. Let's look at a few.

Shortcuts in the Project Panel

You can open or close all the twirly arrows in a bin or in the Project panel with one click. **Alt+Click** (Opt+Click on Mac) on an open twirly to close all the twirlies. **Alt+Click** (Opt+Click) on a closed one to open all of them (Figure 4-19).

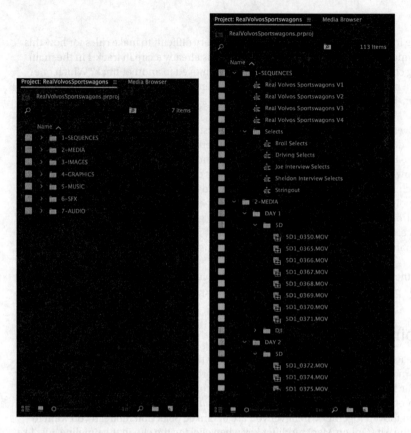

Figure 4-19. *Alt+Click (Opt+Click) one twirly arrow to open or close all of them*

You can **Ctrl+Drag** (Cmd+Drag) a sequence in a bin to make a duplicate of it. This is very handy when making alternative edits of a scene. Just remember to give the duplicate a descriptive name. You can also duplicate anything in the Project panel with the shortcut **Ctrl+Shift+/** (Cmd+Shift+/ on Mac).

To clear all in and out points for many clips in a bin, select them and hit **Ctrl+Shift+X** (Opt+X on Mac). As in the timeline, **Alt+I** or **Alt+O** (Opt+I or Opt+O) clears just the in or out points.

You can use audio gain in a bin. Hit **G**. One way to use this is to select all the clips in your Music bin and normalize the volume to around where you want it so they're all in the ballpark when you start throwing music clips in the timeline.

Shift+H turns Hover Scrubbing on and off in the Project panel. To do the same in the Media Browser panel, you will need to map the panel command for Hover Scrub to **Shift+H** there as well. When Hover Scrubbing is on, if you scrub a clip and then double-click to open it in the Source Monitor, it will keep your playhead in sync with where you were hovering. Thoughtful!

Color coding your clips and bins? You can map shortcuts for each of Premiere's available label colors under the **Edit ► Label** menu or by right-clicking (Figure 4-20). The trick is that you'll need to search by color name in the Keyboard Shortcuts window.

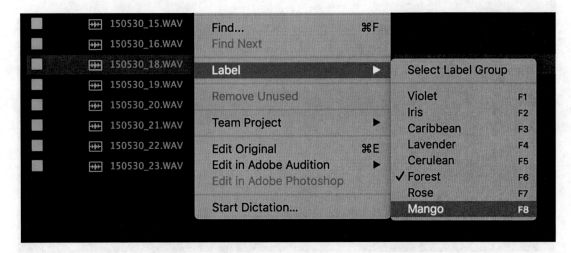

Figure 4-20. *Label colors. In this example, label color shortcuts have been mapped to the function keys*

You can also select a clip and **Edit ➤ Label ➤ Select Label Group** to select all clips with that same color. This option works in the Project panel and the timeline and is worth mapping to a custom keyboard shortcut if you use label colors a lot.

Is it time to save? The asterisk next to your project file name in the window bar indicates unsaved changes. Hit **Ctrl+S** (Cmd+S), and it will go away.

You can quickly find a clip from the timeline in the Project Panel. Right-click the clip in the timeline and choose *Reveal in Project*, or create a shortcut.

Under the panel menu for any sequence, you can choose to *Reveal Sequence in Project.*

Video and Audio Usage Columns

What if you have a clip in your project and want to find every sequence it is used in? The Project panel has two columns for that, but you'll need to add them in.

Go to the Project panel menu and choose *Metadata Display*. Under Premiere Pro Project Metadata, check the two boxes for *Video Usage* and *Audio Usage*. These two columns now appear in the Project panel on the far right, so drag them forward for easier access. Now, for each master clip in your project, the columns will show every instance of that clip in your sequences. When you click on one, it will take you to it in the timeline (Figure 4-21).

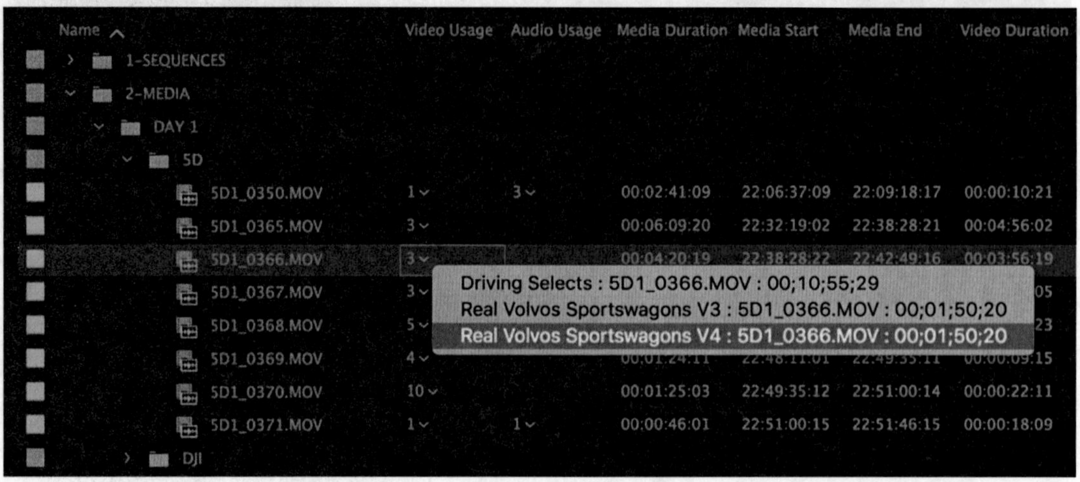

Name ∧	Video Usage	Audio Usage	Media Duration	Media Start	Media End	Video Duration
> 🖿 1-SEQUENCES						
∨ 🖿 2-MEDIA						
∨ 🖿 DAY 1						
∨ 🖿 5D						
🖿 5D1_0350.MOV	1 ∨	3 ∨	00:02:41:09	22:06:37:09	22:09:18:17	00:00:10:21
🖿 5D1_0365.MOV	3 ∨		00:06:09:20	22:32:19:02	22:38:28:21	00:04:56:02
🖿 5D1_0366.MOV	3 ∨		00:04:20:19	22:38:28:22	22:42:49:16	00:03:56:19
🖿 5D1_0367.MOV	3 ∨					05
🖿 5D1_0368.MOV	5 ∨					23
🖿 5D1_0369.MOV	4 ∨		00:01:24:11	22:48:11:01	22:49:35:11	00:00:09:15
🖿 5D1_0370.MOV	10 ∨		00:01:25:03	22:49:35:12	22:51:00:14	00:00:22:11
🖿 5D1_0371.MOV	1 ∨	1 ∨	00:00:46:01	22:51:00:15	22:51:46:15	00:00:18:09
> 🖿 DJI						

Driving Selects : 5D1_0366.MOV : 00;10;55;29
Real Volvos Sportswagons V3 : 5D1_0366.MOV : 00;01;50;20
Real Volvos Sportswagons V4 : 5D1_0366.MOV : 00;01;50;20

Figure 4-21. *Video and audio usage is an extremely useful way to find everywhere you've used a clip*

Want a quick and dirty way to see all the clips you've used in a sequence in the Project panel? Create a new bin named *Used*. Select all clips in the timeline and drag them to the bin. The copies in this bin can be deleted later, as they are new master clips and are not associated with the instances in the sequence.

Keep a TXT File in Your Project

A great way to make notes during editing is to import a TXT file to your Project panel. You cannot use **File ▶ Import**, because TXT files do not appear in the Import dialog. You can use the Media Browser, but you need to click the funnel icon and set File Types Displayed to *All Files*. But the easiest way is probably just to drag and drop it into the Project panel. Once there, you can double click to open it in a text editor, and your notes will stay with the project as long as you don't delete the TXT file from your hard drive.

Don't Underestimate the Media Browser

As we saw in chapter 1, Accelerated Workflow, the Media Browser acts as a Finder window panel within Premiere Pro. You can navigate your drives; find, sort, and scrub clips; and open them in the Source Monitor for further previewing–all without importing them into your project. It can also interpret native card structures and merge spanned clips on import, which is why Adobe recommends importing all camera cards via the Media Browser (Figure 4-22).

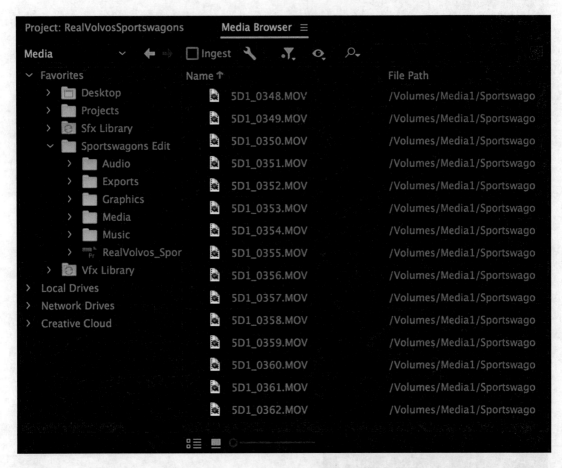

Figure 4-22. *Media Browser panel. In the upper right of the panel you can sort results by file type or directory view, or search to refine what you see. Just remember to clear these selections afterward or you may have a moment of confusion the next time you use the panel. Select any folder, right-click, and choose Add to Favorites for easy access.*

You can have multiple Media Browser panels open at once. Go to the panel menu and choose *New Media Browser Panel*. This way, you can use folders on your drive or even in other projects as bins, taking only what you need for your edit.

Stacked Panel Groups

When you have multiple open bins, Media Browser panels, or any other panel combination, you can dock them together as tabbed panels (the default) or change to a stacked panel group, as shown in Figure 4-23.

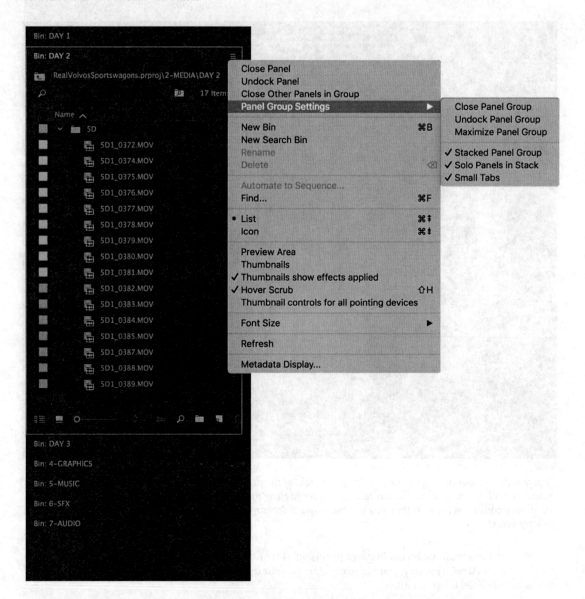

Figure 4-23. *Options for stacked panel groups can be found in the panel menu*

Go to the panel menu and enable **Panel Group Settings ➤ Stacked Panel Group**. The tabs now stack horizontally, and clicking on any one will minimize or expand it. This interface idea comes from Adobe Lightroom and functions just like the Lumetri Color panel.

Ctrl+Click (Cmd+Click) one tab and you will expand them all. If **Panel Group Settings ➤ Solo Panels in Stack** is checked, then you can only click and expand one panel at a time. But **Alt+Click** (Opt+Click) a tab, and you will toggle Solo mode on and off.

Stacked panel groups work best in a long, vertical frame. You can save them with your workspace under the Windows menu.

Open Other Projects and Sequences Using Dynamic Link

Premiere Pro can't have multiple projects open at once, but you can go into other projects using the Media Browser. Simply double-click any .prproj file, and Dynamic Link will open and display everything within that project. You can preview and import bins, assets, or sequences into your own project.

You can also double-click sequences to open them in your timeline. They will automatically open in the Source Monitor, and you'll notice the red playhead. These dynamically linked sequences are read-only, so you can't modify them. But you can set them up using the Pancake Timelines technique described earlier and edit clips into sequences from your current project. When you do, the clips you've added will appear in your own Project panel.

The combination of multiple Media Browser bins, opening other projects and sequences with Dynamic Link, and editing with Pancake Timelines gives you a powerful toolkit for optimizing large projects. *Deadpool*, *Gone Girl*, and other feature films and documentaries edited on Premiere Pro have all used these techniques.

Useful Info About the Premiere Pro Timeline

A timeline is a sequence, but the Timeline panel gives you multiple ways to control your editing. Read on to ensure that you know your way around it.

Choose Your Sequence Settings Wisely

Your sequence settings *do* matter, but how do you decide what settings to use? If you're editing material from just one camera and only want stereo output, you can create a sequence the easy way by dropping a clip into the empty Timeline panel—or dragging it onto the *New Item* button in the bottom right of the Project panel—when you start your project. The Sequence Settings will be matched to your clip specs.

However, if you have other needs, hit **Ctrl+N** (Cmd+N) to bring up the New Sequence dialog and create a sequence with custom settings for video and audio (Figure 4-24). You can read more about these options in chapter 1 on Advanced Workflow, chapter 2 on Audio, and chapter 10 on Customizing Premiere.

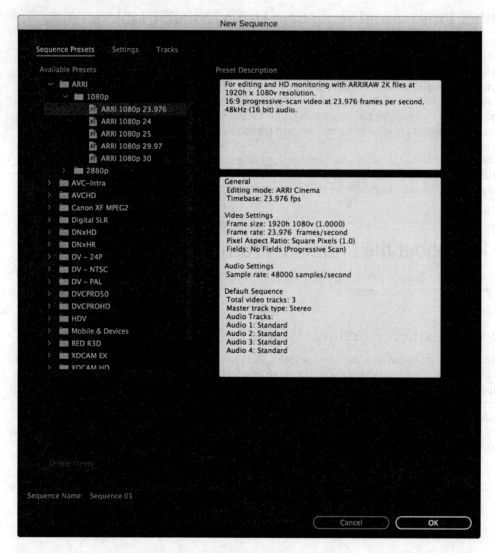

Figure 4-24. *The New Sequence window contains a variety of sequence presets, but you can easily click over to the Settings and Tracks tabs to specify the exact video and audio settings you want for your sequence*

In general, it helps to remember that sequences in Premiere Pro (unlike in many other NLEs) are format-agnostic containers with the frame rate, frame size, and so on that you define in **Sequence ➤ Sequence Settings** (Figure 4-25). There is no format or codec associated with the sequence. The Editing Mode presets in the New Sequence dialog are simply there for your convenience, because the Mercury Playback Engine will attempt to play back everything you throw at it—from compressed .avi files to 8K Red Dragon footage—in real time.

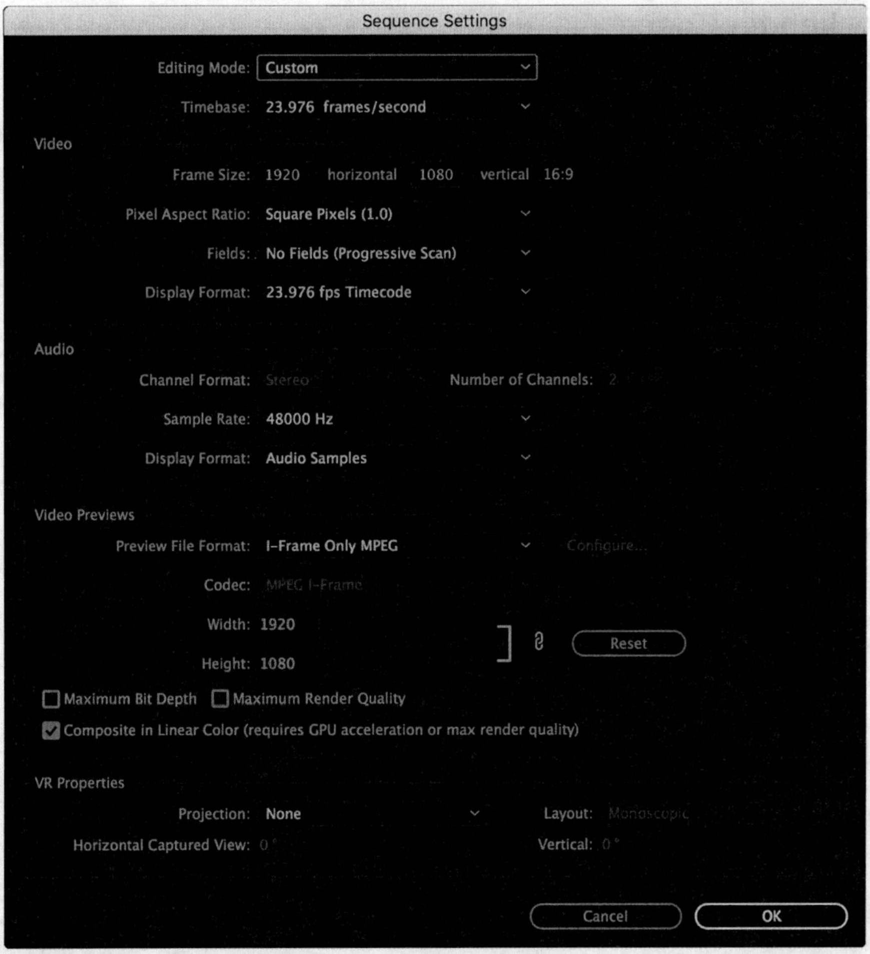

Figure 4-25. *Sequence settings*

So, if you're mixing a lot of formats, frame rates, and frame sizes, take a look at your delivery requirements and create a sequence that matches those. Many broadcast companies have sequence and export presets in place that work with their house format. Whatever your situation, take a moment to create a sequence that you know will suit your workflow—before you start editing in it.

■ **Note** In Premiere Pro, projects and sequences accept all formats and codecs natively. When choosing Sequence settings, compare your source footage specs with your delivery requirements. Create sequences in a frame rate and frame size that will support your end-to-end workflow as smoothly as possible.

Video Preview Render Codec

Under **Sequence ➤ Sequence Settings** you'll notice a third category of settings for Video Previews. This defines the format, codec, and size of any preview files you render for that sequence.

Many of the standard sequence presets use I-frame-only MPEG at a low bit rate as the preview codec for renders, sometimes at a lower resolution than the sequence itself. This makes sense, since they render fast, take up very little disk space, and aren't supposed to be used on export anyway.

If you want to use the preview renders at export time, you need them to be created with a high-quality codec and at full resolution. DNxHD, Go Pro Cineform, and ProRes are the most-used codecs for this purpose. Change **Sequence Settings ➤ Editing Mode** to Custom in order to make this change.

If you have tight deadlines and want Smart Rendering to kick in when you export the finished piece, you need the exact same codec settings for your preview files as for the final export. Read more about Smart Rendering in chapter 12 on Export.

Playback Resolution Is Stored per Sequence

The playback and pause resolution settings are stored per sequence. So, if you have an HD sequence and a 4K sequence in the same project, you can set playback resolution to Full for the HD sequence and ¼ for the 4K sequence. When you switch from one to the other, the playback resolution will switch accordingly.

Resolution changes made by you are also sticky. If you change the playback resolution, the value you select will be used as the default when creating new sequences.

Which Settings Where?

The timeline items that you generally set and forget live in the Timeline panel menu (Figure 4-26), and the ones that you may need to toggle on and off live in the Timeline wrench menu (the official name is Timeline Display Settings) shown in Figure 4-27.

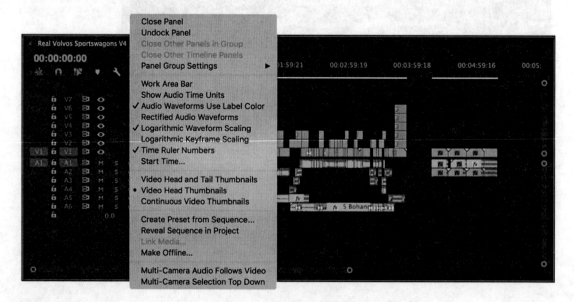

Figure 4-26. *The set-and-forget settings are found in the Timeline panel menu*

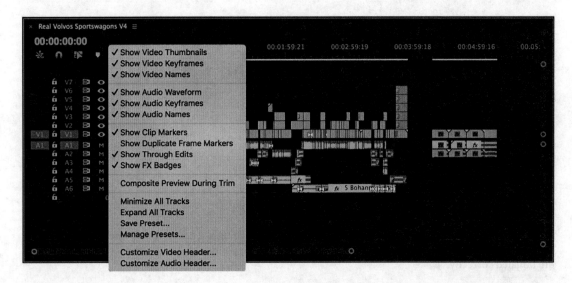

Figure 4-27. *Settings you'll want to switch on and off regularly are found in the Timeline panel wrench menu*

Track Targeting and Source Patching Behavior

You should definitely use custom track targeting and source patching presets and shortcuts as explained in chapter 10 on Customizing Premiere, and chapter 3 on Audio. This tutorial by Dylan Osborn shows how you can speed up your editing with these techniques: dylanosborn.com/2016/11/02/timeline-presets/.

But it also helps to understand how track targeting and source patching are designed to help you by default.

The patching for clips with differing content is remembered and saved at the sequence level. So, once you patch a particular clip type on a sequence, Premiere remembers it until you change it. If you patch a video clip with four audio channels so that tracks 1+2 are added to tracks 3+4 in the timeline, and 3+4 are not used, this will be remembered the next time you use a similar clip as your source. If you patch an audio-only stereo clip to tracks 7+8, Premiere will choose that patching the next time you select a similar clip as your source. Patch a title to video track 5, and that track will be chosen the next time you use a video-only clip. You get the idea.

The intention is to speed up your editing since you only have to patch one particular type of clip once. This is very effective, but can be confusing if you don't know why the patching keeps changing. Now you know.

Some editors like to add transitions and do other stuff to their clips immediately after adding them to the timeline. Say you add a clip to video track 4. If the track is not active/targeted, this means you need to make it active before you can add a transition with a shortcut. We don't like extra clicking, do we? There is a choice if you right-click the track targeting buttons. It's named *Targets Follow Inserts and Overwrites* (Figure 4-28).

Figure 4-28. *Targets Follow Inserts and Overwrites can auto-select tracks after an edit*

This makes the tracks active when you add clips to them with Insert or Overwrite. Then, you can immediately add transitions after adding a clip to your sequence without worrying about whether the tracks are targeted correctly.

Sync Lock Behavior

You can determine which tracks will be affected when you perform an Insert edit, Ripple Delete, Extract, or Ripple Trim operation by toggling Sync Lock on those tracks. By default, all tracks are sync locked. You must click the icon in the track header to disable sync for certain tracks. If the icon has a line through it, Sync Lock is off. Figures 4-29, 4-30, and 4-31 demonstrate this behavior.

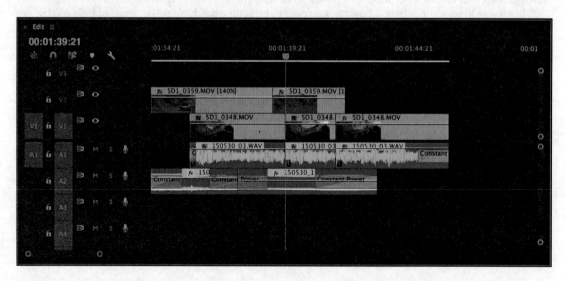

Figure 4-29. *Only sync-locked tracks will ripple when you do inserts, ripple edits, and extracts. Here's the situation before doing an Insert edit.*

Figure 4-30. *Since all tracks were sync locked, the Insert edit on two tracks affected all tracks*

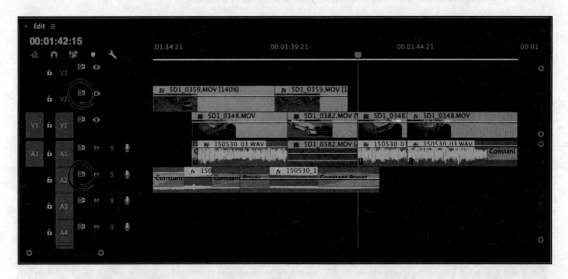

Figure 4-31. *Here, V2 and A2 were not sync locked, and hence were not affected by the Insert edit on the other tracks*

So, leave Sync Lock on in the headers of all tracks you *do* want to shift when a gap is closed, a Ripple edit is performed, and so on, and turn Sync Lock off in the headers of all the tracks that you *don't* want to shift. Of course, the tracks you are performing the actual edit on will always be affected regardless of the Sync Lock setting.

There are no keyboard shortcuts for Sync Lock, but you can **Shift+Click** the icons to turn them all on or off. You can map keyboard shortcuts for track locking, if that helps. Search for Lock/Unlock All Video/Audio Tracks in the Keyboard Shortcuts window.

FX Badge Color Codes

You've probably seen that the FX badges on the clips in your sequence change colors depending on what effects you've applied to them (Figure 4-32).

Figure 4-32. *The different FX badges*

But what do all the colors mean? Here we go:

Gray = Only intrinsic effects; no modified parameters or keyframes

Yellow = Only intrinsic effects, modified parameters, or keyframes

Purple = Intrinsic effects and extra effects; no modified intrinsic parameters

Green = Intrinsic effects and extra effects; modified intrinsic parameters

Red underline = Master Clip effect added

Hide All Effects Button

If you have an effects-heavy sequence and just want to get some editing done, Premiere has a handy button for that situation. It's called *Global FX Mute*. Look for the FX icon in the Program Monitor's Button Editor and drag it to your button bar. When pressed (blue), all clip effects are hidden everywhere in the project, significantly improving performance (Figure 4-33). Even better, you can map Global FX Mute to a keyboard shortcut for easy toggling. It is a panel command, so the Program Monitor must be activated for your shortcut to work.

Figure 4-33. *Global FX Mute is very useful for temporarily hiding all effects, and it's a mean practical joke to play on editors who don't know it exists. Use your knowledge for good!*

Navigating the Timeline

Premiere sticks pretty well to Windows and MacOS standards, so if you know the basics you'll already know a few shortcuts. Of course, **Ctrl+A, Ctrl+C, Ctrl+V, Ctrl+X, Ctrl+Z**, and so on all work as expected (use **Cmd** instead of **Ctrl** on Mac).

End takes you to the end of the sequence, and **Home** takes you to the start, as expected. If you have one or more clips selected and want to go to the beginning or end of the selection, add **Shift. Shift+Home** takes you to the start of the selection, and **Shift+End** takes you to the end of the selection.

While **Up Arrow** and **Down Arrow** take you to the previous or next edit point on active tracks, **Shift+Up Arrow** and **Shift+Down Arrow** will take you to the next edit point regardless of which tracks are active.

Click the blue time display in the timeline and enter *+300* to move three seconds forward. Enter *-20* to move 20 frames back, and so forth.

If you use a mouse with a free-spinning wheel, you can navigate quickly this way. Spin the wheel to move back and forth in time. Hold down **Alt** (Opt) while spinning, and you're zooming in and out in the timeline. Hold down **Ctrl** (Cmd), and you're scrolling vertically in the timeline (when possible).

Zoom to Sequence is \ on the English keyboard. This tends to move around on non-English keyboards. It's very handy to zoom out to see the entire sequence after doing small adjustments at a high zoom level. Press \ again to go back to the previous zoom level.

Just as Zoom to Sequence zooms you all the way out, Zoom to Frame will zoom you all the way in to the frame level. This command does not have a default shortcut, so you'll need to map your own. **Ctrl+** (Cmd+\ on Mac) is easy to remember if you already use \ for Zoom to Sequence.

Making Selections

You can, of course, click a clip with your mouse, marquee-select a range of clips, or **Shift+Click** to select several clips, but using keyboard shortcuts is often quicker.

There is the usual **Ctrl+A** (Cmd+A on Mac) for Select All and its opposite, **Ctrl+Shift+A** (Cmd+Shift+A) for Deselect All. I map Deselect All to **F2**, like in After Effects, since pressing three keys is not very convenient for a shortcut I use all the time.

You can set in and out points around a selected clip or a range of clips by pressing the / (Forward Slash) key for Mark Selection. This often ends up at other keys on non-English keyboards.

Pressing **X** for Mark Clip sets in and out points around all the clips touched by the playhead that are on active/targeted tracks.

To select (rather than mark) all the clips on active/targeted tracks that are touched by the playhead, hit **D** for Select Clip at Playhead. If you edit with Linked Selection mode on, keep in mind that this command *ignores* both linking and grouping and will only select clips actually under the playhead.

To select the next clip in the timeline, hit **Ctrl+Down Arrow** (Cmd+Down Arrow) for Select Next Clip. If you have no clip selected, the playhead jumps to the first clip to the right and then selects it. If you already have a clip selected, it jumps to the next clip on the same track.

Ctrl+Up Arrow (Cmd+Up Arrow) is for Select Previous Clip and works the same way as Select Next Clip—just at the other side of the playhead.

To get properties for a selected clip, hit **Ctrl+Shift+H** (Cmd+Shift+H).

Deleting Multiple Gaps in a Track at Once

Sometimes, you end up having many clips scattered with gaps between them. To quickly delete all the gaps, you could of course use **Sequence ➤ Go to Gap ➤ Next in Sequence (Shift+;)** and delete them one by one, but there is a smarter way.

Put black video, color matte, or any other synthetic clip on an empty track above and make sure it covers all the clips in the target track. Select all clips on the target track and move them up to the synthetic clip, then move them down again. This leaves lots of clips where the gaps were. Select them all and hit **Shift+Delete** (Shift+Forward Delete on Mac) to perform a tipple delete. Poof! The gaps are gone, provided sync lock is enabled for all the tracks involved. Figures 4-34 through 4-38 demonstrate this technique.

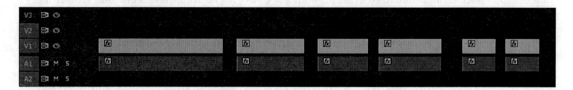

Figure 4-34. *We want to get rid of the gaps between these clips*

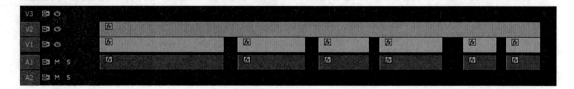

Figure 4-35. *First, we add a synthetic clip (like a color matte) on a track above*

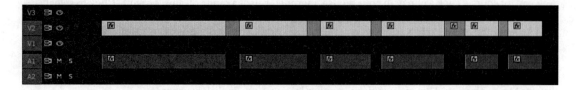

Figure 4-36. *Then, we select the clips and move them up (Alt+Up Arrow)*

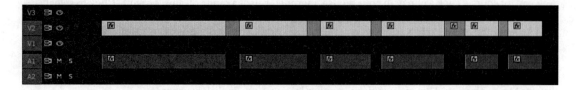

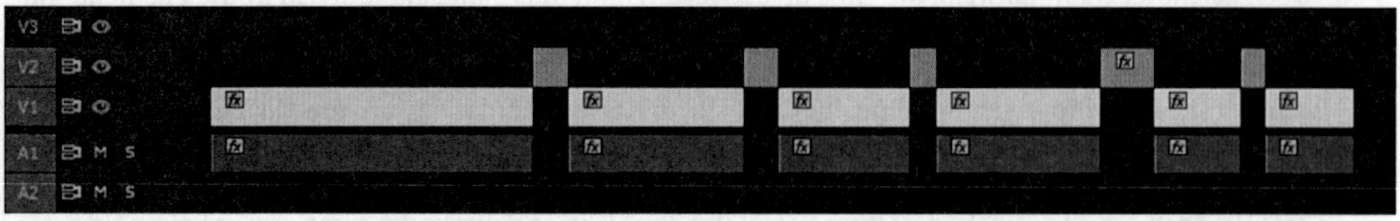

Figure 4-37. *Alt+Down Arrow moves the clips back where they were and leaves lots of short synthetic clips*

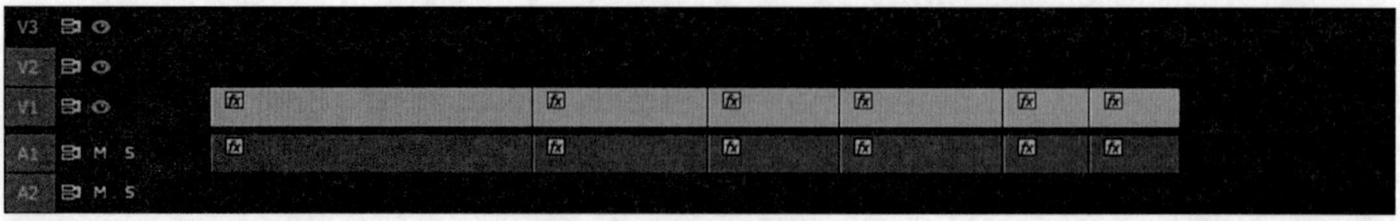

Figure 4-38. *Ripple deleting all the synthetic clips removes the gaps*

If there are no other tracks between the gap track and the synthetic clip track, moving the clips up and down can be done with the Nudge Clip Selection Up/Down shortcuts: **Alt+Up/Down** (Opt+Up/Down).

Adding Gaps

Other times, you have a lot of clips and want to add, for example, 15 frames of black video between them. A fairly quick way is **File ➤ New ➤ Black Video**, open in the Source Monitor, and set an in point at the start and an out point at 15 frames. Then, use your **Down Arrow** to go to the next clip and hit **,** for Insert. Repeat the arrow and comma combination until all the gaps are created.

Delete Many Keyframes

If you need to delete a lot of keyframes, switch over to the Pen tool and just lasso your keyframes, then hit **Delete**, and they'll be removed. You can only lasso one track's keyframes at a time (Figure 4-39).

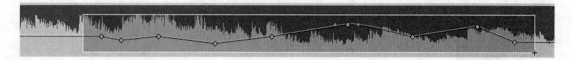

Figure 4-39. *Lasso-select audio keyframes with the Pen tool*

Copy/Paste Transitions to Multiple Edit Points

Audio and video transitions can be pasted to multiple selected edit points while preserving all user-configurable properties. Apply the transition to one edit point, then select it and hit **Ctrl+C** (Cmd+C). Select the edit points where you want to paste the transition by holding down **Ctrl** (Cmd) and **marquee-dragging** around them. With the edit points selected, hit **Ctrl+V** (Cmd+V). You can also select edit points by **Shift-Clicking** them. See Figures 4-40, 4-41, and 4-42.

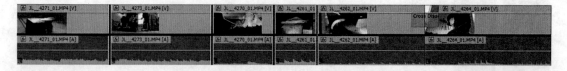

Figure 4-40. *After copying the transition, select the edit points to which you want to paste*

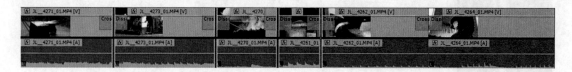

Figure 4-41. *Here, the transitions are pasted*

Figure 4-42. *Deselect the edit points with the Deselect All shortcut*

Moving, Adjusting, and Swapping Clips

This is what most people think of when they hear the word "editing." And it is what most editors spend most of their time doing. So, why not do it efficiently?

The Über Tool

Premiere gives us 16 different editing tools, as shown in Figure 4-43.

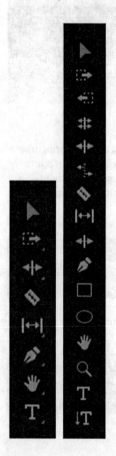

Figure 4-43. *The Tools Palette and its expanded (Photoshopped) version, with the Selection tool active*

I use the Selection tool (**V**) almost all the time. It's the über tool! The modifier keys make this tool so versatile it can be used for almost any kind of edit. **Ctrl** (Cmd) transforms it into a combined Rolling Edit, Extract, and Ripple Edit tool. **Alt** (Opt) makes it a Split Edit tool. **Shift** makes it a Snap-to-Edit-Point tool and a Multiple Selection tool.

The shortcut **Ctrl+K** (Cmd+K) is faster for adding edits than switching to the Razor tool (**C**),and the zoom shortcuts are faster than using the Zoom tool (**Z**). The Hand tool (**H**) isn't needed if your mouse can scroll left and right through the timeline. The Ripple Edit and Rolling Edit tools aren't needed either, and the Slip tool (**Y**) and Slide tool (**U**) are for special situations—although you can also use keyboard shortcuts for slipping and sliding clips around. Once you know everything you can do with the Selection tool, the Tools Palette becomes a waste of valuable screen real estate. Just use the Über tool!

Moving Clips

You may have discovered that you can move clips in the timeline by pressing **Alt** (Cmd) and tapping **Left/Right Arrows**. This is exactly like moving the clip with the mouse and will overwrite existing clips and create gaps. If you press **Alt** (Opt) and tap the **Up/ Down Arrows**, you'll move the clip to another track. Remember to select only the audio or video part of the clip before moving it to other tracks.

You can also move a selected clip a specified number of frames. Type + followed by the number of frames on your numeric keypad, and then hit **Enter**. The clip moves forward the number of frames you typed. So, *+20* moves the clip 20 frames.

If you type *+200*, it will not move 200 frames—that will be interpreted as 2 seconds and 00 frames. *+220* will be interpreted as 2 seconds and 20 frames, and so forth. Of course, typing - instead of + will move the clip backward, so *-115* moves the clip backwards 1 second and 15 frames.

Dragging Video and Audio to Different Tracks

Some editors coming from Final Cut Pro 7 are used to the audio and video parts of a clip moving together when they change tracks. For example, move the video part of the clip to video track 4, and the audio also shifts to audio track 4. If you like this behavior, you can do the same thing in Premiere with the **Shift** modifier key.

Start by dragging the video part of the clip to the desired position on the desired track, then press and hold **Shift**, drag the audio part to its destination track, and let go. You have more direct control over where the clips end up, and this works whether Linked Selection mode is on or off.

What Exactly Are Three- and Four-Point Edits?

A lot of books explain three-point editing in a very complicated way. Let's try an easy way. Every insert or overwrite edit consists of four points: source in and out points, and sequence in and out points (Figure 4-44).

Figure 4-44. *The four points of an insert or overwrite edit*

Computers are good at math, so if you give it only three points, it will automatically figure out the missing fourth point. The missing point can be any of the four points just mentioned. You can give Premiere a Source Out point, a Sequence In, and a Sequence Out, and it will calculate the missing Source In point using the duration you set in your sequence. But the most common practice is to give Premiere the Source In and Out and Sequence In points. That's what happens if you set in and out points in the Source Monitor and drag the clip into a sequence or just hit the Overwrite shortcut. Premiere helps you out by using the playhead position as your third point (the Sequence In point) and calculating the fourth point (the Sequence Out point) for you.

Don't worry if you didn't grasp this in writing. My experience is that people do three-point editing intuitively—they just don't know it's called three-point editing! You probably do it all the time.

But, if you set four points, and the Source and Sequence durations are different, Premiere will display the Fit Clip dialog when you tell it to insert or overwrite (Figure 4-45). Here, you can tell Premiere what you want it to do with the mismatch: ignore one of the four points or change the clip speed.

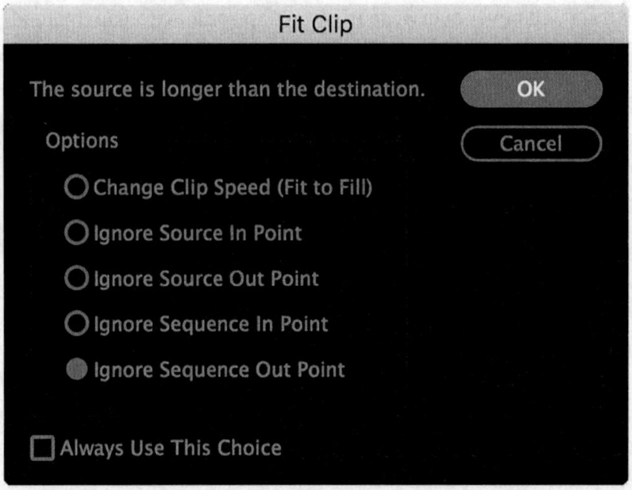

```
┌──────────────────────────────────────────┐
│                 Fit Clip                   │
├──────────────────────────────────────────┤
│                                            │
│  The source is longer than the destination. │  ┌──────┐
│                                            │  │  OK  │
│  Options                                   │  └──────┘
│                                            │  ┌──────────┐
│    ◯ Change Clip Speed (Fit to Fill)       │  │  Cancel  │
│                                            │  └──────────┘
│    ◯ Ignore Source In Point                │
│                                            │
│    ◯ Ignore Source Out Point               │
│                                            │
│    ◯ Ignore Sequence In Point              │
│                                            │
│    ⬤ Ignore Sequence Out Point             │
│                                            │
│                                            │
│  ☐ Always Use This Choice                  │
│                                            │
└──────────────────────────────────────────┘
```

Figure 4-45. *Whenever you have in and out points in both the Source Monitor and the timeline and their durations don't match, you will get the Fit Clip dialog*

The *Change Clip Speed (Fit to Fill)* option is useful if you have a clip of a certain length and want to change its speed to get a different length in your timeline. Set four points, insert or overwrite, choose *Fit to Fill*, and you're done. If you do this a lot, check *Always Use This Choice* and Premiere will fit to fill every time.

If you rarely set in and out points in your timeline, you may never encounter the Fit Clip dialogue. But now you know what three- and four-point edits are.

Rolling Edits

When you select an edit point (or points, by holding down **Shift**), the shortcut for moving it is **Ctrl+Left/Right Arrow** (Opt+Left/Right Arrow). But if that's all you do, you won't get to see the new in and out points as you change them. Try using the standard Trim mode. Hit **Shift+T** to enter Trim mode, and then use **Ctrl+Left/Right Arrow** to roll the edit with visual feedback.

Rolling edits do not affect the duration of your film. If you're cutting head from one clip, you're adding tail to the other.

Ripple Edits

To understand Ripple edits, it helps to think of it as gravity or magnetism that works toward the left—the start of the timeline. When you remove a clip using Ripple Delete or shorten a clip with a Ripple edit, the whole chunk of clips to the right of this point on the timeline will "fall" to the left.

■ **Note**   A Ripple Edit causes a chain reaction through the whole timeline.

The Ripple edit commands Insert and Extract will never overwrite existing clips or leave a gap. Instead, the clips will be forced to the right or "gravitate" to the left on the timeline, making the duration of your film longer or shorter.

Ripple edits can be done with the mouse if you press **Ctrl** (Cmd on Mac) before dragging the edit point. Use **Shift+Ctrl+Click** (Shift+Cmd+Click) to select and ripple drag multiple edit points.

On the keyboard, **Q** and **W** are the commands for Ripple Trim Previous and Next Edit to Playhead. These shortcuts are faster than setting in and out points and performing an Extract edit—especially in the rough-cut stage when your audio and video clips match in the timeline.

To perform a Ripple Delete, mark or select a clip and press **Alt+Backspace** (Opt+Delete) or **Shift+Delete**. This will delete the clip and close the gap.

Extend Edits

I love Extend edits. They let me park the playhead on a frame and then move a selected edit point to that frame—so much faster than clicking and dragging the edit.

You can start with the playhead where you want to move the cut. Simply keep it there, select the edit point, then hit **E**. The edit point is moved to the playhead.

Or, you can do it the other way around. Select the edit point, move the playhead to where you want it to be, and hit **E**.

Extend edits work with Ripple, Roll, and standard edits, and on both the top and tail of a clip.

One great way to use an Extend edit is when you need an adjustment layer that covers all the clips in your timeline. Put the adjustment layer at the start of the timeline on a track above all other clips and select its out point with the mouse. Then, move the playhead to the end of the timeline and hit **E**. The result is shown in Figures 4-46 and 4-47.

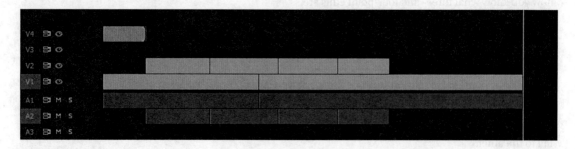

Figure 4-46. Start by selecting the edit point. Then, move the playhead to where you want the edit point to move.

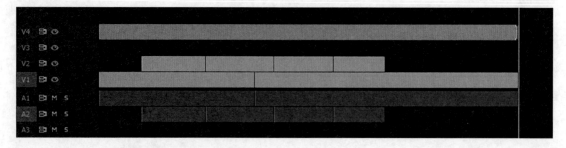

Figure 4-47. Hit E, and the edit point has moved

You can do all this without using the mouse if you want. **Home** is the shortcut to move to the start of the timeline. **Shift+1** takes you to the Project panel, where you can select the adjustment layer (or create a new one with your custom shortcut). **Period (.)** for Overwrite will put the adjustment layer in the timeline, and your custom source patching shortcut makes sure it ends up on the right track. Then, your custom shortcut for Select Nearest Edit Point as Roll (or as Trim Out) will do what the name indicates. Then, **End** will take you to the end of the timeline, and finally **E** will extend the adjustment layer so that it covers the whole film.

See the "Customization" chapter for more ideas on how to set up these and other shortcuts. Although, in many cases like this one a combination of mouse clicks and keyboard shortcuts can be the fastest way to get something done in Premiere Pro.

Slip and Slide Edits

A *Slide edit* means you're sliding a clip along the timeline without changing its in and out points. You use the same content of the clip, but at a different time in the film.

A *Slip edit* means you're keeping the clip in the same place in the timeline, but adjusting the in and out points of the content within it. Neither Slip nor Slide edits alter the length of your clip.

These explanations can be a bit hard to grasp. Let me show this visually using a two-track analogy that I learned from Adobe master trainer Luisa Winters. Even though in the timeline we actually perform Slip and Slide edits with all the clips involved in a single track, it's easier to understand what these edits do if we imagine the clips on two tracks. Check out Figures 4-48 and 4-49.

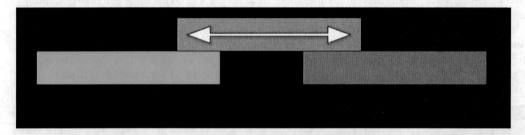

Figure 4-48. *A Slide edit behaves like this*

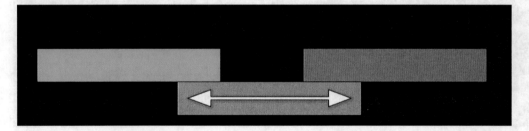

Figure 4-49. *A Slip edit behaves like this*

■ **Note** A Slide edit is like having a clip on a track above two other clips, moving it left and right. A Slip edit is like having a clip on a track beneath two other clips, moving it left and right.

Performing these edits is easy enough using the mouse and the Slip (**Y**) and Slide (**U**) tools, but it can be difficult to get frame accuracy. Learn keyboard-driven slip-n-slide, and you'll work faster.

To slide a clip, select it, then press and hold **Alt** (Opt), tap the **Comma** key to move the clip to the left frame by frame, or the **Period** key to move it to the right frame by frame. To move it five frames with each tap, add **Shift**.

To slip a clip, select it, then press and hold **Ctrl+Alt** (Cmd+Opt) and tap **Left** or **Right Arrows**. This slips the clip frame by frame. As with the Slide edit, add **Shift** to move five frames with each tap.

The disadvantage of doing Slip and Slide edits this way is that you don't see the four-up display in the Program Monitor that appears if you use the dedicated tools. But, I find that if I park my playhead at the in or out points of the clip, I can usually cut to exactly the frames I need.

Remember, Slip and Slide edits do not affect the total duration of your film.

Lift and Extract

These two edit operations involve setting in and out points in the timeline and using track targeting to determine what clips will be removed. Sometimes there are faster ways to do the same edit (like **Q** and **W**), but Lift and Extract will be very familiar to Avid Media Composer editors, and work similarly.

Lift will remove whatever is between the sequence in and out points on all active/targeted tracks without closing the gaps. It also stores the lifted clips in the RAM, so you can paste them somewhere else. There is a Lift button in the Program Monitor, or you can press the **semicolon** key. This shortcut tends to move around to other keys on a non-English keyboard. Figures 4-50 and 4-51 demonstrate a Lift edit.

Figure 4-50. *The Lift edit removes stuff between in and out on targeted tracks and puts it in RAM. The Lift edit does not do a ripple, so a gap will be created.*

Figure 4-51. *Only the content on targeted tracks is lifted*

The Extract command will remove everything on all sync-locked tracks between the sequence in and out points and close the gap. It also stores the deleted portion in RAM so you can paste it elsewhere. If some untargeted tracks are not sync locked, the results can quickly become unpredictable, so watch your targeting and sync-lock buttons carefully. Figures 4-52 and 4-53 demonstrate an Extract edit with Sync Lock on, while Figures 4-54 and 4-55 show different outcomes resulting from Sync Lock's being off on certain tracks.

Figure 4-52. *Same starting point as with the Lift edit, with in and out points in the sequence*

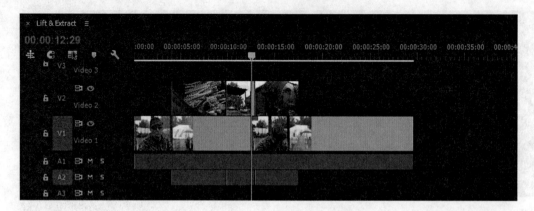

Figure 4-53. *When all tracks have Sync Lock enabled (gray), content on all tracks is extracted, and the gaps are closed*

Figure 4-54. *When some tracks have Sync Lock disabled (blue), the results get a bit unpredictable, as you can see here on track A1*

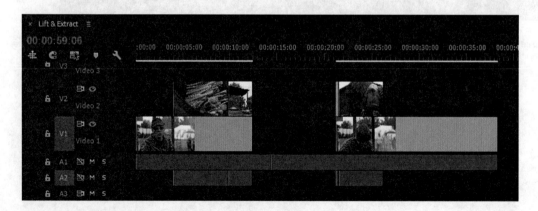

Figure 4-55. *Another Extract edit without Sync Lock. Watch your Sync Lock buttons!*

You can think of Lift and Extract as advanced forms of Cut and Paste operations. If you don't need the Paste part and want to select clips instead of marking ins and outs, you can use **Delete** as a substitute for Lift and **Shift+Delete** as a substitute for Extract (when Sync Lock is on).

Replace with Clip

You can replace a clip in the timeline with a new one from the Source Monitor or a bin, retaining any effects, animation, and other adjustments you've made to the original clip in the timeline. This is commonly known as a Replace edit.

If you right-click a clip in the timeline, or use the menu **Clip ➤ Replace with Clip**, you'll get three choices (Figure 4-56). Of course, you should assign shortcuts to these.

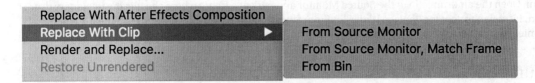

Figure 4-56. *The Replace With Clip menu*

However, when you search for "Replace with Clip" in the Keyboard Shortcuts window, you'll get a surprise: the commands don't show up, because they are in a sub-menu. Instead, you'll need to search "From Source Monitor" or "From Bin" to map them (Figure 4-57).

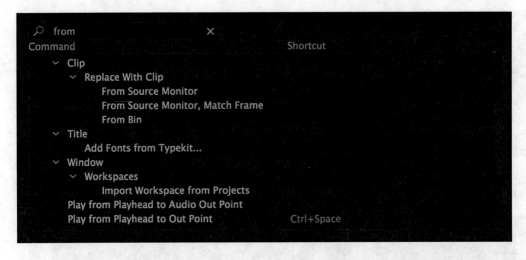

Figure 4-57. *Search "From Source Monitor" and then you can map the Replace With Clip shortcuts*

You can also **Alt-Drag** (Opt-Drag) and drop a clip from the Source Monitor or a bin onto a clip in the timeline to perform a Replace edit. This will use the in point of the new clip. If you want to use the in point of the old clip, add **Shift**.

To replace only video or audio in your Alt-Drag, first select the clip you want to replace in your sequence. If you are editing with Linked Selection mode on, **Alt-Click** (Opt-Click) the audio or video clip to select it out of the linked pair. Then, **Alt-Drag** onto your selection.

You can even Alt-Drag one source clip to replace several clips in the timeline. For example, if you have four instances of clips that you want to replace with the same new source clip, just select them in the timeline and do the standard Alt-drag and drop it on one of the selected clips.

Replace with Clip, Match Frame

The **Clip ➤ Replace with Clip ➤ From Source Monitor, Match Frame** feature can be used when you want an event in the new clip to happen at an exact time in the timeline. Let's say you've cut a music video and you have a boring clip of the drummer that you want to replace with a shot of an audience member stretching her arms toward the sky, playing double air drums. Even though this is shot during another song, we want her air drums to play in sync with the current drummer clip. Here's a way to do this quickly.

Mark the drummer clip in the timeline, then park the playhead at a frame where the drum stick hits the drum. Open the air drum clip in the Source Monitor and park at a frame where she hits the imaginary drum. Then, hit your shortcut for Replace With Clip From Source Monitor, Match Frame, or use the Clip menu. Premiere will replace the old clip with the new clip and match the in points you've specified.

Shuffle Editing

Just like the **Ctrl** (Cmd) modifier enables a Ripple edit, which closes gaps or adds time for additional frames, it can also be used for shuffling clips around without leaving gaps or overwriting existing material.

Ctrl+Drag (Cmd+Drag) a clip, and the gap it leaves is automatically closed. Keep holding **Ctrl** while you drop the clip in its new place, and all the existing clips to the right of that point will ripple further right to make room for it (Figures 4-58 and 4-59). I recommend that you make sure Snap is active when doing this kind of clip shuffling.

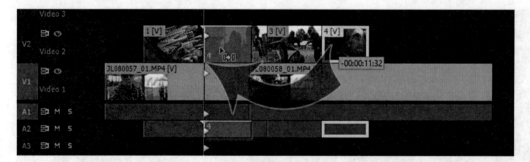

Figure 4-58. *Ctrl-Drag to do a Shuffle edit. The triangles show where the clip(s) will end up and in what tracks content will be shifted.*

Figure 4-59. *Result: The dragged clip has been inserted*

Add **Alt** to the above shuffle edit trick, so you **Alt+Ctrl-Drag** (Opt+Cmd-Drag on Mac), and you'll perform a Rearrange edit (Figures 4-60 and 4-61). It's pretty similar to the previous, but only clips in the destination track are shifted. Clips in other tracks are not affected. This is much faster than locking and unlocking tracks and fiddling around.

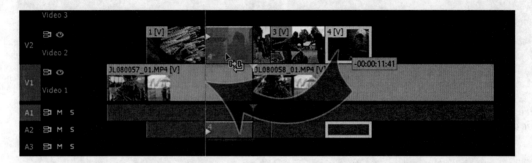

Figure 4-60. *Add the Alt (Opt) key, and you get the Rearrange edit icon*

Figure 4-61. *Result: Only clips in destination tracks are affected. The triangles in the first image clearly indicated this.*

Morph Cut, A New Type of Edit

If you've edited interviews, you've inevitably had to cut out moments where a subject paused too long, said "umm," or took too long to connect their thoughts. Techniques like cutting to a different camera angle (if you have one), covering with b-roll, or even leaving a jump cut are traditional ways of dealing with these edits.

Going to **Effects Panel ➤ Video Transitions ➤ Dissolve** gives you an alternative called Morph Cut. When applied to a cut like any other dissolve, it will identify and track the person's face, generate new in-between frames based on pixel motion, and even search the other frames in the source clip for pixels it can use. The result can be a seamlessly healed jump cut that the viewer will think is a continuous interview shot! Figures 4-62 and 4-63 demonstrate.

Figure 4-62. *These two frames are from different moments in the interview, but we want to put them together as one continuous moment*

Figure 4-63. *The Morph Cut transition generates new in-between frames to make this possible*

Morph Cut works best on "talking head" interview shots that are locked off, are evenly lit with a static background, and frame the subject's head large but not cropped (i.e., medium shot to close up) with their hands out of frame. Excessive head movement, camera movement, lighting changes, subject's face in profile, or big differences in the subject's facial expression can all throw off the algorithm and yield blotchy results (Figure 4-64).

Figure 4-64. *In this case, there was too much head movement between the shots, so Morph Cut could not produce a usable transition*

But, if you place and adjust the transition on a natural pause in speaking or across matching expressions or intonations in speech, you can get remarkably good results. Don't be afraid to try different transition durations; I've found that around ten frames is often the "sweet spot" for a seamless morph.

Remember that Morph Cut is GPU accelerated and processor intensive. It's a good idea to apply clip effects such as color correction on adjustment layers above the joined shots. With keying, try nesting the affected clips and adding the Ultra or Chroma Key to the nest. In extreme cases with interlaced green-screen footage, you may need to export and re-import the Morph Cut shot before applying your key.

Get Back Missing Video or Audio

What to do when you've accidentally or deliberately deleted the video or audio part of a clip and want it back? A quick way is to use a combination of Mark Selection and Match Frame. I'll use a clip with missing audio as my example, since that's the most common scenario.

Select the clip in the timeline and choose **Marker ➤ Mark Selection**, or use the shortcut, which is normally / but tends to move around on non-English keyboards. Then, hit **F** for Match Frame, and the source clip pops up in the Source Monitor.

Now, make sure your audio source patching is set so that the audio track(s) you want from the source end up on the right track(s) in the timeline. Hit **Period** (.) to perform an Overwrite edit, and you're done. Sync audio from the source clip is back!

This took a few words to explain, but you can do it very fast: **Forward Slash ➤ F ➤ Patch Audio ➤ Period**–done. See Figures 4-65, 4-66, and 4-67.

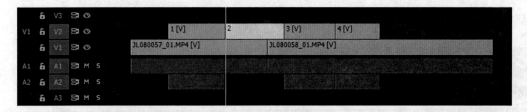

Figure 4-65. *To get back missing audio, first select the video clip*

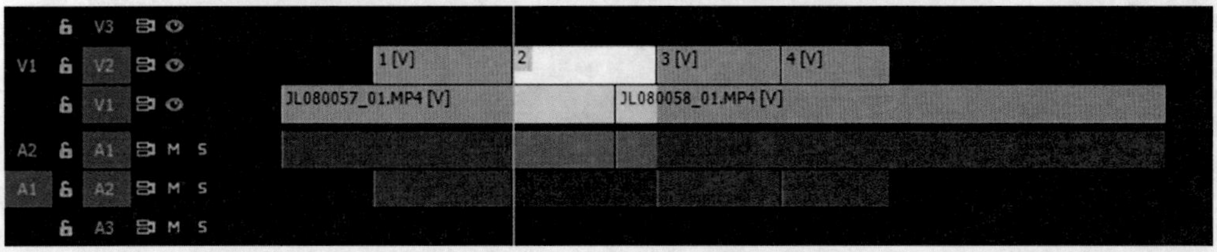

Figure 4-66. *Then, mark in and out points and do a Match Frame*

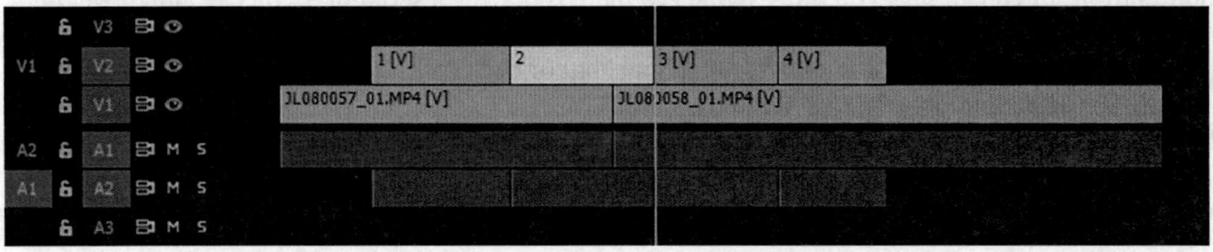

Figure 4-67. *Finally, patch the audio tracks you need and do an Overwrite edit*

This is another situation where you'll want to check the box **Preferences ➤ General ➤ Set focus on the Timeline when performing Insert/Overwrite edits** to perform this technique repeatedly.

Disable, Don't Delete

The Enable Clip feature is great for switching between angles, takes, or alternatives on different tracks (see Figures 4-68 and 4-69). Right-click the clip and toggle the *Enable* option, or use the keyboard shortcut **Shift+E** (Shift+Cmd+E on Mac) if you want to work fast. Enable one clip, disable the other, then select both and toggle between them.

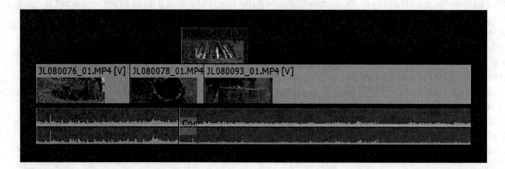

Figure 4-68. *Top clip disabled*

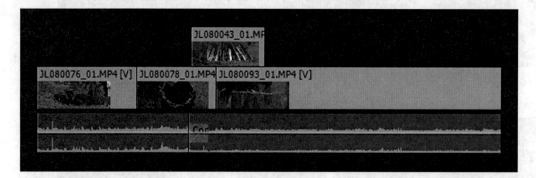

Figure 4-69. *Top clip enabled*

Edit While Playing Back

This is quite simple, but it can save you time. While Premiere is playing a sequence, you can still move the mouse and make adjustments in that timeline. This could include moving clips, trimming with the mouse, adding dissolves, and so on. As long as you don't hit Spacebar or click the playhead bar at the top of the timeline, playback will continue.

Why do this? Let's say you're on a deadline and the producer needs to listen to an interview, but you have to finish adding wipes to all your cuts. Press play, then keep adding the transitions while they watch. Just remember that this additional action will tax your system, so make sure it can handle it.

Advanced Trimming

You can do a lot of editing in Premiere Pro without ever opening Trim mode. Some editors never have! Discover new ways to control and refine your edits using Trim mode (Figure 4-70) and other advanced trimming shortcuts.

Figure 4-70. *Trim mode in Premiere Pro is very powerful. Learn the keyboard shortcuts, and you'll be a faster editor.*

Understanding Trim Mode

In Trim mode, we can trim with the keyboard or the mouse, or use dynamic trimming on the fly while playing back a clip. You enter Trim mode by hitting **Shift+T**, which selects the nearest edit point—and will obey your target track selections when doing so. Trim mode transforms the Program Monitor into a useful two-up display. The left screen is clip A's out point. The right screen is clip B's in point.

In Trim mode, you can use the dedicated keyboard shortcuts for trimming and get instant visual feedback. Here they are:

- Trim Backward by One Frame: **Alt+Left Arrow** (Opt+Left Arrow)

- Trim Backward by Large Trim Offset: **Alt+Shift+Left Arrow** (Opt+Shift+Left Arrow)

- Trim Forward by One Frame: **Alt+Right Arrow** (Opt+Right Arrow)

- Trim Forward by Large Trim Offset: **Alt+Shift+Right Arrow** (Opt+Shift+Right Arrow)

By default, the Large Trim Offset is five frames, but you can change that in **Preferences ➤ Trim.**

When in Trim mode, you can trim with the mouse by dragging directly on the images in the Program Monitor. This is easy to control and includes frame counters for the A and B sides of the edit. You can also trim by entering numbers on the numeric keypad (+8 will trim the edit point eight frames forward, for example).

315

While your edit point is selected, **Ctrl+Shift+T** (Ctrl+T on Mac) toggles through the possible trim types: regular trim (red single arrow), roll trim (red double arrow), and ripple trim (yellow single arrow). You'll also see these options while hovering the mouse in-between the two images in the trim display. Hold down **Ctrl** (Cmd) to get regular trim.

By using combinations of **J**, **K**, and **L** you can perform dynamic trimming while playing back. Press **L** to play forward or **J** to play backward. When you press **K** or **Spacebar** to stop playback, the edit point moves right there. Dynamic trimming works with faster playback speeds as well (press **J** or **L** multiple times in a row).

Hitting **Spacebar** for playback when in Trim mode puts Premiere into a preview loop, and you can add or subtract frames to adjust the edit point while playback continues. Every time you make a trim, Premiere will apply it and restart the preview loop so you can see the revised edit.

Any time you are in this preview loop, you can press either In or Out (**I** or **O**) to make a quick "on the fly" trim to the playhead's position at the moment you hit the key. Try it!

Preroll and postroll times can be set to your liking in **Preferences ➤ Playback**. I recommend setting a long postroll time (for example, three seconds) so you'll have time to enter the new number of frames you want to trim before playback starts again.

You can also create this preview loop around a cut when not in Trim mode. This feature is called Play Around, and the shortcut for it is **Shift+K**.

Pressing the **Up/Down Arrow** takes you to the previous or next edit without leaving Trim mode. This is very useful for continuously refining a scene.

Undo Your Trim Session

To get an edit right, you might make dozens of individual trims. But, what if you want to start over from scratch? Use the *Revert Trim Session* button (Figure 4-71).

Figure 4-71. *At the bottom of the Program Monitor, click the plus icon and add the arrow for Revert Trim Session to your button bar*

This command is a "Trim Mode Undo" that reverts your timeline to the way it was the moment you entered Trim mode. If you close Trim mode, it will forget the trim session.

If you don't use the button bar, Revert Trim Session is also available as a command for you to map under Keyboard Shortcuts.

Trim Preferences

Under **Preferences ➤ Trim** you will find three checkboxes that change trimming behavior (Figure 4-72).

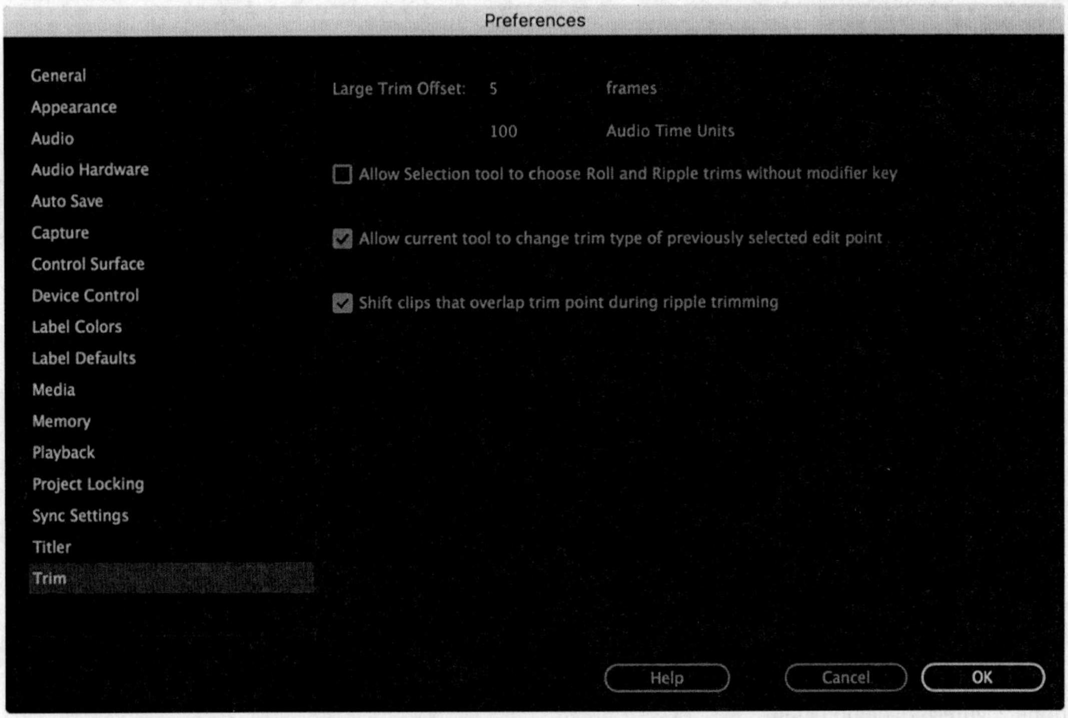

Figure 4-72. *The Trim Preferences dialog lets you customize your trimming options*

The *Allow Selection tool to choose Roll and Ripple trims without modifier key* preference is great if you use Ripple trims more frequently than regular trims. With this preference on, the Selection tool will perform a Rolling edit if you click directly on the edit point and a Ripple edit if you click on either side of the edit point.

Checking this preference also inverts the use of the **Ctrl** (Cmd) modifier, so that you get Ripple In, Roll, Ripple Out without a modifier and Trim In and Trim Out with the modifier. Plus, you get to do Rolling edits with just one click directly on the edit point.

Allow current tool to change trim type of previously selected edit point only matters if you use the Ripple Edit tool and Rolling Edit tool. With this preference checked, the Ripple edit tool will always do a Ripple trim no matter how the edit point has been selected, and the Rolling edit tool will always perform a Rolling edit.

Shift clips that overlap trim point during ripple trimming may not be immediately obvious, but it was added to Premiere Pro by special request from Oscar-winning filmmakers Joel and Ethan Coen. So, I call it "The Coen Brothers Preference." What it does is shift overlapping track items when you perform a Ripple Delete or Ripple Trim. So, if you select a gap in your edit with other clips completely covering it on V2, V3, and so forth, and you hit **Shift+Delete**, those clips above it "fall" to the left with the edit instead of staying where they are. Take a look at Figures 4-73 and 4-74 to see the difference in trimming behavior. If that's useful to you, thank the Coen brothers!

Figure 4-73. *With the shift clips preference off, ripple deleting does not successfully close the gap, because of the clip collision on V2*

Figure 4-74. *With the shift clips preference on, ripple deleting closes the gap and shifts both clips on V2 to the left*

Dynamic Trimming In Depth

When not in Trim mode, **J-K-L** simply shuttle the playhead. But in Trim mode, they will perform an actual trim for you just by playing the timeline. Trimming on the fly!

To be clear: In Trim mode, hitting **Spacebar** will loop playback around the edit point, while hitting **J-K-L** will trim it. And unlike using the **I** and **O** keys to trim in the preview loop, with dynamic trimming you get to see both sides of the cut as you play.

To perform a Dynamic trim in Trim mode, select the edit points you want to adjust with the trim type you want. Let's use a Roll edit as an example. We want to cut one beat after the actor's reaction. To feel the rhythm of the scene, we play it back at normal speed by hitting **L** while editing (after selecting the edit point, of course). When we reach the point where we can feel it's the right beat, we hit **K**, and the edit is already done. Figure 4-75 demonstrates.

Figure 4-75. *In Trim mode, with the edit point selected, hit J or L to play. Hit K to stop, and the edit is done. Notice that the red Rolling Edit indicator in the images has moved after the edit. Footage from Venner i liv og død (Friends In Life and Death) courtesy of Foulwood Film (not color graded).*

Dynamic trimming is the best way to edit when you need to feel the rhythm, pace, and beats of a scene. It works with Ripple edits and standard edits too, of course. The Roll edit in this example is just easy to understand.

You can do frame-by-frame trimming by holding down **K** while tapping **J** and **L**, and variable-speed trimming by holding down **Shift** and tapping **J** and **L**. You can even use Dynamic trim at double or triple speed, which is great for interview rough cuts. You can also trim many tracks and edit points at the same time, which makes this technique even more powerful.

Ripple Trim to Playhead

I highly recommend you use the **Q** and **W** shortcuts for Ripple Trim Previous Edit to Playhead and Ripple Trim Next Edit to Playhead! They're indispensable when doing rough cuts, and I'm proud of being responsible for these shortcuts' making their way into Premiere Pro. It took a couple days of discussions with my friends on the Premiere team before they were convinced that we needed them, but it was definitely worth the effort.

To use these shortcuts, just move the playhead to where you want the Ripple trim and hit **Q** or **W**. The region between the playhead and the previous or next edit will be ripple-deleted away by pressing just one key on the keyboard. What could ever be faster and easier?

If you continue pressing **Q** and **W** after the first Ripple trim, they will keep working by ripple-trimming away one additional frame per key hit–a great way to refine the edit if needed.

This kind of trimming is called Top & Tail Editing and is by far the fastest way to trim away the unwanted parts of a clip. Just be aware that locked tracks, and tracks with sync lock disabled, will not be affected by the **Q** and **W** commands (or any other Ripple edit). See Figures 4-76 and 4-77.

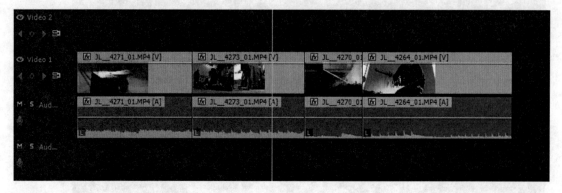

Figure 4-76. Park the playhead at the point you want to Ripple trim to be

Figure 4-77. *Ripple Trim to Playhead (W) removes material between the playhead and the next edit and closes the gap*

Trim or Extend to Playhead

Add **Shift** when you press **Q** and **W** to extend (instead of Ripple trim) the previous or next edit to where the playhead is parked (Figures 4-78 and 4-79). Watch your track targeting!

Figure 4-78. *Park the playhead at the point you want to extend to*

Figure 4-79. *Shift+W extends the next edit to the playhead, performing a Rolling edit*

Somewhat related to this, we also have the Trim Next Edit to Playhead command **Ctrl+Alt+W** (Opt+W on Mac) and the Trim Previous Edit to Playhead command **Ctrl+Alt+Q** (Opt+Q). Since these leave a gap in the timeline, as any standard edit would do, I use these less than the **Q** and **W** shortcuts–but they do have their uses. See Figures 4-80 and 4-81.

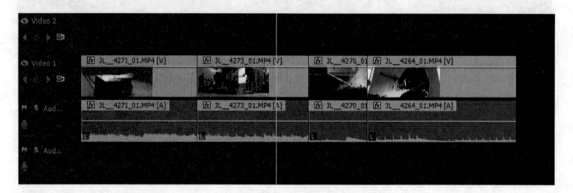

Figure 4-80. *Park the playhead at the point you want to trim to*

Figure 4-81. *Trim Next Edit to Playhead removes the material between playhead and next edit and leaves a gap*

I use the standard Extend Selected Edit to Playhead command **E** much more often than the two shortcuts. It works with any type of trim, including Rolling, Ripple In/Out, and Trim In/Out. To use the Extend Edit command, you have to select the edit points first. But since my brain works best when getting visual feedback, I like the fact that I can see clearly which edit points will be changed before I do the actual trimming. See Figures 4-82 and 4-83.

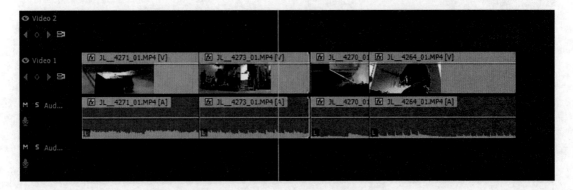

Figure 4-82. *Park the playhead and select the edits you want to move*

Figure 4-83. *Perform an Extend Edit (E), and the edit point shifts to where the playhead was parked. Since this was a regular trim, the edit point was moved to the playhead with no ripple.*

Extend Edit can be used with all the trim types. For a quick "J" or "L" cut in Linked Selection mode, simply **Alt+Click** (Opt+Click) the audio or video cut as a Rolling (double-sided) trim and then hit **E** to extend it to the playhead. Done!

Time-Saving Trim Shortcuts

Instead of toggling between the trim modes with **Ctrl+Shift+T** (Ctrl+T), you can map your own keyboard shortcuts for Select Nearest Edit Point as Ripple In, Ripple Out, Roll, Trim In, and Trim Out (Figure 4-84). Fewer clicks!

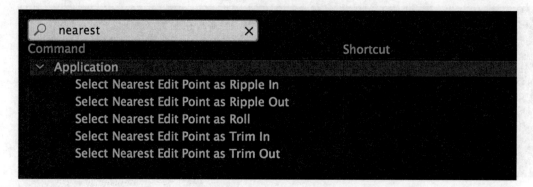

Figure 4-84. Search for "nearest" in the Keyboard Shortcuts dialog and map your own keyboard shortcuts

Trim and Nudge with the Same Shortcut

I'm going to tell you a secret: Trim Backward/Forward and Nudge Left/Right can share the same keyboard shortcut. You may get a warning when mapping them to the same key, but both will work. When an edit point is selected, you will trim it, and when a clip is selected, you will nudge it.

Avid editors appreciate this because Media Composer defaults those commands to the same keys. Also, why remember two shortcuts when you can use just one?

Composite Preview During Trim

In Trim mode, the two-up screens in the Program Monitor give you a composite view of both sides of the selected edit. In other words, Trim mode shows you the resulting output of every video layer in the timeline–including opacity changes, keying, and so on–while you are trimming.

When trimming outside of Trim mode (for example, rolling a cut with the mouse), you'll get a similar but temporary preview in the Program Monitor. In this case, if you want to see a composite preview of your edit, go to the Timeline Settings menu and check the option *Composite Preview During Trim*. If you want your preview to only show the clips on the track you are trimming, uncheck this preference.

Selecting Trim Points with the Mouse

As we've seen, the Selection tool with no modifier keys chooses a regular Trim In or Trim Out depending on which side of the edit point you click on. If you press the **Ctrl** (Cmd) modifier when using the Selection tool, the cursor shows the Ripple or Roll icons and chooses Ripple Out, Roll, or Ripple In depending on whether you are hovering over the left side, center, or right side of the edit point.

After you've selected your first edit point with the trim type you want, hold **Shift** and continue clicking to select multiple audio or video edit points. Use the **Alt** (Opt) key to temporarily ignore linking (if Linked Selection mode is on) or select audio/video pairs (if Linked Selection mode is off).

The three trim tools (Selection, Ripple, or Roll) can also be used to lasso-drag multiple edit points in one step. Press **Ctrl** (Cmd) and click and drag a marquee rectangle. **Ctrl+Shift+T** (Ctrl+T) now toggles the trim type for all of these. Since my brain likes visual feedback, I like using the mouse to select my edit points this way.

Once you've selected all the edits points you want, you can drag any one of them and all the selected clips will be trimmed. Better yet, you can use the trim keyboard shortcuts like **Alt+Left/Right Arrow** (Opt+Left/Right Arrow) to affect them all, enter + or – values on the numeric keypad, or hit **T** to enter Trim mode and do it that way.

Remember that **Shift-Clicking** and **Shift+Ctrl+Clicking** (Shift+Cmd+Clicking) with the Selection tool on edit points enables you to add them to the selection, change them to trims on either side, or change them all to a different trim type. This way, you can do complex edits with ease (Figure 4-85).

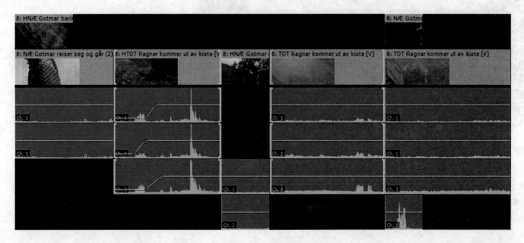

Figure 4-85. *Two Slip edits. When doing complicated trimming, it's easier to select the edit points with the mouse. Ctrl+Drag (Cmd+Drag) to select a bunch, and add Shift to select more edit points individually.*

■ **Note** During your edit sessions, you will use combinations of all the different trimming methods explained here. You should master them all so that you can choose the most efficient one for any given cut in any scene.

Manipulating Time

Premiere has a few different features to help you manipulate time. You can do freeze frames, slow motion, fast motion, fit to fill, and speed ramps. There are good ways to do speed changes, and fast but not-so-good ways to do speed changes. Let's have a look at the different methods and options.

Freeze Frames

There are multiple ways to create a freeze frame, which Premiere calls Frame Hold. Most of them can be found by simply right-clicking on the clip you want to freeze.

If you select *Frame Hold Options* from this context menu, you decide what frame you want Premiere Pro to show. This can be the in point, the out point, or the playhead position. The *Source Timecode* and *Sequence Timecode* options default to the playhead position as well, but they give you a way to enter a specific clip or sequence timecode to freeze on. When you set a Frame Hold this way, the whole clip will become a still image, showing the frame you chose in the options (Figure 4-86).

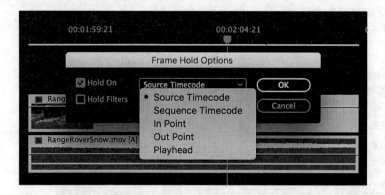

Figure 4-86. *Applying Frame Hold via Frame Hold Options makes the entire clip a still image*

A more common use of Frame Hold is to let the clip play until it reaches a certain frame, and then freeze that frame. To do this, right-click the clip in the timeline and choose *Add Frame Hold* or *Insert Frame Hold Segment*. See Figures 4-87, 4-88, and 4-89.

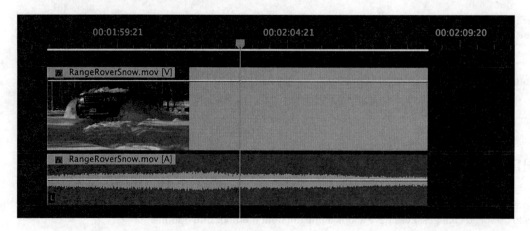

Figure 4-87. *Park the playhead on the frame you want to freeze*

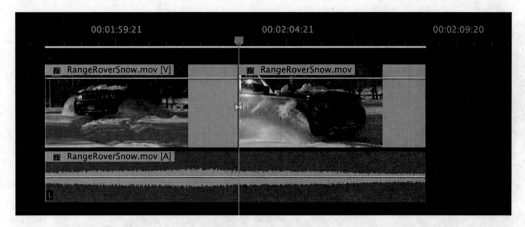

Figure 4-88. *Add Frame Hold creates a freeze frame to the right of the Playhead*

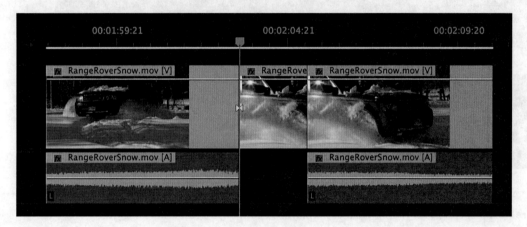

Figure 4-89. *Add Frame Hold Segment inserts a freeze frame*

Add Frame Hold cuts the clip and turns the rest of it into a freeze frame that can be dragged to any duration. Insert Frame Hold Segment inserts a freeze frame clip with a default duration of two seconds and keeps the rest of your video clip in the timeline. Of course, you can adjust the length of the freeze frame clips you create. Clips set to Frame Hold any of these ways also keep their source timecode, so you can continue to freeze them–for example, every five frames for a strobe effect.

What if you do a lot of freezing motion, and when starting it again, how can you preserve sync? Even if you lock tracks, Insert Frame Hold will still ripple the video track. For a quick workaround, try an Add Frame Hold, then **Alt+Drag** (Opt+Drag) to duplicate the frozen clip and place it at the point where you want motion to resume. Then, open Frame Hold Options and uncheck *Hold On* to turn this back into a regular video clip. Voila!

Lastly, if you want the freeze frame to be an image file on your drive, you can export a still image using the Export Frame command. There is a button for this in the Source and Program Monitors (Figure 4-90), or you can use the shortcut **Shift+Ctrl+E** (Shift+E). If you want to use it in your sequence, check *Import into project*.

Figure 4-90. *Export Frame. This button uses the playhead position to create a still image file.*

For a visual demonstration of these options, this tutorial by Dylan Osborn covers them all in three minutes: dylanosborn.com/2016/09/07/freeze-frames/.

Clip Speed/Duration

Open the Speed/Duration dialog (Figure 4-91) by choosing **Clip ➤ Speed/Duration**, right-clicking the clip, or using the shortcut **Ctrl+R** (Cmd+R on Mac).

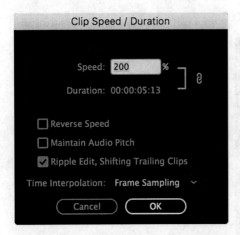

Figure 4-91. *The Clip Speed/Duration dialog has many options for speed changes*

Set it to 200 percent, and you have 2x speed. Premiere just shows every second frame, which is a low bandwidth, easy calculation for any modern editing system. The dialog lets you decide what to do with the audio pitch, and if a Ripple edit should be performed, shifting the following clips. You can also specify the duration, and the speed will be calculated automatically. Be aware that this may cause stuttering playback, just like with the Rate Stretch tool, when some frames are shown twice and some once.

If you click the link symbol to the right of Speed and Duration in the dialog, you can change duration and speed independently.

Adjusting speed also slows down or speeds up the audio. You can choose to *Maintain Audio Pitch*, but Premiere does a very bad job at this compared to Audition. Both nat sound and voices can get badly distorted. Don't even think about doing this to music.

Change Speed/Duration of Many Clips

With multiple clips selected, it may look like the Duration option in the dialog is not available, but you can actually click the field, input a duration, and all the clips will adjust to that length. Tick the *Ripple Edit* checkbox, or else you'll have to close a lot of gaps afterward. This technique works especially well if you have a lot of still images in the timeline and want them all to be the same length. Figure 4-92 demonstrates.

Figure 4-92. *You can change the speed or duration of many clips (or stills) at once*

If you want to copy and paste speed like with other clip attributes, keep reading and learn how to do that with the Time Remapping feature.

Rate Stretch Tool

This tool lets you drag the in or out point of a clip so it fits a certain gap or becomes the duration you want. I must admit I rarely use this, as it often produces non-integer speeds that can cause stuttering playback. On some material, though, the frame-skipping or doubling will not be too visible, and the tool works okay. See Figures 4-93 and 4-94.

Figure 4-93. *Click and drag with the Rate Stretch tool*

Figure 4-94. *The Rate Stretch tool will calculate a speed that makes the clip fit the duration you set by dragging the in or out point*

You can right-click and choose *Speed/Duration* after using this tool to choose what to do with the audio pitch. A similar result to that of the Rate Stretch tool can be achieved with the Fit to Fill option when doing a four-point edit, as covered earlier in this chapter.

Time Remapping for Variable Speed

Variable speed changes such as speed ramps can be achieved with the Time Remapping feature. Time Remapping takes a segment-oriented approach to speed changes, so you divide a single clip into segments with different speeds. You can have a sports clip go very fast until the Big Moment™, where you slow things down until it's over, and then everything goes back to normal speed. The speed changes can be gradual and smooth or abrupt. This is not the most intuitive part of Premiere, but once you understand the interface for Time Remapping, you will find it easy to use. See Figure 4-95.

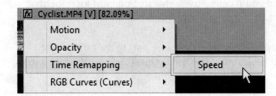

Figure 4-95. *Right-click the FX badge to change the keyframe view from Opacity to Speed*

To use Time Remapping, right-click on the FX icon of a clip and choose **Time Remapping ➤ Speed**. This will show a white line in the center of the clip where you can add keyframes. If you don't see the line, make sure *Show Video Keyframes* is chosen in the Timeline Settings menu. If the FX icon doesn't show either, turn it on in the same wrench menu.

To set keyframes, click with the Pen tool or **Ctrl+Click** (Cmd+Click) on the thin white line in the middle of the clip. The keyframes will show up in the thicker white line above, called the Speed-Control line.

Drag the rubber band between two keyframes upward or downward to increase or decrease the speed of the clip. A tool tip appears showing the change in speed as a percentage of the original speed. As with any speed change, Time Remapping makes the duration of the clip expand or contract. Figures 4-96, 4-97, and 4-98 demonstrate this.

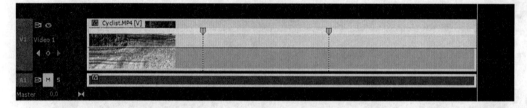

Figure 4-96. *Ctrl-click (Cmd-click) the line to set Time Remapping keyframes*

Figure 4-97. *Drag the line up to increase speed and down to decrease speed*

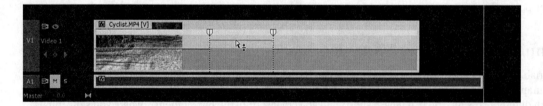

Figure 4-98. *Increasing speed makes the clip shorter; decreasing it makes the clip longer. Audio is not affected.*

If you drag the rubber band segments while holding **Shift**, you'll get snapping to 5 percent increments. The **Ctrl** (Cmd) key, as usual, gives you more control, and you'll get adjustments in 1 percent increments. You cannot go below 1 percent, since 0 percent would result in a timeline of infinite length. Use the freeze frame techniques explained earlier instead.

The Time Remapping keyframes are split in the middle, so you can drag one part to the left or right, creating a speed ramp (Figure 4-99). To move an un-split keyframe, **Alt+Click** (Opt+Click) it and drag it to its new position. To move a split keyframe, drag the gray area between the keyframe halves.

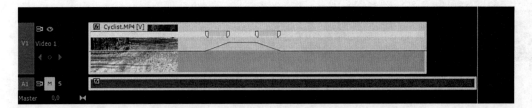

***Figure 4-99.** Split the keyframes to create speed ramps*

Time Remapping has one big disadvantage: it does not affect the audio at all. This means that any speed changes you do with Time Remapping will make your audio go out of sync.

■ **Note**   Even though the audio portion of the clip remains unchanged by Time Remapping, it remains linked to the video portion.

You can also do freeze frames and reverse speed with Time Remapping. **Ctrl+Drag** (Cmd+Drag) a keyframe to make a portion of the clip go backward. **Alt+Ctrl+Drag** (Opt+Cmd-Drag) a keyframe to make a portion of the clip frozen in time. See Figure 4-100.

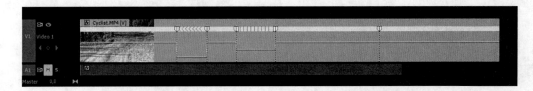

***Figure 4-100.** Small arrows in the white bar indicate backward speed. Vertical lines indicate a still frame.*

Drag the small point at the end of the blue Bezier handle of a ramp keyframe to adjust the ramping shape. This is easier if you zoom in horizontally and vertically in the timeline (Figure 4-101).

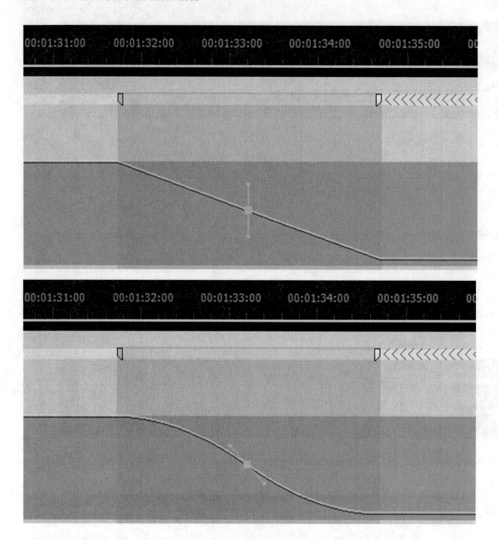

Figure 4-101. *Select a keyframe and drag the Bezier handle to adjust the ramp shape*

Doing Time Remapping in the main timeline has the potential to completely destroy your edit, because the clip you're working on will be shortened or lengthened every time you remap it. Nesting the clip and doing Time Remapping in the nested sequence is a good way to avoid timing issues.

Time Remapping in the Effect Controls Panel

If you have a complex timeline, you might want to do Time Remapping in the Effect Controls panel (Figure 4-102). Time Remapping is an intrinsic effect, so it's already applied to every clip.

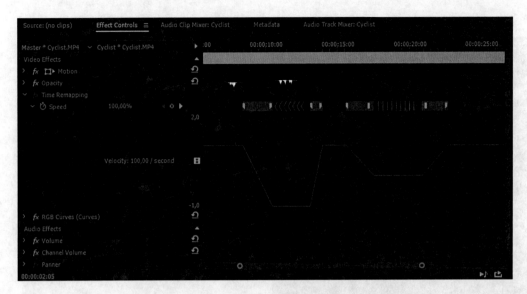

Figure 4-102. *You can also adjust Time Remapping in the Effect Controls panel. Make sure you make the graph tall enough so you can do accurate adjustments.*

Click the triangle next to Time Remapping and the Speed effect to open it. Drag the divider line below the graph to make it taller. Also, make sure the Effect Controls panel is wide enough to make precise adjustments, and that the mini timeline in the Effects Control panel is shown. Now that you can see what you're doing, adjustment is similar to doing it on the clip.

Copy/Paste Time Remapping

As you've seen, Time Remapping is an intrinsic effect on every video clip in Premiere Pro. That means it can be copied and pasted to multiple clips, like any other effect. We do this with the Paste Attributes dialog (Figure 4-103).

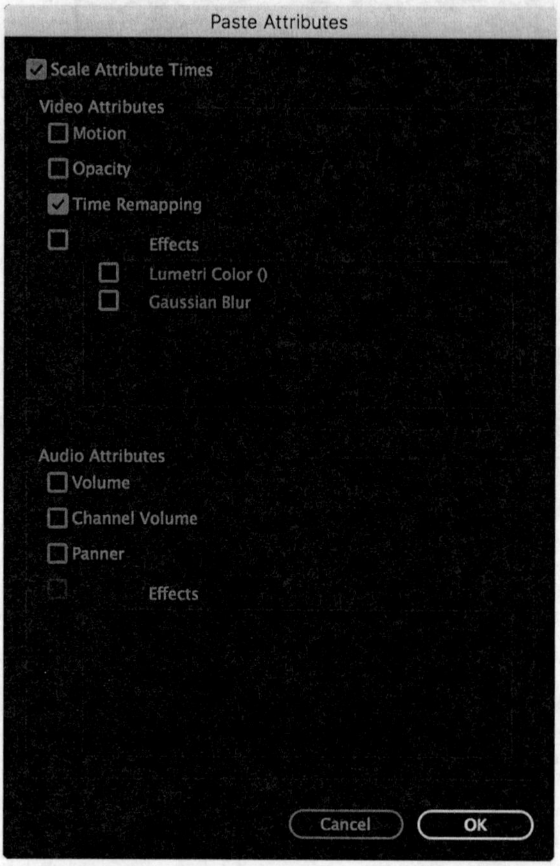

Figure 4-103. *If you work with effects in Premiere Pro, Paste Attributes will save you time*

Select a clip with Time Remapping applied, use **Ctrl+C** (Cmd+C) to copy it, and **Ctrl+Alt+V** (Cmd+Opt+V) to paste attributes to the clips you want. In the Paste Attributes dialog, check *Time Remapping*, and when you click *OK* all the clips will get that speed.

Remove Time Remapping

You cannot toggle the Time Remapping effect on and off like other effects. Enabling and disabling Time Remapping changes the duration of the clip in the timeline, so be careful. Again, nesting the clip before applying the Time Remapping can reduce the risk of timing problems.

In the Effects Control panel, click the *Toggle Animation* button (the stopwatch icon) next to the word *Speed* to turn it off. This deletes all existing Speed keyframes and disables Time Remapping for the clip. To re-enable Time Remapping, click the *Toggle Animation* button again. You cannot use Time Remapping when it's set to off.

Refine Time Remapping in After Effects

If you feel that the frame blending in Premiere isn't good enough, right-click the clip and choose *Replace with After Effects Composition*. This opens the clip in After Effects via Dynamic Link with all your Time Remapping keyframes intact (Figure 4-104).

Figure 4-104. *Time Remapping keyframes from Premiere travel over to After Effects*

Select all the keyframes and hit **F9** to add Easey Ease (easing the change in and out of keyframes) to all of them. Now, go to **Layer ➤ Frame Blending ➤ Pixel Motion** and then click on the Frame Blending Switch of the composition to turn Frame Blending on (Figure 4-105).

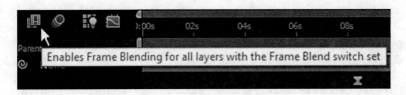

Figure 4-105. *Enable Frame Blending and set the layer to use Pixel Motion for frame blending*

Finally, go to **Composition ➤ Preview ➤ RAM Preview**, or hit **0** on the numeric keypad to do a RAM preview. When After Effects has finished the somewhat CPU-intensive creation of new frames, you should have very nice speed ramps with smooth motion (Figure 4-106).

Figure 4-106. *These keyframes have been set to Ease keyframes by hitting F9 in After Effects*

If you want speed changes to affect the audio too, start the Time Remapping in After Effects and import the composition to Premiere. This is the only way to do it, since the audio doesn't carry through when doing a *Replace with After Effects Composition*.

Time Interpolation and Optical Flow

With all the speed-change methods described in this section, you have a choice about how Premiere Pro will remap the existing frames in your clip across time. Select clips and view your interpolation options under **Clip ➤ Video Options ➤ Time Interpolation**, the same menu via right-click, or in the Time Interpolation pop-up menu of the Clip Speed/Duration dialog (Figure 4-107).

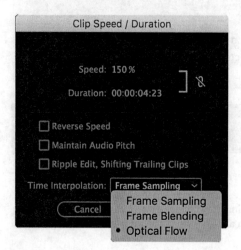

Figure 4-107. *Under the Time Interpolation menu you can choose Optical Flow for your speed changes*

Frame Sampling is the default and will duplicate or throw out whole frames as needed. Frame Blending will create new frames by blending adjacent frames together, which can help motion look smoother but may result in ghosting.

Optical Flow is a different, GPU-accelerated technology that uses motion-vector algorithms to generate new and unique frames based on pixel movement. This is cool, and in many situations you can get very good-looking slow motion from conventional footage. But check your clip after applying it, because the algorithm can create motion artifacts–especially in fast camera moves or areas of low contrast. For a visual comparison of the three time-interpolation methods, see this clip by Michael Heinz: youtube.com/watch?v=m_wfO4fvH8M.

If you select Optical Flow interpolation for your clip, you'll notice a red render bar at the top of your sequence. You'll only see the full quality of Optical Flow after you render effects or export. Otherwise, Premiere shows you Frame Sampling, because Optical Flow is too render-intensive to play back in real-time. And if you are exporting in Software Only mode, the output will use a different rendering method than GPU-accelerated Optical Flow.

One last note: When you export your sequence, you'll notice another Time Interpolation menu at the bottom of the Export Settings window, with the same three options (Figure 4-108). This setting is not for individual clips. It only applies to differences between the frame rate of your sequence (as defined in **Sequence ➤ Sequence Settings ➤ Timebase**) and the export frame rate you've chosen.

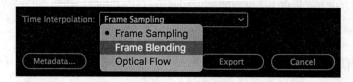

Figure 4-108. *Don't be confused by the Time Interpolation menu under Export Settings. It is asking how you want to handle the conversion of your sequence frame rate to the export frame rate.*

Which Method Gives the Best Slow Motion?

Everyone loves slow motion because it makes even the most mundane activities look dramatic. When learning the different methods for editing slo-mo that we've covered in this section, including Optical Flow, it can be easy to lose sight of this simple truth:

▪ **Note** No slow-motion technique in Premiere will make a slowed down clip look as good as a clip shot in slo-mo—with a higher frame rate than the sequence it is used in. Over-cranking the camera in the field yields far more beautiful slow motion than you'll ever be able to make in post from a standard recording.

If the footage was shot at 29.97 fps and your final output is 29.97, Premiere will need to create in-between frames to get slo-mo. If the footage was shot at 60 fps, there are a lot more frames to work with, and interpreting the clip as 29.97 fps will create perfect slo-mo at (very close to) 50 percent speed, where every frame is a real frame from the shoot.

Some Shutter Speed Science For Shooters

You might want to adjust your shutter speed when shooting in-camera slo-mo. If you double the frame rate, double the shutter speed. At three times the frame rate, reduce the shutter speed to one-third of the standard. If your project is 25 fps and you're shooting with 1/50 second shutter speed, adjust it to 1/100 second when shooting at 50 fps. With these adjustments in the field you will get a more natural-looking motion blur when slowing the footage down in post.

This shutter speed tip only applies when you are shooting slo-mo to be used as slo-mo—not when you are shooting at a high frame rate to be viewed at normal speed (for example, shooting at 50 fps to be watched in 50 fps). In those cases, you'll still want to use 1/50 second shutter. The shutter speed of 1/50 second for video and 1/48 second for film was chosen for technical reasons, and became a standard because the motion blur you get at that shutter speed nicely matches the motion blur we experience with our eyes in real life.

Motion blur has absolutely nothing to do with degrees; it has to do with the time the image sensor catches light. That's because film (up until we recently got High Frame Rate or HFR film) has been shown at 24 fps for many decades. Photographers are used to a 180-degree shutter and know that it creates nice motion blur. At 24 fps, a 180-degree shutter means 1/48 second. That gives us nice, natural-looking motion blur.

At 48 fps, a 180-degree shutter means a 1/96-second shutter—and it does NOT produce natural-looking motion blur, no matter what frame rate you have. The images are too sharp, and we get a kind of strobing effect on fast motion. So, even at 48 or 50 fps, you should shoot with 1/48- or 1/50-second shutter speed to get good, natural-looking motion blur if you're not shooting slow motion. With a film camera, that's not possible, but in a video camera, it is. If you're shooting 60 fps, you'll need to use 1/60-second shutter or the images will start getting too sharp.

When the frame rates get much higher, our eyes aren't able to discern the individual frames, and movement on the screen will start looking like real motion even though the images are very sharp due to fast shutter speeds. But the theater systems that can play back these high frame rates aren't commonplace, so make sure you control your shutter speed for a few years more.

Juggling Frame Rates

Speed changes are one thing, but the variety of normal- and high-frame-rate footage that editors deal with today is quite another. Fortunately, Premiere Pro can play (almost) all of them back natively. But to edit professionally with mixed frame rates, you need to understand your choices and a bit of the science behind them.

Interpreting High-Frame-Rate Footages

You can put a clip with any frame rate into any given timeline in Premiere and press *Play*. It will play back at normal speed. Not necessarily smoothly, if the frame rates are incompatible, but at normal speed–skipping or doubling frames on the fly as needed. So, dropping a 120 fps GoPro clip into a 25 fps timeline will play the recording at normal speed, showing about every fifth frame from the original.

But, if you tell Premiere to interpret that clip as 25 fps, it will play in slow motion and show each frame from the original once. The result is about 21 percent speed. The key to doing this is the **Clip ➤ Modify ➤ Interpret Footage** dialog. Under Frame Rate, you will see the default option, *Use Frame Rate from File*, if Premiere has been able to properly detect it. Select *Assume this frame rate* to type in a new value that matches your sequence, such as 25 fps. See Figure 4-109.

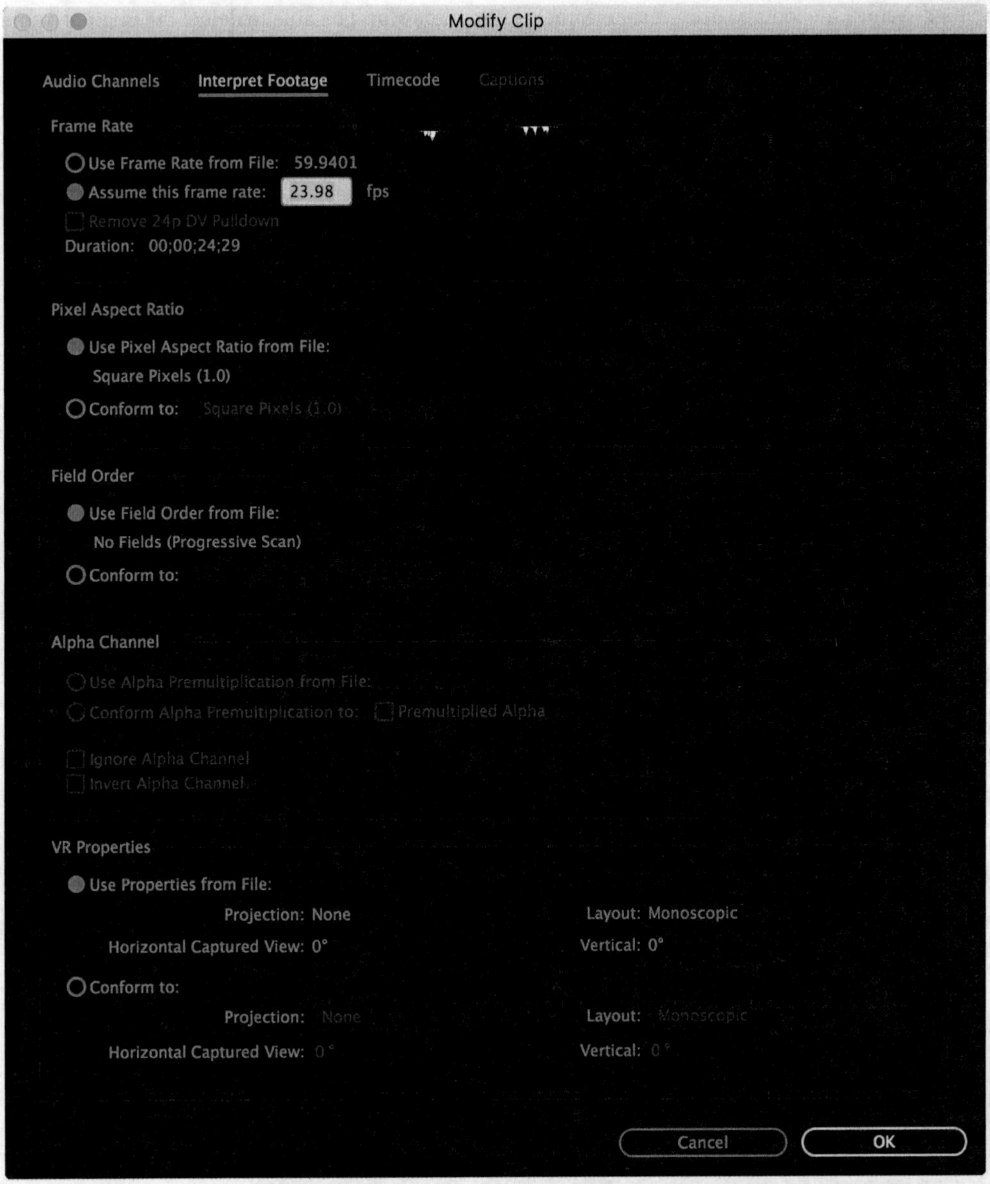

Figure 4-109. *The Interpret Footage dialog gives you control of a clip's playback frame rate. These changes must be made to clips in the Project panel, ideally before you edit them into your sequence.*

You can use slow motion perfectly well without interpreting the clip as 25 fps first. Premiere will still use all the available frames from the source clip and give you great slow motion. I just find it easier to calculate double, triple, and quadruple frame rates if you interpret it to match sequence settings first, then adjust Speed to 200, 300, or 400 percent. We normally want whole numbers (integers) because it results in the smoothest slow motion when played back.

With high-frame-rate footage from certain cameras, Premiere won't be able to detect the original frame rate on import. In these cases, you'll get a clip that plays in slow motion when you put it in the timeline, and the Interpret Footage dialog will show 23.98 fps, 25 fps, or some other regular frame rate. You can work around this if you know the high frame rate that the clip was originally recorded at; for example, 120 fps. Just enter that number under *Assume this frame rate*, and it will play back at normal speed.

Watch for Variable Frame Rates

Another frame rate "gotcha" to be aware of when importing your footage is variable frame rates. Non-traditional recording devices like mobile phones and screen-recording software can produce frame rates that are not constant, either because the frame rate actually does change or because the metadata is inaccurate.

Premiere Pro may have difficulty with variable-frame-rate files. To avoid import or playback errors, Handbrake can be used to transcode these clips to a constant frame rate for editing: handbrake.fr\

A Quick Refresher on Fields and Frame Rates

It used to be that all footage on TV was interlaced. Splitting every frame of video into two fields of horizontal lines was a clever way to compress the signal and send more information through the same bandwidth. The NTSC standard in America broadcast 60 fields per second at 30 frames per second (actually 59.94i at 29.97 fps), whereas the PAL/SECAM standards broadcast 50 fields per second at 25 frames per second (50i at 25 fps) pretty much everywhere else.

The advent of digital video and the switch from analog to digital broadcasting has changed that, and we now see a mix of different recording and broadcasting frame rates–both interlaced (showing alternating fields at 50i, 59.94i) and progressive (showing whole frames at 23.976p, 24p, 25p, 29.97p). For the Premiere Pro editor, it's important to keep in mind that frame rate and field order are two related but distinct properties of your footage.

Where to Check Field Order

After import, you can use the Interpret Footage dialog to see if you are dealing with interlaced sources: **Clip ➤ Modify ➤ Interpret Footage ➤ Field Order**. See Figure 4-110.

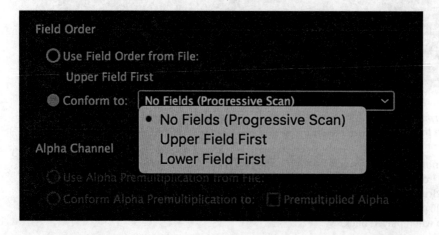

Figure 4-110. *Upper Field First or Lower Field First indicates interlaced Footage. No Fields (Progressive Scan) is, of course, progressive footage.*

Alternatively, you can drag a clip onto the New Item icon in the lower right of the Project panel to have Premiere create a sequence that matches the specs of that clip. Under **Sequence ➤ Sequence Settings ➤ Fields** you'll see if the resulting sequence is interlaced or progressive.

View Interlaced Fields During Playback

To edit interlaced material professionally, you need to see your edit on an interlaced output, such as a broadcast monitor. A progressive monitor like your computer screen won't be able to show you interlacing artifacts such as flickering freeze frames.

However, under the Program Monitor Settings menu (i.e., wrench), Premiere gives you the option to *Display Both Fields*. This will play back interlaced fields sequentially and gives you a backup method of monitoring fielded footage on your computer screen.

Interlaced Footage in an Interlaced Sequence

Assuming you can view your interlaced footage correctly, how do you fix interlacing problems when they occur? Try the Field Options dialog (Figure 4-111).

Figure 4-111. *Dealing with fields is easy using the Field Options dialog*

Go to **Clip ➤ Video Options ➤ Field Options** or right-click your clip in the timeline or Project panel and choose *Field Options*. If your footage is flickering, try the *Flicker Removal* option. If you need to reverse the field dominance (because the edits don't fall on a whole frame), use the *Reverse Field Dominance* option.

A more widely used option is *Always Deinterlace*. This can yield better results if you're scaling or rotating your interlaced footage in the interlaced sequence. Remember that the warp stabilizer effect *will* scale and rotate your footage.

343

Interlaced Footage in a Progressive Sequence

Many users will get interlaced footage but need to deliver progressive files on output. This would be the case if you get 1080i material that you want to put on YouTube, for example. To make this work, just create a progressive sequence and edit. Premiere will automatically de-interlace your footage. The de-interlacing is even GPU accelerated.

Progressive Footage in an Interlaced Sequence

If you put a progressive file in an interlaced sequence, you will have an interlaced output from the sequence. But since both fields are from the same moment in time, the footage will retain the progressive look even after it is interlaced. Essentially, you have created what's called PSF (Progressive Segmented Frame).

Progressive Segmented Frame is basically a method for progressive footage to be disguised as interlaced to retain compatibility with old equipment and standards. So, it will be tagged as interlaced but is in reality progressive, which can potentially confuse Premiere. Yes, there are many strange beasts in the digital video world!

The disguised-as-interlaced footage will make Premiere automatically de-interlace it when you put it in a progressive timeline. This is bad! You'll lose half of the lines, and new lines will be created by interpolation. To avoid this, you need to tell Premiere that the clip isn't what it pretends to be. See Figure 4-112.

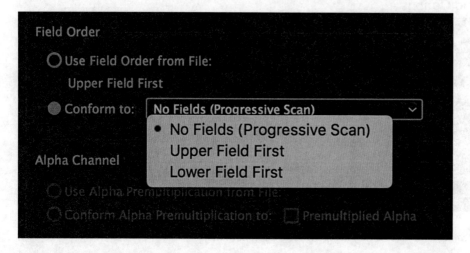

Figure 4-112. *PSF footage is progressive, so tell Premiere this if it hasn't already guessed it*

Use the **Clip ➤ Modify ➤ Interpret Footage** dialog and set it to Progressive. This happens on the Master Clip level, so you can do this even after you've edited the footage in the timeline–but you need to do it from the bin. Now, Premiere will use all the available resolution from the footage.

24p Footage and Pulldown

While cinema material is true 24p, most so-called 24p material is actually 23.976 fps. When this kind of material is placed in a 29.97 fps sequence, Premiere will need to add new frames. This process is called *pulldown*. Premiere auto-manages the 24p pulldown scheme, so in a progressive sequence you'll get Repeat Frame (Figure 4-113), and in an interlaced sequence you'll get Interlaced Frame (Figure 4-114).

Figure 4-113. *Pulldown in a progressive sequence creates whole frames*

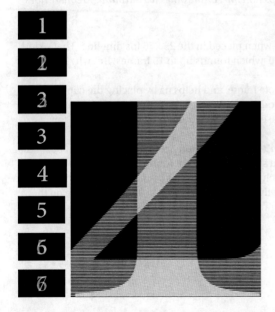

Figure 4-114. *Pulldown in an interlaced sequence creates interlaced frames. Here, you can see the 1 and 2 blended together.*

23.976 in 24 and the Other Way Around

Since true cinema is 24 fps and more video-oriented footage is 23.976 (often called 23.98 for short), you may need to mix and match these. The difference in speed is just 1/1000–one tenth of one percent–so very often you won't even notice it. But the longer the clip, the bigger the difference.

In Figure 4-115, you can see two screenshots. The first shows 24 fps footage in a 23.976 fps timeline. The second shows 23.976 fps footage in a 24 fps timeline. Both timelines are ten minutes five seconds long, counting in at 14,520 frames.

Figure 4-115. *When editing 23.976 fps material in a 24 fps timeline, or the other way around, Premiere does its best to avoid blending frames*

Notice how the 24 fps footage is 15 frames too short when placed in the 23.976 fps timeline. That's kind of logical, since one thousandth of 14520 frames is 14.520, which rounds up to 15 frames. But why isn't it 10:05:00 in length? What's going on here?

Premiere thinks we want to see every frame as a whole frame, and helps us by placing the clip into the timeline frame by frame. This makes the footage look good, because we get no frame blending. But without frame blending, Premiere "runs out" of frames–in this case, about 15 of them–over the course of a ten minute and five second clip.

When the clip is interpreted as 23.976 using the **Clip ➤ Modify ➤ Interpret Footage** dialog, it becomes the right length in the 23.976 sequence. Well, not quite–it seems that the last frame is dropped. Not a big problem, though, since all the other frames seem to match perfectly. With this setting, Premiere will need to duplicate 15 frames in the course of the ten minutes and five seconds. Not too bad, and depending on the footage you may or may not see this. You could turn on frame blending to make those few frames smoother, but then you won't have whole frames any more.

What happens when we go the other way around and put a 23.976 fps clip in a 24 fps timeline? Not surprisingly, it's 14 frames longer than its original length. To sum up:

---

24 fps 10:05:00 clip in 23.976 fps timeline ends up with duration 10:04:09, so 15 frames short.

24 fps 10:05:00 clip interpreted as 23.976 fps in 23.976 fps timeline ends up with duration 10:04:23, so video is 1 frame short—but audio is the perfect length.

23.976 fps 10:05:00 clip in 24 fps timeline ends up with duration 10:05:14, so 14 frames too long.

23.976 fps 10:05:00 clip interpreted as 24 fps in 24 fps timeline ends up with duration 10:05:00, so perfect length.

Now that you know how Premiere handles 24 and 23.976 fps, hopefully you can predict if this will cause any problems for you.

Conforming 23.976 to 24p on Export

If you have trouble with the preceding options and need an alternative workflow for conforming 23.976 deliverables to true 24p, try this method using Adobe Audition.

First, export a 23.976 ProRes 4444 master with synced audio. Then, do a separate audio-only export with 48K 32-bit float settings for your audio master. Import the 23.976 ProRes master into a new project and create a new 24p timeline for it. **Modify ➤ Interpret Footage** and set *Assume this frame rate* to 24 fps. Edit this newly interpreted master file into the 24p timeline and note the exact duration.

Open the audio master in Audition, apply the **Effects ➤ Time and Pitch ➤ Stretch and Pitch (process)** effect, and set Audio Duration to match the exact duration of your program in Premiere (99.9 percent). Export the retimed audio in your desired format (for example, aif) and, finally, import that audio into Premiere and edit it into the master sequence. Now you can export in true 24p.

This multi-export process will take some time, but Audition does a great job of retiming the audio, and your final export should be of high quality.

23.976 in 29.97 Pulldown Issue

What if your source footage is 23.976 progressive and you need to deliver 29.97 interlaced? The frame-rate conversion is one thing–Premiere can handle that in the sequence or on export. But the pulldown involved in going from progressive frames to interlaced fields is another. Here is how your Sequence settings can give you different pulldown results on delivery:

23.976 progressive footage in a 29.97 *progressive* timeline exported to 29.97 interlaced results in 4:1 pulldown (4 progressive frames, 1 repeat frame). Looks choppy.

23.976 progressive footage in a 29.97 *interlaced* timeline exported to 29.97 interlaced results in 3:2 pulldown (3 progressive frames, 2 interlaced frames). Expected result.

It's always a good idea to do a test export well before you are up against a delivery deadline. Again, hopefully this knowledge will assist you in planning your post-production workflow.

Removing Pulldown with After Effects

If you should ever need to remove pulldown from a clip, copy/paste it over to a 23.976 fps comp in After Effects and park on a frame that shows a mix between two frames from the source clip. Right-click the clip in the Project panel and choose **Interpret Footage ➤ Main**, very much like you would in Premiere (Figure 4-116).

Figure 4-116. After Effects gives you great control over pulldown removal

Set the fields to *Upper Field First* and click on **Guess 3:2 Pulldown**. If the comp now shows a single frame and not a mix, click *OK*. If not, try different combinations of settings for *Remove Pulldown* and *Guess Pulldown* until you're left with clean frames only (Figure 4-117).

Figure 4-117. *If you're not sure what settings to use, play around with them until you see whole frames only*

Now, bring the comp over to Premiere Pro via Dynamic Link, or export to an intermediate codec and import the resulting file into Premiere.

Working with Image Sequences

Shooting time-lapse and stop-motion sequences became increasingly popular with the rise of DSLR cameras. Like time-lapse and stop motion, VFX and CGI imagery will also normally be delivered as image sequences. Let's have a look at the best workflows for dealing with these special kinds of footage.

Importing Time-Lapse Footage

If you shoot in RAW format–and you should–you'll need to prepare the files in Adobe Camera RAW via Bridge, After Effects, or Photoshop first. I use Adobe Bridge. Adobe Lightroom is also great for batch-processing large quantities of RAW files and saving out as JPGs.

Premiere can choke on large amounts of big still images, so do not import image sequences as separate stills. Instead, do it the right way and import them as–you guessed it–image sequences.

Navigate in the Media Browser to the folder with your numbered stills. Select the first one in the series. Then, make sure that *Import As Image Sequence* is selected in the panel menu before you right-click and choose *Import* (Figure 4-118).

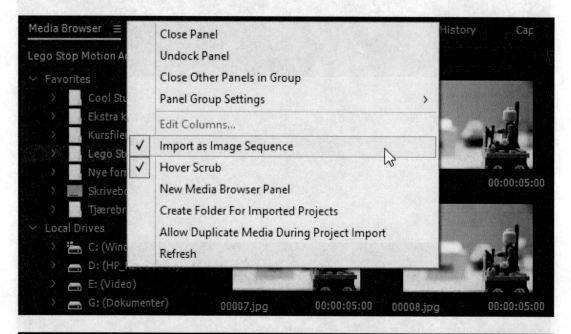

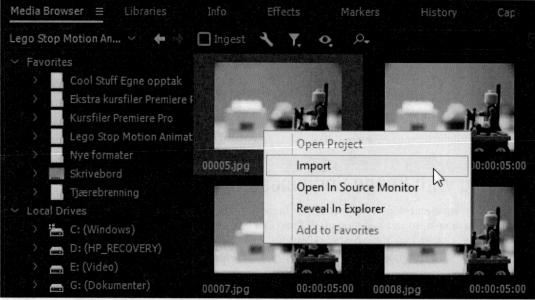

Figure 4-118. *Check that Import as Image Sequence is active, then right-click the first still and choose Import. Stop-motion footage by Per Asbjørn Gundersen and Mark John Cupper.*

The stills will import as one single clip, with each still image one frame in duration (Figure 4-119).

Figure 4-119. *The image sequence shows up in your bin as a video-only clip*

The frame rate will be the one set in **Preferences ➤ Media ➤ Indeterminate Media Timebase**. You can change this by right-clicking the clip, choosing **Modify ➤ Interpret Footage ➤ Assume This Frame Rate**, and setting it to whatever frame rate you want. Also note that the clip has the frame size of the images and takes its name from the first image in the sequence. Rename the clip if it's not a good one.

If the images were shot at the size you want your video to be (such as 1080 × 1920) you can just throw it onto the New Item icon or right-click and choose *New Sequence from Clip* and hit *Play*. If not, you'll need to make a new sequence or throw the clip into your existing sequence and scale and move to reframe it.

■ **Note**   There are some things that need to be in place for this technique to work. All the files must have the same name followed by a number, like Image 1, Image 2, Image 3, etc. Numbers only will also work, as in the preceding example.

There must also be no missing numbers in the sequence. For example, if image 34 is missing in a sequence of 200 stills, Premiere will only import 33 images in the sequence.

I recommend that you use Adobe Bridge to batch rename the stills if there are missing numbers or the images have different names before the numbers. In Bridge, navigate to the still image folder and click **Tools ➤ Batch Rename** (Figure 4-120). You can skip this step if you're using the workflow explained next, as this will be done as part of the batch conversion from RAW to JPG.   •

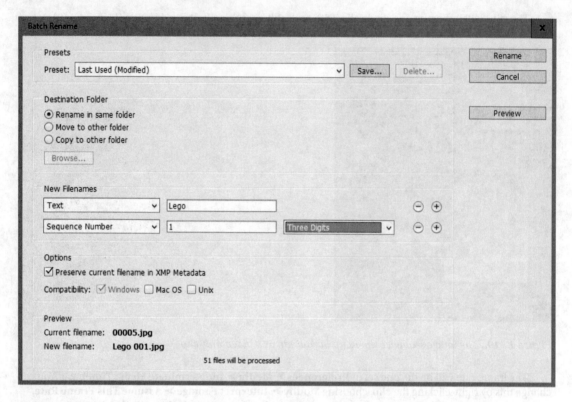

Figure 4-120. *Use Bridge to do a batch rename of all images if there are missing frame numbers in the image sequence*

Editing Time-Lapse Footage

Here's my favorite workflow when editing time-lapse footage. Right-click the folder where you have the RAW files and choose *Browse in Adobe Bridge CC*. If that's not available in your context menu, open Bridge and navigate to the folder manually. Right-click one image that is representative of the scene and choose *Open in Camera RAW*. Adjust the parameters in Camera RAW to your liking and then click *Done*. This saves XMP metadata for that still. See Figures 4-121 and 4-122.

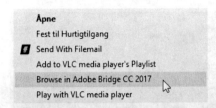

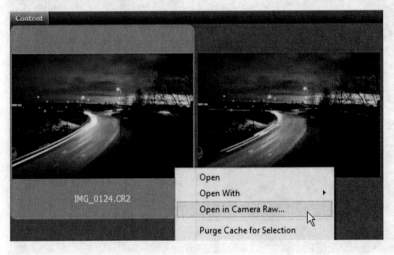

Figure 4-121. *Right-click your folder and choose Browse in Adobe Bridge. Then, open the first image in Camera Raw.*

Figure 4-122. *Adjust the image to your liking in Camera Raw*

Still in Bridge, right-click the image and choose **Develop Settings ➤ Copy Settings**. Then, select all the images, right-click one of them, and choose **Develop Settings ➤ Paste Settings**. See Figure 4-123.

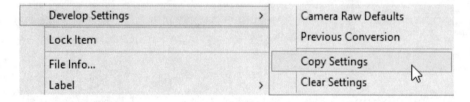

Figure 4-123. *Copy the Develop Settings and paste them onto all the other images*

Still with all images selected in Bridge, click **Tools ➤ Photoshop ➤ Image Processor**. You can do the same directly from Photoshop if you want: **File ➤ Scripts ➤ Image Processor**. See Figure 4-124.

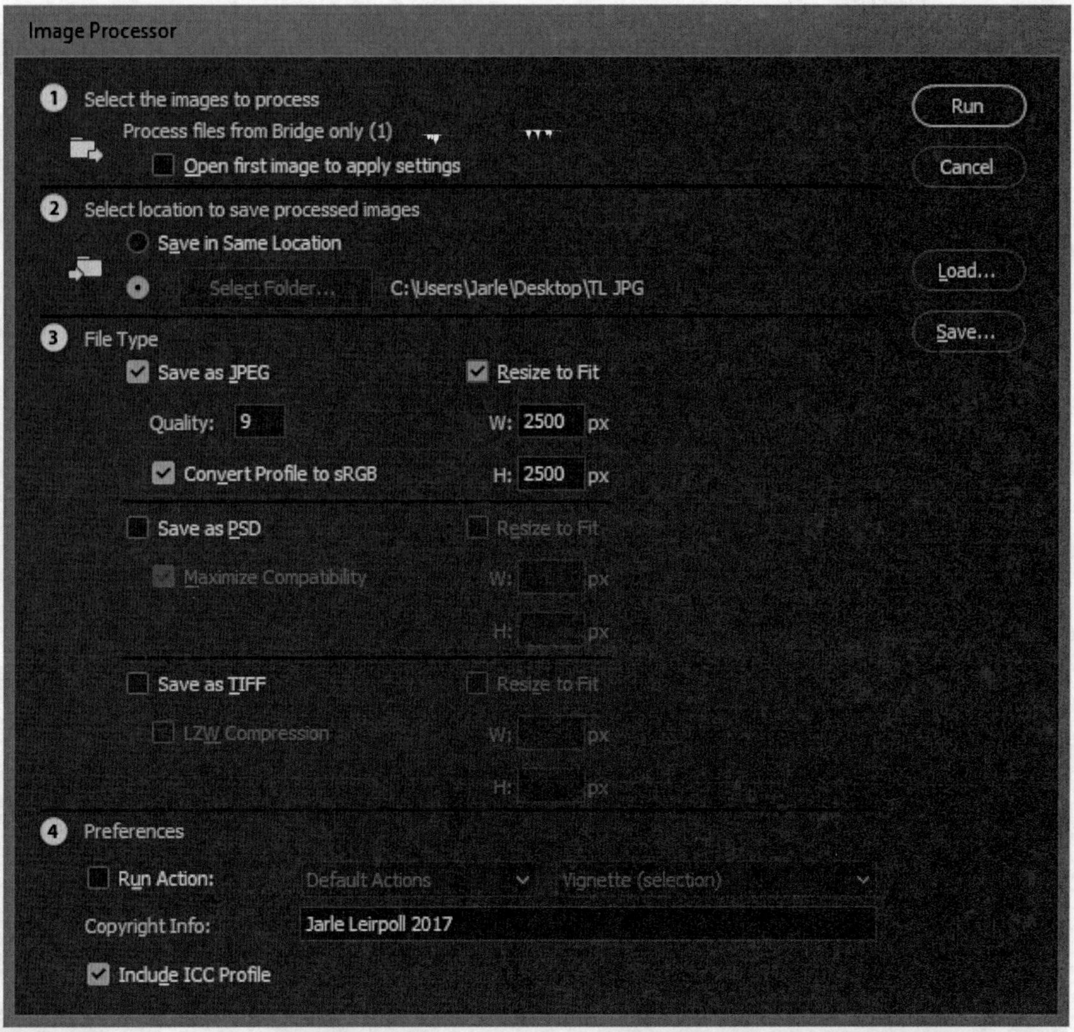

Figure 4-124. *Use the Image Processor from Bridge to batch convert all the images to a format Premiere can read and to a suitable size*

Make clever choices here for size, naming, and so on and export as TIF or JPG. Import as an image sequence as explained earlier, make a new sequence at the size and frame rate you want the final output to be, and cut the imported clip into the timeline.

Since this is now essentially a movie clip inside of Premiere, you can do all the normal stuff to it–scale it so it fits the frame better, do slow zooms with motion, add effects, and so on. See Figure 4-125.

Figure 4-125. *Since the images are bigger than the HD sequence, I could zoom into the time-lapse. Time-lapse footage by Tomas Brekke and Daniel Solbakken.*

If you think the time-lapse needs some smoothing, change its frame rate to about half or one-third of the sequence frame rate and enable frame blending on the clip to get a more fluid time-lapse.

Stabilizing Time-Lapse Footage

Sometimes it's not possible to shoot with a tripod, it's moving because of wind (or an inexperienced photographer touching the camera instead of remote controlling it), or it has to be moved between shots. If you shot a tall building being built over several months, you would end up with non-aligned images. You can try to fix this automatically in Photoshop or with the warp stabilizer in Premiere. To do it in Photoshop, click **File ➤ Scripts ➤ Load Files into Stack** and browse to the folder containing the images (Figure 4-126).

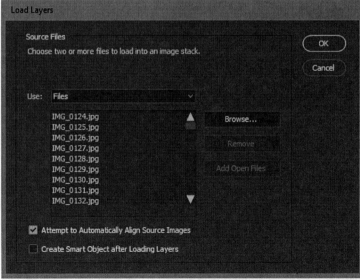

Figure 4-126. Stack mode in Photoshop can be used to stabilize the footage if needed

357

Tick the *Attempt to Automatically Align Source Images* box and click *OK*. This will take a very long time, but I bet it's still faster than doing it manually. There is a limit to how many images Photoshop can open at one time—I believe it's 200 files. Your amount of free RAM will also limit how many images Photoshop can comfortably handle. So, if your time-lapse is longer you'll have to do this in batches.

When the alignment is done, click **File ➤ Export ➤ Export Layers to Files**. Choose a folder and a file format and hit *Run*. From here, follow the earlier instructions for renaming the files, importing them as an image sequence, and so forth. See Figure 4-127.

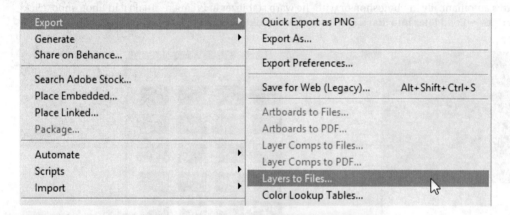

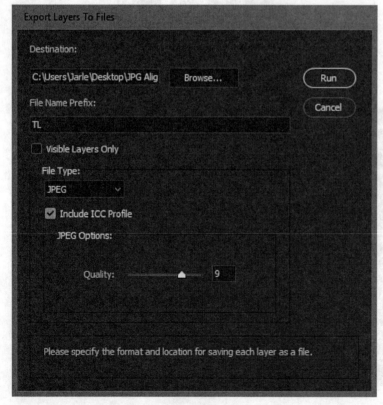

Figure 4-127. After the alignment is done, export the layers as separate image files

The other approach is to import the image sequence as is, without aligning the images, and then use the warp stabilizer effect in Premiere to stabilize the footage. Since the stabilizing part of that effect is GPU accelerated in Premiere, it might actually be faster. The effect also works in the background, so you can continue to edit in Premiere while it's analyzing the clip. You will need to put the clip in a nested sequence that matches its frame size for the warp stabilizer to work. You can see my recommended settings in Figure 4-128.

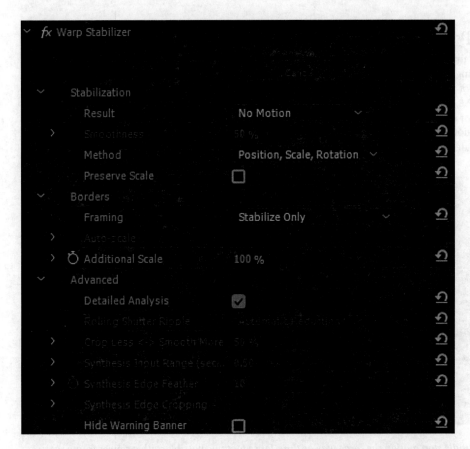

Figure 4-128. *Use Position, Scale, Rotation as the stabilization method to avoid artifacts introduced by the subspace warp*

No Motion is chosen for obvious reasons. If it was a moving camera shot with a motion-controlled slider, choose *Smooth Motion* at a high setting. I don't like the possible artifacts introduced by subspace warp, so I choose *Position, Scale, Rotation*. Since this will be scaled in the main sequence, I also choose to *Preserve Scale*. For the same reason, I choose *Stabilize Only*, so I don't scale the image several times, possibly causing the quality to drop.

When the scene is changing a lot, like it is when going from day to night, you may have to cut the scene into shorter pieces so the warp stabilizer can do a better job. You will then have to manually align the clips at the cuts using Position, Scale, Rotation—but that's better than aligning every single frame.

If you have a very unstable recording, you can try opening the Advanced twirly at the bottom and choosing *Detailed Analysis*, but this will increase the analysis time a lot. There are other possibilities, like masking off areas that should be allowed to move, but if you need these advanced options you're better off sending the whole clip to After Effects via Dynamic Link. The warp stabilizer there has more options.

Remove Flicker from Time-Lapse Footage

If your footage is flickering because of auto-exposure, non-locked mirror, or other reasons, you can try enabling frame blending on the clip. But if it has a lot of flicker you will have to use a third-party plug-in such as Flicker Free from Digital Anarchy, BCC Flicker Fixer from Boris FX, or Neat Video Noise Reduction.

Editing Stop-Motion Animation

Stop motion isn't that different from time-lapse, so the preceding tips on time-lapse editing also relate to stop-motion editing. But to save on the workload when shooting and to achieve a more traditional stop-motion feel, a lot of animators use lower frame rates. 12 fps is a pretty common frame rate for stop-motion animation, but 12.5, 15, 18, 24, and 25 are also used.

Your animator should know the frame rate. If you're not sure, just play the clip in the Source Monitor and see if the motion seems to be at the correct speed. If it's too slow, increase the frame rate; if it's too fast, lower the frame rate in the **Modify ➤ Interpret Footage** dialog (Figure 4-129).

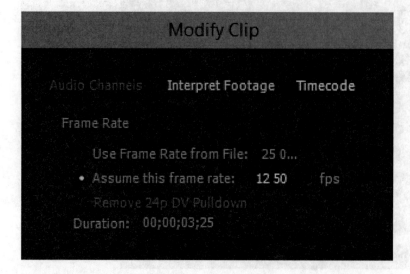

Figure 4-129. *Handle stop motion the same way as time-lapse footage, possibly with a slower frame rate*

The frame rate of your editing sequence may need to differ from the frame rate of your footage; for example, if you want smooth rolling credits on a stop-motion animation film.

Summary

There is great breadth and depth to the editor's toolkit in Premiere Pro. I hope you've seen how learning the available shortcut commands and mouse techniques can make you fast in any editing situation. If you haven't mastered them all just yet, pick a few essentials—like Pancake Timelines, the **Q** and **W** commands, or Replace with Clip—and build them into your workflow.

It's not just shortcuts that save you time; it's also understanding your footage, importing and organizing it correctly, and choosing sequence settings with exporting in mind. We've seen the options Premiere has for interpreting footage and controlling its speed, and how to handle some of the interesting footage conversion situations that modern editors face in the digital world.

Chapter 10 on Customizing Premiere is a logical extension of this one, with even more ways to set up the editing tools in Premiere so they work for your specific needs.

Happy editing!

CHAPTER 5

■ ■ ■

Multi-Camera Editing

By Jarle Leirpoll and Andy Edwards

Multi-camera editing is a very powerful feature built right inside of Premiere. Premiere's audio-syncing feature allows for easy syncing of multiple cameras. You no longer need to buy third-party plug-ins to sync your multi-camera footage. In this chapter, we will dive into the basics of multicam all the way up to advanced features and workflows. Figure 5-1 shows some of the user interface (UI) elements used in multicam.

Figure 5-1. *Multi-camera editing in Premiere*

Traditionally, one scene in a TV show might have three to five different angles. A modern show can have 10 to 20 different angles in every single scene. If it's a reality show, you can have at least five to ten cameras–all with at least four different audio tracks each. Syncing and managing all these angles and audio tracks can be quite a challenge. Fortunately, Premiere has great tools for multi-camera editing.

© Jarle Leirpoll 2017
J. Leirpoll et al., *The Cool Stuff in Premiere Pro*, DOI 10.1007/978-1-4842-2890-6_5

Multi-Camera from Bin

Here's the basic workflow for cutting multicam in Premiere:

1. Select all the source files and choose *Create Multi-Camera Source Sequence* as shown in Figure 5-2.

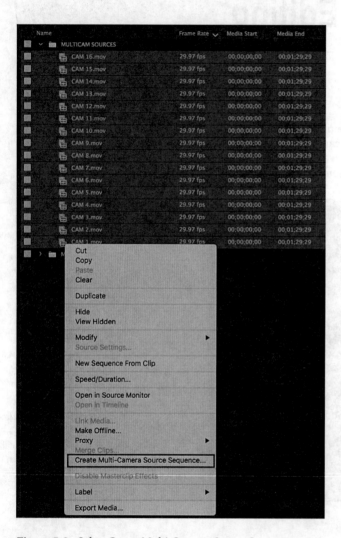

Figure 5-2. Select Create Multi-Camera Source Sequence

2. Choose to sync by audio (or TC, In or Out Points, or Markers) and then watch the magic.

You will get one or more sequences depending on timecode breaks. If no camera or audio recorder was running at a certain point in time, a new sequence will be made for the later clips.

When you select *Automatic for Sequence Preset* as shown in Figure 5-3, the video preset is based on the video format of the Camera 1 clip–meaning the first clip you select if you select them manually, or the one that comes first in alphabetical order if you choose the whole bin.

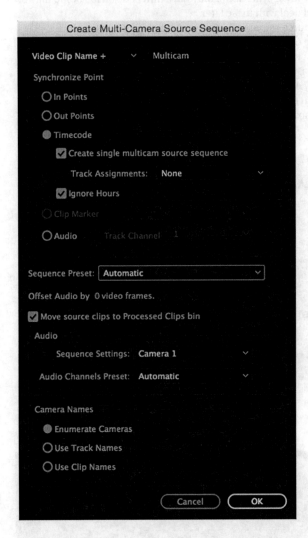

Figure 5-3. Options in the Create Multi-Camera Source Sequence dialog

When you sync by timecode, you can tick the *Create single multicam source sequence* box to keep everything in one source sequence. If the cameras were marked by setting different hours in the timecode, tell Premiere to *Ignore Hours*.

If needed, move the clips to higher or lower tracks. Then, drop this source sequence (or more, if you had breaks) into your cutting sequence and cut using the multicam monitor.

Get More Control over the Multi-Camera Source Sequence

Of course, this is the ideal situation. Sometimes, the source material will not be suitable for this workflow. Some clips may lack audio. Some may have audio out of sync. Some may have timecode offset. Some may be recorded at a different frame rate–and so on. We'll deal with these later.

To get more control over the multi-camera source sequence, you'll want to open it in a timeline. Right-click the newly created sequence and choose *Open in Timeline*, or **Ctrl-double-click** (Cmd-double-click) it–or create a keyboard shortcut for this if you do a lot of multi-camera editing.

When several clips belong to the same camera, you need to move them to the same track manually, then delete empty tracks. Move clips to desired tracks by **Alt-clicking** them, and then tap **Up Arrow** or **Down Arrow** while holding **Alt**, or just drag them in place. If you use the shortcuts, you can lock other tracks first to avoid overwriting existing angles. Figures 5-4 and 5-5 show you a cleaned up multi-camera source sequence.

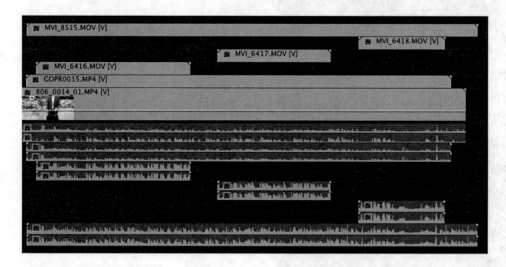

Figure 5-4. *Premiere creates one camera track per video clip*

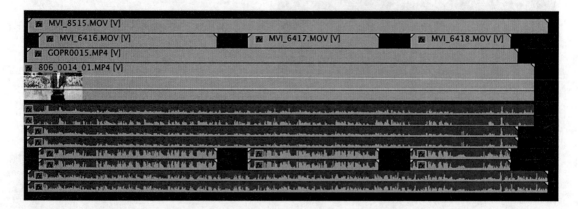

Figure 5-5. *Clean up your tracks so your monitor view does not show black sqaures for empty tracks*

Use Nesting If You Have Lots of Clips

If there are lots of pauses in the recordings from a camera, moving the clips around as just explained will be a lot of work because of all the tracks that are created. I've heard about people ending up with more than 70 tracks. In those cases, I would use nesting instead.

If you select all the clips on all the tracks that make up a camera angle and choose *Nest*, they will be moved over to a new sequence—but not the audio, just the video! You can do a manual nest instead, though, if you want the audio to be nested, too. Park the playhead at the start of the first clip from the camera in question. Select all the clips from that camera and hit **Ctrl+X** (Cmd+X). Create a new sequence and hit **Ctrl+V** (Cmd+V). Provided your source patching was set correctly, all of the clips will be pasted into the new sequence at different layers, as shown in Figure 5-6.

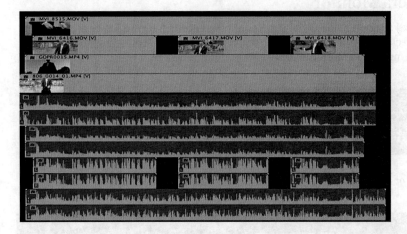

Figure 5-6. *When we expand the audio tracks, we can see that the audio is perfectly synced*

Now, drag this new sequence into your multi-camera source sequence as a nest on the tracks you want that camera on. To finalize the setup, delete all empty audio and video tracks with the dialog you get from right-clicking the track header. Now, this nested sequence will act as an angle in the multi-camera sequence, and you can cut as needed.

■ **Warning**   Don't use this nesting method if you need to flatten your multi-camera edit, as you'll end up with the nested sequence, not the actual camera clips, after flattening. This can cause trouble when exporting XML, OMF, or AAF for further audio mixing or color grading in non-Adobe software.

Nest the Source Sequence into the Edit Sequence

When you put the multi-camera source sequence into your editing sequence, make sure you're nesting. Click the *Nest-or-Not* button (officially named *Insert and Overwrite Sequences as nests or individual clips*) so it's highlighted in blue, as shown in Figure 5-7.

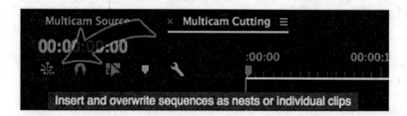

Figure 5-7. Make sure the Nest-or-Not button is activated so you get a nested multi-camera sequence

Use the Multi-Camera Monitor

Click the *Toggle Multi-Camera View* button in the program monitor as shown in Figure 5-8, or use the shortcut **Shift+0**. You can also choose *Multi-Camera* from the wrench menu in the program monitor. Figure 5-9 shows the program monitor in Multi-Camera view.

Figure 5-8. Click this button (or hit Shift+0) to show the Multi-Camera view in the program monitor

Figure 5-9. Multi-Camera view. Multi-Camera footage by Tomas Brekke and Daniel Solbakken. Magician: Rune Carlsen.

The Multi-Camera view in the program monitor shows the cameras/angles. The monitor is divided into 4, 9, 16, etc. based on the number of tracks in the multi-camera source sequence, as shown in Figure 5-10. Empty tracks result in too many cameras with too small thumbnails.

Figure 5-10. *Empty tracks are shown as black squares and should be cleaned up*

For this reason, I recommend that you delete any empty tracks in the sequence after re-ordering the clips, as shown in Figures 5-11 and 5-12.

Figure 5-11. *Bring up the Delete Tracks dialog box and choose All Empty Tracks*

Figure 5-12. *After deleting the empty tracks, the four cameras correctly show as four, and the thumbnails are much bigger*

Use **Q** and **W** to trim Top and Tail, move to the beginning of the clip, and then hit *Play*. Cut between cameras by clicking the images or by hitting the number keys on the keyboard: **1** for Camera 1, **2** for Camera 2, and so forth, as shown in Figure 5-13.

Figure 5-13. *Timeline after cutting*

Now comes the real beauty of multi-camera editing in Premiere; if you make a mistake, just go back to where you need another camera to show and click the preview image of that camera. Done! That's how easy it is to change it. Need to add more edits? Use the Add Edit command or the Razor tool.

Need to move an edit point? Use the Rolling Edit tool or select the edit point and adjust it with the keyboard shortcuts for trimming. I prefer the Rolling Edit tool, since the constant toggle between the trim monitor and multi-camera monitor when using the Trim mode can be confusing and often cause UI glitches. Be very careful when using the Ripple Trim/Delete tool and making Slip edits and Slide edits. If you are not careful, your multicam sequence can end up with a bunch of out of sync media.

View Multicam Source Sequence

To adjust or view the media used in the creation of the multicam sequence, hold the **Control Key** (Command on Mac) and double-click your nested multicam sequence. You can then edit your source media and make audio adjustments like a regular sequence. Changes you make in the source sequence will update in your nested multicam sequence, as shown in Figure 5-14.

Figure 5-14. *Open Multicam Source Sequence in timeline*

Camera Order

The order of the cameras may seem random, but there is some logic behind this. If you are selecting the clips manually, then the order in which you select them sets the camera order. If you're running the *Create Multi-Camera Source Sequence* process on a bin, then Premiere will use alphabetical order.

To change the order, you could move the clips to other tracks, but there is a faster method: click the wrench menu in the program monitor and choose *Edit Cameras* as shown in Figure 5-15. Moving the cameras in this dialog will change their position in the multi-camera monitor. You can also turn the view off for some cameras temporarily.

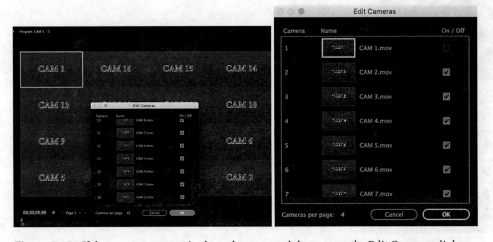

Figure 5-15. *If the cameras are not in the order you need them, open the Edit Cameras dialog*

Once you have completed moving your cameras into the correct order, you should see a proper sequence of cameras, as shown in Figure 5-16.

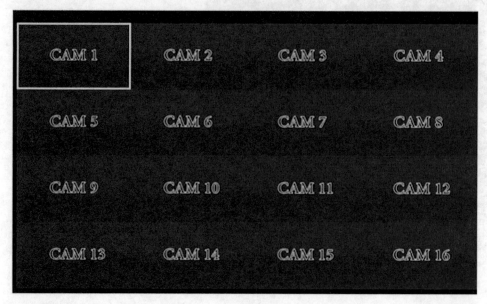

Figure 5-16. After moving the cameras around, the order is changed

Camera Selection Tip

The camera you select first in your bin, as shown in Figure 5-17 (then Shift-select the rest of the cameras), will determine what camera is first in order of your sequence. Premiere will also choose the audio track from this "first chosen" clip to be the main audio you cut with.

Figure 5-17. First-selected clip becomes Camera 1

In the examples in Figure 5-18, CAM 16, CAM 1, CAM 2, and Line Cut were chosen first, then the other cameras.

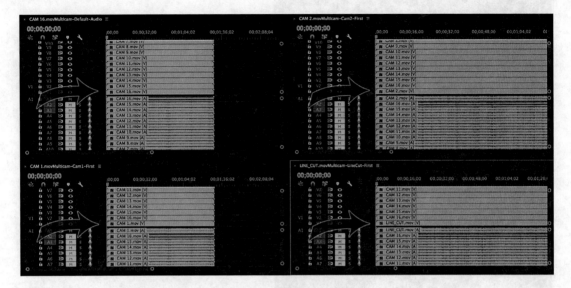

Figure 5-18. *Result with four different first-chosen clips*

Move Source/Processed Bin

When processing your multicam media but you don't want Premiere to move your media into the Processed Bin, uncheck the box *Move source clips to Processed Clips bin*, as shown in Figures 5-19 and 5-20.

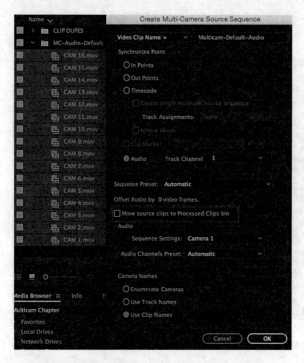

Figure 5-19. *Move source clips option*

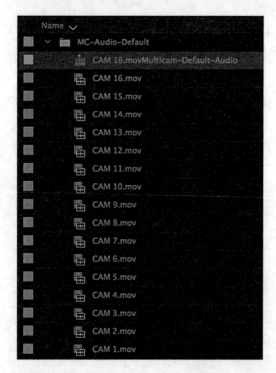

Figure 5-20. *No source clips were moved*

Multicam Time of Day Workflow

Productions that use multiple cameras–for example, reality TV shows, usually choose to record with Time of Day timecode. Not all cameras might be recording at the same time, so this leads to large gaps when trying to sync them in a multicam sequence. Additionally, sound recordings on these shows have a timecode stamped to the wave files that get recorded so they can be used to sync up the camera media. Premiere now features the ability to sync time of day media and field sound recordings in the same sequence by assigning groups of clips a *Camera Label* or *Camera Angle* through the Metadata Display categories, as shown in Figure 5-21. These metadata categories are not shown by default in your project window and must be enabled in the Metadata Display window.

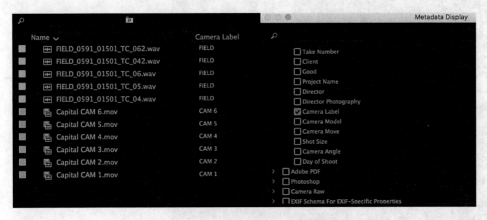

***Figure 5-21.** Turn on the Camera Label category via Metadata Display ➤ Dynamic Media ➤ Camera Label*

Select all your camera clips and field audio in the bin, select *Timecode* to sync your multicam, and under *Track Assignments* choose *Camera Label*, as shown in Figure 5-22. (Do not select bins and attempt to sync your media; it must be the individual elements.)

***Figure 5-22.** Choose Camera Label under Track Assignments*

375

In Figure 5-23, the synced multicam clips and external audio used had timecodes starting at the four o'clock hour, five o'clock hour, and six o'clock hour. Each piece of media is placed on its own track when you create the multicam sequence through this method.

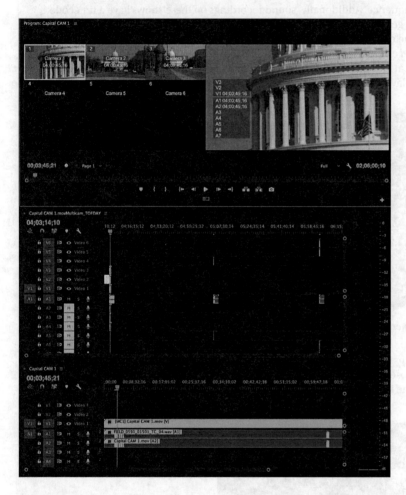

Figure 5-23. *All the clips are synced to time of day*

Field Audio Placement in This workflow

If you use this metadata grouping method, please be aware that field audio (audio-only file) will be placed on track A1 rather than any other camera audio source, as shown in Figure 5-24.

Here is the track layout:

V3	Video 3	Capital CAM 3.mov [V]
V2	Video 2	Capital CAM 2.mov [V]
V1	Video 1	Capital CAM 1.mov [V]
A1	M S	FIELD_0591_01501_TC_04.wav
A2	M S	Capital CAM 1.mov [A]
A3	M S	Capital CAM 2.mov [A]
A4	M S	Capital CAM 3.mov [A]

Figure 5-24. *Field audio will be placed on track 1*

Choose What to Do with Audio

Most tutorials on multi-camera editing in Premiere stop here, which is a shame. Setting up a simple multi-camera sequence and switching video is super easy, so a tutorial is not really needed–but what about the audio? Should it follow the video? Should audio from only one camera be used? Should just one–or a couple–of audio tracks from every camera be available? What about empty tracks?

Really, multi-camera audio is much more complicated than multi-camera video. A proper understanding of audio features and handling is the key to effective multi-camera workflows.

If you're editing a documentary, you may want audio to follow video. If you're editing a reality show, you will definitely want to keep all the audio tracks and edit those separately and individually. If it's a performance piece, like a music video, you will want to use audio from just one camera or from a separate audio recorder.

You can set your audio choices manually or use the Create Multi-Camera Source Sequence dialog. Let's walk through the latter, automatic, method first. We'll get back to the manual approach later.

■ **Note** The following examples and explanations assume that Sequence Preset is set to Automatic. While there are many presets, there are too many variables to cover them here. If you use a custom sequence preset, I recommend that you use the manual approach described later. But Automatic works very well. Every channel will be mapped to a separate output, so you get a one-to-one relationship between source channels and sequence output channels.

When *Audio Sequence Settings* are set to *Camera 1, Mono,* Premiere mutes audio from cameras other than Camera 1, as shown in Figure 5-25. The audio from that camera will be panned left/right to achieve separate outputs for every source channel.

Figure 5-25. *In this example, audio from Camera 1 only is used, and video only is cut*

For some purposes, like performances, this is good. Just remember to make sure that the camera with the good audio is Camera 1. How? Select that camera first–and then **Ctrl-click** (Cmd-click) the other angles–and then create the multi-camera source sequence. The clip you choose first will become Camera 1.

■ **From Help**   Multicam editing is enabled for only the video portion of the source sequence. If you use A/V clips to create this sequence, the audio tracks for all audio associated with video 1 are unmuted. Other audio in the source sequence is muted.

If you use audio-only clips with video or A/V clips, the audio-only clips are placed in the top-most tracks and are unmuted. Other audio (from any linked clips) is muted and placed in lower tracks.

Note that if you have a separate audio-only file selected together with the video files, that audio will be used instead of the audio from Camera 1, even if the Sequence Settings show Camera 1. This might be a bit confusing and unintuitive, but is very helpful, since you usually record separate audio because you want to use it.

If you also need the audio from one or more cameras, you'll need to un-mute these manually in the source sequence.

■ **More from Help**   The channel assignments and panning of each track are set to transfer each source channel to independent output channels (up to 32). The number of unmuted channels of source audio determines the number of active output channels of the sequence.

But what if you want the sound to follow your video edit, as shown in Figure 5-26? When you create the multi-camera source sequence, make sure that Sequence Settings under Audio is set to *Switch Audio*, as shown in Figure 5-27. Then, from the Multi-Camera Monitor panel menu, choose *Audio Follows Video*, as shown in Figure 5-28, and you're good to go.

Figure 5-26. *Here, audio cuts follow video cuts, switching between audio from different cameras*

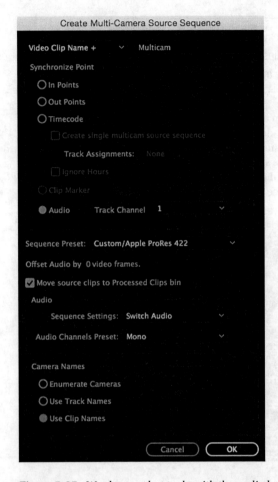

Figure 5-27. *We choose what to do with the audio before we create the multi-camera source sequence*

✓ Multi-Camera Audio Follows Video
 Multi-Camera Selection Top Down
✓ Show Multi-Camera Preview Monitor
 Edit Cameras...

Figure 5-28. *Set audio to follow video in the multi-camera monitor, too*

Think of this as what you do when creating the sequence–enabling the audio of the source sequence to be cut and then activating audio switching in the program monitor wrench menu. Skip one of the steps, and your audio will not be switched.

If you think you'll ever want to switch your audio, choose *Switch Audio*. This will create one adaptive track per camera, so that audio and video can be switched together. The number of outputs will be determined by the camera that has the most audio tracks. You can easily change this later so audio is not switched, but it's a bit harder to change it the other way.

■ **From Help**   This setting also maps multi-mono source audio into a single adaptive audio track. If audio-only clips are included in the selection of clips, the audio-only clips are placed in tracks below any linked clips. Empty video tracks are created to match up with every audio-only track.

Sometimes, you will need to keep all the audio from all the cameras. Of course, to achieve this, you select *All Cameras* in the Audio Sequence Settings drop-down menu.

This will put all audio tracks from all cameras and audio recorders into the multi-camera source sequence. This may result in a huge number of tracks, as shown in Figure 5-29. If there are empty tracks or tracks that will not be used in the final mix, I recommend that you remove these in the **Modify ➤ Audio Channels** dialog before creating the multi-camera source sequence, as shown in Figure 5-30.

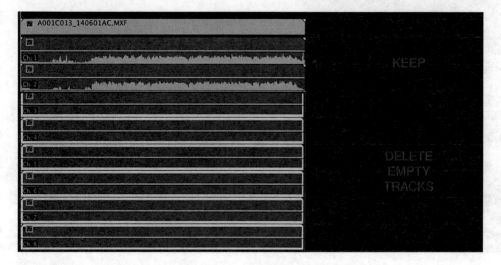

Figure 5-29. Deleting empty audio tracks will help clean up your sequence

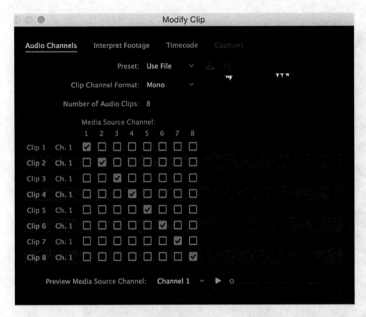

Figure 5-30. *Source Audio shows all eight channels when you only need the first one or two channels of actual recorded audio*

■ **Note** Deleting empty/unnecessary audio tracks prevents a lot of clutter in your timeline, and keeping lots of tracks may also prevent the audio waveforms for the multi-camera source sequence from showing in the main edit timeline.

I recommend removing all unused audio channels in the source clips before adding audio from all cameras to a sequence, as shown in Figure 5-31.

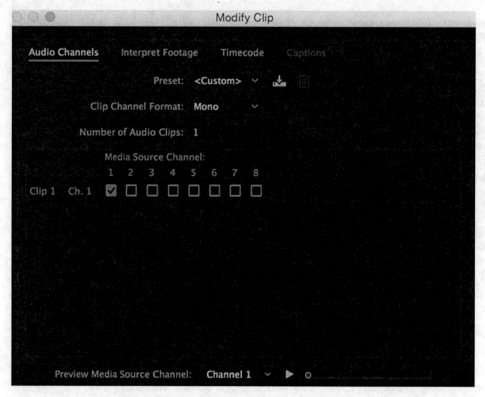

Figure 5-31. *Modify the clip to just show one channel for mono or 1 and 2 for stereo*

■ **From Help**   With this setting, only the video portion of the source sequence is Multicam enabled. All audio is unmuted (up to 32 channels). The number of unmuted channels of source audio determines the number of active output channels of the sequence.

Multi-Camera Audio Channels Preset

The Audio Channels Preset setting determines how the resulting Source Sequence will be dropped into the edit channel. The different audio channel presets map to the chosen type of tracks based on the number of output channels in the source sequence. The choices are mono, stereo, 5.1, adaptive, and automatic. Most people will choose mono.

The *All Cameras, Mono* setting will put all audio tracks from all cameras into the source sequence and map every track to a separate output.

When your sources have mixed audio formats, like two stereo clips and one 5-channel clip, choosing *Automatic* will create as many output channels as needed to route every source track to a separate output.

To check how they are mapped after creating the sequence, choose *Open in Timeline* and open the Audio Track Mixer.

■ **A Little Warning**   If the number of tracks in your source clips outnumber the channels in the preset you choose, the results can be a bit surprising. So, don't use your custom two-track preset when you have four tracks in your sources.

Create a Multi-Camera Source Sequence from Scratch

Sometimes you need more control over audio tracks than you can easily get with the automatic multi-camera source sequence creation. In these cases, I recommend that you start by building your source and editing sequences and then populate them with clips, synchronize, and edit.

   Doing this from scratch can quickly get very, very messy. There are limitations to what different kinds of tracks can do, to what different sequence settings can do, and to what kind of editing can be done to different sources and source sequences. First, a few warnings.

Don't create stereo master sequences. Instead, make them multi-channel and then choose two channels. It will act as stereo, but can easily be changed to more channels later. You cannot change a sequence with a stereo master to multi-channel later. Choosing multi-channel gives you more flexibility.

Don't just enable multi-camera when the sources have more than two audio channels and you want to switch audio. The tracks need to be adaptive for Switch Audio to work.

Do not enable multiple mono audio tracks for multi-camera. Audio will be messed up, and you will see your waveforms disappear.

Preparation and Syncing

Start by creating a sequence with the amount and kind of audio tracks you need, as shown in Figure 5-32. If you want to switch audio with video, you will have to use adaptive tracks and put the audio from each camera on its own separate adaptive track.

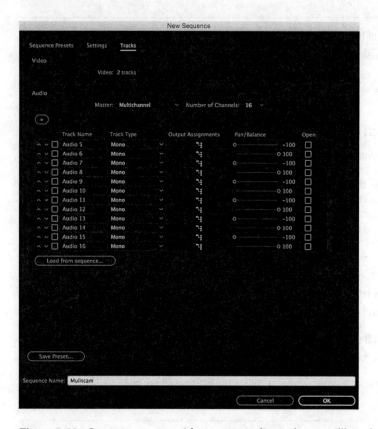

Figure 5-32. *Create a sequence with as many audio tracks as you'll need*

However, most multi-camera editing I've seen at production houses has been done with mono tracks in sequences with multi-channel output. This might be because that's how they used to work in their old NLE, or because they get trouble with OMF export otherwise, or for several other reasons.

If you have eight clips with four tracks of mono audio and you want to continue using mono tracks, you need 32 of them. I have a 16-channel mono sequence preset that I use for this.

Before you put all the source clips in the timeline, make sure that the Audio Channel Mapping is set as you need it. I used a 4 Mono Channels preset I made.

Now, throw all the source clips into your sequence and move them so that all the clips are on different tracks.

▪ **Note** Premiere will not allow you to synchronize several clips on one track so as to avoid collisions. So, to avoid any conflicts, spread the clips to separate tracks, as shown in Figure 5-33.

Then, select them all and click **Clip ➤ Synchronize** or right-click one and choose *Synchronize*, as shown in Figures 5-33, 5-34, and 5-35. Synchronize by audio, in/out points, timecode, or markers, as usual.

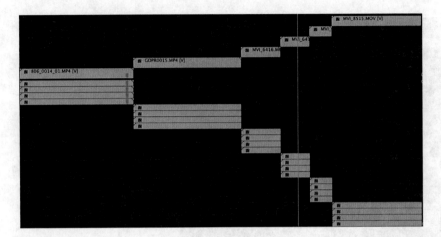

Figure 5-33. *The clips need to be on separate tracks*

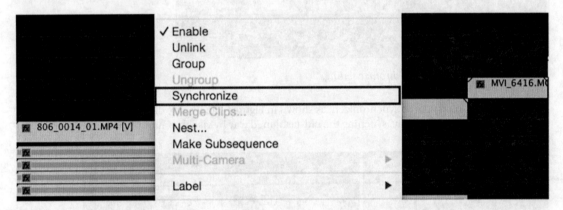

Figure 5-34. *Synchronize the clips from the right-click menu*

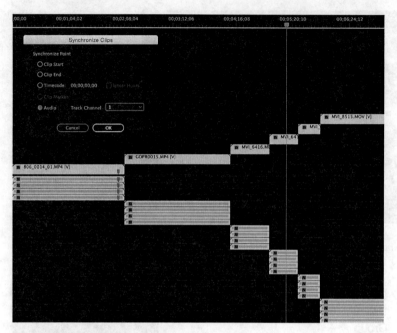

Figure 5-35. *Choose your Synchronize settings*

Your clips should now be synchronized, as shown in Figure 5-36. If some did not get synchronized, move them into place manually, synching the old-fashioned way by visual or audible clues.

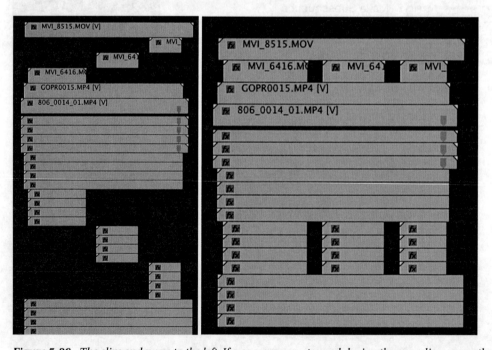

Figure 5-36. *The clips end up as to the left. If a camera was stopped during the recording, move the clips to the tracks where they belong*

386

If you have multiple clips per camera angle because of paused recordings, make sure you move all clips from each camera to the same track. Then, delete all empty tracks as usual. I ended up with four video tracks and sixteen audio tracks.

Cut Video, Keep All Audio

This mimics the *All Cameras* setting in the Create Multi-Camera Source Sequence dialog, where all the tracks from all the cameras are available in the cutting sequence. Having all audio sources available is an advantage if the piece will be sent to audio post-production via AAF or OMF. The person who does the mix can choose between all the audio recordings for the final mix. Make sure all your channels are properly panned, as shown in Figure 5-37.

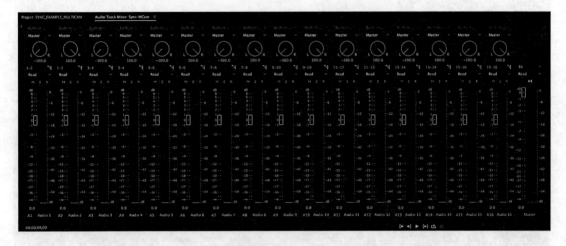

Figure 5-37. *Pan the tracks left and right in the Audio Track Mixer*

This can be set up very quickly. Sync and align your clips in a timeline as explained earlier, then hold down **Alt** and **marquee-select** all the video clips. You can also unlink audio and video and select only the video segments of the clips, as shown in Figure 5-38.

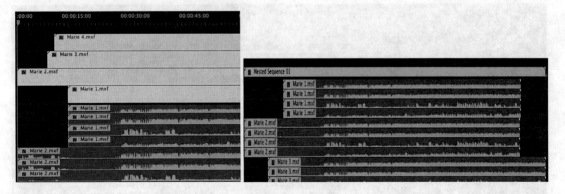

Figure 5-38. *Nest the video portion of the clips and choose Multi-Camera ➤ Enable in the context menu for the nested sequence*

Nest the video clips by clicking **Clip ➤ Nest** or by right-clicking and choosing *Nest* from there. Or, better yet, create a custom shortcut.

Then, click **Clip ➤ Multi-Camera ➤ Enable** with the nested sequence clip selected, or right-click and choose **Multi-Camera ➤ Enable** as shown in Figure 5-39. Switch to multi-camera monitor and start cutting. With this method, you're doing all the work inside one sequence. You never need to open the nested sequence.

Figure 5-39. *Enable multi-camera for the NestCut video, keeping audio from Camera 1*

This mimics the Camera 1 setting in the Create Multi-Camera Source Sequence dialog. One method is to sync and align the clips as explained earlier and then mute all the other tracks. This leaves all the audio tracks available, but it also occupies a lot of tracks, as shown in Figure 5-40. So, if you're absolutely sure that you will never need the audio tracks from the other cameras, go ahead and delete all those clips, as shown in Figure 5-41, leaving you with just the audio clips from Camera 1 (or an external audio recorder). Nest your cameras and begin cutting, as shown in Figure 5-42.

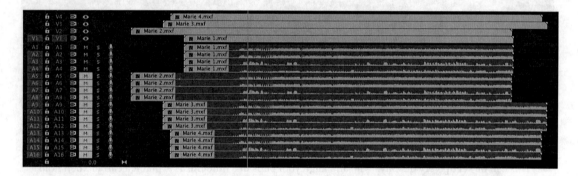

Figure 5-40. *Delete unnecessary audio tracks to avoid clutter if audio from just one camera is used*

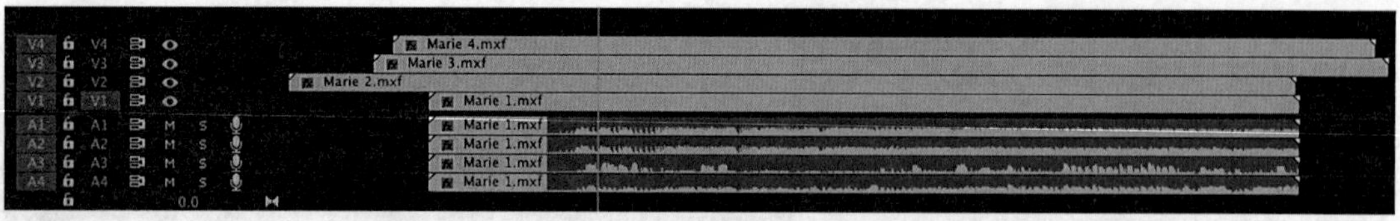

Figure 5-41. *Now you are dealing with only Cam 1 audio*

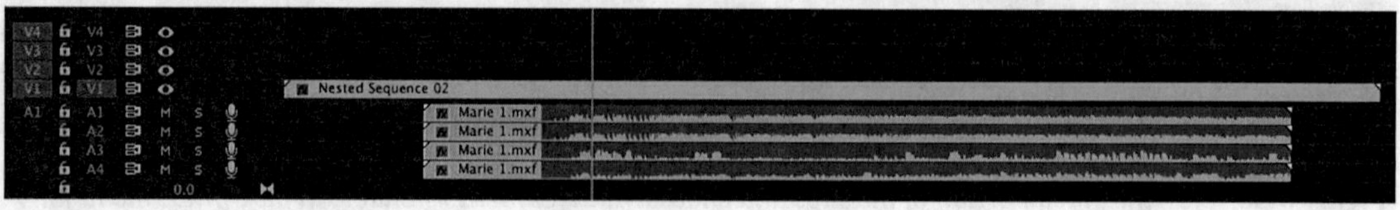

Figure 5-42. *Nest your cameras for a less-cluttered sequence*

Cut Both Audio and Video

If you want to have the audio switch with video from the related camera, you have to make that decision at the time you create the source sequence, and because it's a pretty convoluted process to prepare your clips and sequences for this, I see no reason why you would not want to use the Create Multi-Camera Source Sequence feature with the *Switch Audio* option. It's a lot quicker and easier than doing it manually, and you will not be able to mess up by missing one little setting.

Flatten the Edit

If you need to send the edited piece to non-Adobe software for audio cleanup and color grading, you will need to replace the nested multi-camera source sequence with the actual clips from the cameras and audio recorders.

Select all the clips in the cutting sequence, right-click, and choose **Multi-Camera ➤ Flatten** as shown in Figure 5-43. This step is crucial when you're sending the edit to other software or other intermediate project formats (XML, AAF, and OMF), since some software doesn't understand nested sequences at all–and for sure not Premiere Pro multi-camera sequences.

Figure 5-43. *Choose the flatten menu option*

Flatten the multi-camera clip after editing if you're sending the sequence to other software for audio mixing and color grading. This brings back the original video and audio clips, as shown in Figure 5-44.

Figure 5-44. *All your original audio comes back when you flatten multicam clips*

Manual Sync Offsets

Sadly, not all multi-camera recordings are perfect. You will encounter projects where one or more clips contain audio/video out of sync, as shown in Figure 5-45. You can fix out-of-sync clips by manually moving audio or video clips in the timeline, even whole tracks in a source sequence. **Alt-select** the audio portion of a clip and nudge it a few frames to slip it into sync. The usual red *Out of Sync* warning appears.

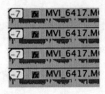

Figure 5-45. *If the audio or video is out of sync, you can manually sync them and drag a new item into the bin*

Under the Metadata Display, you can turn on the *Sync Offset* option so it shows the number of frames your audio is off by (Figure 5-46).

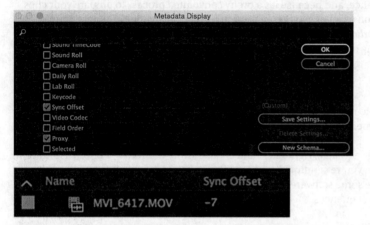

Figure 5-46. *The new item shows the Sync Offset in the metadata field when you show that field*

But, in reality, the audio and video are now in sync, so the warning should not be there. If you drag the synced clip back into the Project panel or a bin, a new project item is created. This item retains the applied offset. You can see this if you display the *Sync Offset* metadata column. If you drag it to a timeline again, the offset is already applied, and there is no Out of Sync warning.

If you're syncing by timecode, and the timecode from one source is consistently off by a given amount, open the clip in the source monitor and click **Clip ➤ Modify ➤ Timecode**. Choose *Set at Current Frame* and enter the correct timecode, as shown in Figure 5-47.

Figure 5-47. *If your audio timecode doesn't match your video timecode, set the offset manually before syncing*

If you use separately recorded audio and it's out of sync, you can use the *Offset Audio* option in the dialog when creating the multi-camera source sequence.

Multi-Camera Color Correction

You can color correct a clip in the multi-camera source sequence, and all the instances of that clip will be corrected in the edit sequence. So, you only need to correct a camera angle in one place.

You can, of course, also apply the color correction to the master clip and get the same result.

Multi-Camera Instead of Merge Clips for Dual-System Sound

Instead of fiddling with the Merge Clips feature for each pair of video and audio recordings, use the multi-camera feature to sync the recordings. Select all the clips in your bin containing the dual-system sound recordings–including the video clips. Click **Clip ➤ Create Multi-Camera Source Sequence** and choose to sync by audio, as shown in Figures 5-48 and 5-49.

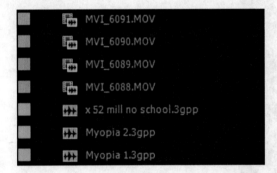

Figure 5-48. *Use multi-camera source sequences instead of merged clips to sync dual-system sound recordings*

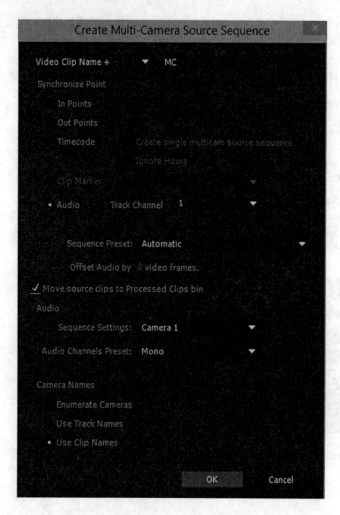

Figure 5-49. *Create Multi-Camera Source Sequence settings*

The *Camera 1* option will use only the audio from the separate audio file, and will mute the camera audio. Move the synced clips to a Processed Clips bin to see what clips were successfully synced, as shown in Figure 5-50.

Figure 5-50. *Move synced clips to a new bin*

You will get one or more multi-camera source sequences, depending on the continuity of the recordings. If, at any given time, no cameras or audio recorder was running, a new multi-camera source sequence will be created. So, if it's fifteen interviews done at separate times, you get fifteen source sequences, automatically synced. If the camera stopped three times during an interview, and the audio recorder was running continuously, you will get one long source sequence.

Use the *Move source clips to Processed Clips bin* choice to easily spot any clips that could not be synced. You will also get a message that informs you if any clips could not be synced, as seen in Figure 5-51.

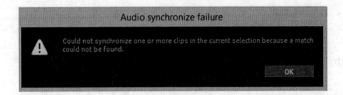

Figure 5-51. *Audio synchronize failure*

When you get this dialog, it's easy to see which clips weren't synced if you chose to move the processed clips to a new bin.

■ **Note** Using multi-camera source sequences has many advantages compared to using merge clips. My favorite shortcuts, **Q** and **W**, work as expected and will not create Out of Sync warnings or result in orphan audio or video clips, as you'd get with merge clips. Also, multi-camera sequences can be flattened, and you'll get the original video and audio clips. This prevents problems when exporting to OMF, XML, and AAF. And the syncing can be done automatically on all clips in one go!

I see absolutely no reason to use merge clips when the multi-camera features in Premiere are far superior. Figure 5-52 shows the same sources synced using multi-camera source sequence (left) and merge clips (right).

Figure 5-52. *Synced with multicam choice (left), and with merge clips (right)*

That doesn't look too bad–but look what happens when we start doing Top and Tail editing. The merged clips now display false out-of-sync warnings and orphaned audio and video clips after using **Q** and **W**. Take a look at Figure 5-53 to see how messy the timeline is after editing with merged clips versus multi-camera clips.

Figure 5-53. *Edited multi-camera clips (left); same clips after flattening (middle); and edited merged clips (right)*

Just so you can see how streamlined the multi-camera way is compared to merged clips, here are the steps to create merged clips.

First, you need to find out which clips belong together. In my example, the clip names gave no clues, so I had to hit *Play* on all of them to sort out which audio clip belonged to which video clip. Incredibly boring and very time consuming!

Then, you'll have to link the pairs one by one and get the dialog and make your syncing choices, as shown in Figure 5-54.

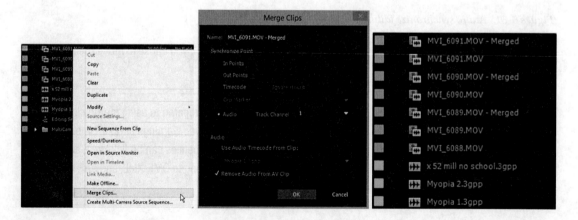

Figure 5-54. *The merge clips feature also clutters the bin a bit more*

After the merge is finished, you have populated the bin with merged clips. There is no automatic way to move the synced clips to a separate bin like we have when going the multi-camera route.

The merge clips trouble doesn't stop here. . . . When you put the merged clips in the timeline and use **Q** and **W** to trim away Top and Tail–the fastest way to edit–you get Out of Sync warnings, even though the clips are not out of sync. Since the clips have different lengths, there will also be leftover parts of audio or video at both ends of the merged clip. You'll have to remove the orphaned clips manually. To top it off, the remaining audio and video parts of all the clips are no longer linked.

Compare this to the multi-camera approach: Sync all clips in one go. Bin is tidy and clean after sync. **Q** and **W** work beautifully. No faulty Out of Sync warnings. No orphan clips to be removed manually. Multi-camera clips can be flattened when the edit is done, and will remain linked until you do so. Oh, joy!

Watch my video tutorial showing this technique at premierepro.net/editing/audio- syncing/.

Multi-Camera Interview Editing

The cost of recording technology has dropped significantly the last few years with the introduction of DSLRs, smartphone cameras, and other cheap equipment. This allows filmmakers to cover interviews and similar controlled situations from two or more angles. Since what the interviewee says is probably more important than from what angle it's filmed, you can cut while watching just one angle and later switch camera angles as needed.

One effective way to edit such interviews is to sync everything as you would any multi-camera sequence and load it into the source monitor, where you set in and out points and put your selected segments down in a Selects timeline. Rename the clips or add markers in the Selects timeline to describe the content of each interview bite.

Use this Selects sequence as the source when cutting the interview into your edit sequence with other material, and make sure you drag copies of the sync sequence into your edit timeline, not a nest of the Selects sequence. You want the multi-camera functionality in the edit sequence so you can change angles.

The Pancake Timeline technique, where you have more than one timeline open, is ideal for this kind of workflow.

The camera angles can easily be changed after the edit is done, since the clips in your edit timeline are multi-camera enabled. Flatten the multi-camera clips after the edit is finished.

Multi-Camera Cooking Show

The preceding technique works well for other material, too. Say you're cutting a cooking show. You could use the same technique, trimming out the best sound bites and explanations, and then do another pass where you pick the angles you need to show the cooking process.

Multi-Camera Reality Shows

Reality shows can lead to quite complicated timelines and workflows. Often, each camera will have two or more audio tracks, and in addition an external multi-channel audio recorder may be used. You end up juggling a lot of audio channels, and you need to keep most of the tracks for the audio editing people further downstream.

There are many ways to approach such an edit. One proven way is to watch your string-out sequence in the source monitor with all angles visible, preferably also on a big external screen.

Put good reaction shots, close-ups, cut-aways, and funny or interesting bits in a separate timeline and make notes or add markers to keep track of them.

When the story foundation is laid down, watch again, and pay attention to all the alternative angles to see if some of them are better than the ones used in the first draft.

Now, if only Premiere would switch more gracefully between the Multi-Camera view and the Trim view. . . . When fine-tuning the edit, Trim mode will be used extensively, but you still need to see all the angles, so you end up constantly switching between Multi-Camera view and Trim view in the program monitor.

Multi-Camera Performance

There is no limit to the number of cameras/angles you can have–but of course your hardware will quickly start to struggle when you tell it to read 20 streams of 4K footage from the disks while showing color-corrected previews of all the cameras. You may have to generate low-res proxies and edit with those, then re-link to the originals after the edit is done.

Different formats will put different strains on your hardware. Cutting a lot of AVC or H.264 material will max out your processors. MPEG-2 (like XDCAM-EX), not so much. DV will be super-easy.

Cutting RAW formats like CinemaDNG will push your drives to the limit, and you'll need a hefty RAID on a good connection. A good GPU will take care of the de-Bayering (creating an actual color image from all the red, green and blue dots from the sensor, which are placed in a Bayer pattern). See en.wikipedia.org/wiki/Bayer_filter for details.

In general, highly compressed formats will saturate your processor power, while lightly compressed formats will depend more on drive read/write speed. The ideal format for multi-camera editing is one where each frame is compressed separately and a lot of info is sacrificed for the sake of speedy editing. If you cut proxies, you need to re-link to high-quality files after the edit is done.

■ **Note**   Adobe engineer Steve Hoeg did a test on one system, and it was able to play four streams of AVC Intra (1080i), six streams of H.264 from a DSLR, eight streams of 4K R3D, fourteen streams of XDCAM-EX (1080i) or DVCProHD (1080p) or HDV (1080i)—and forty streams of DV.

This was measured on a system with 8 x 2.26 GHz Xeon, 10 GB RAM, Nvidia Quadro 5000, and a RAID, and should give you some idea of how different the hardware use is with different formats.

Multi-Camera and Proxies

With the introduction of proxy workflows in Premiere, your multi-camera workflow can benefit from smaller file sizes. Large multicam projects with 10 to 15 cameras can tax a computer system's ability to play back smoothly. With the smaller proxy media files, your multicam playback struggles can be alleviated by using proxy files.

Cut with Proxies, Link to High-Res

Since playing back multiple streams of high-quality 4K (or larger) footage isn't a trivial task, many systems will struggle with multi-camera editing with high-quality sources. A great solution is to transcode the footage to low-quality proxies, edit the proxies, and then re-link to the high-res footage in the multi-camera source sequence after the edit is done.

Please see chapter 2 on Proxy workflows for how to ingest your footage using proxy techniques and tips.

File Metadata and Proxies

When replacing proxy footage with full-res, the clip metadata stays the same, since it's part of the project file, but the file metadata will change. Make sure you have the relevant info in the clip metadata, not in the file metadata only.

Quasi-Proxy Editing

If you do your rough cut with high-quality RAW files and then want to take the edit on the road and work on your laptop, you can render and replace the clips in the timeline to a proxy format and edit with those clips on the road. When you are back on your main computer, select the clips, right-click, and choose *Restore Unrendered* to get your originals back.

Random Multi-Camera Editing Tips

The following are tips from people who've edited quite a lot of multi-camera material in Premiere. Some of these will not be relevant for you, while others may save you from a lot of trouble or just enable you to work faster.

Use Clapper/Slate Both Front and Back

When recording multi-camera material, add a slate or clapper both before and after the actual recording, if possible. That way you have a reference point for any drift in sync.

Multi-Camera Can Be Cut on All Tracks

By default, it may seem that multi-camera can only be cut when the multi-camera source sequence is on track 1 in the cutting sequence. The multi-camera monitor only shows up when the multi-camera source sequence is on track 1, but that's not really the case.

■ **Note**   Premiere displays the multi-camera monitor on the lowest active (targeted) track. So, disable track 1 if you want to see the multi-camera monitor for a multi-camera source sequence on track 2 and so forth. When no video track is targeted, it will show the multi-camera clips on video track 1.

Copy That Sequence

Before making major changes, duplicate your sequence. If something goes wrong, go back to the old version. You can start a whole new edit from the original, or just copy some segments from the old one into your new sequence.

Syncing Long Clips by Audio Waveforms Can Take a Long Time

Audio-waveform syncing is very easy and is fast on small projects, but on more complex projects it can take a long time. If you need to sync very long takes from several cameras, processing the audio waveforms will be a slow process, so other methods may be favorable.

It would be much faster to sync such a project by timecode, if it's available. If not, you could also sync the clips visually by nudging clips while zoomed in on the waveform or by setting common in or out points or markers on all the clips.

Adjusting Sync After the Fact

Adjust sync in a multi-camera source sequence, and the sync will be corrected in all sequences where that multi-camera source sequence is used. If, for some reason, the sync points aren't perfect, you can zoom in all the way to the sample level to do exact waveform matching.

Add More Angles

You can add more angles to an already edited multi-camera segment. Add new clips on extra tracks in the multi-camera source sequence, and new angles show up in the multi-camera monitor for all sequences that use that clip. Now, park over whatever clip you want to swap for the new angle and click on the new camera in the multi-camera monitor.

Scaling Does Not Show in Multi-Camera Preview

If your sources do not match your editing sequence, the preview will look a bit strange, as seen in Figure 5-55. Say you're cutting a 720p source sequence into a 1080 sequence, and apply *Set to Frame Size*.

Figure 5-55.   *To save on resources, scaling does not show in the multi-camera preview monitor. Multi-camera footage by Tomas Brekke and Daniel Solbakken; Magician: Rune Carlsen.*

The source clips will not fill the whole frames in the multi-camera preview monitor, and you get black borders. It's probably done to save on computer resources. The scaling will show in the program monitor and in your output, of course.

It will be even worse when you cut a higher-res source sequence into a lower-res editing sequence, since you will not see the whole frame of each camera.

Cut at Any Speed

Here's something you may not have thought about:

You can cut multi-camera at any playback speed you want. Slow-motion, fast and furious—even backward! So, if you encounter a tricky edit, slow down the playback. Need to get the edit done before dinner? Play at double speed. You can even scrub the playhead and add edits on the fly.

The UI will not always be able to catch up, but when you hit *Stop*, it will update. Of course, your files will need to be read faster, so you'll need a beefy RAID and/or network.

Don't Stop Cutting

If you are editing something that has long segments, play the whole segment through without stopping and make your cuts as best you can. Then, go back and tweak. You will finish faster.

Fill Gaps with Titles

If you're working in a client-over-shoulder situation where the director sits in the room with you, they might be thrown off when they see black in the multi-camera preview monitor. Insert title text in the areas where a camera is not rolling, as seen in Figure 5-56.

Figure 5-56. A title with some explanatory text will tell other people why they're not seeing an image from that camera angle

This will happen if a camera was started and stopped during the shoot for changing memory sticks or to save battery power. To make them understand that there's nothing wrong, add titles in the gaps in the multi-camera source sequence that say "Camera not running" or something along those lines.

You can add the same source sequence more than one time to your editing sequence. This is great when you need to use asynchronous takes or cut-aways from earlier in the same take. Using markers can help highlight bits you want to fix later for a re-cut or a compilation edit.

Display Camera Number, Clip Name, or Track Name

When creating a multi-camera source sequence, you can choose between displaying camera numbers, clip names, or track names. These labels appear in the Multi-Camera submenu and in the monitor overlays, as seen in Figure 5-57.

Figure 5-57. *Multicam overlays*

Depending on your needs, you may want to show camera numbers, clip names, or track names in the multi-camera preview monitor, as seen in Figure 5-58.

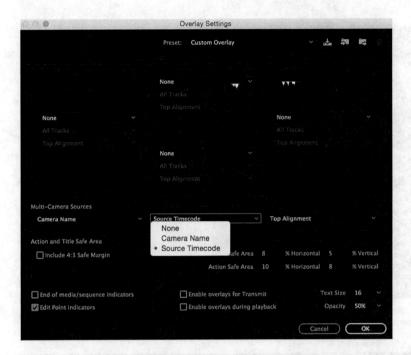

Figure 5-58. *Multicam overlays with additional information*

Show Audio Clip Names

Turn on *Show Audio Names* in the editing timeline wrench menu so you can see if the audio tracks are multi-camera-enabled, as seen in Figure 5-59.

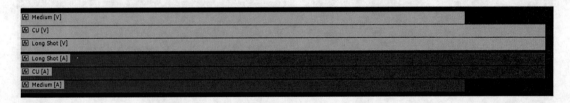

Figure 5-59. *Multicam audio clip names*

Edit Multi-Camera Green Screen Footage

When shooting green screen, as seen in Figures 5-60 and 5-61, you want to see the final result, not just the green screen footage, when cutting. You can do this if you nest all the green screen footage and do the compositing in the nested sequences. Then, create a multi-camera source sequence from the sequences.

Figure 5-60. *Group all your shots into one project bin prior to building your multicam*

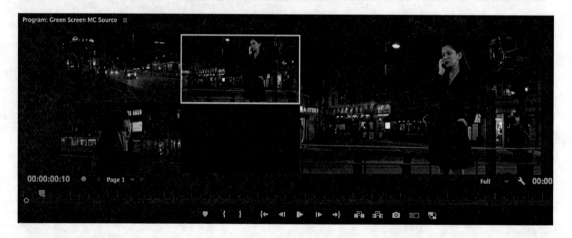

Figure 5-61. *Use the green screen sequences as multicam sources, and you can cut with composite images. Multi-camera footage by Tomas Brekke, Tomas Brekke, Henrik W Møllegård, Stian Løkke Øvrebø, and Daniel Solbakken; Model: Monika Romic.*

Carefully choose your audio options both in the nested sequences and in the multi-camera source sequence.

Import Multiclip Sequences from Final Cut Pro

This is directly from Premiere Pro Help: *You can export a Multiclip project from Final Cut Pro, and import the Final Cut Pro project XML files into Premiere Pro. In Premiere Pro, the Multiclip sequences appear as multi-camera sequences with all the Final Cut Pro project settings intact.*

Use **Multi-Camera ➤ Enable** to un-nest nested sequences that are not multi-camera.

Top-Down Editing

Premiere added a new feature to the multiCam workflow in the 2017 version. Previously, you were stuck with only the lowest-targeted track to create multicam cuts. Now, you can enable top-down multicam editing as seen in Figure 5-62.

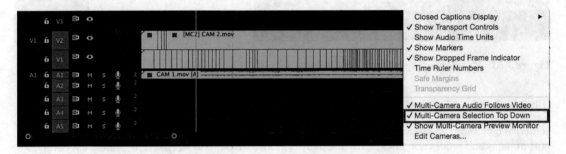

Figure 5-62. Multicam top down

■ **Note** New *Multi-Camera Selection Top Down* item in timeline wing menu to enable top-most targeted track's multicam to show when in multicam mode (default behavior is lowest).

If you enable *Multi-Camera Selection Top Down* from the program monitor gear menu, you can target V2 while making your edits without having to un-target V1. This is very helpful if you have a large amount of cameras and divide up your cameras between multiple multicam nested sequences.

Multicam Un-flatten Tip

Prior to flattening your multicam sequence as seen in Figure 5-63, be sure to duplicate your sequence so you have a safety master to go back to. This will save you from having to search through multiple auto-save versions to get back to the pre-flattened state.

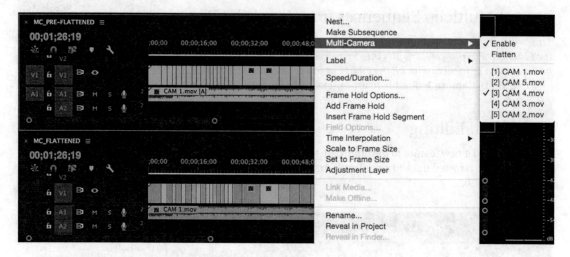

Figure 5-63. *Multicam sequence before and after flattening*

There Is No "Right" Way to Cut Multi-Camera

If there is one thing I've learned from teaching Premiere and After Effects to editors at dozens of broadcast corporations and production houses, it's that there is more than one way to cut multi-camera effectively. What works best for you might not work for another editor because of the source material, the show type, the media management software, the I/O hardware, the network, the way the program will be treated downstream, delivery formats, archive rules, and so on. There are many variables outside of the Premiere Pro timeline that dictate certain workflows.

I have seen people use hybrid workflows where they do use the auto-synchronization part of Create Multi-Camera Source Sequence feature but then flatten all the audio tracks before cutting video only. I've seen editors duplicate all the tracks from the multi-camera source sequence and flatten them before cutting to keep a copy for "the audio people" to work with–multi-camera video with breakout tracks for all the isolated audio, if you want.

I've seen editors create the cutting sequence first, then synchronize the clips in there before nesting the clips and choosing **Multi-camera ➤ Enable.**

I've seen tidy timelines with only a few adaptive tracks, and I've seen timelines with huge numbers of mono tracks. Both ways have advantages and drawbacks.

Now that you have a good understanding of the many possible audio workflows with multi-camera editing, you can build your own workflow that works for you in your ecosystem.

Multi-Camera Gotchas

- One of the most common problems when editing multi-camera is that the editor forgets to make sure the track in the editing sequence that has the multi-camera source sequence on it is not targeted/active.

- Another common problem is that some audio tracks in the multi-camera source sequence are muted without the editor's knowledge.

- Also, quite a few have forgotten to make sure that **Multicam ➤ Enable** is checked on the nested multi-camera source sequence.

- The state of the *Insert and overwrite sequences as nests or individual clips* button in the edit timeline can also be a cause of unexpected behavior.

If you wonder why I haven't mentioned the *Multi-Camera Record* button that's available in the program monitor, it's because I've never found a use for it. I can edit with or without the button active, and I see no difference in behavior. Its only purpose seems to be that it "lights up" when you edit in Multi-Camera mode, which is kind of obsolete since the active camera angle will also have a red border when you edit.

Multicam Undo Gotcha

Hitting *Undo* after performing lots of cuts in a multicam edit will undo **ALL** the edits since you pressed *Play*.

Match to Timecode—Poor Man's Multi-Camera Editing

On a slow system, you may not be able to play back all the angles properly. You can still edit your multicam sources, though, because you can bypass the whole multicam workflow in Premiere! You will not sync the footage, and you will not use the multi-camera monitor. You will not even create a multicam source sequence–just cut linearly using the source monitor as usual.

Use this little-known multi-camera gem found in the source monitor: if you hold down **Ctrl** (Cmd) while switching source clips, you get a Match to Timecode feature. The playhead in the new clip will be parked at the same timecode (TC) as in the one you came from.

So, if you have matching TC on all cameras, this enables you to cut between an unlimited number of cameras even on a slow system! If the shots do not have matching timecode, you can manually set new timecode for the clips with **Clip ➤ Modify ➤ Timecode.**

With a combination of Match Frame editing (**F**) and the Match to Timecode modifier key, you can reliably edit as many streams of video as you want because you only need to play one video stream at a time.

Unfortunately, this doesn't work with the Next and Previous Source Clip keyboard shortcuts for the source monitor, so you'll have to switch sources using the mouse (Figure 5-64).

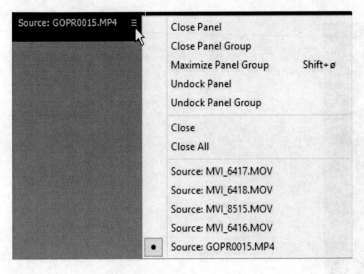

Figure 5-64. *Hold down Ctrl (Cmd) when switching sources from the panel menu in the source monitor and the timecode will match*

Multicam Keyboard Shortcuts

Be sure to customize your keyboard shortcuts when working in multicam mode. The new Keyboard Shortcut interface has many specific multicam shortcuts you can apply to speed up your workflow, as seen in Figures 5-65 and 5-66.

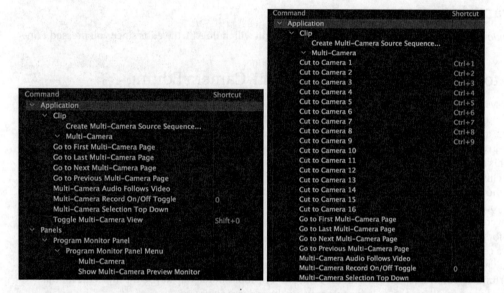

Figure 5-65. *Customizing your shortcut keys can speed up your multicam workflow*

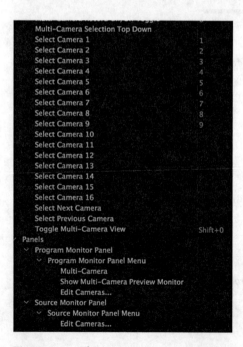

Figure 5-66. *There are many unassigned keyboard shortcuts for multicam in the default keyboard layout*

Convert Multicam Sequence to a Standard Sequence

If you load your multicam nested clip into the source monitor, **Right-click ➤ Multi-Camera➤ uncheck Enable** as seen in Figure 5-67. This step will change your multicam nested clip into a normal sequence in your project panel.

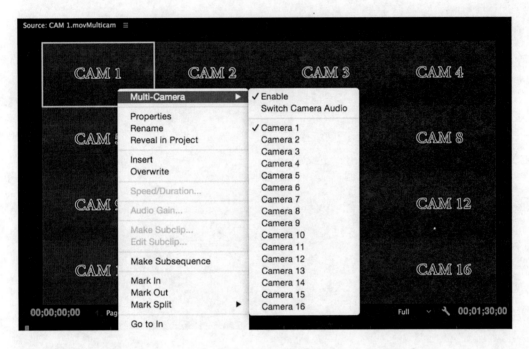

Figure 5-67. *Un-tick Multi-camera ➤ Enable to change the sequence to a normal one*

Multicam with Growing Files

If you are working on a multicam project with growing files, two tips will speed up your workflow. Use Pancake Timelines for your sequences and the keyboard shortcut Extend Previous Edit to Playhead (**Shift+Q**) to update the growing files. This will allow you to bounce between the growing files in one sequence and your multicam in the other. Here is a quick online tutorial by Jon Barrie showing you this technique: youtube.com/watch?v=iWK6vdlezvU.

Summary

The multicam feature in Premiere is very powerful and gets better with each software release. If you edit reality TV, concerts, sports, or any video production with more than one camera, dive into the multicam features to speed up your workflow. Adobe has made syncing multiple camera angles easy. If your camera media has matching timecode or matching audio tracks, or even a slate marker, Adobe Premiere's multicam option gives you the choice on how you want to work.

If you are cutting 4K, 6K, or even 8K multicam, don't forget to use the proxy workflow with your projects so you can cut with faster speed and not bog down your computer system.

CHAPTER 6

■ ■ ■

Color Grading

By Jarle Leirpoll

If your film isn't graded, it isn't finished. Color correction and grading will enhance and stylize your images. Good color grading can make your film shine. Do you think your own films look a bit flat compared to high-end documentaries and blockbuster feature films? That's normal, because you didn't have the same budget for lighting, set design, make-up, and so forth.

But with some clever color grading we can bring some punch back into those shadow areas, enhance or knock back selected color tones, relight the scene, and match scenes shot in different light so they seem to be shot simultaneously. But don't expect miracles. Grading is not a fix-it-all solution for badly shot scenes. It's best when used to enhance a good shot.

We'll take a look at the tools and techniques available for color grading in Premiere (Figure 6-1), and we'll also see how different video formats store color info in different ways–and how this affects how much grading you can do on them. Color grading is a huge topic, so the chapter is long, but in the end, you'll not just know how to correct the white balance; we'll also use color grading as a storytelling tool.

Figure 6-1. *Color grading*

J. Leirpoll et al., *The Cool Stuff in Premiere Pro*, DOI 10.1007/978-1-4842-2890-6_6

Bring Your Images to a New Level of Awesome!

Once, very few people possessed professional color-grading skills. When a proper grading suite cost hundreds of thousands of dollars, naturally there were very few suites, employing very few colorists. Consequently, the whole grading thing was often viewed as a weird science–almost like black magic–not for mere mortals. Today, we all have great color-grading tools inside of Premiere. It's a whole different ballgame!

You Can Use the Monitor You Have

This statement will sound like blasphemy to some colorists, but I'll say it anyway: *You can do pretty good color grading on a pretty standard LED display!* Some high-end colorists will get spasms when they read this. A few of them will disagree loudly because they can afford to disagree. The average filmmaker cannot justify the cost of professional high-end monitors and must make do with what he or she's got. Of course, professional colorists will be able to spot minor flaws in your corrections with their calibrated monitors and scopes, but the average guy might actually think your film looks good!

Of course, a high-end monitor calibrated with a spectrophotometer will offer better viewing, but that doesn't mean you cannot grade on your computer screen. You can–and your footage will look better.

The video camera is a good analogy: even though Arri Alexa and Sony F65 cameras exist, you can still shoot with a Canon DSLR camera and get decent results.

▦ **Note** If your target group is pro colorists or if your films are meant for broadcast, Netflix, or distribution in movie theaters, make sure you do the grading on a professional monitor. If not, use what you have in the best way possible.

Color Correction, Grading, or Look Design?

These terms are used differently by different colorists, and no one owns the right meaning of the word.

▦ **Color correction** can probably best be described as making sure all your shots are consistent and look their best (and that the levels are broadcast safe, if that is important for your distribution/viewing).

The term **color grading** is often used meaning the same as color correction, but some colorists include look creation and secondary color correction in this term.

Look creation is about establishing a time of day, an emotional feeling, a sense of location, or just making the images look cool.

Some will use the term *color correction* for all these processes. So, the confusion is total. Never mind–call it what you want, just make sure your films look good.

Why Do Color Grading in Premiere?

Why not? I have attended both basic and advanced courses on DaVinci Resolve and even on Apple Color back in the day, and there's nothing–I repeat: nothing–that was done during these courses that I cannot do in Premiere. I can do all of it with the same quality and without rendering or conforming. It may take more mouse-clicks and more layers to do it in Premiere, though.

Now that even Premiere can be controlled with sexy control surfaces with nice tracker-ball controls, your choice is one of preference, not necessity. There is one major advantage with dedicated color-grading tools against Premiere, and that is the faster, built-in trackers.

In Premiere, I still need to use the mouse more when grading, and tracking with masks is slow. With the proper use of presets, keyboard shortcuts, and customized workspaces (Figure 6-2), color grading in Premiere works really well.

***Figure 6-2.** A custom color-grading workspace*

Dedicated Grading Software May Cause a Convoluted Workflow

When sending your timelines to most third-party grading software, multi-track timelines, multicam sequences, and nested sequences need to be conformed, meaning you'll have to flatten them into single-layer sequences. Effects need to be removed and recreated. Alternatively, you can render out lossless (or low-loss) video with the effects baked in, and all the cuts must be re-made.

All this conforming takes a lot of time! The round trip is sometimes a bumpy ride and requires lots of manual labor. I prefer spending my time grading instead of conforming and rendering. Why shell out more money, then spend time learning how to use DaVinci, Lustre, Scratch, Baselight, Nucoda, or Pablo and waste time conforming your project to another software, when all the tools you need are there in Premiere?

I'll cover my own color-grading methods in Premiere, but that's certainly not the only way to work. When you know the methods in this chapter, you can develop your own methods and ways to work.

Is This Chapter for You?

This chapter is not for the ultra-high-end users. They already have grading suites with prohibitively expensive monitors, controlled lighting with the right color temperature and brightness, and even the right paint on the walls. They also do their grading in dedicated grading software with dedicated controls. If your high-profile TV series will be aired on national television, or if you're cutting a feature film for cinema release, you should do the grading in a professional, high-end grading suite.

This chapter is written for the other 98 percent of the readers who output their films to the web or Blu-ray and to files for playback on computers and portable devices, and for those who make TV spots, documentaries, or corporate movies. In short: for the rest of us. I'm assuming that buying a new expensive monitor to replace the old one is not an option.

A grading suite is nice, but grading in a normal environment on a standard monitor is still much, much better than no grading at all! If you get rashes at the mere thought of grading on a monitor that costs less than $10,000, this was not written for you.

Want to see my grading techniques in action? Watch my video tutorials on grading in Premiere on premierepro.net.

What About Broadcast-Safe Levels?

■ **Note**   Making the video levels broadcast safe, aka "legalization," is covered in a dedicated section in chapter 10 on Export.

How Much Can You Push It?

This depends heavily on your raw footage. The bit-depth, chroma sampling, and compression all influence how much correction the footage can take. At the low end, DV, HDV, and highly compressed DSLR footage cannot be aggressively corrected because the compression artifacts will limit the headroom you get for correction. Even though the footage looks good before adjustments, artifacts like macro blocks, mosquito noise, posterization, and banding become more visible when you push and pull the colors. Figure 6-3 shows DSLR footage before and after an adjustment, and in the enlarged areas of the man's jacket we see blocks and color noise.

Figure 6-3. *Heavily compressed footage can show severe macro-blocking and banding when levels are raised. (Footage from Egotripp by Kjetil Fredriksen and Jan Olav Nordskog. Actor: Eirik Sandåker)*

In a high-end professional film environment, you will deal with lightly compressed or even RAW formats from Arri Alexa, RED, Sony F65, and other professional cameras with much better chroma sampling, higher bit depth, and sometimes lossless compression.

This kind of material can take a lot of abuse in grading before it falls apart. You can make more extreme adjustments to get better separation between parts of the frame. Figure 6-4 shows 10-bit Log footage with a shadow boost. It has very little blocking and banding when levels are raised as compared to the highly compressed footage in Figure 6-3. To the right is an enlarged portion of the hair and clothing after levels adjustment. That being said, if you have reasonably well-exposed footage even lower quality formats can give nice results.

Figure 6-4. *10-bit Log footage shows very little blocking and banding after raising levels. (Sony PMW-F3 Test Footage courtesy of VortexMedia.com)*

8-bit or 10-bit?

8-bit can look good, and sometimes it's difficult to spot a difference between good 8-bit images and good 10-bit images. But when we start pushing and pulling the material one way or another, the differences quickly show up. The 8-bit material will "fall apart" when we push it too far, but the 10-bit can still look OK due to the much finer increments between levels. 10-bit stores 1024 levels per channel versus the 256 levels of 8-bit. The higher the color bit depth, the higher the color precision.

Karl's "Clicks on a Knob" Analogy

Karl Soulé of Adobe fame used a great analogy to describe the difference between 8-bit and 10-bit video. Think of the bit depth as clicks on a knob. You cannot park the knob between click points. 8-bit gives you 256 clicks, while 10-bit allows for 1024 clicks, resulting in much smaller increments and more precision. See Figure 6-5 for a comparison. 32-bit has an insane four billion plus (4,294,967,296) "clicks on the knob" per channel, and we can even store under-dark and over-bright values. Working at higher bit depth is like having a bigger box of crayons.

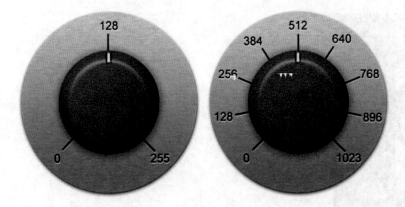

Figure 6-5. *A higher bit depth means more "clicks on the knob" and higher precision when doing adjustments*

What Is YUV?

Most video formats keep the data rate low by sampling the color information less accurately than the luminance (black-and-white info). This is known as chroma subsampling. We can do this because the rods and cones in our eyes give us much more detailed vision for luminance than for colors. So, an image with great luminance detail and low color detail will still look sharp to us.

Since all three R, G, and B channels from the image sensor contribute to the color information, we need a way to separate the luminance info and the color info to treat them independently.

A method for this was already invented to ensure compatibility between analog color TV and black-and-white TV when color TV was introduced. A simple equation calculates the luminance signal, Y, and two color signals, U and V, from the RGB channels. Figures 6-6 and 6-7 show three images separated this way.

Figure 6-6. *The luminance channel and two color channels (color separation images made by Anders T. Leirpoll in MATLAB using code from Michael Tandy)*

Figure 6-7. *Two more images showing how almost all info on detail comes from the luminance channel*

Actually, these are terms used for analog video, and we should use the term YCbCr for digital video, but most of the time people say YUV, even for digital video.

Chroma Compression via Subsampling

When the signal is split into a luminance component (Y) and two color components (U and V), we can use fewer ones and zeros to describe each color channel. This is what chroma subsampling is: resolution compression of the color channels. So, the term *uncompressed video* is very misleading for formats that use 4:2:0 or 4:2:2 sampling, since 1/2 or 3/4 of the chroma channels have already been thrown away when the encoding starts!

You see it everywhere. JPG images and most H.264 material is sampled with 4:2:0; even high-end video formats use 4:2:2 sampling. Only the very best formats use 4:4:4, meaning all the channels have the same resolution, so no subsampling is used.

Chroma subsampling throws away half or one-fourth of the color info. 4:4:4 means that the chroma channels are sampled at the same rate as the luminance channel. 4:2:2 means that the chroma channels are sampled at half the rate of the luminance channel; data rate is reduced by 33.3 percent. 4:2:0 means that the chroma channels are sampled at one-quarter of the rate of the luminance channel; data rate is reduced by 50 percent. Figure 6-8 visualizes chroma subsampling.

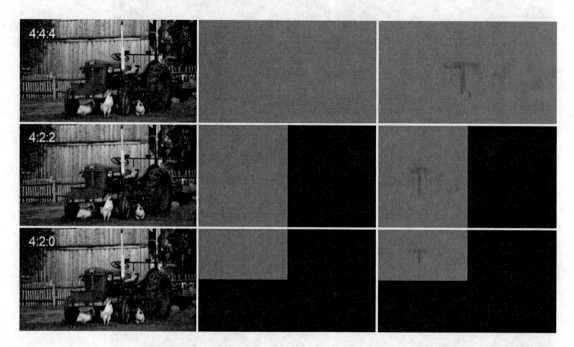

Figure 6-8. *Color subsampling data savings, visualized (color separation images made by Anders T. Leirpoll in MATLAB using code from Michael Tandy)*

4:4:4 RGB sampling is the Gold Standard. If you encounter the term 4:4:4:4, it means that the file also has an alpha channel sampled at full resolution. There are other ways of sampling/compressing the CbCr channels for 4:2:2 and 4:2:0 subsampling (particularly on the 4:2:2); the ones shown here are just the best visual representation of the data rate comparison. Figure 6-9 illustrates how 4:2:0 sampling results in half the data rate.

Figure 6-9. *4:2:0 color subsampling halves the data rate*

For basic viewing of video, 4:2:0 is fine, and for grading, 4:2:2 is preferred. But when we start doing things like chroma keying, reduced chroma resolution will, of course, cause reduced edge quality in the keyed image. Nothing can beat 4:4:4 for keying.

Bit-Depth Confusion

In forums and comment fields you will find endless discussions along the lines of *"What's the best capturing formats for editing, when target is 4K on YouTube"*? Some will recommend ProRes 4444 or ProRes422HQ, some will mention DNxHR, some will speak highly of some special camera, and so on. So, what's the answer? I think Steve Hullfish (author of many books on color correction) put it well in one forum:

> *It all depends on how far you have to push the color correction. End delivery is not the main factor in answering the question.*

The more you want to push the color grading, the higher bit depth you will need.

Lin, Log, and RAW Formats Explained

First, let me say that Log has nothing to do with RAW (it's a common misconception). If you spend any time in professional online forums or groups on color grading, you will quickly see a lot of confusion about RAW formats, Log versus linear capture, bit-depth, and so on. I'll guide you through all this now so you can avoid confusion and make good choices when grading these formats. We'll start with an explanation of Log video.

Why We Get Clipped Highlights and Crushed and Noisy Blacks

Because of the linear nature of most video formats and the limitations in image sensors, the highlights will often be blown out when the midtones are correctly exposed, while the shadows have a lot of noise and lack detail. But why? Linear sampling uses a lot of bits to describe the high levels, while lower levels get very few bits. Result: Noisy shadows and blown-out highs. Figure 6-10 shows a simplified but still somewhat accurate technical introduction to image capture and processing.

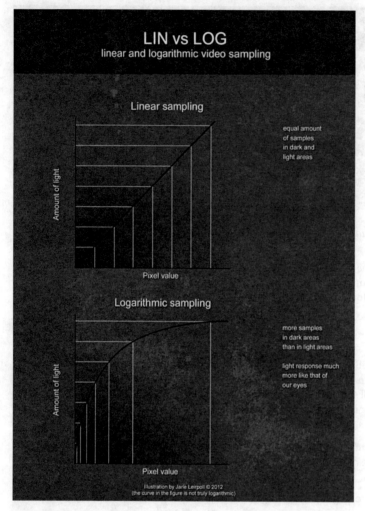

Figure 6-10. *Log and Lin sampling based on amount of light*

How Cameras Interpret Image Data

Most image sensors count photons in a linear way. The analog output voltage of each pixel is determined directly by how many photons it receives. Twice as many photons will double the output voltage. Four times the number of photons means the output voltage is quadrupled, and so forth. This analog voltage is then converted to 8-bit or 10-bit digital numbers.

This would be great if it wasn't for the fact that our eyes don't work in the same way! Our eyes do not interpret twice as many photons as twice as much light. Rather, they work in a logarithmic way, and what image sensors measure as 12.5 percent gray, our eyes may think is around 50 percent gray.

Linear Image Capture

Digital cameras traditionally take this linear analog image data from the sensor and store it in a linear way. The result is that we use a lot of bits sampling the lighter part of the image, while the darkest parts are sampled in very coarse steps. Each f-stop in photography represents twice the light of the previous stop, so half of the bits are used sampling the upper f-stop. Then half the remaining bits are used for the next f-stop, and so on. I've tried to illustrate this in Figure 6-10.

Additionally, very few bits (sometimes none) are used for over-brights and blacker-than-blacks. This is the main reason why low-bit linear video often looks inferior to film–the blacks are crushed and the whites are clipped! That's also why a standard 8-bit video file is often unusable for aggressive grading, especially when underexposed. There are simply too few bits and bytes describing the shadows, so we get lots of noise and artifacts.

Log Image Capture to the Rescue

Digital cinema cameras have a much wider dynamic range than can be shown in sRGB or Rec709, the standards for computer monitors and HD TV screens respectively. Modern camera sensors can capture at least 12–13 bits of image info. This info is often temporarily stored internally as a 16-bit linear image. To capture this image quality with fewer zeros and ones, Log gammas are used, allowing for far more image manipulation in post-production. Logarithmic sampling spreads the bits more evenly so we can get a higher dynamic range with cleaner shadows and more detail in the highlights. See Figure 6-11.

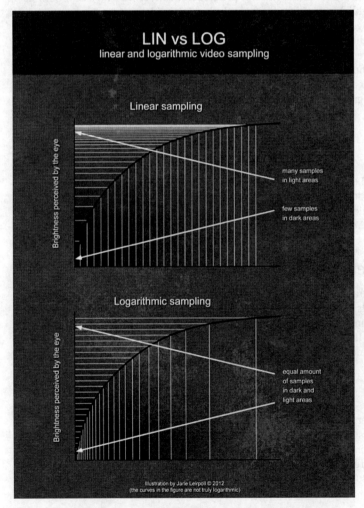

Figure 6-11. Log and Lin sampling based on perceived brightness

421

Log capture mimics the eye's nonlinear response to light. The sampling is done more evenly throughout the whole dynamic range, giving each f-stop a somewhat equal number of values. So, we have a lot more shadow detail that can be retrieved while grading. There's also more room for over-brights and under-blacks; white can be set to 685, not 1023, and black to 95, not zero. Log files are often 10-bit or more, too, and that gives us even more latitude in the grading process. If you want maximum latitude when grading, 10-bit (or higher) Log is the best method to hold that dynamic range. The end result is much better images after grading.

To represent a 16-bit linear image in a 10-bit container, Log is smart when data rates and storage are sparse. Linear files would need to be 13-bit or more to match the latitude of a 10-bit Log file. Visually, 10-bit Log coding is roughly equivalent to 12-bit Rec709 coding.

Some high-end cameras, like the Sony F65, can store their images in 16-bit linear fashion, avoiding the Log-to-Lin conversion. More bits means you'll need more storage, but storage keeps getting cheaper.

Log Is Basically a Gamma Curve

Camera operators are familiar with gamma curves. Even semi-pro cameras can record with a CineGamma setting to get a nicer roll-off in the highlights, avoid clamping in the blacks, and lower contrast to get an image that is more suitable for grading.

The S-Log, Log-C, and REDLog that some cameras offer are essentially extreme gamma curves. A simple S-curve or a LUT in Premiere reverses the Log transform and brings the image back to linear space that computer screens and TVs can show correctly. Recording with Log gamma means you'll *have to* do some grading in post. You will even need to use de-log curves for watching your dailies and getting a general idea of how the footage looks. Before grading, Log looks flat and desaturated, but the blacks and whites are well protected.

Working with Log Material

Quite simple, actually! When editing Log footage, first apply a preset or a LUT that gets the levels in the ballpark. Then, use additional correction tools to tweak as usual. I have made Curves presets for the most common Log formats, which I can quickly apply to an adjustment layer on the entire timeline. These can be downloaded from premierepro.net. You can also find lots of free conversion LUTs on the net.

Tweaking the Camera Settings for Better Grading

You can always add contrast and saturation in post, but it's hard to remove them if they cause clipping, so make sure your camera profile records images with good latitude without crushed blacks and blown-out whites. Most professionals apply a camera setup that captures flat, low-contrast images. Your goal is to protect your highlights and shadows. If you're not shooting your own material, maybe you can talk to the Director of Photography and offer some valuable advice on picture profiles, gamma settings, and exposure.

Standard Gamma Settings

Standard gamma settings in the camera will record punchy images and good contrast so the footage is immediately ready for viewing and distribution without correction. This can be very useful for sports and news stories, especially when using formats where sequences can be smart-rendered out of Premiere when no effects are added. Using these, there's a good chance you'll lose detail in highlights and shadows if the footage isn't perfectly well exposed. But you can work very fast in post.

Cine-like Gamma Settings

Film-like gammas deliver lower contrast, lower saturation images with more dynamic range and latitude. These images need to be color corrected in post to look good. Use film-type gammas for material where image quality is more important than editing speed.

Log Space If Possible

As explained earlier, logarithmic profiles can store the image data in a much more clever way, and as a result you get a better image. There's a downside though: Log-scale images are flat and boring and require grading before you can see how they actually look. Courtesy of the hardware-accelerated color-correction effects in Premiere, this is no longer a problem.

Log isn't just for the ultra-high-end anymore; you can even do Log capture with cheap DSLRs. Pure joy!

Recording Format

If you need maximum control in post, consider shooting in at least 10-bit 4:2:2 or a RAW format like RED, or go crazy and record uncompressed 4:4:4 16-bit Log if your hardware can cope with it and you need the color resolution to get that perfect green-screen key.

If you have more modest demands, 8-bit formats are still used on more budget-friendly cameras. This is OK if you don't need to do aggressive color grading and approach the material with some care. Actually, looking back, I've made most of my films with 8-bit recordings–and I modestly think some of them look pretty darn good. When recording in 8-bit, getting the exposure right is very important.

Expose to the Right

Because of the way sensors translate the light into pixels with linear capture, darkening an image is a much safer operation than lightening it. You may be tempted to underexpose to avoid blown-out highlights, but if you do, you need to raise the gamma in post, introducing noise and posterization in the midtones and shadows–very noticeable when recording 8-bit video.

As a general rule, it's wise to expose as close to blowing out the highlights as you can without actually clipping them. Blown-out isn't always blown-out either! You can often retain some detail in the highlights because many codecs store what's called over-brights or super-whites–levels above 100 percent white.

■ **Note**   Exposing to the right means your highlights fall as close to the right side of the histogram as possible without clipping.

A blown-out window from an 8-bit camera can be darkened with secondary color correction, but there will not be much texture in the exterior. Of course, with native RAW or Log material you may be able to darken that blown-out window and magically get back the people, buildings, foliage, and sky outside.

LUTS

A LUT (look-up table) in its simplest form is a pre-defined table that can be represented by a curve, often an S-curve that brings the flat Log image back to a proper gamma-corrected one. In Figure 6-12, we can see how the 256 different levels in an 8-bit Technicolor's CineStyle S-Log file should be interpreted in linear space. If the level for a pixel is 32 in the Log image, it's displayed as 10. If it's 230, it's displayed as 249.

In	Out	In	Out	In	Out	In	Out	In	Out
0	0	52	26	104	92	156	172	208	235
1	0	53	26	105	93	157	173	209	235
2	0	54	27	106	95	158	175	210	236
3	0	55	28	107	96	159	176	211	237
4	0	56	29	108	98	160	178	212	238
5	0	57	30	109	99	161	179	213	239
6	0	58	32	110	101	162	181	214	239
7	0	59	33	111	102	163	182	215	240
8	0	60	34	112	104	164	183	216	241
9	1	61	35	113	105	165	185	217	242
10	1	62	36	114	107	166	186	218	242
11	1	63	37	115	109	167	188	219	243
12	1	64	38	116	110	168	189	220	244
13	1	65	39	117	112	169	190	221	244
14	2	66	40	118	113	170	192	222	245
15	2	67	41	119	115	171	193	223	246
16	2	68	43	120	116	172	194	224	246
17	3	69	44	121	118	173	196	225	247
18	3	70	45	122	119	174	197	226	247
19	3	71	46	123	121	175	198	227	248
20	4	72	47	124	123	176	200	228	248
21	4	73	49	125	124	177	201	229	249
22	5	74	50	126	126	178	202	230	249
23	5	75	51	127	127	179	204	231	250
24	5	76	52	128	129	180	205	232	250
25	6	77	54	129	130	181	206	233	251
26	6	78	55	130	132	182	207	234	251
27	7	79	56	131	134	183	209	235	252
28	8	80	58	132	135	184	210	236	252
29	8	81	59	133	137	185	211	237	252
30	9	82	60	134	138	186	212	238	253
31	9	83	62	135	140	187	213	239	253
32	10	84	63	136	141	188	214	240	253
33	10	85	64	137	143	189	216	241	253
34	11	86	66	138	145	190	217	242	254
35	12	87	67	139	146	191	218	243	254
36	12	88	68	140	148	192	219	244	254
37	13	89	70	141	149	193	220	245	254
38	14	90	71	142	151	194	221	246	255
39	15	91	73	143	152	195	222	247	255
40	15	92	74	144	154	196	223	248	255
41	16	93	75	145	155	197	224	249	255
42	17	94	77	146	157	198	225	250	255
43	18	95	78	147	158	199	226	251	255
44	18	96	80	148	160	200	227	252	255
45	19	97	81	149	161	201	228	253	255
46	20	98	83	150	163	202	229	254	255
47	21	99	84	151	164	203	230	255	255
48	22	100	86	152	166	204	231		
49	23	101	87	153	167	205	232		
50	24	102	89	154	169	206	233		
51	25	103	90	155	170	207	234		

Figure 6-12. *LUT for Canon Cinestyle*

Don't worry too much about getting *The Perfect LUT.*™ Since the whole point of using Log in the first place is to enhance the quality of the image *after* grading, you'll probably never need a pixel-perfect, accurate representation of the image from the camera. IWLTBAP explain LUTs well on their blog:

A LUT, for Look-Up Table, is a file containing math instructions to replace a color by another one. It's like a color grading preset. This process is done pixel by pixel with a very high accuracy.

You can find their free conversion LUT package on their web site (see Figure 6-13): luts.iwltbap.com/ free-lut-log-to-rec709-and-rec709-to-log-conversion/.

Alexa Log-C to Rec.709

BMDFilm 4K to Alexa Log-C

BMDFilm BMCC to Rec.709

BMDFilm BMPC to Rec.709

BMDFilm BMPCC to Rec.709

BMDFilm URSA to Rec.709

Canon C-Log to Rec.709

Generic LOG to Rec.709

Generic Rec.709 to LOG

GoPro Protune to Video

Panasonic Cine-D to Rec.709

Panasonic V-Log to Rec.709

REDLog to Rec.709

REDLogFilm to Rec.709

Sony S-Log2 to Rec.709

Sony S-Log3 to Rec.709

Technicolor CineStyle to Rec.709

Figure 6-13. *LUTs by IWLTBAP: Free LUTs from IWLTBAP*

A quick Google search will return a huge list of LUT providers. Premiere supports many different LUT formats in Lumetri Color (Figure 6-14). The most common are probably .cube and .3dl.

LUTs (*.cube;*.itx;*.lut;*.ilut;*.irlut;*.fccp;*.3dl;*.txt;*.cc;*.cdl)

Figure 6-14. *LUTs supported: Premiere supports many different LUT formats*

For a fun video explaining LUTs with cats (!), watch youtube.com/watch?v=XgL1Z7tsBz8.

LUTs Are Not Magic

Now, LUTs are not magical and will not make all your shots look great. It kind of assumes that you have a perfectly exposed and white-balanced image–or Log image, if you're applying a Log to Rec709 LUT.

If you apply a LUT to footage that it's not meant for, the results will be poor. For a LUT to work as expected, your image needs to have a certain exposure and saturation, and no color cast. Throwing a LUT on a badly exposed shot or a shot with a color cast will not give you a good result.

■ **Note**   A conversion/correction LUT (also known as Input LUT) should be applied before you do any tweaking. A creative LUT (also known as Look) expects normal levels, color, and contrast and should be applied after you've corrected/tweaked the image.

Working with Input LUTs

Premiere works in Rec709 color space–the color space for HDTV. If you work with footage that's not Rec709, like Log footage, you can apply an Input LUT that converts the footage into the Rec709 color space. If you apply a Lumetri effect with just that input LUT on your master files, rather than on each clip, life gets much easier. With the Input LUT in place, Lumetri will operate as expected.

Some colorists recommend that you apply the conversion LUT on an adjustment layer and do your adjustments on the clips below. I do not recommend this. The controls in Lumetri are expecting standard gamma, not Log, and adjusting parameters under an adjustment layer with the conversion LUT will be difficult because the controls will not be very precise.

Use Input LUTs with Lumetri

To add a technical correction LUT (Input LUT) to a clip, use the Input LUT drop-down menu in the Basic Correction section of the Lumetri Color panel, as shown in Figure 6-15. You can also set this in the Lumetri effect in the Effect Controls panel. Note that the Input LUTs that you apply here are applied before the sliders and other controls.

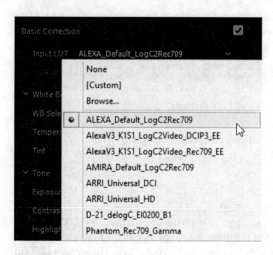

Figure 6-15. *Lumetri Input LUTs*

Find More Input LUTs

There are very few LUTs in the default list in Premiere. It used to be a lot longer. You can still find the old ones if you click the Input LUT pull-down menu and browse to the folder containing the legacy LUTs: C:\Program Files\Adobe\Adobe Premiere Pro CC 2017\Lumetri\LUTs\Legacy. On MacOS, it's Applications/Premiere Pro CC 2015/Show Package Contents/Lumetri/ LUTs/Legacy. See Figure 6-16. You can also copy these to a more convenient folder, like a LUTs folder on your desktop.

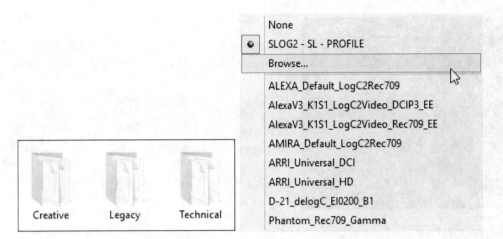

Figure 6-16. *There are three subfolders in the Lumetri LUTs folder. You'll find the old ones in the Legacy folder.*

Using this technique, you can of course navigate to any LUT of your choice. You could also just copy the LUTs you want into the `Technical` folder, and it will appear in the default list, but Adobe advises against this, as some LUTs are known to make Premiere unstable. Also, if you do this, remember to place a duplicate of the same LUTs in Adobe Media Encoder's LUTs folder. See the following.

I prefer to keep the custom LUTs in a dedicated folder elsewhere on my system that can be used by both Premiere and Adobe Media Encoder.

It's about time we take a look at how a LUT can change an image. Log footage looks washed-out and dull before grading. It needs an S-curve or an Input LUT to convert it to linear space. Figure 6-17 shows Log footage before and after adding a correction LUT.

Figure 6-17. *Log footage before and after LUT. Sony PMW-F3 S-Log Test Footage courtesy of VortexMedia.com.*

Use Looks in Lumetri

You can also apply LUTs in the Creative section in the Lumetri Color panel. Here, they're called *looks* to distinguish them from the *Input LUTs* that you add in the Basic Corrections section. To add a creative Look, use the Look drop-down menu in the Creative section of the Lumetri Color panel, or click the arrows to try out the different looks (Figure 6-18). Again, if your desired look is not in the list, click *Browse* and point to your favorite Looks folder.

Figure 6-18. *Creative Look*

A LUT or a Look cannot be edited in Premiere, but you can adjust the intensity of a Look and use all the tools in the Lumetri Color panel to tweak the image after adding LUTs.

Export a LUT from Lumetri

Since a LUT is just a preset, you can create your own LUT by making adjustments to your footage in the Lumetri Color panel and then exporting them as a .cube or .look file from the panel menu (Figure 6-19). The LUTs you export can be used in any color-grading software, so you can exchange LUTs with people who don't use Premiere.

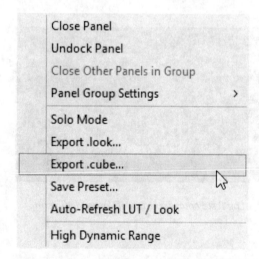

Figure 6-19. *LUTs export*

If you use your LUT as an Input LUT in the Basic Correction section, you can't adjust anything. If you use it as a Look in the Creative section, you can only adjust the intensity. All the sliders and wheels are set to their default settings, so you cannot see what adjustments were made to create that look. To make further adjustments to a clip with a LUT, use any other control in Lumetri.

■ **Note** There's one big difference between LUTs and Lumetri presets: You cannot adjust a LUT!

If you want to see the settings used in your looks, save your adjustments as Lumetri presets instead, using the *Save Preset* choice in the panel menu. The sliders and wheels will then reflect how the Look was achieved, but the preset will only work in Premiere.

Create a LUT in Photoshop

If you're using the color-correction tools in Photoshop on stills, you may want to reuse your corrections in Premiere. Follow these steps to export a LUT and then use it in Lumetri as usual.

First, create your grade in Photoshop. You can use as many adjustments as you like (Figure 6-20). Click **File ➤ Export ➤ Color Lookup Tables**, then choose the format and quality (Figure 6-21).

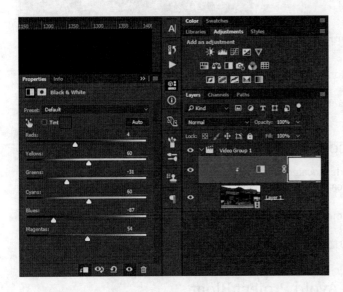

Figure 6-20. *Make your color adjustments in Photoshop*

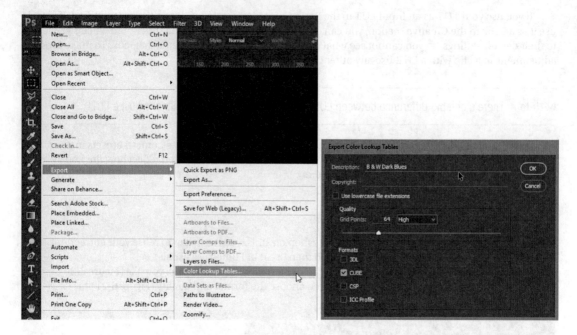

Figure 6-21. *Export the LUT and choose format and quality settings*

For some reason, the file must have a locked Background layer for the LUT export to work. If you don't have one, you can create one. Click **Layer ➤ New ➤ Layer** and move it to the bottom of the layer stack. Then, select it and click **Layer ➤ New ➤ Background from Layer**. Then, export the LUT from the new file.

LUTs and Adobe Media Encoder—A Possible Gotcha

Adobe Media Encoder has its own LUTs folder, located at C:\Program Files\Adobe\Adobe Media Encoder CC 2017\Lumetri\LUTs. On MacOS, Applications/ Adobe Media Encoder CC 2017/Show Package Contents/Lumetri/ LUTs.

So, if you place custom LUTs or move the existing ones around in Premiere's LUTs folders, you must do the same in Adobe Media Encoder's folders. If you don't, the LUTs will be missing in Adobe Media Encoder, and your export will be done without the LUT–and, unfortunately, without a warning.

Remove Arri Amira LUTs to Avoid Project Bloat

Some clips from Arri Amira cameras may have a LUT automatically applied to them at import. This happens when the camera associates a LUT when the recording is done. Sometimes, the camera operator does this without knowing it, and other times it's because they want a certain look on the footage.

These LUTs are big, and if you're running in software-only mode, this could slow down things immensely. If you want to temporarily disable these, select all the clips in a bin, right-click, and choose *Disable Masterclip Effects* (Figure 6-22). Be warned, though–you will have to re-enable Master Clip effects manually on each clip one by one; there is no way to re-enable them all in one go.

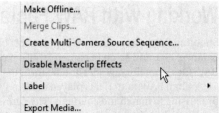

Figure 6-22. *Disable Masterclip Effects on AMIRA footage*

But, you may want to remove the Amira LUT altogether, because they're known to cause project bloat, meaning your project file (.prproj) will increase in size–a lot. This can slow down the project and even cause instability and crashes. To remove a Master Clip effect, you can open the clip in the source monitor and go to the Master tab in the Effects Control panel. Delete the Lumetri effect there.

Or, you can select an Input LUT other than the Amira for one clip, and then change to None. Save a Lumetri preset and add that preset to all clips as a Master Clip effect. Your project bloat should now be gone. Paul Murphy has a good video tutorial on this: vimeo.com/137902501.

Auto-Refresh LUT/Look

Figure 6-23 shows this setting in the Lumetri Color panel menu. This allows the looks and LUTs to be updated every time you open a project. This means you (or someone else on your team) can modify the LUT on your disk, and the changes will auto-update the next time you open the project.

Figure 6-23. *Auto-refresh LUT*

This is an application preference, so it's *not* stored per project. It affects all your projects.

Working with RAW Footage

Shooting RAW means that we bypass most of the in-camera processing. Instead of committing to white balance, ISO, and so on in camera, those parameters are stored as metadata that you can manipulate in post. RAW files store the raw sensor data from the camera without any additional processing.

When RAW material is played back in Premiere, it goes through decoding and de-Bayering, plus color processing to match the channels. The camera has set default settings to all parameters, but you can decide to make other choices for color processing and so forth. This is done in the Source settings.

Source Settings for RAW Formats

The idea of Source settings is to get the levels within a workable range and as good as possible before you start the actual grading. Source settings for all RAW formats are found in the Effect Controls panel under the Master tab.

■ **Note**   If you tweak the Source settings to get a particular look, it's not adding to the CPU or GPU load, and it is using the full bit depth of the file.

The Source settings available for the different formats vary, from the incredibly detailed settings for RED RAW to the very limited settings for Sony RAW. Figures 6-24 and 6-25 show Source settings for four different RAW formats.

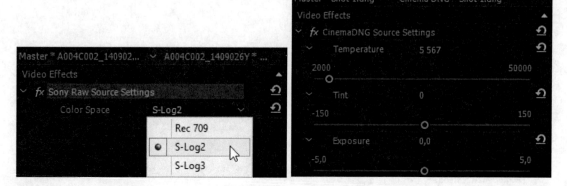

Figure 6-24. *Source settings for Sony RAW and CinemaDNG*

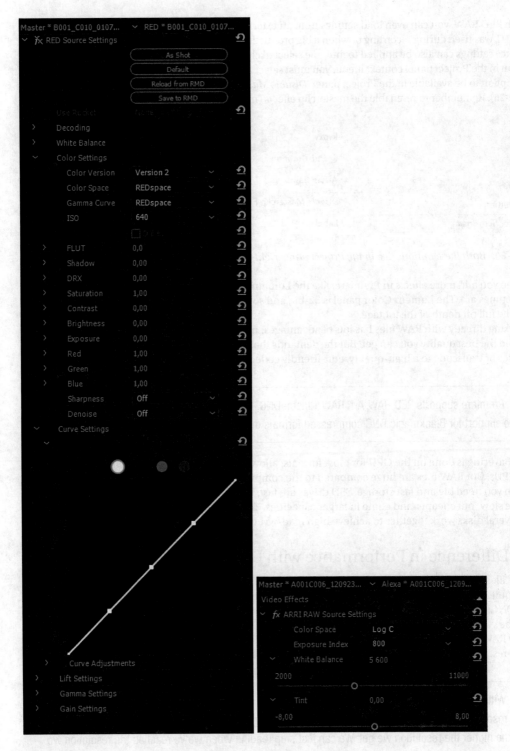

Figure 6-25. Source settings for RED RAW and ArriRAW

With RED RAW, you can even load settings from an external RED metadata file (.rmd). This is useful if a special LUT was used during recording or when a big production requires every editor to use the same settings.

Source settings can also be applied to multiple selected clips in the Project panel. If *Source Settings* is grayed out in the Project panel context menu, you must select *Disable Masterclip Effects* to get the *Source Settings* option to be available in the Project panel. *Disable Masterclip Effects* is found in the same context menu (Figure 6-26). Remember to re-enable the masterclip effects (manually for each clip) when you're done.

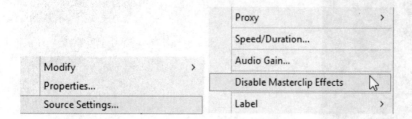

Figure 6-26. *Both these options live in the Project panel right-click menu*

When you add more effects in Premiere, like the Lumetri effect, they will stack on top of whatever your Source settings are. The Lumetri Color panel is 32-bit, and so are many other color-correction effects. These will use the full bit depth of the footage.

Working directly with RAW files has lots of advantages: no transcoding, no extra files to fill up your drives, and the best quality you can get. But the demands that RAW files put on your system may force you to use proxies or transcode to a high-quality, edit-friendly codec.

■ **Note**   Premiere supports RED RAW, Arri RAW, CinemaDNG, Canon RAW, Sony RAW, and Phantom Cine. There's no support for Blackmagic DNG compressed formats or camera, lens, and slate metadata.

De-Bayering is done on the GPU for most formats, allowing RAW editing even on laptops that have decent GPUs. But RAW files are huge compared to the compressed formats that most consumer cameras record, so you need big and fast storage. SSD drives are fast, but quite expensive at large capacities. Hard drives are slow, but cheaper and come in larger capacities. The most cost-effective solution will be a RAID where several disks work together to achieve high read/write speed.

Huge Difference in Performance with Different RAW Formats

Arri RAW files are tough on the system, so you'll probably need to lower the resolution of your program monitor quite a bit to avoid dropping frames, but your system may still struggle just reading the files. Editing CinemaDNG, which is what you get from BlackMagic Cinema cameras, is also a heavy task, and Sony RAW can also be very tough on the system.

RED RAW, on the other hand, uses Wavelets to compress the RAW files, which means it's super easy to read half-res, quarter-res, and lower resolutions. What's the deal with wavelet compression?

■ **Note**   With other compression methods, we must read and decode the whole image, and after this we can lower the resolution in the program monitor. With wavelet compression, it's different. The further into the data we read, the higher the resolution we get. We can just stop reading when we've reached the resolution we need. It's ingenious!

To lower the resolution that Premiere reads, just drop the playback resolution in the program monitor (and source monitor), and it all happens automatically. Very slick.

The same can be achieved with the UltraPix JPEG 2000 codec accelerator from Comprimato, since JPEG 2000 also uses wavelet compression.

Cinestyle vs. RAW

The Cinestyle picture style from Canon has been very popular and is basically a semi-Log curve that gives you more latitude for grading. But don't confuse Cinestyle with RAW. With Magic Lantern (a third-party firmware for some Canon DSLRs; see magiclantern.fm), you can enable video recording in RAW format to your Canon DSLR–and that's when you'll see the difference in resolution, latitude, and quality.

Compare the two images in Figure 6-27; you'll see that, when shooting RAW, it's like you've removed a veil from the lens. The H.264 compression and the applied low-pass filter makes the H.264 Cinestyle footage muddy compared to the RAW footage, which has a lot more clarity. Of course, the DNG RAW files are huge and demand a juicy computer.

Figure 6-27. *Cinestyle and RAW comparison; Canon 5D test footage by Jon Andreas Sanne*

32-bit Magic

When you're color grading, it's your recording codec, not Premiere, that's the weakest link. When using hardware acceleration with CUDA, Metal, or OpenCL, everything is converted to uncompressed 4:4:4:4, 32-bit float before effect calculations are done. You simply can't beat that level of color accuracy and image quality with any existing codec! 32-bit float extended color space is simply unmatched for color fidelity and dynamic range.

Adjusting video degrades it in three ways: clipping, tonal compression, and tonal expansion. If you adjust the black or white sliders in Levels or the obsolete RGB curves, you're clipping the signal. If you drag the gray slider (gamma) to the right, you're compressing the highlights and expanding the shadows, leading to spikes and gaps when you watch the histogram. We need to keep the degradation as low as possible. 32-bit to the rescue!

It's a Matter of Accuracy

Every conversion of material stands the chance of introducing rounding errors. Rounding errors show up in the image as dithering, noise, banding, and general loss of quality, so is to be avoided. Doing the math in 10-bit reduces the errors to a certain extent, but to make them completely negligible, Premiere works in 32-bit. The color accuracy is almost unfathomable, and the only rounding errors will be at the very last stage when we output to an 8-bit or 10-bit file format.

Transcoding Does Not Increase Quality

Most video pros know that 10-bit holds up better in post than 8-bit does. From this very true fact, some make the very wrong assumption that transcoding your 8-bit source material to a 10-bit intermediate format will make it hold up better in post.

Sorry, but transcoding to 10-bit will not magically increase the bit depth of the material. This practice is obsolete knowledge from the time when older NLEs did calculations in 8- or 10-bit, depending on the source material. It's simply not true when working in 32-bit in Premiere.

It will increase your file sizes, waste valuable time, and fill up your disks. Bad idea! Premiere works directly from the source file, and that is the best data you can get. It's the original, and nothing can be better. Quite logical, actually.

You might have other reasons to transcode, of course, like transcoding long-gop material to an intra-frame codec to get smoother scrubbing and better performance on a slow computer, but that's got nothing to do with color precision.

You can read more about this and watch sample videos at premierepro.net/workflow/transcode-not-transcode/.

See the 32-bit Magic in Action

Most people don't see any problems when color grading in 8-bit, so they assume it's OK. This is because they don't know how it would look in 32-bit, and they may not have pushed the grading hard enough to make the differences obvious. Aggressively raising the levels with one correction and then lowering it back with another exposes the huge difference in color accuracy in 8-bit versus 32-bit.

Clipped and Crushed Levels

Put one clip on the timeline and add two copies of the obsolete fast color corrector effect or the levels effect. Now, drag Input White to 128 on the first effect. Your image will be severely blown out in the whites.

Now, on the second effect, drag Output White to 128. This should cancel out the first color corrector, and the image should look normal again, right? Not so in 8-bit. When you set the project to "Software Only," the sequence defaults to 8-bit. Make sure it's not set to Maximum Bit Depth in Sequence settings, and the image is useless, destroyed, after rendering. You've just witnessed the destructive powers of 8-bit video processing. Figure 6-28 shows the original footage and the results after the first and second levels adjustment. Figure 6-29 shows the scopes at each step.

Figure 6-28. *Original footage and the results after two instances of levels adjustment in 8-bit mode*

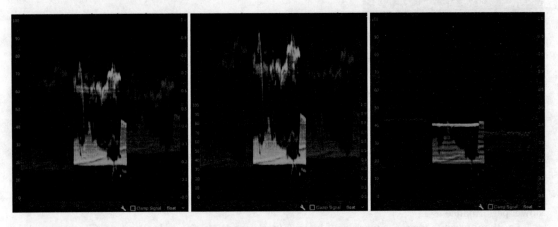

Figure 6-29. *The RGB Parade scope for the steps in Figure 6-27*

So, how can we fix this problem? By working in 32-bit! The best way is by adding an approved graphics card to your system and making sure the Video Rendering and Playback settings are set to *Mercury Playback Engine GPU Acceleration—CUDA* (or *OpenCL* or *Metal*, depending on your card). Then, everything will be rendered in 32-bit with glorious colors by default, and your image will look good again. Figure 6-30 shows the Renderer choice in the Project settings and the scope and final image after switching to GPU rendering. Raising and lowering the levels in 32-bit mode is nondestructive, keeping all the detail in the highlights. Compare this to the 8-bit result in Figure 6-28, and you will never grade in 8-bit again.

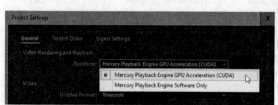

Figure 6-30. *When using GPU acceleration, you're grading in 32-bit and avoid clipping*

If you don't have such a card, salvation is still just a few mouse-clicks away! **Sequence ➤ Sequence Settings** will open a dialog box. Check the *Maximum Bit Depth* box. Premiere will give you a warning, telling you that all preview files will be deleted. Click *OK*, and the good image is back, at least when you park the playhead. When you hit *Play*, it turns bad again, unless you've checked *High-Quality Playback* in the program monitor panel menu. This setting puts a big workload on the CPU. Expect longer render times and slower performance.

So, it's more cumbersome to work in 32-bit in Software mode. You'll need to render to see the actual result on a slow system. You'll also have to check that *Render at Maximum Depth* is checked in the Export settings. If it's not, your export will be rendered in 8-bit and will look different from what you saw in the timeline! See Figure 6-31 for the Sequence settings and Export settings for max bit depth—and the result with and without max bit depth set in Export settings.

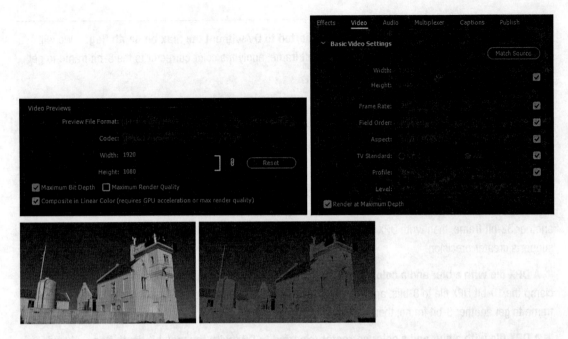

Figure 6-31. *In Software mode, you must set max bit depth in both Sequence settings and Export settings*

In Software mode, this means your render times will be longer and the performance of your system will drop. With an approved GPU, everything just flies, even in 32-bit.

Of course, you wouldn't want to apply two layers of opposite color correction like this. This is an extreme case built to show the difference clearly. But when you use more than one effect or color-correction tool, when you create looks with additional correction on adjustment layers, and when nesting, you'll be working with intermediate clipped and crushed levels. If you're making a trailer of your film, you might even put another Look on that, or maybe some kind of vignette. The possibilities for inadvertently clipping and crushing levels are limitless when working in 8-bit. So don't.

YUV?

As mentioned, technically speaking, the term *YUV* should only be used when describing analog video ($Y'P_BP_R$). In digital video, the signals are different and should be abbreviated $Y'C_BC_R$. But YUV has "stuck." So, I do what everyone else does and use *YUV* incorrectly in this book.

Anyway, if you apply a non-YUV effect to YUV footage, it will cause a format conversion to RGB that can potentially cause minor color differences. But here's the good news: the 32-bit accuracy in Premiere means you can practically ignore this, since the rounding errors are microscopic in floating-point calculations. Many of the effects in Premiere work in YUV, so it's not really a problem.

GPU-Accelerated Color Precision Explained

Steve Hoeg, one of the Premiere Pro engineers at Adobe, has described how Premiere will handle color precision in different scenarios:

■ **A DV file with a blur and a color corrector exported to DV without the max bit depth flag.**   We will import the 8-bit DV file, apply the blur to get an 8-bit frame, apply the color corrector to the 8-bit frame to get another 8-bit frame, then write DV at 8-bit.

■ **A DV file with a blur and a color corrector exported to DV with the max bit depth flag.**   We will import the 8-bit DV file, apply the blur to get a 32-bit frame, apply the color corrector to the 32-bit frame to get another 32-bit frame, then write DV at 8-bit. The color corrector working on the 32-bit blurred frame will be higher quality than in the previous example.

■ **A DV file with a blur and a color corrector exported to DPX with the max bit depth flag.**   We will import the 8-bit DV file, apply the blur to get a 32-bit frame, apply the color corrector to the 32-bit frame to get another 32-bit frame, then write DPX at 10-bit. This will be even higher quality because the final output format supports greater precision.

■ **A DPX file with a blur and a color corrector exported to DPX without the max bit depth flag.**   We will clamp the 10-bit DPX file to 8-bits, apply the blur to get an 8-bit frame, apply the color corrector to the 8-bit frame to get another 8-bit frame, then write 10-bit DPX from 8-bit data.

■ **A DPX file with a blur and a color corrector exported to DPX with the max bit depth flag.**   We will import the 10-bit DPX file, apply the blur to get a 32-bit frame, apply the color corrector to the 32-bit frame to get another 32-bit frame, then write DPX at 10-bit. This will retain full precision through the whole pipeline.

■ **A title with a gradient and a blur on an 8-bit monitor.**   This will display in 8-bit and may show banding.

■ **A title with a gradient and a blur on a 10-bit monitor with hardware acceleration enabled.**   This will render the blur in 32-bit then display at 10-bit. The gradient should be smooth.

Bit-Depth Between AE and Premiere

When you have an After Effects composition in a Premiere sequence via Dynamic Link, the output of the composition will use whatever bit depth you have set the After Effects project to. If you set the After Effects project to 8-bit, you may get clipping and banding issues when you adjust colors further in Premiere.

If you bring the levels above 100, as in the extreme example with the curves effect in After Effects in Figure 6-32, you can still get them back in Premiere if the After Effects project is set to 32-bit. See Figure 6-33. So, make sure you set the After Effects project to 32-bit float if you want to access values that are outside the 0-100 range.

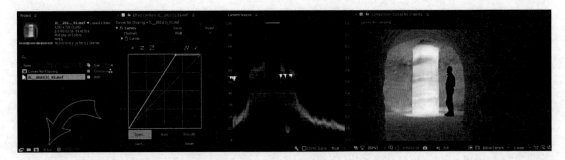

***Figure 6-32.** Set your After Effects project to 32-bit rendering*

***Figure 6-33.** Overbright levels from AE can be retained in Premiere if you're working in 32-bit*

Multi-Generation Production Workflows

If we render stuff out to 8- or 10-bit after working in 32-bit, of course a lot of color info is lost. So, working on material in high bit depth, rendering out in 8-bit, and then re-importing the renders–that's a destructive workflow. Unfortunately, this is the way a lot of people work when sending files to After Effects or other VFX or grading software. It's still a bad idea.

As long as we keep everything in 32-bit internally, and only the final render is in 8-bit, everything is fine. That's the beauty of the dynamic link between After Effects and Premiere–you render out the final result directly from the source files with 32-bit accuracy.

With bigger projects in a multi-user environment, it's not always possible to keep everything inside of the suite on one computer. You'll need to hand off your files to the guy in the other department so he can continue working on it. The workflow that would make sense in a production environment where files are sent from system to system, a true multi-generation workflow, would be this:

- Edit sources natively in Premiere 32-bit, export to a 10-bit or 12-bit file
- Import that 10-bit or 12-bit file in the next system and work in 32-bit
- Export to 10-bit or 12-bit again
- Etc.

Using 10-bit or higher quality for intermediate files results in a much better quality than using 8-bit intermediates. If you can use 16-bit files, that's even better.

8-Bit Effects Advice

Here are a few tips from editor Bart Walczak if you must use 8-bit effects:

1. Try to apply 8-bit effects as the last ones in the row, especially with footage that is 10-bit or more.

2. Avoid performing heavy color correction or image processing after an 8-bit effect has been inserted to avoid banding and posterization, especially with 10-bit or RAW footage.

3. Always perform your technical grade and make your image legal (i.e., not clipping) before you apply any 8-bit effect in the pipeline.

4. Ideally, do all your color correction before any 8-bit effect is applied.

Read more details on the downsides of using 8-bit effects in chapter 12 on "Export."

Understanding the Lumetri Scopes

Our eyes adapt to the image, so we can't trust them to accurately assess our blacks, whites, hue, saturation, and so on. Scopes bypass our brain and will never lie.

You'll use your scopes as guides to place your shadows and highs at "correct" levels, but the midtones you'll mostly have to adjust by eye.

You can select 8-bit, HDR, or float in the drop-down list in the Lumetri Scopes panel. The scales of the scopes change to HDR (High Dynamic Range) level ranges when you select HDR, with the scope scale showing a max range from 0-10000 Nits, instead of the usual 0-100 Nits in 8-bit.

YC Waveform Scope for Noobs

The waveform monitor simply shows the picture's brightness represented as a waveform. You can see how light or dark the image is, and you have a choice of looking at the signal with or without the chroma signal overlaid.

I recommend you set the scope's Brightness to *Bright* and uncheck *Chroma* so you can view luminance only. When watching the waveform scope with the chroma (color signal) overlaid, it can be hard to see the actual levels. So, switch it off.

Figure 6-34 shows a well-exposed shot of a stave church with a lot of info in the shadows and midtones and very little info in the highlights. That's why the trace is concentrated in the lower and the middle parts of the image and very little trace in the top area.

Figure 6-34. *Waveform scope for a well-exposed image*

Figure 6-35 shows a badly exposed image of a factory building. We can see from the trace that the sky is overexposed. There are levels above 100 to the left and in the middle of the frame, resulting in clipping of the whites in those parts of the image. There's very little going on in the midtones, so around 60, there's almost no trace. There's a lot going on the shadows and the highlights, and that's why there's so much tracing in the upper and lower parts of the scope.

Figure 6-35. *Waveform scope for badly exposed image. Clipped highlights and very little trace in midtones.*

But, since the highest levels aren't just a straight line, they're not heavily clipped in the source video, so we can get most of them back! In Figure 6-36, I've dragged the Whites slider in the Lumetri Color panel down until the trace is just below 100. See how much more detail we've got in the clouds now?

Figure 6-36. *When the trace is below 100, we can see more details in the clouds*

If the scope were set to *Clamp Signal*, I would not have seen what was going on above 100, and I would have probably thought there was nothing there. The signal is cut off at 0 and 100. I would have had no idea that there was anything above 100 percent that could be saved. See Figure 6-37. So, I recommend that you never clamp the signal in the Luma Waveform Scope.

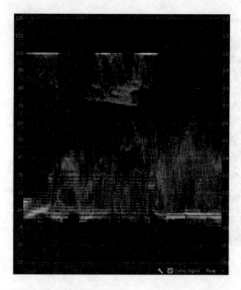

Figure 6-37. *With Clamp Signal on, nothing outside 0 and 100 will be shown*

Vector Scope for Noobs

The vector scope shows the color information about your video. The distance from the center shows how much color you have–the saturation. So, a black and white image would show a small dot in the middle (Figure 6-38), while the trace for an image with crazy-saturated colors could go all the way to the surrounding circle.

Figure 6-38. *Vector Scope for a black and white image–just a tiny dot in the middle of the scope*

The angle of the signal tells you what color the image contains. The more pixels there are in a certain color range in your image, the brighter the signal at that angle of the scope. When watching a color bar, the colors should show up in their respective boxes as shown in Figure 6-39.

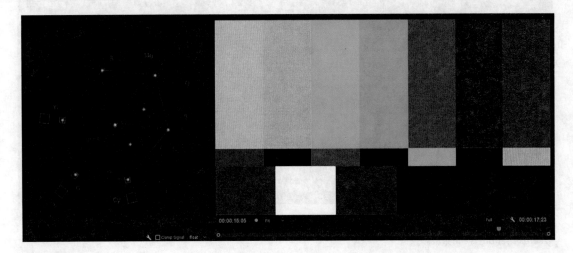

Figure 6-39. *Vector scope for color bars; each color fills its square with a dot*

The vector scope is particularly good for adjusting skin tone and other memory colors and to check the saturation of a color. If the skin color points in the direction of the Skin Tone line in the upper left, as in Figure 6-40, the people in the image will look healthy.

Figure 6-40. *Vector scope with skin color. Footage courtesy of Sean Fulton and Martin Fotland. Model: Marianne Melau.*

Figure 6-41 shows an image with lots of sky, and the vector scope shows that a lot of pixels have a color between cyan and blue. There's also some grass, and that shows in the spike toward green/yellow.

Figure 6-41. *The sky here shows as a spike between blue and cyan on the vector scope. The spike toward a greenish yellow is the grass.*

RGB Parade Scope for Noobs

The RGB Parade is just a way of looking at the waveforms of the three colors separately. I find this scope to be the most useful for color grading.

A grayscale image will show identical levels for R, G, and B in the RGB Parade scope. An image with no color cast should have neutral shadows and highlights, so the RGB Parade scope should have closely aligned tops and bottoms even if the midtones vary. Figure 6-42 has lots of blue in the midtones–the sky. That's why the blue trace is higher in the midtones. The white boat on the right is neutral, as we can see by the equal height of the R, G, and B traces at the very top of the scope. The left side has a lot of orangey yellow, which is why the main red trace goes higher than the green, and the blue trace is lower than the green.

Figure 6-42. *RGB Parade scope*

What I like about the RGB Parade scope is the direct relationship between the adjustment I make in RGB Curves and the result in the RGB Parade scope. It's so easy to understand what needs to be done to each curve, and you'll quickly see when the shadows and highlights are neutral.

This lighthouse in Figure 6-43 was shot close to sunset and has a warm cast. The red trace goes higher than the green, and the blue one is lower than the green. Adjusting the RGB Curves so the upper parts of the traces are equal makes the lighthouse a neutral white (Figure 6-44). Figure 6-45 shows the adjustment I made in RGB Curves. I dragged the top of the blue curve to the left, and I moved the top of the red curve down a bit–all while watching the RGB Parade scope. When the blue and red traces were the same height as the green one, I knew the image was neutral.

Figure 6-43. *Sunset created a warm cast*

Figure 6-44. *Making traces equal at the top creates a neutral white*

Figure 6-45. RGB Curves used in image

■ **Note** There is a direct relationship between adjustments in RGB Curves and the result in the RGB Parades scope. It's a winning combination!

Histogram for Noobs

The histogram in Premiere is turned sideways to the ones in Photoshop, but it still works the same way. The upper part shows the brightest pixels, and the lower part shows the shadows. How many pixels we have at any given brightness for every color is represented by how far to the left the spikes go.

One great thing about the histogram is that it has RGB values for whites and blacks, so you know the exact values of the brightest and the darkest pixel. See Figure 6-46.

Figure 6-46. Histogram

Cropping for Accurate Measurement

Often, we want to look at only a part of the image, like skin tone. For this, we use a temporary crop effect to crop out everything but skin. In an image with different colors, it can be hard to tell just exactly what part of the trace is the skin. Figure 6-47 shows a trace where it hard to identify skin colors.

Figure 6-47. Trace of complete image

Crop away everything but the face, and it's easier to see where the skin tone trace is. You could use masks for this, but since they cannot easily be switched on and off, I prefer using the crop effect. See how much easier it is to identify skin colors in the scope in Figure 6-48.

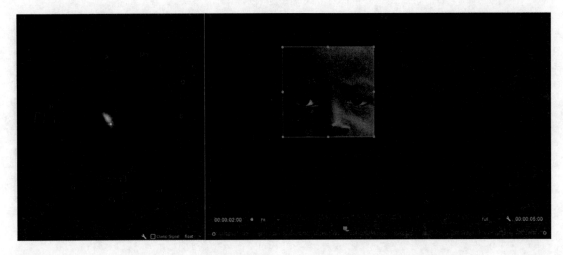

Figure 6-48. *Crop the image to see skin color only*

Want to see if that white shirt, paper, or another object is neutral white? Crop to see just the white area. Figure 6-49 shows how I could tell, with confidence, that the lighthouse was neutral. I isolated the white walls.

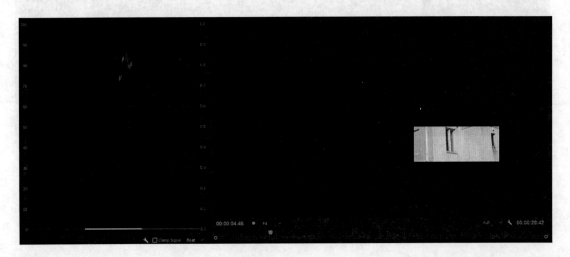

Figure 6-49. *Isolating the white walls makes white balance easy*

Figure 6-50 shows a shot where I've masked out the supposedly neutral white-to-black gradient. The blue outline shows where it was cropped. The rest of the image did of course go black when I turned the mask effect on. This is an "impossible" mock-up. While masking so only the grayscale is showing, we can clearly see that the red trace in the RGB Parade Scope is high, and the blue trace is low. In the vector scope, there is a pronounced spike against orange/yellow.

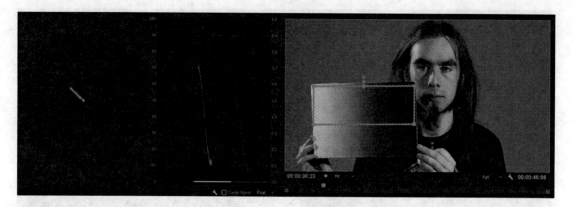

Figure 6-50. *Scopes show that the shot is warm*

In Figure 6-51, the traces in the RGB Parade scope are equal, indicating that the image is now neutral. The vector scope shows a small dot in the middle, another sure sign that there is no color cast. To the right, you can see the RGB Curves adjustments I did.

Figure 6-51. *Scopes after the clip was neutralized. (Footage courtesy of Sean Fulton and Martin Fotland. Model: Sean Fulton)*

An opacity mask can serve as a non-rectangular mask for color correction and scopes, replacing the crop effect for this purpose. But I find it faster to switch the crop effect on and off than to tweak settings in the mask to turn it on and off. Plus, the crop effect has a little-known feature: the zoom (see Figure 6-52).

▦ **Note** When the *Zoom* checkbox in the crop effect is ticked, it fills the frame with whatever is inside the crop. The image will look very strange, but it's a lot easier to read the trace in the scopes.

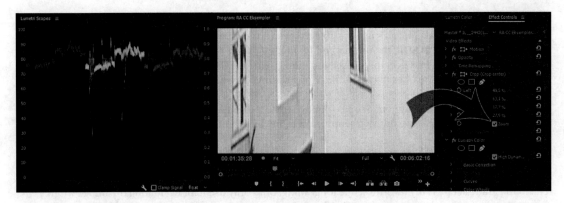

Figure 6-52. *Use the zoom feature in the crop effect to make the trace easy to read*

Beware of the Scopes Presets

The Lumetri Scopes panel conveniently has some presets available in the wrench menu or the right-click menu. Unfortunately, most of the presets in the Lumetri Scopes panel will reset your scopes to 8-bit, clamp the signal, set the color space to Rec709, and give them the default brightness (Figure 6-53). This can be bad.

With the *Clamp Signal* checkbox selected, the scopes behave like traditional hardware scopes. It limits the scope's display to the visible spectrum, showing only values from 0 through 100. If you want to see how much of the signal is being clipped, deselect the *Clamp Signal* checkbox.

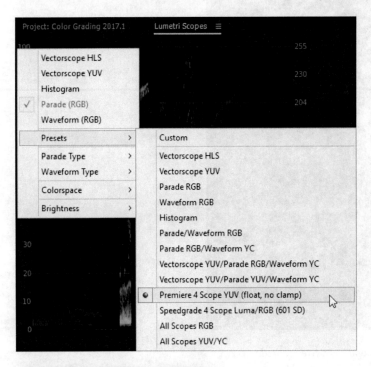

Figure 6-53. *Most presets clamp the signal to 8-bit. Use only the one that's set to Float.*

Even if you're working in Rec709, which is very likely, you wouldn't want to clamp the signal and give the scopes an 8-bit signal. Since it's not possible to save your own presets, there's only one preset I can recommend for grading in SDR: the one named *Premiere 4 Scope YUV (float, no clamp)*.

I recommend that you select this preset and then go to the right-click menu to remove the scopes you don't need and change the ones that have the wrong settings for your needs. I also like to set the brightness to *Bright*.

The presets part of the Lumetri Scopes frankly seems to be just half-baked, Let's hope they'll improve it in later versions. If I could save my own scope presets, my life would be better.

Dancing Scopes

The RGB Parade scope is my favorite scope for grading, but I only use it for evaluating the image when the playhead is parked. When you play a timeline with overbrights or levels below zero, it will jump a lot, trying to scale the reticule to adapt to the signal, making it impossible to read. A lot of YUV material has overbrights. The histogram also jumps in the same fashion.

When you want to evaluate your levels while playing back the timeline, choose the Waveform Luma scope, which has a locked scale, from -20 to 120 (Figure 6-54).

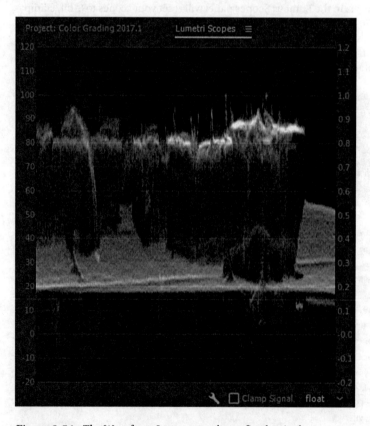

Figure 6-54. *The Waveform Luma scope has a fixed reticule*

I have no idea what the reasoning is behind showing the Waveform Luma scope with a fixed scale from -20 to 120, while the RGB Parade scope scales with the signal.

Reorder the Scopes

When you've chosen a preset or adapted the settings to your needs, the scopes can be reordered by double-clicking on them. This will rotate the scopes view. You cannot set a keyboard shortcut for this "rotate scopes" feature. Whenever you don't need a scope, remove it. Every scope adds more processing, so performance may drop when you show too many.

Yes, There Are More Scopes

If you play with the Lumetri Scopes panel, you will find more scopes. I almost never use them, so I've decided not to describe them here.

Playback Resolution Affects the Scopes

Set your Playback Resolution to *Full* when you watch the scopes. The scopes look very different when the resolution is dropped to ½ or ¼. Figure 6-55 shows the Playback Resolution drop-down menu in the program monitor. The source monitor and the reference monitor have one too.

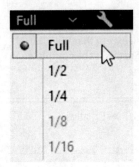

Figure 6-55. Lumetri scopes playback quality

Accurate vs. Pleasing

Ok, enough about scopes. Keep in mind that the scopes are just tools. Don't stare blindly at the scopes when grading. It's more important that the images look good than that all the levels are "accurate."

Great Explanation of Scopes

David Hover, who's a colorist and editor—and also a teacher at the French national cinema school, la FEMIS—has made a series of video tutorials that explains how to read and use the waveform, vector, and RGB Parade scopes in great detail: pixelupdate.com/light-colour/.

The Lumetri Color Panel

The Lumetri Color panel is a remote control for the Lumetri Color effect. When you drag sliders, move points, and adjust curves in the panel, you're affecting the corresponding settings in the Lumetri Color effect. You could do the same adjustments in the Effect Controls panel, but the controls in the Lumetri Color panel are often slicker and easier to adjust.

Lumetri Works in Rec709 Color Space

Premiere Pro uses gamma-encoded 709 throughout, which Lumetri converts to linear for internal processing without touching the primaries and then back to 709 Gamma before spitting it back out. If this was all gobbledygook to you, that's fine, since there's nothing you can do about it.

■ **Note** The *Composite in Linear Color* option in Sequence settings has no effect on Lumetri, because Lumetri is working in linear color internally all the time.

Your monitoring will also be in Rec709. Monitoring in other color spaces is not possible. With the quick move to HDR and Rec2020 in the business, I guess the Premiere team must have plans to support larger color spaces in future versions.

Render Order in Lumetri Color

The render order is almost exactly like the order you see in the Lumetri Color panel, except that the Whites and Blacks sliders in the Basic Correction section come before the other controls. So, this is the complete render pipeline internally in Lumetri:

Input LUT ➤ Basic Correction (Whites and Blacks before other sliders) ➤ Creative LUT ➤ Creative Adjustments ➤ Curves ➤ Color Wheels ➤ HSL Secondary ➤ Vignette

---

Lumetri Helps You a Lot—Sometimes Too Much

The Lumetri controls are designed to help you avoid clipping in both the luma and chroma signals by adding soft "knees" at the extreme highs and lows. So, if you push saturation too far, it will also do something to highlights and the gamma, which is not a standard behavior for a saturation control.

Exposure is not really an exposure adjustment; it "helps" you by compressing the highlights if you raise them high. If you set exposure as high as you can, it will still not let the levels go above 100, provided your levels are within the 0–100 range before you adjust exposure. Again, this is not the standard behavior for exposure controls in color tools from other software–not even for the obsolete color tools in Premiere–so you might be surprised.

If you increase the whites, increase the exposure, and then drag the top of the curves down, you've got a distorted version of your pixel values. In the obsolete RGB Curves and the Three-Way Color Corrector, this does not happen, because all levels above 100 are still there, untouched.

Sometimes, we want to "break" our images intentionally, and I would love to have a checkbox that disables the soft knees. With one mouse click, we could tell Lumetri, *"Hey, I know what I'm doing, please don't try to help."*

Selection Follows Playhead

The Lumetri Color panel is the only panel in Premiere that changes a setting for you automatically. When you open the panel, your sequence is automatically set to *Selection Follows Playhead* (Figure 6-56), no matter what it was set to before you opened the panel. When you close the panel, it's reset to the state it was before you opened the panel. It's the panel, not the workspace, that triggers this setting.

Figure 6-56. Lumetri panel Selection Follows Playhead option

If you want better control over this switch, create a keyboard shortcut to toggle it on and off.

The Panel Works on the Last Instance of Lumetri

If you add another Lumetri Color effect, it appears below the first one in the Effect Controls panel, and the Color panel will switch to inspect the parameters for this second instance. You cannot get it to select the first instance.

To operate additional instances of Lumetri, you must use the Effects Controls panel and operate the controls there. You can put many instances of the effect on each clip, but the Lumetri Color panel will only operate the one at the bottom of the stack in the Effect Controls panel (Figure 6-57).

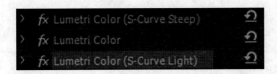

Figure 6-57. Only the last Lumetri Color effect in the stack will be controlled by the Lumetri Color panel

Lumetri Color Can Be a Resource Hog—but You Can Fix That

The Lumetri effect draws a lot more GPU power than the obsolete effects like RGB Curves and the Three-Way Color Corrector. But since it's easier to use, and the older effects will disappear in the future, we're better off using Lumetri. Luckily, there's a way to make use of fewer GPU resources.

Disabling a section in the Lumetri Color panel means that it's not rendered at all, performance should be better, and render times should be faster. See Figure 6-58.

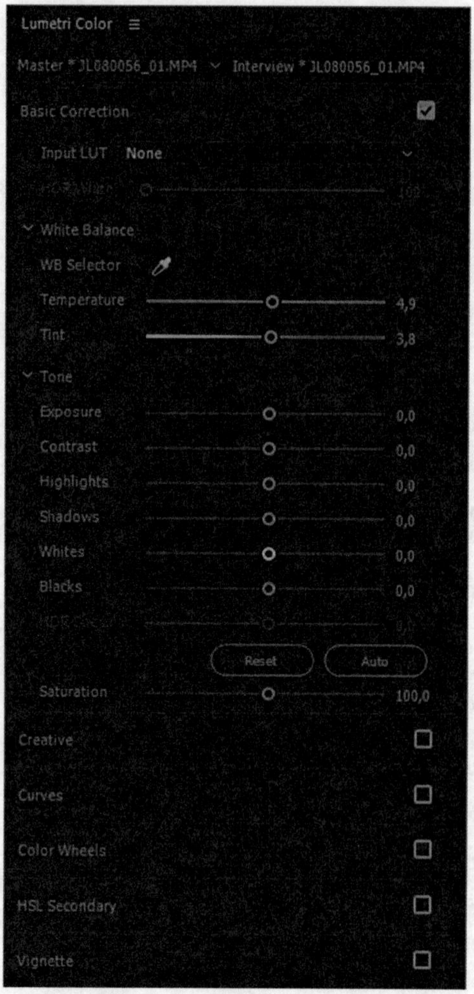

Figure 6-58. *Turn sections off to save some GPU juice*

Knowing this, I've saved presets that mimic my obsolete ones. My S-Curve presets have only the Curves section active. In my Skin Color Qualifier, only the HSL Secondary section is active, and so on. This means I can use several instances of Lumetri on a clip without running into problems like dropped frames.

Lumetri Fix in 2017.1 and Newer Versions

The Lumetri Color engine had a fundamental flaw up until 2017.1 in the way it handled overbrights and super-blacks. When adjusting whites and blacks, only levels within the 0-100 range were affected, and levels below or above this would stay–with the chance of clipping highlights and blacks for YUV material, like XDCAM.

This is now fixed, so the Whites and Blacks sliders in the Basic Correction section work in a broader range, from about -20 to 135, and those sliders will be applied before other controls. OK, great–so the effect is fixed! But to make sure that your old projects still look the same, they will use the old algorithms for the clips that already have a Lumetri Color effect. If you add new ones, these will use the new algorithm.

This means that when you open an old project (made in 2017.02 or older) and do additional color work on it in the new version of Premiere, you will have two different "versions" of the Lumetri algorithms going on. You may be able to save some clips with clipped highlights from the old version by deleting the existing Lumetri effect and adding a new one.

Unfortunately, this fix apparently also seems to have the potential to sometimes by mistake make some clips in old projects darker. I'm sure this bug will get fixed, but for now, make sure you check the colors in old projects before you export, or keep an older version of Premiere installed for old projects.

Use Presets in Lumetri

Unfortunately, the state of the sections in the Lumetri Color panel–meaning if they're open or closed–is not saved with the presets. You may have to open the panel of interest manually. The open/closed state *is* remembered in the Effect Controls panel, though, and the sliders and color wheels can be just as easily adjusted from there. So, make sure you twirl down the arrow for the sections you want to be open in the Effect Controls panel before you save your preset, as I've done in Figures 6-59 and 6-60.

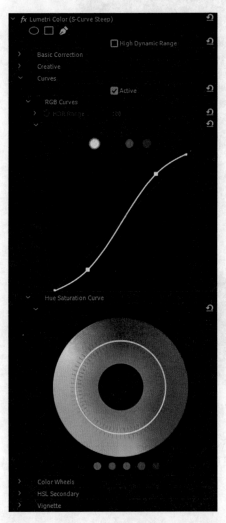

Figure 6-59. *Save your presets with the necessary sections twirled down in the Effect Controls panel*

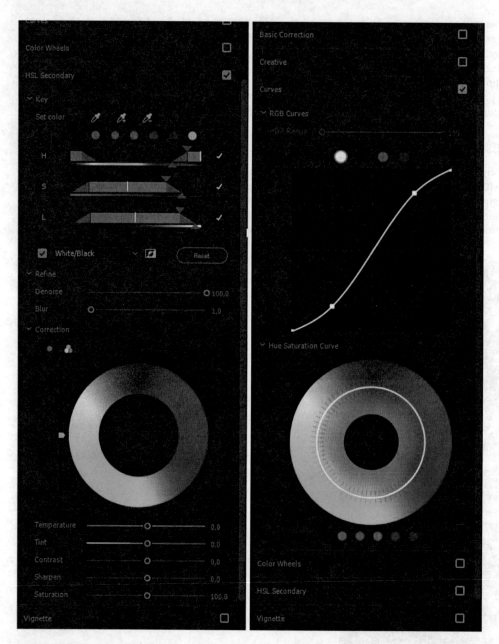

Figure 6-60. *Here are my Skin Tone Qualifier and S-Curve Steep presets*

If you use a control surface for color correction, this means you can adjust the settings on a selected clip without having the Lumetri Color panel open. Throw on a preset and use the control surface while you see the UI update in the Effect Controls panel.

The Panel Menu

The panel menu for the Lumetri Color panel doesn't have too many options. You can save presets, export LUTs, and set it to HDR mode (Figure 6-61).

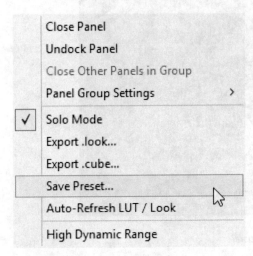

Figure 6-61. *Lumetri Color panel menu*

Great Visual Feedback

The wheels get filled when they're adjusted, and the sliders get a blue color. In the blink of an eye, you know what's been adjusted or not. In Figure 6-62, you can immediately see which controls have been touched. See how the Midtones wheel on the right is filled and the Shadows and Highlights Sliders have turned blue because they're adjusted?

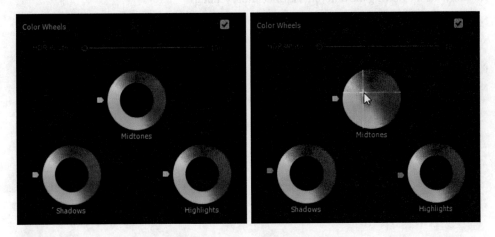

Figure 6-62. *Lumetri Color wheels untouched and adjusted*

461

In Figure 6-63, you can easily see which sliders have been moved from their default values. The default position is in the middle.

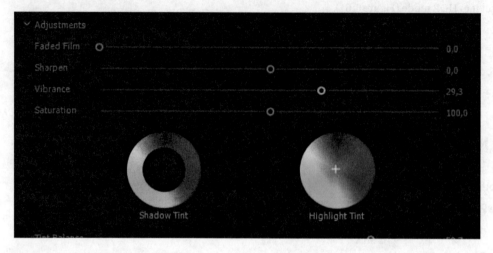

Figure 6-63. *Lumetri Color Creative section with sliders adjusted*

■ **Note**   You can reset each slider, wheel, and curve in Lumetri by double-clicking on them.

Lumetri Shortcuts

Unfortunately, the Lumetri Color panel is hugely mouse-driven. There are very few shortcuts available (Figure 6-64). They largely reflect the panel menu settings.

- No shortcuts for viewing the different HSL Secondary mattes
- No shortcuts for opening and closing sections
- No shortcuts for switching sections on/off
- No shortcuts for resetting the different sections
- No shortcut for switching between multiple instances of Lumetri on a clip

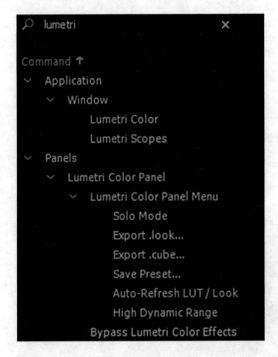

Figure 6-64. *A search for Lumetri in the keyboard shortcuts panel shows how few shortcuts there are for this panel*

The constant mouse-clicking to open and close different sections in the Lumetri Color panel is non-productive. So, at least make sure you set it to Solo mode, which closes other sections when you open a new one.

If you use a control surface to drive Lumetri, it will of course be much less mouse-driven. I highly recommend that you buy a control surface if you do a lot of grading in Premiere.

Bypass Lumetri Color Effects

There's one important feature that I highly recommend that you assign to a one-button shortcut–*Bypass Lumetri Color Effects*–for easy toggling between your grade and the original footage.

This is different from the Global FX Mute feature discussed next, because it only affects the Lumetri Color effect. It will switch off *all* instances of Lumetri Color on the selected clip while you keep the key pressed. When you release the key, the Lumetri Color effects are switched on again.

This shortcut only works when the Lumetri Color panel is active. Use the *fx* button in the Effect Controls panel if you work with the Lumetri Color panel closed.

Global FX Mute

You can assign a keyboard shortcut to the Global FX Mute feature. It switches off rendering of all the effects (except the fixed effects) on all clips. This is great when you want to see the clip before and after all effects and color grading. It's also convenient when your system struggles to play back the timeline. Just hit the shortcut, do your edit changes with no effects, and hit the shortcut again.

It does not affect the export, just the program monitor and monitors connected through Transmit. It only works when the program monitor is active, and you can also add the *fx* button to the Transport Controls area under the monitor. Personally, I hide the Transport Controls to get more space on my screen, so I use the keyboard shortcut.

Use a Control Surface

Any Tangent panel supported by the Tangent Hub software will work in Premiere Pro, including Tangent Elements, Wave, and Ripple. See `tangentwave.co.uk/`. Besides Tangent hardware, you can also use the Palette controller for Lumetri, found at `palettegear.com`. Figures 6-65 and 6-66 show the Tangent Ripple and Palette controllers.

***Figure 6-65.** Tangent Ripple (Image courtesy of Tangent)*

***Figure 6-66.** Palette (Image courtesy of palettegear.com)*

There's only one downside with using a control surface. None of them work with curves, which is fairly logical. You'll have to use the mouse for curves adjustments. But there are lots of other cool things you can do with them. You can cycle through the sections in the Lumetri Color panel and dial in settings for HSL Secondaries (which we will cover later in this chapter) in a much easier way. Figure 6-67 shows the mapping UI for the Tangent Ripple.

Figure 6-67. *Alternate mapping in the Lumetri HSL Secondary mode. (Image courtesy of Premiere Bro, premierebro.com.)*

The Lumetri Color panel doesn't even need to be opened or selected to use the control panel, but the clip you want to adjust to has to be selected, of course.

The Tangent Ripple even adds the option of showing a HUD–a Head-Up Display–that shows the exact values you've set (Figure 6-68). But there's one advantage that tops them all: it frees your eyes from watching the sliders and wheels and allows you to keep your attention where it should be–on the output monitor and the scopes. This is invaluable!

```
Mode: Config
 L Diff-X    G Diff-X    G Diff-X
 L Diff-Y    G Diff-Y    G Diff-Y
 L Master    G Master    G Master
```

Figure 6-68. *Control surface Tangent-HUD*

To connect a control surface to Premiere, add the appropriate Device Class in the Control Surface preferences (Figure 6-69).

Figure 6-69. *Add Control Surface dialog*

The Basic Section

This is where most people will start doing their corrections. The sliders are pretty much self-explanatory. Dragging the Whites slider affects the whites, dragging the Shadows slider adjusts the dark areas, and so on. If you've ever used the Camera RAW module in Photoshop or done color correction in Lightroom, you'll feel at home here.

Input LUT

The purpose of the input LUTs in the Basic Correction section is a conversion to Rec709. So, if your footage is shot in Log or with some custom camera settings, you need to add a LUT before you start adjusting the controls.

White Balance Selector

The Auto White Balance Selector (the eye dropper) can be a quick fix for clips where the white balance is a little bit off. Click it and then pick an area in the picture that's supposed to be white. **Ctrl-click** (Cmd-click) to get a fatter eye dropper that samples a 5 × 5 area, averaging the color of those 25 pixels (Figure 6-70).

Figure 6-70. *BIG Lumetri Color sampler*

Sometimes, the Auto White Balance is a little bit off. I find that I can get better results when I tweak the sliders manually. Figure 6-71 shows the resulting levels in the Parade RGB scope with the auto and manual settings for one clip.

Figure 6-71. *The sliders after using the eye dropper (left) and after manual tweaking (right)*

Figure 6-72 shows the RGB Parade scope for these two results. You can see that the white levels after manual tweaking are more even, probably because the area wasn't completely white.

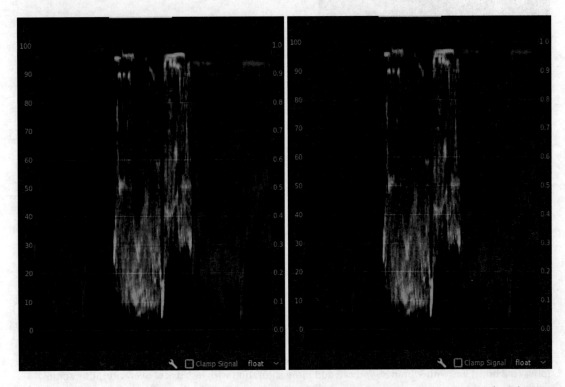

Figure 6-72. *The Parade RGB scope after using the eye dropper (left) and after manual tweaking (right)*

When tweaking the sliders manually for a white balance, adjust the Temperature slider first until you get the red and blue levels the same. Then, adjust the Tint slider until the green matches the two others. There's a reason for the order they have in the UI.

The Tone sliders in the Basic section should be easy to understand. They do what their names indicate.

The Creative Section

The LUTs you can apply here are looks, and are very different from the ones found in the Basic section. The sliders in this section should be self-explanatory. If you don't know what Faded Film or Vibrance mean, just drag the sliders to see. I find myself using this section very little. I only use it when I need to adjust the Vibrance or apply a look/LUT. This section is disabled when you set the panel to HDR. Figure 6-73 shows the Creative section.

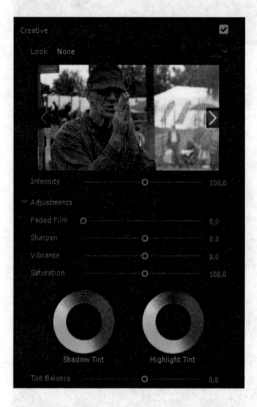

Figure 6-73. *Lumetri Creative section*

You may wonder why there's a Saturation control here, when there's also one in the Basic Correction section. The one in the Basic Correction section is for more technical correction purposes. The one in the Creative section is more like: "I like the *Blue Steel* LUT that I added, but I'd like to desaturate it a bit".

Vibrance works on colors with low saturation, leaving saturated colors aside, as well as protects skin tones (red hues). So, with Vibrance, you can add more saturation with less risk of over-saturating some colors.

The Curves Section

I live and breathe in this section and the Color Wheels section! Combined with the RGB Parade scopes, RGB Curves is a very intuitive way to do color grading.

The Hue Saturation curve lets you control the saturation of every color independently, making it very fast to add saturation to the greens in foliage or to make that red dress "pop."

As with other controls in Lumetri, just double-click to reset the curves. There's no way to reset all four curves in the RGB Curves in one go in the Lumetri Color panel, so they all need to be reset manually. This is possible in the Effect Controls panel, where clicking the *Reset Parameter* button for RGB Curves will reset them all. Figure 6-74 shows the UI for the Curves section.

Figure 6-74. *Lumetri Curves section*

The Color Wheels Section

This section will be the most familiar one if you come from other NLEs. With the three-way color correction, you can adjust the brightness, hue, and saturation for shadows, midtones, and highlights independently.

I love the Lumetri color wheels. When you drag the sliders or the wheels for the first time, you may feel that nothing's happening. This is because there's a "gear" function at work, so you must drag the mouse a lot longer than the distance you want the slider or point to move. This makes it super-easy to make accurate adjustments, even though the wheels are small on the screen. Clever! If you want it to move faster, just press **Shift** while you're dragging. Figure 6-75 shows the UI for the Color Wheels section.

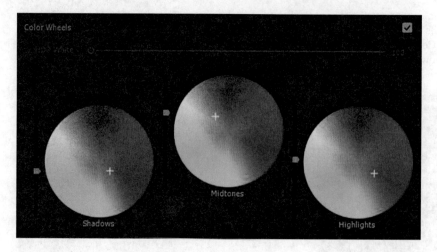

Figure 6-75. *Lumetri Color Wheels*

The HSL Secondaries Section

This is where you get more advanced than most users, and where you can start creating looks, making your viewers focus on the right parts of the image, and so on. You can select pixels within a selected range of hue, saturation, and lightness. You can also hit the *Invert Mask* button to invert the selection.

Adjustments you do in this section will only affect the qualifying pixels and will leave the rest of the pixels untouched. This is where you fix skin tone, make that red dress pop, and so on.

After you've picked the colors you want to change with the eye droppers, you can adjust the sliders to select a wider or narrower range of pixel values.

Let's make the autumn scene in Figure 6-76 look like a nice summer scene. Choose the mask view that best shows your selected pixels (Figure 6-77). This depends on the footage.

Figure 6-76. *Autumn scene*

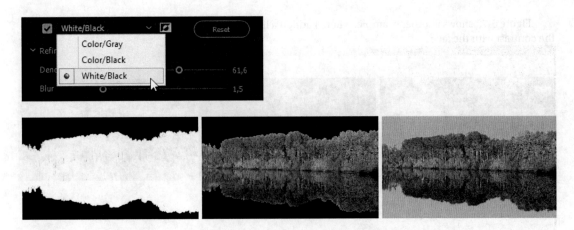

Figure 6-77. *Key views: From left to right: white/black, color/black, color/gray*

Figure 6-78 shows the settings I ended up using for this shot. In a real situation, I would add an adjustment layer above the clip to tweak the overall saturation and contrast in the final image.

Figure 6-78. *HSL Secondaries settings and the final result*

471

Figure 6-79 shows another example, where I added a little bit of extra pop to the blue shirt to increase the contrast with the face.

Figure 6-79. *HSL Secondaries start, mask, and results*

HSL Secondaries Issue

There is one big issue I have with the HSL Secondaries in Lumetri, and that has to do with *when* in the process the qualifier key looks at the pixels. Instead of doing the key on the original footage, it is doing it after the other sections just discussed.

This is a bad thing, because if you tweak the color in sections above the HSL Secondaries in the same Lumetri effect, or on the Master Clip, the HSL keys are gone. So, if you decide to warm up the clip or increase the exposure after you've adjusted the key, all the HSL keying must be done again.

This is a recipe for disaster. It's possible to adjust a Master Clip in one part of the timeline without noticing that a secondary correction on another instance of the clip, later in the timeline, is broken.

In my opinion, HSL keying should be done pre-effects–at the very latest immediately after the Input LUT. Changing the color, sharpness, and so on should not affect the key and should always work based on the original pixels.

The Vignette Section

Although I do use vignettes often, I don't use the Vignette section in Lumetri much. There are no settings for blending modes, and the vignette is always centered. So, I roll my own vignettes as explained elsewhere in this chapter. Figure 6-80 shows the UI for the Vignette section.

Figure 6-80. *Lumetri Vignette section*

Use Masks with Lumetri

Just because we don't have a separate Masks section in Lumetri, that doesn't mean we can't use masks. In the Effect Controls panel, the Lumetri effect has the same mask options as any other effect (Figure 6-81). You can create ellipse, rectangle, and free-draw Bezier masks.

Figure 6-81. *Lumetri color masks*

Combined with the HSL Secondaries and other sections of Lumetri, this is a powerful feature.

In Figure 6-82, I've used the HSL Secondaries on another Lumetri effect on the clip from earlier where the blue shirt has already been corrected. I wanted to make the face brighter and more saturated, but some of the wooden materials in the image were so close to skin tone colors that I needed a mask on the effect to limit it to the area around the face. Yes, I've hugely exaggerated the effect here to better show the difference.

Figure 6-82. *Original image on the left. The right image shows how HSL Secondaries were used to adjust skin colors, and the mask limits the area it affects. Adjustment exaggerated for clarity.*

Gotcha When Stacking Lumetri Color Effects

You should be aware that unless you set the Lumetri Color panel to HDR and adjust the HDR Range up high (something you must do to every clip manually), Lumetri Color will clip any exposure adjustments at 100 percent, so when you stack Lumetri Color effects, you will not be able to get your overbrights back.

Color Correction Workflow Overview

OK, with all that technical stuff out of the way, let's talk about how you should attack a color-grading session.

1. Decide What's Important in the Frame

When you watch a scene, concentrate on the key factors in there. More often than not, it will be a person, but sometimes it can be a logo, an object, or a car in the background. Your job is to make the key elements stand out and maybe separate foreground from background, creating more visual depth–all this so the shortcomings of the scene don't get in the way of the story.

Figure 6-83 shows a blue color cast, so the skin tone of the subject is off. The midtones are a bit low, and the blacks could be lower.

Figure 6-83. *Original image*

2. Make Primary Corrections

First, adjust contrast and exposure. Set your blacks, set your whites, and adjust the midtones to your liking using a gamma curve. Then, correct for color casts in shadows, highlights, or midtones and see if the saturation needs some work. This is what's called *primary color correction*, and the corrections are applied to the whole frame. There will be more on primary color correction later in this chapter. In Figure 6-84, I've corrected for the blue cast, raised the midtones, and lowered the blacks.

Figure 6-84. *Image after primary corrections*

3. Make Secondary Corrections (Optional)

If you think the primary corrections aren't enough, move on to secondary corrections, meaning you adjust some parts of the image independently. Think: local area contrast adjustments. If the skin tones are a bit off after the primary corrections, we can use the built-in qualifier (aka keyer) in the HSL Secondary section of the Lumetri Color panel to make adjustments to skin tones only.

If some areas of the image need more contrast or another gamma, we can use masking and tracking to separate different areas of the frame so they can be dealt with individually. A very common thing to do is to adjust the sky and the rest of the frame individually, or maybe mask out a building to darken it without affecting the rest of the image.

Secondary color correction can be used both to draw attention to important elements in the frame and to blend elements into the surroundings. *"We want the eyes to naturally go to the points of narrative that we want to focus on,"* said Steve Scott, colorist on Birdman. Read more on secondary color correction later in this chapter.

The face was a little dark, so in Figure 6-85 I've raised the midtones in that area using secondary color correction.

Figure 6-85. *Image after secondary correction*

4. Create a Look (Optional)

Now that the image is fully corrected, we can stop grading, or we can go crazy by adding specific looks and effects. The oh-so-popular orange/teal blockbuster look and the bleach bypass look made famous by *Saving Private Ryan* are among the best-known ones. This is where you can add edge and attitude to your footage. In Figure 6-86, I've added a sepia look.

Figure 6-86. *Sepia look added to the corrected image*

This Order Is Not Accidental!

Your contrast adjustments will affect the color adjustments you do later. If you do it the other way around, you'll end up switching back and forth between color and contrast adjustments much more than if you work in the standard order. Applying the look after correcting the shot will save you lots of time, since you can apply presets and copy settings from one shot to another. If the shots are not corrected before you apply a look, the presets will affect the shots differently, since their contrast and colors don't match. If you want to make the deadline, stick to the standard flow. Figure 6-87 shows the image in each step.

Figure 6-87. *Notice how the image changes in each step*

Workflow for Primary Color Correction

So, the first task in a color-grading session is primary color correction. The goal objective is to make sure the blacks, whites, and midtones have proper levels and are free from unwanted color casts. Note that there are images that should never have white levels at 100 percent, blacks at 0 percent, or neutral colors. Images shot in foggy weather should have black levels well above 0 percent and probably no levels at 100 percent. A scene shot during the magic hour should not have neutral colors–they should be warm. Correcting a sunset to a neutral white or gray would take away all the magic.

There are lots of scenarios that differ from the norm, and you'll have to judge every scene separately. Check the scopes to get an idea of where your levels are, but always use your eyes to decide what adjustments to apply.

The usual suspects for primary color correction are whites, blacks, and skin color. Now, let's do another shot, and this time we'll include the actual adjustments I used in the Lumetri Color panel.

Setting Black and White Levels

Watch your image and the RGB Parade scope to decide what needs to be done. Figure 6-88 shows an image with low exposure before any adjustments were done.

Figure 6-88. *Original image before adjustments*

Figure 6-89. *Set black levels*

First, set your black levels. Most shots have something in there that should be fully black. Make sure you bring these areas of the image very close to zero. My favorite tool for this is RGB Curves. I can adjust all colors with the master curve, and I can adjust the colors independently. Set the black levels close to zero, but be careful not to lower them too much. Generally, we want to avoid crushing them. In Figure 6-89, I've moved the bottom of the master curve slightly to the right. Since the green levels were a tiny bit higher than the others, I also dragged the bottom of the green curve to the right. (You can't see that in the figure, because the white curve covers the green one).

Now, look at the lightest parts of the image and adjust the highlights until they look properly white and neutral. If they're not neutral, adjust the upper-right part of the individual color curves until they are. In this particular image, I had to decide how much of the texture in the clouds to sacrifice. Then, adjust the highlights so the spikes reach all the way up to 100. In Figure 6-90, you can see that I've dragged the top of the white curve to the left until the spikes in the scope touched 100 percent.

Figure 6-90. *Set white levels*

Setting Midtone Contrast

Now, concentrate on the midtones. Are they the right brightness? Adjust the midtones to raise or lower their brightness. If the midtones have color casts, you'll adjust the gamma for each color separately. Most professional cinematographers and camera operators will deliver flat images suitable for grading, so more often than not the scenes will need an S-shaped curve to increase midtone contrast.

Finally, adjust the midtones until the image feels like it's nicely balanced and exposed. You'll have to judge this by eye. If necessary, use an S-curve in the midtones to increase midtone contrast. Figure 6-91 shows the curve I used for this shot. Notice that it's got a slight S-form.

Figure 6-91. *Set midtone gamma*

This shot is not finished after primary color correction. It would benefit from a separate adjustment on the sky since it's much brighter than the rest of the image. You'll learn techniques to deal with that when we discuss secondary color correction. For now, just take a look at Figure 6-92 for the finished result and the corrections I did in the HSL Secondary. It's OK if you don't understand what has been done here. You can go back and have another look when you've read the section on secondary color correction.

Figure 6-92. *The sky was greatly improved with secondary color correction. You'll learn this later*

Lift, Gamma, Gain

Books on color grading will use the terms *lift*, *gamma*, and *gain*. Here's a quick explanation:

- Lift: Sets the black level, determining the shadow level and shadow color cast

- Gamma: Adjusts the midtones by darkening or brightening them. If the gamma for each color is adjusted separately, it tweaks the color cast in the midtones.

- Gain: Brightens the whole image, affecting mostly the highlights

All of these can be adjusted in different ways in Premiere. My favorites are RGB Curves and the three-way color wheels.

Avoid the Brightness and Contrast Effect

As you can see, primary color correction is mainly about adjusting brightness and contrast. So, the logical choice is to just apply the obsolete Brightness & Contrast effect and fix it, right? Please don't do that. Be very careful with that effect!

Applying this effect to a reasonably well-exposed image with levels spanning from 0 to 100 percent will always result in some sort of clipping. If you increase brightness, the highlights will be clipped (Figure 6-93). If you lower brightness, you'll clip the black levels. If you increase contrast, you'll clip both black and white levels (Figure 6-94). The only "safe" adjustment in this effect is to decrease contrast, resulting in flat, boring images.

Figure 6-93. *Grayscale gradient with raised brightness*

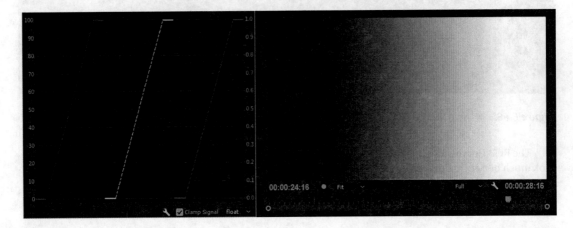

Figure 6-94. *Grayscale gradient with increased contrast*

479

See the flat top and bottom of the curves after applying brightness and contrast? Those are clipped levels, pixels you'll never get back. If that image had a sky with clouds, the texture in the clouds would be gone, leaving a boring white area. Instead, use the Lumetri Color panel and adjust exposure or contrast, which will protect both blacks and whites. See Figures 6-95 and 6-96 for the result using the Lumetri Color effect. No clipped blacks or whites!

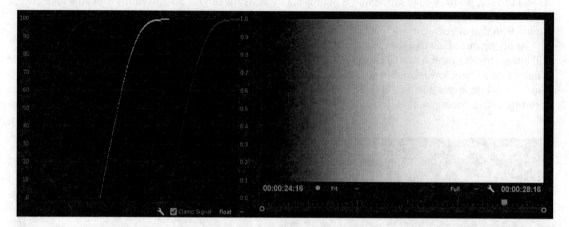

Figure 6-95. *The result of increasing the exposure in the Lumetri Color panel. No clipping.*

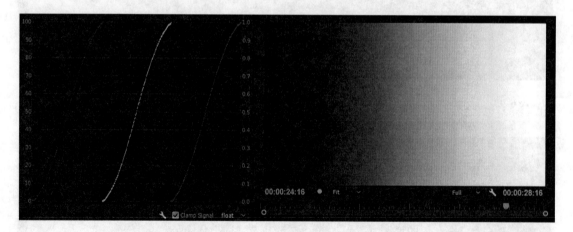

Figure 6-96. *See how the Contrast slider in Lumetri helps you avoid clipping by introducing an S-curve?*

The RGB Curves adjustment also increases contrast, but can do it without clipping. So those clouds will look much better. The Exposure slider and the Contrast slider in the Lumetri Color panel have S-curves built in, so they're safe to use.

Curves—My Grading Tool of Choice

Most of the time, I'll work with the RGB Curves tool while watching the RGB Parade scope. Some pro colorists may not like Curves because they're used to trackball controls and fancy hardware. As a reader of this book, your work is probably more keyboard-and-mouse based. Add to this the fact that the curves in Premiere can be made as large as you want, making precise adjustments very easy, and Curves is the perfect tool! Try maximizing the Lumetri Control panel or the Effect Controls panel, and you get super-big curves.

The RGB Parade scope and RGB Curves work great in tandem. If the Scope shows high levels in the reds, lower the red curve. If it shows low blue levels, raise the blue curve, and so on. It's incredibly intuitive. Figure 6-97 shows the ramp and scope before any adjustments.

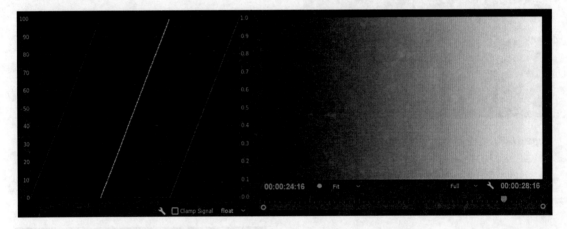

Figure 6-97. *Linear ramp and RGB Parade scope*

Figure 6-98 shows the ramp and scope after the adjustments in Figure 6-99 were made. Notice how the trace in the scope reflects the curves in the scope when applied to a grayscale ramp. There's a direct relation between the R, G, and B curves in the RGB Parade scope and the curves I made in RGB Curves.

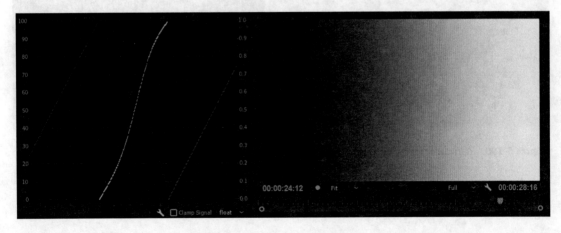

Figure 6-98. *Linear ramp and RGB Parade scope after curves adjustment*

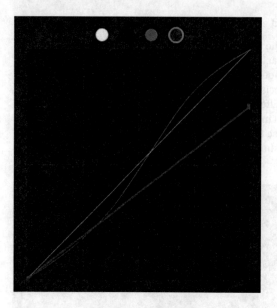

Figure 6-99. *The Curves adjustment used*

Figure 6-100 shows an example with a real image. See how the height of the trace in the Parade scope shows that the highlights have more blue than green, and not much red?

Figure 6-100. *RGB curves before Parade*

By adjusting the curves, this image lost the blue cast in the upper area. This automatically makes the skin tones look better, and the water gets back the proper teal "tropical paradise" look that it had in real life. Figure 6-101 shows the Curves adjustment, the resulting image, and the scope.

Figure 6-101. *Curves adjustment and the resulting image and scope*

A steep curve causes high midtone contrast, while a flatter curve lowers the midtone contrast. Avoid very steep, flat, and inverse curves. Too many points can do a lot of strange things to your footage.

Tweaking brightness, contrast, and gamma is super easy with RGB Curves, which gives you total control over these adjustments. But it has no saturation adjustment, so we use the Saturation slider in the Basic Correction section of Lumetri instead.

This combination of RGB Curves and Saturation is something I use a lot, and I kind of hope you will too. Save a custom preset so you can apply both in one single operation.

If the image needs different saturation adjustments for shadows, midtones, and highlights, you'll want to use the three-way Color Wheels section combined with RGB Curves.

The S-curve

Adding a traditional S-curve to your footage will increase contrast without crushing blacks or clipping whites and generally gives your image more "pop." The S-curve will also increase the saturation, so make sure you add the S-curve before you decide if you need an additional saturation adjustment. Figure 6-102 shows a standard S-curve and the image before and after adding it.

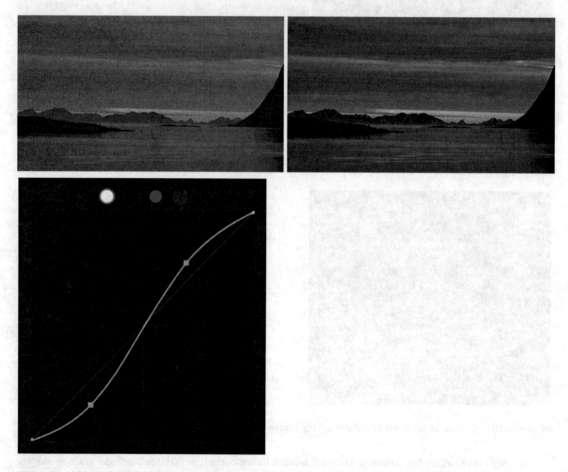

Figure 6-102. *A simple S-Curve increases perceived contrast and saturation without clipping whites and blacks*

In a book, it's hard to convey the feeling of working with RGB Curves and the RGB Parade scope, but the direct link between the tool and the scope, and the immediate feedback you get when dragging the different portions of the curve and watching the same portions in the scope move, is very satisfying. Please try it out yourself.

If you want to see curves in action, watch the video tutorial at premierepro.net.

Memory Colors

Among the most important colors to get right are the colors of skin, sky, and grass. These are very familiar to us, so if they're not right, we feel it very strongly. The color of your jeans or your car will not be that familiar to everyone, and you can get away with a pretty bad match. A colorist friend of mine uses this mantra: *Blacks, whites, midtones, skin.* If there's no skin, but grass and sky, he changes to *Blacks, whites, midtones, sky, grass.*

To determine the right colors, we use the vector scope. The angle tells us the hue, and the saturation can be determined by how far from the center the burst is.

Skin Tone

Skin tones across races fall within a surprisingly narrow angle on the vector scope. In fact, they all fall within a few degrees on the scope. I find this amazing! The only difference between dark skin and light skin is the amount of pigment. The color is the same.

So, you need to make sure the skin tones in your films end up close to that angle. When you want to see skin tone only, use the crop effect to temporarily isolate a face to quickly see where skin tone lies on the vector scope (Figure 6-103). When you're finished tweaking, just disable or delete the crop effect.

Figure 6-103. *Original image, cropped, and vector scope ("Cambelles" test image courtesy of DSC Labs, dsclabs.com)*

Skin tone should end up close to (but not necessarily exactly at) the skin tone line on the vector scope. Cropping away everything that's not skin tone makes it very easy to see the angle and saturation on the vector scope.

Often, we'll warm up the highlights to make the skin warmer, but then we need to cool down the midtones a bit to keep the skin from becoming overly orange. When primary color correction isn't enough, you'll turn to secondary color correction, creating a matte for skin tones and adjusting them separately.

Sky

The sky is mostly blue-cyan, with a gradient that's lighter at the bottom and darker at the top. But our memory of blue sky seems to be more bluish than the real sky color, so if you want the sky to look naturally blue, you may have to overdo it a bit, giving it a deeper, more saturated blue color. As you can see in the collage of sky images in Figure 6-104, the hue of the blue sky doesn't vary much. The saturation and lightness will change, but not the hue.

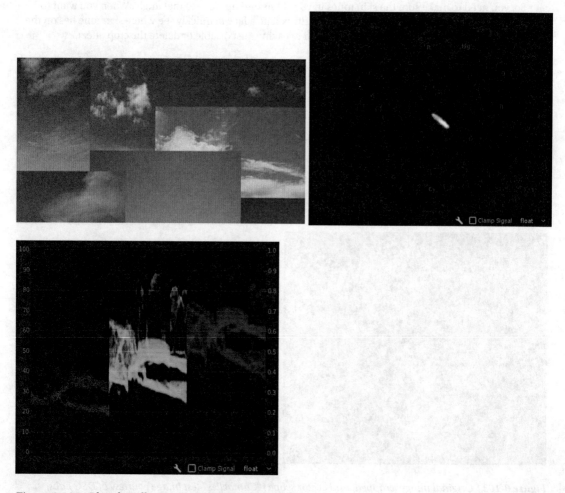

Figure 6-104. *Blue sky collage, vector scope, and Parade scope*

Even though these images of sky all seem quite different, they all fall within the same general angle on the scope. The brightness differs quite a lot, though, as we can see on the RGB Parade scope.

Sunsets

The color of the sunlight changes really quickly from white to orange toward red when the sun approaches the horizon And after the sun sets, the blue sky becomes the dominant light source, and everything turns more blue. See Figure 6-105.

Figure 6-105. *The sun sets at the beautiful Ko Racha Yai in Phuket, Thailand*

You need to establish a reference and correct the rest of the clips to match. If you want to convey the feeling that time has passed, you can adjust the color accordingly.

Foliage and Grass

Foliage and grass also fall within a quite narrow area in the vector scope (Figure 6-106). Young leaves are light green, almost with a yellow cast. Older leaves are darker, and really old leaves (before they turn yellow, red, or orange) can be an almost bluish dark green.

Figure 6-106. *Foliage and grass fall within a narrow area in the vector scope*

Perceived Color and Contrast

Our eyes can't judge absolute contrast, colors, and levels. We always take the surrounding area into account. There are no yellow squares in the left box in Figure 6-107, and there are no blue squares in the middle box. They are all gray like in the right box. But because of the surrounding blue cast in the left box, the gray squares seem yellow, and the yellowish surroundings in the middle box make them seem blue. With a neutral white surrounding, they look gray.

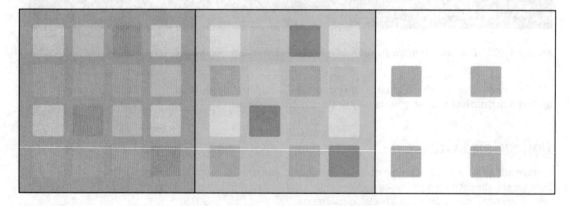

Figure 6-107. *The gray squares seem to change color in different surroundings*

Color constancy is very much a psychological thing and cannot be measured in a way that represents how we perceive it.

We perceive lightness as the difference between image elements, not as an absolute measure. A gray text can look light when placed on a dark background, and still look dark when placed on a white background. See Figure 6-108.

Figure 6-108. *A color seems lighter in dark surroundings than when surrounded by lighter areas*

Secondary Color Correction

Secondary color correction is selective color manipulation, meaning we adjust some colors or certain areas of the frame without affecting others. The usual suspects for secondary color correction are memory colors, like skin tone, grass, and sky, and objects that need to be more visible or less obvious. Secondary color correction can help the subject pop.

Whenever you use secondary color correction, or keying, look at the image with critical eyes. It's easy to apply too much adjustment so the picture screams "fake" because the adjusted parts don't look as if they belong in the picture. They may end up looking as if they're cut out from another scene and pasted into the current frame.

Don't Forget Color Contrast and Saturation Contrast

When doing secondary color correction, we often use contrast to make some objects in the image stand out. This is not limited to different brightness levels and vignettes. Color contrast and saturation contrast are also used a lot in color grading.

If you want to make that blood spill stand out in your action or horror film, you can make it darker and add saturation in the blood. If that's not enough, you can have less saturation and more blue and green in the highlights of the rest of the image. The added contrast in color and saturation will make the blood stand out more.

Qualifiers

The built-in qualifiers in the HSL Secondary section of the Lumetri Color panel are essentially keyers. We can key out pixels based on hue, saturation, and luminance and adjust only the pixels with values that fall within the chosen range.

So, if the object you want to, say, boost the saturation on is different from the rest of the image in terms of the color hue, the color saturation, or the lightness, you can create a good selection. Secondary color correction is also very handy when you want certain colors in the image to pop. Desaturate the overall image and then make some colors more saturated. This creates an interesting look that is often seen in commercials.

In Figure 6-109, I wanted to get some more detail in the sky without affecting the darker parts of the image, so I sampled the clouds and sky and dragged the sliders of the HSL Secondary section until I had a good selection. Note that I switched off the Hue and Saturation sliders, making this a Luminance-only selection. See Figure 6-110. By qualifying the very light pixels only, I could isolate the clouds, sky, and other overexposed areas and bring these down a bit.

489

Figure 6-109. *Only the very bright pixels were qualified and adjusted*

Figure 6-110. *Settings I used in the HSL Secondary section*

OK, so the sky and clouds look a little bit better. Not perfect, because some of the pixels in the upper left of the image are straight-out clipped, with areas that are just solid white. Not much more we can do about that, unless we do a sky replacement.

Ctrl (Cmd) Samples 5 × 5

As a result of noise or grain from the camera sensor and some compression artifacts, neighboring pixels in an image can have quite different values. Clicking with the eye dropper on a seemingly monochromatic area of the image may result in just a few scattered pixels being chosen. Hold down **Ctrl** (Cmd) to sample an area of 5 × 5 pixels, averaging the pixel values from a larger area (Figure 6-111). This eliminates sampling errors caused by noise and variations between neighboring pixels and results in a better key.

490

Figure 6-111. *Hold down the CTRL (Cmd) key while sampling colors to get a 5 × 5 sample*

Refine Your Matte

When using the HSL qualifiers under HSL Secondary to pull a matte, the result will often have noise, chatter, and other artifacts. To fix this, we can use the Denoise and Blur sliders. Don't overdo the blur, or you'll get undesirable halos and glows.

Masking

Often, different parts of the image need different corrections. Enter the art of masking. Other color-grading apps have fancy names for masks and mattes. Resolve uses the term *Power Windows*. But it's just a mask. In Premiere, we call it a mask.

All masks don't have to be perfect. It all depends on what you'll use it for. If you're just adjusting the saturation a little, you'll get away with a really sloppy mask. If you're making extreme corrections to hue or lightness, you'll need a much better mask.

Masks in Premiere are added to the individual effects. To add a mask to an effect, click one of the Create Mask icons in the Effect Controls panel. You can choose between ellipse-shaped, rectangle-shaped, or free-form Bezier-shaped masks. See Figure 6-112.

Figure 6-112. *Click one of the three Create Mask icons to create a mask*

The Bezier masks you draw with the Pen tool work as they do in Illustrator, Photoshop, and After Effects. When you click, you create a corner point, and when you click and drag, you create a Bezier curve. You can move the mask's vertices at any time.

The rectangle is actually a four-point polygon shape, and you can add as many points as you like by clicking on the mask path, remove points by **Ctrl-clicking** (Cmd-clicking) on them, and toggle between Bezier points and corner points by **Alt-clicking** on them. Even the ellipse mask can get more or fewer points this way.

In Figure 6-113, I added RGB Curves and clicked on the Ellipse Mask icon. Then, I dragged the points to adjust the shape to include the red-hot iron. Then, I adjusted the feathering to taste.

Figure 6-113. *An adjustment inside the mask made the red-hot iron darker and more saturated*

Notice how the effect made the hot iron much more saturated and orange, while the area outside the mask is not affected.

When you add an ellipse- or rectangle-shaped mask, it's placed in the center of the frame and has a preset size and feathering. This is just to give you a starting point. Adjust the points to customize the mask to the current image.

When drawing a free-form shape, carefully choose where to create the first point. This is where the handles for mask expansion and feathering will be placed, and you want them in a convenient place. Close the path by clicking on the first point you made (Figure 6-114).

Figure 6-114. *Draw free-form Bezier masks with the Pen tool. Close the mask path by clicking on the first vertex*

To adjust an existing mask shape, drag the points. To adjust the curviness of a Bezier point, drag the Bezier handles on both sides of the point. To adjust mask expansion and feathering, drag the square and the circle on the handle (Figure 6-115). Figure 6-116 shows the image before and after the Curves adjustment with the mask.

Figure 6-115. *Drag the feathering handle to soften the mask*

Figure 6-116. *The image before and after the RGB Curves adjustment*

Combine Qualifiers and Masks

In the preceding explanation of secondary color correction, I used a key to lower the levels of the sky and clouds. However, my adjustment also affected the brightest pixels in the lower part of the image, and I didn't actually want that. I also had a hard time getting the sky to look its best because of the limited corrections available in the HSL Secondary section of Lumetri. Figure 6-117 is a reminder of how it looked after the HSL Secondary corrections.

Figure 6-117. *Secondary result*

So, let's combine secondary color correction with a mask. I prefer to use a three-layer stack for this, with two extra copies of the clip. See Figure 6-118.

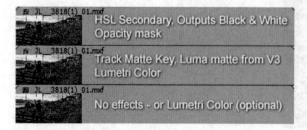

Figure 6-118. *Secondary layer stack*

The source clip is used on three tracks. The lower one has no correction in this example, but it could have one if corrections were required. The upper one has the HSL Secondary section set to output a black and white matte, and I qualified the brightest pixels. It also has a mask that selects the sky, but not the lower parts of the image, as shown in Figure 6-119.

Figure 6-119. *See how the highlights are back in the fence, the house, and the goats?*

The middle layer is where the magic happens. It has the track matte key effect, set to use the luminance values of the upper layer, plus I can use *all* the tools in every section of the Lumetri Color panel for my adjustments.

■ **Note** This layered technique with masks also solves the issue where the HSL Secondary qualifiers look at the modified pixel values, not at the original source pixel values. By using separate layers, we're separating the HSL qualifiers from the other adjustments and can adjust anything in any Lumetri section without breaking our key.

This combination of tracked masks and qualifiers is so flexible, I find myself using it all the time.

Here are some random masking tips:

You can have masks on all video effects except the warp stabilizer.

You can have several masks on each effect.

You can apply the same effect several times with different masks.

You can copy and paste masks, with tracking data, from one effect to another.

You can copy and paste effects, including masking and tracking data, from one clip to another.

You can use the arrow keys to nudge a selected mask vertex. Add **Shift** to move in greater increments.

Place the cursor just outside a vertex and drag to rotate the mask. Press **Shift** to constrain the rotation to 22.5-degree increments.

When you have trouble setting new mask points because the Rotate pointer appears when you're close to another point, use the Maximize Frame feature to make the program monitor go full screen after you've set your first point.

You can also set a new point in another place, and then move it to where it should be—including outside of the frame.

Tracking Masks

When the camera or objects and people in a shot move, we need to move the mask. This is when tracking comes in handy. Tracking in Premiere is incredibly easy. Create a mask, click the wrench icon to choose tracking method (optional), and hit the *Track Forward* or *Track Backward* buttons, then relax and watch the tracking progress. Figure 6-120 shows the tracking options.

Figure 6-120. *Choose between three kinds of tracking. Hit the icon that looks like a Play button to start tracking.*

The tracker adjusts the mask's position, scale, and rotation, and even changes the mask shape itself during the tracking (Figure 6-121).

Figure 6-121. *The tracker adjusts the mask's position, scale, and rotation, and even changes the mask shape itself during the tracking*

When tracking goes wrong, just hit the *Stop* button and go back to the last good tracked frame, then start tracking again from there (Figure 6-122). Use the frame-by-frame tracking buttons and adjust the mask manually for a few frames when required.

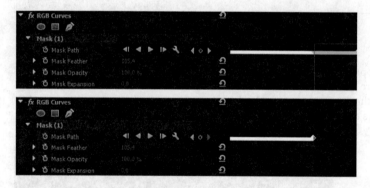

Figure 6-122. *When tracking goes wrong, delete the bad keyframes and track further*

If the tracked element goes out of frame or is obstructed by a person or object moving in front of it, the tracker will start guessing wildly. When this happens, just delete any bad keyframes and start the tracking again later in the clip.

Premiere will interpolate the tracking points between the existing points, and this prevents the mask from moving randomly. You can have as many effects as you want, and add tracked masks to all of them.

Figure 6-123 shows an example where I wanted to lighten up the man's face and also make the eyes even lighter. I used the RGB Curves effect twice and tracked the face for the first instance and the eyes for the other one. Since I was parked on the last frame after tracking the first mask, I chose to track the next mask backward. I used the obsolete RGB Curves effect because I needed two instances, and the obsolete effect uses less GPU power than Lumetri uses to do the same thing. Figures 6-124 to 6-126 show the original image, the result after one RGB Curves effect, and after the second RGB Curves effect.

Figure 6-123. *It's quite amazing that the track follows this movement nicely, even when the eyes are not visible*

Figure 6-124. *Image before any secondary color correction*

Figure 6-125. *Image after one correction where the mask covers the whole face*

Figure 6-126. Image after a second correction where the mask covers just the area around the eyes

■ **Note** When you're editing mask points, a fast way to advance frame by frame is to scroll with the mouse wheel.

Tracking Affects Project File Size

Tracking data is stored in the project file. Since we're tracking several points, and every point gets a keyframe on every frame, tracker data will increase the project file size, and auto-saves will take a lot longer. If you do a lot of tracking, consider doing the tracking in a separate project and export a high-quality video file with the effect baked in. Import this clip in your main project.

Workaround for Variable Feathering

Premiere doesn't have variable feathering on masks, so to achieve different amounts of blur on a mask, we need to use more than one mask with different settings for feathering. Masks in Premiere will be combined in what After Effects would call Add mode.

Use Masks and Curves for Dodge and Burn

If you're familiar with darkroom printing processes, you'll know dodge and burn–to selectively lighten or darken areas of the image. Photoshop has digital versions of these tools, but Premiere doesn't. We can easily make our own, though.

Add two instances of curves to a clip. Use the obsolete RGB Curves or the ones in the Lumetri Color effect. One curve should lighten the image, and one should darken it. Turn both of them off and save this as an effects preset named Dodge & Burn.

Whenever you need dodge and burn, add this effect, turn on the curve you want, and add a mask that covers the area you want to fix. In Figure 6-127, I've dodged his body and burned both sides of the image to separate him better from the background.

Figure 6-127. *Dodged body, burned sides. Before and after. (Footage from Egotripp by Kjetil Fredriksen and Jan Olav Nordskog. Actor: Eirik Sandåker)*

Figure 6-128 shows the curves in my Dodge & Burn preset. One lightening curve and one darkening curve make up the preset. Switch on the curve you need, add a feathered mask to cover the area you want to affect, and adjust the opacity of the mask to taste.

Figure 6-128. *Dodge & Burn curves*

We often use darkened vignetting to draw attention to the subject of the shot. I don't like the built-in one in the Lumetri Color effect. It just darkens everything within the vignette by the same amount, which isn't always what we want.

We can build our own with an adjustment layer, some color correction, and optional blur. I created an opacity mask on an adjustment layer, inverted it, and set Feathering to 250. Then, I added the Lumetri Color effect and adjusted the RGB Curves as shown in Figure 6-129. Finally, I threw on the Gaussian blur effect with a small amount of blurriness and *Repeat Edge Pixels* checked.

***Figure 6-129.** I've made the shadows and midtones darker while keeping most of the highlights*

This is a highly flexible setup where you can adjust the mask shape to any shape you want—even irregular and non-centered shapes. You can also have as much or as little blur as you want in the vignette, and the color, darkness, and blending modes can be adjusted any way you want. Figures 6-130 to 6-133 show some vignettes for comparison.

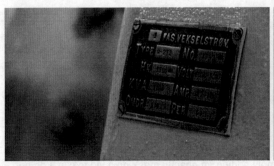 

Figure 6-130. *The original image and the opacity mask*

Figure 6-131. *Standard Lumetri vignette (left); flexible vignette in Normal blending mode (right)*

Figure 6-132. *Flexible vignette in Overlay mode (left); Linear Burn mode (right)*

Figure 6-133. *To draw the attention even more toward the metal plate, I changed the mask. Yes, I exaggerated it, for clarity.*

■ **Note**   Although it's possible to add vignettes by simply adding an opacity mask on a video clip, I do not recommend it. It will only work when you have a black background (or none at all) and export without an alpha channel.

Shot Matching

This is probably the most important skill you can possess as a colorist. If you cannot match the clips within a scene, the audience will not get into the flow of the scene and will be thrown out of the illusion every time we cut because of a lack of visual continuity. So, color consistency is much more important than accuracy.

Shot matching and scene matching are time-consuming tasks, but they are very important and should never be skipped.

Documentaries, corporate movies, and reality shows are among the most labor-intensive shows to grade. Tight budgets and time schedules call for heavy use of available-light shooting and quick lighting setups.

A lot of things must be right: color, contrast, saturation, lightness, and so forth. My favorite two tools to accomplish this are the RGB Curves and the RGB Parade scopes. A winning duo! RGB Curves has no way of adjusting saturation, so I will often use the Saturation slider in the Basic section of Lumetri, too.

Three-Monitor Workspace for Matching Shots

When you're matching shots, you need to see the clips before and after the one you're working on. Here's one way to do that: select the sequence you're working on in the bin and drag it to the source monitor, or use the keyboard shortcut for *Open in source monitor*, **Shift+O**. Then, open the reference monitor. It will show the same sequence as the program monitor.

I've arranged my monitors side-by-side so I can easily switch between them and scrub or play them all. See Figure 6-134. I've also saved this as a workspace and called it *4. Shot Matching*. Yes, I always number my workspaces so I can remember the shortcuts for all of them. When they have numbers, adding a new one doesn't mess with the alphabetic order, and therefore the shortcuts stay the same.

Figure 6-134. *Shot-matching workspace (Swan footage by Vidar Granberg)*

You now have the same sequence open on all three monitors, but you'll only be working on the clips in the timeline, watching the program monitor.

■ **Note**   The scopes and the full-screen view on your second monitor via Transmit will follow the active panel, so switching between the monitors allows you to compare scopes quickly and easily.

Ganging (linking the playhead of two monitors) doesn't work when you have the same sequence on all monitors, so turn it off. You'll have to move the playhead on all three monitors manually by scrubbing or using **JKL**.

It's possible to have four instances of the same sequence with some help from the Icon view in a bin. See Figure 6-135. However, the viewer in the bin is a bit slower to work with. It doesn't update until you let go of the mouse when you drag sliders and do other adjustments. For the scope to show that source, you'll have to play the sequence in the bin or at least move its playhead.

Figure 6-135. *You can have four "monitors" if you show the sequence in a bin with Icon view set to a large size*

So, the bin viewer is a bit limited compared to the three monitors, but it can be helpful in some situations.

Procedure for Matching Shots

Matching shots can be hard–especially if you just start tweaking the colors of the clips without a plan. If you always follow the following steps, you will always be able to match shots, and you will do it fast.

Step 1: Set Your Workspace

To assess the difference between the hero shot and the shot I'm grading, I use the three-monitor workspace just shown and my RGB Parade scopes. I'll also go full screen on my second computer monitor (via Transmit) and cut between the hero shot and the other clips, and sometimes even set up a split screen between them. It will not surprise you by now that I have presets for crop that make mock-up split screens easy.

Step 2: Find a Hero Shot

Find a shot that represents the scene in a good way, ideally a shot that has the potential to communicate the message, feeling, or mood you want for the scene. I try to find one shot that has at least one person and some of the environment and use this as my hero shot.

▓▓ **Note** The hero shot will not always be the best shot! The worst one is never going to look as good as the best one, but it may be possible to make it look as good as another image that's not perfect, but at least acceptable. The best shot then needs to be degraded to look like the other ones. I know, it hurts, but you need to sacrifice something to get a properly balanced scene. What's important is that everything looks consistent—otherwise, the bad shot will stand out, ripping the audience out of the story.

Now, grade this hero shot until it looks good. Then, load your sequence into the source monitor and the reference monitor and match all the other shots, constantly comparing them against the hero shot as follows.

Step 3: Adjust the Clips Using Scopes and Your Eyes

First, match overall contrast by adjusting the contrast in each color channel. Do the white and black points line up for R, G, and B? Probably not, so we'll adjust them until they do. Then, we'll look at the midtones and make sure they align properly. I use the RGB Curves for this because of the close relationship to the waveforms in the RGB Parade scope.

Color adjustments are somewhat trickier than contrast adjustments. Black points and white points can quite easily be determined by looking at the scopes. However, midtone color balance is a more subjective adjustment, and how we perceive color is also determined by what other colors are in the shot. So, you'll be using your skills as an artist here, not just those as a technician.

There can be differences in highlights, midtones, and shadows, and you need to spot them all. But, mostly, the differences will lie in the highlights and midtones. The RGB Parade scope can help you a lot, as the three waveforms will show different levels in the midtones.

Use the scopes to get the levels about right, but the final decision will have to be made based on eyeballing. When the shots are well balanced, but the match still isn't perfect, we'll turn to secondary color correction.

Step 4: Play the Whole Piece

This is very important! Clips that look like a good match on the scopes and when viewing them out of order and as stills may still not look good together when played back. You've not finished your shot matching until you've watched the whole sequence in real-time. If changes are called for, go ahead and tweak some more.

Shot Matching Procedure Summary

To match two or more shots, use your custom shot-matching workspace. Move the playhead in the program monitor to the clip you want to adjust. Now, click the monitor where you have your hero shot. In my case, I chose the one in the source monitor. Watch the scopes. Click the program monitor and see the difference in the scopes. Adjust the clip in the timeline while you watch the scopes and the program monitor.

Match the levels in the scopes first, then do the final adjustments by eye, comparing the two monitors. Click back and forth between the two monitors to better see the difference in the scopes, and on your second computer monitor via Transmit if you have one.

Then, move the playhead over the next clip that needs matching and repeat the procedure. Move the playheads in the other monitors as needed to show the clips you want to compare.

Walkthrough of a Basic Shot-Matching Job

The following image sequence (Figures 6-136 to 6-140) shows the steps I went through to match three clips shot with an iPhone. The automatic white balance varied wildly from shot to shot, so before matching they didn't match at all. I used a combination of RGB Curves, the RGB Parade scope, and the vector scope. Enjoy.

Figure 6-136. *Before matching. Uganda footage courtesy of the Forestry Extension Institute, skogkurs.no*

Figure 6-137. *In the RGB Parade scope and the YUV vector scope we can clearly see how different the colors are. See how tall the blue bar is on the third shot compared to the second one?*

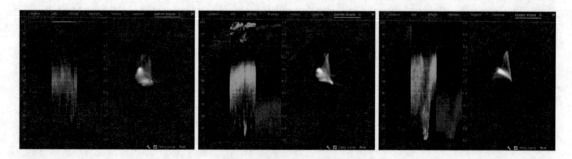

Figure 6-138. *After matching, the scopes are more similar in appearance for each clip*

Figure 6-139. *Here, the shots are matched pretty well*

Figure 6-140. *The saturation and white levels were a bit too hot, so I added an adjustment layer where I fixed this and got them within legal ranges*

Miscellaneous Tips on Shot Matching

What follow here are some random tips that really speed up my workflow when doing shot matching in Premiere.

Crop It

If I have difficulties determining how well skin color or other colors match, I will throw on a Crop preset that crops away everything but skin tones, or–if I'm trying to match the color of a basketball–just the ball. This makes it much easier to see where the waveforms fall, or what angle and strength the color has on the vector scope. You can substitute the crop effect for an opacity mask if you need irregular shapes.

Are More Fixes Needed?

Check to see if noise or other additional effects will be needed. Differences in noise and grain can be disturbing, so you might need to add grain to some shots. You can add noise in Premiere with the noise effect, but for real grain matching you need to fire up After Effects or a third-party plug-in.

Maybe some clips need a little blur or sharpening to better match the others?

Reuse the Grades

When you've graded one shot from a particular angle, chances are that the rest of the shots from that angle will need the same corrections. Copying and pasting the corrections will save you a lot of time.

I also keep many presets of corrections I've done before on other films. After a while, you'll have a great collection of popular and often used corrections that gives you a kickstart when approaching new jobs. If you want to download a small collection of my presets, please visit premierepro.net.

Balance, Then Stylize

Some people like to add a style to the images while they do the balancing. I like to balance my shots first and then apply the style on all the clips at once using an adjustment layer. Why? Because I'm heavily addicted to presets! So, I'll use one of my stored presets and throw it on the adjustment layer. The fact that the clips are all properly balanced before I apply the style means I only need to do very small tweaks on each shot–if any. I find that I work much faster if I balance the shots first and then add the style.

Fixing Problematic Video

Some kinds of fixes are more common than others. The following is a collection of common fixes you need to know. There are limits to what can be done. Aggressive adjustments can reveal the shortcomings of some video formats. Heavily compressed H.264 from DSLRs and 8-bit MPEG-2 from some video cameras will "break" when you do heavy adjustments. There's only so much you can do. If the image is too overexposed, grainy, or underexposed, you will not be able to save it. The following techniques will save the most common problematic footage.

Flat and Dull Images

Bad lighting conditions or a sloppy camera operator can cause flat and dull footage. Maximizing the contrast will give the images more punch. Increased contrast will make the image appear sharper, and you'll get more vivid and saturated colors.

Throw on an S-curve preset to lower the shadows and raise the highlights, then adjust the midtones to taste. You may have to move the lower end of the curve to the right for the blacks to get close to zero, and the upper end to the left for the whites to get close to clipping. Figure 6-141 shows my S-curve and a before and after comparison. See how the yellow flowers are now better separated from the background?

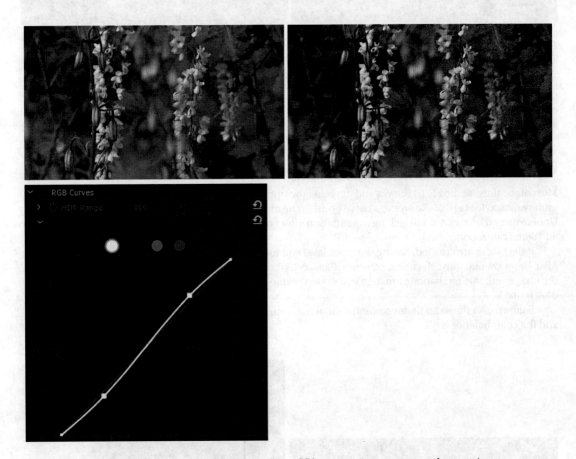

Figure 6-141. *S-curves are great for adding some "punch" by increasing contrast and saturation*

If you get Log footage, it will always look dull. It's supposed to. Apply a Log to Rec709 LUT before doing more corrections.

A well-exposed image with proper white and black levels may still seem to lack contrast. The reason is lack of midtone contrast. The midtones make up the majority of pixels in most images, so adjustments in midtone contrast will make a big difference in the perceived brightness, contrast, time of day, and so forth. S-curve to the rescue! Even good-looking shots can look better with an S-curve. See Figure 6-142.

Figure 6-142. *Good shots can sometimes benefit from an S-curve*

Notice how the S-curve also increases saturation. Even just lowering the shadows a little will give the image more "snap," and it serves the additional purpose of darkening the noisy shadows of highly compressed material, thereby hiding the worst-looking artifacts. Darkening an image overall is often best accomplished by lowering the midtones.

Underexposed Footage

Most of the time, adding RGB Curves and dragging the upper end of the curve to the left will fix underexposed footage. Make an extra curve point in the middle if you need to adjust the gamma. Underexposed images are still lacking in saturation after correcting the contrast, so you'll most likely need to add some saturation.

If the blacks are crushed, raising the black level will turn the blacks into not-so-good-looking gray areas. Also, be aware that most electronic screens (iPads, cell phones, PCs, and TV sets) have a black frame around the image, and raising shadows too high will make the dark parts of the image look milky compared to the dark frame.

Figure 6-143 shows an underexposed shot of two swans before any correction. There are no highlights, and the color balance is off.

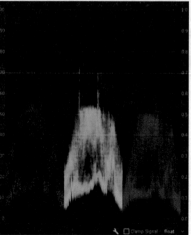

Figure 6-143. *Before adjustments*

Dragging the top of the master curve to the left raises the overall levels, as shown in Figure 6-144. Notice how the lower end of the master curve has been dragged slightly to the right to lower black levels. The green and blue curves have gotten similar treatments, but with different amounts. Figure 6-145 shows the result after I added another instance of Lumetri Color with an S-curve preset.

Figure 6-144. *After corrections*

Figure 6-145. *Additional S-curve gives more pop. Swan footage courtesy of Vidar Granberg*

When you correct underexposed video, you will often get a lot of video noise because of camera-sensor noise and the compression methods used when storing the video. The blue channel is usually the noisiest one. Here's a tip that can help: apply a very small amount of channel blur on just the Blue channel. But beware; the channel blur is not accelerated, does its calculations in 8-bit, and operates in RGB (not YUV), so look out for clipped whites. Putting this effect as the last of your corrections will help preserve the highlights. For better results, dynamic link the clip to AE and do noise reduction there.

Overexposed Footage

This is probably the most common problem you'll run into. Depending on the recording format, slightly overexposed shots can be saved with good results, as there will often be some texture and details hidden in the overbrights. Use RGB Curves and drag the upper curve a bit down. If there are overbrights, they will get below 100, and you'll get some detail in the highlights.

If the codec doesn't store overbrights, you'll just make the blown-out parts darker, but you'll get no extra texture in them. Often, the blacks are also too high and need to be adjusted. If necessary, add a point in the middle, creating a slight gamma curve to lower the midtones.

Figure 6-146 shows how slightly overexposed footage can be rescued by lowering the top of the master curve. Notice how much extra detail I was able to get in the clouds. In this case, I also lowered the highlights in the Basic Correction section to make the blue sky darker.

Figure 6-146. *Slightly overexposed footage rescued by lowering the top of the master curve*

513

Severely overexposed clips are often beyond repair. You need to have some details in the overbrights, or else you'll get large areas of light gray instead of getting back texture and details. If you're editing RED or other RAW source material, you can use a second, darker copy of the clip to replace the highlights using secondary color correction techniques.

Some parts of the image are best left clipping. Reflections in chrome gear, polished cars, and other specular highlights along with light bulbs, LEDs, and other light sources should be left clipped. Their levels are way higher than the rest of the image anyway.

Colored Clipping

Some images will have a color cast to the clipped highlights. Levels near 100 percent will often look very orange or red. This happens because the red channel gets clipped before the other channels when the shot has warm colors. You can deal with this by desaturating only the highlights via secondary color correction.

If only one channel is clipping, we can borrow detail from another channel. This is easier to do with Dynamic Link to After Effects than to build in Premiere. AE has a shift channels effect that can be used to take the info from the green channel and use it in the red channel.

Pushing Skin Tones

Sometimes skin color can be a bit off even though the rest of the image seems OK. Use secondary color correction in the HSL Secondary section to isolate the skin color and apply corrections to it. In Figure 6-147, I've adjusted skin tones to a more normal tone. By isolating the skin tones, I could adjust them while keeping the green cast from the forest in the rest of the image.

Figure 6-147. Isolating the skin tones with HSL Secondary

Get Back the Blue Sky

If there is at least a little bit of blue in the highlights, you can isolate this color in the HSL Secondary section and add saturation and extra color. In Figure 6-148, the blue sky is a bit dull. Figure 6-149 shows how I could isolate the blues in the sky and boost them a little, using HSL Secondary again.

Figure 6-148. *Light blue sky before corrections*

Figure 6-149. *Here, I've boosted saturation and made the blues a bit darker*

Add Some Blue Sky

When the sky is covered by clouds it will often be a sad, white, blown-out thing in the image with no extra texture to fetch in the overbrights. In such cases, you need to fake it. Adding a legacy title with a blue gradient in Overlay or Linear Light blending mode can look quite real in some images, as shown in Figure 6-150. The legacy titler will probably be gone soon, so let's hope we will get gradients in the new graphics engine very soon. If not, we'll have to make our gradients in Photoshop in the future.

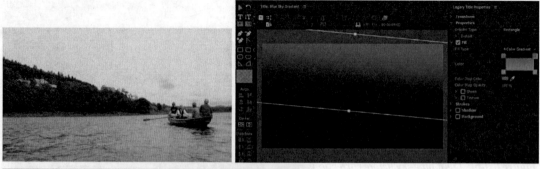

Figure 6-150. *A blue gradient from the legacy titler fixed the sky*

Relighting an Image

The same flexible technique we used for making vignettes can be used to selectively distribute light and shadow areas in an image. Just make a custom mask shape and adjust the levels outside and inside the mask separately to focus the viewer's attention on the important parts of the image.

In Figure 6-151 I've used a mask to protect the girl. Then, I lowered the levels outside of the mask and added some blur, making the girl stand out from the background a bit more.

Figure 6-151. *Lowering levels outside of the mask separated the girl from the background*

Don't Fake It Too Much

Your audience should never be aware that you've manipulated the image, unless it's done for an effect. The earlier autumn-becomes-summer example in the section on the HSL Secondaries in the Lumetri Color panel is one example where it has been pushed too far and looks fake.

Achieving a "Look"

As you've seen by now, color grading is much more than correcting a bad white balance or fixing underexposed footage. Creative looks can create depth, attitude, and drama. Do you want your film to have rich, saturated colors, or do you aim for a more muted, desaturated look? Do you have two different places in your film that need to be recognized without your telling the viewer? A different look for each location will help you tell your story more effectively.

Steven Soderbergh, in his Oscar-winning film *Traffic* (2000), used three different film stocks and film treatments to achieve a distinctive look for each vignette in the story. Quote from IMDB:

> The "Wakefield" story features a colder, bluer tone to match the sad, depressive emotion. The "Ayala" story is bright, shiny, and saturated in primary colors, especially red, to match the glitzy surface of Helena's life. The "Mexican" story appears grainy, rough, and hot to go with the rugged Mexican landscape and congested cities.

This technique of using different looks isn't new at all. Actually, it's been used for almost a century. D. W. Griffith's film *Intolerance: Love's Struggle Throughout the Ages (1916)* is an early example (Figure 6-152). In some of the many released versions, he color tinted the four different parts of his movie in different tones. He gave the Modern story an amber tint, the Judean story got a Blue tint, the French story got a sepia tone, and finally the Babylonian story was tinted gray-green.

Figure 6-152. *Intolerance poster. Image from Wikimedia Commons*

With digital filmmaking, these different looks can easily be created in post. A drama series might have six to ten different looks that they use for different locations, moods, realities, flashbacks, and so on. If you've watched *Game of Thrones*, you know what I mean.

But looks are not just for fiction films. If your documentary film has some historical or archival footage, this can also be processed to stand out as different from the rest of your film. So, a "look" can help the storytelling, or you can use it just because it looks good.

Sepia

This look simulates an old black and white photograph that has taken on a brownish color due to residue chemicals from the developing process. There are several ways to accomplish this look, but the easiest one is the tint effect set to a light brownish color. It's also easily achieved with a combination of desaturation and RGB Curves, which gives you more control. It can be hard to know how much saturation to add back. Always go past the sweet point and then come back. That way, it's much easier to see what works best. You can download this and more "looks" presets from premierepro.net. See Figure 6-153.

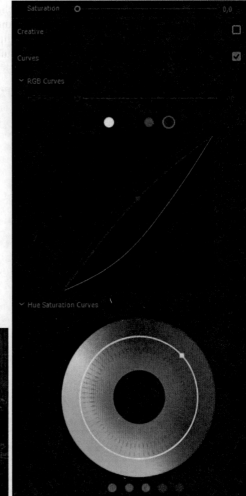

Figure 6-153. *The "old photograph" sepia look*

Bleach Bypass

This was originally a purely chemical look accomplished by skipping or shortening the chemical bleaching stage when developing the film. This look has become very popular. There are several ways to do this chemically, so there is no single look that is the "correct" bleach bypass. Interestingly, the film *Saving Private Ryan* (Steven Spielberg, 1998) is often referred to when explaining bleach bypass. But in that film, they actually used a more expensive process than what was common, so it's not a typical bleach bypass look.

Anyway, the chemical process results in increased contrast, grain, and density and reduced saturation. This means we will be soaking out some saturation and increasing the contrast, clipping whites, and crushing blacks. The examples that follow were all made with the obsolete effects. The same look can be made the same way in the Lumetri Color panel, of course.

Figure 6-154 shows the simplest recipe for bleach bypass, and one of the best-looking ones–S-curve for increased contrast, and saturation lowered quite a bit. If you want to explore more-elaborate versions of bleach bypass, including some with blue highlights, added grain, and so on, then download my free presets from premierepro.net and see how they were built.

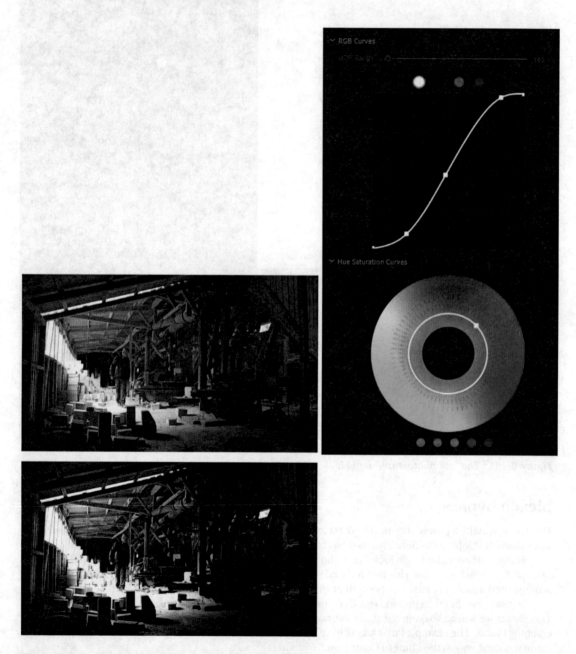

Figure 6-154. *Increased contrast and desaturation is all it takes to create this simple bleach bypass look*

Teal and Orange

This look is very typical for modern action-hero movies; crushed blacks, maybe a bit desaturated, and the background pushed toward a blue-green tone. Still, the skin tones are somewhat correct with an orange-ish tone. Before you expect miracles, be aware of this: this look, like many others, is best made both on set and in post, so trying to create it exclusively in post-production will be a challenge.

Again, the examples here are made with the obsolete effects, but you can use the Lumetri Color panel to do the same thing.

Simple Teal & Orange

The best-known method for teal and orange is to push shadows toward teal and highlights toward orange (Figure 6-155). Personally, I find that this method warms up the highlights a bit too much, so I don't really subscribe to it. I like both the whites and the blacks to be either neutral or just a tiny bit teal-ish.

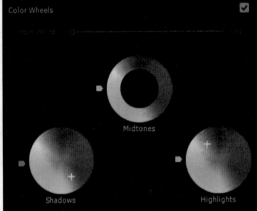

Figure 6-155. Teal and orange in its simplest form

Better Teal & Orange

Figure 6-156 shows my favorite teal and orange preset. First, use RGB Curves to tint the image and add a tiny bit of contrast, but keep the white and black points for all curves. This makes sure the absolute blacks and whites remain neutral. Then, use the HSL Secondaries to bring skin tones back toward normal. You'll need to tweak the secondary color correction to perfectly target skin tones in your images.

Figure 6-156. *My favorite teal and orange preset*

If you want, you can desaturate the image in the Basic Correction section so all colors are desaturated, then add more saturation only to skin tones in the HSL Secondaries. You will need to tweak the key more in this case.

Since we use secondary color correction, you have great control over both skin tones and other colors. By keeping the different adjustments on separate sections of the Lumetri Color effect, it's easier to tweak the result. See Figure 6-157 for another shot where I used the same preset.

Figure 6-157. *Teal and orange before and after*

Working with HDR Video

High dynamic range video is the greatest thing since 4K. Not more, but better pixels! 4K resolution is enough for most screen sizes we use today, provided you're at the correct viewing distance. Increasing the pixel count will not be readily apparent for most viewers, but a brighter image with more color depth will be very noticeable for all viewers.

What Is HDR?

With HDR video, we can have brighter, more saturated images (higher color gamut) with more shadow depth, and they look more natural. To still get good gradients and avoid banding with all that dynamic range, the bit depth has also been increased.

However, let me just make sure you understand this before we continue:

■ **Note**   For a true HDR workflow, you need an HDR monitor and HDR footage. Simulated images of standard versus high dynamic range content? No, I won't even bother. It's like simulating a 4K image on an HD monitor. There is no way to show how HDR looks without an HDR monitor and HDR images, saved in a format that supports HDR. Thank you.

To show all those bright pixels, we can't use the old Rec709 color space (en.wikipedia.org/wiki/Rec._709), so the scopes in Premiere support Rec2020 (en.wikipedia.org/wiki/Rec._2020#System_colorimetry), which is a larger color space but does not support the DCI-P3 color space.

■ Note Premiere still cannot *show* Rec 2020! It's all shown in Rec709 in your monitors, so you will be grading your HDR footage while watching SDR. All color processing also happens in Rec709, but Lumetri converts everything to linear for internal processing and then back to Rec709.

Say what? SDR? Yes, since we now have HDR, we needed a new name for the old dynamic range, and that is now known as SDR, standard dynamic range.

There are a few different HDR standards; Dolby Vision (en.wikipedia.org/wiki/High-dynamic-range_video#Dolby_Vision), Hybrid Log-Gamma (en.wikipedia.org/wiki/High-dynamic-range_video#Hybrid_Log-Gamma), and so on that aren't compatible with each other. Time will tell what standard wins the battle.

■ Note Premiere supports HDR in the following formats: OpenEXR, Dolby Vision (J2K), HEVC, and HLG. This means you cannot take a RED or Arri clip and just start working with it in HDR, even though the cameras are fully capable of capturing HDR. So, you must prepare your media for use in an HDR workflow in Premiere Pro.

You can export HDR to all the supported formats: OpenEXR, Dolby Vision (J2K), HEVC, and HLG.

If you want to play with some HDR material, there are some nice HEVC clips here: demo-uhd3d.com/categorie.php?tag=hevc.

What Is Nits?

Nits is a measurement method for luminance. The Mystery Box blog has a good explanation here: mysterybox.us/blog/2016/10/19/hdr-video-part-3-hdr-video-terms-explained.

■ Nit A unit of brightness density, or luminance. It's the colloquial term for the SI units of *candelas per square meter* (1 nit = 1 cd/m^2). It directly converts with the United States' customary unit of foot-lamberts (1 fl = 1 cd/foot^2), with 1 fl = 3.426 nits = 3.426 cd/m^2.

While some sliders in the Lumetri Color panel go to 10,000 Nits, which is the theoretical limit for HDR monitors, the upper part is not really usable yet. Most consumer monitors can show a maximum of around 600 to 1,500 Nits.

Growing Audience for HDR

You may think that HDR has a small audience—and it's true. But companies like YouTube, Amazon Prime, and Netflix are already showing HDR. With an HDR-compatible SmartTV set with a built-in app for one of these, people have access to an increasing amount of HDR material. Even some 4K Blu-ray movies are HDR. Most new 4K TV models now have HDR panels, and some smartphones have 4K HDR screens, so the potential audience is growing quickly.

For info on how to upload HDR video to YouTube, read more on YouTube Help: support.google.com/youtube/answer/7126552. You must use their free HDR Metadata tool to make sure all the tags are correct: github.com/YouTubeHDR/hdr_metadata.

Color Panel Settings for Working in HDR

To work with HDR footage, turn on the High Dynamic Range switch in the Lumetri Color panel to access the extended range of levels. This disables the *Input LUT* option in the Basic Correction section and activates the HDR White (100-1,000 Nits) and HDR Specular sliders. See Figure 6-158.

■ **Note**   The HDR White slider affects the ranges for shadows/midtones/highlights/etc. The HDR Specular slider controls the brightness of pixels with levels above the HDR White point you've set with the HDR White slider.

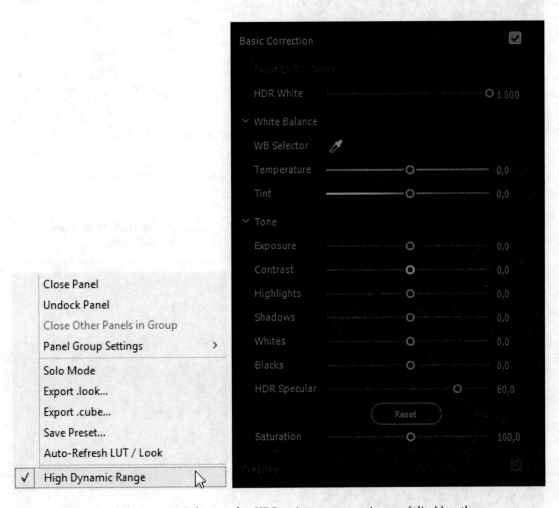

Figure 6-158. *Setting the Lumetri Color panel to HDR activates some options and disables others*

The Creative section is completely disabled when you enable HDR. The Curves section gets an HDR Range slider where you can set the range anywhere between 100 and 10,000 Nits (Figure 6-159).

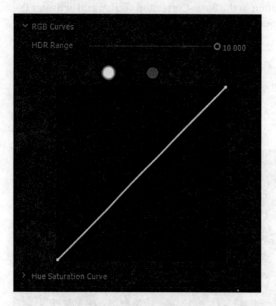

Figure 6-159. *The Curves section gets an HDR Range slider*

The Color Wheels get an extra wheel for the HDR Specular highlights, plus an HDR White slider (100–1,000 Nits) (Figure 6-160). The HSL Secondary and Vignette sections stay the same.

Figure 6-160. *You get an extra color wheel, plus an HDR White slider, in the Color Wheels section*

Scopes Settings for Working in HDR

The scopes also need to be set correctly, which means setting them to HDR mode in the drop-down menu in the lower-right corner of the panel, and switching the Colorspace to Rec2020 in the wrench menu (Figure 6-161).

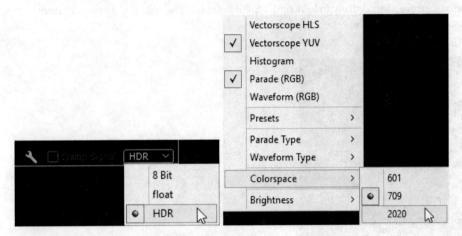

Figure 6-161. *HDR scopes set to Rec2020 color space*

Setting the scopes to HDR deactivates the *Clamp Signal* option and changes the scale, letting you see much brighter levels. Floating-point values (0–100) are displayed on the right-side scale, and to the left is now a Nit scale (0–1,000), replacing the familiar IRE scale (Figure 6-162).

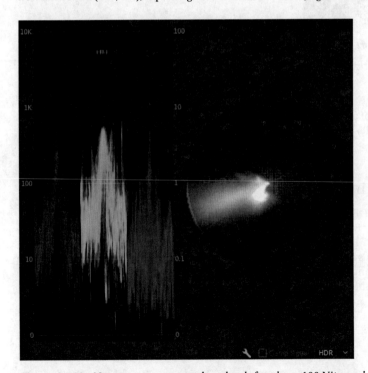

Figure 6-162. *Now your scopes can show levels far above 100 Nits, and the vector scopes can show more-saturated colors*

527

SDR Conform on Export

When you grade in HDR and still have to deliver an SDR version, you can use the *SDR Conform* option in the Export Settings (Figure 6-163). It has a very limited set of controls, though. Since HDR and SDR are so different, an automatic conversion is likely to look bad. I highly recommend that you do two different color-grading passes for HDR and SDR.

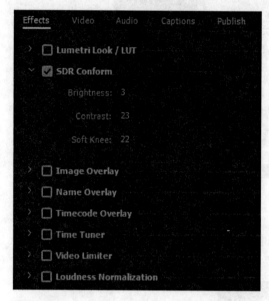

Figure 6-163. *HDR Conform on Export*

HDR Metadata Tools

If you need to change the metadata of a file to make Premiere interpret it correctly as HDR, or need to add HDR metadata to an exported file, try HDRmaster or SEIedit from AVTOP: `hdr.avtop.com/hdr_solutions_avtop`.

Conclusion About HDR in Premiere

As you can tell from this section on HDR, the tools for grading HDR in Premiere are still limited. Until we get proper color management and proper Rec2020 viewing, I don't recommend that you do serious, high-end HDR grading in Premiere yet.

For a quick HDR grading job that's not going to a high-end viewing platform, the tools we have are quite capable, though. I'm sure this will change at a rapid pace in future versions, so maybe the next version of Premiere will have all the HDR tools and support we need.

Presets—Your Secret Weapon

Of course, I've saved presets for all the preceding looks. You should have a storage vault of saved grading and stylizing presets in your arsenal. This saves time, and if you're working with a client, they can be inspired by your existing looks so you can build custom ones together. Colorists often have huge libraries of custom looks that they can quickly add to their shots. (DaVinci Resolve calls the preset a "Power Grade"–a much cooler name than "preset," but it's still a preset. Same difference.)

If you're editing a news story or a reportage and the deadline is close, you will not have the time to correct each shot individually. In such cases, speed is more important than accuracy. With a good selection of presets, you can still make the news story look better by throwing on a preset before export.

More Useful Presets You May Need

In addition to the B&W, sepia, bleach bypass, and orange/teal looks discussed in the previous section, there are lots of other popular looks you may want to know. Here are brief descriptions of how to make looks that I've used over the years. This list is not complete; it's just meant to kickstart your brain.

Presets for all the looks in this chapter can be downloaded from `premierepro.net`.

Black & White

This one's easy–but maybe not as easy as you'd think. Simply desaturating an image by dragging saturation in the Fast Color Corrector or other correction tools will result in a pretty dull B&W image. Adding an S-curve will help, but to get the most control over what colors become lighter or darker, open the video clip in Photoshop and use the superior black-and-white conversion there.

In Figure 6-164, I've used Photoshop's Black & White filter to make the cabin and the grass darker while keeping most of the brightness on the goat, increasing the contrast between the goat and the surroundings. You can also save LUTs from Photoshop that you can use in Premiere.

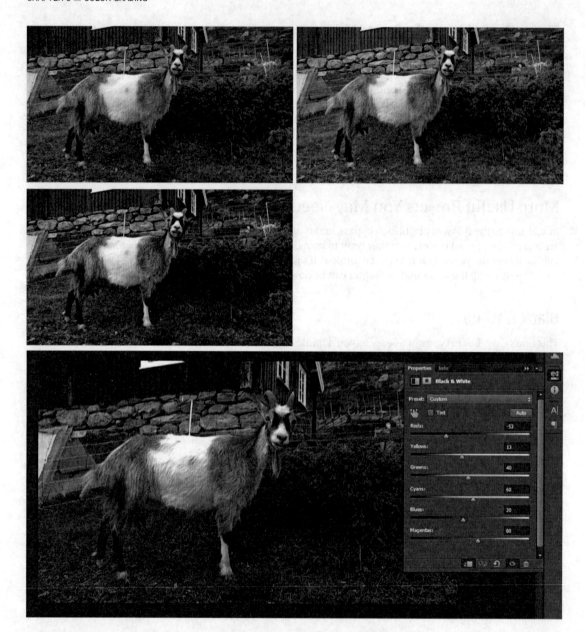

Figure 6-164. *The black-and-white conversion in Photoshop is probably the best one you have, so why not use it? Export LUTs for use in Premiere*

S-curves

S-curves are great! The single most useful of all my color-correction presets is the S-curve preset I made with RGB Curves (Figure 6-165). Quite often, I can make the whole scene look better with a simple drag-n-drop with this preset Of course, every image will probably need to get tweaked a little more independently, but the S-curve is a really good starting point.

Figure 6-165. *You already know how much I like S-curves. They're so useful I thought I'd mention them again.*

Roll-Off

Slightly blown-out highlights can sometimes be restored with a gentle roll-off curve. The curve is set so it doesn't affect the shadows and midtones, just the very top of the highlights. Notice how the clouds in Figure 6-166 get a little bit more texture, especially in the upper left of the frame. The result is subtle, but noticeable in the extreme whites.

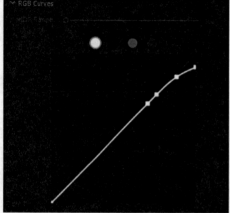

Figure 6-166. *Slightly blown-out highlights can sometimes be restored with a gentle roll-off curve*

Color Negative

Although very stylized and not very useful as a general look on your film, the color negative effect can be used effectively on single clips. You might want to use Luma Curve for this, but that will not work. The difference between inverting with RGB curves and Luma Curve is that Luma Curve does not invert all channels. Only the brightness is inverted, and chroma information remains as is. So, use RGB Curves for this one, too. See Figure 6-167.

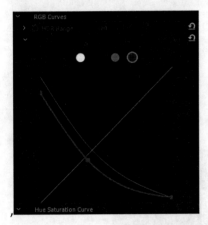

Figure 6-167. *Use inverted curves to simulate color negative film*

Cross Processing

Simulating cross-process film treatment can be fun. Like bleach bypass, this was originally a purely chemical process. By using chemicals intended for other types of film, like positive film processed as negative film or vice versa, strong color casts can be achieved. In brief, you can get a yellowish image with bluish shadows by adding an S-curve to the red and green channel and an inverted S-curve to the blue channel. And so on. The most common use for this effect is to fake an old-faded-miscolored-color-photograph or a 1970s look. See Figure 6-168 for two different cross-process looks.

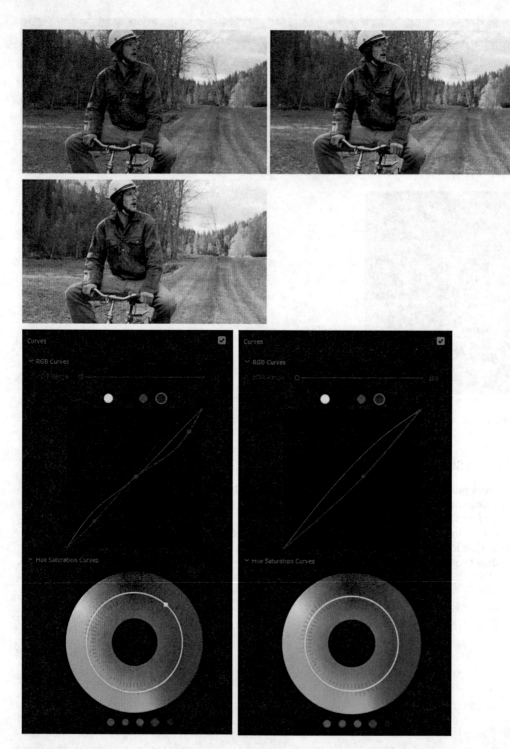

Figure 6-168. *Two cross-process looks. (Footage from Egotripp by Kjetil Fredriksen and Jan Olav Nordskog. Actor: Eirik Sandåker)*

Warming and Cooling Filters

These presets mimic the effect of the ¼ CTO (Color Temperature Orange) and ¼ CTB (Color Temperature Blue) filters used in film and video lighting. Figure 6-169 shows the CTO preset, and Figure 6-170 shows the CTB preset. These two presets are very useful. If you need a stronger effect, just throw on another instance of the preset. They do have some peculiar curves, so don't expect a technically correct image when using these.

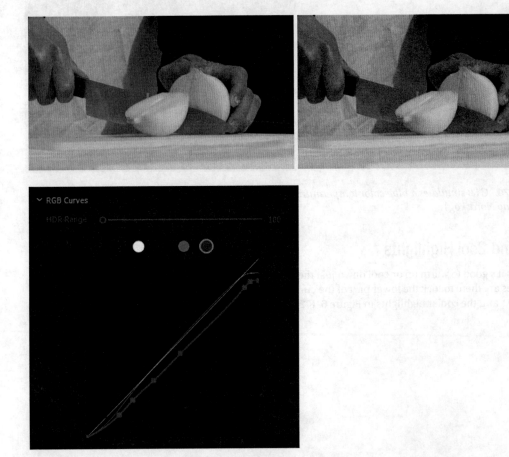

Figure 6-169. CTO Orange simulates an orange color temperature correction filter

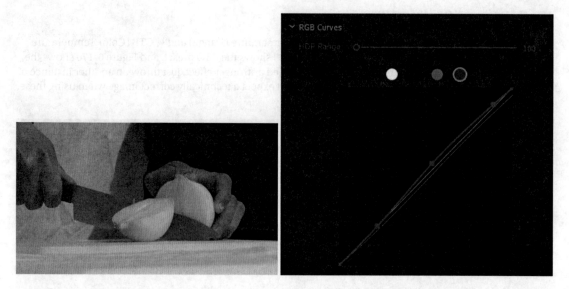

Figure 6-170. *CTB simulates a blue color temperature correction. (Footage from Egotripp by Kjetil Fredriksen and Jan Olav Nordskog)*

Warm and Cool Highlights

Sometimes it's good to warm up or cool down just the highlights. These presets take care of that. The lower curve nodes are there to lock the lower part of the curves to the original levels. Notice the warm highlights in Figure 6-171 and the cooler highlights in Figure 6-172.

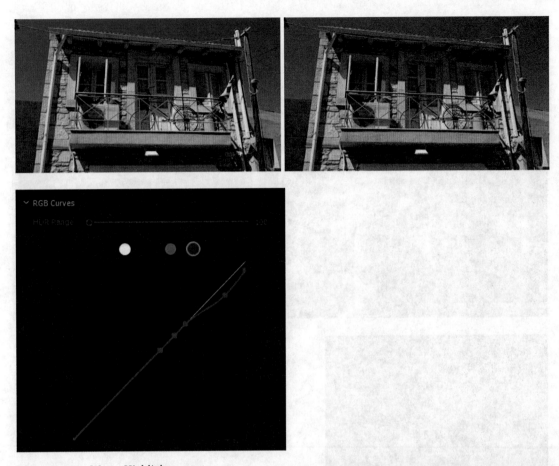

Figure 6-171. *Warm Highlights preset*

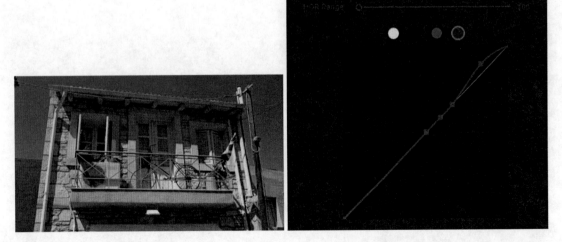

Figure 6-172. *Cool Highlights preset*

Blooming Highlights

Use this preset to introduce some highlight diffusion in your images. This one is meant to be used on an adjustment layer and will not work correctly on a single clip. In Figure 6-173, HSL Secondaries are used to key out the highlights, then the mask is output as black and white and blurred. Because the opacity is set to *Screen blend mode* (not seen in the figure), only the highlights are affected. To tweak the amount of blooming, adjust Blur in the Refine section, as well as Opacity. You may also want to move the handles on the Luma slider for the key to affect more or less of the highlights, depending on your footage.

Figure 6-173. *Clipped highlights are often a problem, especially with 8-bit recordings. These can be made a bit softer with this method.*

In the swan image in Figure 6-174, the preset has been tweaked to give a more extreme look. The Luma slider has been adjusted to affect levels lower into the midtones, and the blur is set higher.

Figure 6-174. Exaggerate the blur and affect lower levels to create a dreamy effect. Swan footage courtesy of Vidar Granberg.

Blooming Blacks

Why not try blooming blacks for a change? Use the preceding method, but add an RGB Curves effect with an inverted master curve before and after the Blooming Highs adjustment, then set the adjustment layer to *Multiply blend mode.*

Crushed Blacks

Sometimes when your footage feels a little dull, crushing the blacks can be an enhancement. Crushing the blacks creates a harder, rougher look with deeper blacks. It can also help hide compression artifacts in the shadows. RGB Curves to the rescue again! See Figure 6-175. The effect only affects the deepest shadows, so it's very subtle on footage that doesn't have much going on in the shadows–but when you play the timeline, you'll see that the blacks are cleaner and the image is rougher and has less noise. Use with care.

Figure 6-175. *Crushing the blacks. (Footage from Egotripp by Kjetil Fredriksen and Jan Olav Nordskog. Actor: Eirik Sandåker)*

Blue, Blurred Highs

On dark footage with some hot highlights, this preset can create a nice effect with blue light streaks. This is made with a combination of Add blend mode, Curves for clipping and isolating highlights, Gaussian blur for separate horizontal and vertical blur, and finally Tint to colorize the whole thing (Figure 6-176). This is actually more an effect than a look, but it's still pretty cool. It's used a lot on commercials, music videos, and action movies. Try it on a scene where the protagonist comes toward the camera with a flashlight, or on a shot of a car passing by with the headlights on.

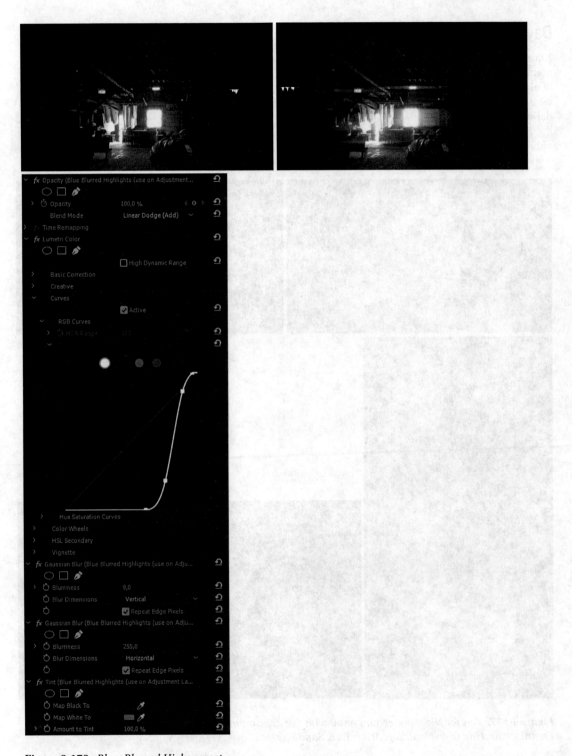

Figure 6-176. Blue, Blurred Highs preset

Day for Night

Naming a preset Day for Night is a bit dangerous! No preset can make all kinds of footage look like it's shot at night. Use this as a starting point, and expect that a lot of tweaking is needed. To create a convincing illusion of night, you'll also need to use adjustment layers with masks to create pools of darkness and light, and tweak contrast and lightness locally to make the important objects in the image stand out from the general darkness.

I've done this in Figure 6-177, which shows the preset and the image before and after–plus the result after adding five adjustment layers with curves with masks for a more convincing illusion of night.

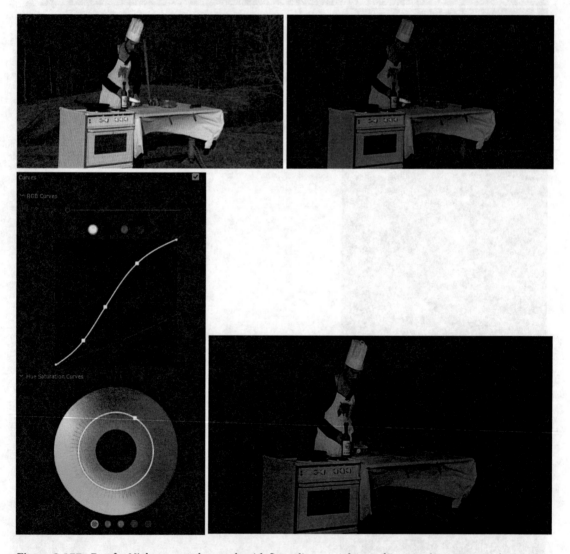

Figure 6-177. *Day for Night preset, plus result with five adjustmant layers. (Footage from Egotripp by Kjetil Fredriksen and Jan Olav Nordskog. Actor: Eirik Sandåker)*

Additional Tips on Color Grading

What follows are a bunch of tips that I felt would not fit in any of the other sections in this chapter. They are very useful in some situations, so I've included them here in random order and with short descriptions. I hope you find at least three tips you'll use.

Get Larger Tools

If you make the Lumetri Color panel wider, some of the controls will get bigger. The color wheels and all the sliders will fill the available space (Figure 6-178). Unfortunately, the RGB Curves and the Hue Saturation curve leave a lot of gray space when you widen the panel, but they do get bigger.

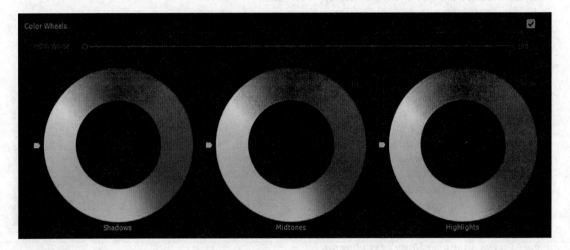

Figure 6-178. Big color wheels

How Much Is Enough?

How aggressively should you grade the images? That depends totally on the genre and type of production. A dream sequence in a feature film can be aggressively stylized without looking cheesy. A 30-second commercial or a music video can also be heavily stylized, but I wouldn't overdo the grading on a documentary or a corporate film unless the theme of the film calls for it. Use your best judgment.

When in Doubt: Overdo It! (Temporarily, That Is!)

Overdo the changes. This way you can see when the highlights start blowing out, when the color is too warm, and so on. The DoP does this all the time: adjusting the exposure until it's too high and then lowering until it's OK, pulling focus too far and then back, and so on. You can do it too when grading your footage.

Keyframed Color Correction

Color correction in Premiere is not always keyframeable, but there is a simple workaround for this. Cut the clip in two with the Razor tool (or use the keyboard shortcut) and make two different color corrections. Then, do a cross dissolve between the two clips, effectively going smoothly from one correction to the other. The length of the cross dissolve simulates the distance between keyframes. This comes in very handy when the sun comes and goes in outdoor footage, and when the camera moves from light to dark areas or from tungsten lighting to outdoor lighting in one shot.

You can also use opacity keyframes on adjustment layers to fade a correction in and out. With multiple adjustment layers, you can make all kinds of adjustments vary over time.

Adjustment Layers as Grading Tracks

Adjustment layers are great and can span several clips when needed. Use them as grading tracks that can easily be switched on and off, and use where you can tweak the color correction for several clips at a time without the need for nesting (Figure 6-179). Adjustment layers will tidy up your timelines, and many tasks can be done much quicker.

Figure 6-179. Adjustment layer as grading track

But there's a caveat. If you add a cross dissolve to the head of an adjustment layer, you might expect the adjustment to be faded in. Instead, the whole image will fade up from black. Use opacity keyframes instead, and it works as expected.

The left sequence in Figure 6-180 will fade in from black–probably not what you expected or wanted. The right sequence will start with the video on Video 1 and gradually fade in the corrections made on the adjustment layer. This opacity trick can be used to vary color correction over time, an easy way to keyframe the adjustments.

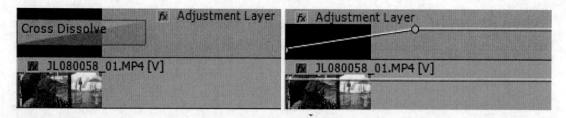

Figure 6-180. Fading in an adjustment layer with opacity keyframes gives a different result than fading it in with a cross dissolve

Use Adjustment Layer as an Effect Preset

If you come from other NLEs, you may be used to having your effects presets in a bin. You can get Premiere to work in somewhat the same way by adding effects to an adjustment layer (or other synthetic clips) in your Project panel. Yep, you can have master clip effects on an adjustment layer and then reuse that adjustment layer like an effect preset.

If you want to use this method for a vignette preset, keep an adjustment layer with the Flexible Vignette preset we made earlier.

Unfortunately, the parameters cannot be adjusted over time in the master clip effect, so you can't save presets with keyframes.

Get Adjustment Layers with a Perfect Duration

If you prefer to use adjustment layers for grading, it can be time consuming to make all of them the correct duration. Here's a quick way to do this, semi-automatically!

Add a video track above the one where you have your footage that needs grading. Name it *Grading* if you want. Now, **Alt-select** all the video clips, dragging a lasso around them. Then, **Alt-drag** them all up to the new track. Now you have a copy of each clip. Select all these clips, right-click on one, and choose *Adjustment Layer*. Now all of them are adjustment layers with a perfect duration. See Figure 6-181.

Figure 6-181. *Get adjustment layers with perfect duration*

Remember to remove all the existing effects on these adjustment layer clips, or the effects will be doubled up. Select the new clips, then click **Edit ➤ Remove Attributes** (or use the keyboard shortcut) and select everything before you hit *OK*. See Figure 6-182. Also, un-target the video tracks below your grading track, so *Selection Follows Playhead* will select the adjustment layers, not the original clips.

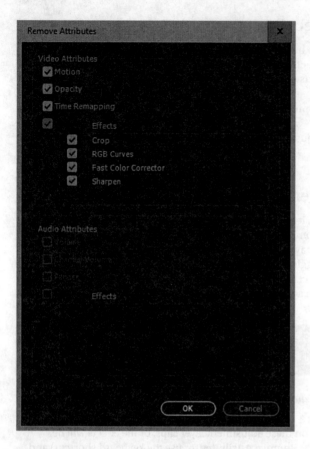

Figure 6-182. Remove attributes

Adobe Color Is Your Friend

If you want to use the color palette of another movie, you can use Adobe Color to capture it. In Figure 6-183, I've used the online version at color.adobe.com to steal the color palette of a frame from the trailer for the Swedish version of *The Girl with the Dragon Tattoo* (Män som hatar kvinnor, 2009). Teal and orange, anyone?

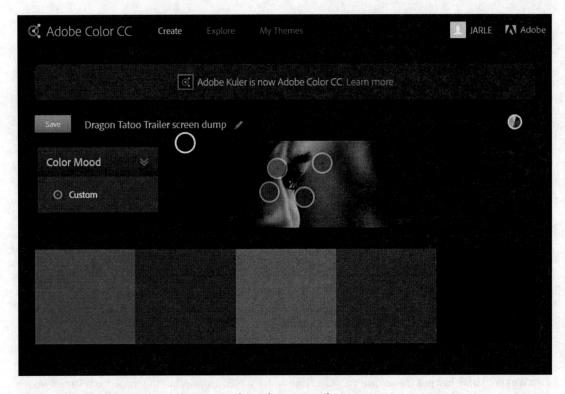

Figure 6-183. *Still image from the Män som hatar kvinnor trailer*

Adobe Color is a great tool with which to capture the color palette of a movie or an image. You can use this palette to imitate the look. Import the color swatches into Premiere and watch where they end up in the scopes. Then tweak your own images to create the same colors.

You can also use the mobile app Adobe Capture and point your camera at any screen. Either way, save the color palette as an image and put it on the timeline to see where the color vectors lie in the scope. Then, tweak your colors to match the palette.

At twitter.com/cinemapalettes, you'll find the color palettes from many movies.

Use Textures to Add Lighting Effects

The lighting effect has an interesting option to use a texture to make the adjustments only apply to part of the image. Unfortunately, the lighting effect is not GPU accelerated, and it also renders with strange banding errors when using textures (Figure 6-184).

Figure 6-184. *The lighting effect is 8-bit only, causes banding, and is not accelerated*

Again, track matte key to the rescue! With a combination of the track matte key and RGB Curves on a duplicate layer, and a texture with added contrast on another layer, we can build the same effect with much better results. With an additional vignette layer, it can look even better.

Again, the current bug with adjustment layers and the track matte key in Premiere forces us to use a copy of the clip instead of an adjustment layer.

We could have just put the texture on a layer and added a blend mode, but the track matte key approach is much more flexible. We can add color, blur, and other effects to the affected areas (or the texture) to further enhance the look. And remember that the texture can be a video clip, not just a still. Using footage of waves and shimmering lights on a wall can lead to very interesting results.

Figure 6-185 shows how the track matte key can be used to accomplish this effect when we place the texture on a separate layer. It's also accelerated, and it's much more flexible. So, you have the original clip on track 1, a darker copy (courtesy of RGB Curves) on track 2, and the black-and-white matte clip on track 3. Track matte key is set to take luma values from video track 3. By tweaking the contrast and levels on the texture image, you can adjust how much to affect the original image, and by using curves on the two video clips, you have endless possibilities for variation.

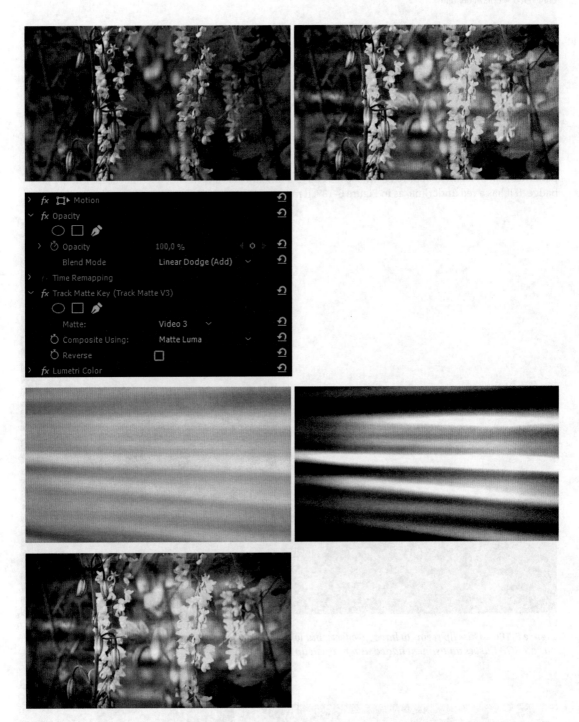

Figure 6-185. The track matte key is GPU accelerated, and is much more flexible than the lighting effect

Master Clip Effects

An effect can be applied on the masterclip level. To add an effect to a master clip, select it in a bin and hit **Shift+O** to open it in the source monitor. Now, watch the Effect Controls panel, where you'll see that it says *Master * Name of Clip* at the top. This means that effects that you add there will be applied at the masterclip level.

When you select a clip in a timeline and watch the Effect Controls panel, it will show the effects that are applied on the clip in that sequence. If none were added in the sequence, it will be empty, so you may wrongly conclude that there are no effects on the clip.

To see any effects added to the master clip, click the word *Master * Name of Clip* in the Effect Controls panel, as seen in Figure 6-186. To easily see if a clip in a timeline has any master clip effects, look at the fx badge. If it has a red underline, as in Figure 6-187, it means the clip has master clip effects added.

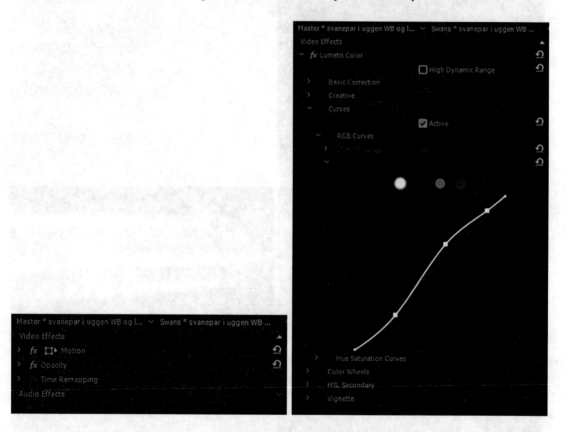

Figure 6-186. *This clip seems to have no effects, but when we click on the Master * name tab, it reveals that it has an RGB Curves adjustment added as a master clip effect*

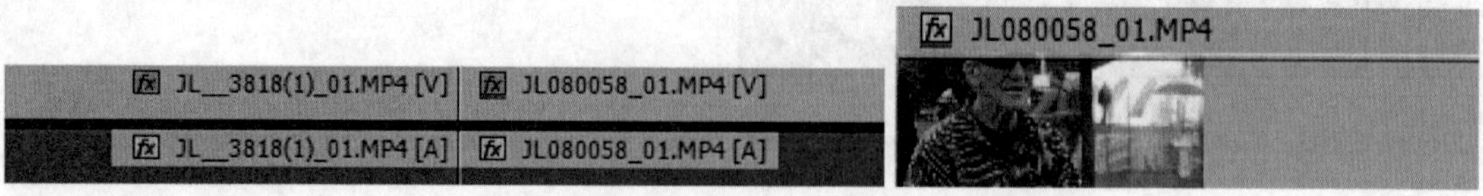

Figure 6-187. *When a clip has a master clip effect, the fx badge gets a red underline*

550

Master clip effects are meant to provide an easy way to add basic color correction to a clip and have that correction affect all instances of the clip in all timelines, very much like how the Source settings on RAW footage work. It's a huge time saver. Keyframes are not supported in master clip effects.

Use a Neutral Image to Assist Your Color Matching

To replicate a look from an image, apply corrections to make it neutral. You don't want to make it grayscale, but rather a normal-looking image with no color casts. The corrections you did to make it look normal can then be applied in reverse on your other clips. If you needed to add orange in the shadows, the original look had blue shadows–and so on. See Figures 6-188 through 6-191.

To make a neutral version of a clip, do adjustments that remove its color cast. In Figure 6-188, I made the midtones and highlights colder to compensate for the warm cast in the lower part of the image. See Figure 6-189. The lower background no longer has such a warm cast, and the glowing metal gets more focus.

Figure 6-188. *Smithy with color cast and with the color cast neutralized*

Figure 6-189. *The adjustments I did to neutralize the warm color cast*

When you've found out which settings are needed to remove the look, add a new correction where you try to reverse the settings (Figure 6-190). If you do this on an adjustment layer, you can switch it on and off to compare your original with the neutralized-then-stylized-again clip.

■ **Note** When the double-corrected clip looks just like the original, this means your last correction will make a neutral clip look just like the original! Copy this second correction to the clips where you want the look from the original (Figure 6-191) or, better yet, use an adjustment layer.

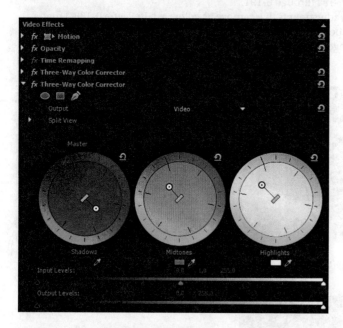

Figure 6-190. *The opposite adjustments*

Figure 6-191. *With both adjustments, the clip looks like the original again*

Use Difference Mode to See What Color You Need to Add

If you want to see what color you need to add to a clip to make a part of it neutral, use a grayscale version of the clip. So, where do you get a grayscale version? **Alt-drag** a copy of the clip to the track above and add the Black & White preset. Then, set Blending Mode to *Difference*.

What you see in your output is an image with the color you need to add. In Figure 6-192, we want the wall behind the blacksmith to be more neutral. With the neutral clip in Difference mode (Figure 6-193), we can see very clearly that we need to add more blue.

Figure 6-192. *A grayscale version in Difference mode reveals that we need to add blue to make the wall neutral*

Figure 6-193. *Black and white copy in Difference mode*

I used the HSL Secondary section in Lumetri Color to isolate the yellow colors of the wall, then dragged the wheel towards blue, decreased saturation, and adjusted temperature and tint. See Figure 6-194.

Figure 6-194. *Now the wall is much more neutral. Note that this correction was done using the secondary color correction qualifiers to isolate the yellow wall.*

Huge Project Size with Warp Stabilizer

OK, this isn't really a color-grading tip, but we often do stabilizing and color grading in the same finishing phase of the project, so I thought I'd mention it here.

When you're doing a lot of stabilizing with the warp stabilizer, it can lead to serious project file-size bloat. Just like tracked masks, the huge number of keyframes are stored in the project and can have a big impact on your project file size. This makes auto-saves take longer and may have other negative effects.

To avoid this, stabilize the footage in a separate helper project and export a high-quality file, like ProRes, DNxHD, JPEG2000, or GoPro Cineform, keeping the same timecode. Place this directly above the original in your main project's timeline. Keeping the original ensures you keep all metadata and so on. Make sure you don't have any other effects on the clip in your helper project–you want to have the effects available in your main project.

Warp Stabilizer Tips

Set Smoothness to a Low Value

Sometimes, setting Smoothness to only 2 to 5 percent gets a good result, without all the warping that can occur with the default 50 percent smoothness.

Turn Off Subspace Warp

When in doubt, turn subspace warp down, or switch it to position, scale, rotation.

Mask Out the foreground

Moving elements in the foreground can confuse the warp stabilizer. We can mask out the parts we don't want the stabilizer to look at and get a much better result.

1. Nest the clip you want to stabilize and open the nested sequence.

2. Add opacity mask with the freeze raw Bezier tool and track the selected mask.

3. In your main sequence, apply warp stabilizer to the nested sequence.

When the stabilizing is done, open the nested sequence and turn off the opacity mask.

Summary

As you've seen in this chapter, color grading is a huge topic! But it's also very interesting, and it's highly rewarding to see your footage get much better with a few presets and some tweaking. I hope you've seen that color grading is much more than just correcting errors–it's a storytelling tool!

I've done training for thousands of editors around the world, and I've often heard the refrain, "*In our daily editing, we're too busy—we don't have time for color correction.*" Those who say so are only fooling themselves. I counter that statement with "So, you don't have time for this?" and drag one of my presets on a slightly overexposed clip, or a warming preset to a group of shots with a cold white balance. Of course, they must admit that they do have time for that. Working with presets, everyone has time for color correction.

Keep your most-used color-grading presets in a custom presets folder in your Effects panel, and they're never more than a drag-n-drop away.

Apart from color grading, there are several other factors that affect contrast, color, and looks in movies. Lighting, set design, make-up, wardrobe, VFX, film stock or camera settings, and so on are all important to create the look that the director wants. All these should be used when possible, but are outside the scope of this book.

Happy grading!

CHAPTER 7

Motion Graphics Inside Premiere Pro

By Jarle Leirpoll and Dylan Osborn

When most users hear *motion graphics* and *Adobe* they probably think of Adobe After Effects, the gold standard for 2D and 3D graphics creation, animation, and rendering. After Effects integrates powerfully with Premiere Pro through Dynamic Link and motion graphics templates, and those features and their workflows are explored in chapter 11 on Integration in this book.

But Premiere Pro has its own powerful tools for applying effects, manipulating video and stills, and creating graphics, titles, subtitles, credits, and captions (Figure 7-1). The Effect Controls panel lets you modify parameters and keyframe them precisely over time. The Legacy Title tool has always given us a lot of options for creating fully-featured still titles, but the new Essential Graphics panel lets you create shapes and text directly in the program monitor and manipulate them as layers. Best of all, these layers can be keyframed individually within a new type of clip called a *graphic object*. And with a good graphics card, the Mercury Playback Engine previews these complex animations for you in real-time without rendering. In fact, there's so much you can do without leaving the application that it's often faster to build your own graphics right inside Premiere Pro!

This chapter will explore the editor's options for handling graphics, effects, text, and stills within Premiere Pro. As a bonus, you'll see some examples and pick up a few design tips for those situations when the editor must "do it all." Read on and discover how Premiere is a much better app for motion graphics than you may have thought.

© Jarle Leirpoll 2017
J. Leirpoll et al., *The Cool Stuff in Premiere Pro*, DOI 10.1007/978-1-4842-2890-6_7

Figure 7-1. Each of these motion graphics examples was built entirely within Premiere Pro

Graphics Workflow Tips

Any kind of work with graphics in Premiere Pro is almost certainly going to tax your computer's GPU and CPU more than the simple editing and playback of video clips does. And when I build graphics, my editor's brain switches over to a "design mode" with different priorities, such as composition, color, and font style. So, before we get into the graphics tools, review these tips to help you optimize your system's performance–and your own.

Check Your Stills

If you're using still images in your graphics builds, check their resolution and consider lowering it before import, because large images may bog down playback and use lots of RAM. In general, 200 percent of the sequence frame size is big enough for most video work.

The Adobe Photoshop image processor can help you batch-convert large stills and get them ready for edit: helpx.adobe.com/photoshop/using/processing-batch-files.html.

16K by 8K (16,384 × 8,192) is the maximum possible frame size of a Premiere Pro sequence at the time of this writing, but you can work with sources that are larger than this. You can import still images that are up to 32K in either dimension, but the image must have less than 256 megapixels total. So, 32K × 8K can be imported, as can 16K × 16K–but not 32K × 32K.

How Much GPU RAM Is Enough?

It depends. It will vary a lot, depending on your source material and your workflow. Puget Systems has some recommendations and guidelines on its web site based on its own tests: pugetsystems.com/recommended/Recommended-Systems-for-Adobe-Premiere-Pro-143/Hardware-Recommendations.

How much GPU memory a frame requires in order to be processed on the GPU will depend on its bit depth and encoding, but there's a formula you can use to calculate whether you have enough GPU RAM for a specific clip to be processed by the GPU acceleration.

▓ **Note**   The approximate amount of GPU memory needed is $\dfrac{Width*Height}{13.107}$.

If your clip is too large and exceeds the amount of GPU memory available, Premiere should fall back to software-only rendering. Premiere should definitely not crash, but there are users who have experienced crashes when they use large still images. Here are some examples of GPU RAM required for common image sizes.

▓ **Note**   A 4K video frame, 4096 × 2160 pixels, requires approximately 675 MB.

Stills from a Canon T2i, 5184 × 3456 pixels, require approximately 1.37 GB, which exceeds the 1 GB available on some laptop systems.

An 8K video frame, 8192 × 4320 pixels, requires approximately 2.7 GB.

Stills from a Canon EOS 5DS, 8688 × 5792 pixels, require approximately 3.84 GB, so you need a GPU with at least 4 GB video RAM.

Often, we'll do a transition from one still to another, which doubles the need–or one still with four other stills in Picture-in-Picture frames–which means five times the GPU RAM needed. You'll easily use all available GPU RAM, even on a beefy system, when combining several large stills or several 8K video clips.

On top of this, your GPU also drives the user interface (UI) on your monitors, and there's little info to be found on how much GPU RAM is needed just for UI display on those fancy 5K displays.

Check Your Fonts

To install a font file on Windows, simply right-click and choose *Install*, and on Mac right-click and go to **Open With ➤ Font Book**.

I prefer OpenType fonts (OTF), since these have better support for ligatures, glyphs, small caps, and alternate characters than TrueType fonts (TTF) have, but will use TTF if the font is not available in OTF format.

Check for Special Character Support

If you work in a non-English-speaking country, make sure your fonts support the whole alphabet in your language. I live in Norway, and we have the special characters Æ, Ø, and Å. I can't use fonts that do not support these (Figures 7-2 and 7-3).

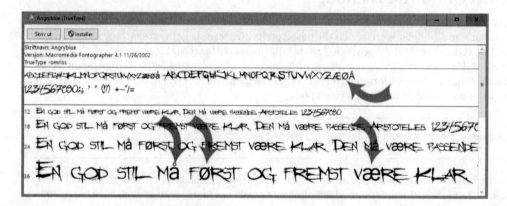

Figure 7-2. *This font lacks the special characters, and they're substituted by characters from a generic font*

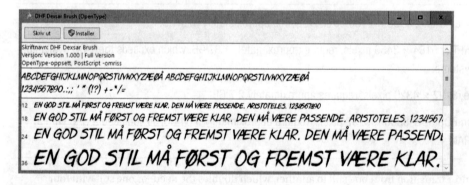

Figure 7-3. *This font has all the special characters, so I can use it*

Use Typekit Fonts

Your Creative Cloud subscription includes access to thousands of fonts through Typekit. To see all the available fonts, open the Creative Cloud app, go to the Resources tab, and choose Fonts, then Manage, or go straight to typekit.com. You can also reach Typekit directly from Premiere via **Graphics ➤ Add Fonts from Typekit**.

Most of the fonts on Typekit are free with your subscription, and some can be bought via Typekit Marketplace (Figure 7-4).

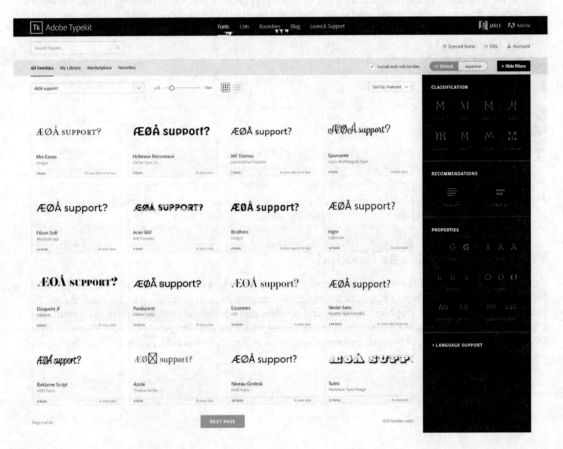

Figure 7-4. *By typing a custom text with the special characters you might need, you can see if the Typekit fonts support them. Only one of these (Azote) had a problem.*

■ **Note**   When working in teams and when you make templates for others, I highly recommend that you use the free Typekit fonts exclusively, if possible. No customer or team leader wants to buy extra fonts to use your templates.

Lower the Playback Resolution

Set preview resolution in the program monitor to ¼ or lower (Figure 7-5) when building complex graphics, adjusting keyframes in animations, and so on. You don't need high resolution to see if a movement is okay or needs tweaking.

Figure 7-5. *1/4 or 1/8 playback resolution will improve performance. This is for playback only and does not affect the quality of your sequence, exports, or preview files.*

Write Preview Files as Needed

One of the advantages of Premiere Pro is that we can usually edit just fine without rendering preview files for our sequences. The Mercury Playback Engine shows us pretty much everything in our timeline in real-time. But to play back graphics smoothly and preview them accurately before export, preview files can be a very good idea. Select a custom sequence preset with a mezzanine preview codec (Figure 7-6) like DNxHD, GoPro Cineform, or ProRes, and go to **Sequence ➤ Render Effects In to Out** for finished parts of a motion graphics–heavy timeline.

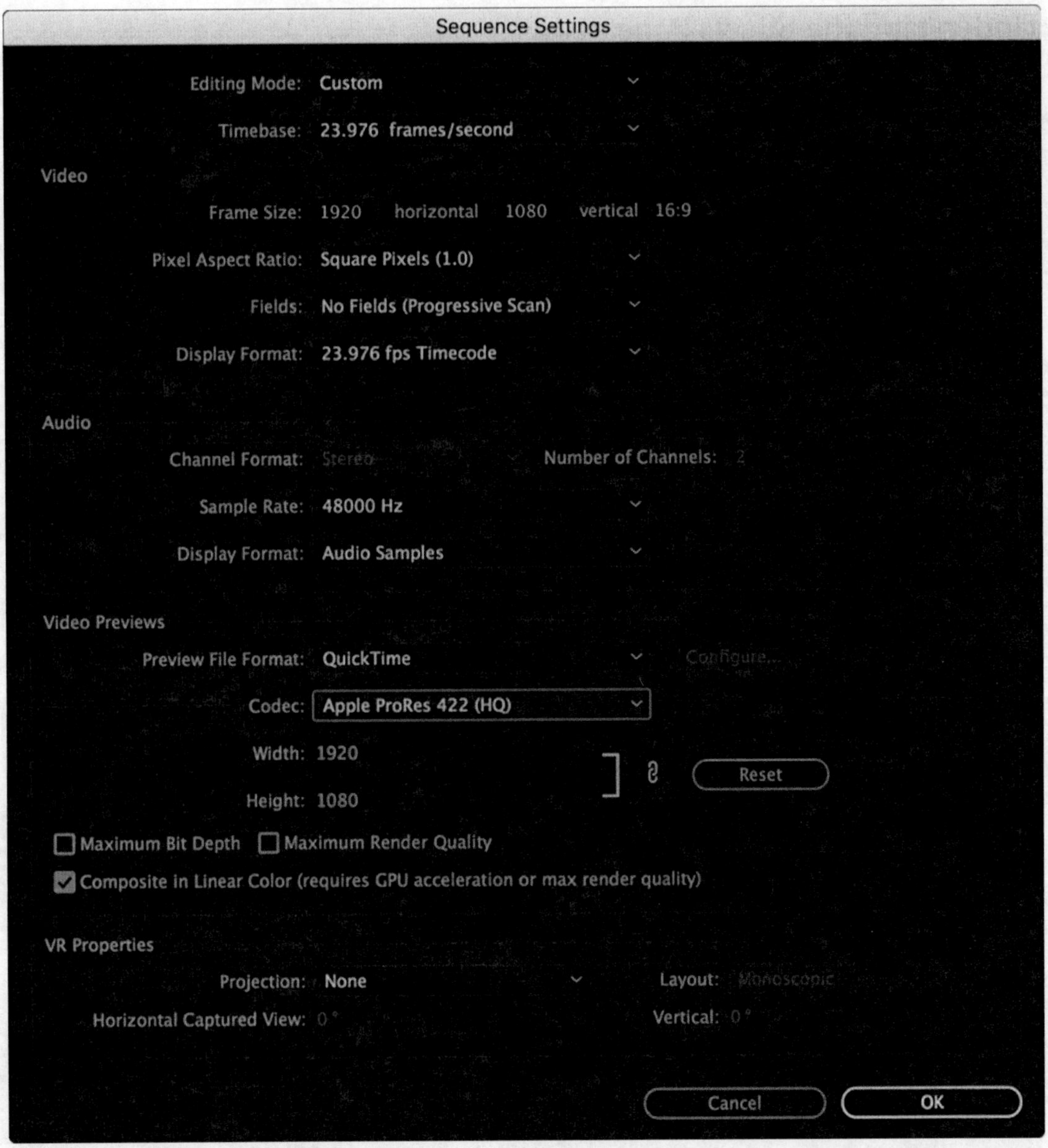

Sequence Settings

Editing Mode:	Custom
Timebase:	23.976 frames/second

Video

Frame Size:	1920 horizontal 1080 vertical 16:9
Pixel Aspect Ratio:	Square Pixels (1.0)
Fields:	No Fields (Progressive Scan)
Display Format:	23.976 fps Timecode

Audio

Channel Format:	Stereo Number of Channels: 2
Sample Rate:	48000 Hz
Display Format:	Audio Samples

Video Previews

Preview File Format:	QuickTime Configure...
Codec:	Apple ProRes 422 (HQ)
Width:	1920
Height:	1080 Reset

☐ Maximum Bit Depth ☐ Maximum Render Quality

☑ Composite in Linear Color (requires GPU acceleration or max render quality)

VR Properties

Projection: None	Layout: Monoscopic
Horizontal Captured View: 0°	Vertical: 0°

Cancel   OK

Figure 7-6. *Change the editing mode to Custom, then select your preview file format under Sequence ➤ Sequence Settings ➤ Video Previews*

Any preview files written will be saved to the location you specified in **File ➤ Project Settings ➤Scratch Disks.**

You can even check *Use Preview Files* in the Export settings, export to the same codec as your preview files, and experience much faster export times.

Understand the Effects Panel Icons

As we've seen in other chapters, not all effects in Premiere Pro are created equal. Many of them are GPU accelerated, so your computer's graphics card will be able to play those effects back for you in real-time. Others are 32-bit effects (which support clips or stills with high bit-depth color) or YUV effects (which support assets in the YUV color space). Look in the Effects panel, and you'll see "Lego brick" icons to the right of each effect indicating which of these three special properties it has. At the top of the panel, the icons act as buttons. Click to enable (blue) and they will filter the effects list for you (Figure 7-7).

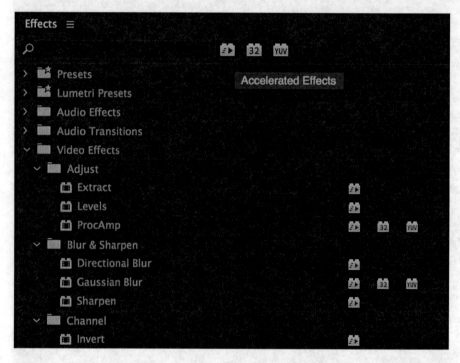

Figure 7-7. Use the three top buttons to filter the effects list by GPU acceleration, 32-bit support, and YUV support

Your need for 32-bit or YUV-enabled effects depends on the type of assets you are working with, but you should always use GPU-accelerated effects in your graphics builds for best performance and quality. There are still some effects that need an Adobe programmer's love to become GPU accelerated. Make feature requests to accelerate effects that you use often: adobe.com/go/wish/.

Use Custom Workspaces

Obviously, you're going to use different panels to work with graphics: Effects, Effect Controls, Graphics, Captions, and the pop-out Legacy Title tool. The new graphics features use the program monitor as their canvas. Give these panels more real estate and speed up your design process by selecting one of Adobe's pre-made workspaces, or configure your own and save it via **Window ➤ Workspaces ➤ Save as New Workspace**.

The custom workspace shown in Figure 7-8 is for working with graphic objects on a small laptop screen. Notice the reduced timeline and source monitor, a full-height frame on the right for the Graphics and Effect Controls panels, and large program monitor for designing in the center.

Figure 7-8. *Graphics workspace*

Pick Colors Like a Pro

The color pickers in Premiere are pretty standard field-and-slider interfaces, with the color value represented for you in HSB (Hue Saturation Brightness), HSL (Hue Saturation Lightness), YUV (luminance and chrominance), and RGB (Red Green Blue–the standard for computer monitors and digital video). If you see a warning triangle pop up when you select a color (Figure 7-9), that means your color is not broadcast safe and could cause problems on a TV signal or DVD. Click the exclamation point, and Premiere will give you the closest color that is safe for broadcast.

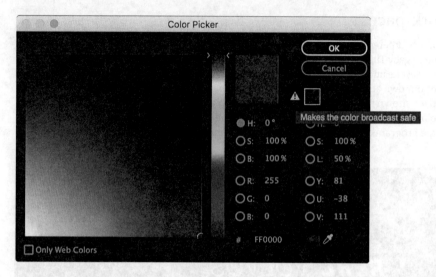

Figure 7-9. *Color warning triangle*

The eye dropper will sample any pixel on your screen, even if it is open in another program–great for pulling colors from other sources, like images, logos, or the web. Hold down **Ctrl** (Cmd), and you'll get the "fat eye dropper," which gives you a 25-pixel average around the point of selection.

If you need to copy the color value from one shape or text to another, use the value from the hexadecimal (#) field (Figure 7-10). Copy the letters and numbers from here to the same field in another title or graphic layer, and they're the same color. This hexadecimal color code also translates between apps.

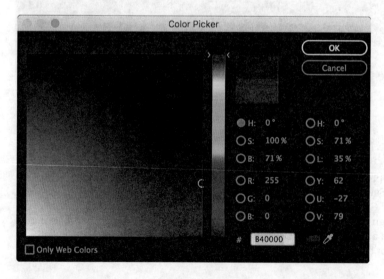

Figure 7-10. *Copy and paste the hexadecimal code instead of the RGB values*

Use the Libraries Panel

If you work across Adobe applications and need a unified workflow for sharing colors and graphic elements, check out the Libraries panel (**Windows ➤ Libraries**; Figure 7-11). Here, you can *Create New Library* under the panel menu or the Libraries drop-down menu at the top. Each library becomes a shareable folder stored on the Assets page of your Creative Cloud account (similar to Dropbox). You can now drag and drop elements to that library in any app that has the panel, including Premiere Pro, After Effects, Photoshop, Illustrator, InDesign, Animate, and Dreamweaver.

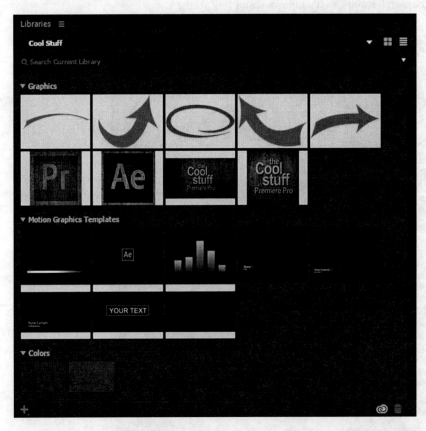

Figure 7-11. *The Libraries panel is a great way to share branded elements across a team designing in different Adobe apps*

These elements can be any graphic (vector graphics from Illustrator will be converted to images in Premiere Pro), hexadecimal colors, looks from the Adobe Color website or the Capture CC mobile app, and layer styles or character styles (Photoshop only). Under the panel menu, you can *Collaborate* (invite others to join the library via email and set user permissions) or *Share Link via email*. Both these options will take you to your Creative Cloud online account, where you can set options for the library. The main benefit is that once you set up and share a library, everyone will have the same graphics and colors ready to go right in their project, in whatever Adobe app they are working in.

The Libraries panel is also a gateway to Adobe Stock, their á la carte service for images, video clips, 3D models, and design templates. Just start typing in the search bar at the top, and you'll see what Adobe has to offer. Choose an element and **Right-click ➤ Save Preview to ➤ Your Library Name**. This uploads a low-resolution, watermarked file to the selected library folder. Use it in your edit, and later you can **right-click ➤License** right in your timeline to replace it with the full-resolution asset. The benefit here (in addition to having Adobe's ever-expanding stock library at your fingertips) is that everyone using that library will be able to access the elements right away.

Figure 7-12 shows the results after searching for "Mountain sunset" in Adobe Stock. It uses artificial intelligence to enhance the search results, so it's super-fast and very accurate.

Figure 7-12. *Adobe has gotten serious about building a high-quality stock library and making it easy to use and license*

Using the Libraries panel in Premiere makes sense if you frequently collaborate with 2D designers in Photoshop and Illustrator, do a lot of brand work, or use Adobe Stock elements in your edits. For purely motion graphics workflows with After Effects, read about template options in chapter 11 on Integration.

To learn more about libraries, go here: helpx.adobe.com/creative-cloud/how-to/creative-cloud-libraries-post-production.html?set=premiere-pro.

Think First, Design Second

Like complex edits, complex graphics builds will get done faster if you spend a little time thinking about how you're going to do them. Here are some planning tips for motion graphics work in any NLE:

1. Find a reference. The content will most likely have a subject, tone, and "vibe" that your graphics should reflect. Searching for visual references (other shows, movies, books, posters, fonts, and so on) can help you agree on this creative direction with your collaborators before you begin. It can also inform the types of elements you'll build.

2. Make a sketch. It doesn't have to be beautiful. Even a rudimentary diagram with arrows will help you decide how an animation is going to happen, what elements you need to animate, and how you'll fill the space in the frame (Figure 7-13). You can figure this out by trial and error while building the graphics, but it will be slower.

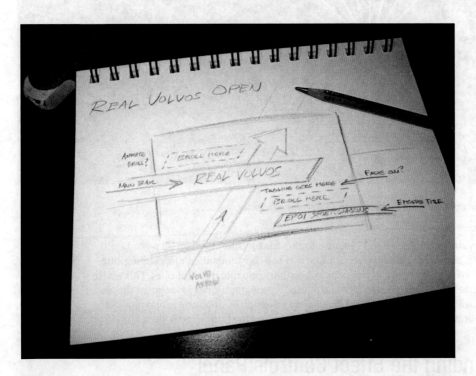

Figure 7-13. *This may not look pretty, but it saved me time designing the animated open you'll see later in this chapter*

3. Build before you animate. When creating a multi-layered animation from scratch, it helps to build all the shape, text, video, and still layers first so you can see them onscreen in their finished positions. Make sure the composition works, then start adding keyframes to bring them on and off screen.

4.   Do the math. Sure, we can drag shapes and text around. But to create and animate something with precision, we need to work with number values. And that means doing math. For example, there is no alignment tool that can distribute things based on rotation. So, if you need even spacing between shapes that are rotated, you need a calculator. Here, I've done my math; I need 12 shapes to be rotated evenly through 180°. 180/12 = 15, so I need to increase the Rotation value by 15° for each new shape (Figure 7-14).

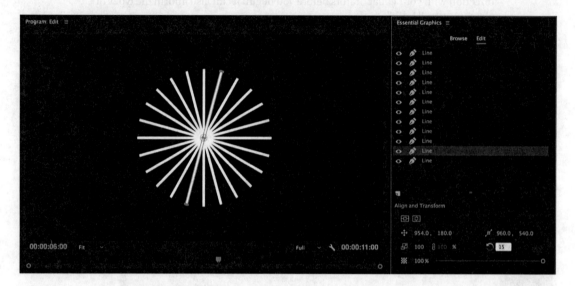

Figure 7-14. *The Rotation was increased by 15 degrees per spoke*

5.   Copy smart. Say you need 12 shapes. You could copy one and then hit paste 11 times. But you could also select the first two and copy both, then the resulting four, and so forth. Try to use as few steps as possible when making duplicates. This advice applies to any work with shapes and effects. If your graphic has four similar shapes that will move in different ways, build one as a template, duplicate it, and modify the duplicates. Anytime you can avoid building something from scratch, do it!

Understanding the Effect Controls Panel

Every clip in your project has "fixed effects" like motion, opacity, and speed already applied to it–all of which you can modify. Applying new effects to a clip is easy enough–simply drag the one you want from the Effects panel onto the clip. Better yet, select a clip or clips and double-click to apply the effect drag-free! Of course, these effects are hardly ever what you need them to be right out of the box. That's where the Effect Controls panel (or ECP, for short) comes in. It is your hub for adjusting parameters, creating keyframes, animating them, and controlling that animation (Figure 7-15).

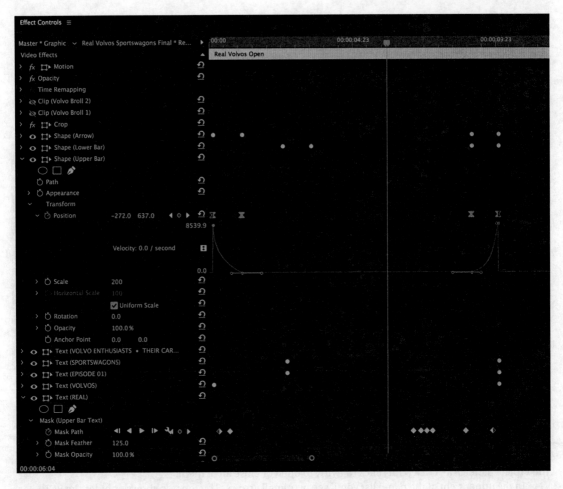

Figure 7-15. *Effect Controls panel in action*

■ **Note** The term *keyframe* comes from the days of hand-drawn animation, when a lead animator would draw the most important frames of character movement—the "key frames"—and then pass those drawings to a junior animator, who drew the in-between frames that completed the animation. Even if you've been animating keyframes in After Effects and Premiere Pro for years, it's important to remember the following principles:

1. You need at least two keyframes to animate any parameter.

2. The computer automatically interpolates the values in-between your keyframes.

3. You can control how it interpolates these in-between values.

4. Effects must be keyframed one parameter at a time.

5. The purpose of keyframes is to represent *change* over *time*.

The ECP Interface

The Effect Controls panel is a list of every effect that is applied to the selected clip. It's important to understand that this list is in reverse order. The last effect in the list is actually the one that's "on top" of the stack, affecting all the ones above it—except for the fixed effects, which are applied after the other effects. Remember this, because color correction, masking, keying, and other effects can give you different results depending on the order in which they are applied (Figure 7-16).

Figure 7-16. *The Lumetri Color effect in this picture is acting on the ones above it, including the lens flare. Add rotation in the Motion section, and it rotates all three added effects.*

Click the twirly arrow next to an effect (like Motion) to see all its parameters (like position, scale, rotation, etc.). Most of these parameters have their own twirly arrows revealing sliders or other tools. As in the Project panel, **Alt+click** (Opt+click) a twirly to open or close all of them.

In the upper right of the panel list you'll see two small arrows. The top one shows or hides the ECP timeline—this part of the panel is essential for keyframing. The other small arrow will expand or hide an entire category of effects (video or audio). If you use this a lot, map custom keyboard shortcuts for the Expand Audio/Video Effects panel commands.

If you have a clip in your sequence selected, you'll also notice two tabs at the top of the ECP (blue text indicates the active tab). The one on the right displays effects for the clip instance you've selected. The one on the left displays effects for the master clip in the project panel. Adding effects to the master clip will add them to every instance of the clip in every sequence in the project. The master clip in Figure 7-17 has a lens distortion effect applied, while the instance has lens flare, directional blur, and Lumetri color effects applied. All these effects can be seen on the clip in the program monitor.

Figure 7-17. ECP master instance–master clip effects preview in the source monitor

As we learned in chapter 4 on Editing techniques a red line underneath the FX icon of a clip instance in your timeline indicates that it has a master clip effect on it.

Adjusting Effect Parameters

All the effect parameters with blue numbers can be adjusted. Click once to get a field for numeric entry. Type in the number you want, or tap the **Up/Down Arrow** keys to increase or decrease its value. Alternatively, **Click+Drag Left/Right** to slide values on the fly. Whether you are adjusting with the arrow keys or dragging with the mouse, modifier keys let you control the adjustment.

Shift gives you increments of ten instead of one. So, **Shift+Up/Down Arrow** or **Shift+Click+Drag Left/Right** accomplishes large adjustments.

Ctrl gives you increments of .1 instead of 1. So, **Ctrl+Up/Down Arrow** (Cmd+Up/Down Arrow) or **Ctrl+Click+Drag Left/Right** (Cmd+Click+Drag Left/Right) accomplishes fine, accurate adjustments.

Use **Tab** to move to the next parameter, and **Shift+Tab** to move to the previous parameter. You can also use the keyboard shortcut for a panel (like **Shift+5** for the Effect Controls panel) to move there, and hit **Tab** to go to the first parameter, letting you work mostly without touching the mouse.

This also works in the Lumetri Color panel, the Audio Track Mixers, the Essential Graphics panel, and other panels where you adjust parameters.

Adjusting Motion

Position, scale, rotation, and anchor point are motion effect parameters that can be adjusted using the number fields as described earlier. Of course, since they move your clip around, you can also adjust them by dragging a wireframe in the program monitor.

With a clip selected, click on the word *Motion* in the ECP to bring up this wireframe, then drag to reposition. You can also double-click the image in the program monitor to select the topmost track item under the cursor and set it for direct manipulation. Holding down **Shift** constrains your drag to the X or Y axis only. Grab a corner and you can scale or rotate the image.

When repositioning, it's helpful to know what the position numbers are telling you. Adobe's coordinate system measures pixels starting from the upper-left corner of the frame. So, 0,0 is always the top left. In a full HD sequence, 1920,1080 would be the bottom-right corner. The point these coordinates are tracking is the anchor point of your clip, which you can change independently of clip position. So, if you dragged your anchor point to the very upper-left corner of the frame, its coordinates would be 0,0–and if the clip's dimensions match the sequence's dimensions, and you haven't moved your clip, its position coordinates would read 0,0 too.

In the left image in Figure 7-18, the clip's anchor point has been moved to coordinates 0,0. The position shows the same coordinates. In the right image, the clip has been dragged, changing the position coordinates but not the anchor point coordinates.

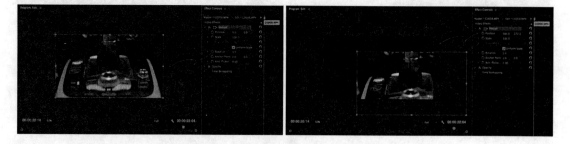

Figure 7-18. *Full HD sequence with different motion parameters*

■ **Note**   When you reposition or animate a clip, image, or other object, use exact coordinates for your landing points. Whole numbers without decimals will yield sharper, clearer pixels.

Adjusting the Anchor Point

Premiere Pro gives you options for moving the anchor point in relation to the object it controls. Consider this question when manipulating graphics: do you want to drag the anchor point itself, or leave it where it is and reposition the object behind it?

When you change number values in the ECP, it moves the frame behind the anchor point. But in the program monitor, you have two options: **Click** to drag the anchor point, or **Alt+Click** (Opt+Click) to drag the frame behind the point. Hold down **Ctrl** (Cmd) in either mode, and snapping boxes will appear when you get near any of the points around the frame or in the center. This is useful if you want to move your anchor point with precision.

The cursor box icon gets a black background when you hold down **Alt** (Opt) to reposition the frame behind the anchor point instead of moving the anchor point itself. See Figure 7-19. This is known as "Kurt Wiley mode" after veteran After Effects tester Kurt Wiley.

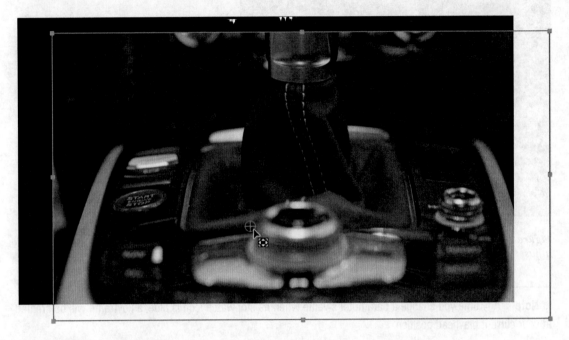

Figure 7-19. *Kurt Wiley mode*

Adding Keyframes

Keyframing is where the magic happens! Or, at least, it's where the motion happens. To change the value of any parameter over time, toggle the stopwatch icon next to its name. If you see blue, you are go for animation (Figure 7-20).

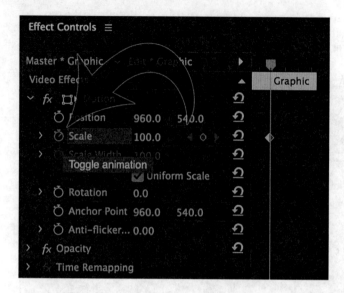

Figure 7-20. *A blue stopwatch means you're setting keyframes where your playhead is parked every time you adjust the parameter*

■ **Note** Any time you change a parameter's value when its stopwatch icon is blue, a keyframe will be created at your current playhead position.

For this reason, it's often smart to "back time" your keyframing. If you have an object flying on screen, turn on the position stopwatch at the moment you want it to land so you capture this default position. Then, go back to the beginning and move it to its offscreen starting position.

You can also "batch keyframe" if you're animating multiple objects landing at the same time. Park your playhead at that spot, select the clips one by one, and toggle *position* on for each. Then, move your playhead to the start and go back through the batch to create keyframes for all their starting positions.

Figure 7-21 shows back timing and batch keyframing in action. By creating all your keyframes in one pass, starting with the default landing position, you save time trying to match start and end points.

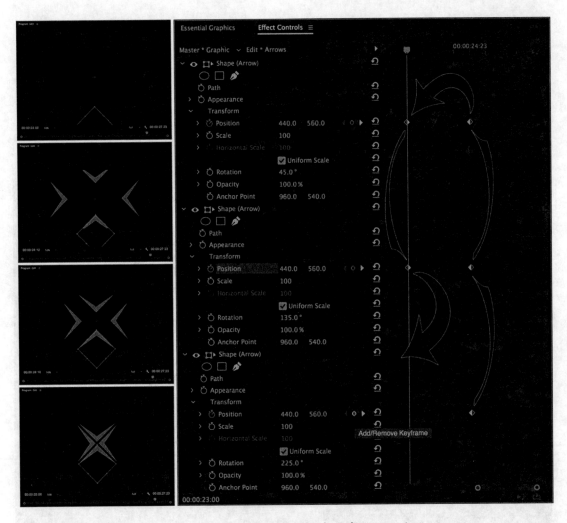

Figure 7-21. *Keyframing backward (starting with the last keyframe) can save time*

Sometimes, you'll adjust a parameter and accidentally add a keyframe when you don't want one. Use the diamond-shaped *Add/Remove Keyframe* button if this happens. Blue means there's already a keyframe at that spot; gray means there is none. Press it to delete the one that's there or to add a new one. Use the left and right arrows to go directly to the next keyframe for adjustment. To drag the ECP playhead to a specific keyframe, hold down **Shift** to snap to it.

The *Reset Parameter* button sets your keyframe back to the default value (for example, Scale to 100) or creates a new default value keyframe at that playhead location. This is useful for resetting part of your animation. If you want to reset everything, toggle the stopwatch back to gray, which will delete all your keyframes.

One keyframing "gotcha" is that certain parameters (for reasons known only to Adobe engineers) have animation toggled on by default. Opacity is one of these, as are audio volume and panner. If you start adjusting opacity without toggling this off, you'll be making new keyframes. So, if you're going to do a lot of opacity adjustments, first create an "opacity keyframe killer" effect by turning off the stopwatch on one clip. Then, copy and paste that opacity effect to all the other clips in your sequence. It will delete any opacity keyframes you currently have and toggle the effect off for hassle-free adjusting.

577

The free download of Jarle's presets includes a ready-made Opacity Keyframe Killer and 97 other useful effects at premierepro.net. Learn how to save effect presets in chapter 10 on Customizing Premiere.

Working with Keyframes

Before you start moving keyframes around, you need room to see what you're doing. Go wide and tall to make room for the graphs. If you don't, you'll never see what's going on with your keyframes.

Figure 7-22 shows how the ECP is set up in this workspace.

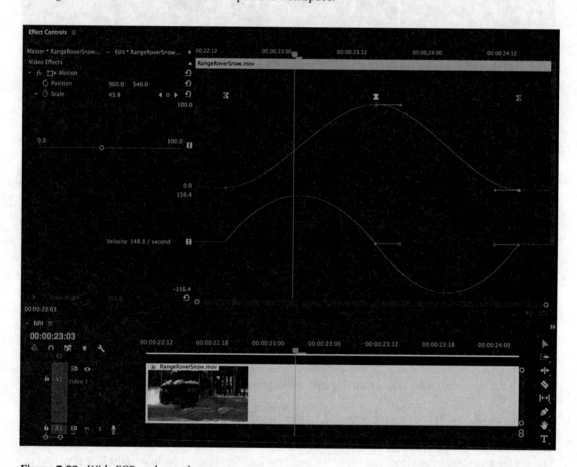

Figure 7-22. *Wide ECP-scale graphs*

First, notice how the ECP has been stretched above the sequence it references. This gives you an excellent idea of where the keyframes are placed in your edit. If you're not using an ECP Timeline/Regular Timeline stack, you can still press the ~ (accent grave) key or double-click the panel name (yes, the words *Effect Controls*), to make your ECP full screen.

Second, notice how the scale parameter has been opened up to reveal two timeline graphs, which have been stretched vertically for a clear view. These are the Value graph and the Velocity graph.

The Value graph shows the change in a parameter's value. In this example, our video is scaling up from 0 to 100 and back down to 0. The graph reflects this. Pretty simple.

The Velocity graph shows the *rate* of change. Do you remember your high school physics class? Measuring an object's velocity tells us if it is accelerating or decelerating. If the movement from 0 to 100 and back is linear, the velocity graph will show a straight line between keyframes; speed is constant. In our case, it's not a straight line, so velocity is changing over time. Read on for more about keyframe interpolation, and you'll see why this graph is so useful.

Once you can see your keyframes, they're easy to move around. Click and drag in the ECP timeline to marquee select, or **Ctrl+Click** (Cmd+Click) to select multiple keyframes. You can drag these together. **Alt+Drag** (Opt+Drag) will duplicate your selection. Press **Shift** to make the keyframes snap to others while you drag.

With motion parameters, you can also use the program monitor to see your object's path. Click the word *Motion* in the ECP to see the frame in the program monitor, and the blue dots will show you the path. If you've animated the object off-screen, zooming the monitor out to 50 percent or less will give you a clearer view, as shown in Figure 7-23.

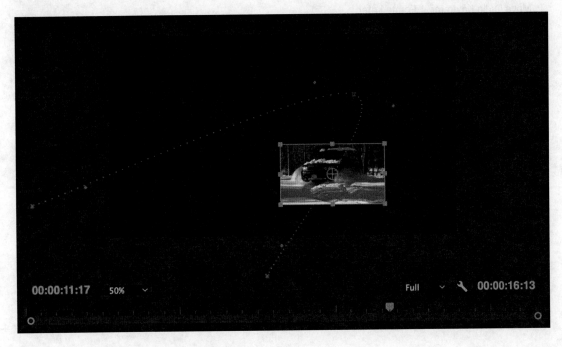

Figure 7-23. Program monitor shows the object's path

Keyframe Shortcuts

Back in the 2015.3 release of Premiere Pro, Adobe engineers gave us a very useful gift: 16 different shortcut commands for keyframing that you can map to your keyboard. Here they are:

Add or Remove Video Keyframe

Decrease Audio Keyframe Value

Decrease Video Keyframe Value

Increase Audio Keyframe Value

Increase Video Keyframe Value

Move Audio Keyframe 1 Frame Earlier

Move Audio Keyframe 1 Frame Later

Move Audio Keyframe 10 Frames Earlier

Move Audio Keyframe 10 Frames Later

Move Video Keyframe 1 Frame Earlier

Move Video Keyframe 1 Frame Later

Move Video Keyframe 10 Frames Earlier

Move Video Keyframe 10 Frames Later

Select Next Keyframe

Select Previous Keyframe

Needless to say, these will save you a lot of time adding, moving, and adjusting keyframes in the ECP and the timeline. But there are so many it can be tricky to map them all to custom shortcuts. With modifiers, you can map a few of them to the J, K, and L keys and the brackets, but if you have a number pad on your keyboard, I've found that a quadrant system combined with modifier keys works well. See Figure 7-24.

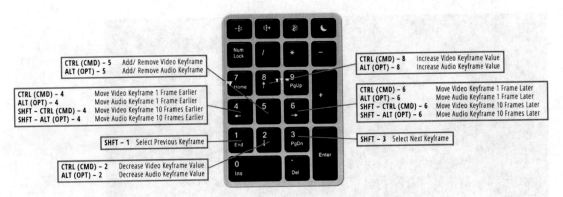

Figure 7-24. *By mapping keyframe shortcuts to the "quadrants" of the number pad and using common modifier keys for video and audio, you can make these shortcuts much more intuitive to use*

Keyframe Interpolation Options

Recall that not only can we add and adjust keyframes, we can also control how Premiere Pro interpolates the "in-between" frames; in other words, how the parameter changes over time. Right-click on any keyframe in the ECP, and you'll see a menu with the interpolation methods. See Figures 7-25 and 7-26.

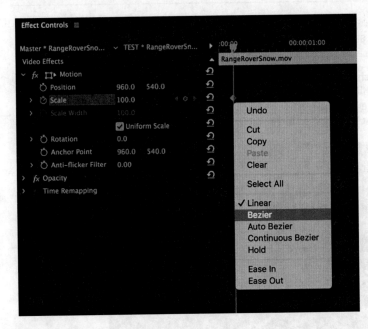

Figure 7-25. *All parameter keyframes have these seven choices*

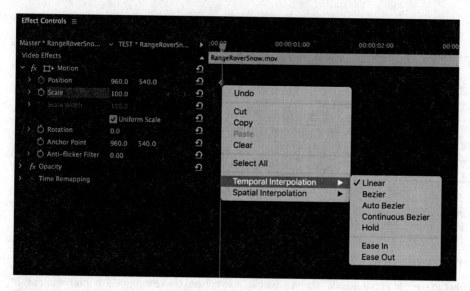

Figure 7-26. *Position keyframes offer the same choices, but split into separate menus for temporal and spatial interpolation*

■ **Note** Let's clarify something before we go any further. There are really only three kinds of keyframe interpolation offered here: linear, hold, and Bezier.

Linear gives us a uniform rate of change. This is the default interpolation and is represented by the diamond-shaped keyframe. Objects will move like Pac-Man and start and stop abruptly. If you keyframe a parameter change from 1 to 100 over ten seconds, at five seconds in Premiere will give you a value of 50. Note that the Velocity graph shows a straight line between linear keyframes because speed is constant (Figure 7-27).

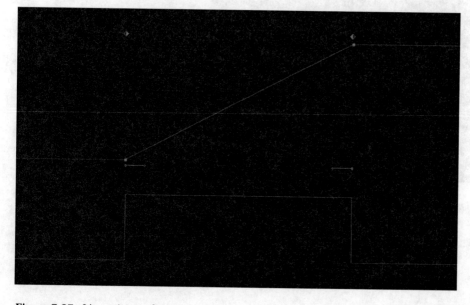

Figure 7-27. *Linear interpolation*

Hold is even simpler: no change at all until you arrive at the keyframe itself. This could be useful if you want flashing Las Vegas neon lights or want to simulate "old film" jitter. Note the half-diamond, half-square keyframe symbol (Figure 7-28).

Figure 7-28. *Hold interpolation: change only occurs at the keyframes*

Bezier is where things get interesting, and Premiere gives us control over the rate of change between keyframes. We can make objects speed up quickly or slow down and stop gently. Notice the curving Velocity graph in Figure 7-29, indicating speed increasing at the start and decreasing toward the end. Note also the blue handles giving us control over the Value and Velocity curves.

Figure 7-29. *Bezier interpolation*

583

When you select an hourglass-shaped Bezier keyframe, blue handles pop up in the graph. Dragging the length and angle of the handle controls the rate of change between your keyframe values. So, if it's that simple, why are there so many options for Bezier interpolation in the menu? And why do their graphs look identical (Figure 7-30)?

Figure 7-30. *Bezier graph comparison. From left to right: Bezier, continuous Bezier, and auto Bezier.*

It's all about control. *Bezier* (the regular one) gives you handles on either side of the keyframe that you can control independently of each other. This way, you can make objects bounce or parameters slowly decrease to a value and then immediately start increasing to another one.

Continuous Bezier locks the two handles together, so your interpolation through a keyframe value will always be pretty smooth. It's especially helpful when animating position to keep paths continuous through keyframe points. When you make a change on one side of the keyframe, it always affects the other side.

Auto Bezier is the same as continuous Bezier, except that it takes away manual control and instead adjusts the handles to "mesh with" the other keyframes around them. This is handy when laying down lots of position keyframes, but be careful, because it can create a "ripple effect" and change the interpolation several keyframes away. Sometimes you might even get movement between two keyframes with the exact same value!

▓ **Note**   Once you adjust an Auto Bezier keyframe it changes to Continuous Bezier.

Figure 7-31 shows three keyframes with different Bezier interpolation settings.

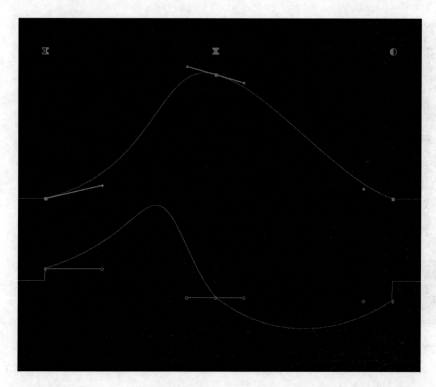

Figure 7-31. *Once you start dragging keyframe handles, you'll understand the difference between Bezier, continuous Bezier, and auto Bezier*

Ease In and *Ease Out* actually work like Bezier presets, and as such they are extremely useful. Ease Out gives you a ready-made, perfectly smooth Bezier ramp from rest to your next value. Use this to start an object moving without any jerkiness or to begin a slow push in on a photo. Ease In gives you an equally smooth ramp from a value to a stop. This is great for bringing an object to rest naturally or easing that slow push in to a stop. Figure 7-32 shows the graphs for Ease In and Ease Out.

Ease In and Out should be your go-to Bezier options for starting and stopping motion smoothly. Just remember:

Use *Ease Out* when you leave a keyframe and *Ease In* when you arrive at one.

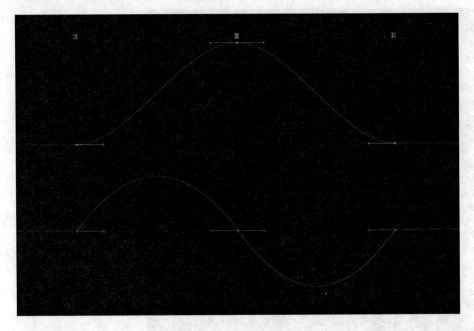

Figure 7-32. Ease Out has been applied to the first keyframe, Ease In to the last. The middle keyframe is Continuous Bezier.

The final point to understand about your options is the one we mentioned at the beginning of this topic: temporal versus spatial interpolation. What's the difference?

Temporal interpolation is about speed. All keyframes have it. You adjust it in the ECP timeline on the Value and Velocity graphs.

Spatial interpolation is about path. Position and anchor point keyframes have it, as do effects with a position parameter within them.

Figure 7-33 shows spatial interpolation choices for the position parameter.

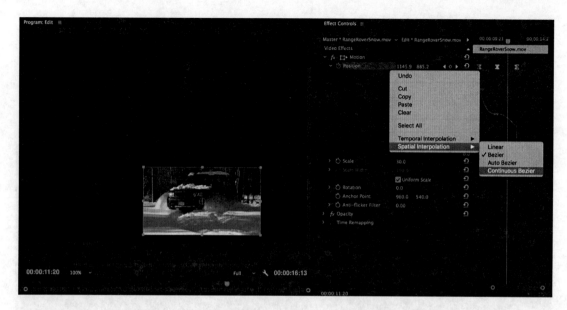

Figure 7-33. *Position keyframes have controls for both temporal and spatial interpolation*

■ **Note**   If you ever get into a "Bezier mess" trying to create smooth paths between your keyframes, just select the ones you want to redo, change them back to linear, and try again.

Interpolation Options in Action

Now that we've covered the interpolation options and what they can do for you, let's see them in action. I've created some "metal" text and want to simulate it hitting the floor, bouncing rapidly like a heavy object, and then slowly being dragged out of frame to the right. See Figure 7-34.

Figure 7-34. *Metal text-frame sequence*

As you can see in the ECP in Figure 7-35, the first two position keyframes when it "drops in" are linear, which is fine for this free fall to the floor. Then, I have a very rapid series (only a couple frames apart) of linear/continuous Bezier/linear keyframes for the bounces. If you look closely at the Velocity graph, you'll see that each time the text hits the floor again, its speed is reduced until it finally comes to rest (i.e., no speed or velocity). It stays there for a couple frames, then an Ease Out keyframe begins the slow slide out to the right. It gets faster and faster until it leaves the frame with a regular Bezier keyframe. This final position movement is easy to see with the blue path dots on the program monitor.

Figure 7-35. *Metal text program monitor and Effect Controls panel*

Remember, objects in real life–especially heavy ones–often move a lot faster than you think when setting keyframes. But that gets into the world of true animation and VFX keyframing, which is a book unto itself!

Pin to Clip

To keyframe consistent motion (or any other parameter change) over the entire length of a clip, you need to create keyframes at its first and last frames. This presents a few small challenges.

First, if you create a keyframe on the cut at the end of a clip, you can navigate to that frame in the ECP, but you won't see it in the program monitor because Premiere Pro always displays the frame to the *right* of the playhead. Second, if you add a dissolve between clips you'll want to place your keyframe before the dissolve begins or the animation will start in the middle of it. This is a common need when doing "Ken Burns–style" photo moves (covered later in this chapter). Third, if you set a bunch of keyframes on a clip and then use only part of it in your timeline, how do you access the ones outside the clip range?

Effect Controls panel menu ➤ Pin to Clip is the option you need. When checked, it restricts your ECP timeline view to the portion of the clip that is actually in your edit timeline. Uncheck it, and you'll be able to move and adjust keyframes before the clip begins and after the clip ends, assuming there is enough media (Figure 7-36). This comes in very handy when working with dissolves and photo moves.

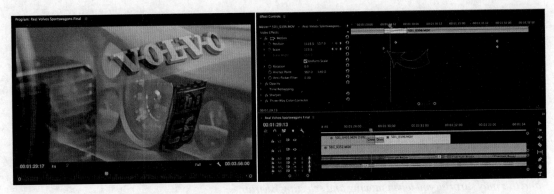

***Figure 7-36.** With Pin to Clip unchecked, you can drag your first keyframe before the dissolve begins*

As for the first and last frame issue, just get in the habit of setting your last keyframe on the frame before the cut. That way, you'll be able to see the results of your adjustments. The **Down Arrow** and **Up Arrow** shortcuts will take you to the start and end of clips on targeted tracks, so **Down Arrow** and then **Left Arrow** will get you to that frame in a flash.

Copy and Paste Effects

The standard cut, copy, and paste commands (**Ctrl+X/C/V** or **Cmd+X/C/V**) *do* work in the Effect Controls panel and are valuable time savers. The ECP can be used to paste effects within the same clip or to other clips. Non-fixed effects will be copied in full and can be pasted multiple times. Fixed effects like scale, position, and so forth will overwrite those properties on the clip they are pasted to.

Alternatively, you can copy and paste attributes to clips in the timeline. Simply select a clip, **Ctrl+C** (Cmd+C), then **Ctrl+Alt+V** (Cmd+Opt+V) to get the Paste Attributes dialog. Select the intrinsic and non-fixed effects you want to paste, and press *OK*. They will now be present in that clip's ECP.

Before we end the ECP section, I want to tell you a secret about keyframes. Okay, it's not a secret–it's something important that you'll learn when you zoom all the way in to the ECP timeline and try to move a keyframe. *Keyframes aren't frames.* In other words, they are not restricted to frame boundaries, because the Premiere Pro (and After Effects) keyframe engine is time-based rather than frame-based. This is a very good thing, because if you copy a set of keyframes from a 23.976 fps clip and paste them onto a 59.94 fps clip, they will still line up in time even though the frame rates are different. Figure 7-37 shows a clip where one keyframe sits between two frame boundaries.

Figure 7-37. *Don't be alarmed; this keyframe is still doing its job. It doesn't have to stick to frame boundaries, and this may surprise you when moving and selecting keyframes.*

Graphic Objects and the Essential Graphics Panel

The Title tool has been part of Premiere Pro for a long time and is based on some very old code. While powerful, it doesn't enable us to animate elements within a title, it requires a separate window for designing, and there is no crossover with other Adobe apps. Knowing this, Adobe's developers created an entirely new system for designing with text, shapes, and even clips right in the timeline and program monitor. Enter graphic objects and the Essential Graphics panel, the future of motion graphics in Premiere Pro!

New Graphics Tools

In Premiere Pro CC 2017.1 and later, graphic objects are the equivalent of titles. They act as clips in the timeline, and you can add many layers of text and shapes within a single graphic object. To create one, look in the tools palette for the new Type tool, select it (or press the default shortcut **T**), and then click in the program monitor. A new graphic object appears in the lowest empty video track in your timeline, and you can begin typing text into the field in the program monitor. Before we dive deeper, let's take inventory of Premiere's new graphics tools and all the places you need to get at them. See Figure 7-38.

Figure 7-38. *Graphics workspace diagram numbers*

1. **Essential Graphics Panel.** The Edit tab is your command center for manipulating the position, contents, look, and order of all layers within the selected graphic object. At the top is the list of layers. Click the eye icons to toggle the layers on or off. Select one, and below it you can modify the transform properties and down into text and appearance. Note also the New Layer menu icon beneath the layer list, used to quickly add a new text, shape, or clip layer. The Browse tab saves graphic objects that can be used as templates.

2. **Graphics Tools.** Bundled with the usual editing tools are the Type tool and, with it, the Vertical Type tool. Click and hold the Pen tool, and you now have Rectangle and Ellipse tools. All three are for creating shapes right in the program monitor. Use the Pen tool to create a freeform shape point by point.

3. **Graphics Menu.** This replaces the old Title menu and contains graphics-related options such as new layer creation (within the selected graphic object or in a new one if none is selected) and advanced options such as *Upgrade to Master Graphic* and *Export to Motion Graphics Template*.

4. **Program Monitor.** Make plenty of room in your workspace for this, because it is the canvas for drawing shapes, entering type, positioning, and animating all the layers together. As Premiere Pro does not yet have a graphics-specific grid or snapping features like in Photoshop, use the program monitor **Settings menu** ➤ **Safe Margins** to display title and action safe guides for design.

5. **Timeline.** Graphic objects are created and edited here as clips. Think of them as a clip container for layers. You create one by creating its first layer using the tools or the **Graphics menu ➤ New Layer** option.

■ **Note**   A crucial difference between graphic objects and legacy titles is that graphic objects only need to exist in the timeline—there won't be a master clip in the Project panel (unless you make it a master graphic, which we'll have a look at later).

Therefore, you can use the Razor tool or **Ctrl+K** (Cmd+K on Mac) to cut one graphic object into two and immediately begin editing the second one as its own instance without having to duplicate it.

6. **Project Panel.** The role of this panel is much reduced with graphic objects since they are one of the only asset types in Premiere Pro that does not require an associated master clip in the Project panel. However, you can still drag master clips here to upgrade them to master graphics, and master text styles are saved here as well. Read on for more about these workflows.

7. **Effect Controls Panel.** The ECP plays a vital role in the new graphics workflow because each layer within a selected graphic object also shows up here as its own effect, enabling you to animate layers independently. In this way, the Graphics panel is similar to the Lumetri Color panel: looks are created and parameters are adjusted in their own dedicated panel, but to animate them over time you can use the ECP.

The Graphics panel–ECP relationship actually works better than Lumetri because the layers are not lumped together into a single effect. Each layer has its own transform, source text, path, or appearance parameters ready for you to control. The only confusing thing about this system is that layers in the ECP and Graphics panels are listed in reverse order. In the Graphics panel, the layer at the top of the list appears at the top of the stack in the program monitor. But switch over to the ECP, and that same top layer will be at the bottom of your effects list (Figure 7-39). The ECP has always handled effect hierarchy this way, but keep it in mind when designing with the new graphics tools.

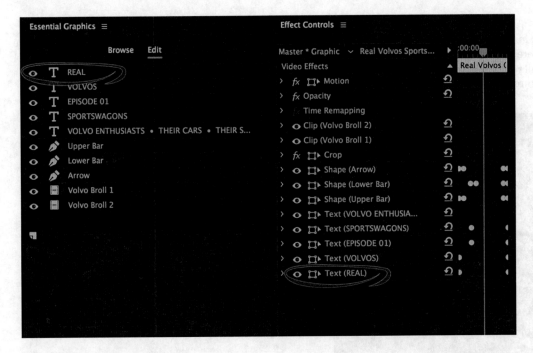

Figure 7-39. *ECP vs. EGP stack*

Working with Different Layer Types

Graphic objects contain shape, text, and clip layers that you edit individually. Using these three layer types, the design options in the Graphics panel, and the keyframing and effect options in the ECP, you can create complex motion graphics that live as a single clip in your timeline.

The animation sequence shown in Figure 7-40, created for a web series about vintage Volvo cars, was made entirely within a single graphic object using layers. Accomplishing the same build with the Legacy Title tool would have required dozens of titles stacked in the timeline, so most users would probably have done it in After Effects. To see the finished episode and its Premiere Pro graphics package, go to vimeo. com/212512406.

Figure 7-40. *Volvos' open frame sequence*

Text layers can be horizontal or vertical, and if you click and drag with the Type tool you will get a text box in the program monitor. New text layers always match the last one selected, so you can select on purpose before creation to easily match styles. After selecting a text layer, scroll down in the graphics panel for control of all your text parameters (Figure 7-41). The default font is Minion Pro, but there's also a "most recent used" feature that remembers which font you used last.

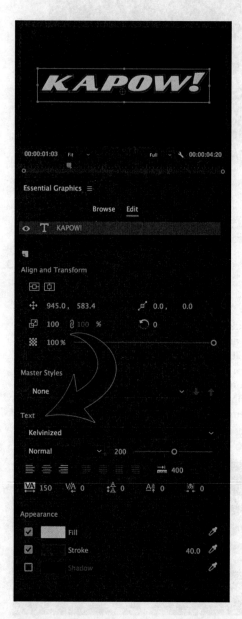

Figure 7-41. *Here, you'll find font, font size, tracking, kerning, leading, baseline shift, and tsume (space around a character) options*

If the Selection tool (**V**) is active, you will change the parameters for all the text in a layer. Unfortunately, double-clicking on a text layer icon won't select all the characters as it does in Photoshop, so you'll need to go back to the Type tool and click into your text box in the program monitor whenever you want to modify the words. Get used to pressing **T** when working with text! To get your anchor point in the exact center of a text layer, click the center text icon. Left and right align will take the anchor point to that edge of the text box.

Shape layers can be rectangle, ellipse, or drawn point by point with the Pen tool. When free-drawing a shape in the program monitor, **Click and drag** to create Bezier handles on each point (Figure 7-42). You can come back and modify this path any time you select the layer, but if you don't create Bezier points at the start, they will always remain fixed. You can scale any graphics layer by selecting it and dragging the outline. To stretch or squeeze it, disable Scale Lock (the chain icon) in the Graphics panel.

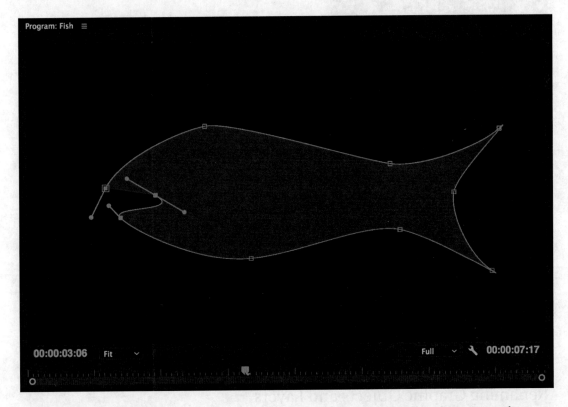

Figure 7-42. *If you need Bezier handles, create them when you first draw a shape's path. You can make complex forms this way.*

Clip layers can be video clips, still images, or Photoshop files imported through the **New Layer ➤ From File** menu (Figure 7-43). Unlike text and shape layers, the clip layer asset will appear in your Project panel as a master clip–and if you delete it there, the layer will disappear from your graphic object. You can also drag clips or images from the Project panel directly to the layer list.

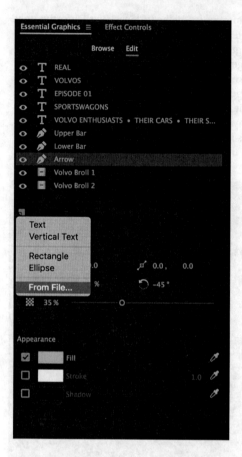

Figure 7-43. *For these opening titles, I used a combination of text, shape, and clip layers to build the finished graphic*

To delete a layer, select it in the Graphics panel and press **Delete** (Forward Delete on Mac). You can also delete layers in the ECP.

Renaming Graphic Objects and Layers

Because graphic objects exist only in the sequence, and you may fill them with a lot of layers to create a complex build, naming both objects and layers is necessary to keep your work organized.

By default, the graphic object takes on the name of your text layer if you started it with a text layer, or just calls itself "Graphic" if you used a Shape or Clip layer. **Right-click ➤ Rename** (Figure 7-44) or use the menu option **Clip ➤ Rename** to change this to something custom. You can map this to a keyboard shortcut if desired.

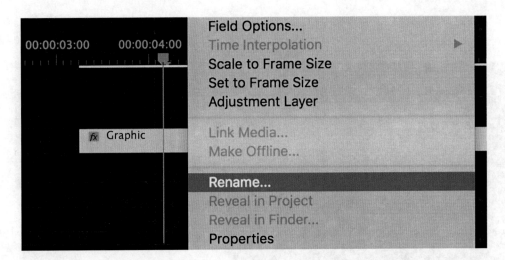

Figure 7-44. *Rename menu*

When first created, text layers are named with the characters you typed in. If the graphic has more than one text layer, the name is taken from the first text layer in the stack (the upper one in the Essential Graphics panel). Clip layers take on the name of the source file. Shape layers are automatically numbered Shape 1, Shape 2, and so on, but can be renamed by **right-click ➤ Rename**. You can also rename them in the Effect Controls panel via the same route.

Also, these "effect names" for your layers will show up in the timeline menu when you right-click on the FX icon in the upper left of the graphic object. Remember, outside of the Essential Graphics panel, Premiere Pro basically treats layers as effects–but more on this as we get into keyframing.

Keyframing Graphic Layers

If you are designing a still graphic, create the layers and modify their parameters in the Graphics panel. There is no need to use the Effect Controls panel. But if you want to keyframe layer parameters (for example, adding motion to text), switch over to the ECP. Shape, text, and clip layers show up here individually, along with any other effects you've applied to the graphic object. Keyframing works the same with graphic layers as it does with regular effects, but there are a few principles to keep in mind.

A series of position and mask keyframes created the motion in Figure 7-45. Although you could break these out into multiple graphic objects and get the same result, having all the layers in one ECP view really speeds up keyframing.

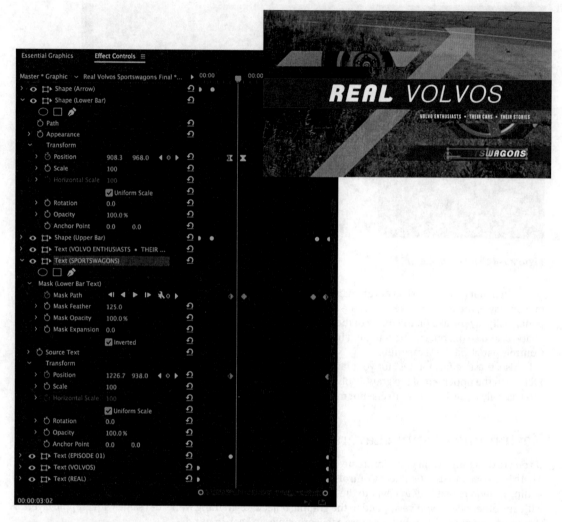

Figure 7-45. *Volvos ECP layer list*

Click the twirly arrows, and you'll see that each layer has its own keyframable transform properties for position, scale, rotation, and so forth. These are not to be confused with the motion, opacity, and time-remapping properties at the top of the ECP, which are for animating the entire graphic object in your timeline (i.e., all the layers together). Remember that layer order is reversed from the Graphics panel to the ECP. Layers and effects on the bottom of the list affect everything *above* them.

Shape layers also have controls for path (the points of the shape) and appearance (the fill, shadow, and so on), while text layers let you toggle animation for source text (the characters and their look). As you'll see when you right-click a keyframe, these properties have no interpolation between values. All the keyframes are Hold keyframes, so they won't change gradually–they will just "cut" at the keyframe you set. Still, this is an effective way to create a flashing font montage or karaoke with just a few keyframes (Figure 7-46).

Figure 7-46. Karaoke sequence

Adding Effects to Graphic Objects

Place a regular effect like blur, crop, or basic 3D into the ECP list, and it will affect all the layers above it. This can be limiting if you can want to apply effects to individual layers. The new graphics features aren't designed to work that way, but by reordering layers you can still use effects within a single graphic object.

Here's an example: In the Real Volvos open, I wanted my clip layers (the video clips of the wheels) to be trapezoid shapes. Using a mask or track matte would have required breaking them out into clips in the timeline, since clip layer masks are not supported at the time of this writing, and a track matte needs a source in the timeline. Doable, but I wanted to keep them contained inside my graphic. The workaround? I ordered them both at the top of the ECP list and applied a crop effect immediately below them, as seen in Figure 7-47. By changing the crop to 50 percent left and 50 percent right, I essentially created a ready-to-go universal mask effect. As soon as I added the first non-inverted mask, everything under the crop appeared except what I wanted to mask out. Four masks and a few keyframes later, I got my trapezoids. Overkill? Maybe, but the point is not to let the order of effects in the ECP prevent you from getting the result you want in a single, tidy graphic object.

Figure 7-47. Masks are your friend if you want to make complex designs in a single graphic object

When to Use Multiple Graphic Objects

One of the benefits of graphics objects is that you don't need a timeline track for each layer. But, as we've already seen, this has some limitations. For example, you can't apply blending modes (multiply, overlay, etc.) to individual layers–you'll need to split them out into their own objects. If the stack gets too large in the timeline, **Clip ➤ Nest** it. This limitation has always applied to the legacy titles, so the nesting workflow should be familiar.

If you need to apply effects to individual layers or groups of layers, you'll also need to break them out into their own objects.

■ **Note** As a general rule, create a new graphic object whenever it saves you time to do so. But keep in mind that containing builds to single objects in the timeline will make them easier to use as templates and easier to save as master graphics.

Saving Master Graphics

As we've seen, graphic objects do not require master clips in the project panel. This makes it very easy to work with them as clip instances in the timeline without worrying about duplicating them in the Project panel. But in certain situations, you may want your graphic to be a master clip so you can save it with the project or update multiple instances of it at once. This is how legacy titles worked, and the functionality exists for graphic objects if you need it.

To turn any graphic into a master clip, select it and choose **Graphics ➤ Upgrade to Master Graphic,** or just drag it from the timeline to the Project panel.

■ **Note** You can't undo this change into a master graphic, so make sure you're ready to upgrade. I usually duplicate the graphic and move it to another sequence before I upgrade it.

Now, you'll see a red line under the clip FX icon in the timeline, and if you double-click the master graphic it will open in the source monitor. To modify it, go into the ECP Master tab, and you'll see that the original layers have been moved here (Figure 7-48). Go to the Graphics panel, and you'll be able to modify them.

■ **Note** When you modify a Master Graphic, it will change every instance of that graphic in every sequence in your project.

As with titles, the inherent motion, opacity, and time-remapping effects are not saved with the master graphic.

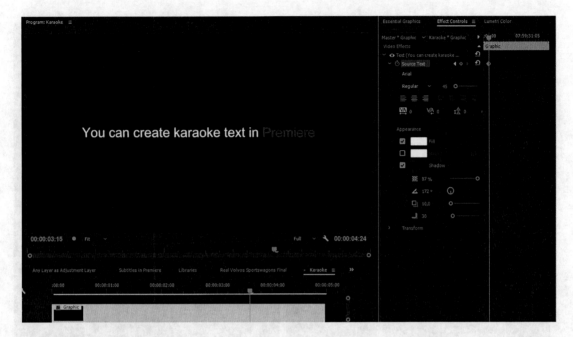

Figure 7-48. *Master graphics are created by dragging a graphic object into the project panel. Updating it in one place updates it everywhere.*

Master graphics are not templates, nor are they great for versioning. I suggest using them when you have a "locked" graphic that you want to share and reuse. Read on to discover better options for template graphic workflows.

Saving Graphic Layers as Effects

Here's an interesting feature: since Premiere Pro treats layers exactly like effects, you can save individual layers as Effect presets. Find the name of the layer in the ECP and **right-click ➤ Save Preset** (Figure 7-49). Type a descriptive name in the dialog and decide if you want any keyframes you've set to be scaled over the length of the clip they are applied to, or kept at their current duration and anchored to the in or out point. Hit OK, and your layer appears in the Effects Panel Presets folder for use in other graphic objects.

■ **Note** Of course, you can copy and paste layers using the Graphics panel or ECP, but as presets your layers are saved with the system and become available in other projects.

Much more on Effect presets in chapter 10 on Customizing Premiere.

Figure 7-49. *If you need to use a layer in another project, consider saving it as an Effects preset*

Master Text Styles

The attributes of a text layer (font, leading, drop shadow, and so on) can be saved together as a master text style, which you can easily apply to text layers in other graphic objects. First, prepare a text layer the way you want it. Remember, all properties in the Text and Appearance sections of the Graphics panel will be saved with the style, but align and transform properties will not. Go to **Master Styles menu ➤ Create Master Text Style**. Name it, and it becomes an option in that menu. The style will also be saved to your Project panel in the active bin. Text styles have a unique "Pr" icon and live with the project, so if you delete this file it removes it from the style list. See Figure 7-50.

Figure 7-50. *Master text style file icon*

To apply the style to other text layers, simply select the layer in the Graphics panel and choose the style you want from the Master Styles menu Figure 7-51). Or, you can drag the style file from the bin onto any text layer in the Graphics panel. You can also drag it onto the entire graphics object in the timeline, which will update *every* text layer to that style.

Figure 7-51. *To create this lower third, master text styles were saved from the opening title graphics and then applied to the new text layers here*

What if you tweak your text layer after applying a master text style? You'll see <modified> next to the style name, and next to the Master Styles menu you'll notice two arrows (Figure 7-52). The down arrow will reset your text layer back to the original style. This "syncing down" from parent to child will erase any changes you've made.

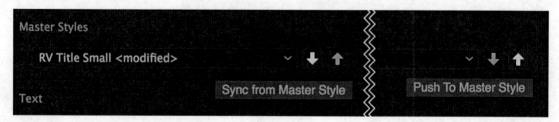

Figure 7-52. *Master text style arrows*

The up arrow will push your changes back to the master style and overwrite it. Think of it as "syncing up" from child to parent. This is very useful if you want to update a lot of text layers within individual graphic objects throughout your project, but be careful! It updates every text layer set to that style the moment you push the up arrow.

This "parent/child" behavior gives you the ability to update your styles in either direction easily–just make sure you push the correct arrow.

■ **Note**   Remember that you can also copy/paste or duplicate text styles in the bin and rename them, and they will show up in the menu. You can use this to make back-up copies of your styles.

Unlike legacy title styles and effect presets, text styles are saved with the project, not the system. So, it makes sense to create a template project with a bin just for text styles so you'll have them at your fingertips.

Master text styles do have some limitations: you can't save any keyframes, and you can't save multiple font sizes, colors, or other parameters within the same style (for example, different lines in a lower third). The settings on your first letter are what the style saves. To get around this, make multiple text layers and save styles for each. Even with these limitations, master text styles are a powerful yet easy way to share text parameters. But the new graphics template workflows don't end here.

Working with Motion Graphic Templates

If you've worked with template graphics in Premiere Pro prior to version CC 2017.1, your options have been title templates (addressed in the next section) or live text templates created in After Effects (as .aep or .aecap files, covered in chapter 11 on Integration). Both workflows are fully featured and ready to go in Premiere Pro. But with the new graphics in CC 2017.1, Adobe introduced motion graphic templates (.mogrt files), an alternative for saving and sharing templates directly from Premiere Pro.

Mogrt Thumbnail

So, what are .mogrts? Program Manager for After Effects, Victoria Nece, has a good explanation: they're encapsulated motion graphics projects with simplified controls; easy to create, share, and customize, and usable in multiple apps on multiple platforms.

To create a motion graphics template in Premiere, select a graphic object in the timeline and choose **Graphics ➤ Export as Motion Graphics Template**. Aside from the name of the template, you can choose where it will be saved (Figure 7-53).

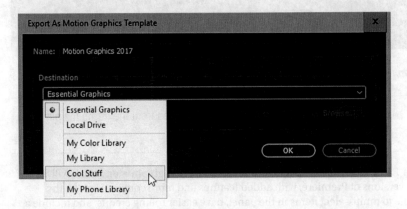

Figure 7-53. *Export as motion graphics template*

By default, it's saved to your local Essential Graphics folder, but you can also save it to a folder on a local drive, or to any of the libraries saved with your Creative Cloud account. A .mogrt file will be saved there containing all the layers, animations, text, and associated media that you used to design it. This is great! No more missing logos!

■ **Note**   The .mogrt files are a great way to share motion graphics templates across teams and projects.

If you export the template to Essential Graphics, it will show up in the panel. And, naturally, if you export it to a library, it shows up there. But when you export to a local file, it's not entirely intuitive how to import it. File-import will fail, and the media browser will not even show it, so how do you use a .mogrt file that someone sends you? You can click **Graphics ➤ Install Motion Graphics Template** or click the little icon with an arrow pointing to a folder in the Browse tab in the Essential Graphics panel.

If you're in a subfolder in the Essential Graphics panel and click the Install Motion Graphics Template icon, you'd think that the template would end up in that folder, but you'll find it in the root folder in the panel, from which you can move it to your chosen folder via the right-click menu.

To use a motion graphics template you've saved or imported, locate it in the Essential Graphics panel under the Browse tab and drag it to the timeline. When you select the clip, the Essential Graphics panel will change to the Edit tab, and you can use the Type tool to edit the text (Figure 7-54). You can, of course, change the font, color and so on, too, but that defeats the purpose of a template.

Figure 7-54. Edit motion graphics template

■ **Note**   When you export a .mogrt file from Premiere, the thumbnail is created from the frame the playhead is parked on.

Obviously, this is version 1.0 of the Essential Graphics panel and the new graphics engine. It will be improved upon in upcoming versions of Premiere, with added features and more control. High on my feature-request list is to be able to multi-select items in the panel, have easier rolling credits, and include a font preview when selecting fonts.

When you want more-advanced graphics, use .mogrts from After Effects, where you can create much more elaborate but still very user-friendly templates for use in Premiere. Learn how to make your own motion graphic templates in After Effects in the chapter on integration.

Resolve Missing Fonts

If you import a motion graphics template that uses a font that's not installed on your system, you'll get the Resolve Fonts dialog. See Figure 7-55.

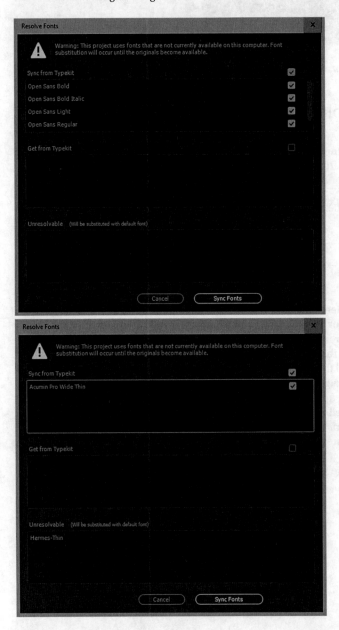

Figure 7-55. *The Resolve Fonts dialog after importing two different .mogrts with missing fonts*

Depending on the availability of the font, you can sync it from Typekit, get it from Typekit, or download it from a third-party web page and install it on your system. If the font is not available, it will be replaced by another font. When syncing fonts, you must restart Premiere once the font is installed (Figure 7-56).

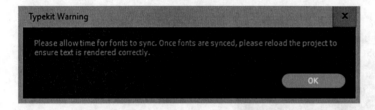

Figure 7-56. *Restart Premiere once the fonts have been synced*

The Motion Graphics Templates Folder

The `.mogrt` files (both from Premiere and After Effects) are installed in this folder on Windows: **C:\Users\<username>\AppData\Roaming\Adobe\Common\Essential Graphics**. On MacOS, it's **/Users/<username>/Library/Application Support/Adobe/Essential Graphics/**.

■ **Note** A pro tip for installing lots of motion graphics templates in one go is to put all the `.mogrt` files directly to the `Essential Graphics` folder.

MOGRT Limitations

The .mogrts in the 2017.2 version of Premiere have some annoying limitations. I'm guessing and hoping that these will be fixed in future updates, but, for now, there are some things you should know.

There's no obvious way to install many motion graphic templates in one operation, although you can drag them directly into the hidden `Essential Graphics` folder where they live. (See previous section.)

Mogrts are great when you first install them, but when you want to replace the mogrt with a new one, you will run into problems. You can **Alt-drag** the new mogrt from the Essential Graphics panel over the old clip in the timeline, and you get the actual new graphics in the timeline and in the program monitor.

Any pre-existing instances in the timeline that are relinked to the updated template do not have access to any newly-added properties. And, surprisingly, the Essential Graphics panel now shows the parameters from the old template, but as long as you are using the same number and type of property controllers, the controllers actually work!

Replacing the mogrt in a bin works the same way, with the same problems.

The Legacy Title Tool

The hardworking Title tool is not going away, although it has become harder to find. Titles created in prior versions of Premiere Pro will function as before, and you can still create new titles by going to **File ➤ New ➤ Legacy Title**.

But the old titler *workflow* in Premiere all but vanished with the 2017.1 update. Surprisingly, they even removed the option to use titler templates, so the only way to use Legacy titler templates now is to import the .prtl files into your project and use them from a bin.

The whole templates workflow in the old titler is gone! It was replaced by the new graphics and the Essential Graphics panel.

This tells us that Adobe is planning to remove support for the titler very soon, so we won't cover the legacy titler here. That's a pity, because the old titler had some nice features that are still not there in the new graphics clips–like gradients and proper alignment tools.

If you want to have a look at the 26 pages in the old version of this book that dealt with the legacy titler, you can download them for free here: premierepro.net/motion-graphics/legacy-titler-premiere-pro/.

We Could Create Anything in the Titler

Okay maybe "anything" is a stretch, but with the title tools you could (and still can) easily create complex compositions from scratch. There are eight kinds of default shapes, including wedges, arcs, and lines, and the Pen tools let you draw freehand with points and then convert them to Bezier at any time with the Convert Anchor Point tool. There are six Type tools, including horizontal and vertical paths, and fourteen different align and distribute options for selecting multiple objects and rearranging them within the title easily (Figure 7-57).

Figure 7-57. Legacy title tools

Best of all, these shape and text objects can be filled with linear, radial, and four-color gradients, bevel, ghost (no fill), sheen, texture (from a file), inner and outer strokes, shadows, and even backgrounds surrounding the object. If you wonder if you can draw something in the titler, analyze it and try to find out what the building blocks of the graphic are. There are so many options for fine-tuning shapes, chances are you can. Match that, Graphics panel (Figure 7-58)!

610

Figure 7-58. *The Title tool is the Chuck Norris of Adobe Premiere Pro graphics tools. Don't call it "basic," or it will roundhouse kick you in the face. It's also old.*

Convert Your Legacy Title to a New Graphic

Instead of starting from scratch when you update your old titler presets to new graphics clips, you can copy and paste from the titler into a graphic object, and it will retain most (but not all) of the appearance parameters for you.

You can find your old templates in this folder: **Documents\Adobe\Premiere Pro\11.0\Profile-[UserName]\Templates**.

Let's hope the new Graphics panel in Premiere can mature and be as good as its predecessor in the future. The Title tool will stick around for a while, but if past precedent is any indication, it's unlikely to be with us forever. Long live the Title tool!

Some Useful Effects

Some effects in Premiere are used more than others when it comes to motion graphics, such as RGB Curves and other color-correction tools in Lumetri for color and contrast adjustments; roughen edges to make text edges grittier; write-on to make travel routes; basic 3D to put stuff in 3D space, and so forth–and, of course, the built-in scale, rotation, and position. And Gaussian blur is our best friend!

Track Matte Key

The mask tools in Premiere are great, but they are restricted to shapes and don't work on pixel values. The track matte key is great for creating transparency based on the luminance values or alpha channels of other layers. The track matte key works great, but it means we need an extra video track with the matte that controls what part of the affected image will be transparent.

Metal Text

Figure 7-59 shows an example where the track matte key makes a metal texture image visible only where there's text. The lower layer has an image of metal with a color effect on it. The upper layer has just some text (Figure 7-60), and the middle layer is where the magic happens. It has the metal texture image with the track matte key effect on it, set to take its matte from the text layer. It also has a bevel alpha effect and a drop shadow to give things a bit more "pop."

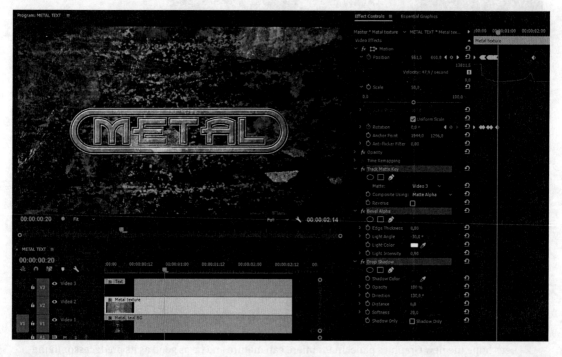

Figure 7-59. *The track matte key makes its layer (the metal texture) visible based on the alpha channel of the text layer*

Figure 7-60. *The cool font EmpireState made this text a bit more interesting than Arial, but the text looks a lot better with a metal texture, courtesy of the track matte key*

Abused Text

The track matte key can also use the luminance of the upper layer, so any source can be used as a matte. In Figure 7-61, the text is made transparent where the concrete wall texture is dark. Quite a few of the standard effects are in use here. Note the use of a texture as a matte for the track matte key and roughen edges to "eat" into the edges of the text. The background gradient and the vignette layer have been applied with the overlay blend mode to create some interesting color variation in the rust texture.

Figure 7-61. *Track matte key and other effects used to create abused text*

613

See chapter 8 on compositing for more details about the track matte key effect.

Gaussian Blur

The Gaussian blur effect is great for creating blurry backgrounds, glows, light leaks, and so on.

Glowing Text

A glow is just a blurred version of a layer, most often achieved with a blending mode. If one copy doesn't give us enough glow, we simply add more. Here, I've plagiarized the look of the TV series *24* using three copies of the same text layer. I found the nice Quartz font at fonts101.com/. See Figures 7-62 and 7-63.

Figure 7-62. *Glowing 25 finished*

Figure 7-63. *Glowing 25 layers*

Blending Modes

Clips on the timeline can be blended into the ones below them in many different ways. The blending modes are just pure mathematical algorithms: adding, subtracting, dividing, and multiplying levels in different and sometimes strange ways.

Blending modes are found under **Motion ➤ Opacity** in the Effect Controls panel in Premiere.

Making a Vintage Map

The world map from vectorworldmap.com fits nicely for an animated travel route, but it's kind of dull. So, let's add some interest by creating a vintage-style map.

We need some textures that can augment the "old map" look. I chose two images of concrete walls and one image of some rough paper from my private texture collection. I placed the paper texture at the bottom of the stack, then the two concrete wall textures with overlay blending mode, and finally the world map image in Color Burn mode. By raising the black level of the map to about 40 percent, I got the look I wanted (Figure 7-64). Figure 7-65 shows the sources I used.

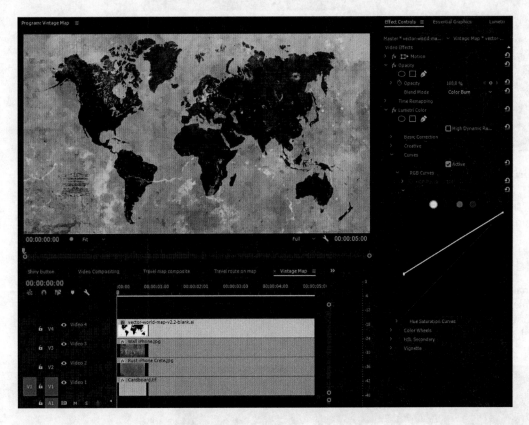

Figure 7-64. *Vintage map finished look*

Figure 7-65. *Vintage map sources*

These images are dull, but when blended together, they look great. Blending modes are an overlooked feature in Premiere. Use them and make your motion graphics stand out from the rest.

Add Some 3D

To make your titles even more interesting, try adding the basic 3D effect. In Figure 7-67, I've used it on the simple graphics clip from Figure 7-66. Figure 7-68 shows the settings I used in the basic 3D effect. If you keyframe some movement in 3D, it looks very After Effects–like. Even the most basic title looks cooler when tilted, swiveled, and animated in 3D.

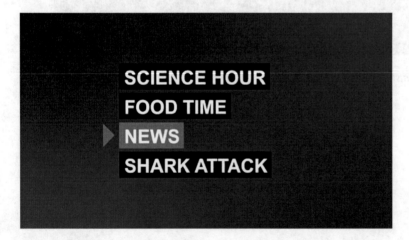

Figure 7-66. *Before adding basic 3D*

Figure 7-67. *After adding basic 3D*

Figure 7-68. *Basic 3D settings*

Add Motion Blur with the Transform Effect

By just unchecking one checkbox, the transform effect gets motion-blur capability! You can even adjust the shutter angle from 0 to 360 degrees. Uncheck *Use Composition's Shutter Angle* (Figure 7-69), which I guess is a leftover from After Effects, since Premiere doesn't have compositions. Then, set the motion blur to whatever you like.

■ **Remember**   Shutter Angle is *not* what affects the amount of motion blur—it's the shutter speed that does so. So, we need to set different shutter angles for different frame rates to get the same amount of motion blur. The old "180-degree shutter angle" rule is *only* valid for 24 and 25 fps.

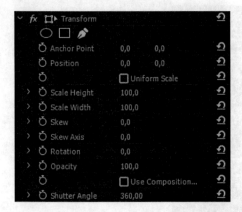

Figure 7-69. *Transform settings for motion blur*

Since this was a 50 fps project, I chose a 360-degree shutter angle. Had it been 25 or 24 fps, I would have set it to 180 degrees. Unfortunately, transform is not GPU accelerated when you turn on the motion blur. Please go ahead and file a feature request for it at adobe.com/go/wish/. Figure 7-70 shows a text that's been animated in horizontally using the transform effect with motion blur settings. Note that it has motion blur when it moves fast.

Figure 7-70. *Transform motion blur*

Never Underestimate Nesting

Every sequence creates an output that can be sent to another sequence. Nesting is when you put one sequence into another and is a great way to "group" clips, to treat them separately.

This is useful when the render order of effects creates problems–like when we rotate a shape with a drop shadow, and the shadow rotates with the shape. With nesting, we can break the render order and rotate the shape in one sequence, put this sequence into another one, and add the drop shadow there. Now the shadow stays where it should.

Another way to accomplish the same thing would be to add the transform effect before the drop shadow effect, but if you've already made the animation using the motion parameters, nesting will be quicker.

Nesting is also great for keeping timelines tidy and for making template projects much more user friendly. Let's have a look at two common motion graphics requests and how to use nesting to achieve them.

Reflections

Everything looks nicer with reflections! In After Effects, it's easy to add reflections with plug-ins, expressions, or scripting. Since Premiere cannot be scripted, and it would be very laborious to keyframe a reflection animation, we must use a workaround; we put the image inside a big sequence and add a flipped, blurred, partly transparent copy of it inside that sequence. Then, we can animate it using basic 3D in the main sequence if we want to. Here's a walk-through.

Start with a Background and a Source

Create an HD sequence. Name it *BG*. Add a clip with whatever you like to use as the background. I used a legacy title with two shapes, which were filled with gradients (Figure 7-71).

Figure 7-71. *Two shapes with gradients make a background*

Create another sequence named *Source* and place a video clip or a still image there.

■ **Note**   These two steps aren't absolutely necessary, but doing this lets you transform the sources separately in their sequences without breaking the layout. It also makes the project much more useful as a template for later recycling of this effect, as you can scale and tweak any material that's not the same size as the project.

Make a New Sequence, Double Height

To make room for a reflection, we'll make a new sequence that's 1920 × 2160 pixels–twice as high as standard HD. Name it *Reflection* and put the Source sequence into it. Set the vertical anchor point at 1080. This moves the clip to the top. Now, **Alt-drag** a copy of the sequence to track 2 and set the vertical anchor point to 0, which moves it to the bottom.

Add the vertical flip effect to the copy and lower the opacity to around 65 percent. Then, add the crop effect to it, with the Bottom parameter set to 95 percent and Edge Feather set to 900. As a final touch to the reflection, add Gaussian blur with *Repeat Edge Pixels* selected to be on, and Blurriness set at around 20. It should look like Figure 7-72.

Figure 7-72. A flipped, cropped, and blurred copy looks like a reflection

Put It All together

To finish up, make a new sequence named *Video Reflection Compositing* and put the BG sequence on track 1 and the Reflection sequence on track 2. Add the basic 3D effect to the Reflection clip and adjust *Distance to Image* and the vertical position under the Motion section until you like the result. Figure 7-73 shows what it looks like with 850 for vertical position and 56 for the Distance to Image parameter, with a 21-degree swivel.

Figure 7-73. *Video reflection compositing*

Everything can now be tweaked and changed to taste. Want to change the background? Open the BG sequence. Need another image? Open the Source sequence. Want to animate the swivel? Set keyframes for swivel in the compositing sequence. Figures 7-74 and 7-75 show two variations made with the same template project.

Figure 7-74. *Frame image from Fuzzimo, fuzzimo.com/free-hi-res-old-picture-frame-images-part-2/*

Figure 7-75. *Video reflection with real frame and floor. Here, I've used a texture as a floor. I used basic 3D to tilt it in the BG sequence.*

See the existing project on `premierepro.net` for an example using this technique. Note: Since that project was posted, we got feathered crop in Premiere Pro CC, so now it's simpler than ever to do this in Premiere!

Cover Flow

The cover flow we've become so used to on smartphones and tablets is a nice way to display a collection of items. When analyzing the cover flow, we'll see that it's just a keyframed movement in 3D space, and we can do that with the basic 3D effect and some position keyframes. Let's build this from scratch so you understand the thinking behind this project and can make your own cool projects later (Figure 7-76).

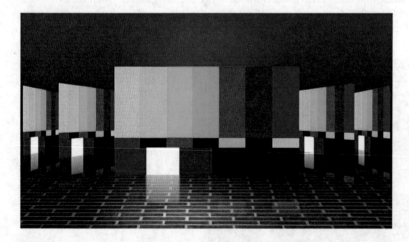

Figure 7-76. *Cover flow main sequence*

The cover flow is just the same movement over and over on many clips on different layers. I used Bars & Tone to create a template project where I can swap in my video material with a simple **Alt-drag-n-drop**.

I made an effect preset using the basic 3D effect and position, where the image moves in standard cover flow–style in steps (Figure 7-77). By throwing this on a stack of color bars, I can see that the movement is OK, but not the order of the layers in 3D space. We'll deal with layer order later.

Figure 7-77. Cover flow movement as ECP keyframes

Nesting for Ease of Use and Extra Features

We could just stack videos and use the preset on all of them. But to make it easier to replace the color bars with your material, we'll introduce source sequences–one sequence for each source. That way, we can just concentrate on one source at a time when building our project, and scaling, doing color correction, adding layers, and so on will be much easier and quicker to do.

■ **Note**   Of course, we need a reflection. Use the technique explained earlier, with sequences that are taller than HD. These reflection sequences are the ones we'll stack to create our cover-flow sequence.

Solving the 3D Problem

The problem we have with the 3D is that Premiere has no idea where the different layers are relative to each other and just places clips in higher tracks in front of clips in lower tracks. But, in a cover flow, an image is only on top when it's the middle, large image. Both when coming in and when going out, it should be lower in the stack. As you can see in Figure 7-78, the right side of the cover flow isn't looking right. Hmmmm. . .

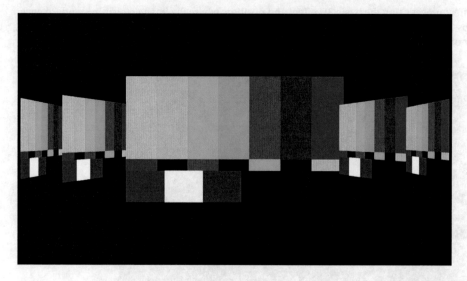

Figure 7-78. *The left part of this animation is correct, but on the right side, the layer order should be exactly the opposite*

My solution is very low-tech: split the animation in half vertically and stack the layers the opposite order in one of them. This works because the images are coming in on one side and going out on the other. Figures 7-79 and 7-80 show what I mean.

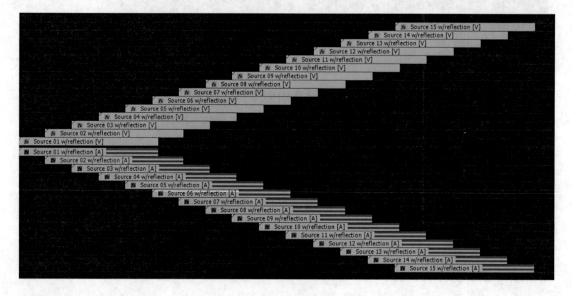

Figure 7-79. *Cover flow left*

The clips are staggered so they come in sequentially. Since we need the layers to switch places in 3D depth mid-way, we need to use two different setups for the left and right side.

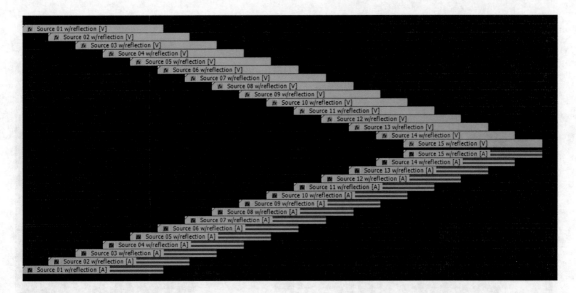

Figure 7-80. *Cover flow right*

These two layer stacks are correct on different sides. One is correct on the right side and one on the left side. So, if they're placed in the main sequence (Figure 7-81) and simply cropped 50 percent from opposite sides (Figure 7-82), together they look perfect! I used opacity masks instead of crop.

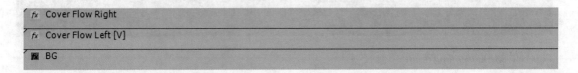

Figure 7-81. *Cover flow main sequence*

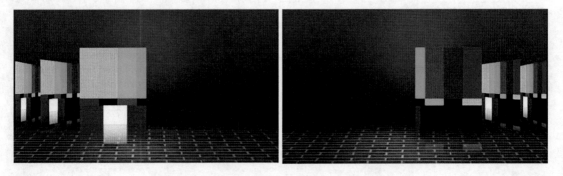

Figure 7-82. *Cover flow left side and cover flow right side*

Wrapping Up

To sum up the effects on the clips in the main sequence: the bottom layer is a background, as in the earlier Reflection example. The two cover flow (right and left) sequences were simply cropped 50 percent from opposite sides with opacity masks (Figure 7-83).

Figure 7-83. *Cover flow result*

This reads like a very complicated thing, but it's actually logical. The source sequences go into the reflection sequences. Those go into the left and right sequences, and those again go into the main sequence with the BG sequence.

To make this user friendly, I sorted everything into bins and made a custom workspace that lets you swap in the source files quickly.

In the Cover Flow template on `PremierePro.net`, I also made a sequence where the image zooms from the front position in the cover flow to full screen, and one that zooms the other way. I used the *Distance to Image* property in the basic 3D effect to accomplish this. By match-framing the source file (**F**) and placing it in a zoom sequence, one can zoom into and out from the cover flow. This project was then saved, and the file was changed to "Read Only" in my OS, making it a useful template project. Figure 7-83 is the result, with some imported material.

I used a "pancake" layout in my template, with two timeline frames showing. All the source sequences are in the upper panels, and the main sequence is in the lower panel (Figure 7-84).

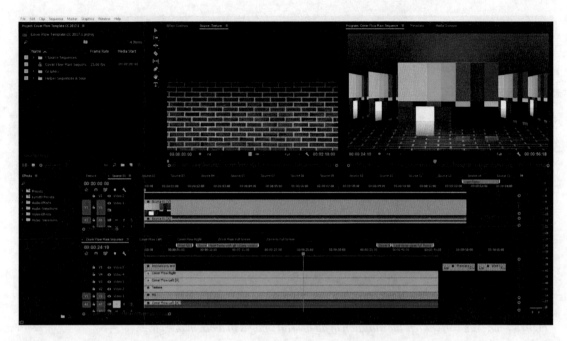

Figure 7-84. *Pancake-style layout*

Use Any Material

Remember, you can put any kind of material you want in here: still images, video, sequences, time-lapse, stop-motion animation, graphics, text, and so on. You can use 720p, 1080p, 1080i, 2K, or 4K. Only if you're zooming in to full screen will the resolution really matter, and if you want to use this in a 720p timeline, just scale the whole sequence down.

■ **Note** I hope these two examples have convinced you that nesting is a great way to organize motion graphics projects, and that nesting makes changes easier.

Working with Still Images

You can import most common image formats into Premiere, but RAW files and files with CMYK colors are not supported. I recommend that you use the media browser for import as usual, as it gives you preview images of all the supported image formats.

Still Image Duration

Let's imagine you want all your still images to be two seconds long. Go to **Preferences ➤ Timeline** and set *Still Image Default Duration* to two seconds. All the stills you import from now on will be two seconds. Setting a new duration here will *not* affect already imported stills, just new ones. The duration is set at import time.

If your stills are already imported and you need to change the duration, select them all in the bin, then right-click one or hit **Ctrl+R** (Cmd+R) and set Duration to two seconds (Figure 7-85).

Figure 7-85. *You can change the duration of all the still images in a bin in one go*

Doing this in the Project panel will still not affect clips already in the timeline. If you need to adjust the duration of stills in the timeline, select them all in the timeline, right-click or use the keyboard shortcut, and set the new duration (Figure 7-86).

Figure 7-86. *You can also change the duration in the timeline, where you get a few more options*

Make sure to check the *Ripple Edit* option to avoid gaps when you change the duration on clips in the timeline. Figures 7-87 and 7-88 show the timeline before and after changing the duration of several still images.

Figure 7-87. *Timeline before changing the duration of stills*

Figure 7-88. *Timeline after changing the duration of stills*

Set Your Rendering Preferences

In the **Preferences ➤ Memory** dialog box, choose *Optimize Rendering for Memory* if you have any memory issues when rendering sequences with a lot of large stills. As the default, it's set to *Performance* (Figure 7-89).

Figure 7-89. *Optimize for memory*

With the default setting of Performance, Premiere will use up to 16 processors for rendering, but sequences requiring large amounts of memory–like sequences with a lot of large stills–will need too much memory to render several frames simultaneously, and your system will potentially starve on RAM. You can make a struggling system more stable by changing this setting to Memory. Remember to change this back to Performance on your next project.

Import Layered Photoshop Files

When you import layered Photoshop files, you can import the image as a flattened file, just a few of the layers as a flattened clip, just one or a few of the layers as separate clips, or all the layers as a sequence.

In Figure 7-90, the media browser shows previews of all supported still image formats.

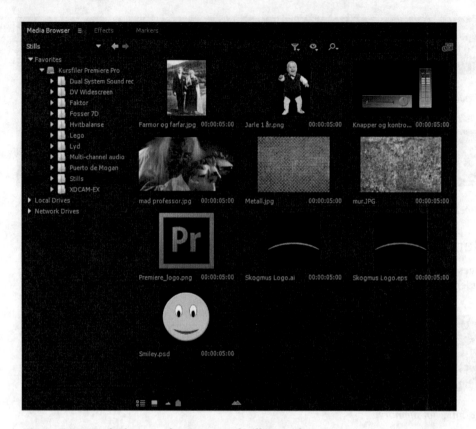

Figure 7-90. *Media browser showing several still image formats*

In Figure 7-91, the media browser shows no preview for JPG, PSD, and TIF images with CMYK colors because you can't import them. NEF (Nikon RAW) and CR2 (Canon RAW) files are not supported and don't show in the media browser at all.

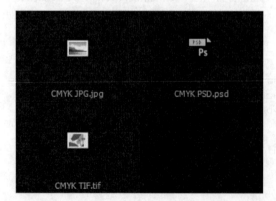

Figure 7-91. *Stills in CMYK and RAW will not show in the media browser because they cannot be imported*

Photoshop PSD files can be imported as one flat image, merging all the layers. If you don't need all the layers, choose which ones to import (Figure 7-92).

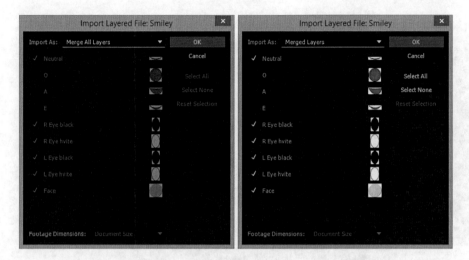

Figure 7-92. *Photoshop (PSD) import all layers versus import merged layers*

Importing the PSD file as a sequence puts all the layers on top of each other in a sequence–great for animations! Elements of a company logo can be animated separately (Figure 7-93).

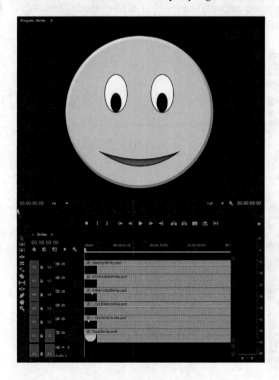

Figure 7-93. *Import PSD file as a sequence*

As shown in Figure 7-94, layers can be set to Document size or Layer size. This affects where the anchor points of the layers end up.

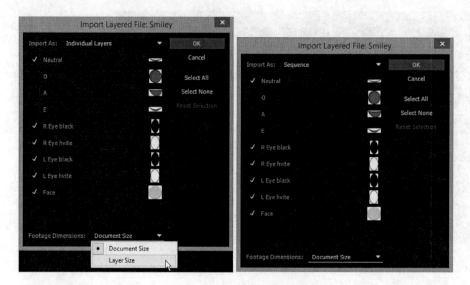

Figure 7-94. *Import PSD as individual layers or as a sequence*

Figure 7-95 shows the result of choosing *Layer Size* when importing a PSD file as a sequence. Probably not what you were expecting. This is a long-standing bug in Premiere.

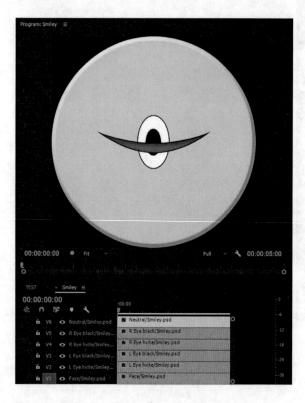

Figure 7-95. *Import PSD, choosing Layer size*

■ **Note**   Don't choose *Layer Size* when you import a PSD file as a sequence. It destroys your layout and places all the layers in the center of the frame. Import at Document size to retain the layout, and then move the anchor points manually for all layers.

After Effects has the same option when importing layered PSDs, and correctly places the anchor points in the middle of each element without destroying the design. So, a current workaround is to import the layers as a composition in After Effects and then copy the layers from the comp in AE and paste into the timeline in Premiere.

Still Image Flicker Removal

Narrow or sharp horizontal lines in stills are not easily displayed in video, especially in interlaced video. They will flicker, most noticeably when you zoom in or otherwise animate them. Adding a small amount of Gaussian blur can help. Use the smallest amount that works, and remember to view the program monitor at full resolution and preferably in full-screen mode to assess the blur. Here's a tip from the technical editor of this book, Colin Brougham, from the Premiere Pro team:

> *It's also useful is to (temporarily) enable the* High Quality Playback *toggle in the program monitor, which will display the sequence in the program monitor using the higher quality algorithm that's usually only used in the paused state. This will help better ascertain the blur (or any other motion, effect, etc., for that matter) during playback, across disparate areas of the image. It's a performance drain, though, so be sure to turn it off for most normal use.*

You don't have to blur the whole image. Mask out the offending items and add blur only to this area (Figure 7-96). Since this is a still image, we don't have to track the mask. It will automatically follow whatever scaling and other motion you apply to the clip.

Figure 7-96. *Here, I've added a small amount of Gaussian Blur to just the offending area of the image. This prevents flicker when the image is moved, rotated, or scaled.*

Remember that blur is resolution dependent, so scaled-down large images may need more blur than smaller ones that are used at 100 percent scale. You can't just copy/paste between different-sized images. Some images don't need blur in both directions. If there are sharp horizontal lines in an image but no vertical ones, you'll only need to blur vertically, keeping the full horizontal resolution.

Storyboarding a Still Image Sequence

Having a visually oriented brain, I like to use the bin as a storyboard (Figure 7-97) and then drag the stills from the bin to the timeline.

Figure 7-97. Use your bin as a storyboard, visually deciding about the order of the images

Still images are often much larger than your average video frame (Figure 7-98), so you will scale them down until they fit. If your images were taken with the same camera, chances are they will need to be scaled by roughly the same amount. You can't choose all the clips and add the same scale amount to all of them, but you can set the scale animation on one clip and then copy the motion to all of them. This will not be perfect for all the images, but it's a good starting point.

Figure 7-98. *Still images are often a lot larger than your sequence frame size*

Pan & Scan Photo Montage

Documentary filmmaker Ken Burns used this effect so much that it was named after him: the Ken Burns Effect. He didn't invent a zoom in on a still image, of course, but he made it popular through his films. Figures 7-99 and 7-100 show the start and end of a still image zoom. Maybe in a few years we'll call lens flare the Michael Bay Effect or the J.J. Abrams Effect?

Figure 7-99. *Still zoom start*

Figure 7-100. *This is how the image looks after the zoom in. The ease keyframes make the movement smooth.*

Personally, I like to do cross dissolves between the animated stills. When you do this, setting the keyframes gets a bit more complicated.

■ **Note** If you set keyframes before adding the transitions, the movement will start and stop in the middle of the dissolve. Not very pretty! You might as well add the transition first and then do the animation.

But, if you adjust a parameter on a keyframe at the very start of a clip that is faded in, you will not see the clip at all. So, you'll have to move the keyframes into the area where there is no transition, adjust the settings, and then move it back again (Figures 7-101 to 7-103). This isn't as much labor as it sounds, but it does add up if you have lots of stills.

Figure 7-101. *Keyframes at both ends*

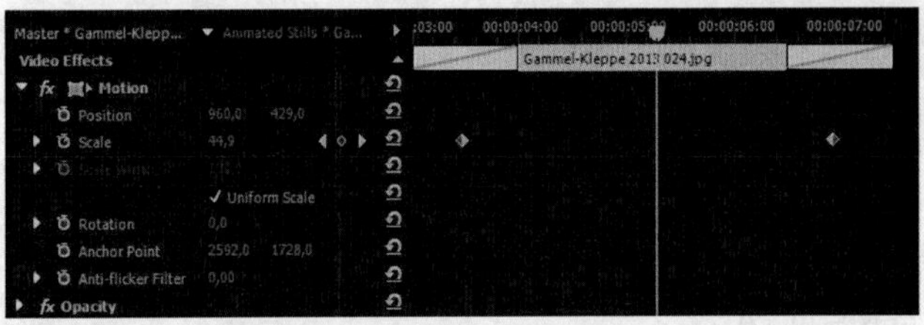

Figure 7-102. *Keyframes after adding transitions*

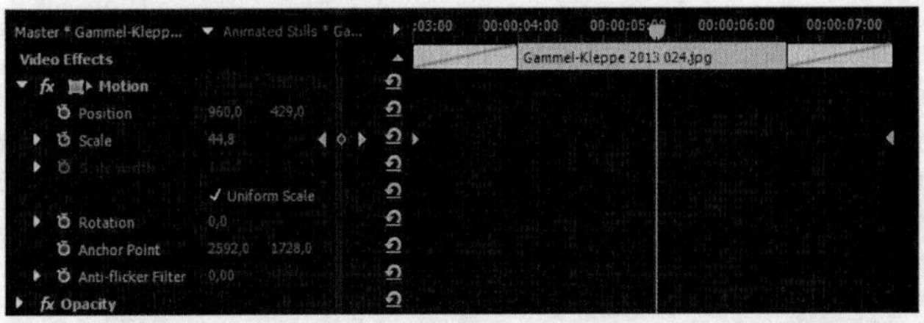

Figure 7-103. *Keyframes moved to start and end of transitions*

When you add cross dissolves or other transitions, you need to move the keyframes so the movement starts at the beginning of the transition in and ends at the end of the transition out.

■ **Note** Another way to get the Ken Burns Effect done quicker is to set both the start and end keyframes in the middle of the clip in the Effect Controls panel. Then, hit **Home** and click the *Add Keyframe* button followed by **End** and *Add Keyframe*. Then, delete the two middle keyframes. Set keyboard shortcuts for keyframe editing (Add/Remove and Select Previous/Next) to speed it up even more.

Don't overdo the movement unless you're aiming for a rough and jarred style. Still montages look classier when the movement is smooth and slow. Hold down **Ctrl** (Cmd) while dragging the parameters to avoid getting too much motion.

If the movement is stopped or started in the middle of the clip, change the keyframes from the default linear to smoother Bezier keyframes by selecting *Ease In* and *Ease Out* (Figure 7-104). See the section on the Effect Controls panel for details.

Figure 7-104. *You find the Ease In and Ease Out options for keyframe interpolation in the right-click menu*

Add music and sit back and watch your masterpiece.

Make Presets

If you do a lot of Ken Burns–style Pan & Scan on stills, I recommend that you make presets for the different image sizes that you use the most–maybe one for 12 megapixels, one for 18 megapixels, and one for 6 megapixels, including both Portrait and Landscape modes for all of them. If you add a few pixels of Gaussian blur to the presets, but leave it turned off, you can very quickly add blur when needed (Figure 7-105).

Figure 7-105. *Give your effect presets good names and add a description so you remember what it does, even after several months*

A handful of such presets will take a lot of work out of your Ken Burns sequences.

Create a Smooth Pan on an Image

Here, we'll move an image sideways, creating a pan-like movement. Of course, we want this to be as smooth as any other movement. We need it to move a whole number of pixels per frame; see the section on rolling end credits for an explanation.

Let's do the math: my image is 11,000 × 2000 px, so I placed it in the timeline, scaled it to fit to the height of the sequence, and moved it all the way to the right, with the left edge just outside the frame, and set a keyframe. Horizontal Position: **2970 px**. Then, I moved it all the way to the left, with the right edge just outside the frame. Horizontal Position: **-1030 px**. Total movement: **4000 px**.

If I want it to move at a speed of 8 px per frame, I will move the last keyframe to frame 500, since 4000/8 = 500 (Figures 7-106 and 7-107).

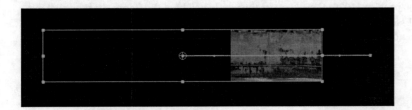

Figure 7-106. *We can create a smooth pan along this large image using the same principles as with the smooth rolling title. The number of pixels it moves per frame needs to be an integer.*

Figure 7-107. *Calculate at which frame you can put the last keyframe and then drag it there*

You can also move a nested sequence the same way, and that way you can add logos, images, and text to the concrete wall with blending modes and so forth. Just be aware that the max width for a sequence is 16K.

Split Screens and PiPs

When you need more than one video frame, you need a nice-looking way to present them. Picture in picture (PiP) and split screens are the most common ways to do this.

The difference between split screens and picture in picture effects can be small, but as a general rule, when we're talking about split screens, the video clips cover the whole screen with no background–just a border between the clips.

Vertical Split Collage

I'll explain the basic technique step by step by explaining how to create a simple four-up split screen. Of course, this could be achieved by cropping or masking each clip and positioning them carefully in the timeline. That would work, but it means that we would need to tweak every clip, and that we would need to do it every time we want to use this kind of effect.

A much smarter approach is to make a template project that can be reused every time you need a split-screen effect with this layout. So, let's do it the proper way, with the track matte key.

Making the Mattes

We need a rectangle that's 480 px wide (1920/4) and covers the whole height of the frame. Start by clicking the *New Layer* button in the Essential Graphics panel or hit the keyboard shortcut for new rectangle. This creates a new rectangle that's not centered and whose size you don't know (Figure 7-108).

Figure 7-108. *Two ways to create a new rectangle. Notice that a keyboard shortcut is also available.*

■ **Note**   For some reason, there's no way to type in an exact size in pixels for rectangles. But default rectangle and ellipse size is 300 × 200 px, so to make one fill the whole width of a 1920 × 1080 sequence, scale 640 percent. To fill the whole height, scale 540 percent.

In our case, we need a rectangle that's 480 px wide, so let's scale it 160 percent horizontally and 540 percent vertically and place it at position 0,0, 0,0 (Figure 7-109). Place this on video track 5.

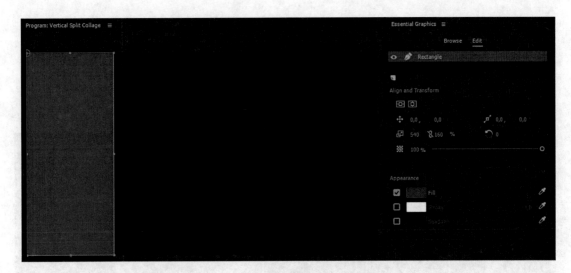

Figure 7-109. *Rectangle graphics are used as mattes for the video clips*

Then, make three copies of this title by **Alt-dragging** copies to the tracks above the original, placing the rectangles at 480, 960, and 1440 px horizontally. These will be used as mattes for the four video clips.

Placing Clips in Nested Sequences

Make four sequences named "Nested Frame" and number them 1 to 4. Put a video clip on the lower track and a rectangle clip above it in each sequence. Lower the opacity of the mattes to about 15-20 percent. Figure 7-110 shows my timeline for my Nested Frame 4. See how easy it is to place the clip in the correct position when the semi-transparent matte is there? When the clip is in place, make sure to turn off the track with the matte on it.

Figure 7-110. *The mattes are also used as guides for placing and framing the video clips correctly. This clip was moved to the right to place the woman inside the matte.*

Stack It All

Now, place the four Nested Frame sequences in the main timeline on tracks 1 to 4, keeping the mattes above them. Use the track matte key on the nested sequences and set it to take the corresponding matte for each sequence. On top of it all, make a new graphic with three narrow black rectangles that cover the seams. Mine were 9 px wide (horizontal scale set to 3 percent), and I've made them white in Figure 7-111 for clarity.

Figure 7-111. *Vertical split with white borders*

I've made the vertical lines white here for clarity. See Figure 7-112 for the final result with black lines.

Figure 7-112. *The complete layer stack, plus a graphic with borders*

If the matte tracks in the nested sequences were not turned off, you'd see it clearly by now. The most common color on the borders between the clips is black, but if you feel that pink looks better, there's no rule against that. Just open the graphic clip and change the color of the narrow rectangles.

Add Animation (Optional)

Of course, the four video clips can be animated in many different ways. Do this in the nested sequences. The opacity can be animated from 0 to 100 sequentially on the four clips so they fade in one by one. They can be animated in vertically–maybe two from the top and two from the bottom. This can happen simultaneously or sequentially. They can get effects or color overlays on them. Two, three, or all four parts can be the same video clip, fading in at different times before the borders fade away to show a complete video frame, like a puzzle. You can build endless variations.

Sample Many-Ups

Now that you've seen the steps, you can easily create any other split-screen layouts you need. Figures 7-113 to 7-118 show a few examples.

Figure 7-113. *Split screen three-up*

Figure 7-114. *Split screen five-up*

Figure 7-115. *Split screen with dotted borders and feathered masks*

Figure 7-116. *Split screen news style*

Figure 7-117. *Split screen slanted*

Figure 7-118. *Basic 3D effect applied to a nested split screen/PiP sequence that is larger than the HD frame*

Captions and Subtitles

Captions can be used in two ways: you can add them to the video file so it's burnt-in (open captions), or you can use a side-car file that the video player can sync to the video file and use to display the text "live" at playback time, like YouTube does (closed captions). When someone mentions subtitles, they most likely mean open captions, at least in Europe.

Captions Standards

CEA-608 (Line 21 captions) is known as the "old" US standard for closed captioning, compatible with analog TV. CEA-708 is the new standard for digital TV. These days, 708 captions are the preferred option and are considered standard by the FCC. Read more here: 3playmedia.com/2015/08/11/whats-the-difference-between-cea-608-line-21-captions-cea-708-captions/.

608 captions always have black-box backgrounds with all-uppercase white text. 708 captions offer more control, allowing the viewer to select from eight font options, three text sizes, sixty-four text colors, and sixty-four background colors, and free positioning. 708 is still quite restricted, compared to open captions.

Teletext is quickly dying, and several broadcasters in many countries have already dropped support for Teletext.

■ **Note**   Unless you're specifically asked to create 608 captions, go for 708.

Adobe has an in-depth overview of closed captioning formats here: adobe.com/content/dam/Adobe/en/devnet/video/pdfs/introduction_to_closed_captions.pdf.

Create Captions Manually

You create a new captions item via **File ➤ New Caption**, or click the New Item icon in a bin and choose *Captions*. Rather unintuitively, there's no way to create captions from the Captions panel or with a keyboard shortcut.

When you create a new captions clip, you must choose the right format (Figure 7-119). It can be changed later, but if you choose the wrong format, you may need to adjust the settings after switching to the right format. The choices you have for text and background formatting will be restricted by the format (Figures 7-120 and 7-121).

Figure 7-119. *Choose captions format*

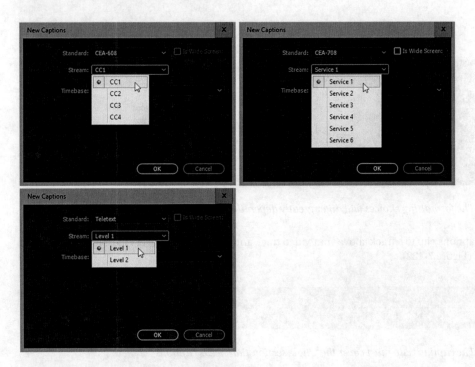

Figure 7-120. *Depending on what captions standard you choose, you get different options*

Figure 7-121. *The formatting choices will differ greatly depending on the standard*

Drag the captions clip to a track above your video track and extend it so it covers the whole section that needs captions (Figure 7-122).

Figure 7-122. *The captions clip must cover the whole section that needs captions*

View Captions in Your Monitors

You need to see your captions in your source and program monitors. You can use the wrench menu and choose **Captions Display ➤ Enable**, or add a button. If you don't normally show the button row, you can assign keyboard shortcuts for this; you can use the same shortcut for both monitors.

Remember to set the Captions Display Settings (Figure 7-123) to show the same type of captions you're creating, or you will not see them.

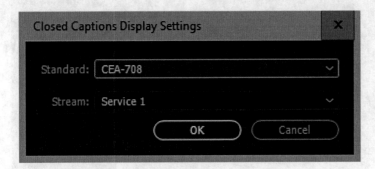

Figure 7-123. Captions Display Settings dialog

Since you can also toggle the video track with captions on and off, we seldom switch the captions display on and off in the monitors. I usually leave it on and toggle the track on and off in the timeline. The settings in the monitors are only for closed captions. Open captions will always show.

Zoom in on the timeline so you can see the captions clips clearly. Also, expand your captions track so you can see the caption blocks and adjust the in and out points, move them, and so on. Use the Captions panel to type text and tweak the format (Figure 7-124). Hit the *Plus* button to add new caption blocks.

■ **Note** When all the captions are in place, I recommend that you group the video clips and the captions clip; select all the video clips and the captions clip and hit Ctrl+G (Cmd+G).

Figure 7-124. *The Captions panel in action*

The Captions panel works great when you import ready-made captions, but I find it rather clumsy to work with when I write new captions. So, if I only need to write open captions (subtitles), I will most likely use a custom motion graphics template from After Effects and type within the Essential Graphics panel instead.

■ **Note**   To modify the formatting for all captions in one go, right-click the preview image for one of the captions and choose *Select All* (Figure 7-125). **Ctrl+A** (Cmd+A) does not work, so you will have to right-click.

Figure 7-125. *You can change the formatting for all captions blocks at once*

Figure 7-126 shows the limited formatting choices for closed captions.

Figure 7-126. *Closed captions have limited formatting choices*

Importing Captions

To detect and automatically import embedded caption data in a media file, tick the checkbox for **Preferences ➤ Media ➤ Include captions on import**. Premiere supports embedded captions in MOV, MXF Op1a, and DNxHD MXF Op1a.

Figure 7-127. *Captions import preference*

■ **Note**   Premiere optimizes performance by scanning the media for caption data only the first time you open that file. Premiere does not rescan for caption data later.

Sidecar caption files must be imported separately. Premiere Pro supports importing closed captioning files in .mcc, .scc, .xml, or .stl formats. When you get a captions sidecar file form a captioning service bureau, just import it to Premiere. The media browser doesn't show a preview, so **File ➤ Import** works just as well.

If the captions look strange, right-click it in the bin and choose **Modify ➤ Captions**. Then, change the text formatting in the Caption section (Figure 7-128). Figure 7-129 shows imported captions before and after fixing the Video Settings in the Captions section of the Modify Clip dialog.

Figure 7-128. *Change settings after the captions have been imported*

Figure 7-129. *Imported captions may look very wrong. Fix the frame size and frame rate via Modify ➤ Captions, and then do the text formatting in the Captions panel.*

■ **Note**   If you ever get a captions file type that's not supported by Premiere, use the free online subtitle converter to convert it: gotranscript.com/subtitle-converter.

Exporting Captions

You can burn in both closed captions and open captions when you export your video. In the Export Settings dialog box, select *Burn Captions Into Video* (Figure 7-130).

Figure 7-130. *Captions burn-in*

■ **Note**   When you import SRT files and XML files with open-caption data in them, Premiere Pro converts these files to CEA-708 CC1 closed captions. You can then edit these files and burn in the captions as subtitles while exporting using Premiere Pro or Adobe Media Encoder.

You can of course also export video with embedded captions. Premiere supports embedded captions in MOV, MXF Op1a, and DNxHD MXF Op1a. In the Captions tab in the Export Settings, select the Export Option *Embed In Output File* (Figure 7-131). You can also choose to create a sidecar file.

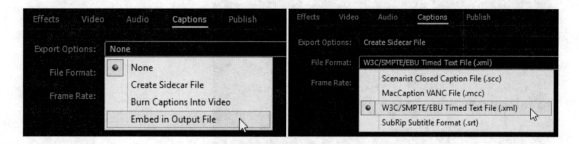

Figure 7-131. *Captions Export Options*

To export a captions sidecar file only–no video–select the captions clip in the bin and click
File ➤ Export ➤ Captions. Choose the format and frame rate (Figure 7-132).

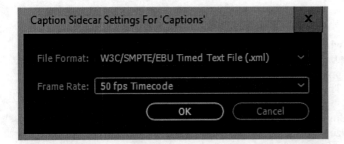

Figure 7-132. *Captions export sidecar*

Captions Limitations

There are some limitations in the Captions feature. There's no option for adjusting leading (the gap between lines), and there's no way to make a fixed-width box. Some people don't like it constantly changing to match the size of the text. Graphics have fewer limitations, so they can be a good alternative for captions when you create open captions (subtitles).

Create Subtitles with Graphics

If you need to add subtitles to a long movie or on a regular basis, you should definitely buy a plug-in. But if you just occasionally need to add subtitles to a short movie and feel that the captions are too limited, you can use the built-in Graphics tools, which can create high-quality subtitles. Figure 7-133 shows built-in captions, and Figure 7-134 shows subtitles made with the Essential Graphics panel.

Maps and drawings are stored in building 124 at the north gate

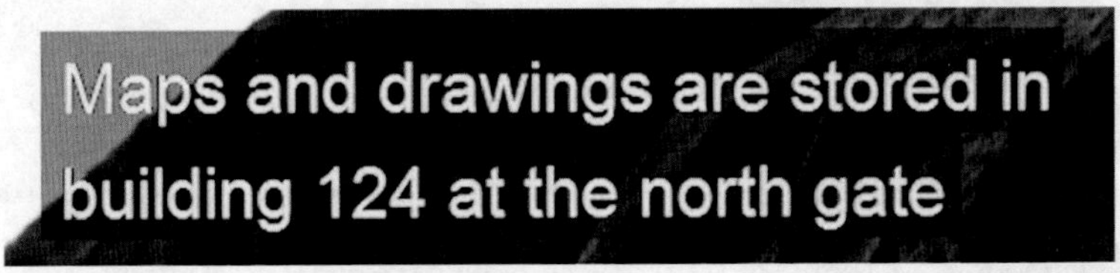

Figure 7-133. *Captions can sometimes get jagged edges*

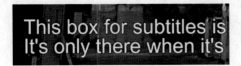

Figure 7-134. *Text made in the Essential Graphics panel has more options for formatting*

Smart Background Boxes

The box behind the text is only necessary when the white text cannot be read against the background video because of too little contrast. So, when the background video is light, we need the box, and if the background video is dark, we don't need it. This is not possible with captions, but we can achieve it by using the Darker Color blending mode on a gray rectangle. The blending mode can be saved with a template, so everything is just drag-n-drop when we use it.

Figure 7-135 shows my Background Box settings. Note that the scale and position parameters are all at even numbers. That makes the edges razor sharp. The best part is the Darker Color blending mode. The opacity can be adjusted to best fit the current image.

Figure 7-135. *Here's my BG box settings. It's gray (68,68,68) with opacity at 60 percent and Darker Color blending mode.*

Make a Text Template

We want all the text to look the same and be at the same size, position, and so forth, so we make a template that we can paste our text into. The most common text color is white, and to increase readability on difficult backgrounds we use a gray outer stroke. Figure 7-136 shows the text settings I used for my subtitles.

Figure 7-136. Subtitle text settings

Combine Them in the Timeline

Now, add the box on one track and the text on the track above it. Type your text and **Alt-drag** copies as needed (Figure 7-137). I like the fact that the boxes I make in Premiere often look better than the ones created by professional subtitling software because I can use the Darker Color, or any other, blending mode (Figures 7-138 and 7-139).

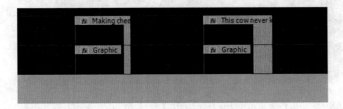

Figure 7-137. Subtitles and background boxes in a timeline

This cow never knew she would be in a book on Premiere Pro! I bet she loves being a model - and hopefully she likes the color grading too.

Figure 7-138. By using Darker Color blending mode, the box is only visible when the image is too light

When the box is not needed, it's not visible! The opacity in the timeline can also be adjusted to taste.

Making cheese the traditional way, with no electricity.

Figure 7-139. Of course, when the text is shorter, you can adjust the box to fit. The right portion of this box is invisible because the image is darker than the box.

More Flexible Subtitles with After Effects

Since working with captions in Premiere is a bit cumbersome and limited, I prefer to use motion graphics templates from After Effects to create my open captions (Figure 7-140). Such templates can be as simple or as advanced as you need. You can also use one of the motion graphics templates for captions and subtitles that comes with Premiere (Figure 7-141).

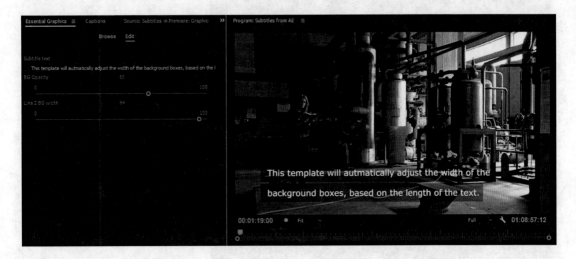

Figure 7-140. *Subtitles from After Effects*

Figure 7-141. Subtitles MOGRTS

Creating Subtitles with Third-party Software

There are many apps to choose from when you want to create subtitles for a film. These apps can output the subtitles in different formats, like an Encore subtitle file, a subtitle file for YouTube, or a .SRT (SubRip) file. Export a video file from the timeline in Premiere and import it into the subtitle software. Type your subtitles and then export a subtitles file. You hit a shortcut every time you want to insert timecode, and there are usually shortcuts for jumping a few seconds backward, spell checking, and so on.

Belle Nuit

Belle Nuit is a subtitling software that went from being cross platform to being MacOS only, and then to being free and open source: belle-nuit.com/Belle_Nuit_Subtitler.

AHD Subtitles Maker Professional

This is open source software. Even though it's free, it's got most of the features you need for subtitling. It can spell check using the dictionaries from OpenOffice.com, and reads and exports to all the common formats: sourceforge.net/projects/ahdsubtitles/.

If you choose the *XML with PNG* option, keeping the imported XML sequence and the PNG files in a separate bin is a good idea, and nesting all the subtitles into a separate sequence will make it easy to place all of them where you want them in one go. They will be centered by default, so you need to move them down. Nesting makes this easier.

Subtitle Edit

Subtitle Edit is a free open source editor for video subtitles and is my favorite. It can use VLC Player for playback, and the spell checker can use the dictionaries from Microsoft Word.

It performs better than any of the other ones on my system. I usually export a .SRT file from Subtitle Edit. It can read, write, and convert between more than 200 subtitle formats and has features like exporting an XML file with PNG images so you can import it into your project and get all the subtitles in place with the correct timing: nikse.dk/subtitleedit/.

SubtitleEdit Online

If you prefer to work online, the most flexible and streamlined option is the free online version of Subtitle Edit at nikse.dk/SubtitleEdit/Online. It's impressively feature rich for being free.

Free Speech Transcripts Using YouTube Subtitle Auto-Sync

Do you have a video speech transcript without timecode? Let YouTube's Subtitle Auto-Sync do the hard work! Then, just download a synced SRT and import it back to Premiere. See YouTube Help for details: support.google.com/youtube/answer/2734796?hl=en.

You can even let YouTube create the transcript automatically. See the same link, or this video tutorial from YouTube: youtube.com/watch?v=CfuchTRTLGU.

Creating SRT Files with Notepad

You can Create SRT files in Notepad or Text Edit if you like. Here's a simple guide: en.wikibooks.org/wiki/Video_Production/Editing_a_subtitle_file_with_a_text_editor.

EZTitles

EZTitles is a software tool for subtitle preparation. It's pricey. EZTitles can use the spell checker from OpenOffice or Microsoft Office, and it has a scene-change detector, WYSIWYG, and a pile of other clever features.

You can buy EZTitles from eztitles.com/.

InqScribe

InqScribe is cross-platform professional software for subtitling found at inqscribe.com/.

It uses QuickTime player or Windows Media Player as its playback engine. InqScribe is cheaper than EZTitles.

Annotation Edit

For Mac people, there's the Annotation Edit software from Zeitanker—also a little pricey: zeitanker.com/content/tools/zeitanker_tools/zeitanker_annotation_edit/

What to Do with the Exported Subtitles File

Some of these software options will only output a captions file. If you put your subtitles directly on YouTube or on a DVD via Encore, this is all you need. But if you want burnt-in subtitles, you'll need to get these files into Premiere.

You can import some captions files and format them in the Captions panel, but it's sometimes very time consuming and can show aliased edges. EZTitles plug-in to the rescue!

EZTitles Plug-in

The EZTitles *plug-in* (not to be confused with the EZTitles program itself) is a Windows-only plug-in for Premiere, and it enables a lot of options when you import subtitles into Premiere.

Import the subtitles file into Premiere, and the Settings dialog from the EZTitles plug-in pops up, allowing you to make some choices regarding video format, fonts, effects, and so on (Figure 7-142). The subtitles appear as a video clip that can be edited just like any other clip and placed on a track above all the video layers.

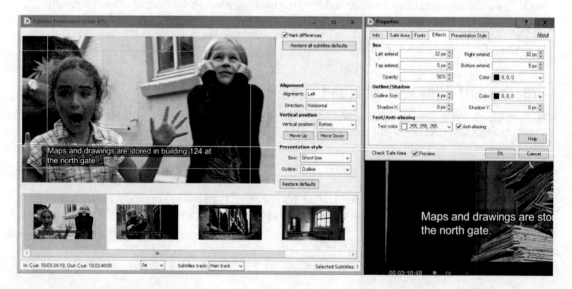

Figure 7-142. Subtitles in the EZTitles plug-in

The EZTitles plug-in is very easy to use and very fast. It is a bit pricey for what it's doing, but if you use subtitles regularly, it's worth the price. You can download the EZTitles plug-in from eztitles.com/.

End Credits

Most films and TV shows have end credits, so you'd think that it's a pretty standard operation to just throw on a credit roll. There are huge amounts of flickering, stuttering, and strobing credit rolls out there to prove you wrong! On TV and film, the rolling credits look much better than on amateur films on the net. Why? Apart from the good ones' being made by professional designers, there are a few other reasons. Welcome to the bizarre world of credit rolls!

Rolling credits will probably become its own option in the Essential Graphics panel in Premiere. Until then, you can build your rolling credits using text, shapes, and clip layers in one single graphic object, and then animate position for that graphic. The whole graphic object will animate as one piece.

Remedy for Jittery and Stuttering Rolling Text or Pans

Let's look at the two simple rules for getting smooth image pans and text movement. When both these are honored, your text or image will move smoothly (provided you're not dropping frames, and you need to render to avoid this).

1. The text or image needs to move a whole number (integer) of pixels per frame.

2. You need to watch your output on a screen that can actually show the frame rate you're using.

If one of these requirements is not met, the text or image movement will stutter. As a matter of fact, *all movement in your project will stutter*, but you only notice it when you have constant movement, like a text crawl/roll, a very smooth-panning camera, or a very smooth-moving object.

Moving clips in integers can be accomplished by animating position (under Motion) in the Effect Controls panel instead of using the built-in text roll and scroll options.

If you're lucky, the screen refresh rate can be set in your GPU driver, but if you're on a laptop, you're probably out of luck. Those are often hard wired to a 60Hz refresh rate. I have an HP Zbook with a DreamColor screen, and it supports several different refresh rates. So, adjustable refresh rates *are* available for laptops, but it's not at all the norm.

Even if your computer monitor doesn't support the frame rate you're working in, you can watch the output correctly on a TV via HDMI. Most HDTV sets are capable of 48Hz, 50Hz, 60Hz, 59.94Hz, 100Hz, and so on. As long as the screen refreshes at a rate that's a whole number (integer) times the frame rate, you'll be fine.

Turn on your *Dropped Frames Indicator* in the program monitor to see if you're actually dropping frames due to a slow system. It's not very likely on a simple crawl, though. But, if you're dropping frames, you'll need to render the timeline before you can do a good quality control.

OK, let's create a sample project so we can dive into the details.

Creating Smooth Rolling Titles

First, we need to make sure your monitor refreshing rate is the same as your frame rate–or an integer of this. Refresh rates and resolutions are connected, since most monitors can do higher refresh rates at lower resolutions.

Computer Screen Setup

If you're on Windows, read this guide on how to adjust the refresh rate: `lifewire.com/how-to-change-monitor-refresh-rate-setting-in-windows-2626207`.

If you're on MacOS, read this: `tekrevue.com/tip/custom-resolution-mac-osx/`.

If the refresh rate you want wasn't available, you may still be able to choose it in the GPU driver settings. If you cannot change the refresh rate here either, you're out of luck. Although it is possible to make custom refresh rates, I've experienced some problems after doing this.

Be aware though–the refresh rates you can set in the driver, but not in Windows' own screen settings, may not work properly. I've also found Premiere to sometimes show jittery movement on the second monitor set to 50Hz when the main monitor is set to 60Hz, so my system seems to like the screens to have the same refresh rate. I've also found HDMI connection to be more reliable than DVI when it comes to refresh rates.

Your HDMI connection and HDTV will almost certainly be able to show the standard HD resolutions and frame rates.

Settings in Premiere

Choose *Enable Transmit* in the wrench menu in the program monitor to watch your output on the second monitor if you have one. If not, make sure you always watch your playback in full screen on your monitor when you evaluate the smoothness of the playback.

Next, we need to set up a sequence with the right frame rate (the one your final delivery will be in) and bring in the graphics. My sequence is set to 1080p at 50fps.

Now for a Smooth Credit Roll—the Easy Way!

We want a credit roll to come from off screen beneath the frame and continue until it's off screen at the top–a very common way to show a credit roll. Do not create a rolling credit title! You'll have no way to control its speed at the granular level we need. Instead, use the Type tool and the Essential Graphics panel. We'll control the "rolling speed" with keyframes for position.

Enter lots of names and details in your graphic, or just copy some random names from `random-name-generator.info` to get some dummy text. Format the text as usual, and then go to the Effect Controls panel and drag the vertical position for the text layer (not for the whole clip) until the text is just below the frame. Click the stopwatch for Source Text Position to enable animation.

Then, move close to the end of the clip and drag the vertical position until the text is just above the frame. Make sure both the start and end positions are round numbers. Mine are now 1130 for start and -1310 for the end (Figure 7-143). Total movement: 2440 pixels.

Figure 7-143. *Credits position keyframes*

Now, we need to know how far apart those keyframes need to be to get a smooth roll. That's much, much easier when we show frames in the timeline instead of timecode. So **Ctrl-click** (Cmd-click) or right-click the timecode in the timeline to change it to frames.

Now, the math is easy. My first keyframe is at frame 0, so if I move the second keyframe to frame 2440, the title will move 2440 px in 2440 frames, a speed of 1 px per frame.

That's very slow, so I choose to move the second keyframe to frame 610. Now it moves 2440 px in 610 frames, a speed of 4 px per frame.

■ **Note**   To check that it really moves a whole number of pixels per frame, scrub through the timeline while watching the position parameter change. The decimal number should always be 0. See Figure 7-144.

Figure 7-144. *The vertical position number should be an integer on every frame*

See how you can choose any frame number that results in a whole number when you divide the position distance in pixels by the time distance measured in frames? In my template for smooth rolling credits, I've added markers at "legal" frames so I can easily move the keyframes there.

■ **Note**   Show frames instead of timecode (Figure 7-145) when calculating smooth rolling titles. It makes the math super easy.

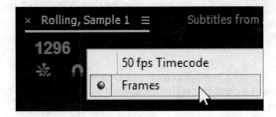

Figure 7-145. *Show frames instead of timecode to make the math easy*

I highly recommend that you set up your rolling credits in a separate sequence like this and then copy it to your edit timeline.

■ **Note** If the total number of pixels of vertical movement can't easily be divided by any number, move the start position until it's better. Say it's 1948 px. Not a very good number, because it cannot be divided by other numbers than 2 and 4. 1880 px is much better, as it can be divided by 2, 4, 5, 8, 10, etc.

Now for a Smooth Credit Roll with a Smooth Slow-down and Stop

OK, so making a rolling credit text stop at the end of its move isn't difficult. It's just a matter of stopping it at another position (and hence at another frame). But if we want it to ease into a stop, it gets more complicated.

Use the same technique we just used, but instead of moving the whole text above the frame, set the vertical position at the end so that the last text line is showing (Figure 7-146).

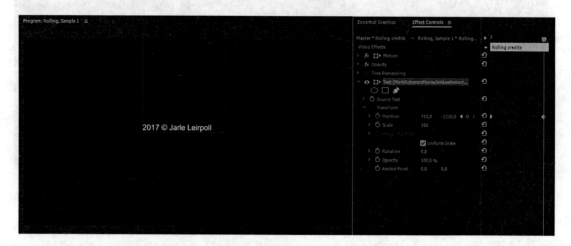

Figure 7-146. Rolling credit stop position

Now, we need to split this clip in two where we want it to begin slowing down. Move the playhead there and cut it in two (Figure 7-147). Select the second clip and immediately set a keyframe at the start of it.

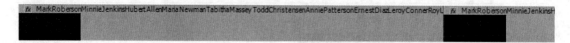

Figure 7-147. Rolling credit split in two

On the second clip, right-click the end keyframe and choose **Temporal Interpolation ➤ Ease In**. Twirl down Position and expand the Velocity graph by dragging the dividing line between the Position and Scale sections in the mini timeline in the Effect Controls panel.

You will see that the graph has a hump upward in the start. This means the speed will increase right after the cutting point. Not good. Note the velocity at the first frame of this clip (355.6/second in my case, as seen in Figure 7-148). We need to get the speed below this on the following frames so we get a deceleration.

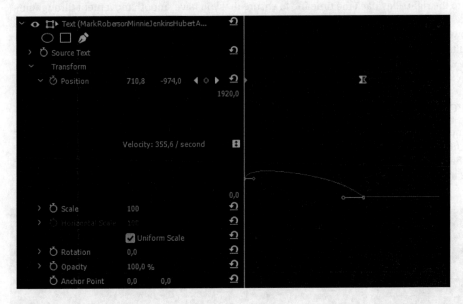

Figure 7-148. *The hump in the Velocity graph means the movement is temporarily accelerating. We need to fix this.*

Select the first keyframe in the clip and drag its Bezier handle to the right, and then up and down until the velocity reads the same number as before or slightly lower. Then, drag the last keyframe to the right until the graph never goes upward (Figure 7-149).

Figure 7-149. *Velocity graph of last clip in rolling credit*

667

Drag the handle on the left keyframe to the right and move it vertically until the velocity is the same or a little less than it used to be. Then, drag the right keyframe to the right until the upward hump goes away.

Step forward frame by frame and watch the velocity. If it ever goes above the start velocity, drag the last keyframe further to the right. Play back the timeline to ensure that you have smooth movement throughout the whole thing.

I know, I know–this sounds like a lot of trouble. Believe me: it takes just a few seconds. And the good news is that if you save this now as a template project, you will never have to do it again. Just import the sequence from the template whenever you need a rolling credit, and reuse the same title by changing its content.

Does It Have to roll?

We're so accustomed to the traditional rolling end credits that we sometimes don't even think of another option. But if you really don't need the movement, given the obstacles we have when attempting to get a smooth roll, it's often better to use static texts that you fade in and out. If you feel crazy, you can animate them in and out, but let them rest long enough to be read. Here are a couple of examples I've used (Figure 7-150).

Figure 7-150. *Use non-moving credits to avoid the whole problem. Fade them in and out, or move them quickly in and out with a blur.*

Roll Slowly

Big letters will need to move fast, or your credit roll will take forever. Using a smaller font size will immediately create more negative space, demand less eye movement to read, and allow for a much slower movement when rolling. That's all good stuff. Just make sure it's readable.

▦ **Note** To avoid judder on linear movement, the rule of thumb is that an object should take seven seconds to travel from one side of the frame to the other at 24 fps. Moving it faster will result in judder. Higher fps will allow for faster pans or crawls.

Motion Graphics for Non-standard Screens

These days, video can be almost any size. Strange solutions have been invented to overcome limitations in video playback hardware and software. Since Premiere is resolution independent, we can make almost any kind of video sizes we want.

▦ **Note** The sequence size limit is 16K by 8K, or 16,384 × 8,192 px (width × height), and we can import source material up to 256 megapixels, with a maximum of 32,768 px in either direction.

For example, an image that is 16,000 × 16,000 pixels is acceptable, as is one that is 32,000 × 8,000, but an image that is 35,000 × 10,000 pixels cannot be used.

The different playback systems have very different ways to achieve the playback. Extremely wide screens will be divided into four or more parts that we need to stack in the output video file. Confused? It gets worse.

Vertical Screen Ads

Many ad companies use standard HDTV sets rotated 90 degrees. Some will use all the available resolution, but it's not uncommon to use lower resolutions because the viewer distance can be quite long. In Figure 7-151, I've made a sequence that is 1080 × 1920 px, and editing it is no different from editing a standard HD project.

Figure 7-151. *Vertical screen ad*

When it comes to export, everything is not necessarily intuitive any more. Some ad systems want vertical video, so we can just make an export preset with the right size. But some want standard horizontal video, so we need to nest the vertical sequence into a horizontal one, and rotate it 90 degrees (Figure 7-152)– most often minus 90 degrees, but not always.

Figure 7-152. Some playback systems require the video to be rotated 90 degrees before export

Stadium Advertising LED Banners

Figure 7-153 shows a sequence for an LED advertising panel at a handball stadium. The screen is 5376 × 72 px in size! This is surprisingly low vertical resolution, but is still pretty common.

Figure 7-153. Handball stadium ad panel wide sequence

Since the sequence size is within the max limits in Premiere, we could work in the main sequence all the time, but it's not very productive. Instead, I've made a simple hierarchy of nests for editing and export. The only full-size sequence in the production chain is the one I use when making long texts that crawl along the whole screen, and other full-screen effects. The wide sequence is nested into all the four smaller sequences, positioned far left, left, right, and far right (Figure 7-154).

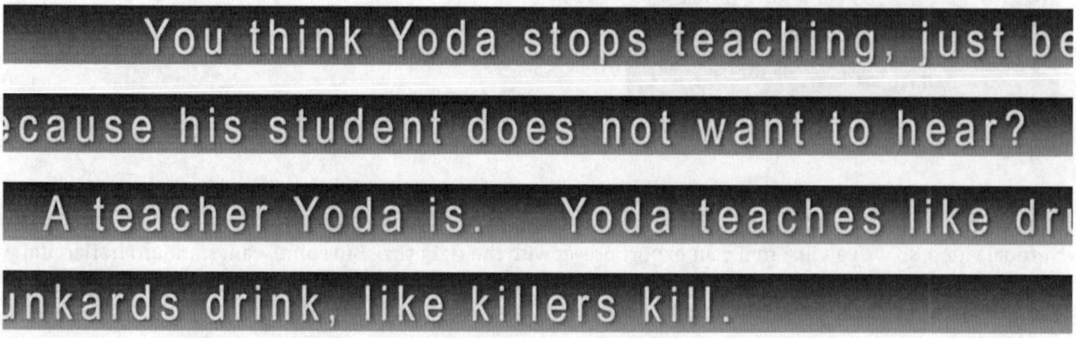

Figure 7-154. Handball stadium ad panel sub-sequences

670

Most of the time, however, the screen will be divided into four parts, sometimes showing different graphics and other times showing the same image (Figure 7-155). Almost all the editing is therefore done in the four small sequences.

Figure 7-155. Handball stadium ad panel. Sometimes all four sequences show the same info.

The exact x positions for the wide sequence in the smaller ones are 2688, 1344, 0, and -1344, and if you do this kind of editing you should definitely make presets for these positions like I have. See Figure 7-156–yes, I made this in an older version of Premiere. When editing, you'll find you're switching a lot between maximized timelines and your special lots-of-timelines layout. See Figures 7-157 and 7-158 for my custom workspace with stacked timelines.

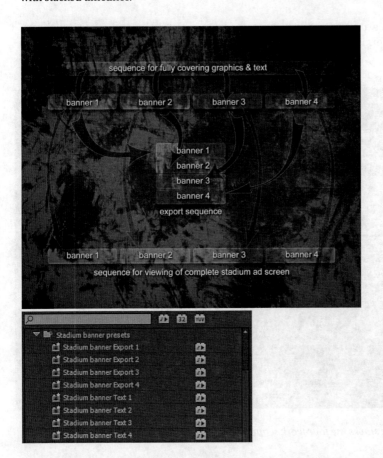

Figure 7-156. If you do this kind of work, make sure to create presets for easy workflow

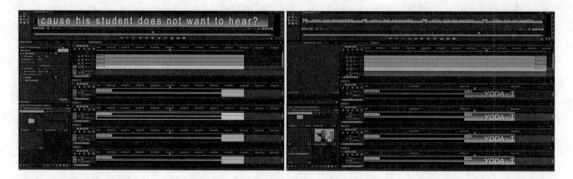

Figure 7-157. *A custom workspace makes the workflow much easier*

In the export/playout sequence, the small sequences are stacked vertically, and the y positions are: 36, 108, 180, and 252 (Figure 7-158). This is how the player software wants the ads to be delivered, so that's what we give them (Figure 7-159).

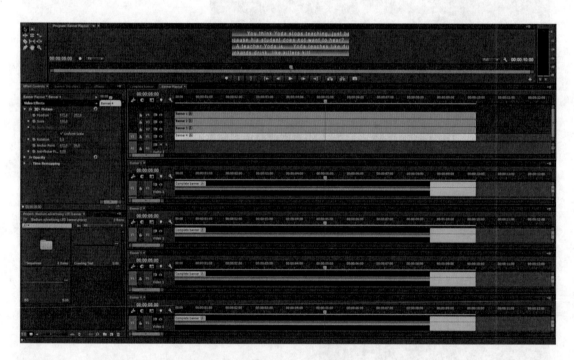

Figure 7-158. *The export sequence stacks the four work sequences*

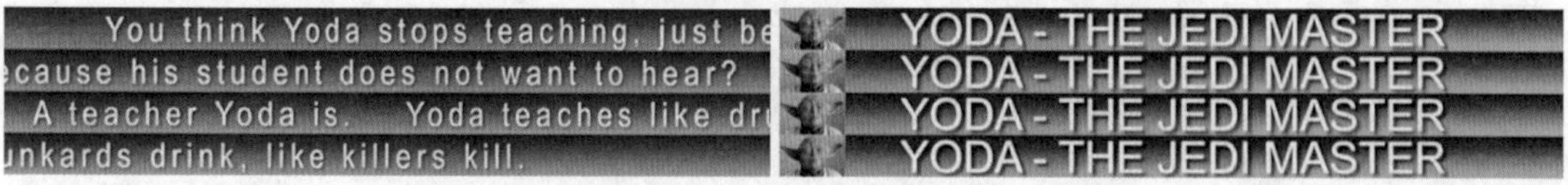

![Handball stadium export sequences showing YODA - THE JEDI MASTER banner]

Figure 7-159. *Handball stadium export sequences*

I don't really need the position presets for the export sequence, because I'll always start from a template project with all the nesting already in place.

What we *do* need is an export preset. In Premiere CC this is pretty simple: just choose H.264 and then the *Match Source - High Bit Rate* preset–and tweak the bit rate if needed. For convenience, I've made a preset named *Stadium Banner Ad 1344 × 288 px 25 fps* (Figure 7-160).

Figure 7-160. *Export to playout device*

The final video and the export sequence look very strange when you play the timeline. To make it easier to watch the finished ad, I've made a viewer sequence where the four parts are placed at x positions 672, 2016, 3360, and 4704 (Figure 7-161). This is never nested or output in any way and is strictly for viewing.

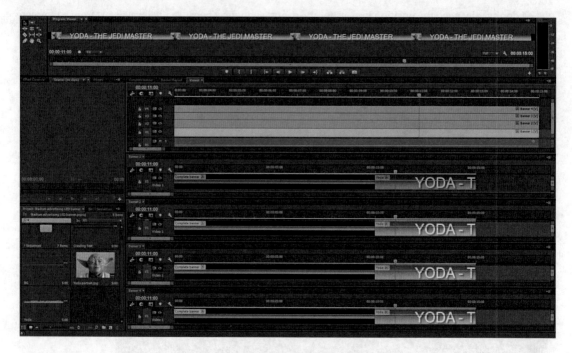

Figure 7-161. *The viewer sequence is strictly for previews; it's never exported*

Output to Video Walls and Other Non-standard Screens

There are lots of different screens and combinations of screens. I've seen clients ask for H.264 video sized 8640 × 1920 px for playback on eight HDTV panels oriented vertically and placed side by side. We can easily make a sequence like that in Premiere. You may even want it to be wider to allow for space between the panels and the width of the bezel. The problem is that H.264 maxes out at 4,096 pixels wide, so it's impossible to export that video file!

Even H.265 maxes out at 8192 px! So, if this is to be H.264, it needs to be split into at least three files. The logical thing to do would be to split it into four files at 2160 × 1920 px, but the playback system dictates the way it is split, so when you get impossible delivery specs like these, you absolutely must talk to the people in charge of technical operations for the event or (preferably) the people that supply the playback system.

■ **Note**   You have to agree on some specs that can actually be met by a codec/format, and you're the one with video knowledge, so it's your job to educate the client.

Getting hold of the people in the know can take some time, but in this case, I would continue working on the piece in my main sequence and worry about the output later. You can output whatever they want later. If deadline is tight, and your render times are getting long, you can export the finished parts of the timeline as image sequences.

That way, you can render only the remaining parts when you're about to do the final output. Then, use the complete image sequence as your master for export. Import it into Premiere, nest it in the output sequences, and export from there.

For client previews during the design process, I would use a downscaled file at 2160 × 480 so they can watch it on their computer screens.

Summary

As you've seen by now, Premiere Pro has very good tools for creating motion graphics. When you add motion graphics templates from After Effects, it's a really good combo.

I've made motion graphics packages for many companies and find it very rewarding to create user-friendly templates that let the users work fast and always get a professional and consistent look. I hope some of my enthusiasm has rubbed off on you so you can get the same joy from this kind of work.

Don't forget to take a look at Appendix C, which is a treasure trove of design resources and techniques for motion graphics design.

CHAPTER 8

Compositing in Premiere Pro

By Jarle Leirpoll

While editing is a horizontal thing in the timeline, compositing is a vertical thing. Compositing means taking two or more elements and blending them into a seamless shot, like when you put a person shot on green screen into a scene in the desert. A good composite shot will most likely be done using a mixture of several techniques.

Let's face it; Premiere is not Adobe's best compositing program–After Effects is. But if you're on a deadline, you may not have the time to learn a new program. You must use the tools you know. The GPU acceleration in Premiere makes it a fast compositing app, so let's dive into it, well aware of the limitations.

To get Premiere to fire on all cylinders when you work on compositing, you need a good GPU. The Software Only mode will slow you down. The GPU-accelerated real-time rendering in Premiere has totally changed my compositing workflow. I can sometimes do advanced compositing quicker in Premiere than in After Effects! Using masks, the track matte key, the ultra keyer, and the blending modes, you can do most of your everyday compositing in Premiere. Figure 8-1 shows some clips before and after compositing.

Figure 8-1. *Layer-upon-layer editing in Premiere Pro is often real-time*

© Jarle Leirpoll 2017
J. Leirpoll et al., *The Cool Stuff in Premiere Pro*, DOI 10.1007/978-1-4842-2890-6_8

This does not mean you don't have to know compositing. To "sell" a composite, you need to create the illusion that the foreground object really exists in the environment you've put it in. This chapter will get you started by discussing the basic principles and techniques used in compositing and how to implement them in Premiere. The tools for compositing in Premiere are surprisingly good for an Non-Linear Editor (NLE), so let's use them!

Opacity Masks

One of the easiest ways of blending layers in Premiere is to use an opacity mask. I've used the Free Draw Bezier tool to draw a mask around the man in Figure 8-2 so we can see the background clip. Because the man was moving, he also needed to be tracked. In Figure 8-3, you can see that I've placed him a bit to the right, so the lady appears to be looking at him.

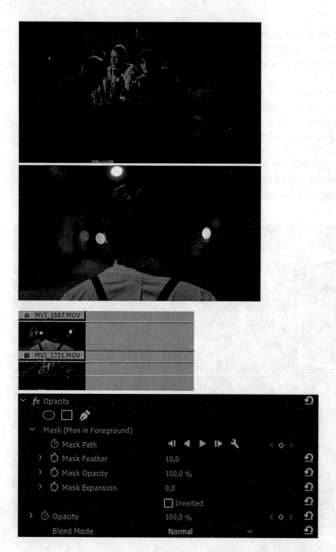

Figure 8-2. Footage from The End, courtesy of Jon Andreas Sanne

Figure 8-3. *The program monitor shows the mask while drawing it. The lower image shows the final composite.*

This super simple compositing technique can work well if the clips are similar in contrast, brightness, and color, but fails spectacularly when they're not. Fortunately, we have many more methods. For more info on creating, adjusting, and animating masks, read chapter 6 on "Color Grading."

■ **Note**   If you liked the now obsolete garbage matte effect better, you can still use it with a little hack. Use an older version of Premiere to save and export a preset with, say, the four-point garbage matte effect. Then, import this preset in your current version of Premiere.

The Wonderful and Versatile Track Matte Key

The track matte key is the Ultimate Cool Tool in Premiere. What it does is simple enough: it makes a clip transparent in certain areas, based upon the alpha channel or the luminance of another clip, so that we can see another clip through these transparent areas. This may sound basic and boring, and in Premiere's Help, it doesn't sound like much of a feature.

Here's the description from Premiere Pro Help.

The Track Matte Key reveals one clip (background clip) through another (superimposed clip), using a third file as a matte that creates transparent areas in the superimposed clip. This effect requires two clips and a matte, each placed on its own track. White areas in the matte are opaque in the superimposed clip, preventing underlying clips from showing through. Black areas in the matte are transparent, and gray areas are partially transparent.

That isn't exactly the sexiest description–and it's partly wrong to boot, as the alpha channel of the matte clip can also be used, not just the luminance signal, which isn't obvious from the description.

What Can the Track Matte Key Do?

It can do some very cool stuff! The track matte key is the effect I use the most in Premiere apart from the color-correction effects. Masks are fantastic, but they can't always give us the kind of transparency control we need. Combined with mattes from secondary color correctors, keying tools, and textures, plus some blurs and color-correction effects, we can do quite interesting things that masks cannot do.

Using the track matte key in combination with adjustment layers or copies of a clip allows for separate treatment of different parts of the image, just like we can with the ordinary masks. I'll explain this basic technique first, and then we'll move on to effects that cannot be done with masks.

In its simplest form in Figure 8-4, the track matte key is used with a title and a logo. But combined with mattes from color correctors, keying tools, and stills or video sources, it provides endless possibilities for creativity.

Figure 8-4. *The classic example for showing the principle behind the track matte key: video inside text*

It's invaluable for compositing. By using procedural masks made with keyers, qualifiers, and certain effects, we can create effects like light wrap in a green-screen key or a sky replacement that makes the weather the same as in the previous shot. We can even smooth out skin to help hide imperfections and pores.

To sum up: The track matte key in combination with other effects and the titler can provide feathered static or animated masks, and even procedural masks that update on every frame. The use of these masks or mattes is limited only by your imagination.

Oh, yes, the track matte key is by far my favorite tool inside Premiere Pro!

Motion graphics and compositing projects can get quite convoluted when we start using track mattes several layers deep with nesting and blend modes all over the place. But it's really fun to work this way–and when you've created such a stack once, you can reuse it forever by saving it as a template project.

Basic Track Matte Setup

The simplest way to build an effect with the track matte key is to have one clip on track 1, another on track 2, and the matte on track 3. This is the method I used for the preceding example. With the track matte key enabled on the clip on track 2, the alpha channel (or the luminance, depending on your needs) of the matte layer will control where the clip on track 2 is visible.

So, start by adding one source clip on video track 1 (BG) and another one on video track 2 (fill). Place the title, logo, or other matte on video track 3 (matte). See Figure 8-5. Now, add the track matte key to the clip on track 2 and set it to use the matte alpha from video 3, as shown in Figure 8-6. Now watch the magic.

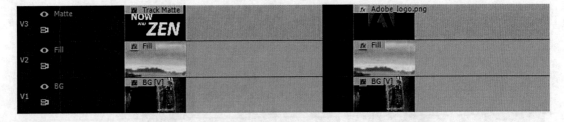

Figure 8-5. *The background clip on track 1, plus a fill clip with the track matte key effect on it on track 2, and a matte layer on top. You can use any image, video, or synthetic clip as your matte.*

Figure 8-6. *The clip on track 2 holds the track matte key effect*

Make a Preset

I use this basic track matte key setup so much that I've made an effects preset for it. In the preset, the track matte key is already set to take the matte from video 3 and to use the matte alpha. See Figure 8-7.

Figure 8-7. *Track matte preset*

Subtle Effects

The setup is very much like the basic track matte setup just explained, but instead of two different sources we'll use two instances of the same clip–plus the logo on track 3. As before, we add our effects to the clip on track 2: the track matte key with the track matte V3 preset on it and an RGB Curves adjustment this time to increase the gamma, as seen in Figure 8-8.

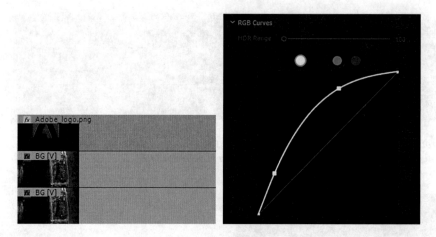

Figure 8-8. *The clip on track 2 has the track matte key and a curves adjustment*

This makes the brightest version of the clip visible only where the logo is. Nice, eh? See Figure 8-9.

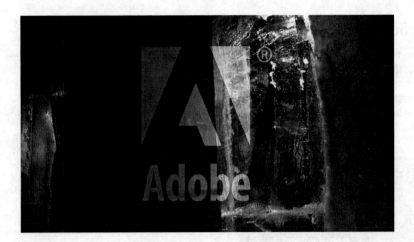

Figure 8-9. *Result of the setup we did in Figure 8-8*

In all fairness, this effect could also be achieved with only two layers. If you put the RGB Curves effect on the logo clip and place it over the background clip, you can make it an adjustment layer via the right-click menu (Figure 8-10). The result is identical.

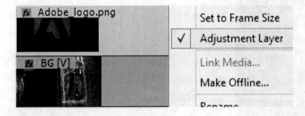

Figure 8-10. *Adjustment layer alternative*

But, if you nest the duplicate clip on track 2 as explained next, you can scale and move it independently, add more effects, animate it, and achieve completely different looks. In Figure 8-11 I've scaled it up and moved it to the left.

Figure 8-11. *By nesting the duplicate clip, you can scale and move it independently in the nested sequence*

Strange Logic When Scaling the Fill Layer

Unlike in After Effects, where you can scale the fill layer independently without affecting the matte, Premiere will scale the matte automatically when you scale the fill layer. In Figure 8-12, I've scaled down the fill layer to 40 percent, and the matte scaled with it. Sometimes this is what you want, but most likely it's not. To prevent auto-scaling of the matte layer when scaling the fill layer, nest the fill layer and scale it in the nested sequence. Use the track matte key on the nested sequence. See the result in Figure 8-13, where I've scaled the fill 200 percent in the nested sequence.

Figure 8-12. *Before (left) and after (right) scaling the fill layer to 40 percent. Matte scaled with the fill.*

Figure 8-13. *Fill layer was nested before scaling 200 percent, and the matte doesn't scale with it*

Nesting Helps When the Brain Hurts

So, when you nest a clip you can resize, rotate, and otherwise manipulate it without impacting the other effects and layers. Moving and scaling an image inside a track matte becomes easy, as do a lot of other things. Nesting is your one-stop solution for situations where the render order of effects messes with your brain.

Track Matte Key as a Custom Wipe Transition

The built-in wipes in Premiere are pretty basic, and they leave very little room for customization, so let's build our own with the track matte key.

Vary the matte shape over time (scale, rotate, move, and so on) so it starts by not covering any part of the frame and changes until it covers the complete frame, and you have a custom wipe. You can use shapes from Photoshop (Figure 8-14), logos from your customer, or shapes, titles, or graphics you create in Premiere.

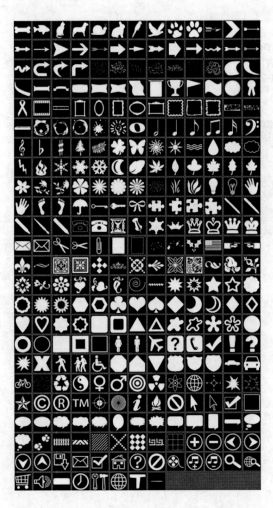

Figure 8-14. Photoshop shapes can be used as track mattes

Use the standard recipe: put the two clips on separate tracks and make sure you have an overlap of the duration you want the wipe to last. Put the matte on the track above them and throw a track matte key on the second clip (Figure 8-15). The matte layer should be the same length as the second clip, or you'll have to split that clip in two. To create the wipe transition, add motion keyframes to the matte clip where you want the wipe to start and end.

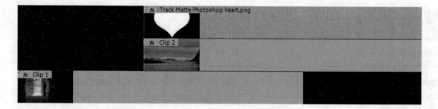

Figure 8-15. *Track setup for custom wipes using graphics*

Since the matte shape can be whatever you want, you can build all the custom wipes you'll ever want with this technique. Want to use a logo as a wipe in a corporate movie? Go ahead and use it as your track matte. Figure 8-16 shows a heart wipe made with a shape from Photoshop (Figure 8-17). I saved it as a PNG to make sure I kept the transparency and then used the PNG file as a matte.

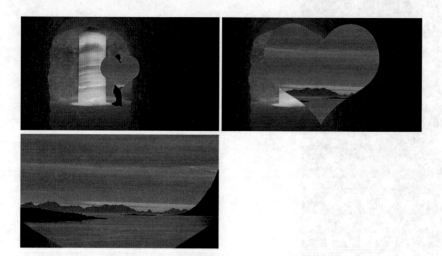

Figure 8-16. *Track matte heart wipe*

Figure 8-17. *Use Photoshop shapes or a company logo to make custom wipe patterns*

686

In this case, I set keyframes for scale for the matte layer so it scaled from zero until it covered the whole frame. You can put a Gaussian blur on the matte and adjust to taste if you want. There you have it: beautiful, customizable, feathered or non-feathered wipes in Premiere! Now, save your matte in a folder and make an effect preset from the motion parameters and the Gaussian blur on the matte layer. The next time you need a custom wipe, just overlap the clips, throw on the matte, put the preset on the matte, and you're done. It literally takes less than ten seconds.

If you want to zoom in to a shape or rotate it, make sure it's larger than the video frame so the edges don't show when rotating and the resolution keeps up with the scaling.

Cover the Wipe with an Image

Wipes can be interesting, but making an image reveal the new video layer is also a good option. To achieve this, create a shape that's black on one side and white on the other, with the line between black and white shaped so that the image will cover it completely. In this example, the wings of the plane will cover the slanted lines (Figure 8-18).

Figure 8-18. *These are the images I used to create an image wipe*

Animating the black and white shape creates a standard track matte wipe. Animating the plane image over it all creates the illusion of the plane revealing the next clip. Figure 8-20 shows the setup in the timeline. Note that the image covering the wipe starts before the first wipe keyframe and ends after the last one. This is because the plane needs to be moving before and after the actual wipe to move into and out of the frame.

As you can see in Figure 8-19, I used the Matte Luma setting in the track matte key for this one, since my matte clip didn't have an alpha channel.

Figure 8-19. *Track matte is set to use the Luma from the matte layer. Plane is animated above everything.*

The plane image covers the wipe. Figures 8-20 and 8-21 show the wipe before and after the plane was animated on top.

Figure 8-20. *Wipes without plane*

Figure 8-21. *Wipe with plane*

Use a Texture or a Video Clip as Your Matte

OK, so we've seen that the track matte key can create some cool-looking composite images combined with shapes and graphics, but they aren't exactly organic. Luckily, the mattes are not limited to shapes and text. If you set the track matte key to use Matte Luma, it will take the luminance values of the matte and make black areas transparent, white areas opaque, and everything in-between semitransparent. Or, you can invert this behavior.

Figure 8-22 shows a setup in which the texture in the matte clip controls where the clip on track 2 is visible. The matte clip is a video clip showing reflections of the early morning sunlight coming from the pool outside through the blinds and onto the wall. It's constantly moving and morphing in a very organic way that can't be visualized in a book. I upped the contrast with color correction to create opaque and transparent areas.

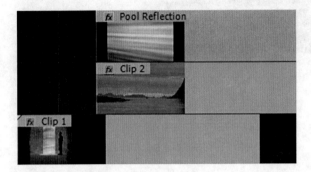

Figure 8-22. Track matte using a video clip

To make this a transition, I used the levels effect and set keyframes for the Input White and Input Black levels on the matte clip. See the sliders in Figure 8-23. It goes from a completely black frame to a fully white one (Figure 8-24), and has a very organic and fluid transition that no longer looks like a common wipe (Figure 8-25).

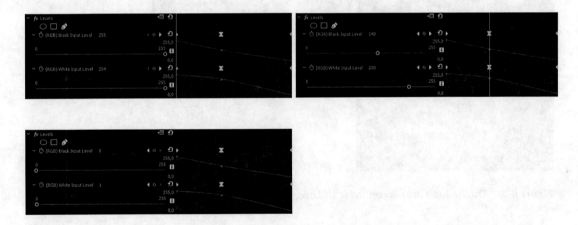

Figure 8-23. Screenshots of the keyframes on the levels effect

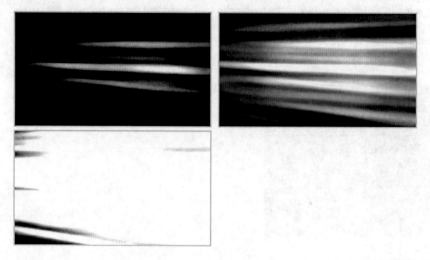

Figure 8-24. *Video clip after levels keyframes*

Figure 8-25. *Track mattes are not limited to still images and titles. Use video clips to create organic, moving mattes.*

Endless Possibilities

So, adding effects to the matte layer can change the nature of the transparency of the matte. Use a texture as your matte and animate the input and output levels in the levels effect to make the image go from black to white, and you have a unique custom track matte transition from one clip to the other. It's easier to do this in the levels effect than in the Lumetri Color panel, and it's a much more lightweight effect for the GPU.

Blurring the matte will have the same effect as feathering a mask, but you can feather it horizontally and vertically independent of each other. Adding the roughen edges effect to the matte layer will, well, roughen the edges of the matte.

If you use a video clip as a matte as we just did, you'll have a living, moving, constantly changing matte. Think of all the combinations of effects you can put on that video clip to tweak the transparency. The possibilities with the track matte key really are limitless!

If you don't want to create your own mattes and transitions, or just don't have the time, there's still hope. Several providers offer matte video packs, one of which is Rampant Design Tools, `rampantdesigntools.com`. At the time of writing, they have several free ones at `4kfree.com`. Figure 8-26 shows one that I got for free.

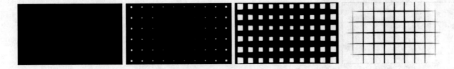

Figure 8-26. Rampant matte transitions

Relighting a Scene with Track Matte Key

You can do all sorts of color-correction adjustments in just parts of the image with the track matte key on an adjustment layer. You can use the ramp effect or just graphics to make your own gradients and shapes to create pools of light and shadow. See chapter 6 on "Color Grading" for more on this.

Shadows from Nowhere

Find a photo or, better yet, video footage of a tree (Figure 8-27) and make a high-contrast mask by adding the black and white effect and tweaking the input and output levels in the levels effect. Then, use the basic 3D effect and position to swivel and place the matte image so it seems to be lying on the ground.

Figure 8-27. Use an image or a video clip to add shadows to your footage

Add a white color matte as background and use the HSL Secondary section of the Lumetri Color panel to key out the sky and clouds and output a White/Black matte. Then, use basic 3D to position and rotate it in 3D space (Figure 8-28).

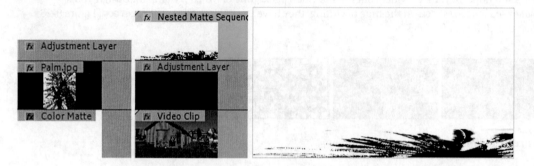

Figure 8-28. *From the left: nested sequence, main timeline, and dhadow matte from nested sequence*

This subtly creates the illusion that this scene was not shot in Norway but rather somewhere much closer to the equator (Figure 8-29). Of course, a video clip where the palms are moving in the wind would make the illusion even better.

Figure 8-29. *Track matte shadows finished*

Using Secondary Color Correction to Create Track Mattes

A good matte is a good matte however you achieve it. Sometimes it's convenient to use secondary color correction to create a matte for further compositing. The HSL Secondary section in the Lumetri Color effect can output a black and white matte.

Simple Sky Replacement

In this example, we'll use the HSL Secondary section in the Lumetri Color panel to create a matte for the blown-out sky. Then, we'll use that matte to feed a track matte key to replace the sky with an image of a darker sky. Figure 8-30 shows the original video clip and the still image that will be our new cloudy sky.

Figure 8-30. *The blown-out sky will be replaced by a more interesting still image of a cloudy sky*

Use secondary color correction in Lumetri Color on a duplicate of the clip to qualify just the sky. Then, use this clip as a track matte for the clouds image. The extreme settings in the Lumetri Color panel in Figure 8-31 gave me a good matte.

■ **Note**   Lumetri needs a lot more processing power than the obsolete effects, so using Lumetri Color for this technique can cause dropped frames on playback on many systems. Make sure you turn off all the sections you don't use in the Lumetri Color effect to save GPU resources.

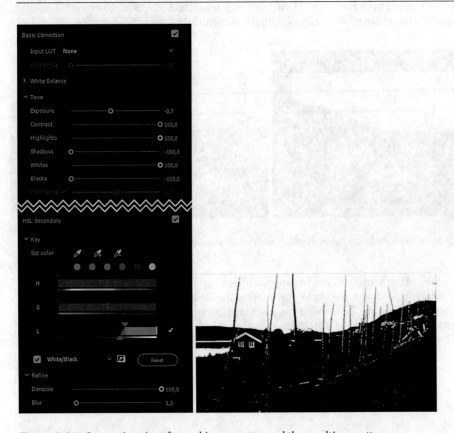

Figure 8-31. *Lumetri settings for making a matte, and the resulting matte*

The important setting here is the *White/Black* checkbox in the Key controls in Lumetri, under HSL Secondary. With the matte showing, adjust the sliders until you get a decent matte. Figure 8-32 shows the layer stack and the result.

Figure 8-32. *The setup in the timeline should look familiar. The upper layer is the matte. The final result is on the right.*

In case you detected the small white areas of the matte that are not part of the sky: yes, in the final image I've combined this matte with another hand-drawn opacity mask on the matte layer to get rid of those areas, so the sky image doesn't show in the lighter parts of the buildings, fence, and lake. See Figure 8-33. From here, I proceeded to color correct the whole composite image using an adjustment layer on top.

Figure 8-33. *I made an opacity mask on the Mmatte. Final composite is on the right.*

Once you have adjusted the matte, you can use any sky image (or video) you like. Figure 8-34 shows another version of this footage with another sky image. I nested the sky image so I could scale and move it around to get the best part of the sky. Note that if you use a replacement sky that differs a lot from the original, you can quickly run into problems with halos and tearing along edges and so on. A small change is easier than a big change. For more advanced sky replacement, use After Effects.

Figure 8-34. With another sky image, the mood of the shot changes

A Tip on Perspective

The perspective in the sky clip needs to match the perspective in the original clip. When shooting from low angles, you should feel that you're looking up at the sky. When shooting toward the horizon, the sky should look just like it normally does when you're looking straight ahead. You will sometimes need to put the basic 3D effect on your sky clip and tilt it so it looks right.

Digital Makeup

Modern filmmakers seem to be allergic to pores and imperfections in people's faces, so as an editor you need to know how to smooth skin, even though it isn't really necessary. We'll accomplish this by making a matte that isolates the skin tones, still keeping the detail around the nose, mouth, and eyes.

Creating the Matte

Start by placing the clip in a new sequence. Call it "Skin tone matte." Use the HSL Secondary section in the Lumetri Color panel on the clip on the lower track, set White/Black in the key output, and tweak the key settings until the skin tones are isolated (Figure 8-35). If needed, add a levels effect and adjust input levels for blacks and whites. Figure 8-36 shows the settings I ended up using in this shot.

Figure 8-35. *Original image and matte from HSL Secondary key (Model: Marianne Melau. Footage courtesy of Sean Fulton and Martin Fotland)*

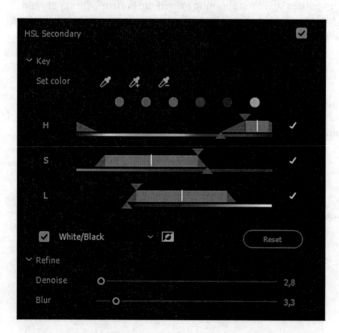

Figure 8-36. *HSL Secondary settings to isolate the skin tones*

Protecting Areas Where We Need to Keep the Sharpness

The resulting matte will not be quite good enough, because the details around the eyes, nose, and mouth will be lost. So, we'll combine it with another matte. Place a copy of the clip on track 2 and add the find edges effect. You'll get thin lines where there was contrast in the image (Figure 8-37). The find edges effect finds areas in the image with high contrast. But the black lines are too thin, so we'll make them fatter with a levels-blur-levels-blur combination.

***Figure 8-37.** Find edges effect applied*

Add the black and white effect to remove color info, then drag the input level for blacks to the right until you get broader black lines. They're still too thin, so add a 10 px Gaussian blur (with *Repeat Edge Pixels* selected), then another levels effect where you increase contrast by dragging the input levels toward the middle (Figure 8-38). Then, add another instance of Gaussian blur. Repeated instances of levels and blur fatten the black areas of the matte. The result is a matte with nice black areas where we need to retain detail in the face (Figure 8-39).

***Figure 8-38.** Levels is used to darken the black lines and increase contrast*

Figure 8-39. *The edges are blurred slightly*

This matte is not restricted to areas of skin tone, so we need to combine it with the one on the lower track. We do this by setting the blend mode of the upper track to *Multiply* (Figure 8-40). Voila! A nice matte constrained to skin tones but still protecting the areas where we need some details (Figure 8-41). Good job!

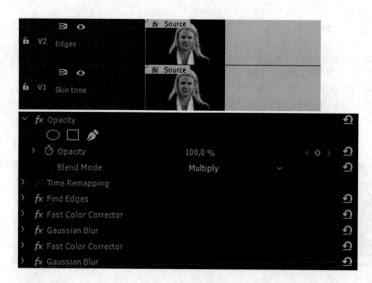

Figure 8-40. *The two mattes are combined by setting the upper clip to Multiply mode*

Figure 8-41. *The combined matte*

If you don't like the levels effect, you can use Curves in the Lumetri Color effect to increase the contrast of the matte.

Using the Matte

Now, make a new sequence named *Smooth Skin* or something similar. Add two instances of the clip to tracks 1 and 2, then place the *Skin tone matte* sequence on track 3 (Figure 8-42). We'll use the matte from that sequence to control what areas of the image will be blurred or not.

Figure 8-42. *The combined matte sequence is used as a track matte for the smoothed clip*

On the clip in track 2, add the Gaussian blur effect and–you guessed it–the track matte key effect. Set the track matte key to take its matte from track 3 and to composite using Matte Luma. Now, tweak the Gaussian blur until the skin looks good or totally unnatural, depending on your (or the director's) preferences. Three pixels of blur is a good starting point, but make sure you watch the result at full res and full size when you're making your decision. Figure 8-43 shows the effects and settings.

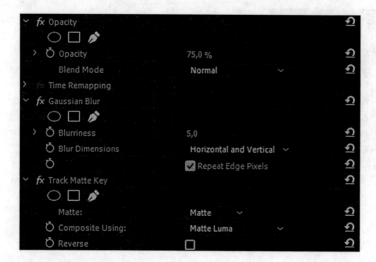

Figure 8-43. *By adjusting the amount of blur and the opacity of the smoothed clip, we can decide how aggressive we want the effect to be*

Turn down the opacity of the blurred layer to get back some of the skin texture. The close-ups in Figure 8-44 clearly show the difference before and after skin smoothing. Yes, this is a bit too much blur–for clarity. Now, you can put this finished sequence into your main timeline and continue editing.

Figure 8-44. *Before and after skin smoothening. Notice that we've kept the details in the eyes, eyelashes, hair, and so on.*

Take It Even Further

If needed, add a sharpen or unsharp mask effect to the bottom layer to exaggerate the sharpness in the areas we're not blurring. You can also use more layers where you protect other colors and combine these with the existing mattes.

Create a Template Project

As you can see, this setup takes some time to build. When you've done it once, save it as a template project and reuse it. Any time in the future when you need this effect, just import the template, swap out the source footage and get the skin tones in the ballpark, then see what needs to be adjusted, if anything at all. Read about template projects in chapter 10 on Customizing Premiere.

Blending Modes

Blending modes are the mathematician's wet dream. Through simple algebra, pixel values in layers can be blended in many different ways. The results can be everything from stunning to ridiculous.

The Five Most Useful Blending Modes

The blending modes I use the most are overlay, linear dodge (add), soft light, multiply, and screen. But what are they doing? Here are the descriptions from Premiere Pro Help.

Screen

Multiplies the complements of the channel values and then takes the complement of the result. The resulting color is never darker than either input color. Using the screen mode is similar to projecting multiple photographic slides simultaneously onto a single screen.

Multiply

For each color channel, multiplies source color channel value with underlying color channel value and divides by maximum value for 8-bpc, 16-bpc, or 32-bpc pixels, depending on the color depth of the project. The resulting color is never brighter than the original. If either input color is black, the resulting color is black. If either input color is white, the resulting color is the other input color. This blending mode simulates drawing with multiple marking pens on paper or placing multiple gels in front of a light. When blending with a color other than black or white, each layer or paint stroke with this blending mode results in a darker color.

Linear Dodge (Add)

Each resulting color channel value is the sum of the corresponding color channel values of the source color and underlying color. The resulting color is never darker than either input color.

Overlay

Multiplies or screens the input color channel values, depending on whether or not the underlying color is lighter than 50 percent gray. The result preserves highlights and shadows in the underlying layer.

Soft Light

Darkens or lightens the color channel values of the underlying layer, depending on the source color. The result is similar to shining a diffused spotlight on the underlying layer. For each color channel value, if the source color is lighter than 50 percent gray, the resulting color is lighter than the underlying color, as if dodged. If the source color is darker than 50 percent gray, the resulting color is darker than the underlying color, as if burned. A layer with pure black or white becomes markedly darker or lighter, but does not become pure black or white.

Cycle Through Blending Modes

Sometimes, it's best to just try out different blending modes until one of them just stands out as the best one for the effect you want. Clicking on the Blend Mode drop-down menu to open the list of available modes (Figure 8-45) every time you need to try a different one is too time-consuming.

Use the scroll wheel instead. Click once to reveal the list, and then click again to close it. Now you can scroll through the modes with your scroll wheel!

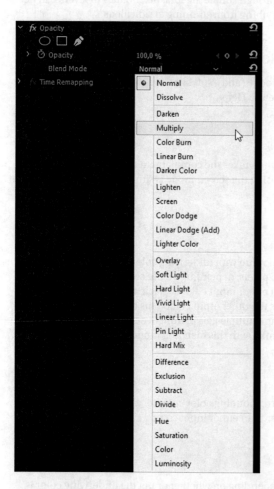

Figure 8-45. *Instead of twirling the list open, browse quickly through the blending modes with your scroll wheel*

Some Cool Uses of Blending Modes

To give you an idea of the versatility of blending modes, let's have a look at a few different uses for them. We'll continue to use blending modes throughout the rest of the chapter, too, so you'll get to know them better.

Grungy Text

In this example, I've created some blood-like writing on the wall using an image of a concrete wall (Figure 8-46), a title generated in Premiere, and a blending mode. Here are the steps I used.

1. I added a vignette on the track above the wall image using the Ellipse tool with this little trick: I set the anchor point of the ellipse to 960,540, and its position to the same. This makes it scale from the center. I added a 100 px black stroke, but no fill. Then, I duplicated the ellipse three times, so I had four copies. Each one was scaled a little bigger than the previous one. This was a workaround to make the black border reach the corners, despite the 100 px limit on the stroke (Figure 8-47).

2. The vignette needs to be feathered, and a bit subtler, so I first added a *Gaussian blur* effect with *blurriness* set to *1000 px* and *Repeat Edge Pixels* checked, then I dropped the *opacity* of the vignette layer to 75 percent (Figure 8-48).

3. Now I set the *blending mode* of the vignette to *overlay* (Figure 8-49). Much nicer than the normal mode!

4. Next, I made a graphic where I wrote the word *BLOOD* in deep red color with the *Chiller* font. This font has a handwritten feel to it, so it could pass as something written with a broad brush on a wall. I also added a few handdrawn shapes with the Pen tool (Figure 8-50). This was placed above the vignette layer.

5. I added the *roughen edges* effect to the text layer to erode the text a little (Figure 8-51). My settings were *Edge Type: Rusty, Border: 150, Complexity: 10.*

6. Next, I wanted the text to be eroded away where the concrete is light, and just be visible where the concrete is dark. To achieve this, I used the same image of a concrete wall as a track matte. I put it on a layer above the text layer and used the *track matte key* on the text layer. Then, I added the *black and white* effect to desaturate the image, and the *levels* effect with adjusted *Input Black* and *Input White* levels to maximize the contrast (Figure 8-52). I watched the image while adjusting these parameters, and ended up at 142 and 177 respectively (Figure 8-53).

7. Finally, I changed the *blending mode* of the text layer to *overlay* to let it blend in nicely with the structure of the concrete (Figure 8-54).

This could pass as a concrete wall with painted text that has been worn away by rough weather over time. Figure 8-55 shows the layer setup.

Figure 8-46. *Concrete wall*

Step 1

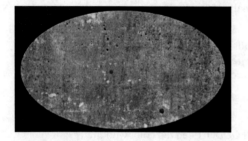

Figure 8-47. *Vignette (graphic)*

Step 2

Figure 8-48. *Vignette with blur and 75 percent Opacity*

Step 3

Figure 8-49. *Vignette set to overlay mode*

Step 4

Figure 8-50. *Type and handdrawn shapes, blending mode normal*

Step 5

Figure 8-51. *Roughen edges effect added to text and shapes*

Step 6

Figure 8-52. *Copy of wall image with black and white and levels effects*

Step 7 Matte

Figure 8-53. *Text with track matte*

Step 7 Result

Figure 8-54. *Text set to overlay mode, and we have a final composite*

Step 8

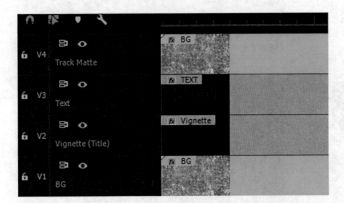

Figure 8-55. *Here's the layer setup. The red render bar is due to the roughen edges effect's not being GPU accelerated.*

Here's a little trick I used, but didn't tell you about; I put the background image in a nested sequence so I could scale it there, and that scaling would ripple through on both the background layer and the track matte layer. Scaling the matte layer itself can lead to some strange and unexpected results, so nesting the texture made everything simple and logical to adjust.

Color Gradient with Blending Mode

We can make gradients with the Rectangle tool in the legacy titler and fill it with a four-color gradient, or use the ramp effect on a black video clip or another synthetic clip. Then, we choose a blending mode to blend the color gradient nicely with the underlying clip or sequence. I've used a rectangle from the legacy titler with a four-color gradient here because it has separate opacity stops for each node. In the future, when the titler is removed from Premiere completely, Photoshop will be our best option for creating transparent gradients. Let's hope we get this feature in the Essential Graphics panel soon.

When you start playing around with different color and lightness of each of the four colors in the gradient and different blending modes and opacity settings on the clip, there are limitless possibilities.

Here, I've used the gradient with slightly different colors and opacity settings on all four corners. I've used four different blending modes just to show how different the clips blend depending on the mode. The normal mode is boring, of course, and it's there just for comparison. The gradient is opaque at the top and around 50 percent transparent at the bottom. That's why the effect is more pronounced at the top—in case you wondered.

Figure 8-56 is the original background clip. Figure 8-57 shows the gradient. Figure 8-58 shows the normal mode for comparison. Figures 8-59 to 8-62 show the different modes: overlay, screen, multiply, and color burn. Notice how different the result is with these blending modes.

Figure 8-56. *Original background clip*

Figure 8-57. *Four-color gradient*

Figure 8-58. *Color gradient normal mode*

Figure 8-59. *Overlay mode*

Figure 8-60. *Screen mode*

Figure 8-61. *Multiply mode*

Figure 8-62. *Color burn mode*

This trick can be used for more subtle effects as well. In chapter 6 on color grading, I used a color gradient with transparency to add some blue back into an overexposed sky.

Muzzle Fire

Here's another example that cannot be done without a blending mode: the oh-so-cool muzzle fire! Most people would turn to After Effects or other compositing software to create effects like this. Not me—I'd rather build it in Premiere, as it's much quicker not to leave the NLE, and most of the time everything will be real-time.

When we're trying to imitate real life, reference material is king! Figure 8-63 shows a frame from a shot (just a tiny bit of pun intended) with real muzzle fire from an MP5 weapon firing blanks. We'll try to imitate this entirely inside of Premiere. It's gonna be fun!

Figure 8-63. *Real muzzle fire from an MP5 machine gun (firing blanks)*

Let's start by drawing some muzzle-fire-like shapes. Use the Pen tool to make irregular shapes that vaguely resemble muzzle fire. The real muzzle fire seemed to have an outer glow around it and a kind of core that's lighter than the main flame. So, we'll make two shapes. One large and fat, and one slimmer (Figure 8-64). They need to be two separate graphic clips, but the color doesn't matter–we'll use a ramp anyway. Add the ramp effect and adjust it so it has a radial ramp that goes from a reddish orange to a yellowish color. Give the inner "core" shape lighter colors than the main flame shape (Figure 8-64).

Figure 8-64. *Draw two shapes with the Pen tool. Add ramp with radial gradients.*

We'll combine these in three layers with different effects on each layer. The lower layer has roughen edges and quite a lot of Gaussian blur (65 px). See Figure 8-65. The second layer is a copy of the lowermost layer, but with less Gaussian blur (15 px) and lowered opacity (80 percent). The upper layer also has roughen edges, lowered opacity (65 percent), and some Gaussian blur (15 px). Figure 8-66 shows the three layers with effects.

Figure 8-65. *Settings for the lower layer. The other layers have the same effects with different settings.*

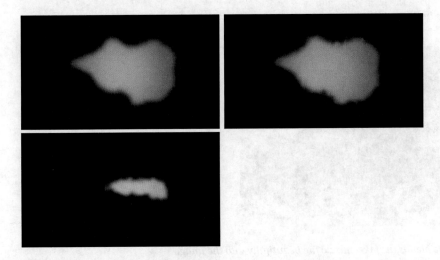

Figure 8-66. *Muzzle fire shapes*

Combining the shapes with blending modes, roughen edges, and some blur, we can make something that starts to look like the real stuff. But it still just vaguely resembles real muzzle fire (Figure 8-67).

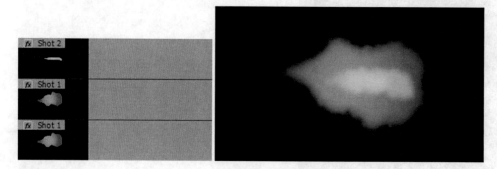

Figure 8-67. Combined shapes with blending modes

Now, let's put these on top of a shot of a person with a weapon. Yep, put the whole *Muzzle Fire Shapes* sequence on top of the shot of the person pretending to fire a weapon. For easy comparison, I used another frame from the same shot as earlier, but with no muzzle fire. Make the muzzle fire one single frame in duration (Figure 8-68). Then, do the magic: change the blending mode of that layer to *add (linear dodge)*. Figure 8-69 shows the result.

Figure 8-68. The setup in the timeline, and result with normal mode

Figure 8-69. Add mode blends the fake muzzle fire beautifully into the image

Not too shabby! And remember that this will only be showing for one single frame, so it doesn't really have to be 100 percent realistic. Besides, most people have no idea how real muzzle fire looks, and those who do often don't know how it looks when captured on film and video. So, I think we're safe.

If you're doing lots of muzzle fire in the same scene, remember to vary the shape, size, and intensity for each time the weapon fires.

Tip for Machine Gun Fire

Animate the evolution parameter in the roughen edges effect in the Muzzle Fire Shapes sequence so the shapes look a little bit different on each shot. Then, animate the opacity, position, and shapes of the muzzle fire layer in the main sequence using hold keyframes so that the opacity changes from 0 percent to 100 percent and back instantly without any interpolation, shapes vary, and the position is correct on every frame. Figure 8-70 shows the timeline, and Figure 8-71 shows the result.

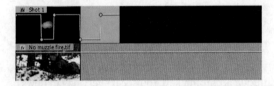

Figure 8-70. *For a machine gun effect, set opacity hold keyframes*

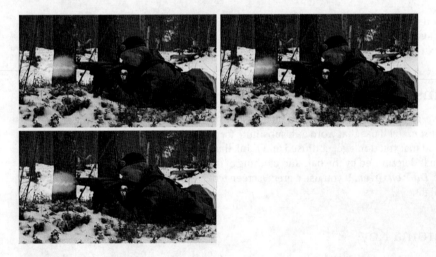

Figure 8-71. *Muzzle fire machine gun. Every shot looks a little different.*

Study real-life muzzle fire to get a more thorough understanding of how it should look. Different weapons have different-looking muzzle fire, and a weapon fired inside a room or at night will have brighter muzzle fire than a weapon fired in full daylight. Why? Because we'll use higher exposure settings (higher ISO/gain, wider aperture, no ND filter) in dark surroundings than we do in bright surroundings. The muzzle fire will still be the same intensity, so it'll appear to be brighter when we use a high exposure than when we shoot with a lower exposure.

Real Muzzle Fire Affects the Surroundings

Even though the muzzle fire itself may look good, in most cases you'd have to take things a bit further. When firing a weapon, especially in dark surroundings, the fire ball will light up objects and persons that are close. So, ideally, we should draw shapes around areas in the image that would be affected, and use those as a track matte for an adjustment layer with color correction to lighten up those areas at the frame where the muzzle fire appears.

Aiming for Realism

OK, realism isn't always the goal. Sometimes just making it look cool is enough. But if you're aiming for realism, that means you'll need to fake some interaction with the environment. Details like adding reflections in windows, shadows from persons and objects, color tints from large, colored objects, creating debris from explosions, and putting elements and spray around feet when someone's running will help fool the eye and make your compositing look real.

Keying Skills

The most known and perhaps most common keying technique is chroma key. You see it every day in news studios, movies, and so forth. Unfortunately, the keying tools in Premiere leave a lot to be desired. The ultra keyer itself is great, but we don't have any tools to refine our mattes, like matte chokers to grow or erode the matte.

So, we need to build this kind of stuff ourselves from scratch. That makes chroma key projects in Premiere a bit more convoluted than in, say, After Effects. But since Premiere can do keying in real-time, it might be worth the extra effort.

I'll Use the Terms *Green Screen* and *Person*

I don't want to write *blue/green screen* all the time, so I'll just use the term *green screen* from now on. The foreground is often a *person*, so I'll use that word as a substitute for *foreground object or person*.

I hope that's OK, and that you don't get confused and think that green is better than blue. It isn't. The color of your screen is determined by the hair and clothing of the talent in front of it. The old rule still applies: *Blonde on Blue, Dark on Green.* If you use a green screen when the person is wearing green clothes, you're not thinking straight.

Lighting for Chroma Key

A lot has been written and said about lighting a green screen, but there are actually just a few things you need to know.

- Light the screen evenly.
- Light the person so that the light on the person matches the light in the image you'll place the person into.
- Avoid green spill on the person.

Light the Screen Evenly

An evenly lit background will make your keying much, much easier, so make sure you light the screen evenly. A green screen shot with uneven lighting can of course be divided into several parts with different keyer settings, and you can use After Effects to rotoscope away almost any problem, but it takes a lot of time and effort. So, go for an evenly lit screen when possible.

Putting up two soft lights that only hit the screen–not the talent–is a good start and may look good in the studio. However, it's impossible to see with the naked eye if the screen is evenly lit or if there's shading from one corner to another (Figure 8-72). Don't guess; use the Zebra function in the camera to measure this.

Figure 8-72. Use the Zebra function in your camera to check if the background is evenly lit

Use Zebra to See If the Lighting Is Even

Point the camera at the screen and open and close the iris slowly. If the zebra pops up in one or more corners or in the middle before it fills the whole frame, it means the lighting is not even. Adjust the lights until you get zebra more or less at the same time over the whole screen when adjusting the iris (Figure 8-72).

This method makes it very easy to spot problems like hot spots, dark areas, and shading. Of course, this is for green-screen lighting control only. When it's time to shoot the scene, you must expose the person like you always do.

Light the Foreground So It Matches the Background Image

There is no way that you can make a scene look real if the light on the subject is hard and comes from below and to the left when the light in the background image is soft and comes from above and to the right. They will never match. It's been said that 90 percent of the success of keying relies on how you light the *foreground*.

Shoot Outdoors Footage Outdoors

Here's a good tip on lighting the scene as if it's shot outside on a cloudy day: *Shoot it outside!* The extremely soft light that we have on a day where the whole sky is covered with clouds is very difficult (but not impossible) to imitate in a studio, but it's very easy to do outside on a cloudy day.

Avoid Green Spill

If the person is too close to the screen, the color of the screen will be reflected from the screen and be very visible in the shadow areas on the person. To avoid this, you'll have to move the person away from the screen. That's why we need a much larger room for green-screen keying than most people think. Moving the person away from the screen will also better defocus the background so that small dents, smudges, and scratches are not visible.

You may be able to use secondary color correction to fix green spill by desaturating the greens or changing the hue, but it's often hard to do so without affecting other areas of the image.

Shooting for Chroma Key

When shooting for a chroma key, there are some settings you can do before you hit "record" that can make a huge impact on the final key. These include detail, ISO, codec, and even camera orientation.

Reduce Detail/Sharpening

Digital cameras always use sharpening of the image. A setting in the menu or in a picture profile will be named *Detail* or *Sharpening*. What this feature does is digitally "enhance" the image by exaggerating the contrast around the edges between dark and light areas (Figure 8-73).

Figure 8-73. Before and after sharpening

The image will look very soft without sharpening, but if the sharpening is set too high you'll get dark and light halos around the person, and keying will be very difficult. To get rid of these halos, you'll have to choke (shrink) the matte, and this will effectively remove all the fine details in the image, often resulting in unwanted haircuts on your talent.

The source in Figure 8-74 was shot with standard detail settings in the camera. Notice the halo around the person, and the white edge after applying the ultra keyer. We will not be able to clean this up without cutting into the edges, losing hair and other fine details.

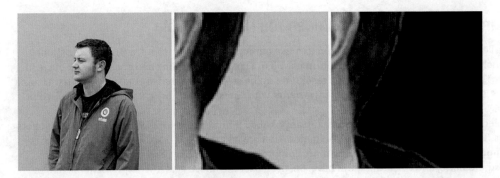

Figure 8-74. *Source shot with standard detail settings in camera*

The source in Figure 8-75 was shot with reduced detail settings in the camera. Notice there's no halo around the person, and the white edge after applying the ultra keyer is reduced to a minimum. These edges can be cleaned up without losing hair and other fine details.

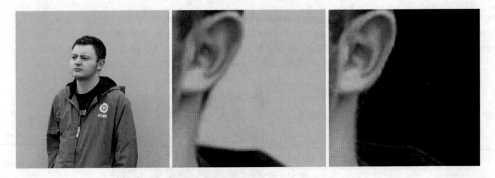

Figure 8-75. *Source shot with reduced detail settings in camera*

When we turn down sharpening/detail on the camera when shooting the green-screen scene, we must resharpen the image using the unsharp mask or sharpen effects after the key is done. But turn the sharpening/detail down too much, and you'll get a muddy image that needs a lot of sharpening post-key, and this will make compression artifacts and noise much more visible. Experiment with your camera to see what amount of sharpening results in a good compromise.

Use Low ISO/Gain

Grainy and noisy footage will result in grainy and noisy edges in your matte, and the constantly varying degrees of green in the screen will create holes in the matte unless you're keying aggressively, meaning you're clipping both low and high levels in the matte with fewer shades of gray in the edges. This is no good, so make sure you use low ISO/gain settings.

Record in the Best Format and Codec You Have Available

In chroma keying we use the color information to make our mattes. It goes without saying that we should have as much color detail as possible. Many formats will use color subsampling and encode the footage in 4:2:0 color. That means we have just ¼ of the resolution in the colors compared to what we have in the Luma signal. This is a bad idea for a chroma key! 4:2:2 is better with ½ resolution, and 4:4:4 is best with full-color resolution.

We need as many shades of gray in the matte as possible. 8-bit will give us 256 levels, while 10-bit offers 1024 levels. The more bits the merrier, so 12-bit and 14-bit are great.

The more compressed the image is, the more compression artifacts like macro blocks, quantization noise, mosquito noise, and smearing it will have. So, the closer the image is to uncompressed, the better. Some cameras have HDMI or SDI outputs with much higher quality than what's recorded on the internal memory cards. Routing this to an external recorder that can record in higher quality is a very good idea.

Ideally, we should all shoot uncompressed RAW 4:4:4 in 12-bit or higher for chroma key purposes, but unfortunately that's not always feasible for everyone.

Turn the Camera 90 Degrees for People Standing Up

Here's a poor man's method to achieve higher resolution when shooting green screen of people standing up: turn the camera 90 degrees! Yeah, you finally get to shoot video in "portrait" mode instead of "landscape" mode (Figure 8-76). This will effectively increase our resolution by making the person fill more of the frame. Of course, it will only work if the person doesn't move too much sideways and out of frame.

Figure 8-76. *Shoot standing-up people with the camera rotated 90 degrees. (Footage by Martin Fotland and Sean Fulton)*

This footage needs to be rotated and scaled down when used (Figure 8-77), and it's the scaling that increases the color resolution. The image needs to be scaled down to 56 percent to fit inside the frame when rotated, effectively raising the resolution to almost double. If you didn't understand this, just look at how much more of the frame a person fills when shooting "vertically" than when shooting "horizontally." Higher pixel count means more resolution.

Figure 8-77. *Source rotated and scaled down*

A similar increase in available color resolution can be achieved by shooting 4K material for an HD production. 4K turned 90 degrees in an HD production can provide awesome keying results!

I highly recommend you do a few test recordings with different settings to decide on the best settings to use with your camera. Turn off all the auto-stuff: no auto-exposure, no auto white balance, no autofocus.

One-click Key? No, It's Never That Easy

If you think that keying is just clicking in the image with an eyedropper, think again. For a key to be successful and look good, there are several things that need to be just right. We'll deal with them in due time. Newbies often think they'll get a great key by just throwing the keying effect on their green-screen clip. This never happens. Never, ever! You will always have to tweak the settings, and you'll often have to use the keying effect more than one time, at least if you're aiming for a great result.

Use More Than One Keyer

The core of the person, the edges, and the area outside the person all need to be treated differently. If you try to get an unevenly lit screen area completely transparent and at the same time get the person to be fully opaque, the edges will have very little detail. Hair, fluffy clothing, motion blur, and other problematic areas will look bad because the matte is too sharp and too smooth.

Choking a matte will very often result in a "digital haircut" that we absolutely don't want. You need to change your keying strategy so you can get the hair back. This means at least doing separate keys on head and body.

Now, let's look at how we can generate three different mattes that, when combined in a clever way, will help us get the best key possible: garbage matte, core matte, and edge matte.

Garbage Mattes

Garbage mattes are used to remove everything in the green screen shot that you don't want to feed to the keyer. This can be poorly lit areas of the green screen, microphones, lighting stands and so on. You only want to keep a small area of green around the person, as this makes the keying a lot easier.

Manually Adjusted Garbage Mattes

We can use the crop effect, opacity masks (my preferred choice), or one of the obsolete garbage matte effects to mask away the areas of the image that should not be present in the final composite (Figure 8-78). That way, we don't have to worry about getting the settings right for those pixels. Why worry about partially transparent pixels in the upper-left corner if the person never goes near that corner?

Figure 8-78. *Use opacity mask as a garbage matte. (Green screen and background shot by Øyvind Osdalen. Model: Håkon Okkenhaug Mathiesen)*

Automatic Garbage Mattes

In addition to the rough garbage mattes we can create manually, we can generate them dynamically, meaning it changes frame by frame based on the movement of the person. This is called a *procedural matte*. The standard procedure is to make a rough key with a high-contrast matte and then expand the matte.

The ultra keyer is the best color keyer in Premiere. It's also the fastest, since it's GPU accelerated, so it's our keyer of choice. Unfortunately, the choke feature will add a lot of chatter and noise to the image at the extreme settings we'll use for our mattes–and it doesn't support negative choke–so we must build our own solution. We'll use two layers and a combination of the ultra keyer, some blur and levels adjustment, and the wonderful track matte key.

Put two copies of the green-screen footage on tracks video 2 and video 3 in the timeline (the background goes on video 1). Name the tracks *Source* and *Garbage Matte* respectively. We'll start with the clip on Garbage Matte track (3). You can use an opacity mask first to remove areas you don't need to worry about. Then, add the ultra key effect and use the key color eye dropper to sample the green screen. Hold down **Ctrl** (Cmd) to get a 5 × 5 pixels sample. Select the Aggressive preset and output the alpha channel.

We actually *don't* want a good key here–we want a rough matte that goes outside the person. Add Gaussian blur (Blurriness 50) and Fast Color Corrector or the levels effect with narrow input levels. Levels is the most future-proof choice. I set *Input Black* to 90 and *Input White* to 100 (Figure 8-79). This expands the white matte around the person (Figure 8-80).

Figure 8-79. *Garbage matte settings*

Figure 8-80. *Alpha channel output from ultra key gets Gaussian blur and levels to expand the matte*

Now, add the track matte key effect to the clip on the Source track (Video 2) and set it to take its matte from the Garbage Matte track we just created (Video 3) and to use the *Matte Luma* (Figure 8-81).

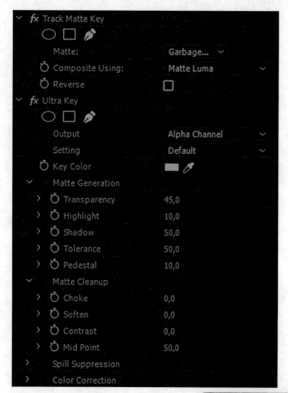

Figure 8-81. *Set the Garbage Matte track to feed the track matte key*

This combination creates a nice dynamic garbage matte that updates on every frame and effectively cuts away everything that isn't close to the person, leaving only the important edge pixels for us to key out (Figure 8-81). Since irrelevant pixels are gone, we can do a much softer key.

Mask Tricks

To scale a rectangle mask, press **Shift** and click just outside one node/point of the mask to drag so the whole mask expands proportionally. **Shift-select** or marquee-select several points to move them all together.

Former Adobe evangelist Colin Smith has a video tutorial on masks, mattes and alpha channels: youtube.com/watch?v=rPk8k8LaXFI.

Core Key

The core matte is easier than the garbage matte, since we can use the choke feature in the ultra key. Put another copy of the footage on Video 4 and name the track *Core*. Since we've used the Aggressive preset, the key is already quite harsh, but to make it absolutely opaque, I've maxed out the Contrast setting. Choke is set to 50 (Figure 8-82).

Figure 8-82. Aggressive preset in ultra key plus max contrast. Choke set to 50.

This creates a completely opaque inner core matte of the person where no transparency exists (Figure 8-83), leaving just the edges for us to worry about in our main key. The result, if you turn off all the other layers, is an eroded version of the person.

Figure 8-83. *Core key*

You may want to add the sharpen effect to the Core track to add some of the detail you lost when shooting with reduced detail/sharpening in the camera. Make sure you watch the image at 100 percent view or full screen when you adjust the amount. Be very conservative with this sharpening, since we'll add more sharpening to the whole image later.

Edge Key

By using the garbage matte and core keys we've isolated the edges and can treat them separately. This makes it super easy to maintain good edges on the foreground clip, which is what really makes a good chroma key.

Figure 8-84 shows the pixels we have left to worry about. Everything but the edges is taken care of, and we can use less aggressive settings, keeping the edges natural, without a digital haircut and with no risk for partly transparent areas in the core or a noisy background. Figure 8-84 is for illustration purposes only–there's no step in this keying process where the image looks like this.

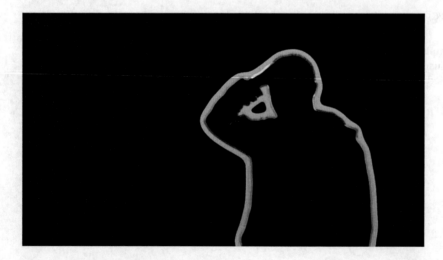

Figure 8-84. *Edge pixels only*

Add the ultra key effect to the clip on the Source track and use the eye dropper to sample the color values inside the green edge around the person. Hold down **Ctrl** (Cmd) again to get a 5 × 5 pixels sample. Now, adjust the parameters while watching the image at 100 percent size. Tweak lightly until you get a nice key with lots of fine details. Figure 8-85 shows the setting I used for this particular footage. I just increased contrast.

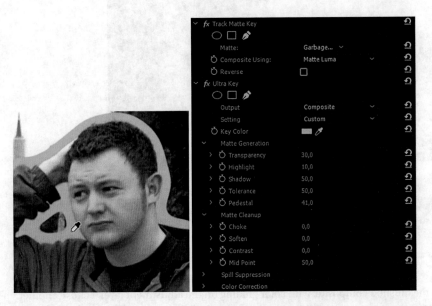

Figure 8-85. *We only have to worry about the edges, making it much easier to get a good key*

Figure 8-88 shows the layer stack in the timeline, in case you lost track.

■ **Note**   This method forces you to use the exact same settings for spill suppression in the ultra key on the clips on the Source and Core tracks, so the edge and core look the same.

The finished key, before color grading, is shown in Figure 8-86.

Figure 8-86. *All mattes combined*

Figure 8-87 shows the finished composite, with color grading on the adjustment layer. I chose another frame where you can see more of his hair sticking up so you can appreciate how good this key is. This is absolutely amazing for a key that plays back without dropping frames–no rendering required. Figure 8-88 shows the final timeline.

Figure 8-87. *After color correction on adjustment layer*

Figure 8-88. *Here's the layer stack with garbage matte, core key, edge key, and background combined*

Have you noticed that the clips in these screenshots are actually nested sequences? That's because I want to reuse this project as a template project later. I also applied the opacity mask on the clip in the nested sequence so I don't have to use it on clips on every layer.

Use Separate Settings on Different Areas of the Image

The edges are partially transparent, and it's here that the difference between a good and a bad key is made. The talent's wispy hair needs different settings than the trousers, and areas with motion blur may need special attention. Most of the time, this means we'll split the image into parts and treat them differently.

If you try to use just one key over the whole image, you'll have to use aggressive settings to avoid transparency where there shouldn't be, and get a key. This will cause huge problems with the edges, especially in hair and other areas with fine detail against the green. The settings that work well for the clothes may not be good for the hair.

Figure 8-89 shows an example where the hair was badly eroded when one setting was used for the whole frame. See the digital haircut in the middle image caused by too-aggressive settings? Not good. When a less-aggressive setting was used, there were semi-transparent areas in the green screen, so the image was unusable. But although the aggressive settings give us a clean key, the loss of edge detail is disastrous.

Figure 8-89. *Original shot (left); hair eroded (middle); hair fixed (right). (Green screen shot by Sean Fulton and Martin Fotland)*

To the right is the same image after applying custom settings to keep the hair detail. This made her trousers go all transparent, so a different setting was needed for the part of the body below the shoulders. So, how do we split the image into different parts?

Unfortunately, opacity masks do not work well with the track matte key, so we need to use more layers.

Add One More Track to Split the Image

Right-click on the track header and choose *Add Tracks. . .* (yes, plural). In the dialog box choose *Add 1 Video Track After the Background Layer* (named BG in my timeline) and no audio tracks (Figure 8-90). This magically keeps track of the settings so that the track matte key still takes its matte from the correct track and everything still looks the same.

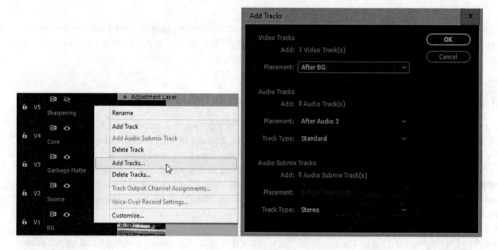

Figure 8-90. Add a new track after the background track

Now, **Alt-drag** a copy of the clip on the Source track (now the third layer) onto the newly created track. Next, name the original Source track *Source (Head)* and give the new layer the name *Source (Body)*.

Add another track above the others, but below the adjustment layer if you added one. Adjustment layers will mess up the track matte keys. Name it *Head & Body Matte*. **Alt-drag** a copy of the clip on the Source layer to this track and delete the ultra key and the track matte key from it. Now, make an opacity mask around the head (Figure 8-91). You can also track the mask, if necessary, when the person moves.

Figure 8-91. *Hair mask*

The image will look a bit strange now, with parts of the green screen visible around the head. This goes away when you add another instance of the track matte key to the Source (Head) and Source (Body) clips, set to take alpha matte from the new matte track. Check *Reverse* on the one on the Source (Body) clip to invert the mask.

Now that you've got two instances of the track matte key on each source clip it's a good idea to rename them so you know which one's doing what. Figure 8-92 shows the layers in the timeline by now. The thumbnails on the right illustrate the output of each layer so you can better grasp what's going on.

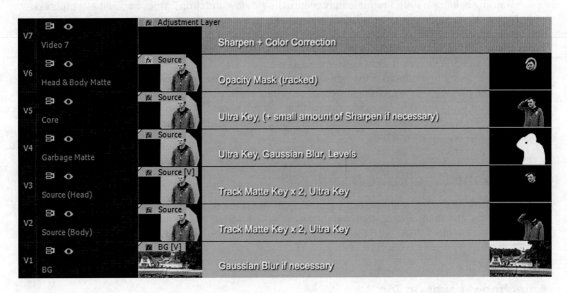

Figure 8-92. *This is the complete layer stack now*

With this setup you can use separate adjustments for the ultra key on the clips in the Source (Head) and the Source (Body) tracks. I made a softer key for the head to avoid a digital haircut. On the Body clip, I adjusted choke to get rid of a light fringe around the edges of the jacket.

If you get some artifacts on the edges of the head mask, you can duplicate the Head and Body matte clip once more and increase the mask expansion on it. Keep the adjustment layer on top. Then, use the two separate matte layers as the track matte for the Head and Body Source layers respectively. Make sure you feather the expanded mask to get a smooth transition between them.

I realize that this whole thing may read like a very complicated maneuver, but it's actually pretty simple once you get the basic idea. And the best part is that you can make a template project, so you only do this once in your life! We go through all this trouble to protect our edges–no matter what–because it's a great way to build a perfect key.

Fine-tuning Your Key

OK, so now we actually have a very decent key, but we could still use a few more tricks of the trade to enhance the result. We'll add a small amount of blur to the edges only, then create some realistic-looking light wrap, and finally color correct everything until we have a perfect composite image.

■ **Note** If you've already built a multi-layered key template as described in this chapter, just copy and paste the green-screen clip from an existing sequence and adjust the ultra key settings so that they correspond with the ones needed in the techniques in this section.

A warning before we start: Premiere may eventually get slow and drop frames as you make progress with these techniques, mainly because of all the blur effects. So, save your mouse clicks for later and be patient. It can take several seconds to update even a single frame in a compositing project like this on a slow system. GPU acceleration helps a lot, so I don't recommend even trying to work seriously with these techniques if you don't have a decent GPU-enabled system.

Don't be allergic to render bars though–you don't have to render just because it's red. You only need to render if the playback isn't smooth enough for adequate previewing. Rendering is boring and should be done when you're not working. You can work with mattes and tweaks without seeing everything in real-time. Then, hit *Render* when you take a break, read your email, talk on the phone, update your status, or leave the room to pretend you have a real life.

Sharpen the Composite Image

You might think we should be able to put an unsharp mask on the edge matte after the final key, and that this would make the clip sharper, cancelling out the blurriness caused by the reduced detail/sharpening setting on the camera. But this will use the pixels outside the mask from the source, so it has the potential to severely destroy the edges.

Adjustment Layer on Top

Instead, we will use an adjustment layer on top with some unsharp mask magic on it. That will sharpen the background layer, too, so we need to add some extra blur to that layer first (or shoot it with reduced sharpening/detail).

Now, the unsharp mask is still not 32-bit and not GPU accelerated and can clip your highlight levels, so the 8-bit-ness of the effect can cause strange things to happen. This will potentially create problems with our garbage matte, which surely has levels beyond 100 percent, especially after sharpening. So, we'll make our own unsharp mask instead of using the built-in 8-bit plug-in.

What Is an Unsharp Mask Anyway?

To build an unsharp mask, we need to understand what it is. The term comes from a photographic darkroom technique where they'd take the original negative film and make a blurred positive copy. An unexposed film frame was covered with a glass plate, and the original film was placed on top. Then, they'd expose this to light for a short time. Using a short exposure time made the copy underexposed and faint, and the glass plate would create enough distance between the films to make the positive contact copy slightly blurred.

Next, they would sandwich these two films together and expose the print paper through them both, resulting in slight halos in the opposite lightness of whatever is on the other side of each edge. Dark areas would get a light halo, and light areas would get a dark halo–which is what the unsharp mask effect mimics digitally.

Bake Your Own 32-bit, Accelerated Unsharp Mask Effect

On an adjustment layer, we'll add a very small amount of Gaussian blur (1.5-2 px for a starting point) and then use the (obsolete) RGB color corrector to lower the gain to 0.50 before we finally set the blend mode to subtract. Then, we'll add another adjustment layer where we use the RGB color corrector to bring the levels back to normal with a gain setting of 2.00 (Figure 8-93). You've just built your own GPU-accelerated unsharp mask effect!

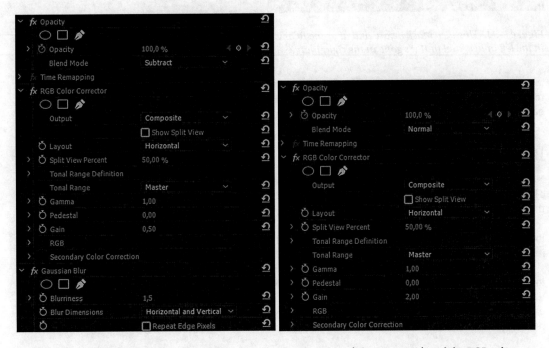

Figure 8-93. *Left*: Lower layer: Subtract blend mode, Gaussian blur (Blurriness 1.5) and the RGB color corrector (Gain 0.50). *Right*: Upper layer, RGB color corrector–Gain setting of 2.00 gets levels back to normal.

Unfortunately, the RGB color corrector is now in the Obsolete folder and will probably be gone in a few years. You can use the Lumetri Color effect instead by setting it to HDR mode and using negative exposure settings for the lower layer and a positive one for the upper layer, but since the Lumetri Color effect always uses some compression to avoid clipping when we do extreme corrections, it's not going to be mathematically correct, and the image will not look the same after these adjustments.

Rather than overdoing this unsharp mask thing on the whole image, I recommend that you put the sharpen effect on the Core layer as explained earlier so the core of the foreground image (the person) gets a tiny bit more sharpness than the edges and the background layer.

Don't go all crazy with these sharpening effects, as they will make the noise more noticeable and may introduce strange contours and halos on the person. Watch everything in full screen when you adjust the settings so you can clearly see all the artifacts they introduce.

If the sharpening introduces halos around dark objects in light surroundings in the background image, add a curve with a nice roll-off at the top to the offending clip(s) to cut off the levels at 100 percent or below (Figure 8-94).

Figure 8-94. *Unsharp mask before and after the RGB Curves adjustment. Notice the halo around the church in the left image, and that it's gone in the right image.*

Just like the standard unsharp mask effect, your home-baked one might introduce some halos as a result of overbrights introduced in the procedure. Use RGB Curves or Lumetri Color to get the highlights back into legal levels, and the halos will disappear.

Blur the Edge

Natural images have a natural softness around hard edges because of limitations in lenses and sensors. This is what we need to replicate when we're compositing. This does *not* have the same effect as blurring the matte in the ultra keyer, which will make the foreground layer partly transparent in the soft edge.

A subtle blur of just the boundary between the foreground and background elements will make the key look more realistic. The pixels of the background and the foreground will be blurred together, and will blend in with the edges of the person, very much like it would if shooting the scene for real.

We'll use the find edges effect to make a matte for an adjustment layer where you blur the edges together ever so slightly. Again, be subtle. Don't overdo this technique–a little goes a long way.

Use the find edges effect to, well, find the edges of the alpha channel output from the ultra key. Then, use a blur-levels-blur combination to fatten the edge matte. Figure 8-95 shows the effect settings and the resulting matte.

Figure 8-95. *Edge-blur matte*

This matte is then used as a track matte for an adjustment layer with some blur. See Figure 8-96. The image to the right shows the subtle result of adding edge blur. It doesn't show as well in a still image as it does on video playback, but you should be able to see that the edge is slightly blurred, and that there's less aliasing.

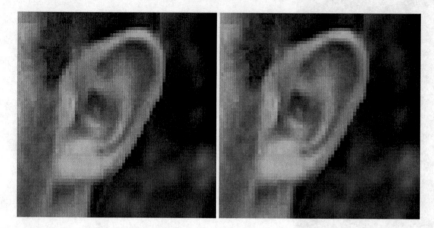

Figure 8-96. *Edge blur off (left) and edge blur on (right)*

Edge Blur, Step by Step

1. Create a new video track and name it *Edge Blur*; put an adjustment layer there. We'll come back to this later.

2. **Alt-drag** a copy of the green-screen clip with the ultra key effect from the Source (body) track and put it above everything on its own track. Name the track *Edge Blur Matte.*

3. Set the ultra key on this clip to output the alpha channel and delete the track matte key effects.

4. Add the following effects to the ultra key already on the clip:

    a. An *opacity mask* to mask off unwanted areas, if you haven't done this in a nested sequence as I did. Copy the one from the garbage matte.

    b. *Find edges,* to create a black line around the person

    c. *Gaussian blur* to blur the line. Adjust *Blurriness* to around *2 pixels* and select *Repeat Edges.*

    d. *Fast color corrector* or *levels* with *Input White* adjusted to 200 to make the matte from the find edges effect thinner. Set the *Saturation* to 0.

    e. *Gaussian blur* with a *2 px* blur and *Repeat Edge Pixels* selected

    f. If you want the outline to be even thinner, add copies of fast color corrector (or levels) and Gaussian blur and adjust the parameters until it has the desired thinness.

5. On the adjustment layer, add the following effects:

    a. *Track matte key* set to take the matte from the *Edge Blur Matte* track and to use *Matte Luma,* and *with the Reverse switch activated.*

    b. *Gaussian blur* with a *2 px* blur and *Repeat Edge Pixels* selected

Now the edges will be blurred, but everything else will be untouched from the original sequence. If you want a less pronounced effect, lower the opacity of the Edge Blur track. Unfortunately, you'll probably have to render this sequence to watch it in real-time without dropping frames. As always, make presets for this kind of stuff if you use the techniques often.

For reference, Figure 8-97 shows the layer stack after adding the Unsharp Mask and Edge Blur layers.

Figure 8-97. *All layers, including Unsharp Mask and Edge Blur layers*

Light Wrap

In a real image, because of the nature of light, diffraction causes light areas of the background to bend, or "wrap" around, the edges of a foreground element. Consequently, a person shot against a sunset would have slightly orange-colored edges. For a green-screen key to look natural, we should imitate this phenomenon.

We'll basically combine a normal matte from the keyer with a blurred version of itself to get a matte with a sharp outer edge and a smooth inner edge. Then, we'll use this combined matte as a track matte for a blurred version of the BG clip. If you think this sounds complicated, read on–it will all make sense very soon.

Making a Light Wrap Matte

Create a new sequence, name it *Light Wrap Matte*, and place two copies of your green-screen footage in there. Rename your tracks so it's easier to understand later what they do. The lower clip should have the *ultra key*, tweaked for a good key and set to output the alpha channel (Figure 8-98). Copy the ultra key from an existing green-screen clip in the previous section so you don't need to tweak too much.

Figure 8-98. *Light wrap layer setup, and the ultra key on the lower layer set to output alpha channel*

The upper clip should have these effects to create a blurred negative version of the matte (Figure 8-99):

- *Ultra key* as earlier

- *Gaussian blur*, set to about 100 px and to repeat edge pixels

- *Invert*, with the default settings

- Opacity set to *Multiply* blending mode

Figure 8-99. *The upper layer has an added Gaussian blur and the invert effect, and is set to the multiply blending mode*

734

The combination of these layers should output a matte that has nice edges on the outside and blurred inner edges. If you want a whiter matte, add an adjustment layer with fast color corrector or levels, and set Input White as low as necessary to get a whiter matte (Figure 8-100). If needed, you can also add a very small amount of Gaussian blur–maybe Blurriness set to 2.

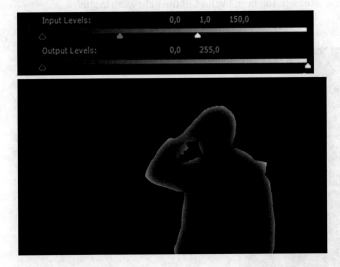

Figure 8-100. *The final light wrap matte has a nice outer edge and a feathered inner edge*

Using the Light Wrap Matte

Create a new sequence and name it *Light Wrap*. Put a copy of the background clip (not the green-screen clip) on V1 and rename the track to *BG Blurred*. Put the *Light Wrap Matte* sequence on V2 and name the track *Light Wrap Matte* (Figure 8-101).

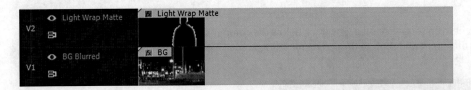

Figure 8-101. *The Light Wrap Matte sequence is used as a track matte for a blurred version of the background clip*

The Light Wrap Matte clip needs no effects. The copy of the background clip should have these effects on it to create a blurred version and make it visible only where the light wrap matte is white (Figure 8-102).

- *Gaussian blur*, set to around 15–40 px, and repeat pixels

- *Track matte key*, set to take the matte from the Luma values of the light wrap matte track.

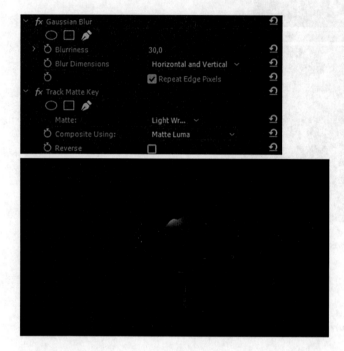

Figure 8-102. *This is how the light wrap sequence looks now. We'll add this on top of the existing layer stack.*

Place the light wrap sequence on a new track below the color grading track. Now, adjust opacity to 50 percent as a starting point and set it to the screen blending mode (Figure 8-103).

Figure 8-103. *Light wrap set to screen mode*

Figure 8-104 shows the complete layer stack with garbage matte, core, and edge layers, sharpening, edge blur, and light wrap. That's quite a few layers, with quite a few instances of ultra key, track matte key, blurs, and other effects.

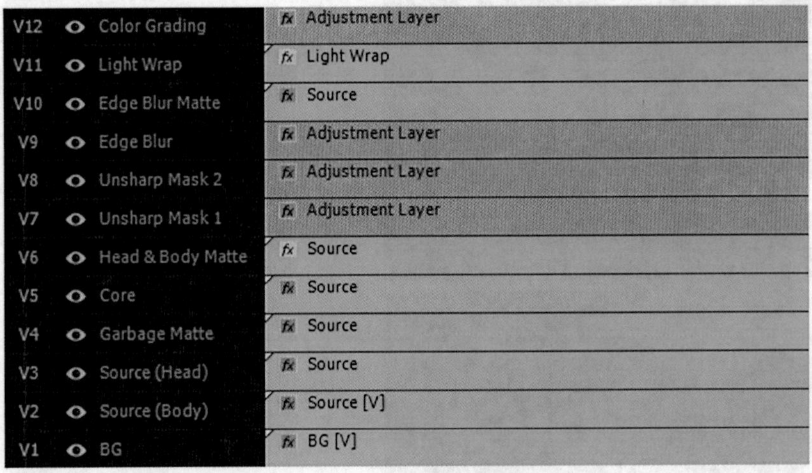

V12	⊙	Color Grading	*fx* Adjustment Layer
V11	⊙	Light Wrap	*fx* Light Wrap
V10	⊙	Edge Blur Matte	*fx* Source
V9	⊙	Edge Blur	*fx* Adjustment Layer
V8	⊙	Unsharp Mask 2	*fx* Adjustment Layer
V7	⊙	Unsharp Mask 1	*fx* Adjustment Layer
V6	⊙	Head & Body Matte	*fx* Source
V5	⊙	Core	*fx* Source
V4	⊙	Garbage Matte	*fx* Source
V3	⊙	Source (Head)	*fx* Source
V2	⊙	Source (Body)	*fx* Source [V]
V1	⊙	BG	*fx* BG [V]

Figure 8-104. *Full layer stack for advanced keying*

You must experiment with blend modes and different blur and opacity settings for different footage. Tweak the settings to taste as needed, and enjoy your light wrap. You'll be amazed how much it adds to the illusion. Don't add too much light wrap, though, or it can quickly start to look cheesy.

The light wrap effect is very subtle, especially in a daytime scene, but will make the final composite look more realistic. You will probably not see it in the still image in Figure 8-105, but if you were to turn the light wrap layer on and off, you would see a noticeable difference.

Figure 8-105. *Upper image*: Before applying light wrap; *Lower image*: After applying light wrap

Figure 8-106 shows the shot on a darker background. It should be easier (but still hard) to see on this dark background. Try to notice how the jacket gets lighter where the background is lighter. Above the lifted arm, where there's a light in the BG layer, it should be visible.

Figure 8-106. *Upper image*: Before applying light wrap; *Lower image*: After applying light wrap

What Have We Achieved with All This?

Figure 8-107 shows the result after combining all the techniques in this chapter. That's a very decent key considering the sources are 8-bit 4:2:0 highly compressed MPEG-2 encoded XDCAM-EX 35 Mbps material where the camera was not even turned 90 degrees.

Figure 8-107. *Green screen final composite*

Miscellaneous Tips on Compositing

This section has a lot of tips on keying and compositing. Think of it as a way to expand your knowledge base so you can improve your workflow, analyze your keys, and quickly pick the right tool or know the right way to correct a problem.

Ultra Key Tips

The ultra keyer differs from other keyers in several ways. This may throw you off at first if you're used to other keyers, like *Keylight* in After Effects.

Some users say that, as a rule, it's best to pick the key color from a darker part of the screen, as this is easier to correct with some tweaking later. Wherever you decide to click, remember to hold down **Ctrl** (Cmd) as you sample the green screen to enable the 5 × 5 pixels eye dropper trick. This makes sure that you don't accidentally get a lighter or darker color than anticipated as a result of video noise.

Use the Scopes to Fine-tune Your Mattes

When tweaking the settings to make a perfect matte, I recommend that you use the scopes to watch the levels as you create your mattes. You'll see clearly if there are completely white areas or completely black and partly transparent pixels, making the tweaking of the parameters much easier.

To help you understand what the parameters in the ultra key are, here's a description from Premiere Pro Help.

From Premiere Pro Help: Ultra Key Effect Parameters

Matte generation, matte cleanup, spill suppression, and color correction sections explained.

Matte Generation

Transparency

Controls the transparency of the source when keyed over a background. Values range from 0 through 100. 100 is fully transparent. 0 is opaque. The default value is 45.

Highlight

Increases the opacity of light areas of the source image. You can use Highlight to extract details like specular highlights on transparent objects. Values range from 0 through 100. The default value is 50. 0 does not affect the image.

Shadow

Increases the opacity of dark areas of the source image. You can use Shadow to correct a dark element that became transparent because of color spill. Values range from 0 through 100. The default value is 50. 0 does not affect the image.

Tolerance

Filters out colors in the foreground image from the background. Increases tolerance to variation from the key color. You can use Tolerance to remove artifacts caused by color shift. You can also use Tolerance to control spill on skin tones and dark areas.

Values range from 0 through 100. The default value is 50. 0 does not affect the image.

Pedestal

Filters out noise, often caused by grainy or low-light footage, from the alpha channel. Values range from 0 through 100.

The default value is 10. 0 does not affect the image. The higher the quality of your source image, the lower you can set Pedestal.

Matte Cleanup

Choke

Shrinks the size of the alpha channel matte. Performs a morphological Erode (fractional kernel size). Choke level values range from 0 through 100. 100 represents a 9×9 kernel. 0 does not affect the image. The default value is 0.

Soften

Blurs the edge of the alpha channel matte. Performs a box blur filter (fractional kernel size). Blur level values range from 0 through 100. 0 does not affect the image. The default value is 0. 100 represents a 9 × 9 kernel.

Contrast

Adjusts the contrast of the alpha channel. Values range from 0 through 100. 0 does not affect the image. The default value is 0.

Mid-point

Chooses the balance point for the contrast value. Values range from 0 through 100. 0 does not affect the image. The default value is 50.

Spill Suppression

Desaturate

Controls the saturation of the color channel background color. Desaturates colors that are close to being fully transparent. Values range from 0 through 50. 0 does not affect the image. The default value is 25.

Range

Controls the amount of spill that is corrected. Values range from 0 through 100. 0 does not affect the image. The default value is 50.

Spill

Adjusts the amount of spill compensation. Values range from 0 through 100. 0 does not affect the image. The default value is 50

Luma

Works with the alpha channel to restore the original luminance of the source. Values range from 0 through 100. 0 does not affect the image. The default value is 50.

Color Correction

Saturation

Controls the saturation of the foreground source. Values range from 0 through 100. 0 removes all chroma. The default value is 100.

Hue

Controls the hue. Values range from -180° to +180°. The default value is 0°.

Luminance

Controls the luminance of the foreground source. Values range from 0 through 200. 0 is black. 100 is 4x. The default value is 100.

Knowing how the parameters work, the following workflow in the ultra keyer is one possible way to approach a key.

- If your person has some gray or black scattered around in the white matte after picking the key color, adjust the *Transparency* slider to clean up.

- To clean up the blacks in the matte, adjust the *Pedestal* and—if needed—the *Shadow* parameter.

- Next, tweak *Choke* and *Soften* until the edges look good.

- If there's some green spill, especially in the hair, adjust the *Spill Suppression* settings.

Now, continue setting up garbage matte, core and edge keys, head and body masks, edge blur and light wrap as explained earlier.

Premultiplied and Straight Alpha

Footage with alpha channels can store the transparency info as straight or premultiplied alpha. If this is interpreted wrongly, you will get jagged edges with a color edge. A white or black fringe around the edges of a clip is an indication of a wrongly interpreted alpha channel (Figure 8-108).

Figure 8-108. *A fringe around the edges indicates a wrongly interpreted alpha channel*

Select the clip in a bin and choose **Modify ➤ Interpret Footage** in the right-click menu. Under *Alpha Channel*, conform the alpha to Premultiplied or Straight (Figure 8-109).

Figure 8-109. *Alpha Interpret options*

Need Camera Shake?

Since we don't have advanced tracking tools in Premiere, we need locked-off green-screen shots. If you need a handheld camera-look on the composite image, just nest the whole sequence into another sequence and add one of my *Deadpool* handheld camera presets, found here: `premierepro.net/editing/deadpool-handheld-camera-presets/`. Yes, these are actual presets I made for the editors who cut the *Deadpool* movie, and you can download them for free.

If you want to create similar presets yourself, here's the recipe: shoot handheld, track in AE, copy keyframes to Premiere, and you have real camera shake in Premiere. There will be no motion blur when you use these in Premiere, though, so you may want to add the camera shake in After Effects.

Track Matte Workaround

A problem with the way Premiere works with track mattes is that the matte scales with the clip where the track matte key effect is added. This is almost never what you want. You can, of course, use nesting and scale in the nested sequence like we've done a couple of times in this chapter.

You can also use the transform effect instead of the fixed motion effect. Add it *before* the track matte key in the Effect Controls panel, and you can scale the clip without affecting the matte.

Current Bug with Adjustment Layers and Track Matte Key

As mentioned a few times, there is a bug in Premiere CC 2017 where adjustment layers do strange things when combined with the track matte key. Until Adobe fixes that problem, use a duplicate of the clip instead of an adjustment layer, or use nesting like we've done in this chapter.

Composite in Linear Mode

Premiere will composite in linear color when the checkbox is checked in Sequence settings and either *Max Render Quality* or *GPU Acceleration* is enabled. Linear processing fixes the math for processes such as blurs and blend modes, and blends more like natural light would do.

Unfortunately, it also creates unexpected results when adding built-in video cross dissolves and fades. Read and watch my explanation of why you should use the free impact dissolve instead at `premierepro.net/editing/impact-dissolve/`.

It can be challenging to understand how Max Render Quality, Max Bit Depth, and Composite in Linear Color work together. Here are some facts and rules.

For CPU

- Max Bit Depth switches between using 8-bit and 32-bit effects and processing.

- Max Bit Depth switches some importers between 8-bit and 32-bit imported frames.

- Max Render Quality switches scaling to use a higher quality bicubic re-sampler.

- Max Render Quality, in addition to the sequence setting, also switches compositing, Gaussian blur, and frame blending to linear color.

- Max Render Quality switches some importers to use larger resolutions.

For GPU

- GPU effects are always 32-bit.

- Scaling is always best quality.

- Linear compositing controlled only by the sequence setting.

- Max Bit Depth switches some importers between 8-bit and 32-bit imported frames.

- Max Render Quality switches some importers to use larger resolutions.

- Unaccelerated effects follow the rules from CPU section.

And remember: It's enough to have just one non-GPU filter on a clip to turn rendering of the frame into non-GPU mode.

Matching Color

The colors of the foreground image need to match the colors of the background image. When colors, white and black levels, and contrast in the foreground and background don't match, there's no way to make the key believable. A foreground image with a blue cast on a background with an orange cast will never look realistic. This goes without saying, but nevertheless we often see green-screen scenes where the colors don't match (Figure 8-110).

Figure 8-110. *Black levels in foreground image don't match black levels in background*

Match White Levels

If there is something white in the foreground image, it should have the same overall level and the same color (if there is a color cast, intentional or accidentally) as any white objects in the environment (the background image).

Use your Parade (RGB) scope and vector scope (YUV) to watch the levels as you tweak the color correction on the foreground image. Read more on shot matching in chapter 6 on color grading.

Match Black Levels

Your black levels in the foreground and background images also need to match. This is where most composites fall apart. It's far too common to see a foreground image with high black levels on a background with low black levels and vice versa. This is partly because two monitors are never the same. So, people adjust their black levels by eye on their own monitor, and when watched on a screen with higher black levels, the differences suddenly stand out.

So, what can you do about this? Apart from using the Parade (RGB) scope and not trusting your eyes too much, you can use a gamma slammer, soon to be explained, to temporarily raise your black levels.

Color and Contrast Balancing

When white and black levels are matched, move on to matching midtone colors, gamma, and midtone contrast. A light S-curve or an inverted S-curve, or maybe just a slightly raised or lowered curve, can work wonders when matching two images.

Pay special attention to the shadows. Shadows are lit by reflections from their surroundings, not by the direct light source. So, when we put people in an environment, the shadows should be tinted the same color as the environment's overall colors. Look for shadows in the background plate and try to match these in color, saturation, and intensity.

Gamma slamming

A gamma slammer is a method used by compositors to check that their levels will work on different monitors. Watching your sequence at a range of exposures will indicate if a layer is brighter or darker than it should be.

In dedicated compositing software, this would be done by raising the exposure. Premiere doesn't have a proper exposure setting (the one in the Lumetri Color panel is helping you by compressing the highlights to avoid clipping), so we'll make our own again.

Make Your Own Gamma Slammer Presets

Add an adjustment layer to the top of the track stack in your sequence. Add four copies of the RGB Curves from Lumetri such that one has a raised gamma and one has a lowered gamma, and the two others have raised and lowered overall levels. See the images in Figure 8-112, and you'll get the idea. I highly recommend you save a preset with all these effects and with all of them turned off.

Figure 8-111 shows the original green-screen composite. Figure 8-112 shows the four gamma slammer curves and the result of each one.

Figure 8-111. *Original composite*

Figure 8-112. *Use RGB Curves to make your own gamma slamming presets. (Footage by Geir Rossebø)*

Now Match Everything Else

Careful matching of foreground and background elements is crucial to avoid the stuck-on look that sometimes can make an otherwise good composite look fake.

To really sell the illusion that the composited scene is real, a lot of stuff needs to match in the foreground image and the background plate. There's a long list of things to take into consideration if you want a perfect illusion.

In addition to the obvious color matching just explained, this also includes on-set lighting, grain matching, focal length, depth of field, camera position/angle, shutter speed and motion blur, lens distortions like vignetting, flare, chromatic and geometric distortions, and more. If one of these things is "off" enough to create a visible difference, the illusion can fall apart.

Lighting

Matching the lighting to the light in the background image is probably the most important thing you do in a green-screen scene. Lighting for green screen was explained in some detail earlier.

Re-light

If necessary, create pools of light and darkness using masks on color-correction effects. Try to make the lighting in the foreground and the background match better. You can't do real magic, but at least you can make it look better.

Frame Rate

When shooting green screen, you need to match the frame rate of the background image. It could be any of these: 12, 23.976, 24, 25, 29.97, 30, 50, 59.94, or 60 fps or other, nonstandard, frame rates–or even a variable frame rate (which Premiere doesn't like at all). Make sure you know what the frame rate is.

If you get footage where the frame rates don't match, use Optical Flow in the Speed setting in Premiere, or interpret the footage to matching frame rate if there's no movement that will reveal the speed change.

Shutter Speed

If the background footage is shot with a shutter speed of, say, 1/50th second, you should shoot the foreground with the same shutter speed, or one as close as possible, to match the motion blur.

If there's a lot of movement in the foreground clip, the motion blur may cause trouble for the keyer if it has partially transparent areas and so forth. You may consider shooting with a faster shutter speed to avoid this, but then you'll have to do the keying in After Effects and add fake motion blur after the key.

Camera Shake and Camera Movement

If there's camera movement in the background image, this isn't a job for Premiere. Send it over to After Effects and use tracking to make your foreground image stick to the background, following the movements of the camera that shot the background. Camera shake will introduce some motion blur, and this needs to be added to the foreground image in After Effects. If it's supposed to be a locked-off shot, but the foreground and/or background have a little bit of movement, stabilize the shot(s) with the warp stabilizer effect before keying in Premiere.

Camera and Lens Properties

When shooting, take care to match the perspective (camera height and distance relative to the object), focal length (field of view), aperture settings, and so on; depth of field will also match if the cameras have the same sensor size.

Lens distortions like color fringing, shading, lens flares, and geometric distortions should also match as closely as possible. This is a job for After Effects.

Edge Quality

Here's a setting you should not match while shooting. As explained earlier, sharpening/detail in the camera will create halos around the person and should be avoided. It needs to be added in post. That's why we created the unsharp mask layers.

After adding sharpness in post, the sources should match. If they don't, you need to blur sources that are too sharp or sharpen footage that's too soft.

Compression Artifacts

Cameras record video with a lot of compression. As a general rule, the cheaper the camera, the more compressed the signal is. This introduces artifacts like macro blocks, mosquito noise, blurring, and so on, and chroma subsampling (4:1:1, 4:2:0, 4:2:2) will decrease the color resolution.

These compression artifacts and the results of chroma subsampling can be hard to match with effects in Premiere. The good news is that you don't have to. Say you want to give some footage a "shot on DV" look, complete with macro blocks, ringing, and mosquito noise. Just export the clip as DV and reimport it, and you'll have all the degradation you need. Don't use the degraded clip to make mattes, though.

Instead, use the original to make the matte, and fill with the degraded clip. Yeah, the track matte key saves your butt again.

Grain Matching

Are the sources shot on video or film? Did they use high or low ISO/gain settings? The answers will dictate how you proceed when matching grain or noise. To match two sources, it may be necessary to remove noise from noisy footage or to add noise to overly clean sources. This is best done in After Effects.

The add grain effect in AE is better than the noise effect in Premiere when imitating the grain in motion picture footage. Noise is better when replicating digital video noise as found in digital cameras.

Try using channel blur on just the blue channel to remove video noise. The blue channel often has the most noise, and blurring just that channel will degrade the image very little, while sometimes effectively reducing the noise.

Match Motion Blur

Motion blur can be faked with the use of directional blur or even with just Gaussian blur if the movement is horizontal or vertical. You can also use the transform effect with some clever settings. See my tutorial here: premierepro.net/editing/motion-blur/. But these should be considered workarounds or cheats, and can only take you so far.

For more advanced options, use pixel motion blur in After Effects, if necessary in combination with CC force motion blur. Set the shutter angle to a value that matches the background footage. The render time gets longer the higher you set shutter samples and vector detail. Add the CC force motion blur effect if timewarp doesn't get you all the way.

In Figure 8-113, pixel motion blur in timewarp is used in combination with CC force motion blur to increase the amount of motion blur in the clip.

Figure 8-113.   Timewarp and CC force motion blur in After Effects

Motion Blur or not?

■ **Note**   Some people advise that we should shoot green-screen scenes at the shortest shutter speed available to avoid problematic motion blur. If so, you must add it back after the keying. If you go for "perfect" compositing, the motion blur of the green-screen footage should match the shutter speed of the background.

You *need* motion blur on the foreground if the background plate and the rest of your scenes have motion blur. Otherwise, it will stand out, not blend in, which is the point of the whole green-screen game after all.

Yes, shooting with motion blur does make it harder to get a great key. So, in some cases, it may be a better choice to shoot with a faster shutter and add fake motion blur in post. But as we've seen in this chapter, a perfect key is so much more than a clean cut-out of the person.

Interaction with the Surroundings

A person or an object in an environment will interact in several ways with the surroundings. They will cast shadows and create contact shadows where they touch the ground.

If it's a hit, explosion, or collision, analyze what would happen during and after impact. Elements should fly around immediately after the impact, and debris should continue flying and dropping for a while. Shock waves might be deforming objects close to the bang. Don't forget what happens outside the frame–this might also affect objects in the image.

Creating debris digitally can be hard. Try Ghetto Pyro instead. Throw objects and debris in front of the camera while shooting, and save lots of work in post.

Add Reflections

If a person stands beside or walks past a shiny object, a mirror, or a window, there should be a reflection. You could fake this in Premiere, but with complex environments, head to After Effects and use displacement maps for this.

Use References

Don't try too hard to imagine what a scene would look like. Instead, take a look at the real thing so you know what you're trying to recreate. Google Image Search and YouTube are great resources for finding this kind of stuff. But don't be a slave to realism. Sometimes you'll want the effects to be larger than life.

The 180-Degree Shutter Myth

If you talk to cinematographers or spend time in forums, someone will eventually mention the 180-degree shutter rule. They will tell you that you need to shoot at 180 degrees to get natural-looking motion blur. A 180-degree shutter meant the image was projected onto the celluloid film half the time duration of one film frame–which is 1/48th, since a whole frame is 1/24th second. The opening in the rotating shutter is 180 degrees, as shown in Figure 8-114.

Figure 8-114. *180-degree shutter*

Why do people think that a 180-degree shutter is mandatory? Because in traditional 24 fps celluloid film, at 1/48th second, it closely mimics the motion blur we experience in real life with our eyes, as did 1/50th second used in PAL video for ages, and (almost, but not as good) 1/60th second in NTSC video. We like the look of these shutter speeds. Coincidence? Nope, it's because they look natural.

But the 180-degree shutter rule is dated! It's great for 24 and 25 fps footage, but looks bad on 50 fps footage unless you're shooting at 50 fps for slo-mo. The 180-degree rule was actually a 1/48th second shutter rule, but since film was always shown at 24 fps, they were the same. If you shot 48 fps it was because you wanted slo-mo, and the 180-degree rule still worked.

When shooting 50 fps that will also be viewed at 50 fps, I always use a 1/50th second shutter (yes, this is possible with digital cameras) because the motion blur you get with 1/48th or 1/50th second is very close to the motion blur in human eyes. No one complains about it being "too real," "looking like TV," etc. like they usually do when watching 48 or 50 fps. It's the shutter speed, not the shutter angle, that affects the motion blur! The shutter angle varies with the fps. Shutter speed does not.

180-degree shutter on 50 fps footage is 1/100th second. 180-degree shutter on 60 fps is 1/120th second. These shutter speeds will result in images with very little motion blur–much less than we see with our eyes in real life, so it looks unnatural. 1/48th and 1/50th second matches our eyes very well, and looks good. (For a video that shows the 180-degree shutter visually, visit vimeo.com/204328432.)

But, if you want a sharper image in order to make it easier to stabilize, track, or key the footage, then go ahead and shoot at faster speeds, but remember to add motion blur in After Effects in post. Adding motion blur in post will add to your render times, and it's not as accurate as the real thing.

Compositing in AE

If you have found this compositing stuff interesting, you should also learn After Effects (AE), which is made for this kind of work and consequently has better tools that let you work faster. With AE, there are no limits to what can be done with moving pixels! Now that you know some of the techniques used for compositing in Premiere Pro, you have a good foundation to learn AE, as a lot of the tools work the same way.

Choose the Right Blur

The blur effects in Premiere are OK, but compared to the camera lens blur in After Effects, they look dull and flat. If you need your blur to look more like a lens-out-of-focus blur, send the clip to After Effects via Dynamic Link and add the camera lens blur effect. It's quite processor intensive, so expect long render times, but it will totally be worth it! Figures 8-115 to 8-117 show the original image, the image with Gaussian blur, and the image with camera lens blur.

Figure 8-115. *No blur*

Figure 8-116. *Gaussian blur*

Figure 8-117. *After Effects camera lens blur*

RAW Formats in VFX

For some RAW formats, you can choose settings for de-Bayering in post. If you can, duplicate the master clip and choose a soft de-Bayer for the green-screen key signal and a sharper one for the fill. You can use the track matte key effect to use the alpha output from the keyer as a track matte for the fill clip.

You can also choose different white balance settings for the two clips. This is useful when the green screen was lit by daylight LED light and the foreground was lit using traditional warmer lights.

Don't Key in Log

If the material was shot in Log, add a Log-to-Lin LUT before starting the compositing. Keyers work best in linear color space.

Remove Noise Before Keying

De-graining or de-noising before keying is often required to avoid chatter in the edges. You can do this in After Effects, or in Premiere with third-party plug-ins, but it's a slow process, so budget with more rendering time.

Free Green-Screen Plates

If you don't have any green-screen material, but want to try out some keying techniques, you can download free green-screen plates here: hollywoodcamerawork.com/green-screen-plates.html. Figure 8-118 shows one of the shots you can download to train your keying skills.

Figure 8-118. *Footage from hollywoodcamerawork.com*

Third-party Plug-ins

Some editors love plug-in collections, while others don't own any. Personally, I don't use too many third-party plug-ins, mainly because I can get my work done without them. Using the built-in effects and a lot of presets and template projects, I can do most of the stuff that third-party plug-ins do–but a dedicated plug-in might get the job done quicker.

There's another reason that I don't use too many plug-ins; I like to upgrade Premiere when new versions are released. Some plug-in creators are very slow to upgrade their plug-ins to new versions of Premiere. That stops me from using old projects with such plug-ins until they decide to release an upgrade. Or, I must keep several versions of Premiere on my system to be able to open old projects.

Of course, both purchasing and upgrading the plug-ins cost money too, so you need to weigh the benefits against the cost. If a plug-in enables you to work faster and save several hours on your next project, it's definitely worth the cost.

Some Good Ones

Twixtor gets good reviews for its ability to convert NTSC to PAL and PAL to NTSC, and to de-interlace footage. Twixtor also intelligently slows down, speeds up, or changes the frame rate of your footage. Find it here: revisionfx.com/products/twixtor/.

The *Magic Bullet Suite* is used by many editors, especially Magic Bullet Looks, which makes creating a look on your movie very easy. A lot of editors will tell you that they use Magic Bullet Colorista daily, and the Magic Bullet plug-ins in general are great tools. Magic Bullet Suite supports the Mercury Playback Engine in Adobe Premiere Pro, so it will not slow you down with renders and slow exports. Find it here: redgiant.com/products/magic-bullet-suite/.

Neat Video can remove noise and grain from your footage: neatvideo.com/.

Sapphire has lots of nice lens flares, glow effects, light rays, transitions, and some compositing-effects goodness. Most effects are Nvidia CUDA GPU-accelerated, so you need an Nvidia GPU to get the most out of these: borisfx.com/products/sapphire/

Boris has a whole range of plug-ins for Premiere that can do all sorts of cool stuff. *Boris Continuum* is an extensive set of effects used by a lot of filmmakers. Boris has other effects packages, too, and it owns the Sapphire plug-ins. Find out more here: borisfx.com/products/continuum/.

Digieffects Damage can simulate bad video and film damage–great for that Old Film look and for "surveillance" monitors: digieffects.com/products/damage/.

FilmImpact.net has some great transition packs for Premiere. They are Nvidia CUDA GPU-accelerated, which is great: filmimpact.net/.

These are just some of the most popular ones. There are many more, and you can spend all the money you want on plug-ins. There are more plug-ins packages available to Premiere than you'll think when searching the web; a lot of AE plug-ins also work in Premiere, and there are thousands of plug-ins for AE out there.

Summary

If you're new to compositing, this chapter was probably a lot to take in. But if you try the techniques and follow the instructions, you should be able to build your own keying and compositing templates, which make it easy to get started on new projects. Just change the source material and tweak the settings.

I hope that by now you have a good understanding of what can be done with keying, blending modes, masks, and track mattes. You should be able to tackle basic and intermediate compositing jobs on your own and get the best out of the material, with a decent result.

Compositing skills count more than the software when you're working with keying and compositing, and the tools in Premiere are quite capable. But if you want to take your compositing to a higher level, you should definitely learn After Effects, too.

CHAPTER 9

■■■

VR Video Editing

By Jarle Leirpoll

Even though Virtual Reality (VR) Video is inherently challenging as a storytelling tool; adds a lot of restraints on how we can light, direct, and shoot audio and video; puts huge demands on streaming bandwidth; and requires special hardware to really get the full VR experience, VR is still gaining popularity fast.

When you start editing 360-degree VR, you will bump into new words and terms like *equirectangular video* (Adobe has a good explanation at blogs.adobe.com/creativecloud/working-with-immersive-vr-video), *ambisonics Audio* (see Wikipedia: en.wikipedia.org/wiki/Ambisonics), *head-mounted display* (Wikipedia again: en.wikipedia.org/wiki/Head-mounted_display), and *true north*. Don't worry–it's not hard once you try it.

In Premiere, you can work with stitched equirectangular video, watch the footage in a VR viewer environment while editing (Figure 9-1), and export VR tagged video for YouTube, Facebook, Vimeo, and other destinations. Premiere automatically detects if the media is monoscopic or stereoscopic over/under or left/right.

Figure 9-1. *Footage from 360° Star Wars, The Great Escape, courtesy of Charbel Koussaifi, charbel.work*

Before You Edit

If you get your hands on some 360/VR material, it will most likely not be ready for editing. If you have video files from several cameras in a VR rig, these need to be merged into one VR clip before you can edit them in Premiere. This procedure is called *stitching*, and Premiere does not do stitching.

© Jarle Leirpoll 2017
J. Leirpoll et al., *The Cool Stuff in Premiere Pro*, DOI 10.1007/978-1-4842-2890-6_9

Stitching

A 360-degree camera rig can have anywhere from 2 to 6, 12, or more camera angles (Figure 9-2). These cameras/angles will be recorded as separate video files. You can't just import these files into Premiere and get VR video–they need to be stitched first.

Figure 9-2. *The GoPro Omni Sync Rig holds six cameras, pointing in all directions*

Stitching is the process of merging all the different camera angles in a 360-degree camera rig into one 360-degree equirectangular video file. Some 360-degree cameras will do the stitching in-camera, and some will provide a stitching app. There are also more-advanced stitching apps like Autopano Video from Kolor/GoPro (kolor.com/autopano-video/) and VideoStitch Studio from Orah (orah.co/software/videostitch-studio/).

In short, you import your 360-degree video angles recordings to the stitching app and export as an equirectangular video that Premiere can interpret as VR video. Stitching is outside the scope of this book.

Filling the Nadir Hole

Say what? The *nadir hole* is the region at the bottom of the 360-degree sphere where either the camera rig can't see or, if it does, just sees the tripod. In some productions, it's OK to see the tripod, but in others it must be removed.

Here's a tutorial that explains how to patch the nadir hole using After Effects and the Mettle SkyBox Studio plugin: youtube.com/watch?v=gUM5Dkx9h_0.

Consider Using UltraPix for Auto-Proxy

360-degree VR editing takes a lot of computer power. You're dealing with 4K or 8K material, even though the part of it that you see at any given time is smaller. To push all those pixels through your system, you either need a super-high-end system or a clever codec. JPEG2000 is a very clever codec. It uses Wavelet encoding (see Wikipedia: en.wikipedia.org/wiki/Wavelet_transform), and you can easily and instantly switch between full or lower resolutions while editing.

Comprimato UltraPix provides GPU acceleration of JPEG2000 codec in an MXF container. They claim to have the world's fastest JPEG2000 encoder/decoder, and it really is fast, as it uses both the GPU and the CPU for encoding and decoding. Find out more here: comprimato.com/products/ultrapix/.

■ Note   If you save your 8K VR videos in this format after stitching, you will have a very high-quality master file with 8K, 4K, HD, and SD resolutions in one single file.

VR Video Settings in Premiere

Premiere reads VR tags in metadata for some formats, and it also has some built-in interpretation rules for VR based on frame sizes.

Source Clip Settings

The VR properties of imported clips are probably OK, since Premiere will auto-detect if the footage is monoscopic or stereoscopic and so forth.

VR properties are automatically assigned to clips when VR properties are present in the clip metadata. If there are no VR properties in the metadata, the importer detects, based on frame dimensions, if it's a VR clip. The auto-detection is limited to specific frame heights of 960, 1920, 2048, 2880, 4096, 5760, 6000, and 8192.

If the frame size dimensions are 1:1, the clip is interpreted to be stereoscopic over/under VR.

If the dimensions are 2:1, the clip is interpreted as monoscopic VR.

If the dimensions are 4:1, the clip is interpreted as stereoscopic side-by-side VR.

If the file is not tagged and interpreted correctly, you can change the properties in the **Clip ➤ Modify ➤ Interpret Footage** dialog seen in Figure 9-3).

Figure 9-3.   *VR modify clip settings*

759

Enable VR in the Sequence

If you create a new sequence from a VR clip, the sequence will automatically get the correct VR properties. If you create your sequence manually, you'll need to do the VR settings manually in **Sequence ➤ Sequence Settings** (Figure 9-4).

Figure 9-4. VR sequence settings

These settings need to be correct, since the source and program monitors' settings options for VR Video are disabled when a sequence that does not have VR properties is viewed.

Source and Program Monitors' Settings for VR video

Both the source monitor and the program monitor can play back VR video. They also have the same set of VR settings and choices available in their wrench menus (Figure 9-5).

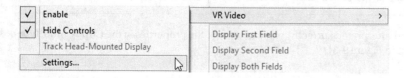

Figure 9-5. The source and program monitors have VR video choices

To navigate around in VR mode, use the sliders along the right and lower edges of the frame, adjust the blue numbers, or click and drag in the frame. If you've ever played VR on YouTube, Facebook, Vimeo, and so forth, you'll have no problem using the controls.

You can enable the VR video display mode in several ways. If you've added the *Toggle VR Video Display* button (Figure 9-6) to your button row under the program monitor, just click it so it turns blue. You can also use the wrench menu in the program monitor, and choose **VR Video ➤ Enable**. Or, create a keyboard shortcut for *Toggle VR Video Display*. Figure 9-7 shows the available keyboard shortcuts for VR.

Figure 9-6. Toggle VR Video Display button

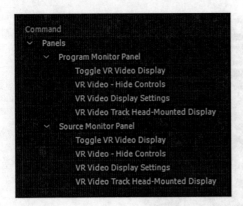

Figure 9-7. *Available keyboard shortcuts for VR in source and program monitors*

By default, Premiere will show VR controls alongside the image in the program monitor (Figure 9-8). If you choose to hide these VR Controls, you will get a much larger image (Figure 9-9). You can still pan around by dragging in the image, but you lose the numbers that indicate in which direction you're looking.

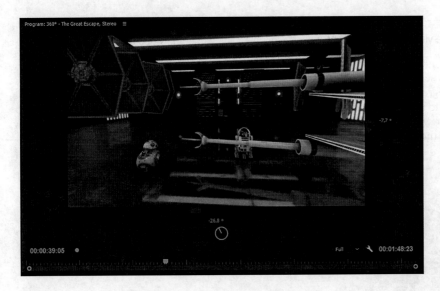

Figure 9-8. *VR controls in program monitor showing*

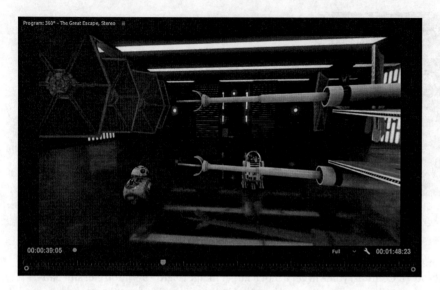

Figure 9-9. VR controls in program monitor hidden

■ **Note**   To center the view and get back to true north, double-click within the video frame in the monitor.

The Monitor View settings in the VR Video Settings dialog determine how much you see of the whole image, measured in degrees, horizontally and vertically. Set to 160 × 90 if you want to match YouTube (Figure 9-10), 180 × 90 to match Vimeo, and 90 × 60 to match the Oculus Rift. The info on this is sparse, so do some tests and compare with your target viewer to make sure your settings are accurate. These Monitor View settings are saved with the project.

Figure 9-10. VR Video Settings dialog

You often need to see a localized view and a global view simultaneously to edit in context. Say you want to create a title inside your footage; you'll discover that the graphics tools do not work when the program monitor is in VR viewing mode. So, you need an extra viewer to see the text in place while you're typing and placing it.

I use the source monitor as my second viewer. Just open the same sequence in the source monitor as in the program monitor, and you have both localized view and global view (Figure 9-11).

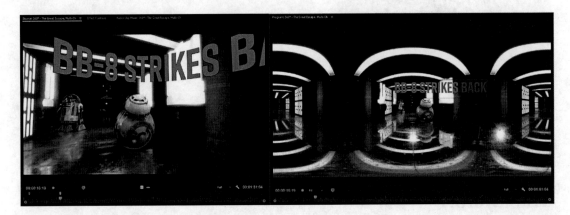

Figure 9-11. *The Type tool doesn't work with VR viewing mode, so I open the sequence in the source monitor to see the text in context while editing it*

Track Your VR Headset

If you have a VR headset (aka HMD), tick the *Track Head-Mounted Display* feature in the VR Video menu to watch everything in true VR while editing. This option gets highlighted only when you install a VR headset (Figures 9-12 and 9-13) along with supporting plug-ins, such as Mettle for Premiere Pro.

Figure 9-12. *HTC Vive VR Headset. Image courtesy of HTC.*

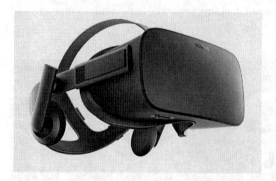

Figure 9-13. *Oculus Rift VR Headset. Image courtesy of Oculus.*

VR Players

There are some free VR players that you can use in Premiere. You may wonder why you'd want an extra VR player when Premiere has built-in VR viewing in two monitors (the reference monitor does not have VR viewing).

Sometimes you need three views of the same sequence! Say you want your new text to look like a previous one in the same sequence (or another one)–then you need two monitors to edit the text and watch it simultaneously, plus another monitor to see the previous text (Figure 9-14).

Figure 9-14. *Footage from 360° Star Wars, The Great Escape, courtesy of Charbel Koussaifi, charbel.work*

With an extra player, you don't have to constantly toggle the program monitor VR view on and off. To enable the VR player, first select *Enable Mercury Transmit* in the Playback preferences (Figure 9-15).

Figure 9-15. *You enable the VR players by first enabling Mercury Transmit in the Playback preferences*

Mettle Skybox VR Player

The Mettle Skybox VR Player (Figure 9-16) can be used as a third VR viewer, and it also supports Oculus Rift and HTC Vive VR headsets.

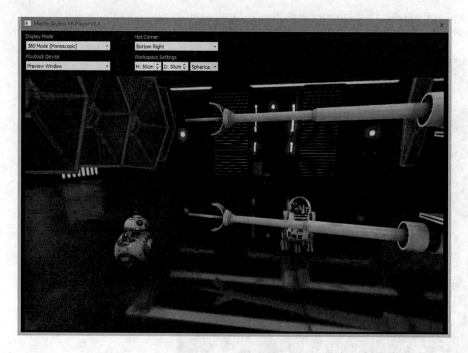

Figure 9-16. *VR Mettle Player 360 Mode*

The Workspace mode in the Mettle SkyBox VR Player lets you see your computer screen(s) in your head-mounted display, so you don't have to take it off to see what you're doing (Figure 9-17). You can switch from Workspace mode to 360-degree mode by placing your cursor in the "hot corner" of your display. You can decide which corner is the "hot" one. The Workspace mode even includes a virtual keyboard.

Figure 9-17. *The Workspace mode in the Mettle SkyBox VR player. Footage from Hawaii 360 video courtesy of Matt Givot.*

You can scroll within the image to move along the Z-axis, and to recenter the Rift's orientation, press **Spacebar** with the SkyBox VR Player window selected.

At the time of writing, the Mettle VR Player can be found at `mettle.com/product/skybox-vr-player/`. But since Adobe has now acquired Mettle, the VR tools will soon be included in the Creative Cloud subscription.

GoPro VR Player

The GoPro VR Player plug-in for Adobe Premiere Pro also supports Oculus Rift and HTC Vive VR headsets. It has more VR projection modes (GoPro VR, Rectilinear, Little Planet, Fisheye) than the Mettle SkyBox VR Player has, but I have never felt the need for all of them.

The user interface is even more minimalistic than that in the SkyBox player (Figure 9-18), and unlike the former, the GoPro VR Player has a *Minimize* button that comes in handy when you want to hide it away.

Figure 9-18. *The GoPro VR player has a very minimalistic UI*

As with the SkyBox player, you can scroll in the image to zoom in and out, but you can also zoom with the + and – keys.

To go full screen, double-click the image. To reset camera orientation to zero, hit **Z**. To move camera up/down/left/right, use the **Arrow keys**.

See more at kolor.com/gopro-vr-player/download/.

Effects for VR Video

The built-in effects for VR in Premiere are limited. A major player on the third-party market is Mettle. They offer great tools for VR editing in Premiere, and I can't imagine anyone doing serious VR editing in Premiere without their plug-ins. That's probably why Adobe recently acquired Mettle. That's good news, since we'll now get these plugins for free! Let's have a look at both the built-in ones and the ones from Mettle.

The VR Projection Effect

In the early days of VR in Premiere, we used the super simple offset effect to pan the footage (Figure 9-19), but the newer VR projection effect is a lot more flexible and offers three-axis rotation for VR (Figure 9-20). It has pan, tilt, and toll, and it shows the properties in degrees, not pixel values. Pan and tilt are often used to control the focus of the audience. The roll could be used to induce nausea, but it's better to make it correct the zero angle–to adjust for improper camera placement.

Figure 9-19. *Offset effect*

768

Figure 9-20. *VR projection effect*

As a bonus, the VR projection effect also offers conversion between monoscopic, stereoscopic L/R, and stereoscopic over/under, allowing for the mix and match of different resolutions and stereoscopic/ monoscopic layouts in the same sequence.

The VR projection effect ties in nicely with the ambisonics panner effect for VR audio to control the point of interest.

Like the offset effect, the VR projection effect is GPU accelerated, so with a modern GPU you could get real-time performance.

You will use this effect to change the point of interest–and to animate it. It's not just a technical tool; it's for storytelling! This effect is great if you want to make sure your viewer is looking at the right part of the image before you do transitions. Combine a pan with audio cues to make sure the audience looks were you want them to.

Avoid Effects That Affect the Edges

All the traditional effects that affect the edges will sometimes fail in VR. You will see the edge in the 180° position, where the left and right edges of the equirectangular frame meet. Figures 9-21 and 9-22 show how the standard Gaussian blur looks when applied to VR footage. The same problem will show up with sharpen, glow, and de-noise effects.

Figure 9-21. *With* many *of the traditional effects, you will see the seam in the VR footage*

Figure 9-22. *Repeat edges in the Gaussian blur effect makes the edge less visible, but it's still not right*

■ **Note**   Transformational effects like position, scale, rotation, and the warp stabilizer will also fail with 360-degree footage, as the edges will get all messed up.

But fear not—help is near! You can use the effects from the Mettle SkyBox 360/VR tools instead of the built-in ones, and everything will work as expected.

Mettle SkyBox 360/VR Tools

This is an essential plug-in collection if you're serious about editing 360-degree video in Premiere. It has 360 Post FX that were designed for 360-degree footage, and they are all seamless when applied. All the effects are mono and stereo compatible, as well as GPU accelerated in the Mercury Playback Engine (Figure 9-23).

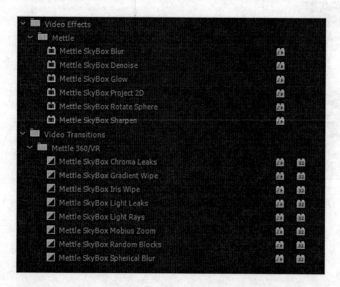

Figure 9-23. *Mettle SkyBox effects*

770

■ **Note**   Since Adobe has now acquired Mettle, the plug-ins will soon be part of the Premiere Pro installation. Read this blog post to find out how you can get the plug-ins for free before the next update: `blogs.adobe.com/creativecloud/the-latest-and-greatest-in-vr/`.

Figure 9-24 shows the Mettle SkyBox blur on the same footage as previously, and it has no visible seams!

Figure 9-24. *SkyBox blur. No seams!*

SkyBox Blur, Glow, Sharpen, and Denoise

The choice of effects in the plug-ins may seem random at first, but these are all essential tools in VR.

There's often lots of noise in VR footage because of low light. You can't hide the lighting anywhere! So, denoise and sharpen are important before compressing the VR video and uploading to YouTube and other VR web viewers. You can use these on adjustment layers.

The blur and glow effects are as popular in VR as in other films, both for controlling attention and for fun–and the ones in this plug-in collection are of course seamless.

SkyBox Rotate Sphere

This works very much like the built-in VR projection effect in Premiere, except it has an *Invert Rotation* checkbox (Figure 9-25).

Figure 9-25. *SkyBox Rotate Sphere*

360/VR Transitions

A lot of traditional video transitions will fail miserably in VR. The Mettle SkyBox 360/VR Tools offer eight transitions that work well. These are Chroma Leaks, Gradient Wipe (create your own gradients to make custom transitions!), Iris Wipe, Light Leaks, Light Rays, Mobius Zoom, Random Blocks, and Spherical Blur.

Like the SkyBox effects, the SkyBox transitions are also 360/VR aware and will be seamless.

All of these look cool, but, more important, they can be used as good storytelling tools, giving the audience cues to look in a special direction before a scene change and so forth. There are both technical and narrative reasons for effects and transitions.

The SkyBox Iris Wipe (Figure 9-26) can influence the gaze and make people look there. The SkyBox Gradient Wipe (Figure 9-28) is extremely customizable. You can use the built-in presets or create your own gradients in Photoshop. You can assign a video track as the gradient, even a duplicate of one layer. The SkyBox Mobius Zoom (Figure 9-32) is like a 3D zoom. You can also change point of interest with this one.

Figure 9-26. SkyBox Iris Wipe

Most of these transitions have XYZ controls, so you can make sure you're leading the gaze to the right area. Figures 9-26 to 9-34 show the settings available in the Mettle effects.

Figure 9-27. SkyBox Chroma Leaks

Figure 9-28. SkyBox Gradient Wipe

Abstract1.png
Abstract2.png
Abstract3.png
Abstract4.png
Box.png
Circles.png
Default.png
Fire.png
METTLE
MettleText.png
Noise1.png
Noise2.png

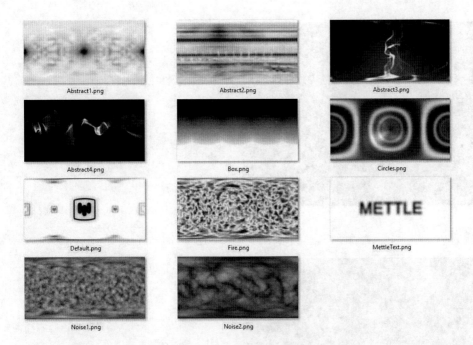

Figure 9-29. *These gradients come with the SkyBox Gradient Wipe, but you can also make your own in Photoshop*

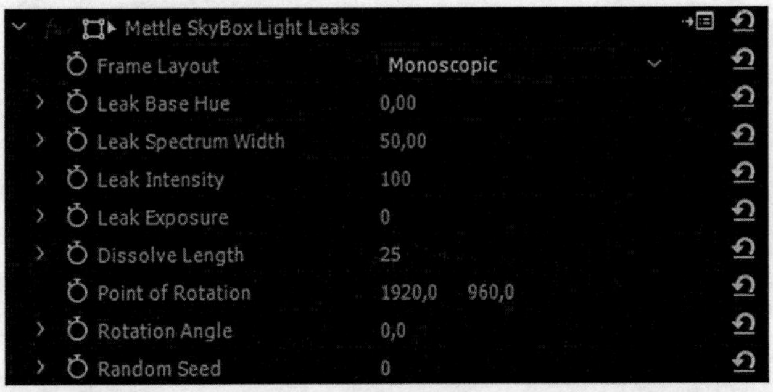

Mettle SkyBox Light Leaks
Frame Layout
Monoscopic
Leak Base Hue
0,00
Leak Spectrum Width
50,00
Leak Intensity
100
Leak Exposure
0
Dissolve Length
25
Point of Rotation
1920,0
960,0
Rotation Angle
0,0
Random Seed
0

Figure 9-30. *SkyBox Light Leaks*

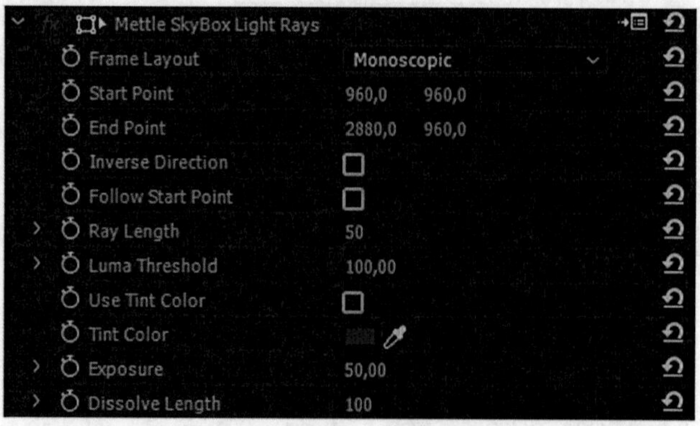

Figure 9-31. SkyBox Light Rays

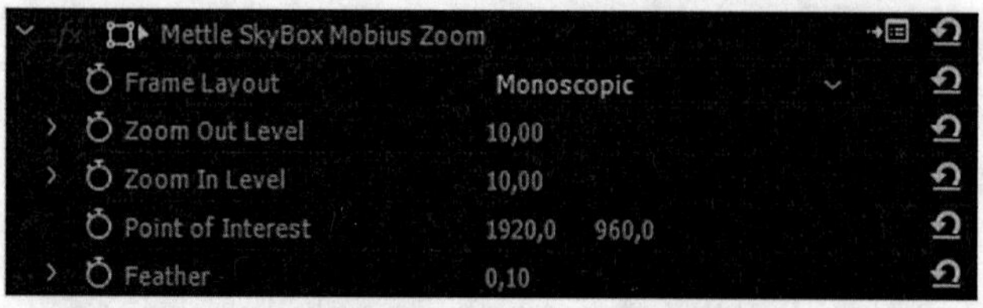

Figure 9-32. SkyBox Mobius Zoom

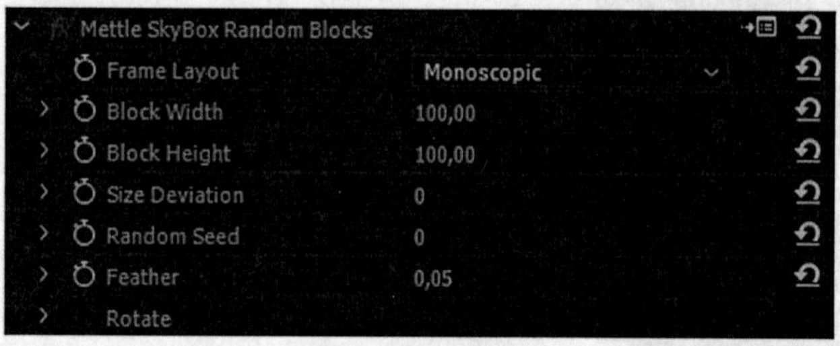

Figure 9-33. SkyBox Random Blocks

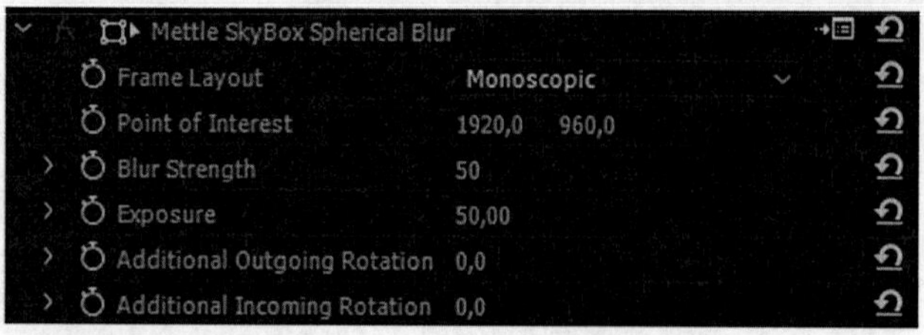

Figure 9-34. SkyBox Spherical Blur

If you want to try the Mettle plug-ins, you can get a free trial at mettle.com/free-demo/. To watch the Mettle SkyBox 360/VR transitions in action, watch these two videos on YouTube: youtube.com/watch?v=AN2DH4mOOWk and youtube.com/watch?v=jjv3ZKDx5eQ. As mentioned earlier, these plug-ins will soon be part of your Creative Cloud subscription.

Use 360° Footage in a Standard HD Production

Using the SkyBox Viewer from Mettle, you can convert equirectangular 360-degree format to HD flat video in After Effects. Create an HD comp (**Ctrl/Cmd+N**) and throw the 360-degree footage in. It will be much larger than the HD comp, and straight lines will be curved (Figures 9-35 and 9-36).

Figure 9-35. *The VR footage is much larger than the HD comp*

Figure 9-36. *This is how the image looks now. The lights in the ceiling should not be curved*

Add the SkyBox viewer effect to the clip, set input format to Equirectangular, and adjust Output Frame Width and Output Frame Ratio to fit your HD comp settings (Figure 9-37).

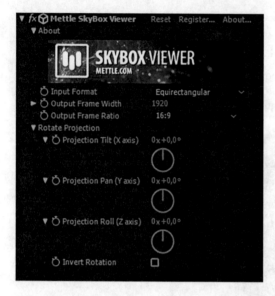

Figure 9-37. *VR in HD SkyBox Viewer*

Now, add an After Effects camera (**Layer ➤ New ➤ Camera**) and choose one of the wide-angle presets. I used the 15mm preset in my example. Now, you can use the Unified Camera tool to pan and scan around in the 360-degree footage, or adjust the Rotate Projection parameters in the SkyBox viewer. Zoom with the Track Z Camera tool or by adjusting the zoom parameter on the camera (Figures 9-38 and 9-39). You can toggle between different camera tools in After Effects by hitting **C**.

Figure 9-38. *Camera zoom set to wide angle (128.3° horizontal)*

Figure 9-39. *Camera zoom set to 100.4° horizontal*

If you want this HD comp in Premiere, just import it to Premiere and enjoy the Dynamic Link integration.

VR Graphics

We need to add text and graphics to our VR videos, but if you add a text or a logo to the VR timeline, they get spherical and look strange–especially when we move them (Figure 9-40, left). Here's where the project 2D effect from Skybox 360 VR tools comes to good use.

Figure 9-40. *2D graphics in a VR sequence are spherical in the VR view (to the left), which does not look right*

Just add Mettle Skybox project 2D to texts or graphics, and they straighten (Figure 9-40, right). You still have a yellow render bar in Premiere, which is great. Figures 9-41 and 9-42 show how text and graphics look in VR when the SkyBox project 2D effect is added.

Figure 9-41. *With the SkyBox project 2D effect, it looks straight and correct in the VR view (to the left)*

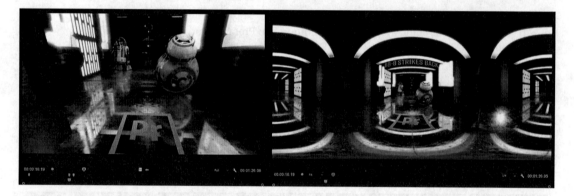

Figure 9-42. *Logos and other still images (and video, of course) also look correct in the VR view (to the left) when we use the SkyBox project 2D effect*

Grading 360-degree VR Video

To work with masks in 360-degree video, you must turn off the VR view in the program monitor, just like when working with graphics (Figure 9-43). Well, actually, it is possible to draw masks in the VR view, but they will be distorted, and you won't be able to trace anything.

Figure 9-43. *This is the correct mask (in VR view) to trace around the floor. Stick to the standard view so you can see what you're doing.*

Draw your masks in the equirectangular image in the program monitor and use a VR player or the source monitor to view the result as you do adjustments in the Lumetri Color panel (Figures 9-44 and 9-45).

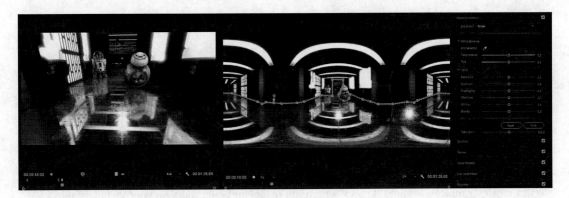

Figure 9-44. *Draw your masks with VR view off. Footage from 360° Star Wars, The Great Escape, courtesy of Charbel Koussaifi, charbel.work.*

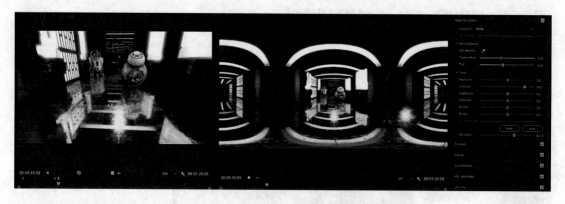

Figure 9-45. Result after adjustments with mask. The floor is now darker.

Ambisonics Audio

Ambi means "on both sides" and also "all around," and *sonic* means "audio," so ambisonics just means surround sound—or sound all around you. Ambisonics sound (en.wikipedia.org/wiki/Ambisonics) is captured with a full-sphere surround sound microphone, like the TetraMic from Core Sound (Figure 9-46).

Figure 9-46. TetraMic. Image courtesy of Core Sound, core-sound.com

But ambisonics audio is not just like your old surround sound system where you watch Blu-rays and Netflix movies. Ambisonics audio "knows" where you're looking when you wear your VR headset—like Oculus Rift (oculus.com/rift) or HTC Vive (vive.com)—and the audio is panned in 360 degrees when you move your head.

To really experience ambisonics audio, you need to wear a VR headset. To just listen to it while you edit, you can also use a set of headphones.

■ **Note**   Audio is very important in VR video. In real life, we tend to hear things before we see them. If you're walking down the street, and a dog barks at the other side of the street, you first hear it, then you turn around to see it. When an alarm goes off, you hear it, then you turn to see the red blinking light. This is the reason we use audio splits a lot in traditional editing. In VR, we use audio cues to make people look where we want them to look.

Ambisonics Audio in Premiere

OK, so high-quality spatial sound is important. How do we deal with it in Premiere?

First, you should note that Premiere and its audio filters work with VR clips or AIFF or WAV audio files with first-order ambisonics audio streams that have four channels in ACN channel ordering (WYZX) and have SN3D normalization applied. Files in this format are typically called AmbiX files and are pretty similar to first-order B-format files, with the exception that B-format has WXYZ channel ordering as opposed to WYZX. In practice, the difference in normalization (gain) does not matter too much.

There are two audio effects available specifically for ambisonics in Premiere: the panner and the binauralizer (Figure 9-47). The panner is used on audio clips, while the binauralizer is mostly used on the master track in the Audio Track Mixer.

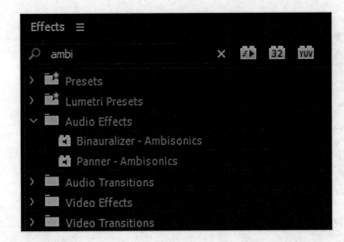

Figure 9-47. *Ambisonics Audio FX*

Placing Mono Sources in the Mix

In addition to the ambisonics audio recording taken from the camera's position, you will probably get mono sources from additional lavaliers and hidden microphones with dialogue and close-up sounds. You must decide where to place these into the mix.

Using the ambisonics panner (Figure 9-48), you can move the audio sphere in all directions to align it with the camera's true north position. This is mostly done to compensate for any offset between the camera and the microphone orientations. You could also go crazy and use the panner to generate spatial audio animations.

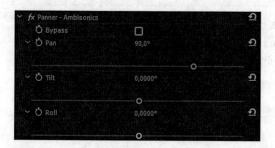

Figure 9-48. *Ambisonics panner*

■ **Note**   The panner only works on audio clips with adaptive tracks, and those require adaptive tracks in the sequence

---

This means you need to tell Premiere that the four-channel audio clips should be treated as adaptive tracks. Select all your ambisonics audio clips and hit **Shift+G** to reveal the **Clip ➤ Modify ➤Audio Channels** dialog (Figure 9-49).

Figure 9-49. *Choose adaptive tracks, four channels per clip, and one audio clip*

If you do a lot of VR editing, you may want to avoid the trouble of interpreting all your four-channel audio. You can set a default rule to interpret all multi-channel mono clips as adaptive tracks, as shown in Figure 9-50.

Figure 9-50. *Audio default tracks*

Choose Your Sequence Settings

You need a sequence with a multi-channel master track with four channels and at least one adaptive track (Figure 9-51).

Figure 9-51. *VR audio sequence settings*

To listen to the audio mix, you'll want to add the binauralizer effect in the Audio Track Mixer (Figure 9-52). This blends the four output tracks down to a two-channel binaural format. It's not normal stereo, since it represents the signal as actually experienced/heard by the listener (e.g., filtered by the head-shadow and pinna (the outer part) of each ear).

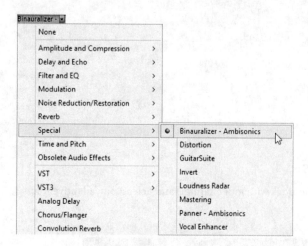

Figure 9-52. *Ambisonics–Binauralizer*

Because the binauralizer effect outputs two channels, only stereo effects can be applied after it. So, the ambisonics panner cannot be applied after the binauralizer, only before it.

The binauralizer is dependent on the listener's head position, so it also has a built-in panner with independent pan, tilt, and yaw controls.

▓ **Note**   Make sure you turn the binauralizer effect off before you export your VR video.

The ambisonics panner and binauralizer are general audio filters, so they can be applied directly to clips as well as to tracks in the track mixer. Mixing non-ambisonics with ambisonics effects may yield unpredictable results.

Where to Find Ambisonics Audio Clips

If you have never experienced ambisonics audio, you can listen to a handful of clips here: `ambisonic.xyz`. If you need clips for testing in Premiere, or some atmosphere sound for a real production, try the links here:

`shop.prosoundeffects.com/collections/ambisonics`

`ambisonic.info/tetramic/samples.html`

`ambisonictoolkit.net/download/recordings/`

`asoundeffect.com/sound-category/misc-sounds/ambisonics/`
`spheric-collection.com/`

Get VR Audio Help

Adobe has some info about using ambisonics audio in Premiere Pro on their online help pages:
`helpx.adobe.com/premiere-pro/using/VRSupport.html#main-pars_header_1711869371`

Export VR Video

VR video can be exported in H.264, HEVC, or QuickTime formats. To make sure the VR metadata is written into the file, make sure the *Video Is VR* checkbox is active and that the correct frame layout is chosen (Figure 9-53).

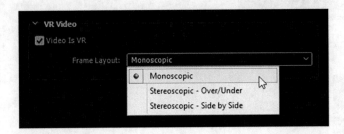

Figure 9-53. *VR Export: VR Frame Layout in Video Settings.*

I recommend using one of the VR Export presets for H.264 as a starting point. This will check the *Video Is VR* checkbox, set the scaling to *Stretch to Fill*, and enable *Ambisonics Audio* if applicable (Figures 9-54 and 9-55).

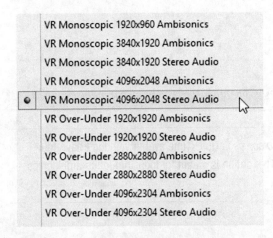

Figure 9-54. *VR Export: Presets*

Figure 9-55. *VR Export: Stretch to Fill*

To export ambisonics audio, hit the *Audio Is Ambisonics* checkbox (Figure 9-56). Ambisonics audio export (and the checkbox) is only available for H.264 and QuickTime (Figure 9-57). For ambisonics audio, you need to export four audio channels.

Figure 9-56. *VR Export: Audio Is Ambisonics*

Figure 9-57. *To enable the ambisonics audio export for AAC or QuickTime, you need four audio channels*

▓ **Note**   Beware that it's possible to check *Audio Is Ambisonics* in QuickTime even if you don't have four audio channels, but the output might *not* be ambisonics. This option is meant for loop-through of ambisonics audio. Make sure you have four channels (Figure 9-58).

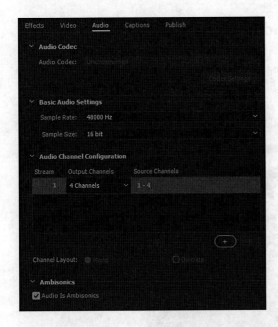

Figure 9-58. *VR Export: QuickTime four channels*

Make sure you export in a format combination that your destination supports. Facebook supports H.264 format with AAC audio. YouTube supports H.264 with AAC audio, and QuickTime with ProRes or DNxHR HQ (8-bit) and Uncompressed audio.

Here are the recommended settings from Facebook: facebook.com/facebookmedia/get-started/360/#recommended-video-upload-specs

Check Your Video Before You Upload It

I like to check my VR video quality in a VR player before I publish it (Figure 9-59). If you want to live dangerously, use the *Publish* settings in the Export dialog to automatically upload the file when the export is done and skip the quality control.

Figure 9-59. *Test the exported video in a VR video player before you upload it*

Upload!

If the file works OK in the VR player, you can upload it to any service that supports 360-degree VR video. Since the VR checkboxes are all set by the export presets, the VR metadata will be baked in. Vimeo, Facebook, and YouTube will recognize the metadata (Figure 9-60) and display the video in 360/VR. Figures 9-61 and 9-62 are screenshots from Vimeo.

Upload complete! | 360 detected

Figure 9-60. *Vimeo has found 360/VR metadata*

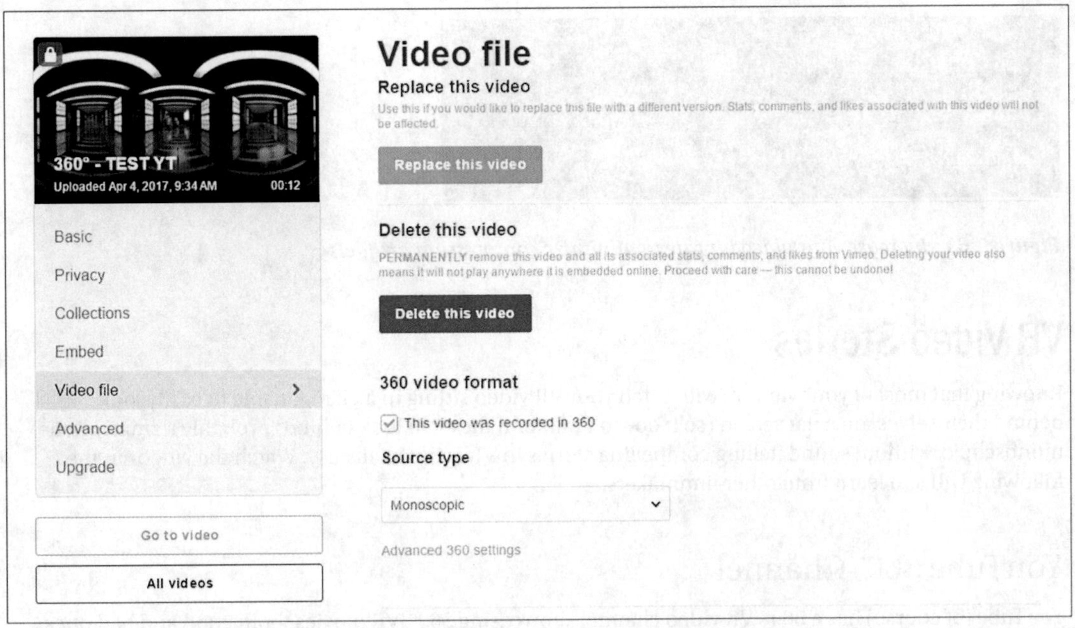

Video file

Replace this video

Use this if you would like to replace this file with a different version. Stats, comments, and likes associated with this video will not be affected.

    Replace this video

Delete this video

PERMANENTLY remove this video and all its associated stats, comments, and likes from Vimeo. Deleting your video also means it will not play anywhere it is embedded online. Proceed with care — this cannot be undone!

    Delete this video

360 video format

☑ This video was recorded in 360

Source type

    Monoscopic   ⌄

Advanced 360 settings

Basic
Privacy
Collections
Embed
Video file   >
Advanced
Upgrade

    Go to video

    All videos

360° - TEST YT
Uploaded Apr 4, 2017, 9:34 AM   00:12

Figure 9-61. *Basic VR settings in Vimeo*

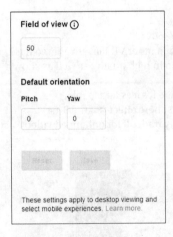

Field of view ⓘ

    50

Default orientation

Pitch   Yaw

    0   0

    Reset   Save

These settings apply to desktop viewing and select mobile experiences. Learn more.

Figure 9-62. *Advanced VR settings in Vimeo have settings for default field of view and orientation*

If the VR video gets artifacts after you've uploaded it, adding Mettle SkyBox denoise and sharpen effects may be necessary to fight the noise, especially in low-light scenes. Noise has a severe impact on video quality. You should also increase the bit depth. Facebook recommends bit rates up to 150 mbps for H.264 if necessary (Figure 9-63).

Bitrate Settings

Bitrate Encoding:	VBR, 1 pass	⌄
Target Bitrate [Mbps]:	———O———————	80
Maximum Bitrate [Mbps]:	——————O——————	150

Figure 9-63. *Increase your video bit rate to minimize compression artifacts*

VR Video Stories

Knowing that most of your viewers will watch your VR video sitting in a chair, unable to easily look behind themselves, on a flat screen (so it doesn't matter if they can look behind) probably a smartphone, monoscopic, without sound, telling compelling stories in VR is not at all easy. Watch the videos in the following URLs to learn from other filmmakers.

YouTube 360° Channel

YouTube (of course) has a 360°/VR video channel showcasing 360°/VR movies–both good and bad ones: youtube.com/channel/UCzuqhhs6NWbgTzMuMO9WKDQ.

Vimeo 360° Cinema

Vimeo (of course) also has a 360°/VR video channel: vimeo.com/channels/360vr.

Be aware, though, that your VR video will look different on Vimeo than in other VR Players. Vimeo has chosen a default field of view that's pretty wide, so they can render the video in high quality as well as show a large portion of the frame.

Most 360-degree players show distortion on the sides of the video, where it's less noticeable. In an effort to eliminate overall distortion, Vimeo has chosen to accept the sphere effect (Figure 9-64). According to Vimeo support, they decided that "the sphere effect is a worthy tradeoff for enhanced video quality all around."

Figure 9-64. *Default view on Vimeo for 360-degree VR video*

But then, in the full-screen view they crop off the sides, so when you fill your screen with pixels, they choose to show a narrower view of the full 360-degree sphere (Figure 9-65). My guess is that their player will change and be more like other VR players.

Figure 9-65. *Full-screen view on Vimeo for 360-degree VR video*

360° Star Wars, The Great Escape VR 4K

Lebanese film maker Charbel Koussaifi made a nice 360-degree short movie using the free Star Wars model pack from Video Copilot (videocopilot.net/blog/2016/05/free-star-wars-model-pack/). Watch the film at youtube.com/watch?v=-segJswzIZw (Figure 9-66) and see more of his work at charbel.work. This movie was used in a lot of screen dumps in this chapter.

Figure 9-66. *Footage from 360° Star Wars, The Great Escape, courtesy of Charbel Koussaifi, charbel.work.*

Hawaii: The Pace of Formation 360—in 8K

Matt Givot, CEO at Givot Media, shot some beautiful scenery in Hawaii in 8K VR (Figure 9-67). This film too has been used in screenshots in this chapter. Visit Matt's web pages at `mattgivot.com`. Watch the film in glorious 8K on YouTube: `youtube.com/watch?v=c858UGeCeG4` or in 4K on Vimeo: `vimeo.com/203191496`.

Figure 9-67. Footage from Hawaii. The Pace of Formation 360, courtesy of Matt Givot.

They even made a non-VR companion film: `vimeo.com/202955663`. I can't help but think that it looks a lot better than the 360-degree version. It's a great idea to make both a traditional film with close-ups and traditional cutting and a VR experience version. The best of both worlds!

You can watch more of Matt's work on his Vimeo channel: `vimeo.com/tmatthewgivot`.

Summary

Storytelling in 360-degree VR is still a huge challenge. Let's hope VR soon grows out of the "experience" state that it's currently in so editors can do more narrative choices and not just technical choices.

Premiere already has the tools that enable you to make professional 360-degree VR video, especially if you use the VR tools from Mettle. So, if you can find a good way to tell stories using VR, Premiere will not stop you.

Good luck with your 360-degree VR endeavors!

CHAPTER 10

■ ■■ ■

Customizing Premiere Pro

By Jarle Leirpoll and Paul Murphy

Editing is just a continuous series of thousands of small tasks, and the more of these you can automate, the more efficient your workflow will be. Small savings on every task add up to significant savings when doing so many operations daily. Unless you're paid by the hour, you'll want to work as efficiently as possible.

Thankfully, there are many different ways to customize Premiere and eliminate these tasks, or at the very least, minimize the time they take. The default settings are just that, and it's well worth looking at your own workflow and considering where you can save time. It can be as simple as customizing the appearance of Premiere to maximize screen space, creating presets and custom keyboard shortcuts to reduce the number of clicks per task, or making template projects where a lot of the setup work that comes with every new project has already been done. If you factor in your Creative Cloud settings, you can customize Premiere not just for one machine, but for every machine you log into, wherever it is. For the more advanced user, you can even hack Premiere's system files to customize it beyond anything you could possibly do inside the software itself.

These are just a few examples, but the possibilities for customizing Premiere are far-reaching, and we're going to cover as many as we can. Be warned: this is a very lengthy chapter, but the time you spend reading it will be rewarded with time you save on editing!

Sync Settings

Basically, Sync Settings synchronize the contents of your Profile folder and the same (hidden) folder in your personal cloud storage on Adobe's servers. The folder shown in Figure 10-1 is located at **Documents\Adobe\Premiere Pro\11.0\Profile-CreativeCloud-[Adobe ID]**, and on Mac it's **Users/[User]/Documents/Adobe/Premiere Pro/11.0/Profile-[Adobe ID]**.

Name	^	Date Modified	Size	Kind
Adobe Premiere Pro Prefs		Yesterday, 7:45 AM	175 KB	TextEdit Document
▶ ArchivedLayouts		2/14/17, 6:40 AM	--	Folder
Effect Presets and Custom Items.prfpset		Yesterday, 6:59 AM	1.9 MB	Adobe Premie...17 Document
▶ Layouts		Yesterday, 6:59 AM	--	Folder
LocateDialog Column Settings		3/2/17, 12:39 PM	483 bytes	TextEdit Document
▶ Mac		11/5/16, 1:12 PM	--	Folder
Media Browser Provider Exception		Yesterday, 6:59 AM	435 bytes	TextEdit Document
▶ Metadata Preferences		11/5/16, 1:12 PM	--	Folder
Recent Directories		Yesterday, 6:59 AM	14 KB	TextEdit Document
▶ Settings		2/28/17, 12:51 PM	--	Folder
SharedView Column Settings		Yesterday, 6:59 AM	10 KB	TextEdit Document
▶ Styles		11/5/16, 1:12 PM	--	Folder

Figure 10-1. This folder gets synced to the Creative Cloud

© Jarle Leirpoll 2017
J. Leirpoll et al., *The Cool Stuff in Premiere Pro*, DOI 10.1007/978-1-4842-2890-6_10

I recommend that you do backups of this folder as a part of your regular backup routine. You can accidentally overwrite these files if you're not paying attention while syncing.

If someone else has used a system before you, they may have downloaded their settings, so you could click *Clear User Profile* in the Welcome dialog. This switches to the local settings, and then you can choose *Download* to get your own user profile from the server.

These items will be stored in the cloud for you: workspaces, metadata view settings, sequence presets, monitor overlays, source patcher presets, track height presets, keyboard shortcuts, preferences, effects presets and custom effects bins, recent directories.

There might be even more, and I'm sure that more custom items will be synced in future versions.

Custom Workspaces

The default workspaces are quite useful, but if you find yourself shuffling the windows and panels in Premiere around a lot, you should consider making yourself a few custom workspaces. Arrange the panels and frames the way you need them, and click **Window ➤ Workspace ➤ New Workspace**. They're super easy to make, and you can switch between them lightning fast with keyboard shortcuts.

Your custom workspaces will be hidden as XML files in **Documents\Adobe\Premiere Pro\11.0\ Profile-[Adobe ID]\Layouts (/Users/[User]/Documents/Adobe/Premiere Pro/11.0/Profile-[Adobe ID]/ Layouts)**. These files can also be distributed to all the workstations on your network in a larger facility.

The XML files get some not-very-useful names like UserWorkspace1.xml, UserWorkspace2.xml, and so on. But you can find out which workspace is what layout if you open the file and search the XML. In Figure 10-2, I've opened the file UserWorkspace5.xml in my Layouts folder, and when I search for the phrase *UserName*, the name of the layout appears just below that line. So, this is a custom-made *logging* workspace.

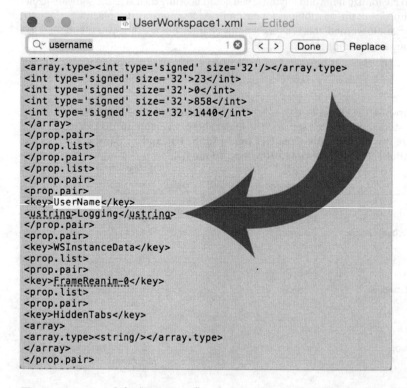

Figure 10-2. *Search for "UserName" in the XML file, and you'll find its name on the next line*

Use Clever Names for Workspaces

The workspaces are always shown in alphabetical order in **Window ➤ Workspace**, and the shortcuts are distributed in the same order. That means that if you add a workspace named *! My Workspace* (yes, with the exclamation mark) it will be the first one in the list–and it will also be workspace shortcut number one. This also means that all the other workspaces have now got new shortcuts, making it impossible to remember what shortcut is associated with what workspace.

So, I recommend using numbers when you create your workspaces, as in Figure 10-3. That way, you can decide where in the list a new workspace should live, and you will remember—and actually use—the shortcuts.

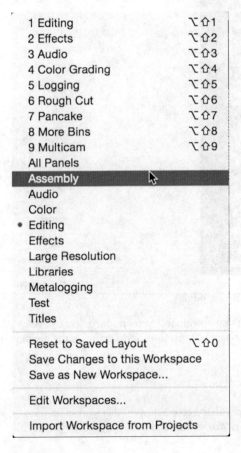

Figure 10-3. *Start names of workspaces with a number so they always get the same keyboard shortcut*

The Workspaces Panel

As well as using keyboard shortcuts to switch between shortcuts, you can use the Workspaces panel to quickly click between workspaces. If you can't see it at the top of the application window, then choose **Window ➤ Workspaces** (at the bottom of the list of panels). Any new workspaces you create will be added to this panel. You also customize which workspaces are displayed here by going to **Window ➤ Workspaces ➤ Edit Workspaces**, as seen in Figure 10-4.

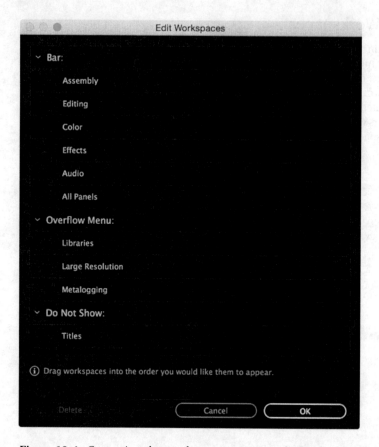

Figure 10-4. *Customize what workspaces you see via the Workspace panel*

Otherwise, if you find that the Workspaces panel is just taking up valuable screen space, you can get rid of it by right-clicking an empty portion of the panel and choosing *Close Panel* or dragging up the divider between the panel and the panel group below it.

The Fast Way to Share a Workspace

When you save a project file, it also saves the current workspace with it. You can import this workspace onto another machine by going to **Window ➤ Workspaces ➤ Import Workspace** and then opening the project file.

Tweaking the UI

Beyond the layout of your panels, there are lots of other things you can do to optimize your Premiere interface.

Hide the Title Bar

Screen real estate is precious, especially on a laptop. At the very top of the application window is the title bar, which displays the name and location of the project file you're working on. If you want to get rid of this in favor of giving more space to other panels, just use the keyboard shortcut **Ctrl+** (Cmd+\) to toggle the title bar on and off.

Get Rid of the Button Row

Similarly, you don't need the transport controls below the source and program monitors. They take up space that you could use for a taller timeline or bigger image instead (compare Figure 10-5 with 10-6). Most buttons have keyboard shortcuts anyway, and you can make some for the ones that don't—most notably, *Export Frame*.

Figure 10-5. *Transport controls waste valuable screen estate*

Figure 10-6. *Cleaner screen without transport controls*

Hidden Secrets in Panel Menus

Explore the panel menus and settings to customize each panel. Look for the little icon in the upper-left corner of most panels, and the wrench icon on the Source, Program, and Timeline panels. These have different options depending on what panel you're in. You can also use these to learn the shortcuts for some of the features in the panel. Here's a small collection.

The program monitor has options for warning about dropped frames (see Figure 10-7) and for showing a transparency grid, alpha channel, and safe margins—among lots of other stuff.

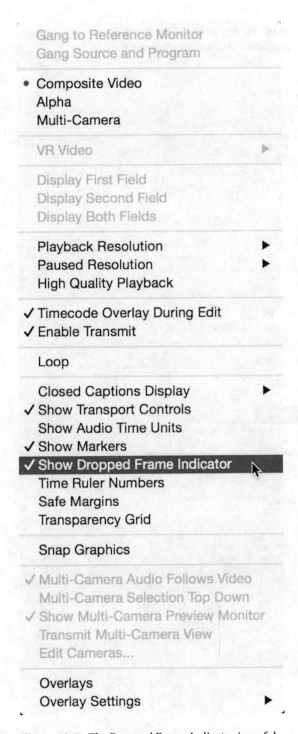

Gang to Reference Monitor
Gang Source and Program

• Composite Video
Alpha
Multi-Camera

VR Video ▶

Display First Field
Display Second Field
Display Both Fields

Playback Resolution ▶
Paused Resolution ▶
High Quality Playback

✓ Timecode Overlay During Edit
✓ Enable Transmit

Loop

Closed Captions Display ▶
✓ Show Transport Controls
Show Audio Time Units
✓ Show Markers
✓ Show Dropped Frame Indicator
Time Ruler Numbers
Safe Margins
Transparency Grid

Snap Graphics

✓ Multi-Camera Audio Follows Video
Multi-Camera Selection Top Down
✓ Show Multi-Camera Preview Monitor
Transmit Multi-Camera View
Edit Cameras...

Overlays
Overlay Settings ▶

Figure 10-7. *The Dropped Frame Indicator is useful*

The Effect Controls panel has a secret feature: Pin to Clip, shown in Figure 10-8. Unchecking this will allow you to edit keyframes before or after the clip—an invaluable time saver when needed.

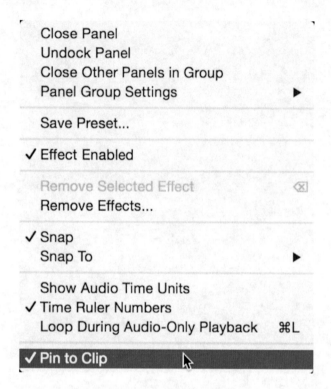

Figure 10-8. *Deselect Pin to Clip to see keyframes outside the clip's in and out points*

Did you know that the audio meters can be tweaked to show the scale you want and the kind of peaking you want, and to allow you to solo or mute audio channels as pairs or individual tracks? For these panel options, you need to right-click the panel itself, as shown in Figure 10-9.

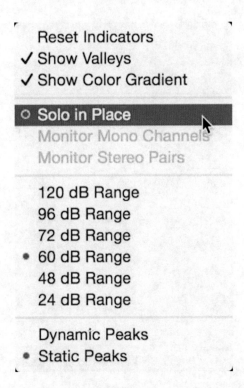

Figure 10-9. *The audio meters have some interesting options*

In the Project panel and bins, you can choose to show thumbnails even in List view, and choose *Metadata Display* to decide which columns to show and in what order (see Figure 10-10).

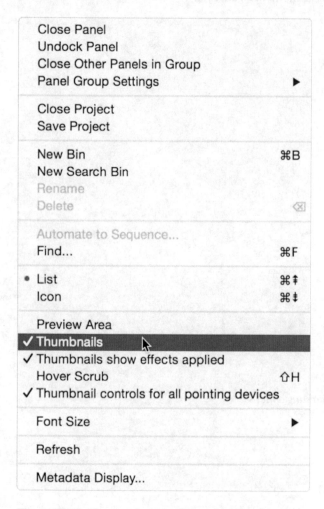

Figure 10-10. You can show small thumbnails in List view, too

Stacked Panel Groups

The classic way to display multiple panels on top of each other (what's known as a *panel group*) is by using tabs. The other way to do this is by *stacking*, which offers a bit more flexibility and space. Just click the menu of any panel in a group and choose **Panel Group Settings ➤ Stacked Panel Group,** as seen in Figure 10-11. Now the panel group becomes a vertical list of tabs, and you can click any one to expand its panel. You'll probably recognize this layout if you've used the Lumetri panel before.

The other advantage of stacked panels is that if you go to the Panel Group Settings, you can choose whether to expand only one panel at a time (*Solo Panels in Stack*) or reduce the size of the tabs.

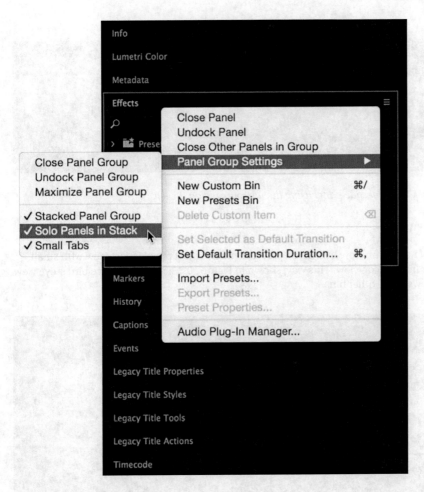

Figure 10-11. *Stacked panels offer more flexibility and space*

Dock the Timecode Panel

By default, the Timecode panel floats above the application window. It's not immediately clear how to dock this panel, since it doesn't have a tab you can drag like other panels. If you select the panel to highlight it, you'll notice there is a narrow area outlined on the left (see Figure 10-12). Just click and drag this area to dock the panel to the application window.

Figure 10-12. *You can dock the Timecode panel using the narrow area on the left*

Icon View vs. List View

Personally, I'm a big fan of having multiple bins on display, the main Project panel in List view with small thumbnails, and the other bins in Icon view. This way, shown in Figure 10-13, gives me a nice bird's-eye view and scrubbable source views in the other bins.

Figure 10-13. *I usually keep my main Project panel in List view and other bins in Icon view*

Unfortunately, these bin views you develop so carefully cannot really be saved with the workspaces, since each project will have different amounts of bins and so forth. When you have a project open and change to a new workspace, the panels will have bins in them, but it's kind of unpredictable if they will be in List view or Icon view, and what bin that will show.

In some projects, you will have only one bin, and that one will show in all your panels. It can still make sense to use two or more bin panels. Having the same bin in both Icon view and List view at the same time gives you a lot of control.

Of course, you can easily toggle between List view and Icon view with the keyboard shortcut **Shift+**. Also note that the bin views are saved with the project. So, if you start your projects from a Premiere Pro template project you can quickly get the views you want.

Thumbnail Controls

If you have a trackpad or tablet, or just prefer using a mouse, you can enable some handy controls for scrubbing and marking footage in the Project panel. Click the context menu for the panel and check *Thumbnail controls for all pointing devices* (Figure 10-14), and now you can use the onscreen icons (Figure 10-15) rather than keyboard shortcuts.

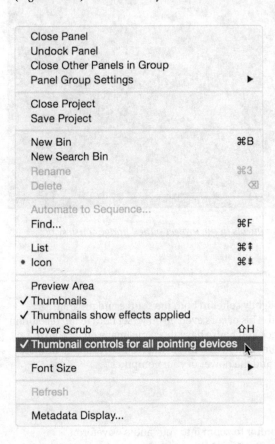

Figure 10-14. Enable thumbnail controls in the Project panel

shutterstock_v515833_1.mov   750

Figure 10-15. *Scrub and mark footage with thumbnail controls in the Project panel. Image courtesy of Shutterstock.*

High-Quality Playback

With Premiere's default settings, playback will appear slightly softer in both the source and program monitors compared to when the same footage is paused. This occurs even if you've set both to full resolution in the wrench settings. If it's important that both playback and pause have the same image quality, go to the wrench settings and check *High-Quality Playback*. Be warned that this could result in dropped frames during playback, depending on the media you're using and the power of your computer.

Zoom Your UI

Use those tiny zoom bars that you find in the source monitor to zoom into your audio waveforms (Figures 10-16a and 10-16b) so you can find out where that vacuum cleaner starts in the background, or where the little bird sings. It's important to note that although the peaks appear taller when you do this, you're not boosting the volume of the clip, only zooming in on the waveforms as a visual aid. Of course, you can also zoom in horizontally to see tiny details on the waveform by hitting + and -, or you can use the zoom bar all the way to the bottom of the monitor (Figures 10-16c and 10-16d).

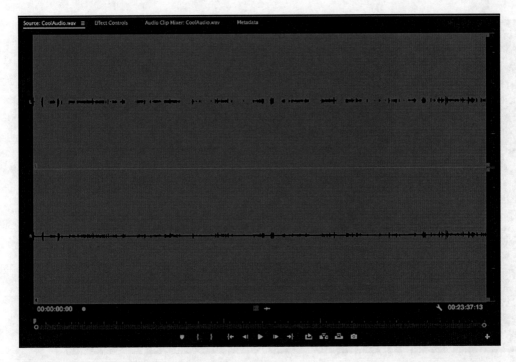

Figure 10-16a. *Zoom vertically to see waveforms better*

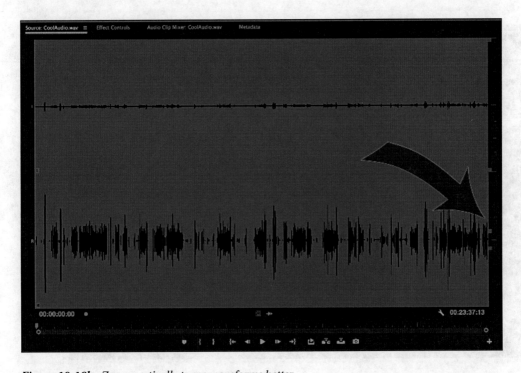

Figure 10-16b. *Zoom vertically to see waveforms better*

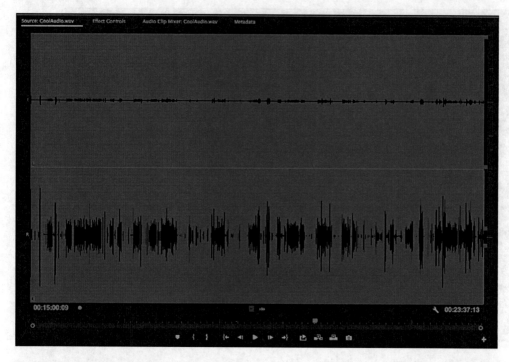

Figure 10-16c. *Zoom horizontally to see details*

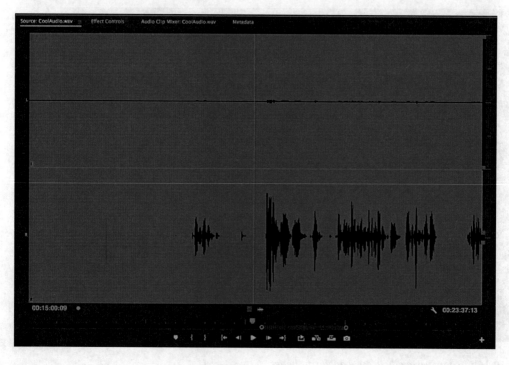

Figure 10-16d. *Zoom horizontally to see details*

The Effect Controls panel (ECP) also needs to be tweaked to fit the task at hand. Need more space to read the parameter names in your effect? Get rid of the mini timeline in the ECP, as shown in Figures 10-17a and 10-17b.

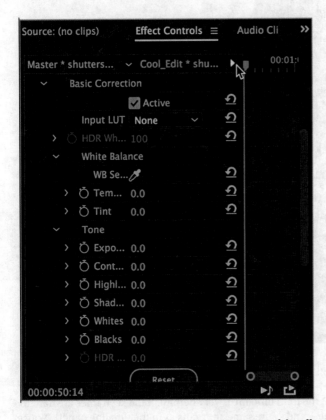

Figure 10-17a. *Hide the mini timeline to see more of the effect parameters*

Figure 10-17b. *Hide the mini timeline to see more of the effect parameters*

When working with keyframes in the ECP, the mini timeline is very helpful. If the keyframes are hard to see, just zoom in to the mini timeline by hitting + and – (the same shortcuts as in the timeline panel). Notice the difference before and after in Figures 10-18a and 10-18b.

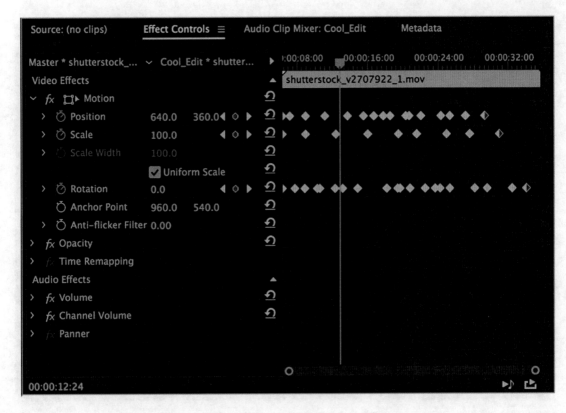

Figure 10-18a. *Zoom in to see keyframes that are close*

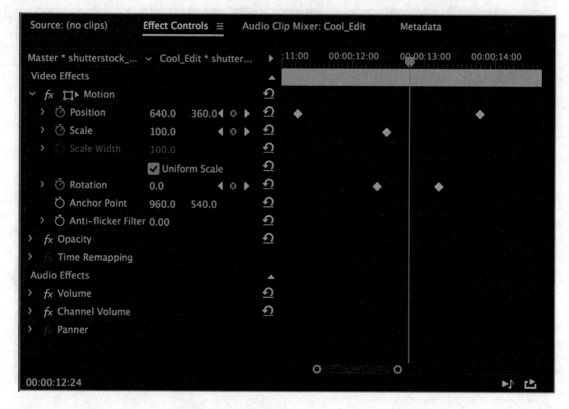

Figure 10-18b. *Zoom in to see keyframes that are close*

The same rules apply to the main timeline window; please don't fiddle with tiny little clips on the timeline while doing minute adjustments to edit points, keyframes, or clip placement! Moving your mouse a millimeter will move the clip many frames, and you'll struggle with every little adjustment.

Instead, zoom in both vertically and horizontally to see everything clearly, and moving the mouse four millimeters will just move the clip one frame. Perfect little tweaks are suddenly extremely easy to do.

Scale Your UI

If you have a very high-res monitor or retina display screen, the UI elements can feel very small. In this case, you have the option to scale up the entire UI so that all text and icons become bigger. This also applies to Premiere, with the exception of the old audio plug-ins, which may not scale properly, and some controls that may also be obscured in the Effect dialog box.

Customize the Media Browser

Editors often have a lot of media files in many different folders stored on different drives. Don't waste time clicking your way through the hierarchy every time you need to import media. Add your most used folders and drives to the Favorites list (see Figures 10-19a and 10-19b) to get immediate access to them.

Figure 10-19a. *The media browser's Favorites list is a timesaver*

Figure 10-19b. *Quick access to folders you often grab material from*

Custom Metadata Columns in Media Browser

The media browser is great in Thumbnail view, but if you switch to List view, you get additional options for sorting your material, such as by date created, frame size, and video compressor. Select *Edit Columns* in the Media Browser panel menu to choose columns and order, as seen in Figures 10-20a and 10-20b. The views are stored with each Directory Viewer setting.

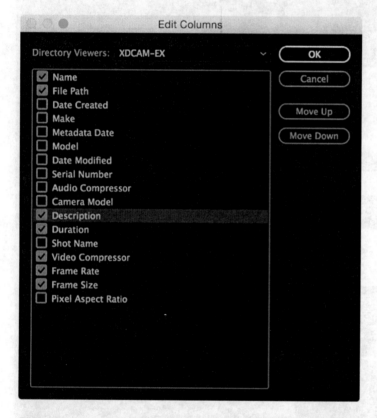

Figure 10-20a. *Metadata views are stored per Directory Viewer setting. These are the settings I use for XDCAM-EX.*

Figure 10-20b. *Here, we're viewing a P2 directory, showing other columns than the XDCAM-EX viewer. Note that the Pixel Aspect Ratio column is showing.*

The changes you do here are stored in the file named SharedView Column Settings in your Profile folder. This means they're global changes and are not stored in your workspaces, project file, or preferences.

Don't forget the Search field in the media browser. Want to see the voiceover files only? Search for them and filter out everything else—assuming your voiceover files are named *Voiceover*, of course. Note that the Search field remembers your latest searches, so you can just enter the first few letters and then hit the **Arrow** key to go down to the one you want.

This ability to see the metadata is yet another reason I prefer the media browser over the **File ➤ Import** feature. Sorting and searching metadata fields makes it a lot easier to select your media—especially in huge folders.

Custom Labels

The default label names aren't very helpful. They do describe the colors, but names like Cerulean and Lavender don't mean much while editing. Why not change them to more editing-related names, like B-roll, Interviews, and so on? You can easily do this in the Label Colors tab in Preferences, as seen in Figure 10-21a. Changing the label names also makes it easy to set up the label defaults that are applied on import (Figure 10-21b).

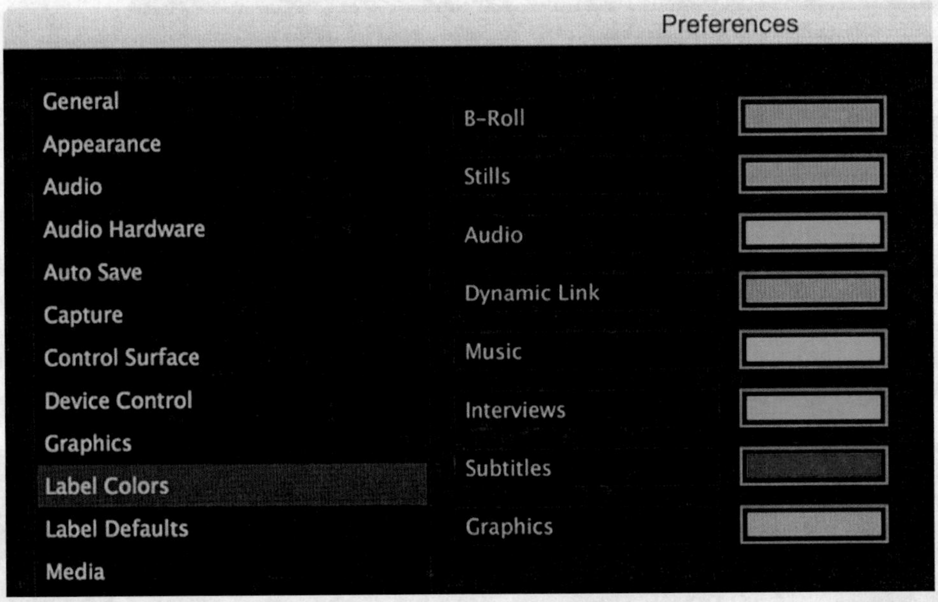

Figure 10-21a. *The default label names are not very intuitive. Change them to more meaningful editing-related names.*

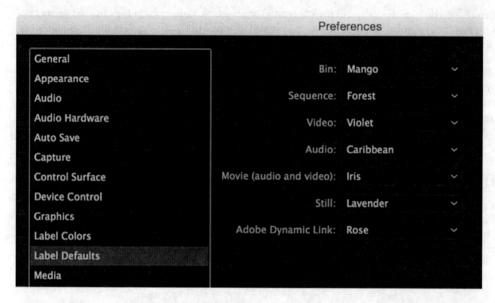

Figure 10-21b. *You can also change the default colors Premiere assigns to different media types*

Premiere has no way to know if a video clip is an interview or a beauty shot, so for all this customization of labels to help, you will need to manually set labels for the different clip types. I prefer doing this in my bins. Select all the clips in the Interviews bin and label them *Interviews*. Select all the clips in your Graphics bin and label them *Graphics*, and so on. Quick and easy!

You can also apply labels with a right-click in the timeline, but if you have tidy bins, labeling clips in the bins before adding them to the timeline is much faster.

Using meaningful labels makes the timeline navigation much easier, as shown in Figure 10-21c. If all the interviews are orange, masks and vignettes are green, and so on, you can very quickly find them and do the necessary tweaks. The visual feedback you get from the colors helps a lot. If you don't like the colors, just change them in Preferences by clicking on the colored rectangles (Figure 10-21d).

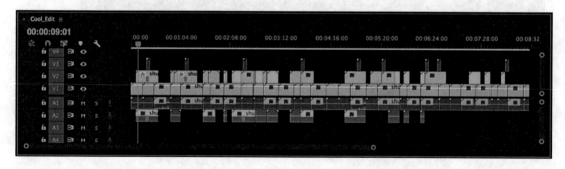

Figure 10-21c. *Labeling clips will make your timeline much easier to decipher*

Preferences

General

Appearance

Audio

Audio Hardware

Auto Save

Capture

Control Surface

Device Control

Graphics

Label Colors

Label Defaults

Media

Violet

Iris

Caribbean

Lavender

Cerulean

Forest

Rose

Mango

Figure 10-21d. *Change the colors of each label if you're not happy with the defaults*

By default, Premiere does not change the color of a clip label or the clip name in the timeline when you change them in a bin—and the other way around. Go to **File ➤ Project Settings** and check *Display the project items name and label color for all instances.* This tells Premiere to always sync them. Most of the time, this is desirable, but if you need the clip names to match your log notes, don't activate this setting!

Custom Label Keyboard Shortcuts

If you use labels a lot, you will want to add keyboard shortcuts to the different colors so you can assign them quickly (see Figure 10-22).

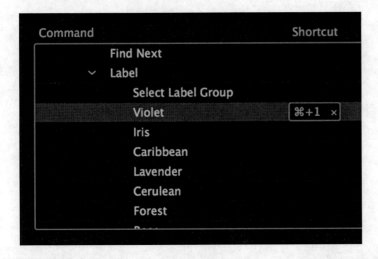

Command	Shortcut
Find Next	
∨ Label	
Select Label Group	
Violet	⌘+1 ✕
Iris	
Caribbean	
Lavender	
Cerulean	
Forest	

Figure 10-22. *Select clips and hit your custom shortcut to change their color*

Customize Metadata

Before you customize the metadata schemas and views, you need to understand exactly how the different types of metadata are stored and managed in Premiere. If you don't understand this properly, you will lose metadata one day. Here's a quick list of important stuff to know.

- Clip metadata is stored in the Premiere Pro project file and is not available for other applications like After Effects, or even for Premiere (if you import the file into another project, the metadata is not there).

- File metadata is stored in the actual media file or in a sidecar XMP file stored alongside the media file.

- You can link Clip and File metadata so that changing one changes the other.

- Many video file formats support XMP, and File metadata will be stored directly in the source files.

- Some formats (MXF is one example) do not support XMP, and File metadata will be stored in sidecar XMP files.

The Metadata panel shows both Clip metadata and XMP File metadata for selected assets.

File Metadata vs. Clip Metadata

In short, *Clip* metadata is only available in the Premiere Pro project you're working in. *File* metadata will be available for any software you have that reads it, and it's stored in the file or in a sidecar file. As long as the sidecar file is stored in the same folder as the media file, the metadata will always follow. The Metadata panel in Premiere shows both types of metadata (Figures 10-23a and 10-23b), and both types can be added and altered in the panel. *These two different types can be linked, but this only changes future metadata you insert, not the metadata already in there.*

Figure 10-23a. *An example of Clip metadata in the Metadata panel*

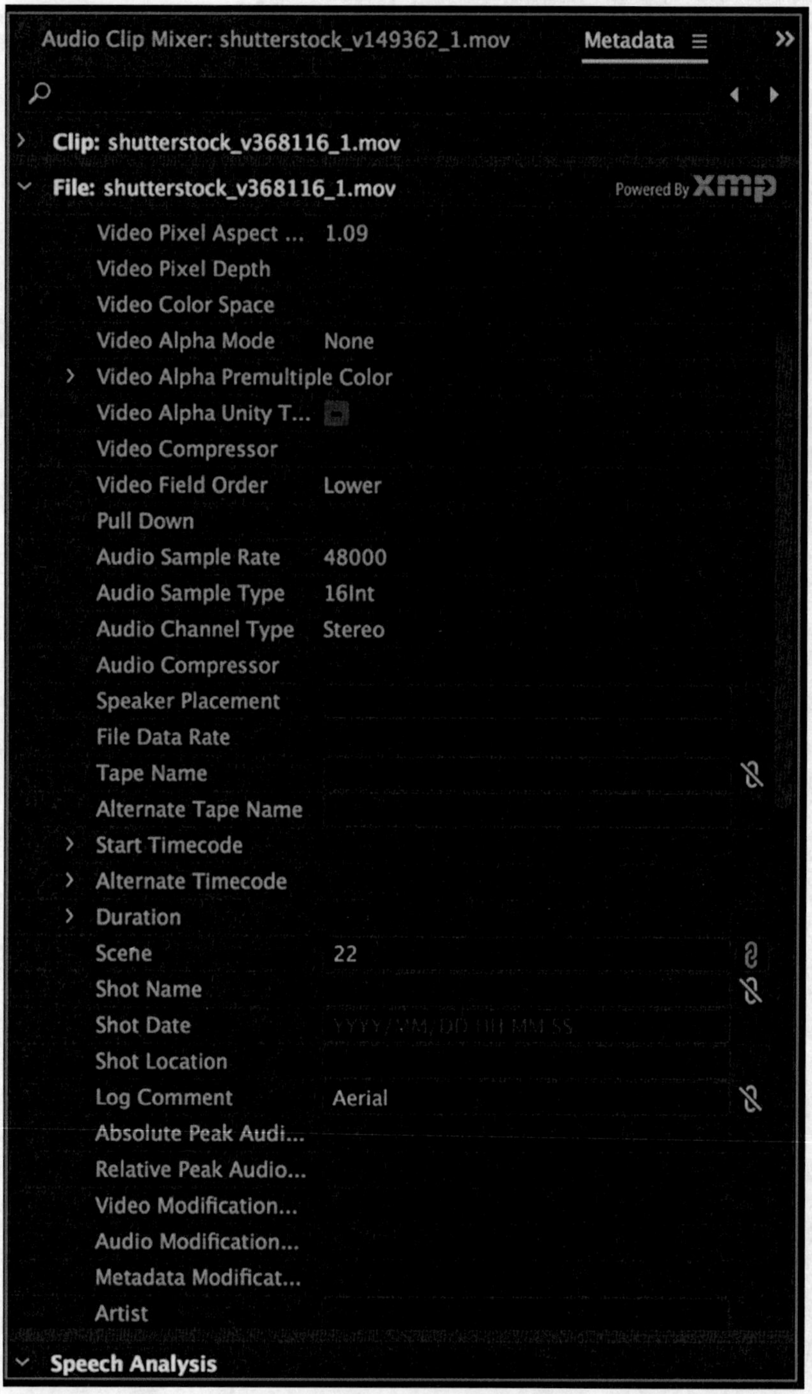

| Audio Clip Mixer: shutterstock_v149362_1.mov | | **Metadata** ≡ | ≫ |

🔍 ◀ ▶

> **Clip: shutterstock_v368116_1.mov**

∨ **File: shutterstock_v368116_1.mov** Powered By **xmp**

     Video Pixel Aspect ...   1.09

     Video Pixel Depth

     Video Color Space

     Video Alpha Mode   None

   > Video Alpha Premultiple Color

     Video Alpha Unity T... 🔲

     Video Compressor

     Video Field Order   Lower

     Pull Down

     Audio Sample Rate   48000

     Audio Sample Type   16Int

     Audio Channel Type   Stereo

     Audio Compressor

     Speaker Placement

     File Data Rate

     Tape Name   🔗

     Alternate Tape Name

  > Start Timecode

  > Alternate Timecode

  > Duration

     Scene   22   🔗

     Shot Name   🔗

     Shot Date   YYYY/MM/DD HH:MM:SS

     Shot Location

     Log Comment   Aerial   🔗

     Absolute Peak Audi...

     Relative Peak Audio...

     Video Modification...

     Audio Modification...

     Metadata Modificat...

     Artist

∨ **Speech Analysis**

Figure 10-23b. *An example of File metadata in the Metadata panel*

File Metadata Can Cause Slow Backups

Since File metadata is written to the actual media file when possible, the media file is altered, and incremental backups will see this change. So, the whole file is copied, even if just one word of metadata is changed.

File metadata stored in sidecar XMP files will of course only change the XMP file, which is a tiny little thing compared to the media file, and back-ups will be quick.

Metadata Preferences

In **Preferences ➤ Media**, ticking *Write XMP ID to Files on Import* will write a unique ID into the file so that all Adobe apps use the same cached previews and conformed audio files. This prevents unnecessary rendering and conforming when using the file in more than one Adobe app. It's a global setting, meaning it is set in all apps when you tick it in Premiere.

Of course, since the file is altered, the file modification date is also changed. Again, this will lead to backup software including the file in incremental backups.

Link Clip Data to XMP Metadata

In **Preferences ➤ Media**, ticking *Enable Clip and XMP Metadata Linking* (seen in Figure 10-24) and the *Link* checkbox will make anything you input in Clip metadata also appear in File metadata, and vice versa.

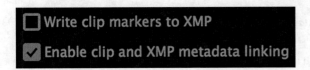

Figure 10-24. *You can link Clip and File metadata by ticking this checkbox in Preferences ➤ Media*

Most users will benefit from this, as it makes metadata available for other applications and also for other Premiere projects. However, it will also change the modification date of files and make incremental backups slower, as described earlier.

Note that this does not duplicate already existing metadata—just the metadata that you input from that point on that will be duplicated.

Most fields have the same names in Clip and File metadata, but the Name field in Clip metadata is copied to the Title field in the Dublin Core schema, and Log Note in Clip metadata is copied to Log Comment in the Dynamic Media schema.

Custom Metadata Fields and Schemas

You might want to create your custom schemas and properties to avoid wading through the long lists of irrelevant metadata you can choose from. First, make a new schema by clicking the *New Schema* button in the Metadata Display panel. Give it a clever name, then start adding properties by clicking the *Add Properties* link to the right of its name.

There are four kinds of metadata fields you can choose from, shown in Figure 10-25:

- Text fields can contain any kinds of text.

- Integer fields can contain only whole numbers.

- Real fields can contain numbers with decimals up to two digits.

- Boolean fields give you a checkbox that can be checked and unchecked.

You will use mostly text fields, but the other ones can come in handy for some kinds of footage. Make sure you give the fields names that are clear so as to avoid confusion.

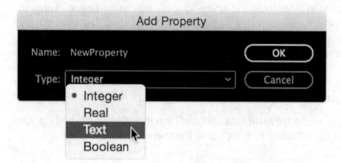

Figure 10-25. *You can add four kinds of metadata fields*

When you've created all your properties, you have a custom schema. This schema can now be used as part of your new custom Metadata Display settings.

The schema file is saved as an XML file in the folder **C:\Users\[User]\AppData\Roaming\Adobe\ XMP\Custom File Info Panels\4.0\custom** on a Windows system, and in **Users/[User]/Library/ Application Support/Adobe/XMP/Custom File Info Panels/4.0/custom/** on MacOS. Let's hope they're moved in the future so they can be synced via Sync Settings.

To share custom metadata between systems, you'll need to copy the same custom schema XML files to all the systems and enable them in Premiere.

Once the XML files are in place, select Metadata Display in the panel menu of the Metadata panel. The new schemas will be at the bottom, and you can tick the ones you want to enable.

Manage Metadata Sets

From the panel menu for the Metadata panel, select *Metadata Display*. Here, you can choose saved presets from the drop-down menu or save a customized set of displayed metadata as a new preset (Figure 10-26a).

The new Metadata Display setting will contain all the ticked properties in the list on the left, so choose only the ones you want or need to see (Figure 10-26b).

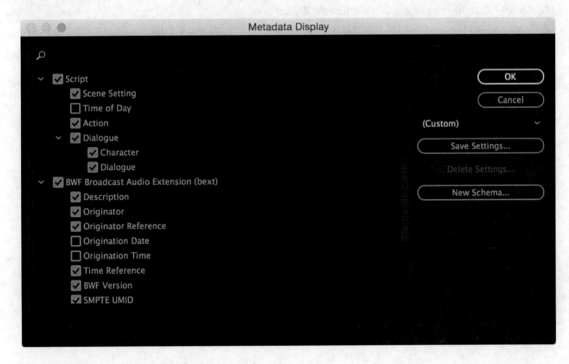

Figure 10-26a. *Give your settings meaningful names*

Figure 10-26b. *Display only the fields you need to see*

Customize the Metadata View in Bins

OK, so the settings we just made will dictate what columns are shown in your bins in List view, but the order and width of each column can be adjusted directly in the bin.

By default, the Project panel and bins display only the clip properties, but since we've chosen our own Metadata Display settings, it will now show just the columns we wanted. To adjust the order, drag the column header to where you want it. Adjust the width by dragging the divider between the headers. Maximize the panel while doing this so as to avoid unnecessary scrolling. For an example of a custom Metadata view, see Figure 10-27.

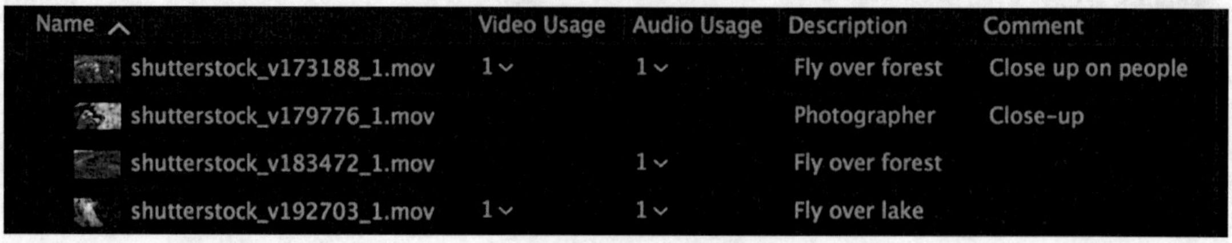

Name ∧	Video Usage	Audio Usage	Description	Comment
shutterstock_v173188_1.mov	1 ∨	1 ∨	Fly over forest	Close up on people
shutterstock_v179776_1.mov			Photographer	Close-up
shutterstock_v183472_1.mov		1 ∨	Fly over forest	
shutterstock_v192703_1.mov	1 ∨	1 ∨	Fly over lake	

Figure 10-27. *A much more useful view than the default ones*

Metadata Display Settings Are Saved with the Workspace

You might wonder where you can save these Metadata views. Actually, you can't save them separately, as they're saved with the workspace. So, make sure you have your Metadata Display just the way you want it before saving your workspaces. See Figures 10-28a and 10-28b for examples of different Metadata views that use the same workspace.

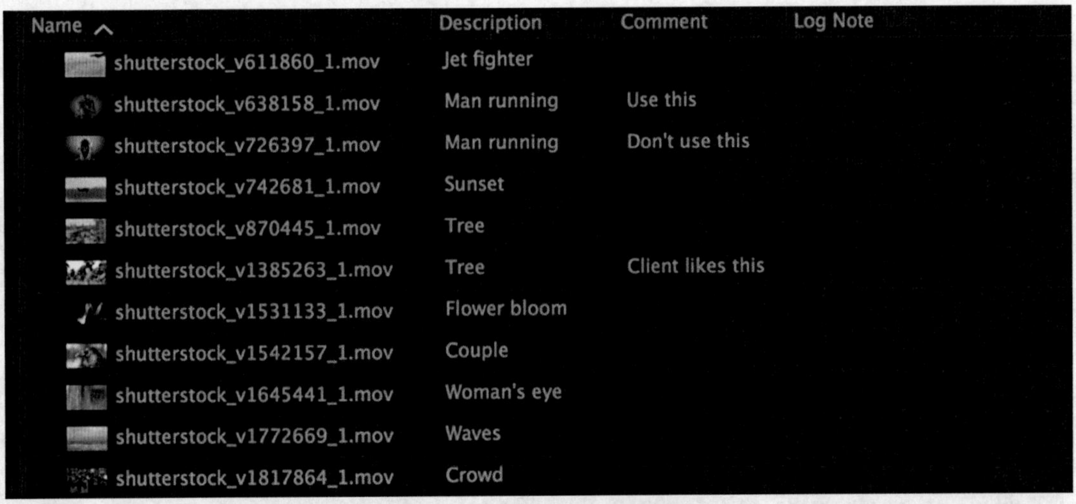

Name ∧	Description	Comment	Log Note
shutterstock_v611860_1.mov	Jet fighter		
shutterstock_v638158_1.mov	Man running	Use this	
shutterstock_v726397_1.mov	Man running	Don't use this	
shutterstock_v742681_1.mov	Sunset		
shutterstock_v870445_1.mov	Tree		
shutterstock_v1385263_1.mov	Tree	Client likes this	
shutterstock_v1531133_1.mov	Flower bloom		
shutterstock_v1542157_1.mov	Couple		
shutterstock_v1645441_1.mov	Woman's eye		
shutterstock_v1772669_1.mov	Waves		
shutterstock_v1817864_1.mov	Crowd		

Figure 10-28a. *Metadata views are stored in workspaces, so you may need to make workspaces that show different metadata*

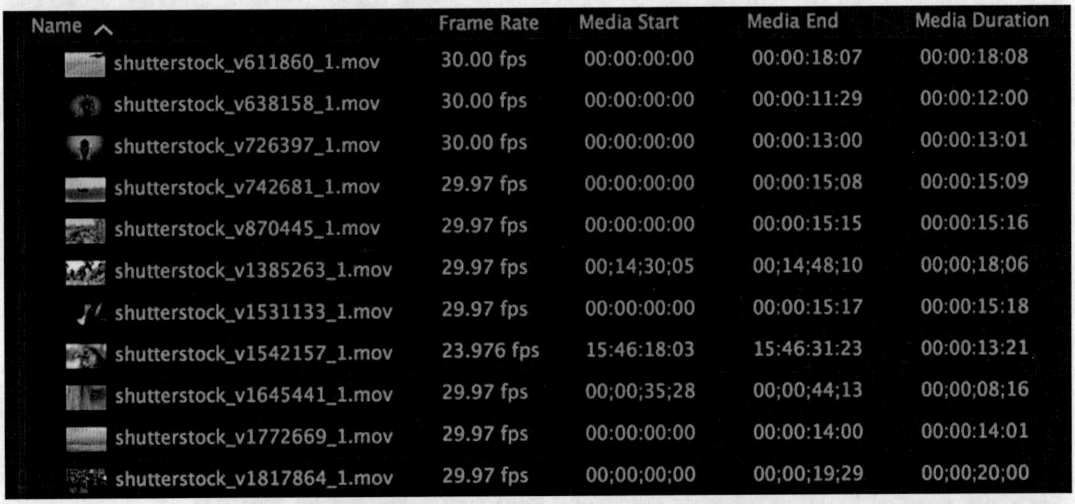

Name ∧	Frame Rate	Media Start	Media End	Media Duration
shutterstock_v611860_1.mov	30.00 fps	00:00:00:00	00:00:18:07	00:00:18:08
shutterstock_v638158_1.mov	30.00 fps	00:00:00:00	00:00:11:29	00:00:12:00
shutterstock_v726397_1.mov	30.00 fps	00:00:00:00	00:00:13:00	00:00:13:01
shutterstock_v742681_1.mov	29.97 fps	00:00:00:00	00:00:15:08	00:00:15:09
shutterstock_v870445_1.mov	29.97 fps	00:00:00:00	00:00:15:15	00:00:15:16
shutterstock_v1385263_1.mov	29.97 fps	00;14;30;05	00;14;48;10	00;00;18;06
shutterstock_v1531133_1.mov	29.97 fps	00:00:00:00	00:00:15:17	00:00:15:18
shutterstock_v1542157_1.mov	23.976 fps	15:46:18:03	15:46:31:23	00:00:13:21
shutterstock_v1645441_1.mov	29.97 fps	00;00;35;28	00;00;44;13	00;00;08;16
shutterstock_v1772669_1.mov	29.97 fps	00:00:00:00	00:00:14:00	00:00:14:01
shutterstock_v1817864_1.mov	29.97 fps	00;00;00;00	00;00;19;29	00;00;20;00

Figure 10-28b. *Here's an alternative view from another workspace. Other than the metadata views, the workspaces are identical.*

Adding Metadata to Clips

Now, let's use these new schemas and views to our advantage. To quickly add metadata to lots of clips, select them in a bin and add metadata in the Metadata panel. Start by adding metadata that all clips have in common (Figure 10-29), then move on to smaller groups, and then to individual clips.

Project: CoolStuff
Media Browser
Libraries
Info
CoolStuff.prproj
5 of 72 items selected
Name
Description
Scene01
Scene02
shutterstock_v173188_1.mov
shutterstock_v639262_1.mov
shutterstock_v198697_1.mov
shutterstock_v427183_1.mov Forest Shots
shutterstock_v198694_1.mov Forest Shots
shutterstock_v183472_1.mov Forest Shots
shutterstock_v179776_1.mov Forest Shots
shutterstock_v496930_1.mov Forest Shots
shutterstock_v192703_1.mov
shutterstock_v246010_1.mov
shutterstock_v192709_1.mov
Scene03
shutterstock_v5470289_1.mov
shutterstock_v2280635_1.mov
shutterstock_v9636986_1.mov
Metadata
Clip: <Multiple selected>
Name <Multiple Values>
Label
Media Type Movie
Frame Rate 29.97 fps
Media Start 00:00:00:00
Media End <Multiple Values>
Media Duration <Multiple Values>
Video In Point
Video Out Point
Video Duration <Multiple Values>
Audio In Point
Audio Out Point
Audio Duration <Multiple Values>
Video Info <Multiple Values>
Audio Info 48000 Hz - 16-bit - Stereo
Video Usage
Audio Usage
Tape Name
Description Forest Shots
Comment
Log Note
File Path <Multiple Values>
Capture Settings
File: <Multiple selected>
Powered By xmp
Speech Analysis

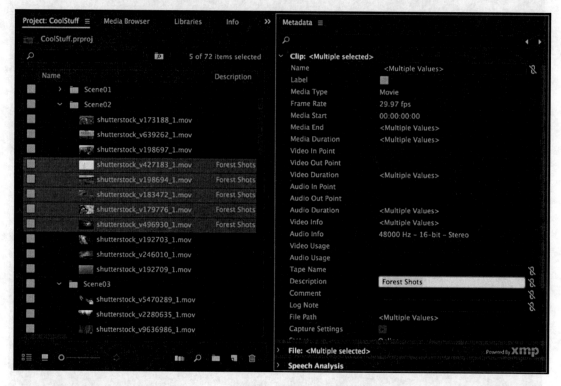

Figure 10-29. *In the Metadata panel you can add metadata to many clips in one go*

I prefer adding metadata to individual clips directly in the bin (Figure 10-30a), but it can also be added in the Metadata panel (Figure 10-30b).

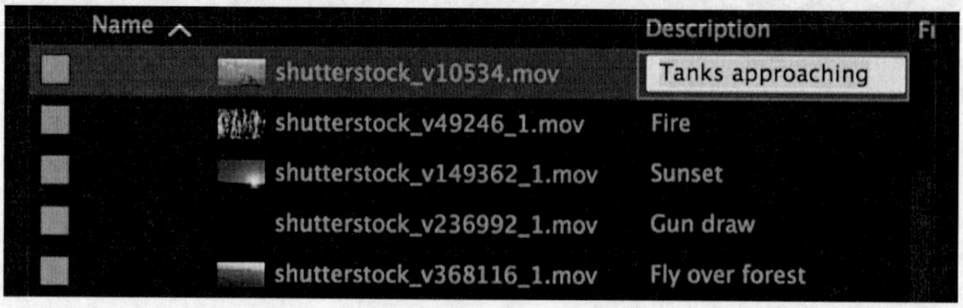

Name
Description
shutterstock_v10534.mov Tanks approaching
shutterstock_v49246_1.mov Fire
shutterstock_v149362_1.mov Sunset
shutterstock_v236992_1.mov Gun draw
shutterstock_v368116_1.mov Fly over forest

Figure 10-30a. *I prefer adding metadata to individual clips in the bin*

Figure 10-30b. *Metadata for individual clips can also be added in the Metadata panel*

Custom Project Templates

Don't get confused by the term *template*. These are just ordinary Premiere project files (`*.prproj`) that you have saved for the purpose of reusing them. Custom projects can be used as start-up projects or to quickly access ready-made motion graphics projects, compositing projects, and other kinds of projects you use every now and then. The whole point is to save time. If you've created a project before, and you need the same setup or the same motion graphics, recreating it is a waste of time.

Of course, you run the risk of saving over a template, so set the project files to *Read Only* in Finder or Windows Explorer, depending on your OS.

Custom Startup Projects

In larger production studios, it's not uncommon to create a project template that contains already created bins, starter timelines, a shared layout, and so forth. Even though I'm a one-man band myself, I use project templates for the simple reason that it saves time, and I don't have to do this boring bit of creating bins and so forth on every project. You can see a sample of one of my own project templates in Figure 10-31.

If you use the same folder structure in every project, the same sequence presets, and even the same countdown, header clip, and bars and tone, these can be saved in a ready-made template project. If you throw in your lower-third templates and templates for credit roll, logos, and other graphics, you'll have everything but the dailies already in place when you start.

So, take five minutes now and make a custom project with all the good stuff you need in every project. Then, save it. If you're working with other people, this folder should live on a network drive along with the assets so everyone can access it.

After this, you can either start your new projects by importing the template project into your new project or by opening the template project and immediately going to **File ➤ Save As**. You'll save several minutes on every project by doing this, minutes that can be spent on more important stuff—like telling that story right.

Figure 10-31. Template projects can hold all the relevant bins, graphics, media browser folders, sequence settings, and so on that you need

Audio Templates

If you do multi-channel audio, your startup template could include a sequence with the entire track-patching already in place, compression on the voiceover track, and even a limiter on the master audio track. Setting this up from scratch every time is just a waste of time.

Custom Helper Projects

If you don't want to have a crowded project template, and if you have projects you only use once in a while, make small helper projects. I use a lot of these helper template projects in the middle of my editing, and, as a result, I edit a lot faster! Even quite complex compositing and motion graphics tasks, such as those seen in Figure 10-32, can easily be done in mere seconds. I kid you not! In just seconds!

When you need something, just import that project file into your main project and let it sit nicely in its own bin in the Project panel with all its stuff ready for use.

Say you have a Lower Thirds and Credit Roll template project. Just import it and edit the text. Everything else—the graphics, the logos, the fonts, the colors, and the tab stops—is already finished, so you only need to change the actual names and the text. You'll actually make it home before dinner today!

Combining helper projects with the Replace Clip feature in Premiere lets you make self-contained, ready-made, drag-n-drop template projects with mostly Premiere-generated synthetics like bars and tone.

Read more about template projects in chapter 7 on motion graphics, and download sample projects from premierepro.net.

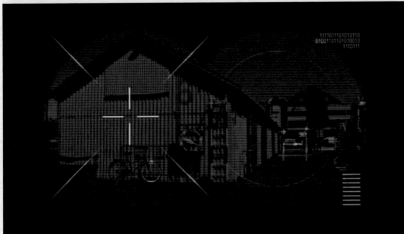

Figure 10-32. *Creating these from scratch can take a long time. Use a template project, and you'll be done in a couple of minutes.*

Making a Self-Contained Template Project

Let me walk you through the making of a template project for a nice reflection effect on a video rotated in 3D. See the image in Figure 10-33, and you'll get the idea.

The video is rotated using a basic 3D effect, and the reflection follows. The reflection has a lowered opacity, and it's blurred. The opacity gets lower as the distance from the original image increases. This was probably a bad explanation, so take a look at `premierepro.net/templates/video-reflection/` to watch a video. The details of making this template are explained in chapter 7 on Motion Graphics, but let's do a quick recap.

To make the template self-contained, I use Bars & Tone as my source (see Figure 10-34). I always put the "source" into a sequence named *Source*, and nest that sequence into the other timelines in the template, as shown in Figure 10-35. This makes it much easier to use the template, as the source only needs to be added to the Source sequence, and all the effects and animation will ripple through the whole thing.

The Source sequence in this template is placed in a bigger sequence where there's room for both the source and the reflection—one on top of the other. So, it's double the height of the HD Source sequence at 2160 × 1920 pixels, and is named *Reflection*. This size isn't strictly necessary if the source will never be shown at full screen, but keeping it this big allows for more creative animations where you can zoom in to let the source cover the whole frame.

The reflection layer has Opacity set to 60 percent, and it also has a feathered crop. This is what makes the opacity of the reflection lower as the distance increases. It also has a Gaussian blur effect on it. The amount of blur here will affect how high we perceive the surface's reflectiveness to be.

Figure 10-33. *Quickly create this reflection effect using a self-contained template project*

Figure 10-34. *Use Bars & Tone to make the template entirely self-contained*

This big sequence is then taken into a standard 1080p sequence named *Animated Reflection on BG* and placed above a simple background made from two instances of a title with a four-color gradient fill. A basic 3D effect with a simple animation of the swivel parameter (-20 to +20 degrees) is applied, and position and scale are adjusted to taste.

Voila! A self-contained template project! The whole process is quite quick and easy—and it will save you from having to start from scratch every time you need a 3D-rotated reflection in the future.

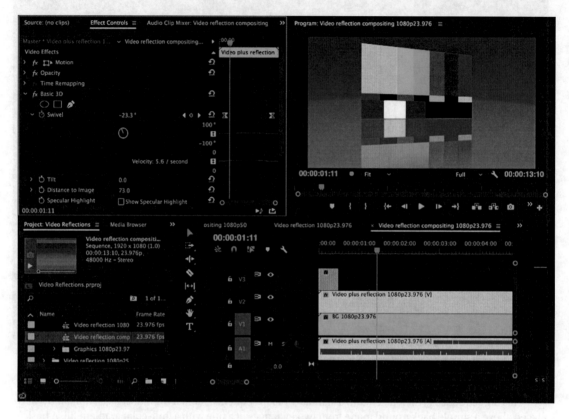

Figure 10-35. *With the use of nesting, the sequences are tidy*

Make sure you do some housekeeping, putting everything into properly named bins, before you permanently save it in your `Template Projects` folder on your computer. See Figure 10-35.

Using the Template Project

To use the template project, import it into an existing project where you want this effect. Drag the *Animated Reflection on BG* sequence into your main timeline. Set an in point in your source footage and then drag it onto the Bars & Tone clip in the Source sequence, like in Figure 10-36, and watch the magic in the main timeline!

Of course, you can adjust the settings when you use the template. The colors of the background are probably not right for the new film, so adding an adjustment layer above the background layers may be necessary—or you could change the colors of the title, but that's more work.

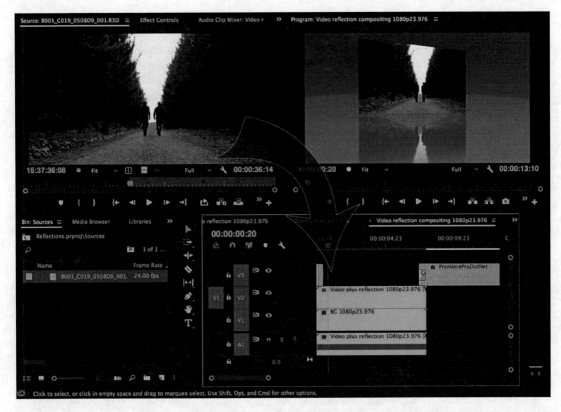

Figure 10-36. *Alt-drag-n-drop your own source clips onto the Bars & Tone clips. Incredibly fast and easy!*

Maybe you'll use a blurred video clip or a texture instead of the gradients? And you may want to have the image closer or farther away, and maybe rotate more, or less, or quicker? Feel free to tweak the settings to your taste.

Even if you need to alter some settings, you'll use a lot less time than if you build the effect from scratch. And that's the whole point of using template projects!

Guidelines for Template Projects

- Save time by using your existing projects to build your templates. If you've created an effect in a project, copy it to its own sequence, select it, and choose **File ➤ Export ➤ Selection as Premiere Project** to create a project file that contains only this sequence and any media used in it.

- Nest source material into source sequences so you only need to replace the media in one place, even though it's used several times in the composite.

- Remove all the actual media, replacing it with Premiere Pro's built-in synthetic media, like Bars & Tone. Synthetic media is extremely lightweight, keeping the template files both small and self-contained.

- If a texture is used to enhance the look, feel free to use one, but save a copy of it in the same folder as the template project so it doesn't get lost. Also, remember to copy this image file to your project folder so it follows the project.

Share Your Templates on PremierePro.net

Free sample templates can be downloaded from `premierepro.net`. My hope is that other editors will share their template projects, too, so this website can become a cool collection of time-saving template projects that everyone can benefit from! Please shoot me an email with your template project, and I'll consider sharing it! All contributors will be duly credited, of course.

Sample Project: The Evening News

If you're making the opening for the evening news, you can import a helper project with all the titles, nesting, and effects ready made. This is a fairly complex project that makes up the opening headlines sequence of a news show (see Figure 10-37). You just change the words in the titles, import the new video clips, set in points, and replace the old clips. Hit *Export Media*, and you're done! You can literally do this in less than a minute.

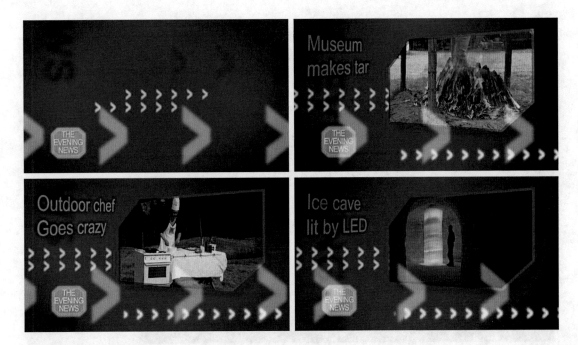

Figure 10-37. *This is what we'll create*

As you'll notice in Figure 10-38, the background elements are kept in a separate nested sequence, and the sources have all been nested to make it easy to swap the footage each day. The nested sequence with all three spots is where the frame around the videos is added. The rest is just some layers of graphical elements with blending modes. Everything in this project is made entirely in Premiere Pro.

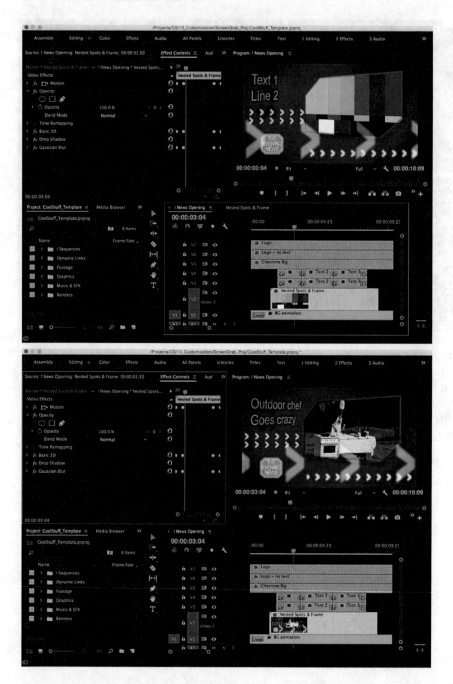

Figure 10-38. *You don't need to understand how a template was made. Just Alt-drag-n-drop your sources onto the Bars & Tone clips and it Just Works.*™

Pre-Render Complex Stuff

Because of all the blurs, blend modes, 3D effects, and animation in the News Opener project, this will take quite a while to render. So, if this were a real evening news show, you would want to render out the background animation, the logo animation, and the chevrons as high-quality video files, some with alpha channels, and swap these with their sequences so the whole package could render much faster.

Custom Preferences

In Preferences, you can change behaviors that range from being just a little annoying to driving you nuts. Stuff you can change includes the default lengths of audio and video transitions, how often Auto Save should kick in and if it should be synced to Creative Cloud, length of preroll and postroll, and more.

If you feel that Premiere acts a bit silly in some situations, and wish that it could be smarter, chances are there's a setting for that. I urge you to spend a couple of minutes checking out the different Preferences tabs. There are some real gems in there! Here are a few that I've changed on my system.

Audio and Video Transition Default Duration

In the **Preferences ➤ General** panel for video and audio transitions, in addition to choosing the default duration for still images, you can choose a duration measured in seconds or frames. Setting this to seconds makes the most sense, especially when you deal with footage of different frame rates, since a 25-frame transition is half a second in a 50 fps sequence and a whole second in a 25 fps sequence.

Do Not Play After Rendering

In **Preferences ➤ General**, the *Play work area after rendering previews* setting is one that really drives me crazy. Why would I like Premiere to jump back and play the whole work area if I just want to see the transition I just tweaked and rendered? No, I want to place my playhead where I want it myself, thank you. So, I untick that setting, and life is OK again.

Maintain Pitch While Shuttling

Tired of the chipmunk sound when you shuttle? Tick this box, and Premiere will try to maintain the pitch, making it easier to hear what people are saying when playing back fast.

Want Those Pop-ups to Go Away?

When Premiere encounters a problem, by default it will display a brightly colored pop-up message in the lower right of the application, as well as logging it in the Events panel. You can disable these pop-ups by unchecking the *Show Event Indicator* option in **Preferences ➤ General**.

Default Audio Tracks

Here's where FCP and Avid editors can make Premiere treat audio just like they're used to. In **Preferences ➤ Audio**, set Stereo Media to import as Mono, and you'll get two mono tracks instead of one stereo track—and you'll understand what's happening again.

Actually, I recommend that everyone does this, as we almost never record stereo, but rather use dual mono, on a camera.

Save Media Cache Files Next to Originals When Possible

This one is very important if you're moving projects around between different systems. If you don't check this box in **Preferences ➤ Media**, media cache files will save in your local Media Cache folder. Of course, that folder cannot be seen by other computers, even on the same network, so the media cache files need to be recreated when the project is moved to another system.

Check that box, and media cache files will be stored next to the media files and will follow them when you take that drive to another system.

Set Tour Video Device

If you have a two-screen setup, you can show the output video in full screen on one monitor while editing. In **Preferences ➤ Playback**, choose one of your monitors in the Video Device list. When doing my final tweaks to a show, I always watch it in full screen on one monitor.

Since I have an HP DreamColor monitor, I can watch my output in full screen 1080p50, 10-bit mode with beautiful and correct colors on the right monitor, while adjusting the color-correction parameters in the Premiere Pro UI on the left monitor.

Auto-save Location

This is not found in Preferences as you might expect. Instead, it's found in **File ➤ Project Settings ➤ Scratch Disks** (see Figure 10-39). This means it's a project-based setting, not a global preference. The default when creating a new project will be the same as in your most recent project. Again, starting from a template project will ensure your scratch disks are set the way you want. Setting the auto-save location to your DropBox folder can't hurt—even though you can also sync it to your Creative Cloud. Two copies in the sky is better than none.

Figure 10-39. Auto-save location is project based

Delete Preferences and the Plug-in Cache

As a freelance editor who regularly shares machines with others, one of the first things I'll do when I start a new job is delete the preferences of the previous user. Hold down **Alt** (Option) when you load Premiere until you see the Start screen. This will set everything back to its default settings and clear the list of recent projects.

Deleting your preferences can also be a useful step when troubleshooting Premiere if it's behaving weirdly. In this case, it's also worthwhile to delete the plug-in cache, which is used to speed up loading plug-ins when you open Premiere. You can do this by holding down **Shift** until you see the Start screen, or add **Alt** (Option) to delete both.

You can also delete your Adobe Media Encoder preferences by opening the application and holding down **Ctrl+Alt+Shift** (Shift+Opt+Cmd).

Custom Ingest Settings

For more information on how to customize your ingest and proxy file settings, check out Chapter 1 on workflow.

Custom Sequence Presets

Premiere is pretty much format agnostic and will handle almost anything you throw at it. However, there may still be good reasons to make a custom sequence preset, as in Figure 10-40. In the New Sequence dialog box, choose *Settings*. Here, you can adjust any settings you want, though there might be some restrictions on the preview codec and editing mode you choose.

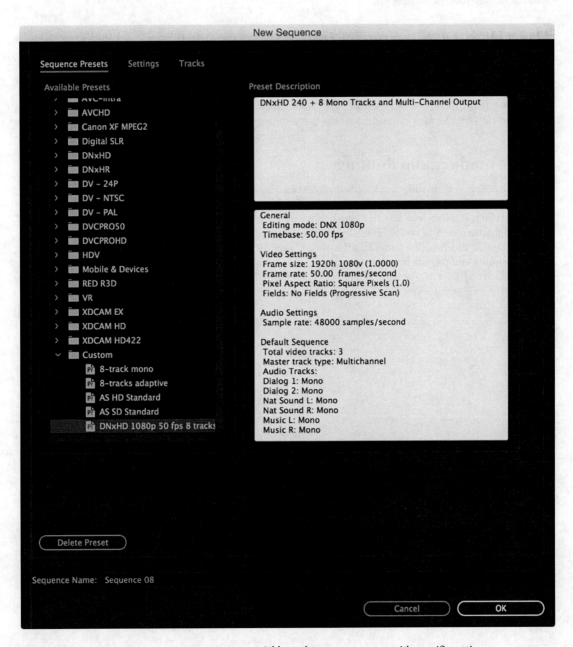

Figure 10-40. *Use custom sequence settings to quickly make new sequences with specific settings*

Use a High-Quality Preview Codec

Using a high-quality preview codec is (of course) important if you need to see rendered areas in high quality. Some formats will get the not-very-good (because the bit rate is set too low) *I-Frame Only MPEG* format as the preview codec by default. After rendering your effects and transitions, you will see compression artifacts in that format. Using quality codecs like *DNxHD, GoPro Cineform*, or *ProRes* instead will give you much higher quality preview/render files for rendered areas in the timeline, which can also be used for faster exports.

Ready-made Audio Routing

Some editors build their audio tracks, panning and routing from scratch in every project. Using a preset is much faster. To set up and make sequence presets for multi-track audio, I recommend that after you create a sequence that you like, load it in the Timeline panel, click the panel's context menu, and choose *Create Preset from Sequence*. You could build it in the New Sequence dialog, as in Figure 10-41, but I just think it's easier to do it in the Timeline panel and the Audio Track Mixer. Now you'll never have to build your audio tracks, panning and routing from scratch, again.

The Custom folder can be renamed in your OS. I named mine *Cool Stuff Sequence Presets* after I took the screen grabs in Figure 10-41.

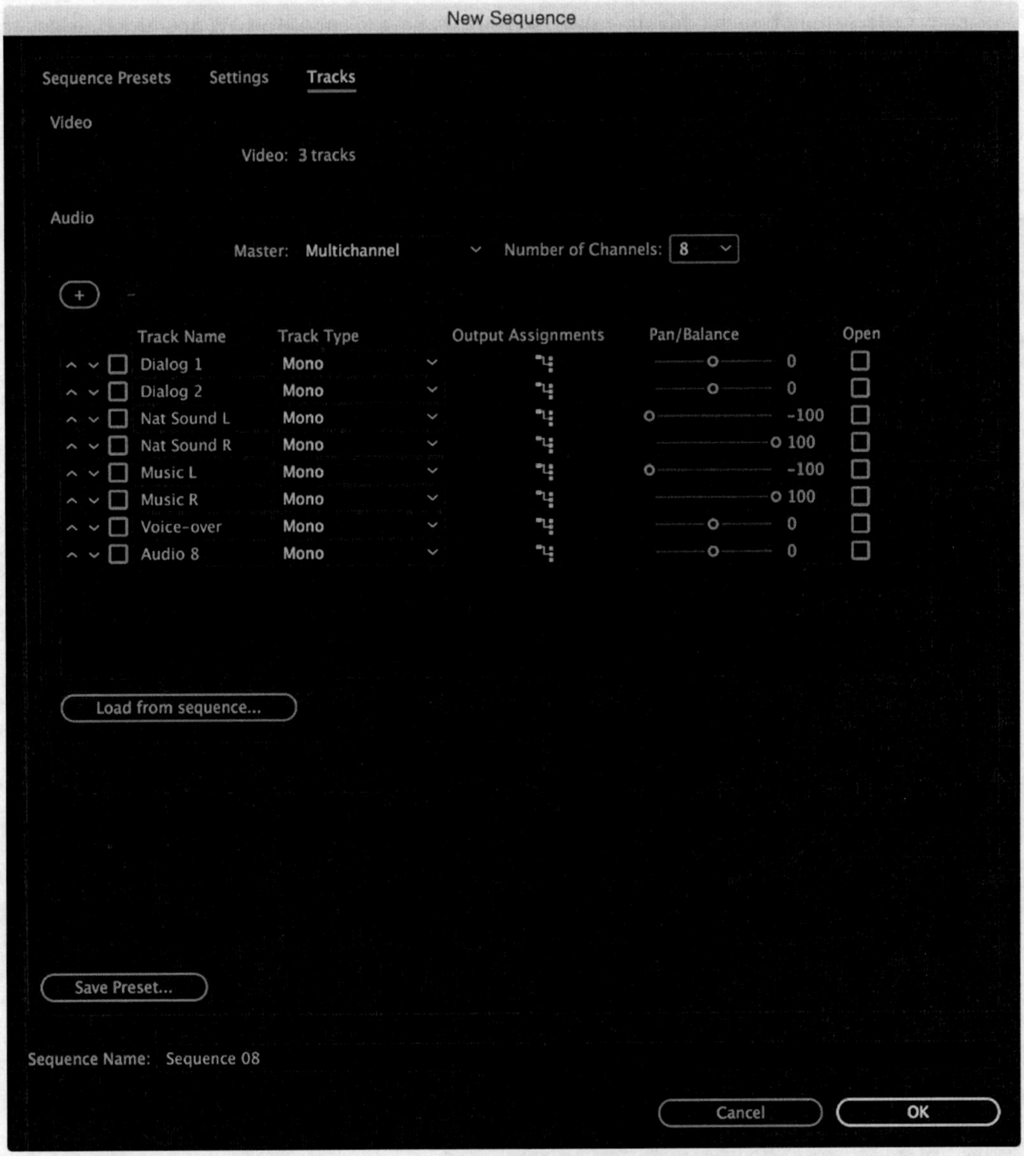

Figure 10-41. Audio routing takes time, so start from a preset

Custom Frame Sizes

If you choose *Custom* as your editing mode in the Settings tab, you can make your video any frame size you want, like the image in Figure 10-42. Need to create video for a four-screen setup with 5376 × 288 pixels? No problem—just set that size in the Video settings. The maximum sequence frame size in pixels is 16,384 × 8,192 (width × height), and that should be enough for most of us.

Not many codecs support such odd frame sizes, so you may have to choose an AVI or QuickTime codec with no or very little compression. If necessary, lower the resolution of the video previews. In this case, Uncompressed AVI UYVY 422 8-bit will let us set the preview size to 1344 × 72, which equals ¼ resolution.

Read more about custom frames sizes in chapter 7 on motion graphics. Here's a video created in Premiere for a handball stadium.

Figure 10-42. *You can make sequences with very strange sizes. Vertical video or super-wide video ads are easy to build.*

Getting Rid of Sequence Presets

The New Sequence window can scare the living daylights out of editors who haven't studied video formats. You also have a very good chance at creating a timeline with the wrong settings, and that can cause all kinds of trouble downstream.

Some broadcasters will only use one format for all their productions, and having all the presets available is just another source of errors. So, let's remove them. They can be found in the Premiere Pro folder under **C:\Program Files\Adobe\Adobe Premiere Pro CC 2017\Settings\SequencePresets** (Applications/Adobe Premiere Pro CC 2017/Adobe Premiere Pro CC 2017.app/Contents/Settings/SequencePresets).

■ **Note**   To access the Premiere Pro application files on a Mac, you need to right-click the Premiere Pro application and choose *Show Package Contents*.

The folders inside that folder match the folders in the New Sequence dialog, as seen in Figure 10-43, and each preset is stored in a separate *.sqpreset file. Removing the file or folder will remove it from the list in the New Sequence dialog.

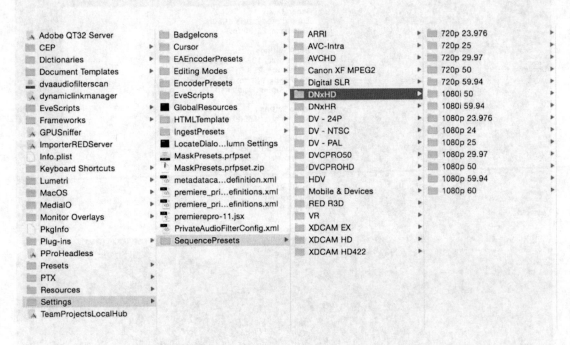

Figure 10-43. *You can remove all the sequence presets you'll never use to lower the risk of your choosing a wrong one*

Remove all 29.97 fps presets if you work in a 25/50 fps area—or the other way around—and while you're at it, remove all the non-square pixels presets and the other bad stuff. Only keep the presets you will actually need and use. As you'll notice in Figure 10-44, now the chance of making a fatal error when creating a sequence is very slim.

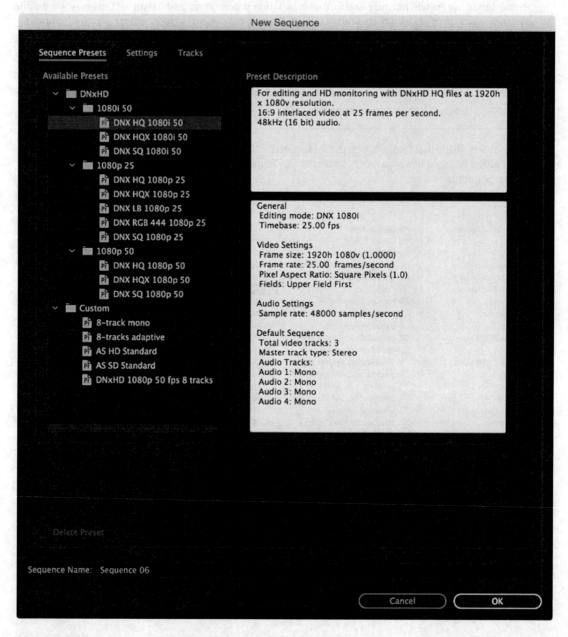

Figure 10-44. Removing irrelevant presets leaves few choices

Speed Up Your Preview Renders

For most editors, preview renders are exactly that—previews. They are not a way to see the final product, and the renders will not be used on export anyway. Often, we don't need to render at all, but when we need to, it's because we've used an effect or transition that's not accelerated by the GPU. The purpose of the preview will—in most cases—be to see if the timing of an animation is right, or if the timing of a transition or cut is precise.

We don't need a full-resolution preview in a lossless codec to see if the timing is right, so we can use a lower quality, faster codec at a lower resolution. Even at half res, the render time is reduced to 25 percent. Remember, it's half resolution both vertically and horizontally, so the renders are almost four times faster! At quarter resolution, as in Figure 10-45, the previews will be almost 16 times faster.

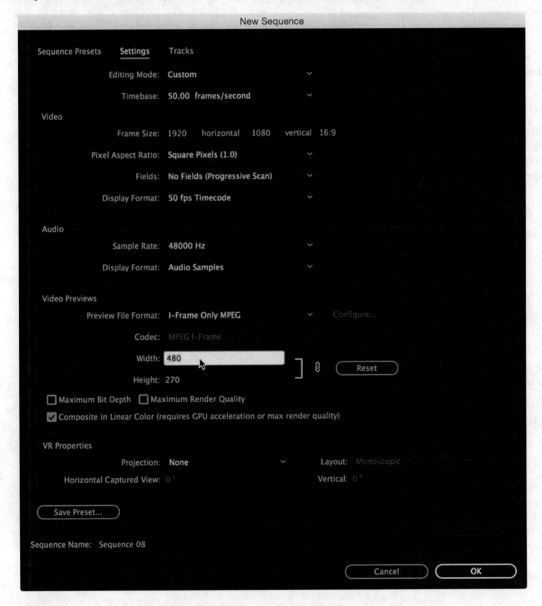

Figure 10-45. Preview files at ¼ res will render almost 16 times faster

Invoke Smart Rendering to Speed Up Your Exports

Smart rendering is a feature that's pretty intelligent at export time. If there is unaltered source footage (meaning just cuts, and no effects or scaling) or preview renders in the timeline with a codec that matches the output, those parts will just be copied into the new exported file, and not be re-rendered. It's a bit-for-bit copy operation, so there's no quality loss, and it's also very fast.

So, if your source footage is ProRes 422 HQ and your previews are ProRes 422 HQ, exporting to ProRes 422 HQ will be very fast, and there will be no quality loss. The same goes for the supported flavors of DNxHD, of course.

For I-frame-only formats, there is no loss. For long-GOP formats, there will still be a re-render near most cutting points. Unless you're cutting on an I-frame, the last GOP before a cut and the first GOP after a cut will need to be re-rendered, so for long-GOP formats there is a bit of quality loss.

If you want to use your preview render files to shorten export, make sure your preview file format is set to exactly the format you're outputting to. This will enable smart rendering when possible, and can dramatically shorten your export times.

Smart Rendering Even with Non-Matching Material

This feature can even be helpful when the source material does not match the output. Say you're doing a simple, but longish, project with just a lot of interviews and a little B-roll footage. If you work natively and do color correction on every clip and use some cool motion graphics effects, the final export will take some time. If you're on a tight deadline, you may want to shorten that export time.

If your preview file format matches the output, you can render bits of the timeline whenever you have the chance—when you talk on the phone, when you walk away from the computer for bio breaks, coffee and lunch, and so on. When you export the final movie, use smart rendering, and the final export will be dramatically faster. Yes, this is how we used to work in the old days, but it still has its advantages in some situations.

See the chapter 12 on export for more info on smart rendering, supported codecs and flavors, and so on.

Dig Deeper

There are ways to customize sequence presets even further. See the section on extreme customization with XML for more of a hacker's approach to customization. That section is not for the faint-hearted.

Customize the Timeline

Of course, customizing your sequence doesn't end with presets. There's even more you can do once you load it in the timeline.

Custom Track Heights

Here's a BIG timesaver! Make presets and shortcuts for the track heights—especially the audio track heights. If you're like most editors, you actually spend much more time editing audio clips than video clips. Split edits, audio fades, effect sounds, music, nat sound, and voiceovers all overlap and interact, while most of the time video just gets a straight cut between clips. So, having a quick way to change the height of the different audio tracks is very handy.

Combined with the custom source-mapping presets that we'll deal with later in this chapter, these presets allow for much faster audio editing.

Let's say you keep sync audio on tracks 1 and 2, interviews and voiceover on tracks 3 and 4, effect sounds on tracks 5 and 6, and music on 7 and 8. Using these presets, you can swiftly have a closer look at the ones you want using only one keystroke (Figures 10-46a and 10-46b).

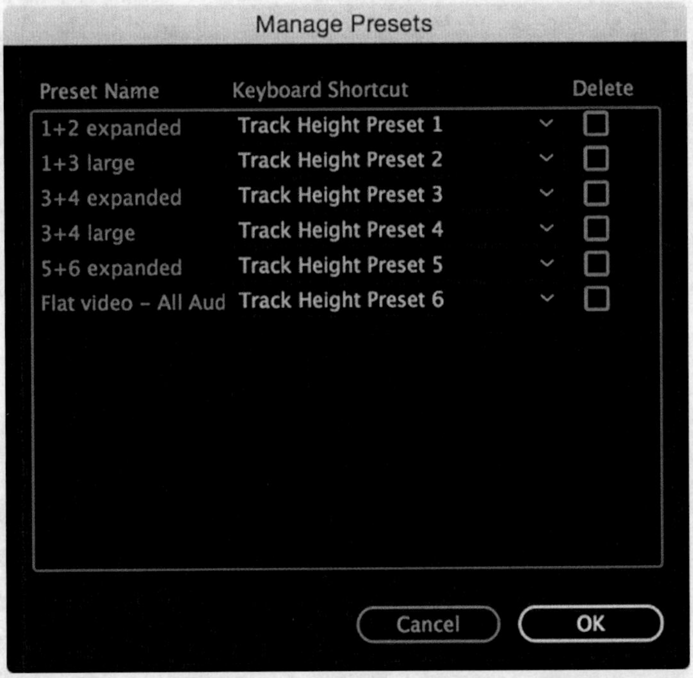
Manage Presets
Preset Name
Keyboard Shortcut
Delete
1+2 expanded
Track Height Preset 1
1+3 large
Track Height Preset 2
3+4 expanded
Track Height Preset 3
3+4 large
Track Height Preset 4
5+6 expanded
Track Height Preset 5
Flat video - All Aud
Track Height Preset 6
Cancel
OK

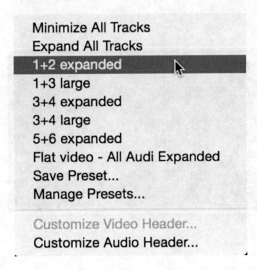

Figure 10-46a. *Assign shortcuts to all your custom track height presets. It's a huge timesaver!*

Minimize All Tracks
Expand All Tracks
1+2 expanded
1+3 large
3+4 expanded
3+4 large
5+6 expanded
Flat video - All Audi Expanded
Save Preset...
Manage Presets...
Customize Video Header...
Customize Audio Header...

Figure 10-46b. *Some of my presets. I've used all the presets just described in the following timeline.*

Figures 10-47a, 10-47b, 10-47c, 10-47d, 10-47e, and 10-47f should be pretty much self-explanatory.

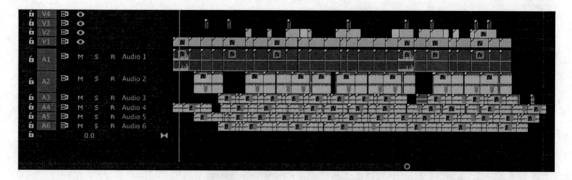

Figure 10-47a. *Only tracks 1 and 2 expanded*

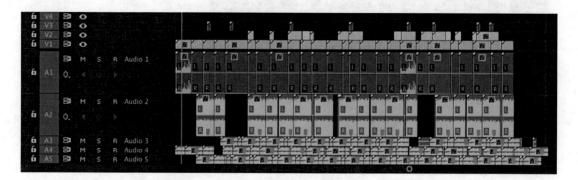

Figure 10-47b. *Tracks 1 and 2 expanded more*

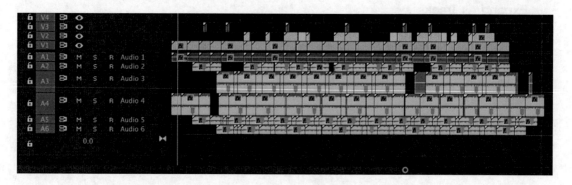

Figure 10-47c. *Only tracks 3 and 4 expanded*

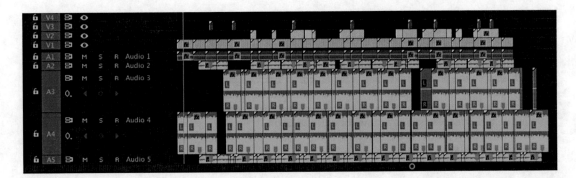

Figure 10-47d. *Tracks 3 and 4 expanded more*

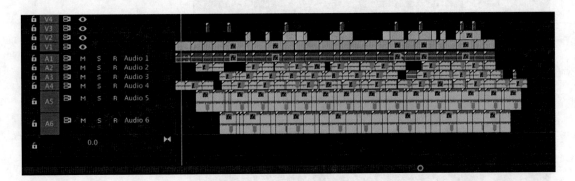

Figure 10-47e. *Only tracks 5 and 6 expanded*

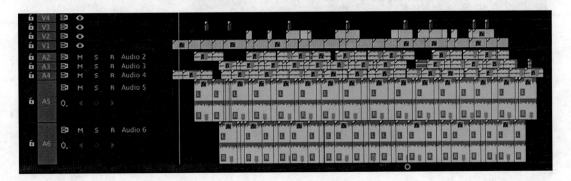

Figure 10-47f. *Tracks 5 and 6 expanded more*

Customize the Track Headers

Click the wrench icon in the timeline and choose *Customize Audio Header*. In the dialog, you can add or remove buttons by dragging into or out of the highlighted track header (Figure 10-48). The upper row will be visible first, then the second, and so on as you increase track height.

In Figure 10-49, I've added the audio meter to my track header so I can see the levels of the individual tracks. You can also add the track name, a one-click voiceover button, a record button, and a left/right balance button, choose to see keyframes or not, and so on.

The video track header doesn't have as many choices, and I've never bothered to customize it. But if you need to, it's available via the wrench menu.

Figure 10-48. Add new features by dragging the icons onto the track header

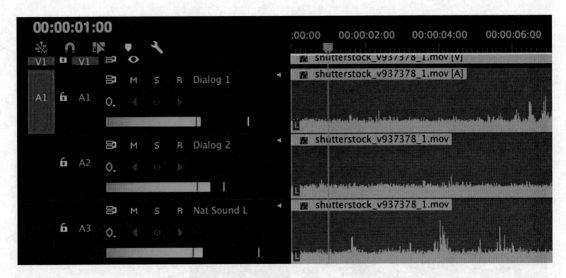

Figure 10-49. *The audio track headers are highly customizable*

Custom Source Channel Assignment Presets

By clicking on the "buttons" in the *Source Patching* column in the timeline, you can easily decide which channels from the source you want to go on which tracks when you do insert and overwrite edits. These will override the track target patches just to the right of them. Nice, but using the mouse to do this will slow you down.

Using presets for this patching instead of the mouse will really speed up your editing! Track selection is vital to every editing operation done with the keyboard, and once you start using these presets and shortcuts, you will wonder how you ever edited without them. Right-click the Source Assignment area to get to the settings, as seen in Figure 10-50.

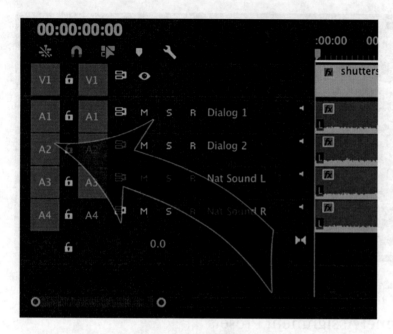

Figure 10-50. Right-click here to find settings

In Figure 10-51, I've made presets for the combinations of video and audio tracks that I use the most, and you can see each of these assignments on the timeline in Figure 10-52. When I need other combinations, I'll use the mouse to manually click on the source. Since I have a numeric keyboard, I use **Shift** combined with the numbers on the numeric keyboard.

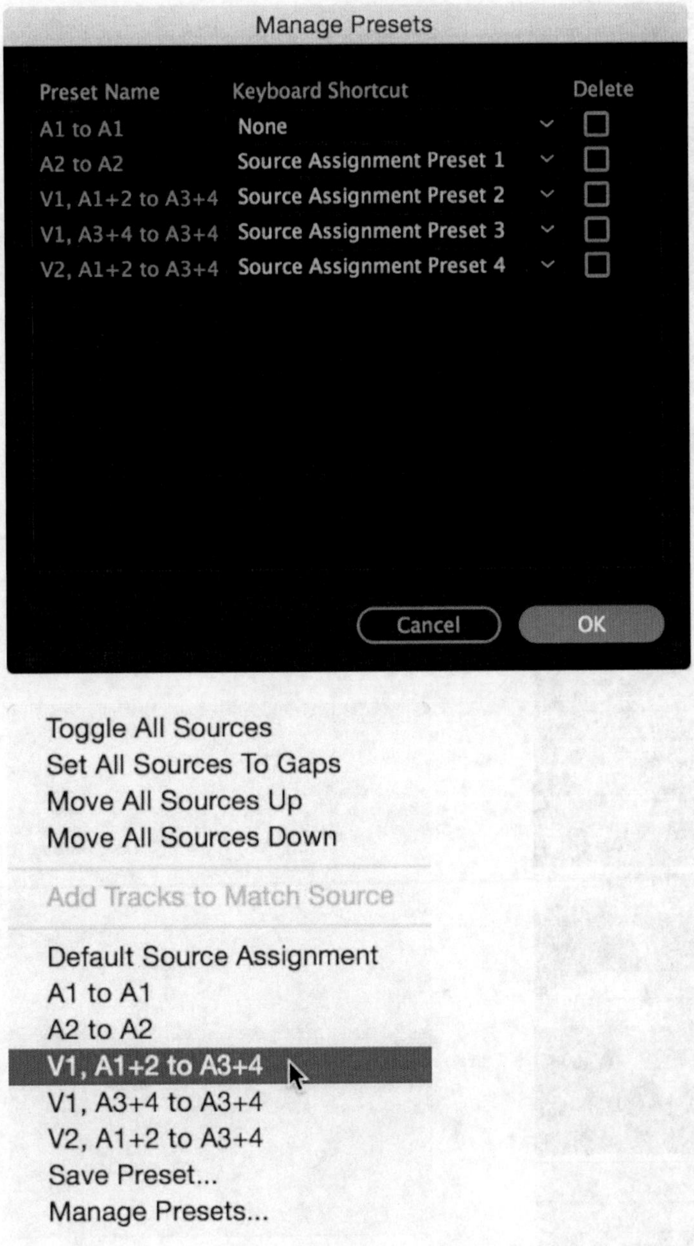

Manage Presets

Preset Name	Keyboard Shortcut		Delete
A1 to A1	None	⌄	☐
A2 to A2	Source Assignment Preset 1	⌄	☐
V1, A1+2 to A3+4	Source Assignment Preset 2	⌄	☐
V1, A3+4 to A3+4	Source Assignment Preset 3	⌄	☐
V2, A1+2 to A3+4	Source Assignment Preset 4	⌄	☐

Cancel   OK

Toggle All Sources
Set All Sources To Gaps
Move All Sources Up
Move All Sources Down

Add Tracks to Match Source

Default Source Assignment
A1 to A1
A2 to A2
V1, A1+2 to A3+4
V1, A3+4 to A3+4
V2, A1+2 to A3+4
Save Preset...
Manage Presets...

Figure 10-51. Give your presets good names and quick and easy shortcuts

Notice that the source tracks that are available in your clips here will, of course, be influenced by the audio channel mapping you've done on the master clips in the bins, and your Default Audio Tracks settings in Audio Preferences.

As you will discover, you can also set keyboard shortcuts for toggling all audio and video tracks on or off, moving all sources up and down, and so on. You can also toggle all audio sources on and off by **Shift-clicking** on the patches.

Figure 10-52. *Using these shortcuts, you can change your source channel assignments instantly and without a single mouse-click*

Custom Monitor Overlays

A limited choice of metadata can be shown in the monitor overlays. The Monitor Overlay Settings dialog allows you to customize the layout of overlays in the monitors (see Figure 10-53). Click the wrench icon in the source or program monitor and choose **Overlay Settings ➤ Settings**.

The overlay settings are shared by the source and program monitors, so they will display the same info. You find the overlay presets files in the Settings folder inside your Profile-CreativeCloud folder as .OLP files.

You can choose whether you want the overlays to show on your external broadcast monitor via Transmit or not. If you have a director or client watching the external monitor, you probably want to turn overlays off for Transmit.

The overlays display can quickly become crowded when you have complex timelines, as in Figure 10-54, so make sure you only show the info you need.

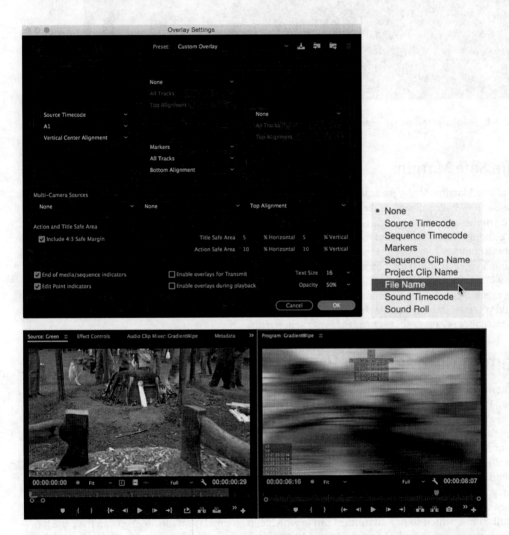

Figure 10-53. *The Monitor Overlay Settings dialog allows you to customize the layout of overlays in the monitors*

Figure 10-54. *Don't use too many overlays—you also need to see the image*

Custom Safe Margins

You can set Safe Margins display parameters in the same dialog as where you set the overlay settings. This makes sense, but is somewhat confusing, since Safe Margins are turned on and off separately from the other overlays.

To add to this confusion, you can also set the Action and Title Safe areas in **File ➤ Project Settings ➤ General**, although these don't seem to update the values in the overlay settings, so be aware of where you're making these changes.

Although you can adjust the percentages for Action and Title Safe areas, you don't have the same flexibility with center-cut settings, which show what will be cropped from a 16:9 frame on a 4:3 screen. In Premiere, this is a checkbox you can turn on or off, whereas in After Effects you can also specify a percentage. Why would you ever want to change them? Because broadcast-safe areas have actually been redefined in recent years: nab.org/xert/scitech/pdfs/tv031510.pdf.

Custom Audio-Mapping Presets

Audio channel mapping can be done at three different stages in your editing. In **Preferences ➤ Audio**, you can tell Premiere to treat audio files differently from the original source at import time. Mono files can behave like stereo or 5.1, or stereo files like mono, and so forth.

Then, there's the Audio Channel Mapping dialog, where you can choose what tracks from the source you want to use. This can be reached from a right-click in a bin (**Modify ➤ Audio Channels**) or via a right-click on a clip in the timeline. You can even use the shortcut **Shift+G** from both places. When you do this on a master clip in a bin, you can use the presets, as explained in the next section.

When you go to the same Audio Channel Mapping dialog from a clip instance in a timeline, the presets will be grayed out, and you cannot change the format. So, a stereo file cannot be changed to mono, but you can still choose which source channel to put in which clip channel from the file. You can have the left channel from the source in both channels (Figure 10-55), or the right channel from the source in the left channel and none in the right (Figure 10-56), if that makes you happy.

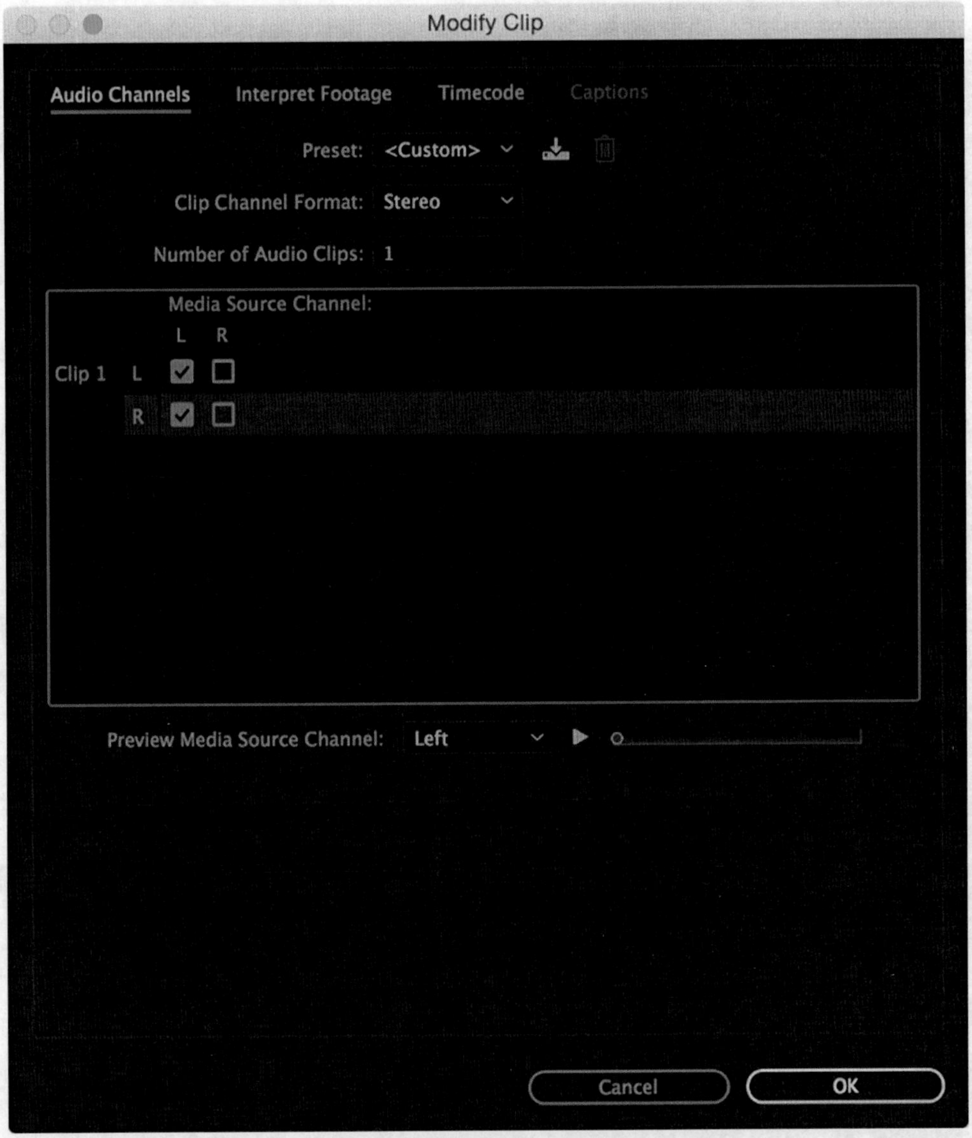

Figure 10-55. *You can have the left channel from the source in both channels*

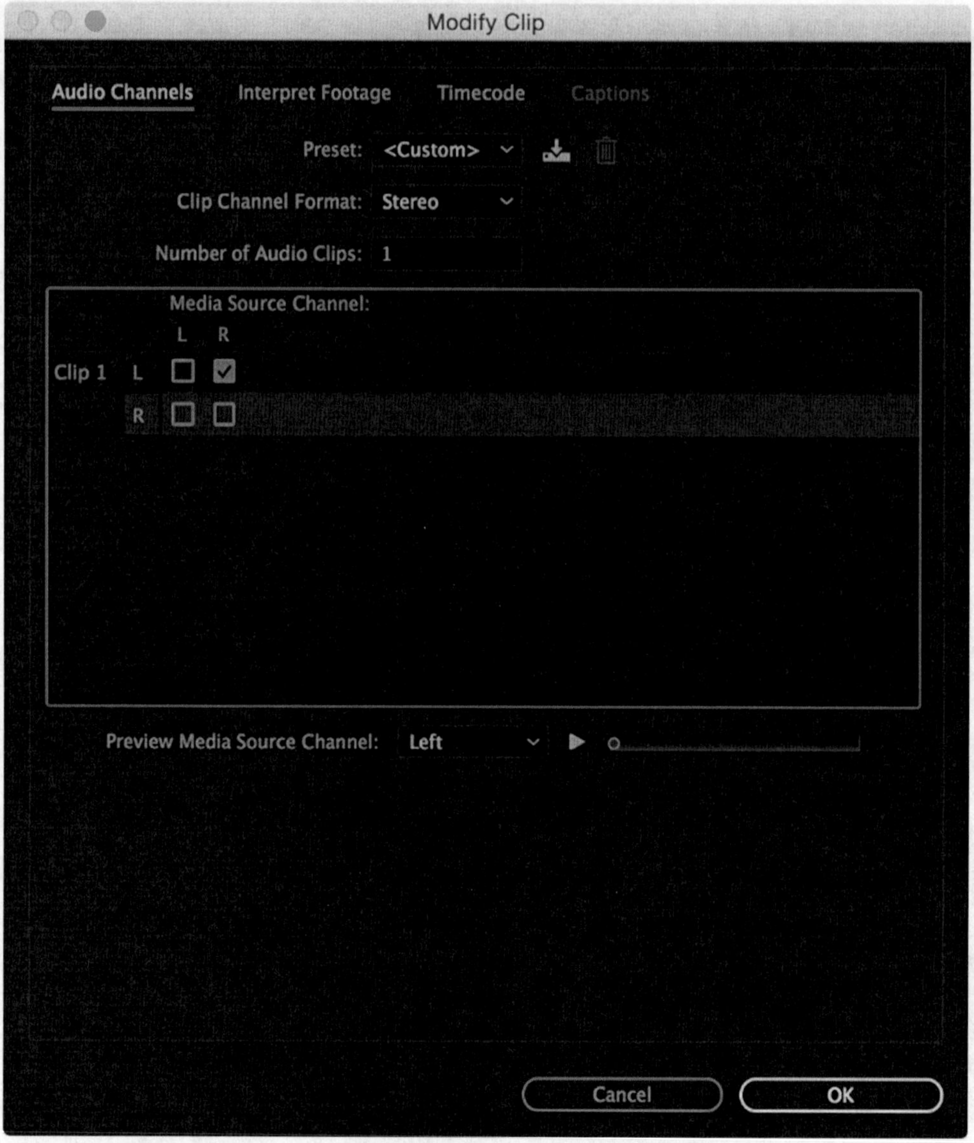

Figure 10-56. *Remove irrelevant audio channels*

Custom Audio Channel Mapping Presets

Right-click on a file containing audio in a bin and choose **Modify ➤ Audio Channels**, or just mark it and hit **Shift+G**. This is where you can choose what channels from the source file to use, and what kind of audio you want that source file to have: stereo, mono, and so forth. You can make stereo sources behave like mono files, eight-channel audio behave like two-channel stereo files, and so on.

Of course, to save a few seconds every time you use this dialog, you should make your own presets, as in Figure 10-57. I recommend using a file with the maximum number of channels that you expect to be editing. This way, you can create all the presets you need without opening more than one file. Choose the channels and format you want, then save the preset with a descriptive name like *Mono, 1 Only*.

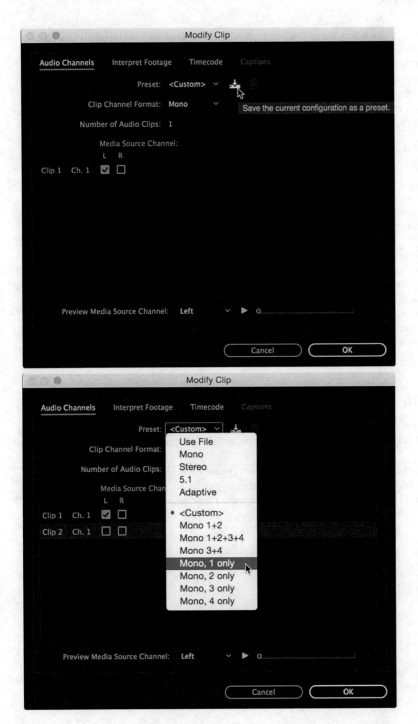

Figure 10-57. *Save presets to save time. They appear in the drop-down menu.*

These presets cannot be set directly using keyboard shortcuts, but at least you can open the dialog box with the shortcut. If you really want to avoid using the mouse to choose presets, the following keyboard sequence will work: **Shift+G ➤ Tab ➤ Tab ➤ Tab** to highlight the Preset drop-down menu, then use the **Up Arrow** or **Down Arrow** to select the preset you need, then hit **Enter**.

These presets (named .acpreset) are found in **Documents\Adobe\Premiere Pro\11.0\Profile-[Adobe ID]\ Audio Channels Presets**, (Users/[User]/Documents/Adobe/Premiere Pro/11.0/Profile-[Adobe ID]/Audio Channels Presets).

Custom Effects

You'll find after you've done some editing that you use many of the same effects over and over, even with the same settings. Building these from scratch every time is a big waste of time. When I edit, I almost never search for effects or scroll through the Effects panel to find effects. I use effects presets extensively to speed up my workflow dramatically. I think you should do so, too!

Everybody's got a deadline, so why spend your time recreating stuff you've done before or manually doing something that can be done automatically? After customizing your effects presets for a while, your Favorites folder will be populated with presets for things you use most often, and you'll gain a reputation as a fast editor because you can do complex stuff with just a couple of mouse-clicks.

You've automated tedious, repetitive, non-creative tasks so you can focus on the creative part of editing—the most important part. And that's the whole point of this chapter.

Effects presets and the contents of your Favorites folder will be saved to the Effect Presets and Custom Items.prfpset file in your Profile folder and will be synced to Creative Cloud with Sync Settings.

Make a Favorite Effects Bin

Tired of wading through all the effects and presets in the Effects panel to find the effects you need? Searching can help, but then you need to type. What if you could just show only the effects and presets you use often? Well, you can!

Right-click in the Effects panel to create a new custom bin (Figure 10-58). Name it *Favorites* and drag all your frequently used effects and effects presets into it, as seen in Figure 10-59. Maximizing the Effects panel to fill the whole screen will make this easy. The panel is too short to show the complete list, so you might need to search for the effects and presets you want to drag there.

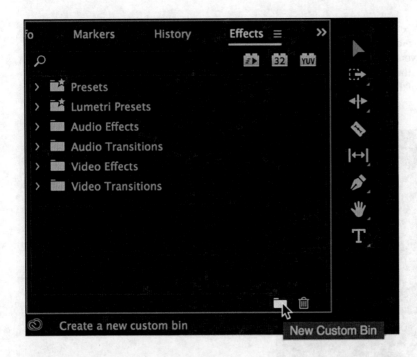

Figure 10-58. *Keep your favorite presets in a custom bin*

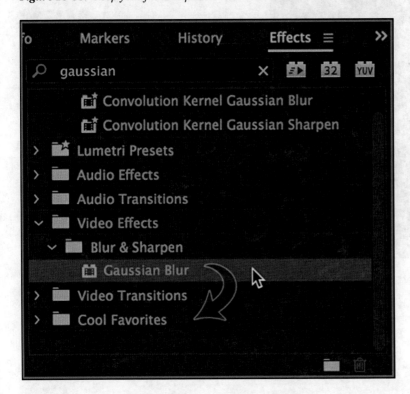

Figure 10-59. *Drag presets to the new bin to add them there*

863

Now, scroll the panel so you only see the Favorites bin, as shown in Figure 10-60, and you have a fast, clutter-free Effects panel. No more searching or browsing effects folders to get the effects you need most often! This bin is saved with your profile, so you can use Sync Settings to carry it wherever you go.

Read more about customizing the Effects panel in the section on extreme customization with XML, where you'll learn to get rid of the factory presets.

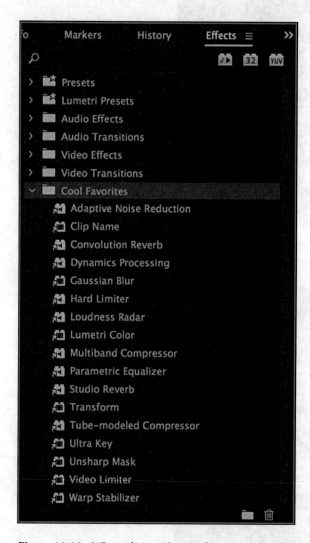

Figure 10-60. *When editing, I keep only my Favorites bin open*

Create Custom Presets in Existing Effect Presets Bin

You're not allowed to drag a custom preset to one of the factory preset bins, but you can select the bin first, then save the preset, and it's saved in the bin. So, if you want to keep your custom Blur presets with the factory defaults, you can.

Custom LUTs in the Lumetri Color Panel

One of the great things about the Lumetri Color panel is the ability to load your own custom LUTs (look-up tables) in both the Basic Correction and Creative sections. The only problem is if you're working with the same custom LUTs on a regular basis, having to repeatedly click *Browse* and locate these files can be a complete waste of time.

The workaround for this is to add your custom LUTs to the list that ships with Premiere. That way, you can just choose it from either the Input LUT or Look drop-down lists, or even preview it in the Creative section.

These LUTs are stored in the folder **C:\Program Files\Adobe\Adobe Premiere Pro CC 2015\Lumetri\ LUTs** (Applications/Adobe Premiere Pro CC 2017/Adobe Premiere Pro CC 2017.app/Contents/Lumetri/LUTs/).

For Inputs LUTs, add them to the Technical folder, and for Creative LUTs, add them to the Creative folder. You will need to restart Premiere for these to be included in their respective lists.

If you create a look in the Lumetri Color panel that you'd like to include in these drop-down lists, all you need to do is click the context menu for the panel and choose *Export .cube*, then save it to the appropriate folder.

■ **Warning**   AME doesn't necessarily see these presets, so you can get surprises when exporting. Use direct export, or copy the presets to Adobe Media Encoder's folders as well if you want to export via AME.

Custom LUTs in the Library Panel

Another way to quickly apply a custom LUT is by adding it to your Libraries panel. To do this, load your custom LUT in the Lumetri Color panel, then go over to your Libraries panel, click the plus icon in the bottom left, and choose *Add LUT*. Now you can drag this LUT directly onto your footage in the timeline, and it will be available to you wherever you're signed into your Adobe ID.

Custom Effect Presets

If you do some color correction, an S-curve and a highlight roll-off effect will be very useful. Saving these settings as presets (see Figure 10-61) instead of starting from scratch every time will save a lot of time. They might not be perfect for every clip, of course, but they will take you very close to what you're trying to achieve, and using a preset will be faster than starting from a straight curve.

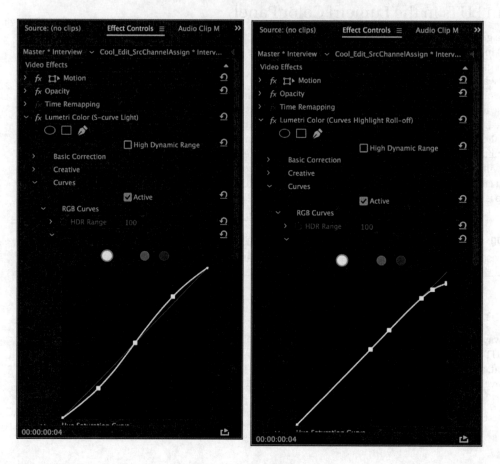

Figure 10-61. *Save effect presets for settings you use often*

Custom Multiple-Effects Presets

Effects presets aren't limited to single effects. We can save combinations of several effects with all their settings, and even animation, as one preset.

First, **Ctrl-click** (Cmd-click) on the name of all the effects you want in the Effects Control panel to choose them. Then, right-click on one of them to get the context menu. You can also use the panel menu in the top-right corner of the Effect Controls panel. Choose *Save Preset* and enter a name and some descriptive details, as in Figure 10-62.

This effect preset shows up in the Presets folder in the Effects panel. The details you added will show up as a tool tip if you hover the mouse on it (see Figure 10-63). Trust me—you need that tool tip a few months later.

Now you can easily add multiple effects in one go, to one or several clips, or to an adjustment layer. For an example of a preset with multiple effects applied to a clip, see Figure 10-64. If timesavers like these, where you do stuff in a fraction of the time, are not appealing to you, then you've got way too much time on your hands.

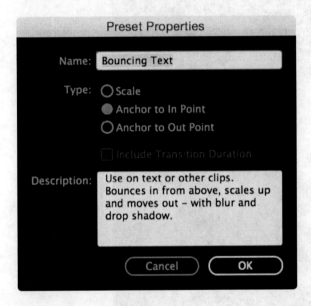

Figure 10-62. *A good name and a description help you find the right preset later*

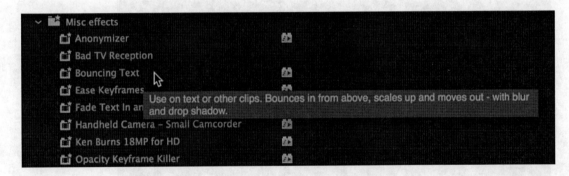

Figure 10-63. *The description shows as a tool tip when you hover over the preset*

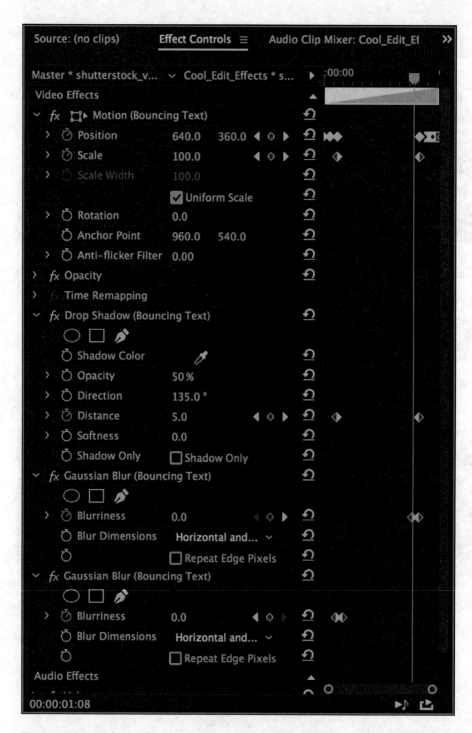

Figure 10-64. *Multiple effects can be saved in one preset. Imagine doing this with a drag-n-drop instead of building it from scratch.*

Bouncing Text

If you're working on a motion graphics project and create a novel bounce effect to animate your text into the image, you don't want to recreate this for every text item. Of course, you can copy the animation over to new text, but a smarter approach is to save the effects as a preset so it can be recycled in future projects.

Rich Voiceover

Audio effects can, of course, be saved as presets too. A preset for a rich voiceover effect can come in handy, so create the effect like the one in Figure 10-65 and save it as a preset for later use.

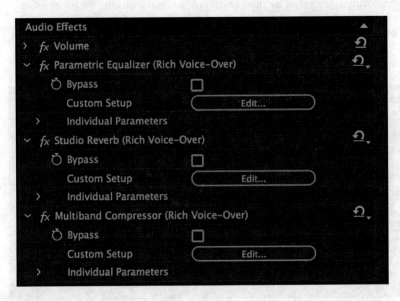

Figure 10-65. *Don't forget to make presets for your favorite audio effects, too*

Custom Keyframe Behavior Presets

Intrinsic effects like opacity and motion don't always behave the way you want. Some intrinsic effects have animation already turned on, and all effects have linear keyframes as standard. This isn't necessarily what you want. So, let's have a look at ways to fix this.

Opacity Keyframe Killer

Opacity already has an active *Toggle Animation* stopwatch icon. This means that you will automatically set a keyframe when you adjust opacity. This is not the standard behavior of effects and can throw you off if you're not paying close attention.

If you adjust opacity, then play back your animation, stop the playback, and adjust opacity again, you will have created an animated opacity adjustment—even if that wasn't what you intended to do. Personally, I hate this behavior, so I've created a preset that sets the animation to Off and Opacity to 100 percent.

I discovered that fellow Premiere Pro test pilot Colin Brougham also had a preset like this, and his name for that preset was so good that I adopted it. Say hello to the *Opacity Keyframe Killer™*!

This can easily be created from a clip where you haven't touched opacity at all. Just click the stopwatch icon for opacity to turn animation off. Then, save this as a preset by right-clicking on *Opacity* and choosing *Save Preset*. *Opacity Keyframe Killer*™ is a very good name. For my audio, I've also made the *Volume Keyframe Killer*. Guess what that one does?

Ease Keyframes

Default keyframe interpolation is linear, and that makes a lot of sense. However, sometimes we need ease in and ease out in order to get more professional-looking animations. Let's save a preset that already has ease keyframes for position, scale, and rotation.

On a synthetic clip, add four position, scale, and rotation keyframes without adjusting the parameters, as in Figure 10-66. This creates four linear keyframes for each property. I recommend that you have more time between the middle two keyframes than between the rest so you can easily see what's animation in and animation out.

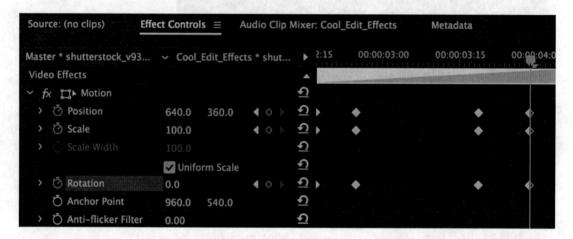

Figure 10-66. *To create a preset with ease keyframes by default, add four position, scale, and rotation keyframes without adjusting the parameters*

Now, right-click the first keyframe for each property and select *Ease Out* (Figure 10-67). Right-click the second keyframe for each property and choose *Ease In*. Then, make the third keyframe *Ease Out* and the last keyframe *Ease In*. Your Effect Controls panel should now look like Figure 10-68.

Right-click on the word *Motion*, save this as a preset, and name it *Ease Keyframes*.

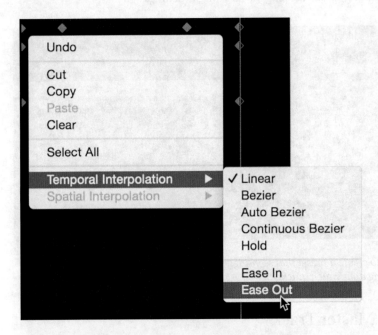

Figure 10-67. *Set easing by right-clicking the keyframes*

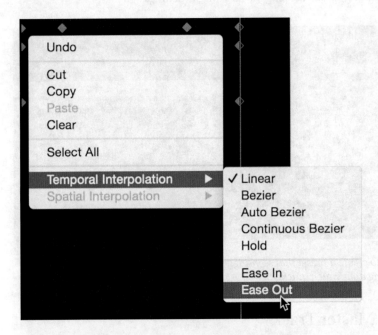

Figure 10-68. *Your keyframes should look like this after setting them to ease in and ease out*

When you apply this preset to a clip (see Figure 10-69), there is no motion, but when you start changing the parameters while parked at a keyframe, you will see that the easing is built into the preset, making it super easy to quickly make natural-looking motion effects. You can easily move the keyframes to the time where you want animations to start and stop, still keeping the Ease In/Out settings.

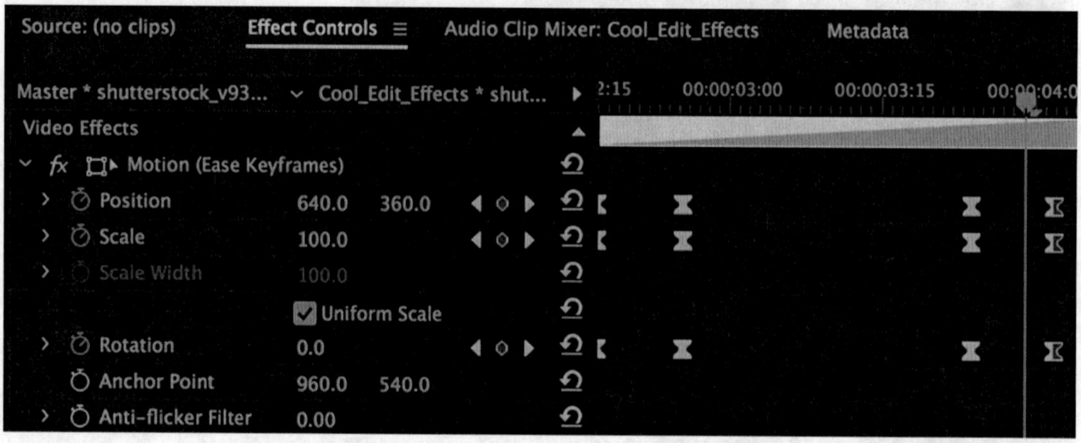

Figure 10-69. *It might feel strange to create a preset that seemingly does nothing, but by using this as a starting point you will get your easing done much quicker!*

Custom Presets for the Master Track

Unfortunately, when you add effects in the Audio Track Mixer—for example, the hard limiter in Figure 10-70— your effects presets cannot be used. Only the built-in presets from each plug-in can be applied. So, the workaround is to save a template project with a sequence where you've already added the effect you want and tweaked it to taste.

In chapter 3 on Audio, we cover the use of compression and limiting on the master track. Read that paragraph, tweak the settings on the master track, and save the project as a template.

Figure 10-70. *You can't save presets for the Audio Track Mixer, but it can be part of your template project*

Now, Share the Presets with Friends

In the **Effects ➤ Presets** folder, right-click and choose **Export Preset** (Figure 10-71), or use the panel menu. Save to a folder where you can easily find it again, like the desktop. Now, mail it to your friend or colleague.

When your friend gets the preset, she can import it via the same panel menu or a right-click, choosing *Import Preset*. When the preset is imported, she can delete the original file. Premiere Pro saves a copy in the Presets folder. If she wants to, she can edit the name, properties, and description of the preset to better suit her needs via the same context menu.

Even though these presets are saved in the cloud when you do Sync Settings, you probably want to keep backups of your preset files somewhere so you can easily get them back when you upgrade Premiere, reinstall your OS, cancel your subscription, or generally screw up your computer—or buy a new one.

Figure 10-71. Export and import presets with a right-click

Download Jarle's Presets

To quickly get insight into the possibilities of effects presets, download Jarle's presets from `premierepro. net/customizing/jarles-premiere-pro-presets-version-4/`.

All the presets mentioned in this section are part of this preset collection.

Custom Keyboard Shortcuts

I highly recommend customizing your keyboard shortcuts. If you're used to Final Cut Pro or Avid, you might want to use the ready-made custom sets that come with Premiere. The downside of customization is that all the shortcuts you learn from tutorials will be wrong. But even if you're used to editing in Premiere, you should make custom keyboard shortcuts for stuff you do often.

Knowing your keyboard shortcuts will save you from a lot of wading through menus and clicking with your mouse. There are even some features that can only be used via shortcuts. There is no doubt that learning to use keyboard shortcuts for tasks that you do often is one of the best things you can do for increased editing speed.

If your keyboard doesn't have these keys, I recommend getting one that has, or getting a separate numeric keyboard that you can connect when you edit. You'll get at least 16 extra keys, and used alone and with combinations of Shift, Ctrl, Cmd, and Alt, you can have more than 100 new shortcuts available!

Don't get too carried away with keyboard shortcuts, though. I use the mouse whenever it enables me to work faster than with the keyboard.

It's the Grave Accent Key folks, not the Tilde Key

Among the most useful functions in Premiere are *Maximize or Restore Frame Under Cursor* and *Toggle Full Screen*. They both involve the Grave Accent key (`` ` ``). For some reason, a lot of tutorials and books will tell you to use the Tilde key (~) when they should really tell you to use the Grave Accent key.

Now, on an English keyboard, this isn't too bad, as they both appear on the same key. Technically, you should press **Shift+`** to get the Tilde, and if you don't press **Shift**, you'll get the Grave Accent. When told to "hit the Tilde key" most people will hit the Grave key, and everything works, even though the key is misnamed.

But this creates some trouble for non-English keyboards where these two characters are on different keys. So, if you're not using an English keyboard, don't be confused.

To be clear: Pressing the Grave key (`` ` ``) alone on an English keyboard blows up the panel under your cursor to full screen, and pressing **Ctrl** while hitting Grave (**Ctrl+`**) shows full-screen video. The Tilde is not involved.

Change Multi-Key Shortcuts to Single-Key Shortcuts

Operations that you use a lot should be mapped to single keystroke shortcuts. Some of the most used functions already have this, like **Q** and **W**. But some functions I use often are mapped to multi-key shortcuts by default, and I change them to better suit my workflow.

Clear in and out is one example. After doing an operation where I intentionally use in and out points in the sequence, I find that it leads to mistakes if I keep them. They quickly get out of sight in the timeline, and I stand the risk of accidentally editing parts of the timeline that I don't see and didn't intend to change. So, I clear the in and out points as soon as I've used them and don't need them anymore. The default **Ctrl+Shift+X** (Cmd+X) is not fast enough, so I've mapped this to **F1**.

Yes, that means that I have to click **Help ➤ Adobe Premiere Pro Help** using my mouse to go to Help. Luckily for me, I need to clear in and out points far more often than I need to read Help documents.

Deselect All is another feature I use a lot, especially after we got the advanced trimming features. I often need to get quickly out of Trim mode. I refuse to press **Ctrl+Shift+A** (Shift+Cmd+A) to do this. Instead, I've mapped this to **F2**, like in After Effects.

There are many more, but you get the idea. If you find yourself using complicated or time-consuming multi-key combinations, take a moment and see if you can replace them with single-key shortcuts.

Assign the Same Shortcut to Multiple Commands

There are two types of keyboard shortcuts you can assign: application-wide and panel shortcuts. Panel shortcuts will only work if the panel is selected, but application shortcuts will work regardless. This not only means that panel shortcuts can override application shortcuts, but also that you can reuse the same key across different panels.

For example, both the program and source monitor panels can be assigned shortcuts for zoom in and zoom out, but rather than having to remember different shortcuts for each panel, you can use the same for each. I use **Ctrl+-** and **Ctrl+=** (Cmd+- and Cmd+=). Similarly, if you regularly use the pancake layout for your sequences, you can assign the same shortcut for both Open in Source Monitor and Open Sequence in Timeline.

As well as being able to share shortcuts between panels, you can also share them between specific commands in the same panel. In the Timeline panel, you can assign the same shortcut to both nudging a clip and trimming a clip. For this, I use the default shortcut for nudging for both, which is **Ctrl+Left/ Ctrl+Right** (Cmd+Left/Cmd+Right). If you select the clip, the shortcut will move it. If you select the edit point, the shortcut will trim it.

Assign Two Shortcuts to a Command

If you regularly switch between using a tablet pen and the keyboard, you may want to assign more than one shortcut to a command based on whether you have both hands on the keyboard or not. For example, the default key to mark an in point is **I**, but if you're holding a pen in your right hand, it would make sense to also assign a key on the left side of the keyboard. To do this, go to the command list in the Keyboard Shortcuts panel and click the blank space to the right of the first keyboard shortcut, as in Figure 10-72. Now you can type in another shortcut. Add as many as you want!

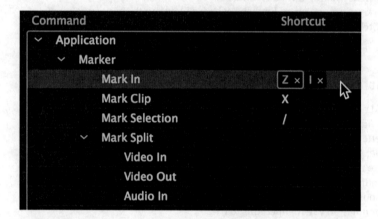

Figure 10-72. *Assign more than one shortcut key if you regularly switch between a tablet pen and the keyboard*

Custom Transition Shortcuts

If you type *Apply* in the search field in the Keyboard Shortcuts panel, you will see all the available transition shortcuts (Figure 10-73). These are the familiar Apply Video Transition and Apply Audio Transition, plus Audio Crossfade, Video Crossfade, Dip to White, and Wipe. Four often overlooked shortcuts are the ones that apply the default video and audio crossfades to or from the playhead.

Since the default transitions are Audio Crossfade and Video Crossfade—and those have their own shortcuts—you will want to change the defaults to other transitions.

Say you change the default audio transition to *Exponential Fade* and the default video transition to *Dip to Black* (Figure 10-74). Then, you'll have a total of four video transitions and two audio transitions available with custom keyboard shortcuts.

Figure 10-73. *Several keyboard shortcuts are available for transitions*

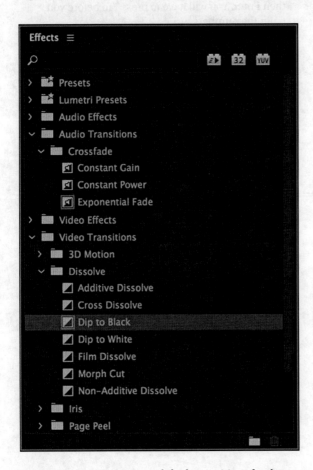

Figure 10-74. *Reserve your default transitions for those not already included in the keyboard shortcut list*

Candidates for Replacement

Very few of the F-keys are used by Premiere by default, so let's put them to good use. When was the last time you hit F1 for Help? You clicked the Help menu, didn't you? And when was the last time you captured from tape? If you don't use Help or Capture often, why not use the F-keys for more useful features?

If you find that features you use very seldom have nice shortcuts, consider stealing them for use with more frequently used features. Table 10-1 lists some good candidates you can assign to functions you use more than the ones they're assigned to by default.

Table 10-1. *Most of Us Can Live Without These*

Win	Mac	Command
F1-F9	**F1-F9**	Help, Capture—but most of them are not in use
Numeric keyboard 1-9	**Numeric keyboard 1-9**	Mostly unused—but you will lose the ability to jump directly to a timecode by hitting the numbers and then Enter. You will have to press Tab before you enter the numbers.
R	**R**	Rate Stretch tool
H	**H**	Hand tool
B	**B**	Ripple Edit tool
Z	**Z**	Zoom tool
Shift+Ctrl+.	**Shift+Cmd+.**	Select Next Panel
Shift+Ctrl+,	**Shift+Cmd+,**	Select Previous Panel
Ctrl+Shift+P	**Option+P**	Clear Poster Frame
Ctrl+Q	**Cmd+Q**	Exit

Searching for Shortcuts

If you want to know if a shortcut is available for a feature you use often, open the Keyboard Shortcuts panel and look at the visual keyboard layout, shown in Figure 10-75. Each key is color coded to indicate whether it has been assigned or not. Purple is an application-wide shortcut, green is a panel-specific shortcut, and gray means the key is unassigned.

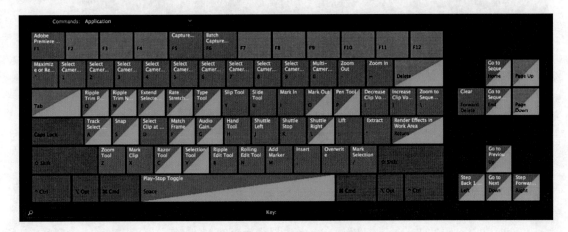

Figure 10-75. *The visual keyboard in the Keyboard Shortcuts panel makes it easy to see which keys are already being used*

If you select a key, you'll see all its modifier keys and their assigned commands in the bottom right, as in Figure 10-76. You can also select a combination of modifier keys on the keyboard to see which keys are being used by those modifiers.

Figure 10-76. *See which keys are being used by modifiers, like shift+option. To see what command has been assigned, hover you mouse over the key, and it will appear as a tool tip.*

You can also use the search box to look for commands (Figure 10-77). Did you know that you can assign a shortcut to *Replace with After Effects Composition*? Search for After Effects, and you'll find out.

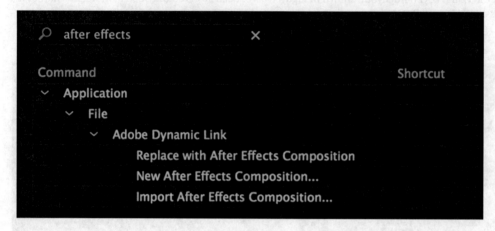

Figure 10-77. Search to find existing and available shortcuts

Tables 10-2 and 10-3 list some additional shortcuts you may find helpful.

Table 10-2. *Useful Shortcuts You May Not Know*

Win	PC	Command
Ctrl+G	Cmd+G	Group
Shift+Ctrl+G	Shift+Cmd+G	Ungroup
Shift+Ctrl+E	Shift+E	Export Frame (source and program monitors)
F	F	Match Frame
Ctrl+K	Cmd+K	Add Edit
Shift+Ctrl+K	Shift+Cmd+K	Add Edit to All Tracks
Shift+T	Shift+T	Trim Edit
E	E	Extend Edit to Playhead
Shift+K	Shift+K	Play Around
Ctrl+Shift+Space	Opt+K	Play In to Out
Shift+F	Shift+F	Select Find Box
Shift+Ctrl+F	Shift+Ctrl+F	Reveal Nested Sequence
Shift+\	Shift+\	Toggle View (Icon/List)
Shift+Ctrl+A	Shift+Cmd+A	Deselect All
Ctrl+Alt+W	Opt+W	Trim Next Edit to Playhead
Ctrl+Alt+Q	Opt+W	Trim Previous Edit to Playhead
Shift+W	Shift+W	Extend Next Edit to Playhead

(*continued*)

Table 10-2. (*continued*)

Win	PC	Command
Shift+Q	**Shift+Q**	Extend Previous Edit To Playhead
Shift+R	**Shift+R**	Reverse Match Frame
Ctrl+Up	**Ctrl+Up**	Select Previous Clip
Ctrl+Down	**Ctrl+Down**	Select Next Clip
Shift+Up	**Shift+Up**	Go to Previous Edit Point on Any Track
Shift+Down	**Shift+Down**	Go to Next Edit Point on Any Track
Alt+Up	**Opt+Up**	Nudge Clip Selection Up
Alt+Down	**Opt+Down**	Nudge Clip Selection Up
Alt+click	**Opt+click**	Expand/Close All Bins
Shift+S	**Shift+S**	Toggle Audio While Scrubbing

Table 10-3. *Some New Shortcuts I've Made (Windows)*

Ctrl+Alt+C	New Sequence from Clip
Shift+A	New Adjustment Layer
Ctrl+P	Preferences
Shift+Ctrl+R	Replace with Clip from Source Monitor
Alt+Ctrl+R	Replace with Clip from Source Monitor, Match Frame
Shift+Ctrl+S	Select Nearest Edit Point as Ripple In
Shift+Ctrl+A	Select Nearest Edit Point as Ripple Out
Shift+Ctrl+	Zoom to Frame
Alt+R	Optical Flow (set as your time interpolation)

A Shortcut You May Have a Hard Time Finding: *Find in Timeline*

Ironically, this is one of the least discoverable features in Premiere. It's not available from a menu, so you'll have to use the keyboard shortcut, **Ctrl+F** (Cmd+F).

Hitting this Find in Timeline command opens a dialog box (see Figure 10-78) where you can specify your search. When you've entered the search criteria and hit *Find*, it will find the first clip that matches the criteria. If you hit *Find All*, it will select all matching clips, making it easier to do things like move them all to another track or change their label color.

You can also set a keyboard shortcut for the command *Find Next*, which will find the next matching clip without having to open the dialog box again. Great timesaver!

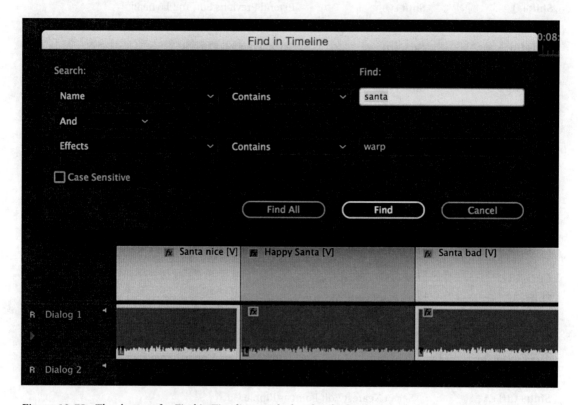

Figure 10-78. *The shortcut for Find in Timeline can be hard to find*

Adjusting the Track Header Height

You may already know that you can resize the height of your track header by scrolling your mouse wheel over it. If you hold down **Ctrl** (Cmd), you will have finer control of the adjustment. If you hold down **Shift**, you can adjust all the other audio or video tracks proportionately, and double-clicking the header will quickly expand and collapse the track.

Print a Spreadsheet of the Keyboard Shortcuts

By copying the keyboard shortcuts list to the clipboard, you can paste it into a spreadsheet document, do some formatting, and then print it.

Choose **Edit ➤ Keyboard Shortcuts** (Premiere Pro ➤ Keyboard Shortcuts). Click the *Copy To Clipboard* button (Figure 10-79), then go to your spreadsheet or text document and paste (Figure 10-80), format, and print.

Now, study your list to see what other features you can customize shortcuts for. If you can't sleep, take this print-out to bed to learn it by heart. That should help.

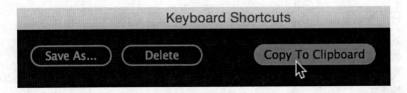

Figure 10-79. *Copy your list of keyboard shortcuts*

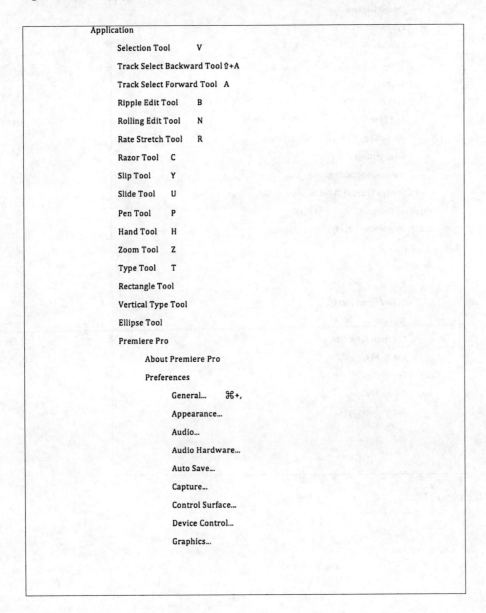

Figure 10-80. *Paste your keyboard shortcuts to a spreadsheet or text document*

Label Colors...

Label Defaults...

Media...

Media Cache...

Memory...

Playback...

Project Locking...

Sync Settings...

Timeline...

Trim...

Sync Settings

Sync Settings Now

Last Sync

Use Settings from a Different Account...

Clear Settings...

Manage Sync Settings...

Manage Creative Cloud Account...

Keyboard Shortcuts...   ⌥+⌘+K

Quit Premiere Pro   ⌘+Q

File

New

Project...   ⌥+⌘+N

Team Project (Beta)...

Sequence...   ⌘+N

Sequence From Clip

Bin   ⌘+/

Search Bin

Offline File...

Adjustment Layer...

Figure 10-80. (*continued*)

Print a PDF of the Default Keyboard Shortcuts

You can print PDFs of the existing keyboard shortcuts from the Help articles online: helpx.adobe.com/
premiere-pro/using/print-premiere-pro-cc-shortcuts-windows.html and helpx.adobe.com/
premiere-pro/using/print-premiere-pro-cc-shortcuts-mac.html.

Sharing the Custom Keyboard Shortcuts

Keyboard shortcuts are saved in .kys files in your Profile folder and will be synced to the cloud. Your
Windows shortcuts can be found in the Win subfolder and your MacOS shortcuts in the other one.

If you're working in a larger facility, you would probably like to have the same shortcuts on all the
computers on your network, as in Figure 10-81. The .kys file can be distributed to all the editing stations in
your company. The new shortcuts preset can then easily be chosen via the drop-down list in the Keyboard
Shortcuts dialog.

.kys files can't be shared across different platforms, because keyboard shortcuts created for Windows
will not work on a Mac. This is true even if you're using Sync Settings.

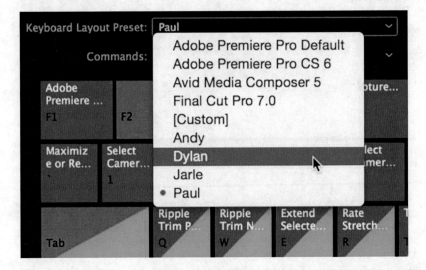

Figure 10-81. *You can have several sets of custom shortcuts on the same machine for different editors*

NRKs Custom Shortcuts

NRK, the Norwegian Broadcasting Corporation, has kindly shared an image of their default custom shortcuts in Figure 10-82. Their editors can customize this further, of course.

This should give you an idea of how they've adjusted this to the Norwegian keyboard layout and to their specific needs as a broadcaster.

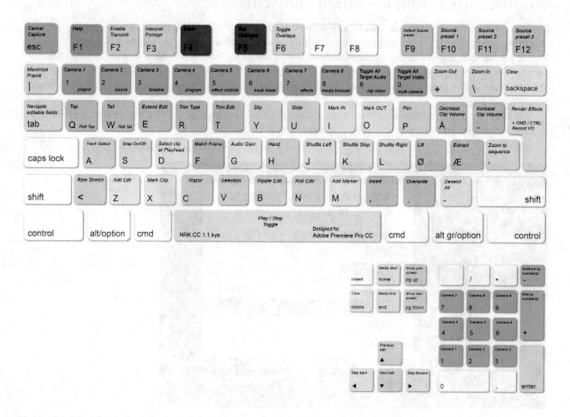

Figure 10-82. *The custom keyboard shortcuts used at NRK, the Norwegian Broadcasting Corporation*

Switch Language When Keyboard Shortcuts Stop Working

I'm on a Norwegian Win 10 system, and on Windows, there's a keyboard shortcut combo (**Alt+Shift**) that changes the keyboard layout between installed languages. I can switch between Norwegian and English.

This shortcut is very similar to some shortcuts I use in Premiere, and I will sometimes accidentally hit the keyboard combo without realizing and switch the keyboard layout. A whole bunch of keyboard shortcuts will suddenly not work anymore. Switching back is very easy, though.

If you want to disable this Windows shortcut, go to **Control Panel** ➤ **Language** ➤ **Advanced Settings** ➤ **Change language bar hot keys**. Here, you can change or remove the shortcut.

Details can be found here: `winaero.com/blog/configuring-language-settings-in-windows-8/`.

This can also be an issue on OS X, where the shortcut for switching languages is **Cmd+Spacebar**. You can change this shortcut by going to **System Preferences** ➤ **Keyboard** ➤ **Shortcuts** ➤ **Input Sources**.

Custom Transition Presets

The cross-dissolve transition and a few others can be saved as presets. For cross-dissolve, click the Effect Controls panel menu and choose *Save Preset,* as shown in Figure 10-83. For other third-party transitions, right-click on the transition's name to save your current settings as a transition preset. Make sure that *Include Transition Duration* is checked.

You can save presets with different lengths, of course. All your preset transitions can be found in your Effects Presets bin (Figure 10-84).

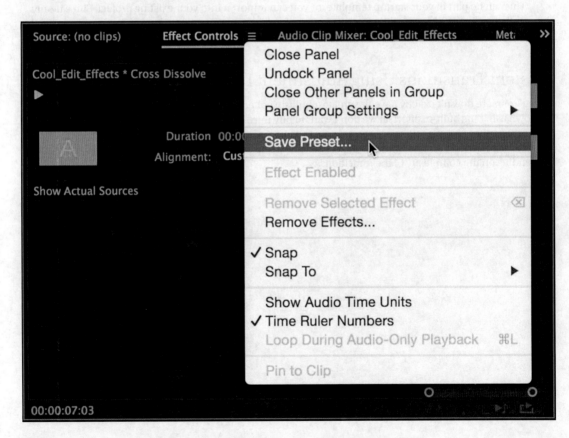

Figure 10-83. *The cross-dissolve transition can be saved as different presets*

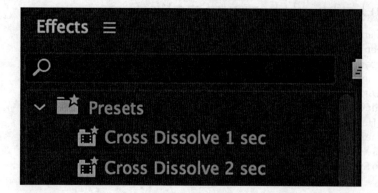

Figure 10-84. *Your transition presets end up in the Effects Presets bin, just like other effect presets*

Copy/Paste Your Favorite Transitions from a Template Sequence

Many transitions are still not preset-capable, so the preceding method doesn't always work. However, since we can copy/paste transitions, you can have a sequence with synthetic clips only with all your favorite transitions in it. If you use a pancake layout for your timelines, you won't even need to continually jump between them.

This can be part of your startup template, or you can import it into your existing project. Since it only has synthetic clips, it adds very little to your project size. Adding sequence markers makes it easy to find the different transitions.

Custom Transitions Using Adjustment Layers

Since Premiere doesn't exactly have the greatest built-in collection of transitions, we often end up rolling our own using the built-in effects if we don't want to buy third-party collections. But since we don't have a way to store these as transitions, we can save them as part of a sequence in a template project, or just save them as effect presets and add them to adjustment layers, to color mattes, or to the actual clips themselves, depending on the complexity of the transitions.

S-Curves on Your Cross-Dissolves

If the standard fade is not smooth enough, you can always use opacity keyframes and make the transition smooth. To get total control over your video dissolves, adjust the opacity of a clip with ease out and ease in keyframes. Drag the Bezier handles if you need to tweak the transition curve.

Save these as two separate presets, *Opacity S-Curve In* (anchored to in point) and *Opacity S-Curve Out* (anchored to out point), as shown in Figure 10-85.

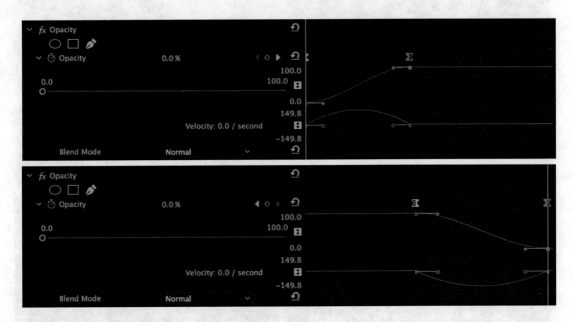

***Figure 10-85.** Make two opacity ease presets for smoother cross-dissolves*

Another option is to install the demo of Film Impact's Transition Pack 1, which includes a free "proper" GPU-accelerated dissolve transition: `filmimpact.net/blog/impact-dissolve-in-depth-video-tutorial/`.

Camera Flash Transition

We have a dip to white transition, but it doesn't behave like a camera flash, so we need to create one ourselves. An old-school flash bulb would fade in in an instant and fade out quickly and in a somewhat non-linear fashion. We can mimic this using a white color matte with opacity keyframes and a blend mode.

Go to **File ➤ New ➤ Color Matte** and choose a white color. Name it *Camera Flash*. Put the clip on the timeline above a cut between two clips so it starts three frames before the cut. I would do this by placing it at the cutting point and then moving it to the left by pressing the **Left Arrow** three times while holding down the **Alt** key.

The ideal duration will depend on your frame rate, but if you're editing at 24 or 25 fps, make it about 20 frames long. Right-click on the clip and choose *Speed/Duration* to set duration to 20 frames. For an example of this effect, see Figure 10-86.

Figure 10-86. *A better-looking camera flash transition than dip to white. Adjust the opacity curve in the Effects Control panel to make the flash fade-in and fade-out as long as you want.*

I decided to make opacity go from 0 to 100 in three frames, stay at 100 for one frame more, then fade out over 16 frames with a Bezier curve (see Figure 10-87).

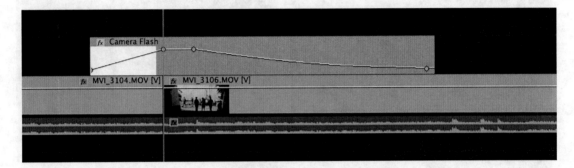

Figure 10-87. *Opacity keyframes show how the flash has a quick fade-in and a slow fade-out*

I used the linear light blending mode to give it much more punch, completely clipping the lighter colors. To view how the effect appears in the Effect Controls panel, see Figure 10-88.

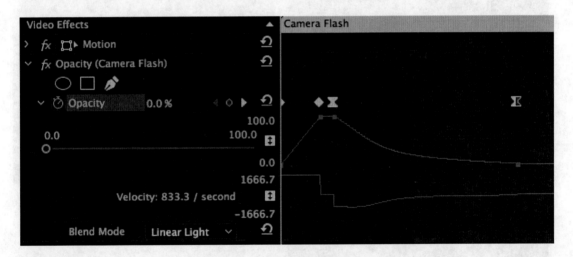

Figure 10-88. *This is how it looks in the Effect Controls panel*

The Oh-so-popular Glow and Blur Transition

A glow and blur transition (Figure 10-89) is basically just some levels and color adjustment combined with a blur. We'll build this on an adjustment layer so it can be easily copied from your Transitions sequence to the sequence where you need it.

Figure 10-89. *You see this kind of transition everywhere*

Create an adjustment layer that is about half a second long. Put it on the timeline above the two clips you want a transition between. I've even put a cross-dissolve transition between them (Figure 10-90), but this doesn't have to be as long as the adjustment layer.

Figure 10-90. *Add a cross-dissolve transition under the adjustment layer*

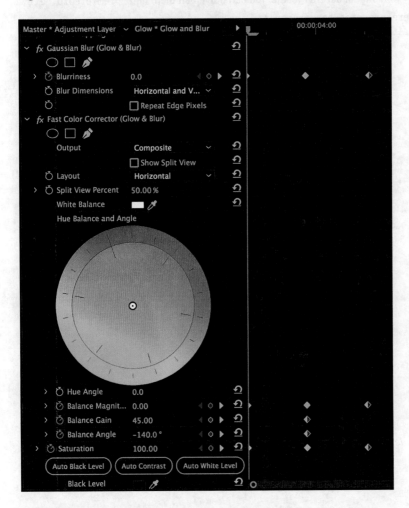

Figure 10-91. *The whole stack of effects and their keyframes*

Add Gaussian blur to the clip and set keyframes for *Blurriness* from 0 to 150 and then back to 0. Check *Repeat Edge Pixels*.

Then, add the fast color corrector and set keyframes for Input White Level to 255, then 2, and back to 255. Now you have a standard blur-to-white-and-back-again transition. To make it a bit more interesting, we can add some color during the transition. I adjusted Saturation from 100 to 200 and back to 100.

This gave it a bit more punch, but let's also set Balance Angle to -140 and Balance Gain to 45, and animate Balance Magnitude from 0 to 75 and back to 0. Now we also get some colorization. You can view these effect settings in the Effect Controls panel in Figure 10-91.

As you can see, this transition can be tweaked in many ways by adding more effects. If you add in some opacity keyframes and play with blending modes, too, you can get very different results. Normal will appear quite soft and with vivid colors (Figure 10-92). Screen mode (Figure 10-93) will make the original images blend through more sharply even when there's quite a lot of blur, making the whole transition more dream-like. Hard Light (Figure 10-94) mode will add contrast and saturation.

■ **Note**   It's possible to recreate this transition using Lumetri Color instead of the fast color correction effect. I've done so, and included it in version 4 of Jarle's Presets. You can download them here: `premierepro.net/ customizing/jarles-premiere-pro-presets-version-4/`

Figure 10-92. *Normal mode*

Figure 10-93. *Screen mode*

Figure 10-94. *Hard Light mode*

Swish-Pan Transition

We can build the swish-pan transition in Figure 10-95 from some position animation and Gaussian blur. For the position animation, we could use the push transition, but that one doesn't have any settings apart from duration, and it moves in a linear fashion, with constant speed. So, we cannot make it simulate a natural panning movement with acceleration and deceleration. Let's use our built-in position for the animation, and use ease in/out and some Bezier curves.

Figure 10-95. *Homemade swish-pan transition*

Since it involves two clips, and both of them need to be visible at once, we have to put them on separate tracks. So, we'll put one clip over the other and extend their in and out points, respectively, to create an overlap where we can do the transition, just like in the early days of NLE editing. I made my overlap a little over half a second long.

We want the two clips to move together to the left (or right, of course, but we'll move them to the left in this example). We set position keyframes at the start and end of the overlap for both clips. The outgoing clip is easy: just add a keyframe at the start of the transition overlap without changing the position at all. Then, add a minus (-) before the existing position at the end of the clip. This will move the clip so it's just outside the frame at the end.

For the incoming clip, we'll need some math. It should end up perfectly aligned in the middle of the frame, of course, but it should start completely out of the frame to the right, so we'll add the width of the clip to the existing position at the start keyframe. In my example, I had 720 × 1280 footage, so I entered 640 + 1280 into my calculator and got 1920. For 1080 × 1920 footage, it would be 960 + 1920 = 2880.

This creates a linear movement, but we could have achieved this by adding the push transition, so we'll need to tweak this further. Go to the Effects Control panel and change the start keyframes to ease out and the end keyframes to ease in for both clips. Now the movement is much more natural.

You may have to zoom in a lot in the Effects Control panel to get access to the keyframes, depending on the length of your clips. I recommend using your keyboard shortcuts to zoom in, since the zoom bars at the bottom of the panel behave, well, kind of illogically and even erratically.

Now we need some simulated motion blur on this. Add an adjustment layer above the overlapping clips and name it *Swish Pan*. Add Gaussian blur, then make sure *Repeat Edge Pixels* is checked and that the blur is set to horizontal blur only.

Add three blurriness keyframes—at the start, at the end, and in the middle. Adjust the blurriness to about 270 in the middle keyframe. Now, make the start and end keyframes Bezier (right-click on keyframe, then choose *Bezier*) and drag the handles so the curve gets steeper at both ends. Then, change the middle keyframe to Bezier, and we've made an upward arch in the curve, which means the blurriness will increase faster at the start, be more static in the middle, and decrease faster toward the end. This will correlate somewhat to the speed of the movement in the two clips.

No one can keep the camera perfectly horizontal while panning, so we should also introduce a bit of vertical blur. Add another instance of Gaussian blur, this time set to *Repeat Edge Pixels* and *Vertical blur only*. Repeat the same procedure with the blurriness keyframes, but set the middle one to around 15 pixels. Click *Play* and enjoy.

To view all these settings in the Effect Controls panel, see Figure 10-96.

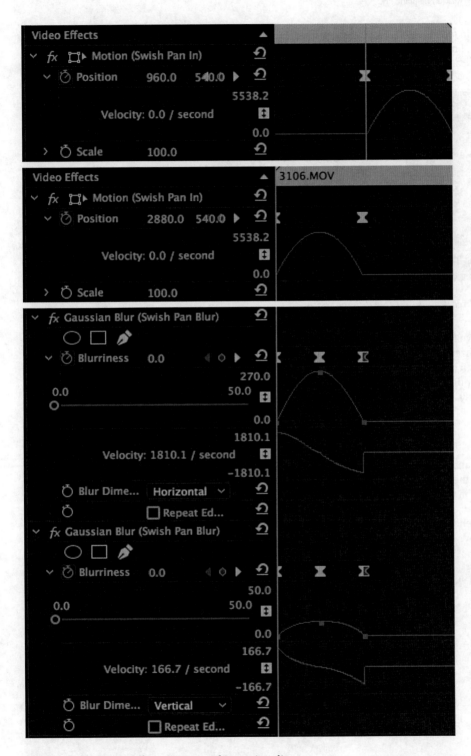

Figure 10-96. *Settings for outgoing and incoming clips*

897

You can avoid too much copy and pasting when you want to use this transition by saving the animations as effects presets. I named mine *Swish Pan Out* (anchor to out point), *Swish Pan In* (anchor to in point), and *Swish Pan Blur* (scale), as shown in Figure 10-97.

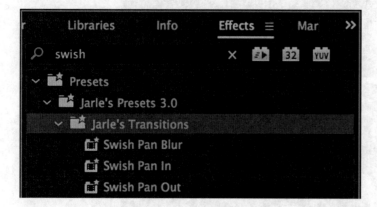

Figure 10-97. *Three presets for three different clips*

A little-known fact is that Premiere Pro is smart enough to adapt presets like these to different frame rates and frame sizes. I made my preset in a 720p50 sequence, and when I use it in a 1080p25 sequence, the length is still about half a second, and the movement of the clips still goes all the way to the left and the right of the frame, adapting both the duration (measured in frames) and the position animation (measured in pixels). So, we only need one preset to cover all frame rates and sizes. Clever!

Jarred Cuts

The swish-pan transition can be tweaked to have only linear keyframes, as well as to move the clips unpredictably to the left, then right, and at irregular speeds several times before it finishes. This will result in a twitchy transition that creates some confusion and grunge to the transition.

If you want an even more messy transition, use a complex nested sequence and speed it up like crazy without frame blending. This will show many different clips for the duration of the transition, with random frames flashing by.

You can also change the motion parameters on every frame with hold keyframes on the incoming or outgoing clip to create a jarred cut (Figure 10-98). Change the parameters wildly so you see very different parts of the image on every frame.

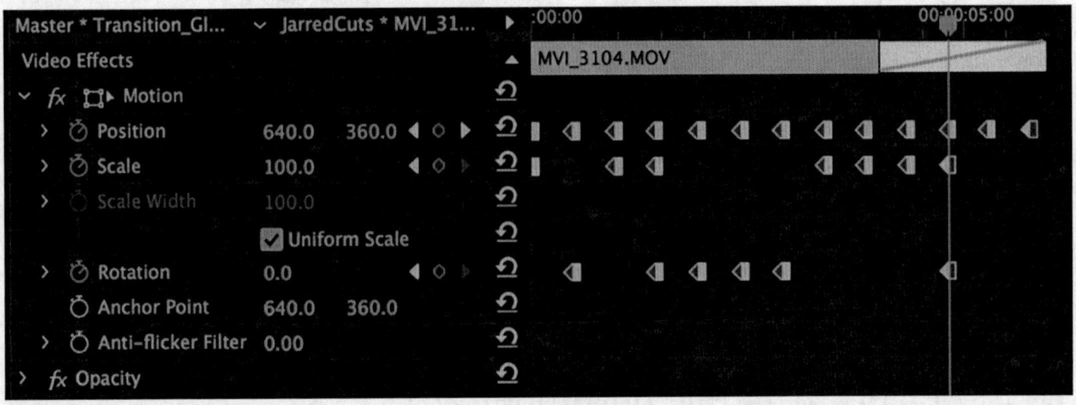

Figure 10-98. *Hold keyframes for motion create highly irregular movement and chaos*

Logos as Wipes

If you have a high-res logo file, you can make it cover the screen from top to bottom, and hide a mask animation behind it. In my example, I've used the logo for Movies on War (Figure 10-99), a film festival in my area.

I got an Illustrator file so I could make the logo as big as I needed it in Photoshop and save a PNG file (Figure 10-100). I settled for 2930 × 1929 pixels—enough to cover the whole HD frame top to bottom while animating it from the right to the left, and then some.

Figure 10-99. *Make sure you get the logo in a format that supports alpha channels. Logo design by Eivind Høimyr.*

Figure 10-100. *Scaled logo on transparent background*

Of course, if we wanted to make this easy, we could just do a standard horizontal wipe behind the logo, but it looks cooler if the new image isn't revealed with a straight wipe, but rather in different parts at different times. Let's use Premiere's masks to achieve this. View the complete layer stack in Figure 10-101 and mask settings in Figure 10-102.

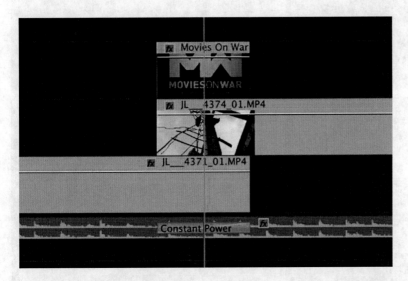

Figure 10-101. *The complete layer stack that makes up the logo wipe*

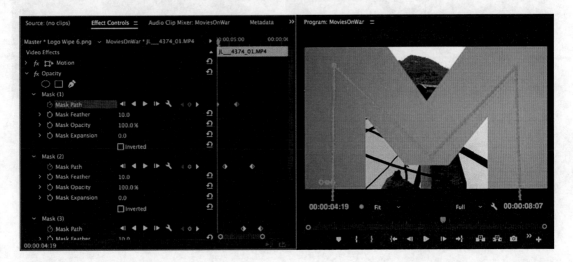

Figure 10-102. *Masks follow the logo shape*

All the masks are animated from the right side of the frame to the left side of the frame, timed to the opening in the logo that they're supposed to reveal the image in. The last mask covers the whole frame when it stops. For the resulting transition, see Figure 10-103.

Figure 10-103. *The logo reveals a new image as it's moving*

Logo Reveals

You can get away with effects and transitions on text and logos that would look extremely cheesy on normal video footage. Try adding lens flares (as shown in Figure 10-104), 3D motion, Venetian blinds, splits, horizontal Gaussian blur, and other effects to logos to reveal them in fancy ways.

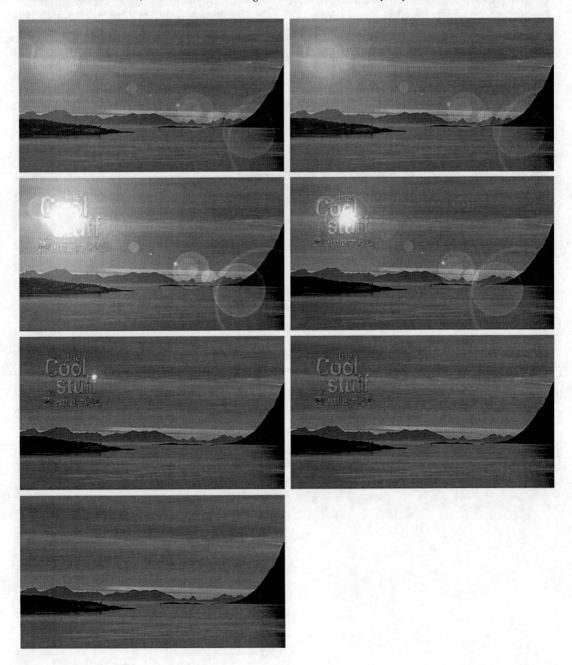

Figure 10-104. *Lens flare reveals logo*

Organic Wipes with Gradient Wipe

We have two gradient wipe effects in Premiere. One is a true transition that can be put on the cutting point between tow clips, like any other transition. If you put it on, you will be asked to choose an image to use as the gradient map. We don't want that—we want a much more organic and dynamic transition. Luckily, we also have the other gradient wipe effect, found in **Video Effects ➤ Transition ➤ Gradient Wipe** (see Figure 10-105).

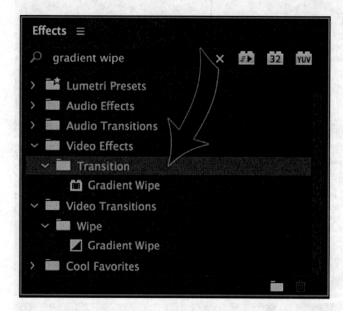

Figure 10-105. *Use the gradient wipe from the Video Effects folder, not the one from the Video Transitions folder*

This effect has a choice for which layer you want to use for the gradient map. Note that it says *layer*, not *image*. This means that anything you put on a layer can be your gradient map, including live video and nested sequences! We'll use a nested sequence.

First, we need to build a nice, grungy texture, so let's put three very different textures on separate tracks in an empty sequence named *Gradient Wipe Nest*. Then, we set the blending mode for the two top ones to *Overlay* and put an adjustment layer on top of them with the tint effect to make everything black and white. Now we have a quite unique texture to build from, shown in Figure 10-106.

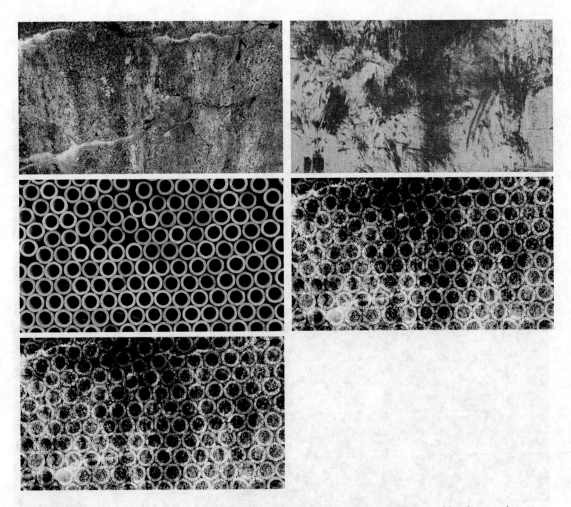

Figure 10-106. *The three first texture images are combined into a unique matte uising blending modes*

We create a black video clip and put it on top of all the other layers, then add the four-color gradient effect and set keyframes for the four colors. We start with all of them white. Then, in the middle, we make the two color points to the right black, and those to the left white. At the end, all of them should be black. These settings (see Figure 10-107) create an animated gradient that goes from right to left, getting darker and darker.

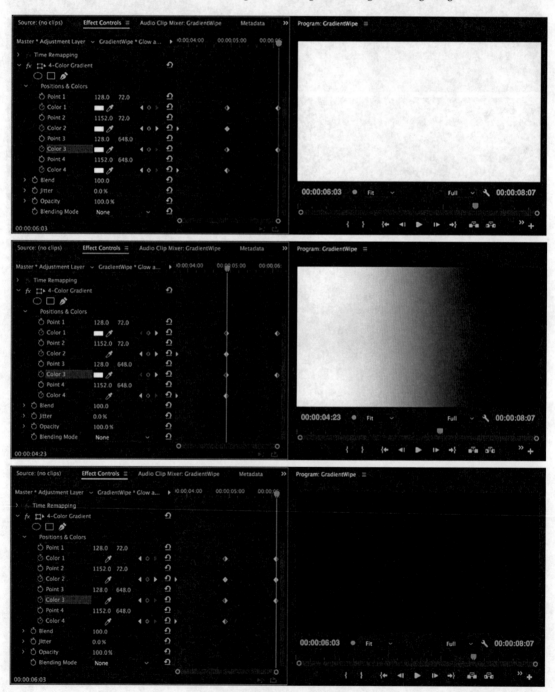

Figure 10-107. *The gradient is animated from completely white to completely black*

We set this layer to the vivid light blending mode and scrub through it. The effect, shown in Figure 10-108, is a very organic transition from white to black.

To get rid of some stray black noise at the beginning, we throw on another adjustment layer, using the fast color corrector to set the Input White Level to 200. This may or may not be necessary, depending on the settings you've done on other layers, and the textures themselves. The levels effect could have been used instead of the obsolete fast color corrector effect.

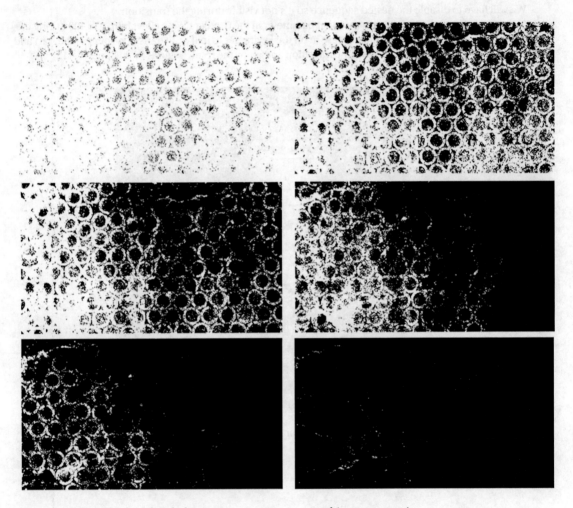

Figure 10-108. Combined with the texture matte, we get something very organic

OK, so we have a beautiful white-to-black transition. We want to use this as the source for our gradient wipe effect.

Again, we make an overlap between the two clips where we can do the transition in our main timeline. Then, we put the gradient wipe effect on the upper clip and place the Gradient Wipe Nest sequence we just made on a track above it. We tell the gradient wipe effect to use Video 3 as its *gradient layer*—or any other video track you've placed your nested sequence on. The stacked clips should look like Figure 10-109.

We will have to disable the nested sequence so it's not visible during the transition.

Now, we keyframe the *transition completion* parameter in the Gradient Wipe effect from 0 to 100 during the length of the transition. I used ease out and ease in on the keyframes to make the transition softer at the start and the end (shown in Figure 10-110). Render the transition and enjoy the result (Figures 10-111 and 10-112).

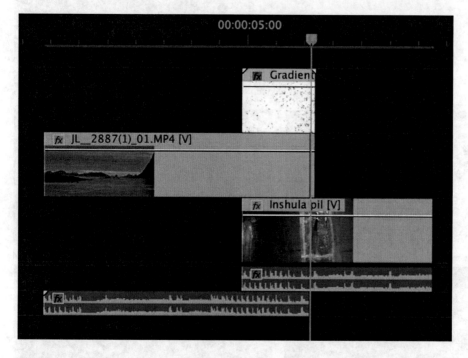

Figure 10-109. *This is how your stacked clips should look on the timeline*

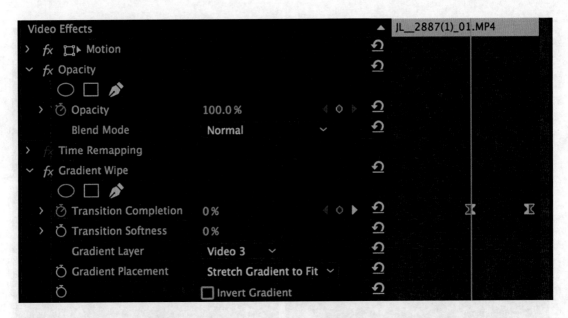

Figure 10-110. *The gradient wipe effect uses the organic animated matte sequence as its gradient layer*

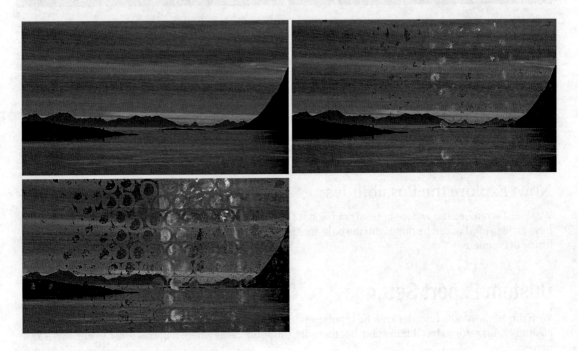

Figure 10-111. *The start of the transition*

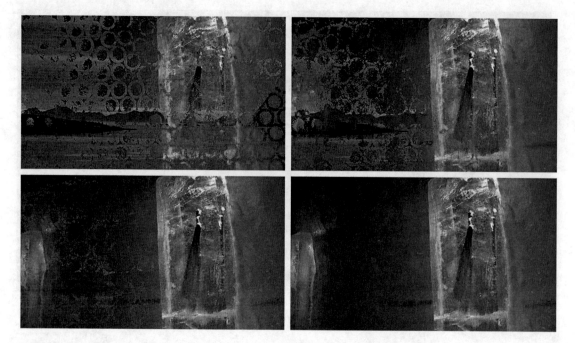

Figure 10-112. *The end of the transition*

You can tweak this transition in many ways. You can animate the textures; you can make it softer with blurs—even animated blurs; you can use other blending modes; you can use masks on the layers; and you can animate the four points in the gradient so they start and finish at different times, creating movement toward or from one corner, and so on.

Unfortunately, both the gradient wipe effect and the four-color gradient effect lack GPU acceleration, so you'll have to render this transition. If you want to avoid rendering the whole outgoing clip, make an invisible cut at the start of the transition and delete the effect from the first part of it.

Now, Explore the Possibilities

We've just scratched the surface here, of course, but I hope you got a glimpse of something interesting and have an idea of what can be done with the built-in effects to create presets for clever and creative transitions inside of Premiere.

Custom Export Settings

With the Adobe Media Encoder and the export presets maturing steadily over several versions, the need for custom export settings has diminished, but there are still some cases where it makes sense to create custom presets.

Adobe's engineers can't possibly know the needs of all their customers. Some of the default presets are good, while some can get better with a little tweaking. Some are buried in long lists, and some are just not there. So, let's customize!

Avoid Long Lists and Minimize Errors

Some formats have a huge number of built-in presets. The DNxHD format has more than 60 presets, as shown in Figure 10-113, and having to scroll through them all each time you export a file is a time waster. Say you're often using the DNX 120 1080p25 preset for archive versions; it would be nice if that one was on the top of the list, right?

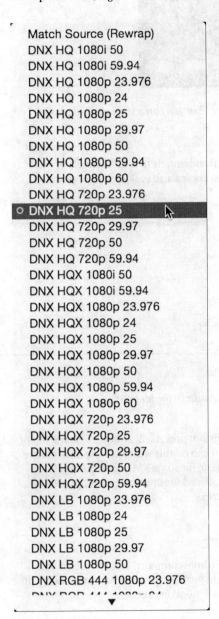

Figure 10-113. *Long lists are cumbersome and can be a source of user errors*

If you try to click the Save Preset icon to the right of the preset name, you will get a warning that it's a system preset (Figure 10-114) and can't be overwritten. So, we will trick Premiere into thinking we've altered it.

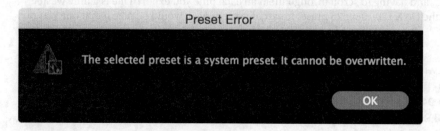

Figure 10-114. *Premiere won't allow you to overwrite system presets, but you can trick it to think you've altered it*

First, choose the preset, then click the Audio tab and change the channels to four channels. If this is what you want, leave it like this. If not, go back to the default stereo choice and look at the preset name. Now it says *Custom*, and we can save it.

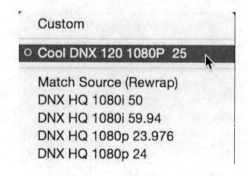

Figure 10-115. *Custom export settings are easier to find than the defaults in the long list*

Save the new preset with a clever name. From now on, your custom preset will always be on the top of the list, above all the factory presets, as shown in Figure 10-115. You can do this with any format, of course. The list for H.264 export presets is even longer, so it's a good candidate for some XML file trashing.

If you save your export presets with *Match Sequence Settings* selected for the most important settings, one preset can cover your needs for many frame rates and frame sizes.

Quality-Controlled Exports Company-Wide

The preceding technique is a nice way to foolproof the exports in a whole company. Make presets with simple, easy-to-understand names, so everyone will choose the right format settings on exports—every time.

Read more about foolproofing the company's exports in the XML tweaking section.

Better Quality H.264 Exports

It turns out I have a different understanding of the phrase *High Bitrate* than the ones who created the factory-export presets. When you export to the H.264 format, the default preset is Match Source–High Bitrate. Nice, but when we look at the bit rate, it's set to a mere 10 Mbps target and 12 Mbps Max. For a 1080p25 clip, that's not very high at all. It's also set to VBR, 1pass.

We want better quality than that, so let's change the Bitrate Encoding field to VBR, 2 pass, Target Bitrate to 12 Mbps, and Max Bitrate to 15 Mbps, as shown in Figure 10-116. This will yield better quality, but can still easily be played back on any modern computer. Yes, it will result in a larger file, and, yes, it will take longer to export, but it will make your work really shine at the next company presentation. Less banding, less noise, and less blocking.

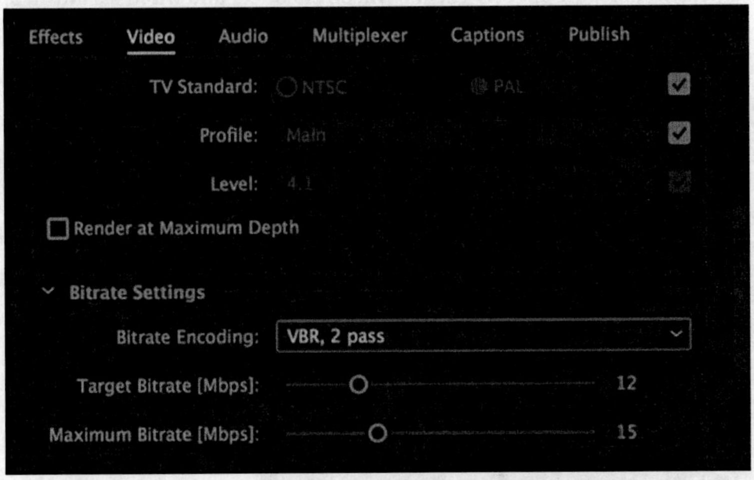

| Effects | Video | Audio | Multiplexer | Captions | Publish |

TV Standard: ○ NTSC   PAL   ☑

Profile: Main   ☑

Level: 4.1   ☑

☐ Render at Maximum Depth

∨ **Bitrate Settings**

Bitrate Encoding: VBR, 2 pass ∨

Target Bitrate [Mbps]: ———○——— 12

Maximum Bitrate [Mbps]: ———○——— 15

Figure 10-116. These settings will yield better quality than the High Bitrate preset

Export Your Preset

Of course, if you work in a company with more than one system, you want to spread your custom presets to all your colleagues. If there are lots of presets, you could just copy them to the same folder on all systems.

The custom export presets are stored in this location: **Documents\Adobe\Adobe Media Encoder\11.0\Presets** (Users/[User]/Documents/Adobe/Adobe Media Encoder/11.0/Presets).

Sometimes, you've created just a couple of new export presets and want to share them. This is when you export them one by one and send them to others who need them. Here's a little-known secret: you can export a copy of the preset file to whatever folder you want if you hold down the **Alt** (Option) key while clicking the Save Preset icon. The preset is saved as an .EPR file.

Give your presets logical names and descriptions so you know what they are—even after several months.

Import Presets

Directly to the right of the Save Preset icon in the Export Settings panel is the Import Preset icon. Click it and navigate to the location of the preset. Type a good name for the imported preset and tweak other options if necessary.

Transfer Your Files to YouTube, Vimeo, or FTP Servers While You Sleep

Yes, even your user names and passwords on an FTP server, YouTube, Facebook, or Vimeo account can be saved as part of an export preset, as shown in Figure 10-117. The file will be encoded, and when it's finished, Premiere will log in and transfer your files. You can auto-publish while you're sleeping.

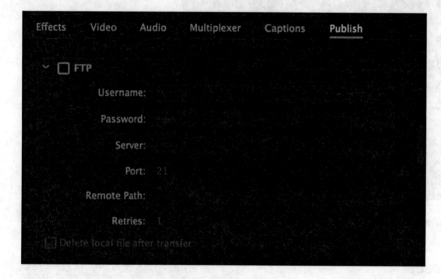

Figure 10-117. *FTP, YouTube, Facebook, and Vimeo passwords can be built into a preset so it automatically uploads the file when encoding is done*

Add Effects to the Exported Video

You can add Lumetri looks/LUTs, logo overlays, file name overlays, and timecode to your output files like the example in Figure 10-118 using the Effects tab in your Export settings (Figure 10-119). This is extremely useful when sending files for review and feedback. You can save these as part of your export presets and name them *HQ with TC and Logo*, or similar describing names.

Figure 10-118. *This output file includes a logo overlay, timecode, and file name overlay*

Figure 10-119. *Use the Effects tab in your Export settings to add overlays of your choice, then save them as custom presets*

Closed Captions Export

You can also save settings for closed captions export, but since I've never used closed captions, I'll leave this for you to explore on your own.

Custom Metadata Export

In the Metadata Export panel, you can create and use custom presets for what metadata to preserve from the source files, and what metadata to add to the output file at export. Your custom settings are saved as XMP files in subfolders inside the same folder as the other export presets.

The files end up here: **Documents\Adobe\Adobe Media Encoder\11.0\Export Templates** (Users/ [User]/Documents/Adobe/Adobe Media Encoder/11.0/Export Templates) and **Documents\Adobe\Adobe Media Encoder\11.0\Preservation Rules** (Users/[User]/Documents/Adobe/Adobe Media Encoder/11.0/ Preservation Rules).

To get to the Metadata Export panel shown in Figure 10-120, click the *Metadata* button all the way down in your Export Settings panel. Under Export Options, choose the way you want your metadata to be saved—embedded in the video file, as a sidecar file, as both, or not at all.

Then, concentrate on the source metadata. What kind of metadata do you want to stick around from the source files? Do some qualified guessing around what you'll need, and then save these choices as a new *source metadata preservation rule*.

Figure 10-120. You can decide what metadata to keep in the exported file

Now, let's have a look at the output file metadata. What do we want to add to the output file? Again, do some well-founded guessing and save a new *output file metadata export template*. In the example in Figure 10-121, I've added a clip description and a starred rating.

■ **Note** These settings are *not* stored as part of your export presets, so you need to make a deliberate choice for every new export you make from Premiere.

To use these presets, just use the drop-down lists to find the desired preset and then click *OK*. At export, the metadata will be saved embedded in the video file or as a sidecar, depending on your settings, and of course only if the format supports embedded metadata. When you import the exported files in Premiere or any other XMP-savvy program, the metadata fields will be available for display and for searching, as shown in Figure 10-122.

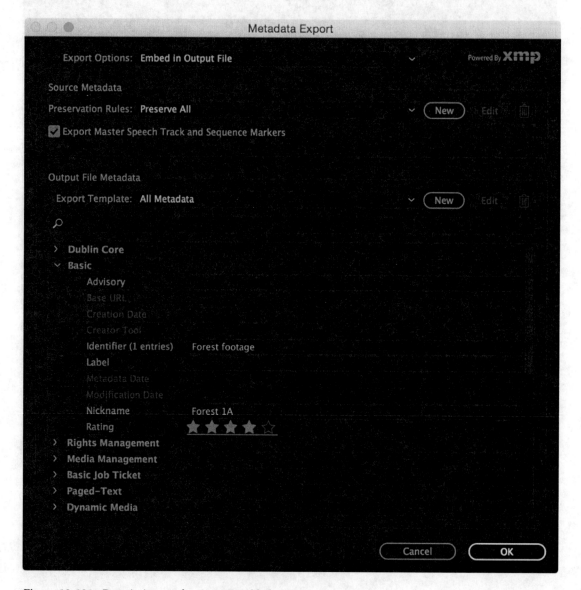

Figure 10-121. Descriptions and ratings are added at export

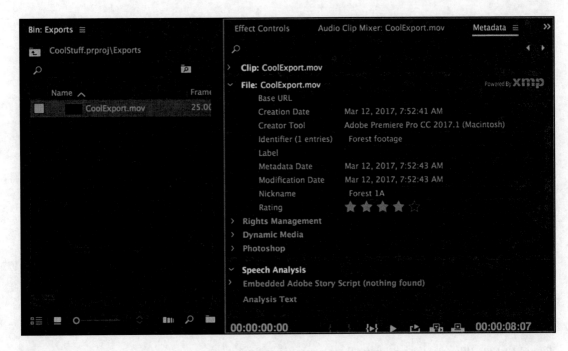

Figure 10-122. *Metadata you include in the export can be read by Premiere and other XMP-capable software*

Custom Proxy Presets

For information on how to create custom presets for your proxy files, including how to add metadata and watermarks, refer to Chapter 1 on workflow.

Custom Project Manager Presets

If you're archiving your project with the Project Manager, you have the option to transcode all your media to a single codec. Premiere provides some default presets for MXF OP1a, DNXHD, or QuickTime, but you also have the ability to import your own.

The laborious way to do this is to go to Media Encoder, create a preset, jump back into Premiere, and then import the preset through the Project Manager window. There is an easier way, however!

Simply create a new preset, then click *Save Preset* while holding down the **Alt** (Option) key. Save the new preset to the folder **Documents/Adobe/Premiere Pro/11.0/Profile-[Adobe ID]/Settings/ Consolidate And Transcode Presets** (/Users/[User]/Documents/Adobe/Premiere Pro/11.0/Profile-knowr/ Settings/Consolidate And Transcode Presets) and the preset will show up in the list. Keep in mind, for your transcodes to match the original dimensions of the clips or of your sequence, you'll need to tick *Match Source* in the preset.

Any presets in this folder with Match Source checked will also be used when you select *Render and Replace* for your timeline.

Customize the Default Presets

The default presets for transcoding and consolidating are kind of cryptic, and are shown in Figure 10-123. The only information they offer about their settings are their preset names. Did you know that the Apple Pro Res 422 preset only encodes audio at 16-bit? What if your original audio had been recorded at 24-bit? You would lose all that detail in your archived files.

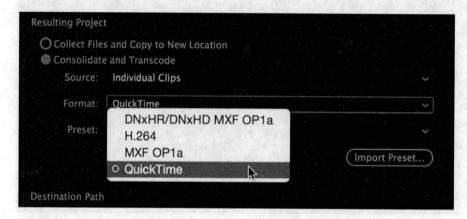

Figure 10-123. *What are the settings for these transcode presets?*

There is a way to check these settings. If you go to the Export window, you can import these presets from the folder **Program Files\Adobe\Adobe Premiere Pro CC 2017\Settings\/EncoderPresets/ ConsolidateAndTranscode** (Applications/Adobe Premiere Pro CC 2017/Adobe Premiere Pro CC 2017.app/ Contents/Settings/EncoderPresets/ConsolidateAndTranscode). This will load all the settings in the window. If there's anything you want to change, just save the preset over the original.

Custom Thumbnails for Motion Graphics Templates

Thumbnails in mogrts from Premiere are 1422 × 800 pixels, while the ones from After Effects are 800 × 600 pixels. This means that widescreen After Effects mogrts are shown smaller than Premiere mogrts in the browser in the Essential Graphics panel, with letterboxing. Plus, they get gray space on both sides—so, in effect, they're both pillarboxed and letterboxed. What a waste of space!

If you want to change the thumbnail image you can create a PNG file in Photoshop that is 1422 × 800 pixels and save it as thumb.png. Rename the .mogrt file to .zip and open it. Drag the new image into the zip folder and confirm that you want to overwrite the old image. Rename the .zip file to .mogrt again, and import into Premiere as usual. Your AE mogrt now has a 33 percent larger widescreen thumbnail, as shown in Figure 10-124.

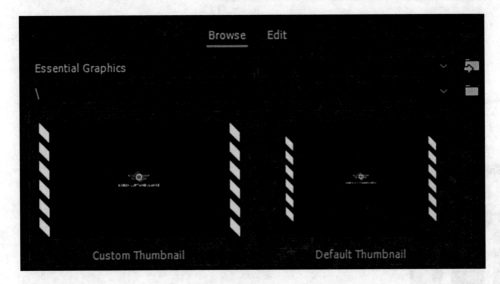

Figure 10-124. *Custom thumbnail on the left, default on the right*

Of course, the same method can be used to change the thumbnail in a mogrt made in Premiere, but in this case you would keep the size and just change the image.

Custom Icons

Iain Faulkner of OneOne2 Media (oneone2.co.uk) was tired of opening After Effects projects when he wanted to open Premiere projects, which he did because of the color similarity between the Premiere and the After Effects project icons. And yes, they really are quite similar, especially when displayed at small sizes, as you can see in Figure 10-125a.

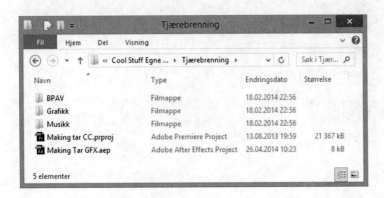

Figure 10-125a. *Original icons*

Iain decided to replace the default icon with one that's more distinctive (Figure 10-125b), and now he can easily tell one from the other.

Figure 10-125b. *Iain Faulkner's custom Premiere Pro icon can easily be told from the After Effects icon, even at small sizes*

Creating Custom Icons

If you have a minimum of Photoshop skills, you can create your own icons. Just use the old icons—or screenshots of them—as a starting point and create your own look. I decided to go for a grungy look on my Premiere icons, as shown in Figure 10-126.

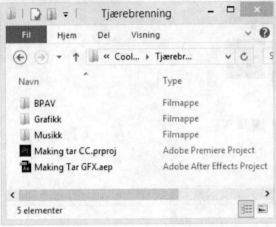

Figure 10-126. *My custom icon*

Start by creating a new Photoshop document that's at least 512 × 512 pixels. When you have the look you want, save the file as a PNG and navigate your browser to iconverticons.com/online/. Drag your PNG file to the drop zone in the browser, and the web page will provide download links for MacOS and Windows icons (Figure 10-127).

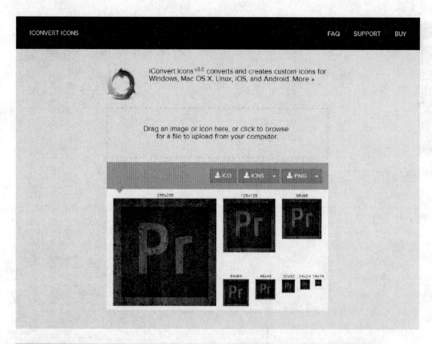

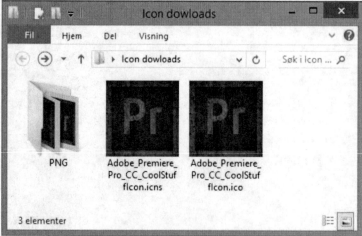

Figure 10-127. *Upload your PNG file and get icons in many sizes back. Super easy!*

Custom Premiere Icons on a MacOS System

Iain is on a Mac, so replacing the icons is easy. In his words: Just navigate to the application, right-click, choose *Show Package Contents*, enter the Contents and then the Resources sub-folders—and there are all the icons. Replace the project icon pr_proj_primary.icns with a revised version, and it's a global and immediate change on that particular computer.

Custom Premiere Project Icons on a Windows System

On a Windows system, the icons are built into the Premiere Pro.exe file, so we cannot change the default icons without hacking the exe file—something I strongly advise you not to do. But, if you're willing to go out on a limb and open RegEdit—the Registry Editor—you can change the path where Windows looks for the icon to use when displaying Premiere projects.

In RegEdit, go to **HKEY_CLASSES_ROOT ➤ Adobe.Premiere.Pro.Project.8 ➤ DefaultIcon** and double-click the value in the right panel. By default, it's set to **C:\Program Files\Adobe\Adobe Premiere Pro CC 2017\Adobe Premiere Pro.exe**. You can change this path so it points to your custom .ico file.

This change requires a system restart to become active, so you will not see the change before you restart the system.

Custom Premiere Icons in Windows Quick Launch

You can change the icon used in the Windows Quick-Launch bar too. You don't even have to use RegEdit. It's just a shortcut, and you can easily change icons for shortcuts. Navigate to the **Adobe Premiere Pro.exe** file in your **Program Files\Adobe\Adobe Premiere Pro CC 2017** folder. Right-click it and choose **Send to ➤ Desktop** (create shortcut).

Then, right-click on the shortcut you just made on the desktop and choose **Properties ➤ Shortcut ➤ Change icon**. Browse to your custom icon file and use that for the shortcut. Now, drag it onto your Windows task bar, and you have a custom icon that launches Premiere (Figure 10-128).

Figure 10-128. *This icon stands out from the rest*

Extreme Customization with XML

This section is not for wimps! It involves some hacks that can possibly make things unstable or cause strange problems if you mess up. Most of the stuff is pretty safe, but you should always make copies of the original files before you start fiddling with the XML.

Now that you've been duly warned, let's get on with the fun! We'll start with some easy hacks where you just move particular XML files out of their folders, and then we'll advance into actual XML tweaking and a hostile take-over.

Get Rid of the Factory Presets

The factory presets in PP are an incredibly strange selection of bad-taste effects. It's like a lame joke, really. I can't imagine any film being better after adding solarize (Figure 10-129) in or mosaic out. The convolution kernel is actually a nice plug-in, but the user interface is even more convoluted than the name implies, and you'd better be a mathematician if you want to know what the settings actually do. So, my recommendation is: Ditch them!

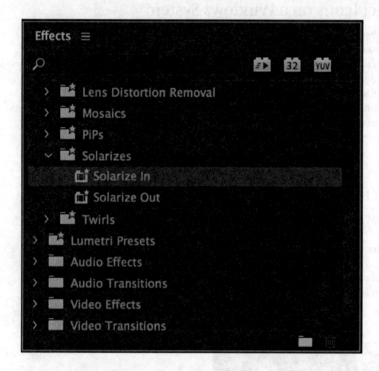

Figure 10-129. *When was the last time you used solarize in/out? I hope never...*

But, if you try to right-click one of the factory presets in PP, the *Delete* choice is grayed out so you can't delete them. Let's do a quick hack: locate Premiere's Effect Presets folder. You can find it here: **Program Files\Adobe\Adobe Premiere Pro CC 2017\Plug-ins\en_US\Effect Presets** (Applications/Adobe Premiere Pro CC 2017/Adobe Premiere Pro CC 2017.app/Contents/Plug-ins/en_US/Effect Presets). Just move the Factory Presets.prfpset file out of there, restart Premiere, and the pesky presets will no longer take up valuable screen estate in the Effects panel, as in Figure 10-130. Oh, joy!

Figure 10-130. It's much cleaner without the default presets

You'll have to move the file out of the folder—renaming it will not work. You may also need to be logged in as Administrator to do this.

Re-import Presets You Want to Keep

Want to keep a few of the factory presets for some reason? OK, no problem; navigate to the `Factory Presets.prfpset` file you moved and import it. The presets will now be imported, but now they can be deleted like any other custom preset. Delete the ones you don't want, and you're good.

Keep the Lens Distortion Removal Presets

These are the only ones I find useful from the default presets, and, luckily, they're saved in a separate file from the factory presets and are not deleted when you remove the others. The lens distortion removal presets are found in the `LensDistortionRemoval.prfpset` file. I found it here on a Windows system: **Program Files\Adobe\Adobe Premiere Pro CC 2017\Plug-ins\Common\Effect Presets** (Applications/ Adobe Premiere Pro CC 2017/Adobe Premiere Pro CC 2017.app/Contents/Plug-ins/Common/Effect Presets).

Ditch the Lumetri Presets Too

If you don't use them, why show them? The `Lumetri Presets.prfpset` file is in the same folder as the `Factory Presets.prfpset` file. Move it, then restart Premiere, and they're gone. The `Lumetri Looks` folder will still show up in the Effects panel, but it will be empty.

Need to Idiot-Proof a Preset?

If you're adding presets for a whole organization, and you want everyone to have the exact same presets, you want them to be non-removable. Since the factory presets are meant to be undeletable, you should be able to add presets to that XML file (and maybe remove the default ones) if you want. Since I am a one-man band, I never tried this, so I don't really know.

It might take some XML-file scrolling to understand the syntax so you know where to copy from your existing `Effect Presets` and `Custom Items.prfpset` files and where to paste the XML info into `Factory Presets.prfpset`. But, it should be doable. I do recommend that you make backup copies of the files before trying, though.

Unless the users have read this book, they will not be able to accidentally remove these presets. Even if they know how to do it, it takes a lot more effort than just deleting it in the Effects panel.

Custom Mask Defaults

You can edit the default settings for both the ellipse and four-point polygon masks in the file **Program Files\ Adobe\Adobe Premiere Pro CC 2017\Settings\MaskPresets.prfpset** (Applications/Adobe Premiere Pro CC 2017/Adobe Premiere Pro CC 2017.app/Contents/Settings MaskPresets.prfpset).

Open the file in a text editor, then do a search on the words "Mask Feather," "Mask Opacity," and "Mask Expansion." The element you want to change is five lines above these words in the node named `<StartKeyframe>` (skip the first value, which is a really long number starting with -9). For example, the default value for Mask Feather is set to 10, but you could change this to 0, or anything you want, as in Figure 10-131.

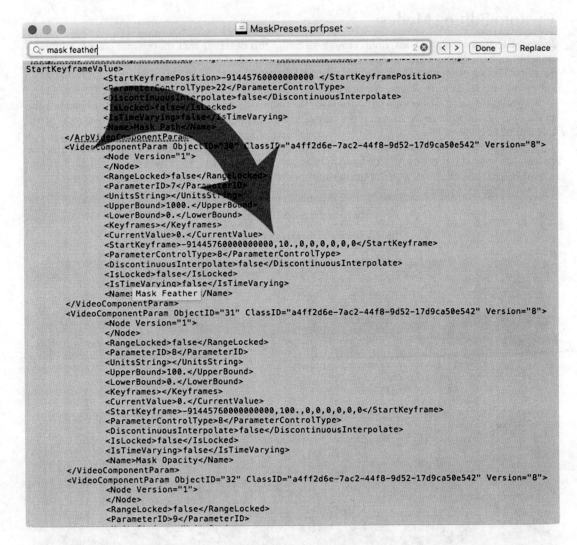

Figure 10-131. *Do you find yourself turning off the mask feather more than turning it on? Why not turn it off by default?*

The VideoComponentParam node, underneath the mask expansion, controls whether the mask is inverted or not. So, if you find you mostly work with inverted masks, change this value from false to true.

Also note, you'll need to search for these settings in two places in the document to change them for both mask types.

Custom Editing Modes

From the tech editor of this book, Colin Brougham comes this neat little trick that creates custom editing modes. Open the Adobe Editing Modes.xml file in **Program Files\Adobe\Adobe Premiere Pro CC 2017\ Settings\Editing Modes** (Applications/Adobe Premiere Pro CC 2017/Adobe Premiere Pro CC 2017.app/ Contents/Settings/Editing Modes). Make a copy first, of course.

The file has some localization parameters for the names of the editing modes, so if you're changing the name of the mode, change the name for the language version of Premiere that you're using. For most of us, this will be English, en_US.

Let's add an editing mode with higher frame rates than Premiere has by default. Take a look at how the default Adobe Editing Modes.xml file looks at lines 133-136 (Figure 10-132). These lines describe the frame rate of 60 fps. The one above, with the strange number 1001 as the denominator, describes 59.94 fps.

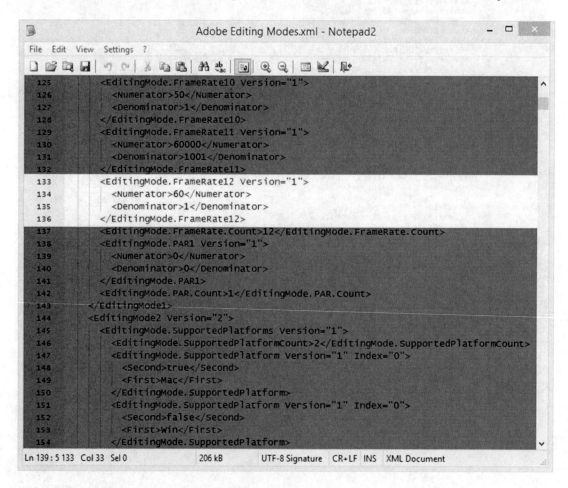

Figure 10-132. Find these lines in the XML file and copy them

Copy the highlighted lines twice and change them so they look like Figure 10-133. Also, change the `<EditingMode.FrameRate.Count>` from 12 to 14.

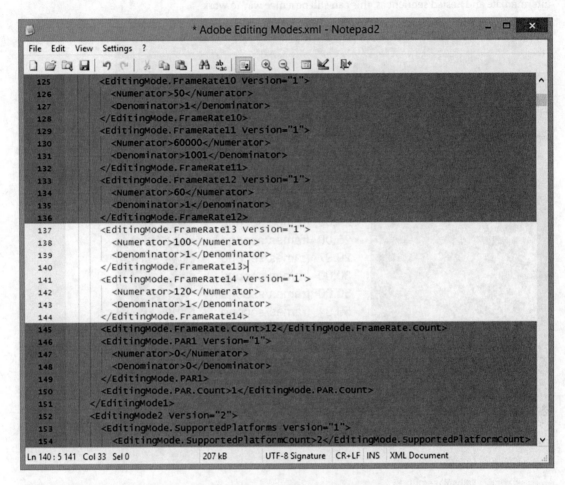

Figure 10-133. *Change the frame rate on the copy, then change the frame rate count below*

On my system, I'm not allowed to save a file to this location, so I have to edit a copy of the file and then move it to the folder. Now, restart Premiere, and when you create a new sequence and choose Custom editing mode, the new frame rates will be available, as in Figure 10-134. Create a new custom sequence preset using these presets.

Now, Premiere doesn't know how to count anything smaller than 60 frames per second, so you're stuck using frames for timecode, and only select codecs like HEVC (H.265) can export more than 60 fps. But, for intermediate and nested sequences, this can still be a nice way to work.

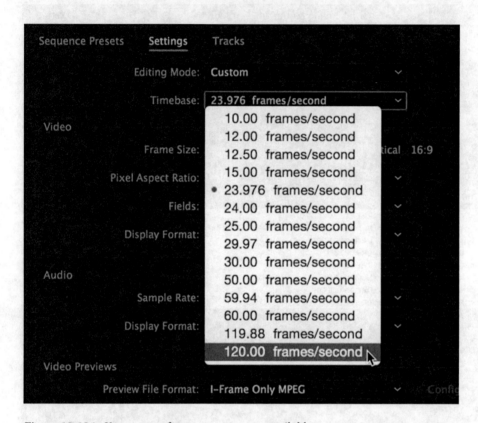

Figure 10-134. *Your custom frame rates are now available*

Custom Preview Codecs

Now that we have DNxHD as an editing mode, the need for this hack has diminished, but there are still some situations where this might be useful. Even if you choose a DNxHD editing mode, you're stuck with what the editing mode offers. Premiere doesn't support DNxHD rendering in the Custom editing mode (as you can see in Figure 10-135), but we can fix that.

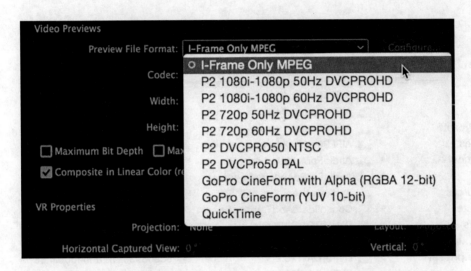

Figure 10-135. *No support for DNxHD as a preview format in Custom mode*

The preview formats are stored as separate XML files in the **Program Files\Adobe\Adobe Premiere Pro CC 2017\Settings\EncoderPresets\SequencePreview** (Applications/Adobe Premiere Pro CC 2017/ Adobe Premiere Pro CC 2017.app/Contents/Settings/EncoderPresets/SequencePreview) folder with an .EPR extension. This means they're actually Adobe Media Encoder encoding presets! The folder contains more than 50 folders with strange names, as seen in Figure 10-136. However, the .EPR files inside them have straightforward names like XDCAMHD 50 PAL 720.epr, so we're in luck.

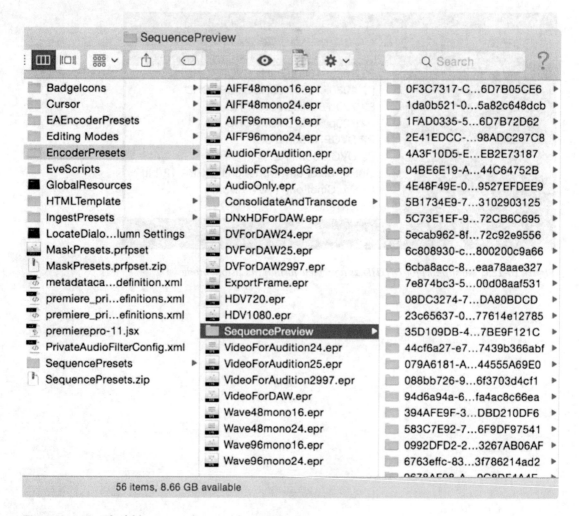

Figure 10-136. *The folder names do not make much sense*

So, how do we know which one is the Custom folder? We'll find the answer in the `Adobe Editing Modes.xml` file we used for adding custom frame rates earlier. Search for *Custom* in that file, and you'll find the editing mode IDs for Mac and Windows (see Figure 10-137).

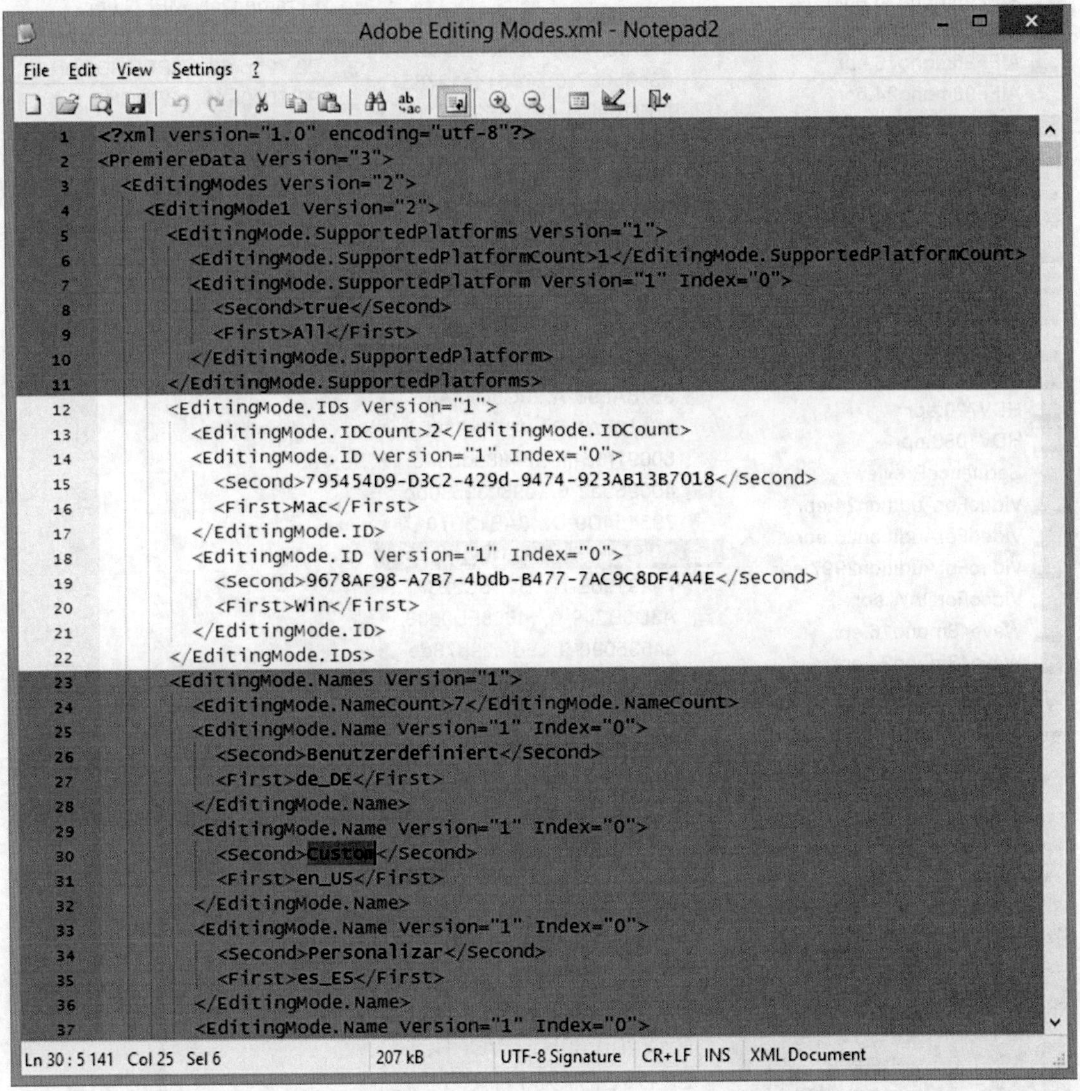


```
<?xml version="1.0" encoding="utf-8"?>
<PremiereData Version="3">
  <EditingModes Version="2">
    <EditingMode1 Version="2">
      <EditingMode.SupportedPlatforms Version="1">
        <EditingMode.SupportedPlatformCount>1</EditingMode.SupportedPlatformCount>
        <EditingMode.SupportedPlatform Version="1" Index="0">
          <Second>true</Second>
          <First>All</First>
        </EditingMode.SupportedPlatform>
      </EditingMode.SupportedPlatforms>
      <EditingMode.IDs Version="1">
        <EditingMode.IDCount>2</EditingMode.IDCount>
        <EditingMode.ID Version="1" Index="0">
          <Second>795454D9-D3C2-429d-9474-923AB13B7018</Second>
          <First>Mac</First>
        </EditingMode.ID>
        <EditingMode.ID Version="1" Index="0">
          <Second>9678AF98-A7B7-4bdb-B477-7AC9C8DF4A4E</Second>
          <First>Win</First>
        </EditingMode.ID>
      </EditingMode.IDs>
      <EditingMode.Names Version="1">
        <EditingMode.NameCount>7</EditingMode.NameCount>
        <EditingMode.Name Version="1" Index="0">
          <Second>Benutzerdefiniert</Second>
          <First>de_DE</First>
        </EditingMode.Name>
        <EditingMode.Name Version="1" Index="0">
          <Second>Custom</Second>
          <First>en_US</First>
        </EditingMode.Name>
        <EditingMode.Name Version="1" Index="0">
          <Second>Personalizar</Second>
          <First>es_ES</First>
        </EditingMode.Name>
        <EditingMode.Name Version="1" Index="0">
```

Figure 10-137. *This is where you find the custom folder names*

In the `<EditingMode.IDs>` section, you'll find that the Custom folder for Mac is `795454D9-D3C2-429d-9474-923AB13B7018` and the Custom folder for Windows is `9678AF98-A7B7-4bdb-B477-7AC9C8DF4A4E`.

So, let's go into these subfolders in the **EncoderPresets\SequencePreview** folder. You can see the Mac version in Figure 10-138.

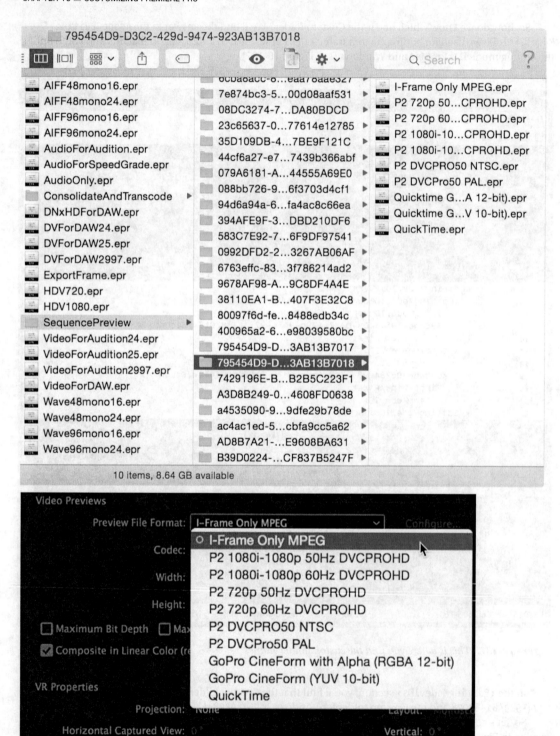

Figure 10-138. *See how the .epr files show up in the preview formats list in Premiere?*

There are no DNxHD presets here, so let's make some!

Search the SequencePreview folder for *dnx*, and you'll find a lot of presets from different subfolders. Copy the ones you want and paste them into the 9678AF98-A7B7-4bdb-B477-7AC9C8DF4A4E folder (because this example is in MacOS; use the 795454D9-D3C2-429d-9474-923AB13B7018 folder on Windows). Restart Premiere, and you've got access to DNxHD as your preview codec in Custom mode (Figure 10-139).

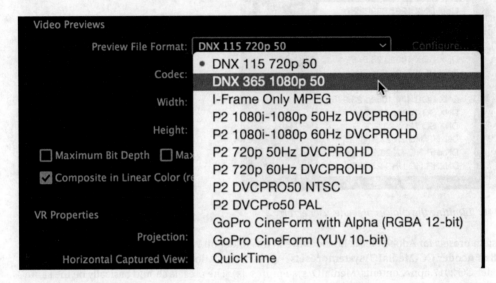

Figure 10-139. Our new preview formats are now available

Using the Custom Preview Codecs

So, why would you want to do this? One way to use this little hack is to use a fast, low bit rate codec during the first steps of your production, and then switch to a high bit rate version when the project is closer to being finished.

Note that you'll see all the presets that correspond with your frame rate, so be careful that you don't choose a frame size for the preview codec that's different from your sequence frame size—unless you want to in order to save render time or for other reasons.

Foolproof the Exports Presets Company-Wide

When people with less-than-average video-format knowledge export their final output file, a lot of things can go wrong. If they choose the wrong format or settings, the spot may not make it to the air.

The system export presets for Premiere are found here: **Program Files\Adobe\Adobe Premiere Pro CC 2017\MediaIO\systempresets** (Applications/Adobe Premiere Pro CC 2017/Adobe Premiere Pro CC 2017.app/Contents/MediaIO/systempresets). The folders in there have strange names, but if you look inside them, it's pretty easy to find out which presets are in which folder. The EPR files are just XML and can be viewed in a text editor. I use Notepad 2. If you delete the folders, or just some presets inside them, these presets will no longer show up in the Export Settings panel.

The format choices will still be in the Export Settings, but the only presets available will be the ones you left in their folders and your custom ones. In the example in Figure 10-140, I've removed all DNxHD presets that are not 25p or 50p, so no one can export a wrong frame rate by mistake.

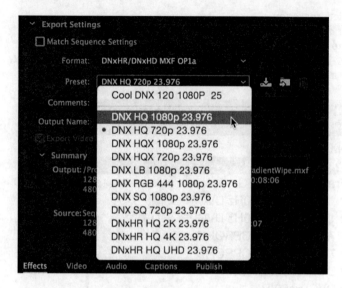

Figure 10-140. *Limiting the choices prevents user errors*

The system presets for Adobe Media Encoder live in this folder on Windows: **Program Files\Adobe\ Adobe Media Encoder CC\MediaIO\systempresets** (Applications/Adobe Media Encoder CC 2017/Adobe Media Encoder CC 2017.app/Contents/MediaIO/systempresets). The presets should basically be the same as for Premiere. Your custom presets will show up both in Premiere's Export panel and in AME.

In **C:\Users\[User]\AppData\Roaming\Adobe\Common\AME\11.0\Presets** (/Users/[User]/ Documents/Adobe/Adobe Media Encoder/11.0/Presets), you'll find the file PresetTree.xml. This is the file that tells Premiere what export formats and presets to display. You might be able to tweak this file to show exactly what you want it to, but take care and save a copy before you start.

The Console

■ **Warning** Fiddling around here can seriously damage your installation, and you shouldn't expect everything to work if you alter the settings!

This little tool is for developers doing debugging and is probably meant to be a secret. However, by now it has been revealed on so many web pages, forums, Facebook groups, and blogs that I feel that it's OK to describe it. So, here we go: If you hit **Ctrl+F12** (Cmd+F12), the Console window opens, and if you choose *Debug Database View* from the panel menu, you get a list of options as shown in Figure 10-141.

You'll see that you can enable things you thought were lost from Premiere, like the Time Warp filter from CS4. Well, you can enable it, but it will not perform very well, it will render slowly, and you'll most likely experience crashes. Not much fun in that. There is a very good reason they've not enabled it in the current version. And since we can use Dynamic Link to AE and add the Time Warp effect there, the Console hack simply isn't worth the trouble.

Have you ever switched to the Color workspace and been annoyed by your playhead suddenly selecting clips underneath it? You can actually disable this behavior here by ticking *Color. AutoSelectionFollowsPlayhead*.

Some of the features are quite useful for problem solving. Generally, though, you should stay away from the Console, as you will possibly create much worse problems than the one you're trying to solve.

Console ≡		
AddDebugClipInfoToTimelineTooltips	☐	false
AddTimestampToLogFileNames	☐	false
AddUTCTimestampToTraces	☐	false
AEResolveQTDataRefs	☑	true
AllowDynamicLinkToOwnProjectType	☐	false
AllowMergedClipsToBeOpenedAsSequences	☐	false
AME.EnableNonStillVideoForOverlay	☐	false
AME.EnablePresetDB	☐	false
AME.EncoderHost.NoXMP	☐	false
AME.UseExportProgressCallback	☑	true
ApplicationLanguage		en_US
ApplicationLanguageBilingual	☐	false
ASL.AsyncBlockSize		0
ASL.DisableReadAhead	☐	false
ASL.NoCache	☐	false
assert.enabled	☐	false
AudioClockOffsetThreshold		0.20000000000000001
AudioClockSkewCompensation	☐	false
AudioClockSkewOffsetThreshold		0.10000000000000001
AudioClockSkewSmoothingConstant		0.01
AudioDropoutDiskReadFallback	☐	false
AudioFadeOutOnStop	☐	false
AudioFilters.SuppressDeprecatedWarnings	☐	false
AudioForceNoDevices	☐	false
AudioIgnoreSetIOSettings	☐	false
AudioIOPreventSuspending	☐	false
AudioMaxShuttleSpeed		4
AudioOutputOnlyUI	☐	false
AudioPrefetchDefaultTime		2
AudioPrefetchDelayDisk		0
AudioPrefetchOverloadThreshold		110
AudioProcessingBypassingEnabled	☑	true
BE.CompressProjects	☑	true
BE.DisableCS7RelinkUpdate	☐	false
BE.EnableNewSerializer	☑	true
BE.Media.GetProperties.GetImporterTestingInfo	☐	false

Figure 10-141. *Lots of crazy stuff can be done in the Console*

Enable Dog Ears

There is a feature used by developers called *EnableDogEars*, which shows how many frames there are in the buffer when playing, what field is displayed, what importer is being used, and so on. For an example of this, see Figure 10-142. Dog Ears can be enabled in the Console, or just use the shortcut **Ctrl+Shift+F11** (Cmd+Shift+F11).

Figure 10-142. *Enable Dog Ears to see what importer is being used, what render size is used, and so forth*

Custom Panels and Add-ons

Panels are a way of augmenting the functionality of Adobe applications using HTML, JavaScript, ExtendScript, and CSS.

Premiere Pro can be extended in different ways by third-party developers. Media Asset Management system (MAM) manufacturers can make custom panels that make importing material from their MAM easier, and news-desk systems can integrate with Premiere through custom panels and scripting, to name just a few.

Quoting Bruce Bullis from the Premiere Pro team about one example, "Panels can get and set XMP metadata for project items. Panels can display whatever they want (they're a web page), so they could (conceivably) display the metadata field(s) they care about, let the user change them, then set the metadata to match those changes."

Sample Panel: PProPanel

You can download Bruce's own sample panel here: github.com/Adobe-CEP/Samples/tree/master/PProPanel. The panel demonstrates the many functions available to custom panels, as well as how to install them.

Sample Panel: PDFViewer

If you're constantly referring to PDF documents (scripts, notes, etc.) while you're editing, you'll love PDFViewer (Figure 10-143). As the title suggests, it allows you to view any PDF document inside Premiere (it's also available for After Effects and Audition). You can open multiple documents at the same time and keep them in tabs, dock them to your workspace layout, or have them float above the application. It also includes a PDF toolbar for adjusting your view, flipping pages, searching, and even copying and pasting text from your PDFs into Premiere.

Figure 10-143. *PDFViewer allows you to view any PDF document inside Premiere, After Effects, and Audition*

Sample Panel: Google Keep

This panel, created by colorist Julien Chichignoud, connects to Google Keep, allowing you to manage a to-do list directly inside Premiere. All you need is a Google account and a label in Google Keep called "Premiere." You can even search Google inside the panel. Download it for free here: julien.chichignoud.com/blog/google-keep-premiere-panel.

Sample Panel: Helpr

Helpr makes it easy to create and customize markers and bins (Figure 10-144). It has two tabs—Markr and Binr. Markr will help you create and modify clip and sequence markers, save marker templates, adjust marker in/out points, and use all of the supported marker colors. Binr is for generating and saving complex bin structures with one click. To learn more, visit brysonmichael.com/helpr.

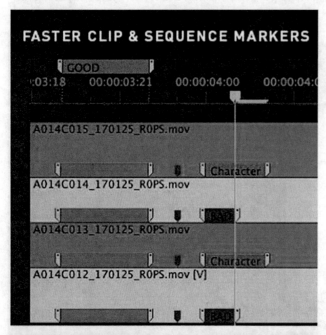

Figure 10-144. *Helpr makes it easy to create and customize markers and bins*

942

Sample Panel: SpeedScriber

Adobe removed Premiere's built-in speech-recognition tool in an earlier version, but with SpeedScriber's dedicated panel, you can get transcripts of your footage in real-time or faster. The idea is that you pay for the transcription, which is then available through your account in the SpeedScriber panel. The transcript is synced with your media and then searchable in the Speech Recognition section of the Metadata panel. You can also export transcripts to PDF, .srt for captioning, and other formats. SpeedScriber is still in beta at the time of writing this book. For more information, visit `speedscriber.com`.

Sample Panel: Screenlight

Screenlight is a video review and approval platform. With their free panel (Figure 10-145), you can import feedback from clients directly into your timeline. The client reviews the edit on the Screenlight web site, making notes at specific times in the video. Then, you can export these comments from the website and import them into Premiere as markers in your timeline. Say goodbye to burnt-in timecode and vague descriptions from your customers!

Figure 10-145. *Import feedback from clients directly into your timeline with Screenlight's free panel*

Sample Panel: Vimeo

If you regularly upload your videos to Vimeo, you can now do it directly from the timeline using the Vimeo panel. This also includes the ability to track client feedback for Pro and Business users. Download the Vimeo panel from `join.vimeo.com/adobe-premiere-panel/`.

Sample Panel: Adobe Time-Tracking Widget

The Adobe Time-Tracking Widget from Workflow Max will track your time as you work (Figure 10-146), not only in Premiere, but in many other Adobe apps as well. When it comes time to bill your client for time spent on a project, your timesheet is already filled out for you!

Learn more at `workflowmax.com/add-ons/time-tracking-software/adobe-widget`.

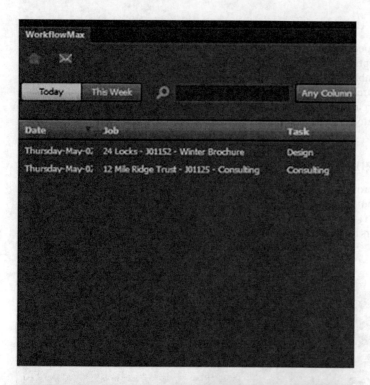

Figure 10-146. Track your billable time as you work in Premiere using the Adobe Time-Tracking Widget from Worklflow Max.

Sample Panel: MediaSilo's Edit Companion

MediaSilo is an online video sharing, collaboration, and asset-management platform. With their Edit Companion for Adobe Premiere Pro, you'll be able to browse and download the assets in your MediaSilo cloud account from directly within Premiere Pro. You can browse the online assets just like you browse a local drive.

With Edit Companion, you can also upload your source footage or mezzanine files to MediaSilo and then import proxies directly into Premiere Pro. After cutting proxies on the go, you can easily match back to source assets back at your workstation.

At the end of your editing session, you can export previews from the panel in Premiere and make them available for your team on different platforms and devices.

Add-Ons

Clicking **Window ➤ Browse Add-ons** takes you to a web page where you can download add-ons for Premiere and other Adobe apps, both paid and free (Figure 10-147). These add-ons can expand the capabilities of Premiere (creative.adobe.com/addons). I recommend that you browse add-ons now and then to see if a new super-plug-in, motion graphics template, or other stuff have been released.

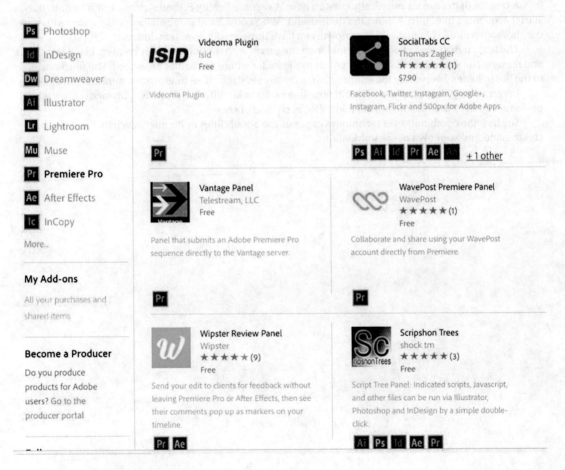

Figure 10-147. *The number of available add-ons is increasing*

945

Create Your Own Panels and Add-ons

There is a pretty detailed manual on how to create new panels at adobe.com/devnet/creativesuite/articles/a-short-guide-to-HTML5-extensions.html. You'll need to install some software and follow the instructions in the manual. Prospective developers of Premiere Pro panels should contact Bruce Bullis at Adobe directly (bbb@adobe.com).

Summary

OK, now you know everything I know about customizing Premiere. Thank you for your patience!

We've covered a lot of different ways to speed up your workflow through customization, but remember that faster editing isn't about choosing just one of these techniques—it's a combination of many small timesavers that amounts to a job being finished sooner than later. When you combine all the techniques in this chapter, there are endless possibilities.

You know that you can save workspaces in template projects. You also know that you can have multiple instances of some windows—like we did with the Pancake Timeline. And you know that panels can add some great functionality. Here's a way to combine those three techniques.

A custom panel can automatically create a new "Awesome Reality Episode" project with custom bins, starter sequences like "Intro," "Meet the dudes," and "Who's out?," and some elements like end credits and the show open already in place. This template can have three media browser windows.

The first media browser points to a folder on the server with motion graphics content, like lower thirds and teasers. The second media browser points to the folder where the dailies are stored. The third one points to the Music folder. Everything the editor needs is readily available at all times with a minimum of clicking.

Larger editing shops can use different template projects for different projects, with media browser panels set up to look at the most-used folders for each kind of show.

See how the combination of techniques expands the possibilities in Premiere even further? Now, get creative and find your own new combinations.

CHAPTER 11

Integration

By Jarle Leirpoll and Paul Murphy

During an editing project, I will use many apps other than just Premiere, and the real power of Premiere lies in its tight integration with other Adobe apps and third-party software. Adobe provides several features and techniques to make the integration seamless. In this chapter, we'll dive into features like Dynamic Link, Edit Original, and motion graphics templates, and take a closer look at the different ways these can speed up your workflow. We'll also cover how to export to and import from other, non-Adobe software.

Premiere as Your Editing Hub

When you have access to all the apps in the Creative Cloud (Figure 11-1), there isn't much you can't do with video and audio. You can edit still images with Photoshop, change vector graphics with Illustrator, fix audio problems with Audition, and add advanced effects with After Effects.

© Jarle Leirpoll 2017
J. Leirpoll et al., *The Cool Stuff in Premiere Pro*, DOI 10.1007/978-1-4842-2890-6_11

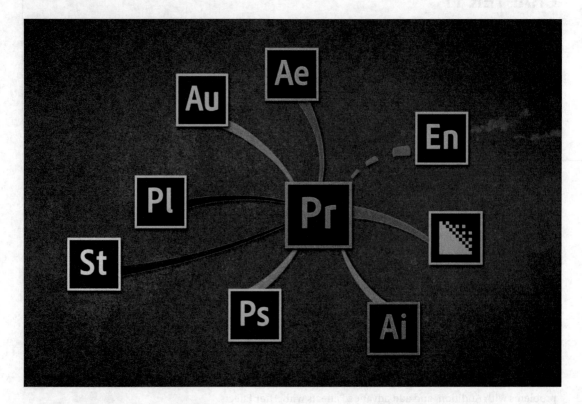

Figure 11-1. *Premiere as your editing hub*

Add Story and Prelude and the workflow before you start, and the editing will also be simplified.

The type of integration varies with the different apps, and here we'll cover Dynamic Link, Edit Original, and more. Don't be afraid to experiment—you can't break the apps.

Dynamic Link

Dynamic Link is a frame server. Think of it as a traffic cop. *"Hey, someone needs a frame in Premiere, but it's now in After Effects. I'll send that frame to Premiere."* So, it's basically just sending the frames from After Effects to Premiere, one by one, as Premiere asks for them. This way, you can add any of the effects that After Effects offers and get instant previews in Premiere.

After Effects can do amazing things that Premiere can't, like the per-character text animation shown in Figure 11-2. With Dynamic Link, advanced effects are just a right-click away from your Premiere Pro timeline.

Figure 11-2. *After Effects per-character text animation*

The huge advantage of Dynamic Link is that everything is *live*. You can right-click a clip in Premiere's timeline and send it to After Effects. You can do whatever you want in After Effects and just switch back to Premiere and watch how it looks when played with the other clips on your timeline. If you don't like what you see, switch back to After Effects, tweak a little, and then switch back again. The switching is super quick, and you only render once. You don't even have to know where the files are on your system.

If you have enough RAM to keep both applications active at the same time, Dynamic Link is a fantastic tool. I use Dynamic Link a lot because it saves me time. What might have taken me 20 minutes before can now pretty much be done instantly, so what's not to love? There are a few limitations that we'll come back to later.

Dynamic Link Workflow

There are many ways to establish a dynamic link between After Effects and Premiere. In Premiere, you can click **File▶ Adobe Dynamic Link▶ New After Effects Composition**. Or, you can import an existing After Effects composition with **File▶ Adobe Dynamic Link▶ Import After Effects Composition**.

The most common way is probably to select one or more clips in the Premiere Pro timeline, right-click, and choose *Replace with After Effects Composition*.

The result is that all the clips you sent to After Effects are replaced with one single dynamically linked clip (Figure 11-3).

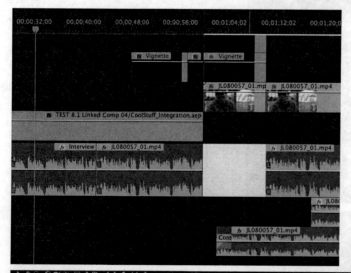

Figure 11-3. *After sending clips to After Effects via Dynamic Link, they are replaced by a linked comp in the Premiere timeline, and the comp opens automatically in After Effects*

This is good, and it's bad. Good because the link is live and updates instantly. The problem is that the original files are gone from the timeline (Figure 11-4), and that can create some problems if you want to go back to them, or if you send the project to other facilities via XML, AAF, or EDL.

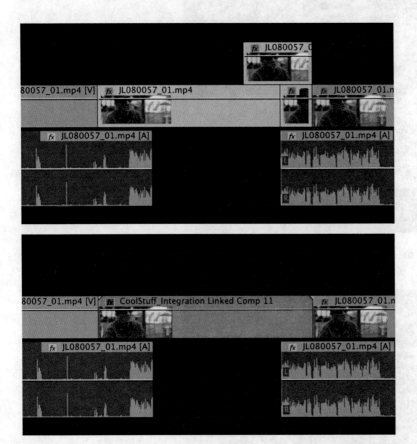

Figure 11-4. *The selected clips in the timeline are replaced by a linked After Effects composition*

Make a Copy Before Dynamic Linking

To keep a copy of the original clips in the timeline, just make copies in the timeline before you create the dynamic link. You can copy/paste or just **Alt-drag** (Option-drag) the clips to make copies (Figure 11-5). Then, group them together so they move as one, and then disable the clips. Disable the copies and keep them as a "backup" if you need to go back to the original clips (Figure 11-6).

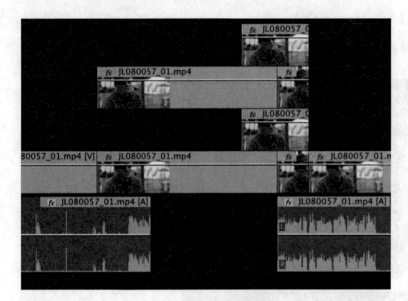

Figure 11-5. *Make copies of the clips before creating the dynamic link*

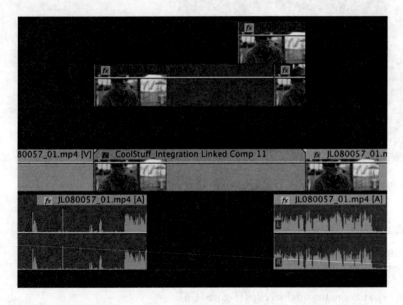

Figure 11-6. *Disable the copies*

Dynamic Link Undo

Another way to keep the original clips in the timeline is to right-click and replace the clips with an After Effects composition, and when After Effects has opened, just go back to Premiere and hit *Undo*. The clips are now in After Effects, but there is no dynamic link.

Then, you can do your thing in After Effects and drag the After Effects comp to Premiere and place it over the original clips in the timeline. Some even prefer to render out the After Effects comp as a video clip and place that video clip above the originals. If you do so, I recommend that you make a copy of the original clips before creating the dynamic link. Copy/paste can save your bacon.

If you've forgotten to make copies or undo, and the clips are lost from your timeline, don't despair. You can copy and paste clips both ways between Premiere and After Effects (Figure 11-7). So, just select the clips in After Effects, hit *Copy*, go to Premiere, and paste them in on a higher track. The result is the same as before—except for the label color of the clips, perhaps.

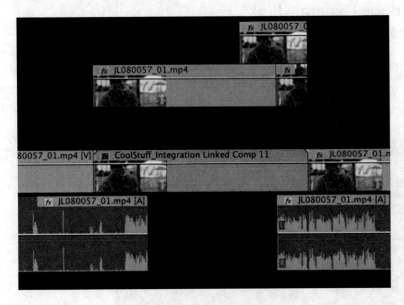

Figure 11-7. *You can copy the clips from the After Effects composition and paste them into Premiere's timeline*

When copying new clips from Premiere to After Effects, you can change them to guide layers in After Effects so they don't render in the dynamic link. Also, any graphic elements from Premiere with text or shapes will be editable in After Effects.

Note that pasting items from Premiere will actually place the clips at their corresponding sequence timecode in the comp. To place them at the playhead's current time instead, use the shortcut **Ctrl+Alt+V** (Cmd+Option+V).

Dynamic Linking and Proxies

If you transfer a clip that has a proxy attached using either *Replace with After Effects Composition* or simply copying/pasting, you will still be able to toggle proxies in After Effects. It will display the original media by default in After Effects, but if you locate the clip in your Project panel, you'll notice there is a checkbox to the left of the file name (Figure 11-8). Click this, and it will display the proxy file instead throughout the project.

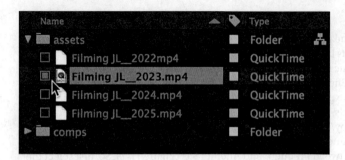

Figure 11-8. *Toggle this checkbox to switch between proxies and your original media in After Effects*

Color Spaces and Adobe Dynamic Link

If you want your After Effects comps to look the same in Premiere, it's important to match their color and color-depth settings.

To set After Effects' color settings to be as close to Premiere's as possible, choose **File➤ Project Settings**, go to the Color Settings tab, change Depth to 32-bit, set Working Space to HDTV (Rec.709), and check *Linearize Working Space* (Figure 11-9).

Figure 11-9. *Make sure you work in 32-bit in After Effects if you need the extra headroom*

Render and Replace

If you want to free up some computer resources, or need to send the project to another system, or even just to keep a copy of the project on the shelf, replacing the dynamically linked comp in the timeline with a rendered video file can be a good idea. Right-click the clip and choose *Render and Replace*. You get a dialog where you can choose render settings and where the file is stored (Figure 11-10).

You can match the sequence settings, individual clips, or use a preset. Make sure you create video files of high quality when you do a render and replace. To get back to the dynamically linked comp if you need to make changes, just right-click and choose *Restore Unrendered* (Figure 11-10).

Figure 11-10. *Even after doing a render and replace, you can still get back to the original clips*

Render and replace is not a background process; it will lock you out of Premiere while it's processing. If you have a lot of comps in your project, the last thing you want to do is sit there while you render each individual one. A better way to do this is to select all your comps in your sequence by using Find in Timeline (**Ctrl+F/Cmd+F**), search for *.aep*, and make sure you click *Find All*. Now you can render and replace all of them at once while you're out to lunch or at home overnight. If you've renamed all your dynamically linked comps, but you've kept their default label colors, you can also use **Label➤ Select Label Group**.

When all your comps are spread across different sequences in your project, another way to render everything at once is to drag them into a single sequence and render them there, then copy the rendered files back into their original sequences.

Dynamic Link Gotchas

If you close both After Effects and Premiere, then open Premiere and do another dynamic link to After Effects, a new After Effects project will be created, which is most likely not what you wanted. You'll want all the dynamically linked comps in one After Effects project.

To ensure that this happens, whenever you close After Effects, open it again by right-clicking a dynamically linked clip in the timeline in Premiere and choosing **Edit➤ Original**. Now the After Effects project you've already used will open, and you can send more clips to the same After Effects project with a dynamic link.

Some After Effects users like to use **File➤ Increment and Save** when saving their projects. This will automatically save a new copy of the project with a version number appended to the file name (i.e., CoolStuff 01.aep). It's a great way to keep backups of previous versions, but with After Effects' default settings, Premiere will continue to link to the previous version. To get around this, you need to open After Effects on the same machine that is using Premiere, choose **Preferences➤ General**, and tick *Dynamic Link with After Effects Uses Project File Name with Highest Number* (Figure 11-11).

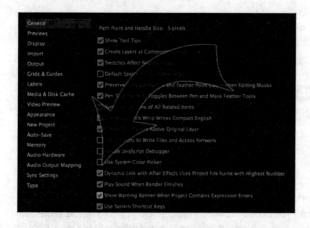

Figure 11-11. *With this preference ticked in After Effects, Premiere will assume these are versions of the same project and import the highest number*

Conversely, if this preference is already ticked, you need to be aware of how you're naming your files. For example, if you have all your After Effects files in the same folder, and they're named Episode01 and Episode02, even if you select the first file when dynamically linking, Premiere will automatically choose Episode02. You would either need to uncheck this preference in After Effects or add something unique to the file name to prevent Premiere from thinking they're incremental versions.

At the same time, you should also make sure your dynamically linked comps have unique names. Firewalls may also prevent Dynamic Link from doing its magic. Make sure the firewall allows all the Adobe apps plus the Creative Cloud app.

If you see the wrong portion of a comp is showing in your Premiere timeline, try deleting the render files or trashing your media cache files. To make your dynamically linked comps perform much better, use an SSD disk and turn on Disk Cache in After Effects (Figure 11-12).

Figure 11-12. Enabling Disk Cache lets After Effects store RAM previews and rendered frames on SSDs or spinning disks

Don't Overestimate Your System

Even though Dynamic Link works great, it's best for short comps and is not really designed for long clips. It eats a lot of RAM. If you can't RAM preview the comp in After Effects, you're better off rendering out the comp to a video file with a mezzanine video codec.

Project Link

As an alternative to Dynamic Link, you can export your comp out of After Effects with a project link embedded, which allows you to easily open the After Effects project that the video file was rendered from directly from the timeline in Premiere!

With your comp active in After Effects, go to **Composition➤ Add to Render Queue**, and the Render Queue opens. Make sure Render Settings is set to Best Settings (Figure 11-13).

Figure 11-13. After Effects Render Queue panel

Click the *Output Module* link and make sure *Include Project Link* is checked (Figure 11-14). An After Effects project file path is embedded in the file. If the format doesn't support embedded XMP metadata, the link will be stored in a sidecar file.

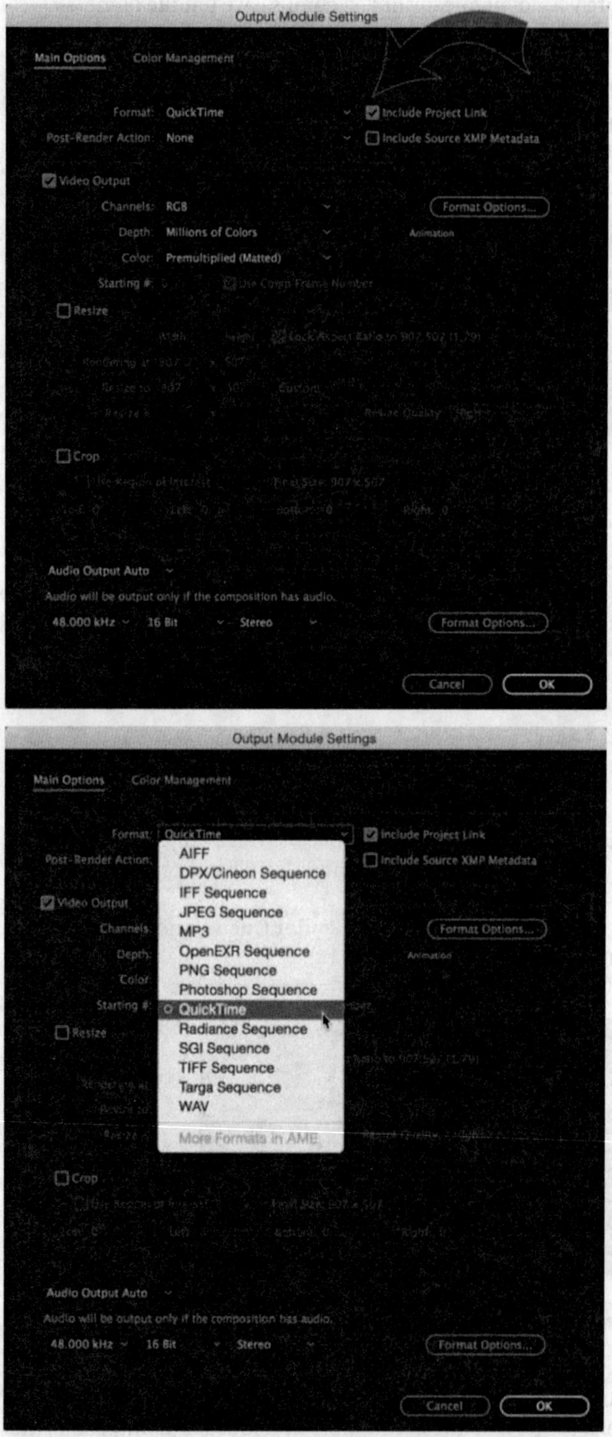

Figure 11-14. *Including a project link enables the Edit Original command to access the After Effects comp directly*

Then, choose your output format. You can, of course, use any format in the list. The image is just one example.

Click the *Output To* link to tell After Effects where to save the file, and then click the *Render* button in the upper-right corner of the Render Queue panel.

Now, when you use the file in Premiere and feel the urge to change anything, just select the clip and hit **Ctrl+E** (Cmd+E) (or right-click and choose *Edit Original*) to open the After Effects project. Do your changes and render out a new file. If you overwrite the original file, it will be automatically updated in the Premiere timeline.

Project Link in tandem with *Edit Original* is a nifty little timesaver.

Motion Graphics Templates from After Effects

This is a very special kind of dynamic linking. With motion graphics templates, you can edit text layers, color, or other parameters in an After Effects comp directly from the Effects Control panel in Premiere! That means a motion graphics artist can make cool text templates in After Effects, and the editor can use the template and input text like names, titles, tag lines, and so on, and change colors, sizes, and almost any other parameter without even knowing After Effects!

Exporting Templates from After Effects

To make a comp into a motion graphics template, right-click it in the Project panel and select *Open In Essential Graphics* (Figure 11-15). Now you can drag any supported parameter from a layer in your comp timeline into the Essential Graphics panel (Figure 11-16). If a parameter isn't supported, you'll get an error message. These are the parameters that will be editable when you import the template into Premiere. You can even drag parameters from layers in other comps so long as they're nested in the loaded comp.

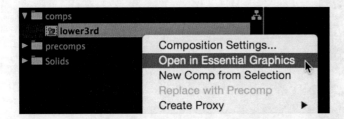

Figure 11-15. *Right-click your comp and choose "Open in Essential Graphics"*

Figure 11-16. *Drag a parameter from the timeline to the Essential Graphics panel*

Make sure you drag the actual parameter and not the parameter group name. For example, if you twirl down the properties for a text layer and drag the word Text, nothing happens—you need to drag the *Source Text* parameter, which is in the Text group. If you get tired of having to dig down into layer properties like this, there's a handy *Solo Supported Properties* button at the top of the Essential Graphics panel. Click this, and it will only display the supported properties of each layer in your timeline (Figure 11-17).

Even in the simple comp in Figure 11-17, the list of properties that can be made available in the template is surprisingly long. In complex AE projects, the possibilities are endless—especially if you combine sliders, checkboxes, color pickers, and so on with expressions.

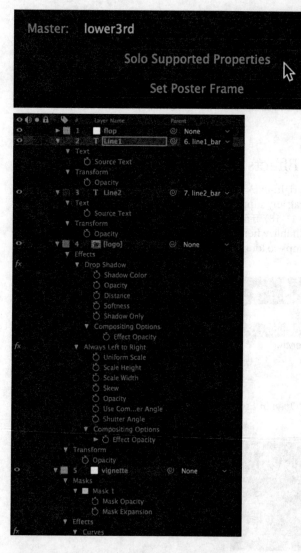

Figure 11-17. *Click "Solo Supported Properties" to quickly view only the parameters you can add to your motion graphics template*

You have the option to rename the parameters to make them clearer to the person who will be working with them in Premiere (e.g., change *Source Text* to *Interview Name*). You can also add comments to help guide them through the template, or divide the parameters up into sections. The default parameter names in After Effects don't offer much information to users in Premiere (Figure 11-18).

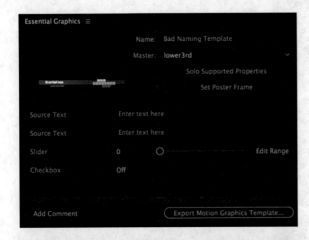

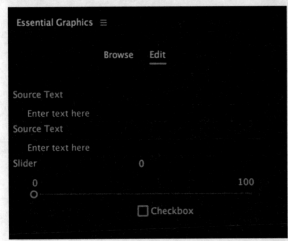

Figure 11-18. *Default parameter names*

Renaming your properties and using comments will make your template much more user-friendly. *Name* and *Title* make much more sense for the user than having two fields named *Source Text* (Figure 11-19).

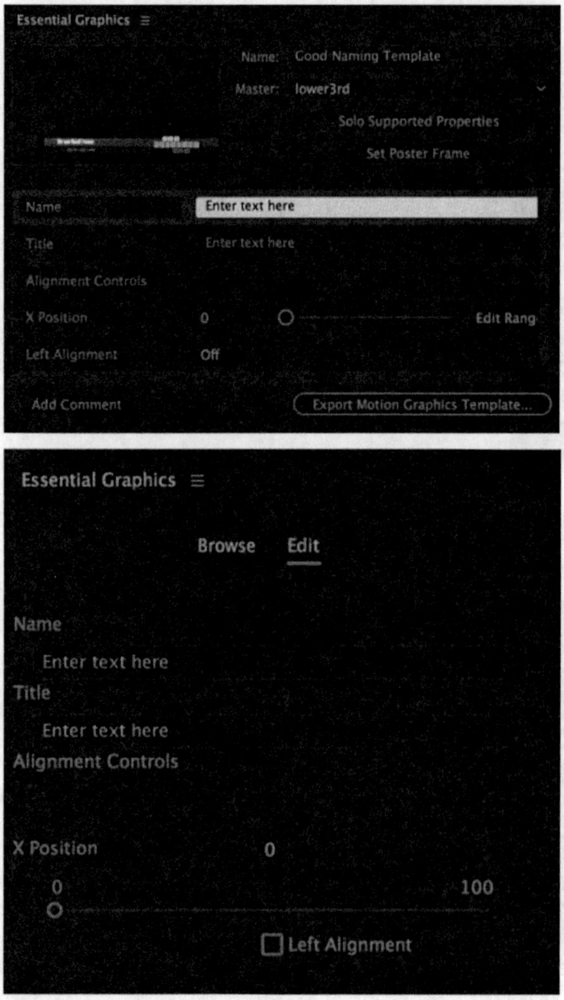

Figure 11-19. Renamed properties

Once you're finished setting up the controls, give the template a name and export it by clicking the *Export Motion Graphics Template* button at the bottom of the panel. This will give you the option to save the file to your local drive, to your Essential Graphics folder, or to a Creative Cloud library. After Effects exports a .mogrt file, which will include the comp as well as any assets it's using, like video or images.

■ **Note** The max file size of a .mogrt from After Effects is 1 GB.

Importing Templates into Premiere

To import the template file into Premiere, you can't just use the usual **File➤ Import**, or even the media browser. If you get a .mogrt file from a designer, you can import it into the Essential Graphics folder by clicking **Graphics➤ Install Motion Graphics Template**.

If you export a .mogrt from After Effects on your own computer and choose to install in the Essential Graphics folder, it will automatically populate the Essential Graphics panel in Premiere (Figure 11-20). Locate it there and then drag it directly to your sequence (Figure 11-21).

If the .mogrt was exported to a library, open the Libraries panel and drag it to the sequence from there.

Either way, this will create a new bin called Motion Graphics Template Media, with your template file inside it. Simply select the template in your timeline and click the Edit tab in the Essential Graphics panel to adjust any of the parameters added in After Effects (Figure 11-22).

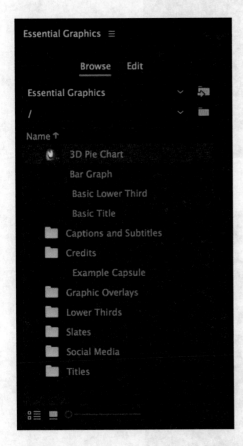

Figure 11-20. Locate your motion graphics template in the Essential Graphics panel

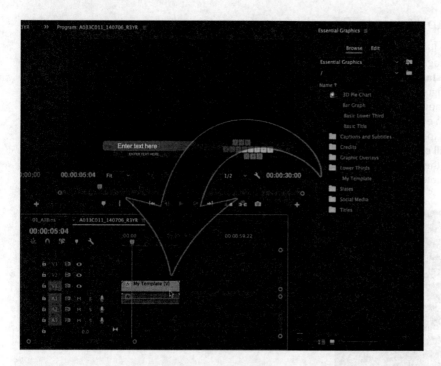

Figure 11-21. *Drag your template onto the timeline*

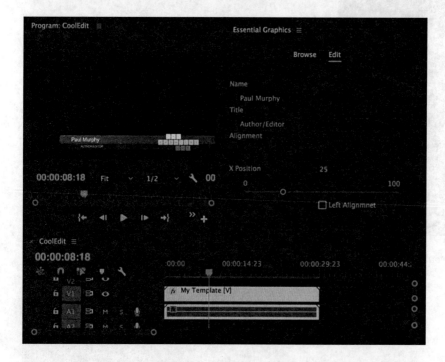

Figure 11-22. *Edit your template using the Edit tab in the Essential Graphics panel*

If you need to create multiple versions of the same template, **Alt-drag** (Option-drag) the clip in the timeline to create a new instance of it.

Control Templates with Expressions

As well as being able to change things like text and color with motion graphics templates, you can also use text layers and expression controls to make changes to After Effects expressions. This means just about *any* parameter in After Effects can be set in Premiere! Here are some examples of the sorts of things you can do with expressions.

Control the Size of a Bar Graph from Premiere

In this example, we'll control the size of a bar in a bar graph. The scale property is not yet supported in the Essential Graphics panel, so we'll use a slider control instead.

Create a solid and name it *Bar*. Mine is 100 × 800 pixels, with the anchor point of the bar set to the bottom, so it scales upward from there (Figure 11-23).

Figure 11-23. *Control the height of this bar inside Premiere Pro*

With the Bar layer selected, choose **Effects➤ Expression Controls➤ Slider Control**. This adds a slider to your layer, but it won't actually change anything about its appearance just yet.

Now, twirl down the properties for the Bar layer, then **Alt-click** (Option-click) the stopwatch next to the Scale field so you can start writing the expression. Write **[100,]**, then move the text cursor after the comma and use the curly icon below the Scale numbers, called the pickwhip, to select the Slider in the Effects Controls panel (Figure 11-24). Make sure you select Slider and not Slider Control—Slider Control is just the name of the control. After Effects has filled in all the information for the Slider automatically! See Figure 11-25.

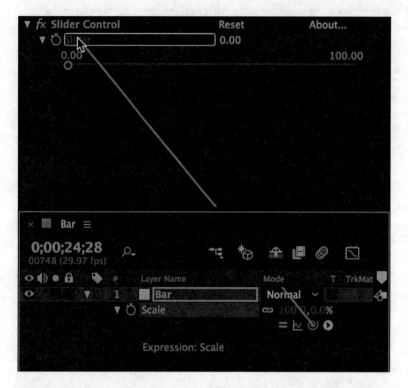

Figure 11-24. *Use the pickwhip to select the Slider value in the Effects panel*

Figure 11-25. *The Scale expression for the Bar layer*

From the timeline panel, drag the slider property to the Essential Graphics panel and export the comp as a motion graphics template.

The nice thing about using this in Premiere is you can either enter a number or drag the slider for the bar height (Figure 11-26). Great! It only scales vertically, since we set the first parameter to 100. This locks the horizontal scale to 100 percent.

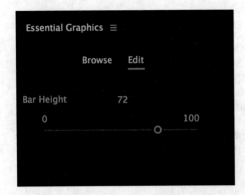

Figure 11-26. *Adjust the height of the bar by dragging the slider or entering a number in Premiere*

Figure 11-27 shows a more advanced project where I used the same expression on three bars.

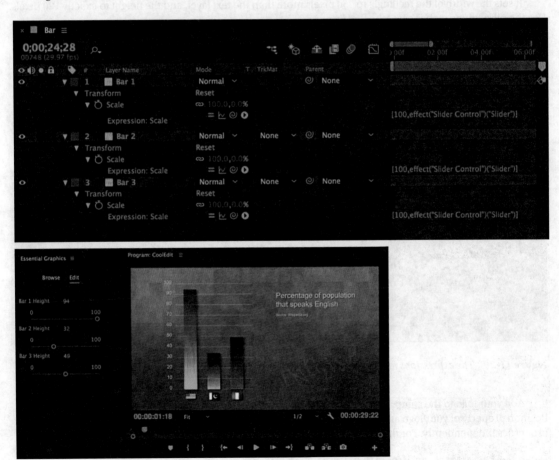

Figure 11-27. *Same expression used on three bars. Moksha font by MisprintedType.com, Flags from Wikipedia Commons.*

Dynamically Adaptive Background for Lower Thirds

Here, we'll make a lower-third background automatically scale according to the length of the text. We'll also make a logo automatically adjust its position so it always stays at the same distance from the lower-third background. The expressions that follow lean heavily on the expressions shared by motion graphics artist Evan Abrams: youtube.com/watch?v=kI3yzx6CATg

First, we'll create a shape layer named *Text BG Matte* as our background and a text layer named *Credit*. Add some random text to the text layer for now.

With Text BG Matte selected, draw a rectangle and twirl down the shape Contents section until you get to the properties for *Rectangle Path 1*. Enter this expression for the Size property of Rectangle 1 in the shape layer:

```
s=thisComp.layer("Credit");
x=s.sourceRectAtTime(time-s.inPoint,true).width+250;
[x,120]
```

It sets the width of the rectangle to 250 pixels more than the text layer, and the height to exactly 120 pixels. Use the pickwhip to grab most of the first line.

Now, enter the following expression for the Position property of the same Rectangle 1 in the shape layer. This makes sure that it scales from its top-left corner:

```
content("Rectangle 1").content("Rectangle Path 1").size/2
```

See Figure 11-28 where the two expressions are used. Manually move the shape layer so it aligns with the left side of the frame. The position of the rectangle and the position of the whole shape layer are two different parameters, so you can freely move it around without breaking the expression. Nice.

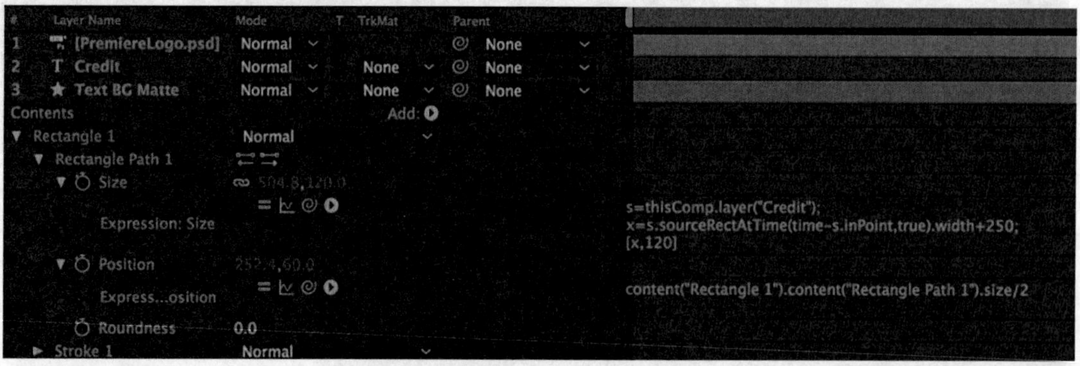

Figure 11-28. *The expressions for the shape layer*

Add your logo to the comp. This needs to move according to the width of Text BG Matte. Right-click the Position property of your logo and select *Separate Dimensions* (Figure 11-29). Now we can adjust the X and Y properties independently. For the X position, add this expression:

```
thisComp.layer("Text BG Matte").sourceRectAtTime(time,true).width+30
```

See Figure 11-30. Again, the pickwhip can be used to automatically write most of the code. This places the logo 30 pixels to the right of the lower-third background. Because we separated the X and Y values, you can still freely move the logo up or down.

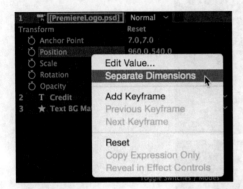

Figure 11-29. *Right-click the Position property to adjust the X and Y properties separately*

Figure 11-30. *The expression for the logo*

Figure 11-31 has some examples that show how this works in Premiere. I added an animated background with some turbulent noise, tint, and fast blur to the comp and used the Text BG Matte layer as a track matte for this.

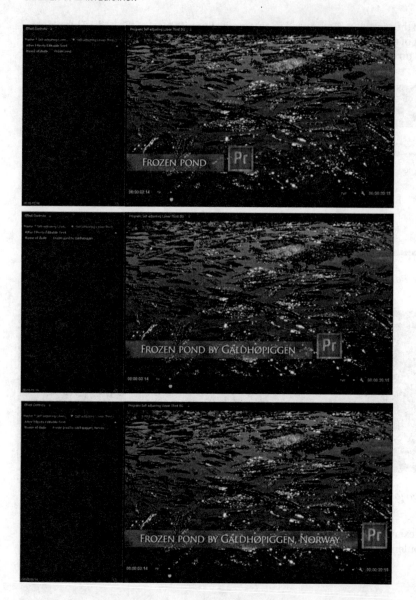

Figure 11-31. *Doing this without expressions would require a different comp for each background length*

Want to Learn More About Expressions?

Adobe has a very useful language reference for expressions in After Effects: helpx.adobe.com/after-effects/using/expression-language-reference.html. I also highly recommend expressions guru Dan Ebberts' AE Expressions and Scripting Resource: motionscript.com.

OK, So What Can We Use After Effects For?

All this talk about Dynamic Link and motion graphics templates is nice, but why would we send a clip to After Effects in the first place? Because After Effects has so many advanced tools and features that Premiere doesn't. Here are a few examples to trigger your imagination.

Animation That Requires Motion Blur

As you've seen in chapter 7 on motion graphics, you can do pretty advanced motion graphics stuff in Premiere. However, there is one feature that makes After Effects animations look much nicer than the ones in Premiere: motion blur. Yes, you can add motion blur in Premiere with the transform effect (premierepro.net/editing/motion-blur/), but the motion blur in AE is much more flexible and can look a lot better.

Figure 11-32 shows an animation I made in Premiere. It's a wooden texture and a world map, plus a graphic that moves quickly across the screen and stops in the middle. In Premiere, there's no motion blur. We could fake it, but it would be time consuming, so I sent this to After Effects to add some motion blur magic.

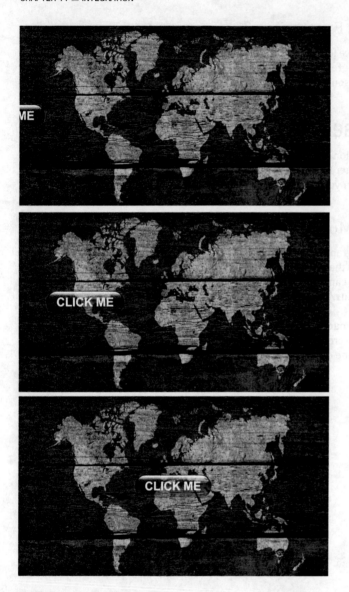

Figure 11-32. *Button animated in Premiere. Note that there is no motion blur*

Most of what you do in Premiere comes over to After Effects without a problem, including blend modes, ease keyframes, scaling, opacity, markers, time remapping, and so on.

To apply motion blur to a layer in After Effects, click the *Motion Blur* switch for the graphic layer. After Effects doesn't preview motion blur by default; to do this, you need to click the *Enable Motion Blur* button at the top of the timeline.

The animation with motion blur from After Effects just looks way better than the original when you see it in motion (Figure 11-33).

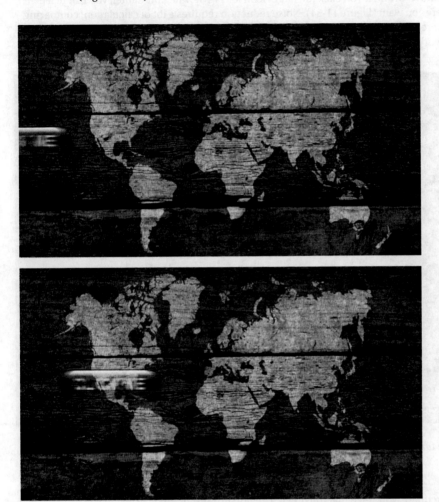

Figure 11-33. *Same animation in After Effects, with Motion Blur switch on*

Noise Reduction

As you've seen in chapter 6 on color grading, increasing the brightness of an image will make the noise from the darker areas of the image much more visible. Noise is the enemy of every video codec, so sometimes we need to do some noise reduction. Premiere doesn't come with good noise-reduction tools, so again we move to After Effects.

Send your footage to AE via Dynamic Link, select the clip in the AE timeline, and then go to **Effects ➤ Noise & Grain ➤ Remove Grain**. If you click the target icon for Preview Region Center, you can place the preview region where you want (Figure 11-34). Noise reduction requires a lot of calculation, comparing pixels in the frames before and after, predicting movement, and so forth. AE shows us just a small region of the footage so we can work much faster.

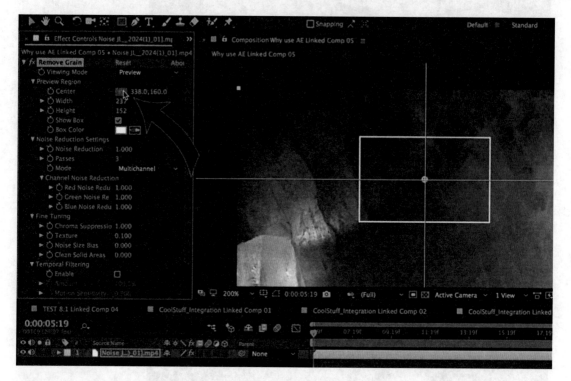

Figure 11-34. *Click the target icon for the preview region and then click where you need it in the composition window*

If you go back to Premiere, you'll see that the preview region box is rendered. So, when you've tweaked the settings, make sure you set the viewing mode to Final Output.

Noise reduction takes a lot of processor power, so don't expect real-time performance here. Render the clip in the Premiere timeline to see the cleaned-up video in real-time. Figures 11-35 and 11-36 show a clip before and after noise reduction. It may be hard to see the difference in a still image.

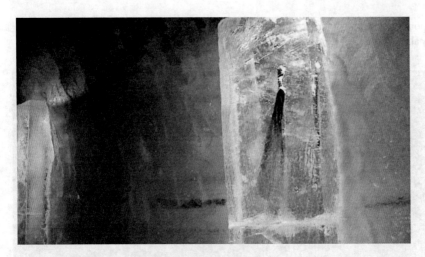

Figure 11-35. *After making a clip brighter and more contrasty, the noise became visible. (It looks a lot worse when played back than on a still grab like this.)*

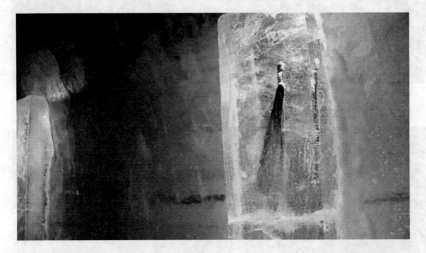

Figure 11-36. *After removing the noise, the clip looks better, though we may have lost some of the finer details*

Go easy on the reduction, or you'll lose too much detail in the image. You can also introduce heavy banding if you overdo the noise reduction. AE also has another effect called *match grain* that lets you add grain to computer-generated sources so they match the video or film material you mix them with.

Warp Stabilizer VFX

The warp stabilizer in Premiere uses the same technology as the one in AE, but the AE one has a few more options and is called the Warp Stabilizer VFX. One great feature is its ability to do reverse stabilization.

With your clip selected in the AE timeline, go to **Animation➤ Warp Stabilizer VFX**. The effect takes some time to analyze the shot. Tell the effect to show tracking points; delete the bad ones by **Ctrl+dragging** (Cmd+dragging) around the ones you want to remove, and hit **Delete** (Figure 11-37). You need to do this at short intervals in the shot if the camera is moving a lot.

You want to keep the points on just the objects you want to stabilize—the phone in my example here (Figure 11-38). Don't worry about a few stray tracking points; they will be outweighed by the proper ones anyway.

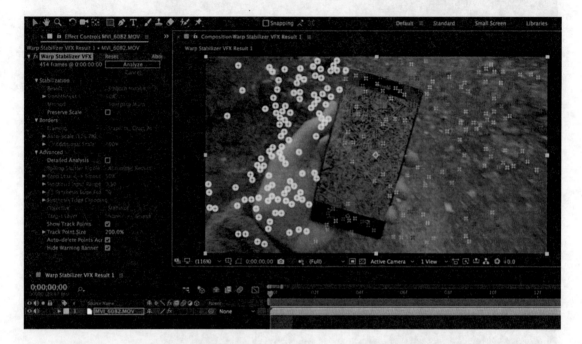

Figure 11-37. *Delete the tracking points outside the phone*

Figure 11-38. *Here, only the good points remain. If the camera or the background moves, you will have to delete new points that appear during the shot*

■ **Note**   Nothing affects stabilization more than objects moving in your footage, so another way to improve the tracking is by masking out anything that moves (e.g., your actors), pre-composing your footage, and then applying the warp stabilizer effect to your pre-comp. Disable the mask once you're happy with the result.

Turn the visibility of the tracking points off and set the Stabilization Result to *No Motion*. Now you have an eerie shot where the phone is kept still in the frame, while the whole shot moves around it (Figure 11-39).

Figure 11-39. *The phone is stabilized, while the rest of the image moves around it*

Add the image or video clip you want to add to the phone's display on a layer above the tracked shot, right-click it, and choose *Pre-Compose*. This moves the clip to another comp and places the comp where the clip was—and nothing has changed visually. Then, change the Objective to *Apply Motion to Target Over Original* (Figure 11-40), choose the pre-comp you made, and watch the magic; the content of the layer above follows the movement of the phone!

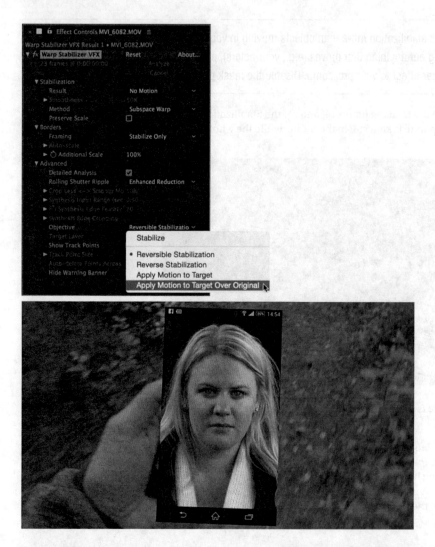

Figure 11-40. *Apply the Reverse Stabilized Motion to the pre-comp with the screen replacement image*

Well, the clip isn't aligned to the phone display yet. To fix that, we'll use the CC power pin effect and the optics compensation effect on the screen content. But the Warp Stabilizer VFX strips out all the effects when we use the *Apply Motion to Target Over Original* feature, so we need to add the effects before the stabilizer does its thing in the render order. That's why we pre-comped the clip—so we can add the effects in the pre-comp. Since the pre-comp has no effects, there will be no missing effects when we add the Warp Stabilizer VFX to it. Clever, eh?

To work in one comp while we're looking at the other, we need to set up an edit-this-look-at-that (ETLAT) workspace. We do this by clicking the little padlock icon in the Composition panel (Figure 11-41) to lock it, and then click on the name of the nested comp beside it to open another viewer containing the nested comp.

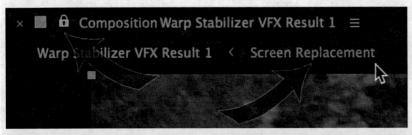

Figure 11-41. *Lock one comp view so you can see it while editing the other comp*

Now we can add and adjust the CC power pin and optics compensation effects, plus add a little fast blur to match the reduced sharpness of the phone shot, all while watching both the comp we're working in and the end result (Figure 11-42).

Figure 11-42. *Add optics compensation and blur and adjust the CC power pin to match the screen perfectly*

Go back to Premiere, and, courtesy of the dynamic link, the final result instantly shows up in the timeline. Figure 11-43 shows my final result after tweaking the parameters.

Figure 11-43. *Three screen shots showing the final result*

Now, if you look closely, this result is lacking a few things before it's a convincing composite. The reflections in the screen are gone, covered by the new screen content, and there is no motion blur when the phone moves quickly like there should be. I just wanted to show how you can easily do quite advanced compositing even if you're not an AE pro, using tools that you already know from Premiere.

The aforementioned problems can be fixed by shooting the phone with a black screen with a few tracking points (Figure 11-44) rather than with a screen with an image on it, cloning away the dots, and using a blending mode like Screen to show the reflections. By converting the warp stabilizer data to keyframes that can drive the motion of the new screen image/video, AE can add motion blur automatically.

Figure 11-44. *This would be a better screen-tracking image*

Figure 11-45. *The Warp To Keys script converts stabilizer data to keyframes*

Warp To Keys is an After Effects script (by Jesse Toula) that converts warp stabilizer data to keyframes: batchframe.com/extras/info/Warp%2520To%2520Keys. See Figure 11-45.

RotoBrush

The RotoBrush in After Effects combined with the Refine Edge feature is very close to real magic. By just painting with broad strokes on what you want to separate from the background in a shot, you can make very accurate masks that automatically (well, almost) track the shape and movement in the shot.

After you've sent your clip to AE, duplicate the clip in the comp and double-click the upper one to open it in the Layer monitor. We'll be working on the layer itself, not in the comp. Park at the first frame of the clip, find the RotoBrush tool, and start painting on the object you want to keep in the image. As you can see in Figure 11-46, I just kind of drew some strokes on the girl. When you let go, After Effects makes a guess based on the pixels and creates a mask around the object, or person in my case.

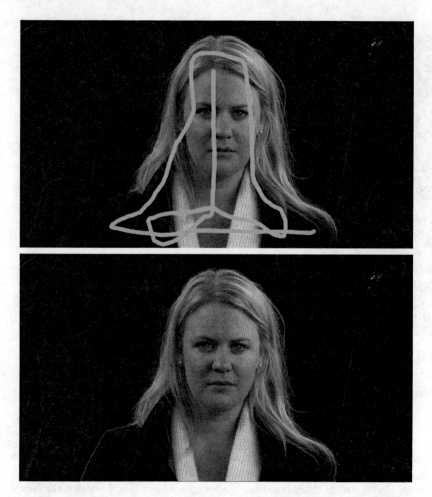

Figure 11-46. *Draw on the person/object you want to keep, and After Effects finds the edges. Model: Marianne Melau, Footage courtesy of Sean Fulton and Martin Fotland*

If you find that there are areas you did not want to include, hold down **Alt** (Option) and paint on them with the red "minus" brush. If you want to include more areas, just paint on them with the green "plus" brush. You will need to do this at intervals during the shot. The mask will propagate until it hits the end of the *Propagate* area in the timeline below the Layer panel (Figure 11-47). Drag the end of the Propagate area to the ring to extend the mask-creation period.

Figure 11-47. *Drag the Propagate area longer to roto the whole clip*

984

Now, change to the Refine Edge tool and paint around the edges in the image (Figure 11-48), still in the Layer panel. When you let go, After Effects creates a much better and more detailed mask (Figure 11-49).

Figure 11-48. Switch to the Refine Edge Tool, and draw around soft edges like hair, fur, etc

Figure 11-49. The Refine Edge tool does a really good job of guessing where the edges are and creating a mask

I wanted a text layer to go behind the girl, so I placed a text layer between the two other layers. Then, I tweaked the settings of the Refine Edge tool in the Effect Controls panel until things looked good, animated the text, and added an adjustment layer with color correction on top.

Just for the record, Figure 11-50 shows the settings I used on the Text layer behind the girl.

Figure 11-50. Text layer effects

Figure 11-51 shows the final result. I find it amazing that we can separate the girl from the background like this, almost as if it were a green-screen shot.

Figure 11-51. Final result

   If you want to practice Screen Replacement, download the free tracking clips from Adam Everett Miller at vimeo.com/87612978.

3D Camera

In After Effects, you can create virtual cameras to simulate 3D camera movement, and this can be used to create a variety of cool effects. Figure 11-52 shows a simple camera movement over a map that I made for the Norwegian Directorate for Cultural Heritage.

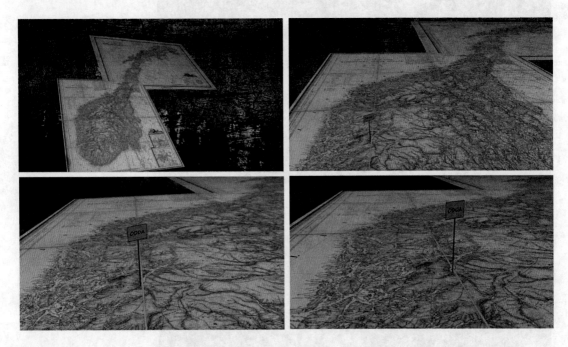

Figure 11-52. *Four screenshots from the clip where a virtual camera is moved over the map in 3D space*

3D Text and Shapes

Text and vector shapes can be turned into shape layers, which can be edited, animated, and extruded. Now you can make golden text and glass-like logos (Figures 11-53 and 11-54).

Figure 11-53. *Screenshot from John Dickinson's 3D material template project*

Figure 11-54. *Movies on War logo designed by Eivind Høimyr*

To enable 3D shapes in After Effects, you need to choose *CINEMA 4D* in the 3D Renderer tab of your Composition Settings panel (Figure 11-55). You also have the option of choosing Ray-traced 3D, but this is an older and slower renderer. To set the quality of the renders, click on *Options* in the dialog. Basically, the higher you set the quality, the longer the render time will be.

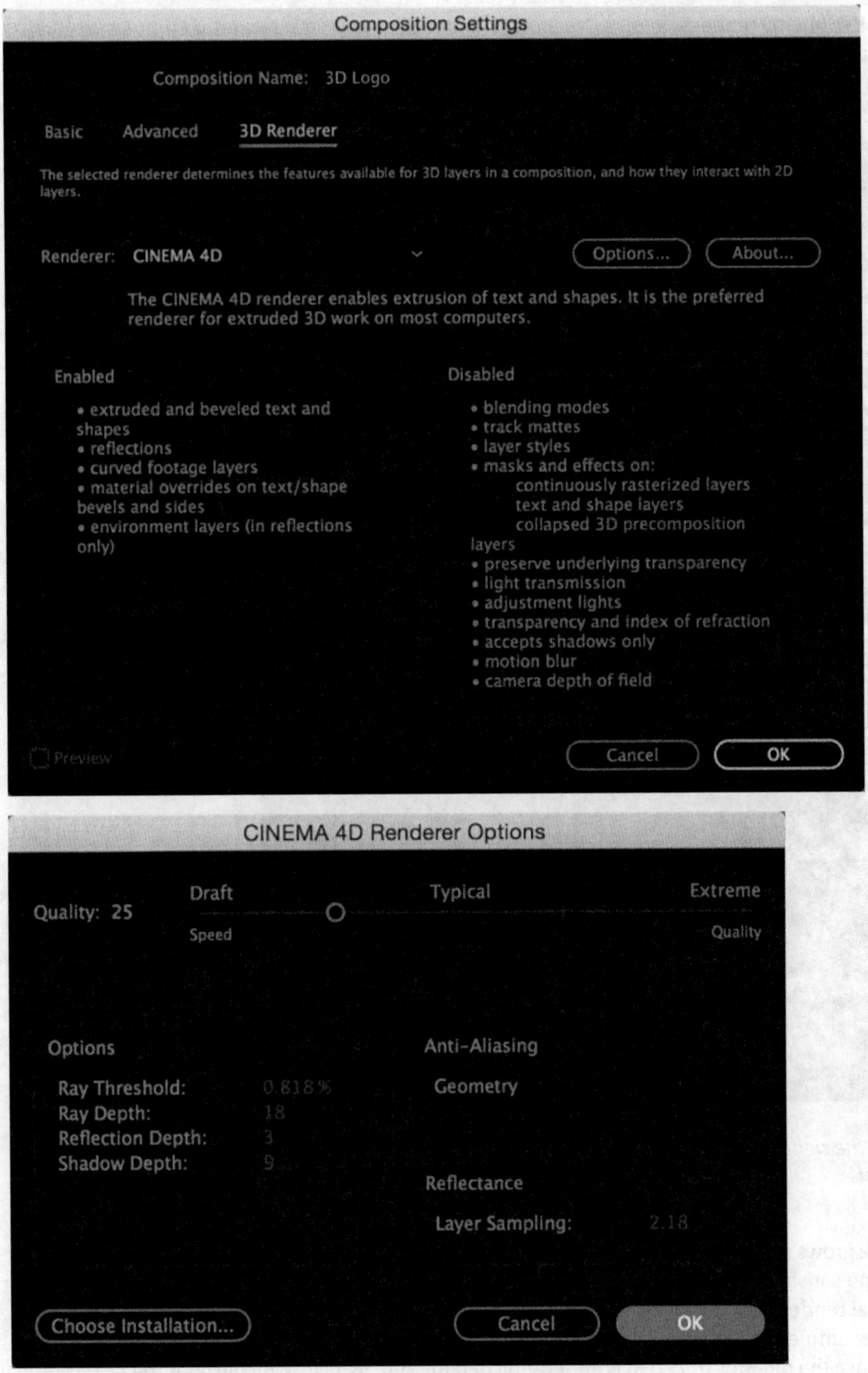

Composition Settings

Composition Name: 3D Logo

Basic   Advanced   **3D Renderer**

The selected renderer determines the features available for 3D layers in a composition, and how they interact with 2D layers.

Renderer: **CINEMA 4D**   ⌄   (Options...)   (About...)

The CINEMA 4D renderer enables extrusion of text and shapes. It is the preferred renderer for extruded 3D work on most computers.

Enabled

- extruded and beveled text and shapes
- reflections
- curved footage layers
- material overrides on text/shape bevels and sides
- environment layers (in reflections only)

Disabled

- blending modes
- track mattes
- layer styles
- masks and effects on:
  - continuously rasterized layers
  - text and shape layers
  - collapsed 3D precomposition layers
- preserve underlying transparency
- light transmission
- adjustment lights
- transparency and index of refraction
- accepts shadows only
- motion blur
- camera depth of field

☐ Preview   (Cancel)   (OK)

CINEMA 4D Renderer Options

Quality: **25**   Draft   ○   Typical   Extreme
                    Speed   Quality

Options   Anti-Aliasing

Ray Threshold: 0.818 %   Geometry
Ray Depth: 18
Reflection Depth: 3
Shadow Depth: 9

                                    Reflectance

                                    Layer Sampling: 2.18

(Choose Installation...)   (Cancel)   (OK)

Figure 11-55. *Select the CINEMA 4D renderer and set the quality*

Enabling the CINEMA 4D renderer gives new choices under *Geometry* and *Material Options* for each shape layer or text layer (Figure 11-56), including vector logos you've converted to shapes, and also lets you convert images into environment layers that can be reflected in the 3D shapes.

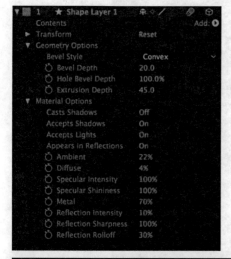

Figure 11-56. *With the right combination of material options, lights, and environment, you can get much better results than this*

The render time grows almost exponentially when you increase the quality, so keep it at the lowest number that gives you satisfactory results. To save time, keep it low while composing and animating, then set it higher for your final render.

The preceding examples were made using comps from John Dickinson's *3D Material Template* as a starting point. They use the old Ray-traced 3D renderer by default, but also work nicely with the CINEMA 4D renderer: motionworks.net/after-effects-cs6-3d-template/.

3D Camera Tracking

Use a video clip where the camera moves. The more the camera moves, the better the tracker works, so don't use a clip with very little movement. An almost static shot would actually benefit from a camera move before its in point. With the video layer selected in a comp, go to **Animation▶ Track Camera**, or open the Tracker panel and click on *Track Camera*.

Does the banner in Figure 11-57 seem familiar? Yep, it looks very much like the banner we get in the warp stabilizer in Premiere. That's not a coincidence, since the technologies behind them are pretty similar.

Figure 11-57. *You can continue to work with other parts of the comp while the camera tracker is analyzing and solving the camera moves*

The 3D camera tracker in After Effects analyzes your 2D video footage and creates a virtual 3D camera to match the camera movement from when the video was recorded. On top of this, it adds 3D tracking so you can add more 3D layers and lock them into place in the scene. If you create shadow-catcher layers and set some lights, the 3D objects can even cast shadows onto the video footage.

In Figure 11-58, I dragged to select a few tracking points, right-clicked one of them, and chose to create a *shadow catcher*, a *light*, and a *camera*. Why a light? Well, without a light, 3D text and shapes are just boring—very boring. To see the depth, we need a light, so why not let After Effects create it? Then, I right-clicked again and told After Effects to create a text layer. Since the text layer is created parallel to the ground plane, I rotated it 90 degrees so it would stand upright. I also scaled it down to make it fit better in the frame.

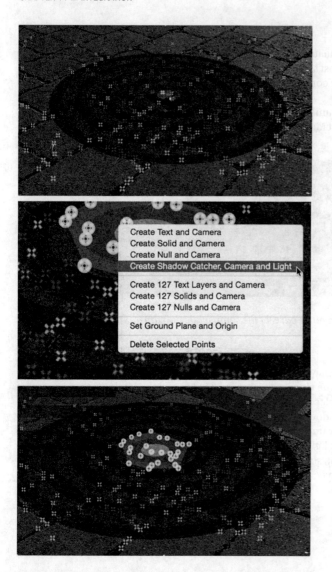

Figure 11-58. *Select a few points to define a ground plane, then right-click to create a camera, a light, and a shadow catcher*

To achieve the look seen in Figure 11-59, I set another light directly above the text to create a kind of contact shadow, and I tweaked the material options to make the text semi-transparent. I also added a solid with a ramp effect and made it an Environment layer.

The CINEMA 4D renderer that I've used here has some limitations. When it's enabled, you will not get motion blur, blending modes, or track mattes to work. You can see that the text is a little bit too sharp against the blurry video. This can be fixed by adding artificial motion blur to the text and shadows only, but that's beyond the scope of this book.

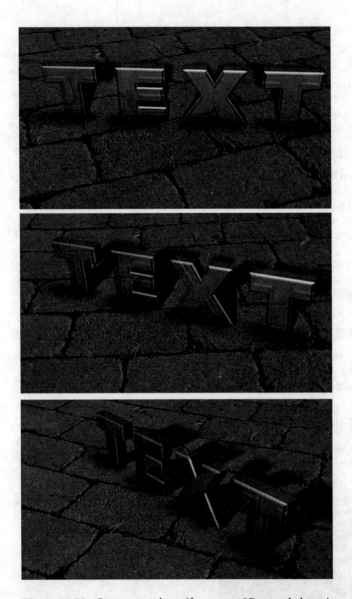

Figure 11-59. Create a text layer if you want 3D extruded text in your shot. Add more lights if necessary

Explore After Effects Further on Your Own

The preceding projects can by no means show the vast capabilities of After Effects, but I think it gives the impression you can do a lot in this software.

After Effects is one of my favorite apps, and I love to do After Effects training. People tend to get very excited when they see that they can do pretty advanced effects even with limited knowledge. With thorough knowledge on motion graphics and compositing, you can do pretty much anything you want to do with moving pixels. Have fun!

Photoshop Magic

Photoshop is an invaluable tool for film and video production. I use it a lot to create graphics and to prepare still images before import, but it also has some great tools for fixing video footage.

What many users don't know is that Photoshop can automate a lot of common tasks with scripting, and this can be a huge timesaver. Let's have a look at some common tasks and workflows with Photoshop.

Make PSD Files from Premiere Pro

In Premiere, click **File➤ New➤ Photoshop file**. You get a Photoshop document (PSD) file with guides for title safe and action safe, with the right pixel aspect ratio and size already set. Nice.

Sometimes this is a good idea, but if you're working in a timeline with non-square pixels, your graphics will also be created with non-square pixels, which is not a good idea, because they can easily get jaggies around the edges or look too soft. I recommend that you work in square pixel timelines with square pixel graphics whenever possible.

Also, you will have no extra room for pushing into the image. The text and graphics will go soft when you zoom in past 100 percent. So, I tend to not create my Photoshop files from Premiere, and rather create them in Photoshop at a larger size than I think I'll need.

Edit Original in Photoshop

When you have a PSD file in your timeline and you need to change it, just right-click it and choose *Edit Original in Photoshop*. Do whatever changes you want in Photoshop and hit *Save*. When you go back to the timeline in Premiere, the image is automatically updated. Very handy, and very powerful.

Gotcha with Layered PSD Files

Sometimes it's necessary to import a PSD file as a sequence or as individual layers (Figure 11-60). This enables us to manipulate, animate, or adjust the layers separately in Premiere.

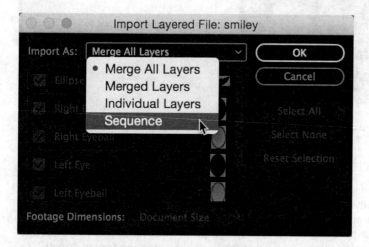

Figure 11-60. *Import PSD files as a sequence to animate the layers individually*

This is great, but when you do an *Edit Original* or *Edit in Adobe Photoshop* you can get into trouble. Say you want to add an adjustment layer to change the colors a bit (Figure 11-61). When you save the file from Photoshop, you'll see your new colors, but when you go back to Premiere, the change is not seen. What's up with that?

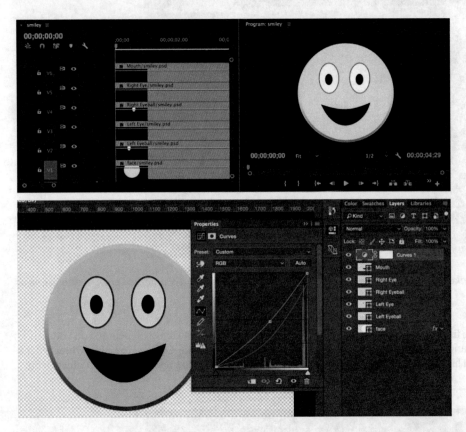

Figure 11-61. *The added adjustment does not show in Premiere because the layer wasn't there when the file was imported and does not exist in Premiere*

The problem is that the new layer you just added was never imported to Premiere and will not be rendered as part of the file, nor is there an option to add that extra layer from Photoshop in Premiere automatically. The workaround is to reimport the file with the new layer and replace the old version in the timeline—or to bake the adjustment into the file.

Import Camera RAW Footage

Premiere doesn't support RAW still image formats like Nikon NEF and Canon CR2. They don't even show up in the Import dialog or in the media browser. If you try to import a folder with RAW files, you'll get an error message but no images.

Photoshop does, of course, support these formats, and we can open a RAW file in Photoshop and keep it as an editable *smart object,* letting us resize and adjust everything without losing quality. So, open Photoshop and go to **File➤ Open** and point to the RAW file you need in your project. This opens the file in the Camera RAW module, where you can tweak all the settings as usual (Figure 11-62).

Figure 11-62. *Make the necessary adjustments to your image in Camera RAW and then open in Photoshop as a smart object*

When you've finished your adjustments, hit the *Open Image* (or Open Object, depending on your settings) button, and it opens in Photoshop. Click **Layer➤ Smart Objects➤ Convert to Smart Objects** if it's not already one. This changes nothing visually other than that the layer icon turns into a smart object icon (Figure 11-63).

Figure 11-63. *The small icon tells us that this is a smart object*

Now, save the file as a Photoshop document. Go to **File➤ Save** and accept the default PSD format suggestion. Import this PSD file into Premiere, and you can use it like any other PSD file. Keep in mind that RAW files are quite big and quite RAM hungry, so consider making a lower-res copy unless you really need the latitude and extra leeway you get from the RAW format.

Stitch Panorama Files

Photoshop can also be used to stitch together your panorama stills automatically, and you can use the settings to adjust the whole image easily. Select your photos in Bridge and choose **Tools➤ Photoshop➤ Photomerge** (Figure 11-64). This will take you to Photoshop and the Photomerge window. Choose your layout (*Auto* is the default), any other settings (Figure 11-65), and click *OK*. Just like that, you've stitched all your photos together (Figure 11-66)!

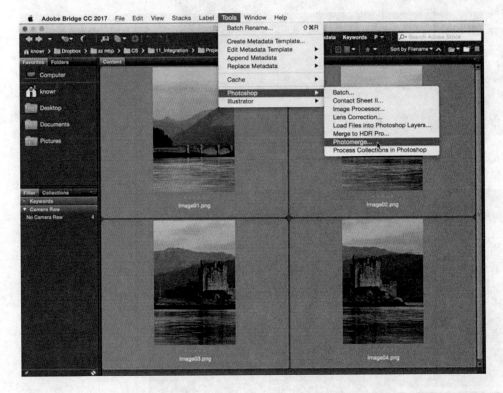

Figure 11-64. *Select all your panorama stills in Adobe Bridge and choose Tools ➤ Photoshop ➤ Photomerge*

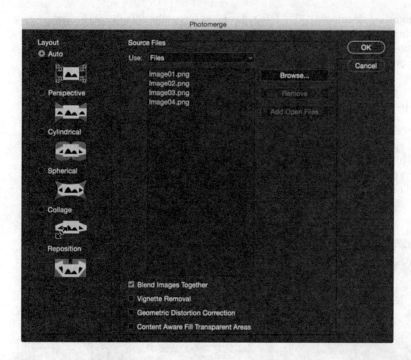

Figure 11-65. *Select your layout in the Photomerge window*

Figure 11-66. *All the photos are now stitched together! Photos courtesy of Shutterstock*

Video Clip Fixes with Photoshop

We can't send a video clip from Premiere to Photoshop, but we can import a video clip in Photoshop and save a PSD or video file that can then be imported into Premiere.

Why would we use Photoshop to fix a video clip? It has better lens distortion tools, it can clone away unwanted objects, it has lots of filters, and most of the great features that we normally use only on still images can be used with video too (Figure 11-67). What you can achieve will probably be limited only by your own imagination.

Figure 11-67. *Photoshop is not just limited to still images—you can apply Photoshop filters to your video footage*

Median Magic—Making a Clean Plate in Photoshop

Imagine this: The director of a documentary has shot heavy traffic on a busy street and wants you to slowly fade away the traffic and end with no cars. What's your first thought? I bet most editors would jump over to After Effects and start cloning away cars, tracking them over time, and covering them with road texture from earlier or later in the shot. Others would do the cloning in Photoshop, creating a clean plate.

Both the preceding methods include a lot of elbow grease. Let's do this much quicker and easier. Start by importing the traffic shot into Photoshop as layers by clicking **File➤ Import➤ Video Frames to Layers**. Find the video file with the traffic and click *OK*.

Make sure you untick the *Make Frame Animation* option. We just want separate layers, not an animation. We don't need to analyze all the frames, so I told Photoshop to import every 15 frames (Figure 11-68). Since this wasn't a very long clip, I ended up with 27 layers (Figure 11-69).

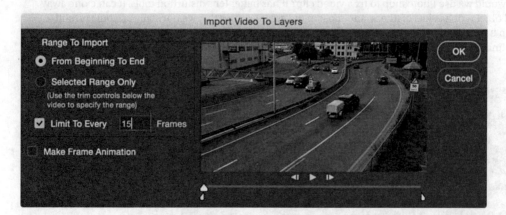

Figure 11-68. *You can import video frames as separate layers. In this case, we don't need all the layers, so we'll skip some*

Figure 11-69. *In my case, I ended up with 27 layers. We'll convert these into one smart object*

Select all the layers (click on the first one and **Shift-click** on the last one) and go to **Layer ➤ Smart Objects ➤ Convert to Smart Object**. This merges all the layers into one. Select this layer and click **Layer➤ Smart Objects ➤ Stack Mode ➤ Median**. Photoshop thinks for a couple of seconds, and then shows what you see in Figure 11-70. The Median filter in Stack mode automatically creates a clean plate for us with just a couple of mouse-clicks!

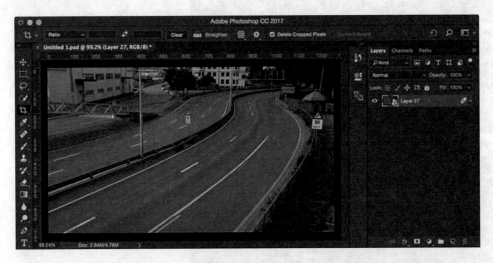

Figure 11-70. *After conversion to smart object, we have just one layer, but all the original layers are still available inside this smart object*

Poof—the cars have vanished. Magic! How did that happen? Well, the Stack mode filters are used by scientists to get statistics from images taken over time. The Median algorithm is used by these scientists to provide robust statistics—*robust* since it doesn't change with big deviations in values, so a few—or even many—wrongly measured numbers will not destroy a scientific experiment.

It's not like the mean value, which will be all the values of one pixel on all layers, divided by the number of layers. Mean would have given us ghost cars on the road in our example. No, median is the middle number in a sorted list of numbers. So, we measure the value on all the layers for each pixel. Then, the pixel values are arranged from lowest to highest, and the middle number is the median.

I found a very simple explanation of median here if you're interested: mathsisfun.com/definitions/median.html.

Median isn't the only filter available in Stack mode. Figure 11-71 shows the results of running the Maximum, Minimum, and Deviance filters.

Figure 11-71. *Maximum, Minimum, and Deviance filters*

The median value for our road clip will be whatever is there most often. Well, actually, that would take a Mode filter, which Photoshop doesn't have, but now we're going way too far into science. Let's get back to video production. The Median filter lets us get rid of people and cars passing by and gives us a nice, clean plate. This method doesn't necessarily work well with leaves blowing in the wind, but can auto-delete a lot of moving objects from a shot.

We don't need the Photoshop document itself any more, but we have to save that image as a still. I like the lossless PNG format, so I did **File ➤ Save As** and chose *PNG*.

Now, jump to Premiere and import the cars-on-road clip and your new PNG file with no cars. Add a cross-dissolve between them and put an exponential fade on the audio track to get a smooth fade out (Figure 11-72). This makes the cars fade away nicely, but if you look closely, you'll see that the still image doesn't look like video. It's too perfect! The still image has no noise, but video always has some, so let's add some noise to match the noise in the video clip.

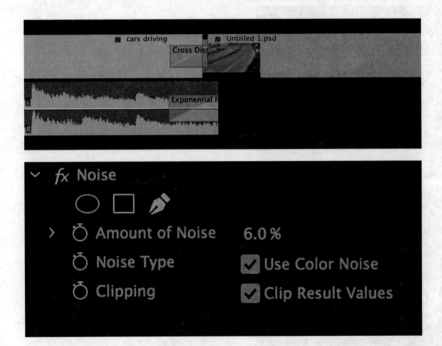

Figure 11-72. Do a cross-dissolve from the live video to the clean plate and add noise to match the video noise

Add the noise effect to your still image clip and tweak to taste. I ended up with 6 percent noise, but you really have to watch your video in full screen to get the right amount, and your video absolutely needs to be playing. So, toggle on full-screen playback and hit *Play*. Then, tweak a bit and play again until it looks good. Now we have a "natural"-looking clip where the cars gradually disappear. See Figure 11-73 for the final result.

Figure 11-73. *Quick and perfect result! The Stack mode in Photoshop just saved us from a lot of manual cloning and patching*

This method will obviously just work with a locked-off camera. A little bit of shake can probably be fixed by using the **Edit ➤ Auto-Align Layers** feature in Photoshop before you create the smart object. It will take a while to align them, but the computer is doing the work, not you. With a moving camera, this method will not work, and you'll have to do some manual clone fixing.

Export LUTs from Photoshop for Use in Premiere

If you've made adjustments to the color of an image in Photoshop using adjustment layers, you can export these same changes as a single LUT for use in Premiere.

In Photoshop, load your image and then click **File ➤ Export ➤ Color Lookup Tables**. Give the LUT a name and choose either the 3DL or Cube format.

■ **Note**   To successfully export a LUT from Photoshop, the image needs to have a background layer.

In Premiere, go to the Creative section of the Lumetri Color panel and browse for the LUT.

Spreadsheets to Lower Thirds

Spreadsheets are great for holding data, like names, and if you share them via Dropbox, Google Drive, or other online sharing sites they can easily be reviewed and controlled by a lot of people to make sure that every name and title is correct. This is all great, but they're still kind of boring-looking.

Photoshop documents can look really good, but are bad at storing lots of data. Combined, a spreadsheet and a Photoshop document offer the best of both worlds, so here's a method that I developed when I needed 83 lower thirds for a corporate movie I made.

Say you're making a documentary about magicians and magic shops in Scandinavia (Figure 11-74). You have lots of interviews with Scandinavian magicians, shop owners, and so on. You've even talked to some American magicians. You want the flag of each interviewee's country to show on the lower third, and of course their name and occupation. You've collected all this info in a spreadsheet, and you've gathered the necessary flag images. Now, let's make Photoshop do all the hard work for you.

Figure 11-74. *Photo of Johan Ståhl by Alex&Martin, alexochmartin.se*

Data Preparation

We'll use a Google Drive spreadsheet as our starting point and make Photoshop generate our lower thirds automatically! We'll combine the flags and the list of names in Figure 11-75 with a Photoshop document and create our lower thirds automatically.

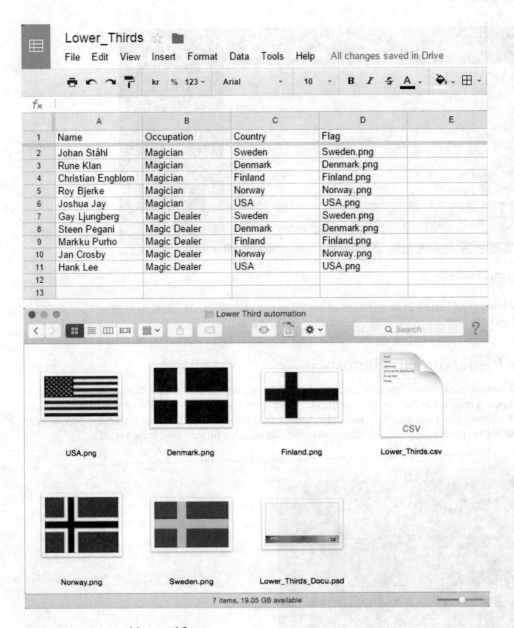

Figure 11-75. *Spreadsheet and flags*

Make sure the columns in the spreadsheet have proper names. We need to save the data in a format that Photoshop can import—CSV or TXT. Google Drive cannot save in TXT format, so we'll stick to CSV. In Google Drive, click **File ➤ Download as ➤ Comma-separated values**. Give your downloaded file a meaningful name. I very creatively named mine Lower_Thirds.csv.

You need a PSD with layers that correspond to the spreadsheet columns. My Photoshop document in Figure 11-76 has five layers: Background, Flag, Name, Occupation, and Country. Also, make sure you have all the flag images in the same folder as your CSV and PSD files.

You can download the sample files from premierepro.net/editing/spreadsheets-to-lower-thirds/.

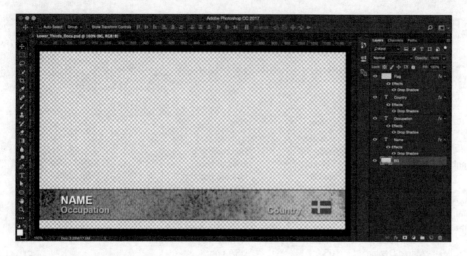

Figure 11-76. *Photoshop file*

Your lower third can be as simple or as advanced as you like. All the design tools in Photoshop are now at your disposal!

Image Preparation in Photoshop

Now, let's jump to the fun part. We need to define four of these layers as fields that will be altered.
Click **Image ➤ Variables ➤ Define.** Choose the Flag layer and choose *Pixel Replacement* from the drop-down menu. Give it the name *Flag*, just like it had in the spreadsheet (Figure 11-77). Photoshop is very picky about this, so the names need to be exactly the same as in the spreadsheet, upper-/lowercase and all.

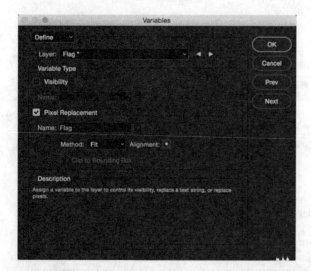

Figure 11-77. *Define the variables in the PSD file one by one*

Now, click the triangle pointing to the right in the dialog to do the same thing with the three text layers, but choose *Text Replacement* from the drop-down menu. Name them *Name*, *Occupation*, and *Country* respectively—again, exactly like in the spreadsheet. Do not set a variable for the BG layer, but click *OK* once you've set the variables for all the other layers.

Get the Data and Export Files

Now, it's time to import our data. Go to **File ➤ Import ➤ Variable Data Sets**. Change the format to CSV and choose our downloaded Lower_Thirds.csv file and click *Load*. Make sure your settings look exactly like mine in Figure 11-78. Choose *Unicode (UTF-8)* for encoding, or else characters like the Norwegian Æ, Ø, and Å will be interpreted incorrectly. Å becomes Ã¥ and so forth.

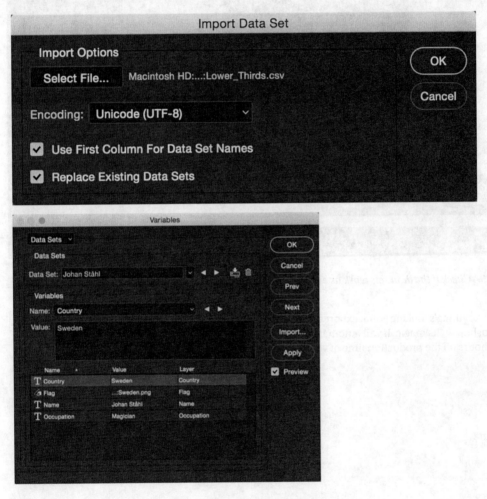

***Figure 11-78.** Import the CSV or TXT file and check that everything works*

Go to **Image ➤ Variables ➤ Data Sets**. Now you can see each of the different rows from the spreadsheet as a separate data set.

Tick the *Preview* box (not to be confused with the *Prev* button) to see how each data set will look (Figure 11-79). Click the left/right arrows to switch between entries. Try viewing a few just to see if everything is working OK. If not, the problem is probably the pixel replacement. Go to the Flag entry, click on *Select File*, and point to the correct flag image for each entry.

Figure 11-79. *Check if the data sets work as expected*

When everything's looking good, export the files: **File ➤ Export ➤ Data Sets as Files** (Figure 11-80). Watch Photoshop do its magic. It will automatically spit out all the lower thirds you need in your film. You just shaved hours off the production time of your documentary with a few clicks!

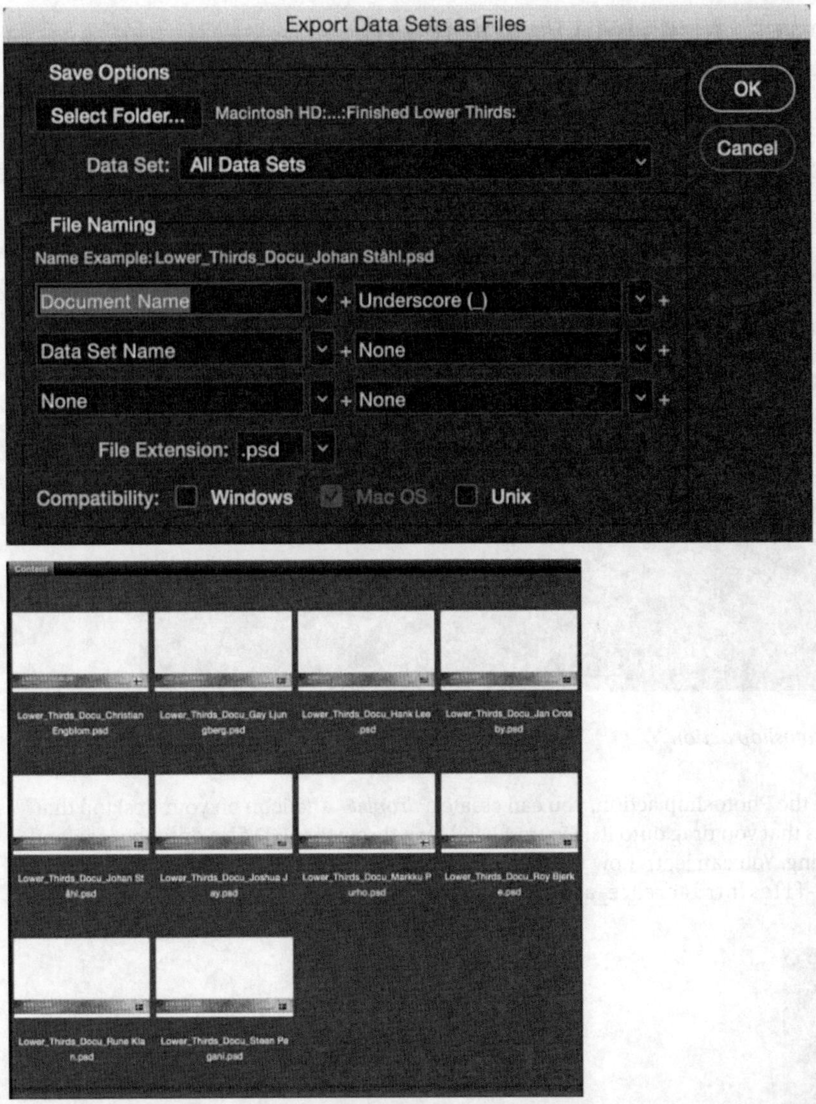

Figure 11-80. *Export settings and finished lower thirds, viewed in Bridge*

Every lower third is ready to be imported into Premiere Pro, complete with name, occupation, country, flag, and all. Photoshop automation is really, really cool stuff! Imagine the amount of work this will save on a TV documentary series with 150 lower thirds.

There's an added bonus: they will all be correct. Why? Because you can share the spreadsheet in Google Drive with everyone who needs to check the spelling and get corrections directly from the source. So, say goodbye to wrongly spelled names!

Importing the Lower Thirds into Premiere Pro

Import the whole folder with your lower thirds into Premiere Pro, then hit **Enter** to confirm the choice to *Merge All Layers* for every PSD file you made. If you don't want to hit **Enter** that many times, you can make an *action* in Photoshop that merges the layers of every file and run that in batch mode before you import the files into Premiere (Figure 11-81). To learn more about Photoshop actions, read more in the online Photoshop Help: helpx.adobe.com/photoshop/using/creating-actions.html.

Figure 11-81. *Create a Photoshop action*

When you have made the Photoshop action, you can create a *droplet* - and icon on your desktop that applies an action to images that you drag onto it. (Figure 11-82). Just throw the PSD files onto the icon and watch Photoshop do its thing. You can learn how to make droplets here: helpx.adobe.com/photoshop/using/processing-batch-files.html#create_a_droplet_from_an_action.

Figure 11-82. *Photoshop droplet*

Inside a bin in Premiere Pro, you'll find that the files show up with black where they're transparent. You might want to set your Default Still Duration to, say, five seconds in **Edit ➤ Preferences ➤ General** before you import the stills. Now, drop the files onto the timeline where they belong.

If you've placed some markers where they need to go, you can even automate this part! Read on!

Automate Lower Thirds to the Timeline

A great way to place lower thirds is to set sequence markers. Hit **M** to set markers on the fly while playing, or when paused, where you need a lower third. With all the sequence markers in place, lock all tracks but your Titles track (just in case). Then, sort the PSD files in the bin in the order they need to appear in the timeline.

You could also have added an extra *Order* column in your spreadsheet with a number that corresponds to the order in which the persons appear in the film, plus an invisible text layer (Opacity set to 0) in your PSD. This way, the files would already be sorted correctly in your bin at import. In a large project with lots of lower thirds, it may be worth the extra two minutes of setup time in Photoshop.

When they're sorted, select all of the clips in the bin and click the *Automate to Sequence* button at the bottom of the bin, or go to **Clip ➤ Automate to Sequence** (Figure 11-83). Choose *Sort Order* and *At Unnumbered Markers*, and Premiere Pro will put every file on its marker so all the people have a lower third.

Figure 11-83. *Automate To Sequence dialog*

Animate In/Out

Finish the almost automatic lower-third generation by selecting all the clips in your Lower Thirds video track and throwing your favorite custom animation preset on one of them.

Don't have a favorite preset? Save a fancy position, opacity, and blur animation in a preset and name it *Lower Third Animation*. The preset used in Figure 11-84 even has the hard light blending mode applied.

Figure 11-84. *Throw an animation preset on all the lower thirds in one go*

Easy Changes

OK, so what if you want to change just one of the lower thirds? Easy—just click **File ➤ Export ➤ Data Sets as Files** and, instead of exporting all of them, choose the one you want to export in the drop-down menu (Figure 11-85). If the file name is the same as before and you overwrite the old file, it will auto-update in the timeline in Premiere.

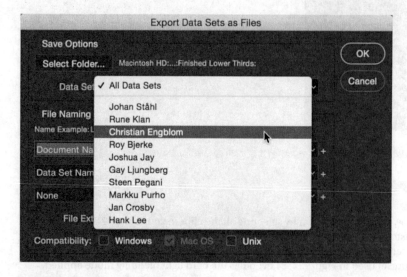

Figure 11-85. *You can change one or all the lower thirds quickly by running the export again, overwriting the existing files*

If you've changed a dataset that's part of the file name, you'll need to swap the files manually with an **Alt-Drag-n-Drop** (Option-Drag-n-Drop) in Premiere.

A big bonus with this method is that you can also do changes to all the lower thirds in one go! Just make the design changes you want, then export your data sets as PSD files again and tell Photoshop to overwrite the old ones. When the files are overwritten, everything just automatically appears in the timeline in Premiere.

Use Your Favorite Spreadsheet App

Don't want to use Google Drive? No problem—use your favorite spreadsheet app. Of course, using Google Drive has several advantages. You can send a link to the people involved so they can check the spelling and whatnot without having any spreadsheet software installed. Or, you can send it as an Excel or PDF email attachment.

There might be reasons why you want to use Excel, Numbers, or OpenOffice. By all means do so. I've had some problems with the CSV from Excel in the past, so you might want to export to TXT, not CSV, if you use Excel.

Credit Where Credit's Due

I want to give credit to Marcel Izidoro from Brazil, who created a tutorial about variables in Photoshop for the Pixel Corps to share his knowledge with fellow PXC members back in July 2007. That's where I learned the basics of using variables in Photoshop. The rest I learned from the section on variables in Adobe's online *Photoshop Reference* documentation at helpx.adobe.com/pdf/photoshop_reference.pdf.

Just so you know, there's one kind of variable that we haven't used in this tutorial: *Visibility*. You can make a layer visible or invisible based on a *True/False* entry in the spreadsheet. In our case, we could have a shiny gold medal appear only for world champion magicians in our documentary.

Random Tips

Make sure your Photoshop file is the same size as your Premiere Pro sequence. Choosing a video format preset like HDTV 1080p or 2K and 4K Film is a pretty safe way to start.

I recommend saving the original PSD file, the CSV file, and the replacement files (flag PNGs, in our case) in the same folder so Photoshop, and you, can easily locate them.

Remember to re-import the Data Set file if you make changes to it, and make sure *Replace Existing Data Sets* is ticked so you don't get duplicates.

Gotchas

Keep the spreadsheet tidy to avoid trouble. Empty fields and wrong column names, among other things, can trigger error messages.

You can have no empty fields in the spreadsheet, or you'll get this kind of message: *Could not parse the file contents as a data set. Data set 2 was incomplete.* But you can make this work if you enter a double quotation mark (") and a space ( ) into a field where you want nothing to print.

This message will pop up when your first row has more entries than the number of variables you've defined in the PSD file: *Could not parse the file contents as a data set. There were too many variable names in the first line of the file.*

If you have too few, the text will change to *Could not parse the file contents as a data set. There were not enough variable names in the first line of the file.*

You'll get this kind of message if one row has an extra column that's not present in the first row: *Could not parse the file contents as a data set. Too many values were listed for data set 2.*

This type of message means your column names and your variables do not match: *Could not parse the file contents as a data set. The name "Test Column" is not a variable in the current document.*

No replacement layer can be a smart object, or you'll only get one choice for variable—Visibility. You'll also need to rasterize a layer before you can use pixel replacement.

Illustrator Vector Graphic Fixes

Photoshop is great for working with pixel-based images, but when it comes to vector images, Illustrator is the king. When working on corporate movies or documentaries, I get a lot of logos and other graphics from designers and marketing people. Generally, the graphics and logos are designed for print and need to be altered for video purposes.

Extracting Vector Graphics from PDF Files

Sometimes, the only available format is PDF, so we need to be able to extract what we want from these files, adapt the content for video use, and save it as a new, video-optimized file.

Acrobat Reader will not cut it—you'll need Acrobat Pro, which is a part of the Creative Cloud. When you open a file in Acrobat, you can edit the contents by clicking the Tools tab and then the Content Editing tab. Here, you'll find the Edit Text and Images tool, and you can choose the elements you want to extract from the PDF. In the example in Figure 11-86, I just marquee-selected the elements that I wanted and clicked **Edit Using ➤ Adobe Illustrator.**

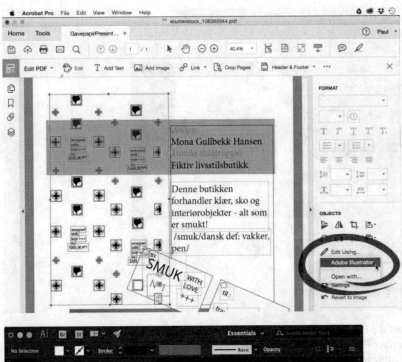

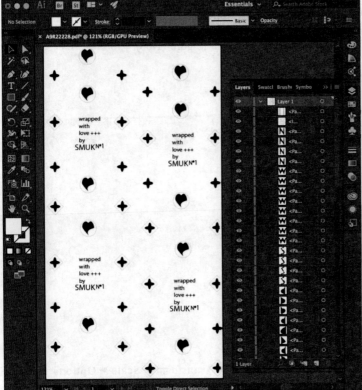

Figure 11-86. Edit the selected items in Illustrator to get access to the layers. Wrapping paper design by Mona Gullbekk Hansen

The size of the AI artboard will match the size of the original PDF, so we need to make it fit just the selected graphics. This is simple: **Object ➤ Artboards ➤ Fit to Artwork Bounds**. See Figure 11-87.

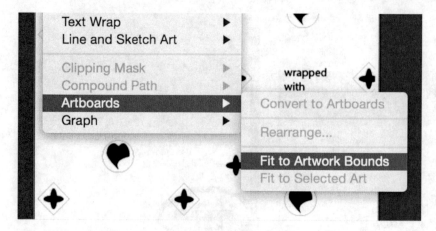

Figure 11-87. *Fit the artboard to artwork bounds*

We want to see the size of the file in pixels, not millimeters or inches, so right-click on the Info panel's top bar and choose *User Interface Preferences*. Choose *Pixels for the General Units* display mode. If the Info panel is not showing, click **Window ➤ Info**. Now we can see how much we need to scale the graphics for it to fit the whole frame—or part of the frame, depending on our needs (Figure 11-88).

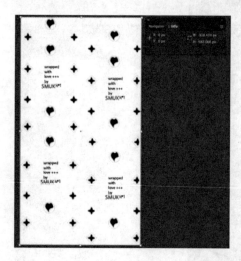

Figure 11-88. *Show the Info panel to see the size in pixels*

Calculate how much scaling is needed, and then hit **Edit ➤ Transform ➤ Scale ➤ Options** and enter this value. Make sure *Scale Strokes & Effects* is selected, or the whole look of the graphics will change (Figure 11-89).

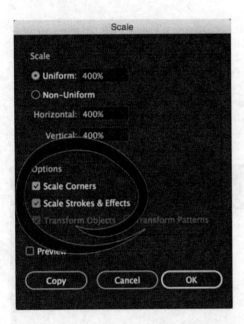

Figure 11-89. *Inspect the Scale options before scaling the artwork*

Scale to whatever size you need, measured in pixels, and, again, choose **Object ➤ Artboards ➤ Fit to Artwork Bounds**. If you need to get rid of any backgrounds or unwanted objects, now is the time to delete them. Use the Layers panel to select and delete layers.

To show the graphic with a transparent background, go to **View ➤ Show Transparency Grid**. As you can see in Figure 11-90, this design has an opaque white fill in some of the elements—something that will influence how it reacts to effects and blending modes.

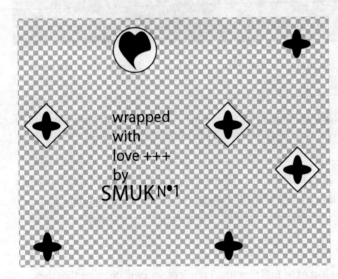

Figure 11-90. *Show the transparency grid so you can see what parts of the artwork are transparent*

Your final step is to go to **File ➤ Document Color Mode** and make sure it's set to *RGB*. Chances are it's made for print and is CMYK. If so, change it from CMYK to RGB by clicking **File ➤ Document Color Mode ➤ RGB Color**.

When you've finished editing the design, hit **File ➤ Save As**, choose *AI* as the format, and give the file a good name.

Figure 11-91 shows the extracted and scaled graphics, which are being used as a background element on which I can put text, bar charts, and so forth. I added some blur, movement, and colorization to get the look I wanted.

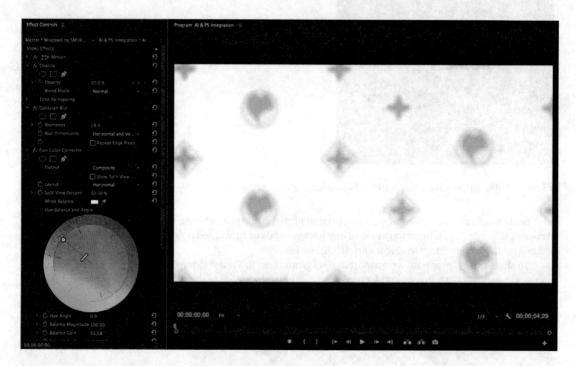

Figure 11-91. *Some blur, position keyframes, and colorization made this a nice background for text and graphics*

If you want to, you can of course also save the image as a PNG or PSD file, but keeping it as a vector file will give you more opportunities for manipulation in After Effects, like depth extrusion, should you so desire.

■ **Note**   To get logos from PDF files, they need to be editable. If a PDF file is protected, you'll not be able to get the vectors out of it, but you can still scale the view in Acrobat to fill the screen and get a pretty high-res screen grab.

Resize Vector Graphics

Sometimes when you import vector graphics like AI or EPS files into Premiere, you will discover that they are too small. What's worse is that they look bad and pixelated when you scale them up to the size you need. The reason is that Premiere rasterizes vector graphics on import, so they end up effectively being pixels, not vectors. The vector image in Figure 11-92 doesn't fill the entire frame. Scaling to fit in Premiere means we'll be up-scaling pixels, thus losing quality.

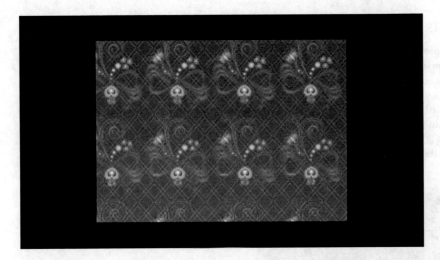

Figure 11-92. *This vector graphic file is too small. Design by Janne Marete Grødum, mittdigitalegalleri. blogspot.com*

Luckily, we can use Edit Original on AI and EPS files to resize them in Illustrator. Back in Premiere, they'll be updated automatically. Great! So, let's have a look at the workflow.

Right-click the vector clip in the timeline in Premiere and choose *Edit Original* (or hit the shortcut). It opens in Illustrator. Show the Layers panel and make sure no layers are locked. Unlock them if necessary.

Click **Select ➤ All** and then **Object ➤ Transform ➤ Scale**. Make sure you scale strokes and effects as in the preceding example.

Do an **Object ➤ Artboards ➤ Fit to Artwork Bounds** routine like before, and then save the file. It automatically updates in the Premiere Pro timeline (Figure 11-93).

Figure 11-93. *Scaling in Illustrator kept all the details sharp, and I was even able to create an infinite pattern with ease*

Isolate Elements to Treat Them Separately

If the graphic designer has built the AI file with only one layer, there is no way to separate them in Premiere or After Effects. However, opening the file in Illustrator gives you access to all the elements, and you can put them on as many layers as you want, or even remove unwanted elements.

For this example, I used the beautiful wrapping paper design by Janne Marete Grødum (mittdigitalegalleri.blogspot.com) again. I wanted to isolate the elements on different layers so they could be animated separately in Premiere. I opened the file and clicked **Window ➤ Layers,** and as you can see in Figure 11-94, everything is kept on the same layer in the original file. I made new layers by clicking the New Layer icon, then moved the elements to the different layers and gave them proper names before I saved the file.

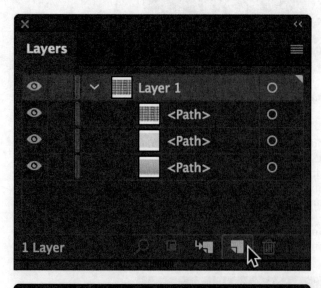

Figure 11-94. *Move elements to separate layers so you can animate them independently*

If I would have imported it to After Effects at this point, I could have chosen to have the layers from Illustrator as separate layers in After Effects, too (Figures 11-95 and 11-96).

Figure 11-95. *After Effects can import Illustrator layers separately*

Figure 11-96. *After Effects can also create a comp automatically*

Premiere will not see the separate layers like After Effects does, so I needed to export the layered artwork to a Photoshop file. To do this, I went to the Illustrator menu and selected **File ➤ Export ➤ Export as**, chose the Photoshop format, and made sure to tick *Write Layers* in the Export dialog (Figure 11-97).

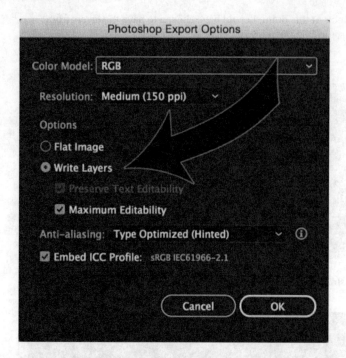

Figure 11-97. *For Premiere, export to a layered Photoshop file*

Join Elements in Vector Files

As kind of the opposite of isolating elements, we also have the possibility to join separate paths into one. **Window ➤ Pathfinder** takes you to the Pathfinder panel. Select the paths that you want to join and click the Unite icon in the Pathfinder panel to join the paths into one.

Trace Images into Vectors

You can only do this with still images, so start by exporting your video out from Premiere to an image sequence format like PNG or TIF. Now, open one image and click **Window ➤ Image Trace**. This brings up the Image Trace dialog (Figure 11-98). Tweak the settings to taste, save the settings as a new preset, and export to a still image format.

Figure 11-98. *Export your video as a still image sequence so you can trace the images in Adobe Illustrator. To batch process all the frames of your video, start the automation from Bridge*

Here's how to do it from Bridge: open the folder with the image sequence in Adobe Bridge, select all the files, and then click **Tools ➤ Illustrator ➤ Image Trace**. Figure 11-99 shows the settings I used.

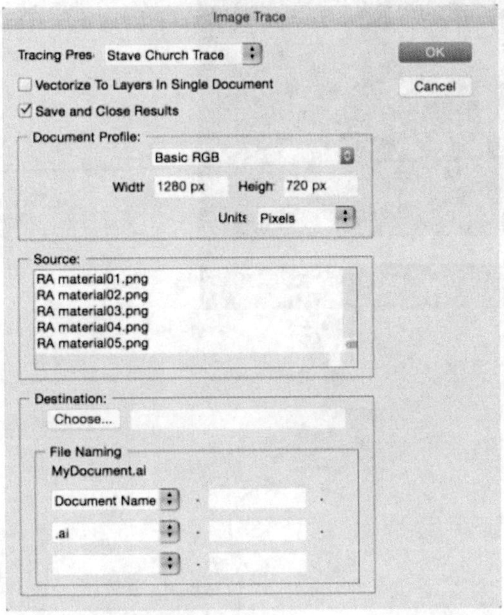

Figure 11-99. *You can start a batch Image Trace process from Bridge*

This creates an AI file with lots of layers. It's quite a heavy process, so it will take a while. The resulting layers can be exported as previously described and imported as an image sequence in Premiere.

You can also try image tracing if you're unable to get a proper vector logo from a client and you're forced to use a pixel-based format. Tracing it and saving it as a vector image will sometimes allow you to create a vector-based logo or other graphic elements with a decent result.

Make Vector Patterns

Create a new Illustrator document and make it as big as you need it. That often means larger than your video frame. Also make sure you have your Swatches panel open—**Window ➤ Swatches**. Copy the shape or element you want to repeat from the pattern from another document.

Note that you cannot have guides in a pattern, so turn any guides off in the Layers panel before making the pattern from the object.

Select it in your new document and click **Object ➤ Pattern ➤ Make**. You could also drag the selected element over to the Swatches panel and let go when you see the + sign to create a new pattern.

Make sure you have nothing selected, then double-click the new pattern in the Swatches panel, and the Pattern Options panel opens. Give it a good name and play with the settings, like those for tile type and spacing. When you're finished, click *Done* up in the bar just below the menu bar (Figure 11-100).

Figure 11-100. *Copy the shape to a new document and make a pattern. Then, set your preferred pattern options*

Delete the shapes so you have an empty document. With the custom pattern selected in the Swatches panel, create a new rectangle using the Rectangle tool. It automatically fills with your new pattern. Save the Illustrator file and import into Premiere as usual (Figure 11-101). The resulting pattern can be treated in many ways in Premiere. In Figure 11-101, I've placed a blurred copy beneath it on a black background.

Figure 11-101. *Pattern used in Premiere. Design by Janne Marete Grødum, mittdigitalegalleri.blogspot.com*

Patterns like these can be very helpful when you work with motion graphics and need a bit more texture and detail.

Unlimited Scaling of Vector Graphics

As we discussed, Premiere rasterizes vector graphics on import, so once imported, it's no longer a vector graphic—it's pixel based. You can send the vector image to Illustrator and enlarge it, as explained in the preceding Illustrator section, but it will still be a pixel-based image—just larger. Figure 11-102 shows a vector image scaled to 500 percent in Premiere. Note the ugly jagged edges.

Figure 11-102. Premiere rasterizes vector graphics on import, which can create jagged edges like this

After Effects can "continuously rasterize" an image, create pixels from the vectors for every frame, which makes it a fully scalable vector graphic. Via Dynamic Link, we can get the perfectly smooth image back in the timeline in Premiere. Start by adding the vector graphic to the timeline in Premiere and scaling it to the preferred size, then send it to After Effects by right-clicking the clip and choosing *Replace with After Effects Composition*.

Now, click the icon on the layer in AE that looks a bit like a sun on the vector graphic layer (Figure 11-103) to enable *Continuously Rasterize*. Suddenly, the image is razor sharp—even back in Premiere (Figure 11-104).

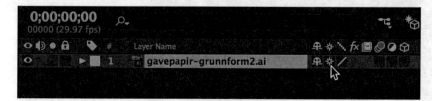

Figure 11-103. Click the layer's "sun" icon to continuously rasterize in After Effects

Figure 11-104. The graphic looks much sharper now

Integration with Audition

Audition has great tools for audio clean-up and finishing. Using a brush to "paint away" the noise is so intuitive that anyone can do it.

When you right-click a clip in Premiere and choose *Edit Clip in Audition*, it's not like the *Edit Original* workflow we have with Photoshop and Illustrator. Edit Clip in Audition creates a new audio file and replaces the original in the timeline, so the original is not changed. But just like Render and Replace, you have the option of right-clicking and choosing *Restore Unrendered* to revert back to the original audio.

In the chapter 3 on audio, you'll find lots of ways to use Audition for audio clean-up, noise removal, and sound effects creation, as well as how to use the Speech Volume Leveler and other tools to fix volume differences and loudness issues.

You'll also need Audition for some surround-sound jobs. Premiere can export 5.1 surround audio, but if you need Dolby Digital 7.1, you will have to mix and output this from Audition.

Import Premiere Sequences

Besides editing individual clips, you can also send your entire sequence to Audition for the final mix. Select the sequence and choose **Edit ➤ Edit in Audition ➤ Sequence** (Figure 11-105).

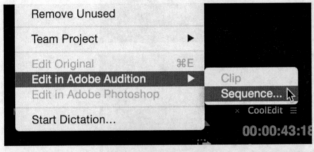

Figure 11-105. *Export your sequence from Premiere to Audition*

This will create duplicates of your original audio files using "handles" (audio from beyond the in and out points, which you can set to be anywhere from 0 to 9.99 seconds) and transfer all volume and pan adjustments, Essential Sound panel parameters, clip and track effects, label colors, track names, and submix routing for further tweaking in Audition (Figure 11-106).

Figure 11-106. *The session in Audition will have all your clip and track effects, submix routing, and a dynamically linked video*

The real advantage of working this way is that the full-resolution video for your Audition session will be dynamically linked from the Premiere project, so there's no need to render proxy video references for your sequence every time you make a change. Just like After Effects, any adjustments to the video will be updated automatically.

Generate Temp VO

It's often the case that I'll be working on an edit before the voiceover has been finalized. Usually, this means grabbing a microphone and recording the temp VO myself, but there is another way to generate this—with a synthetic voice in Audition.

Choose **Effects ➤ Generate ➤ Speech**. Enter the settings for your new file, then paste the text for your voiceover into the text box (Figure 11-107). You can choose a language, gender, and different types of voices—these will all depend on the voice libraries available to your operating system. Once you're happy with it, save the file and import it into Premiere.

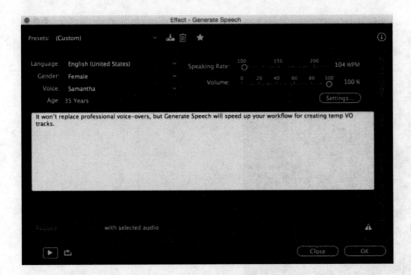

Figure 11-107. *Generate speech in Audition*

Side-chaining (Automatic Ducking) in Audition

If you have a voiceover with a music track underneath it, you'll often want to turn the volume of the music down while the voice is speaking, and up again every time there's a gap in the voiceover. This can be a very repetitive and manual task if you're keyframing the music in Premiere, but it can actually be done automatically in Audition using a technique called *side-chaining*.

Send your voice and music tracks to Audition, then select the music track (not the music clip) and choose **Effects ➤ Amplitude and Compression ➤ Dynamics Processing**.

■ **Note**   Dynamics Processing is the only native effect in Audition that utilizes side-chaining, although some third-party VST or audio unit effects also support it.

If you look at the graph in the Dynamics tab in Figure 11-108, the straight line moving from the lower left to the upper right indicates that there is no change to the audio at the moment. Click the control point at the upper right of the line and drag it down to -20 on the vertical axis (Figure 11-109). This will turn the music down by 20 dB whenever the voice is speaking.

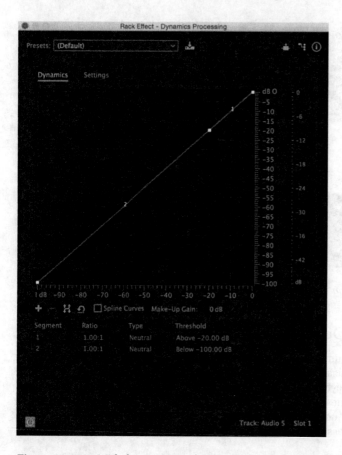

Figure 11-108. *With these settings, there is no change to the audio*

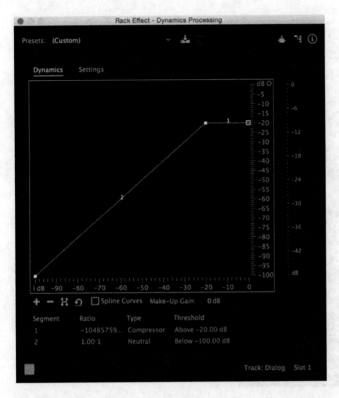

Figure 11-109. *These settings will turn the music down by 20 db*

At the top right of the effect dialog is an icon called Set Side-Chain Input—click this and choose the number of channels on your voiceover track (most likely mono). See Figure 11-110.

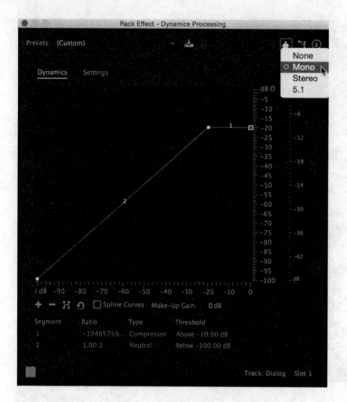

Figure 11-110. *Choose the number of channels in your voiceover track*

The final step is to send your voiceover to the effect. Select the voiceover track and switch to the Sends view by clicking the arrows icon at the top left of the Editor panel (Figure 11-111). Click the drop-down list for S1 and choose **Side-Chain ➤ Dynamics Processing** (Figure 11-112).

Figure 11-111. *Click the Sends icon to display the sends menu in your track headers*

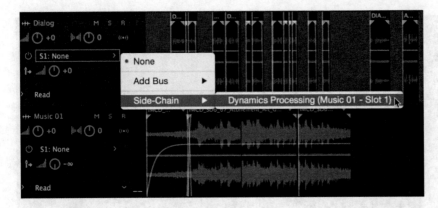

Figure 11-112. *Choose Side-Chain ➤ Dynamics Processing to send your voiceover to the dynamics effect on the music track*

Now, play the session, and you should hear the music automatically ducking when the voiceover starts speaking. You can solo just the music track to hear only the music and the changes in volume.

If you want to tweak this further, play around with the control points on the Dynamics graph, as well as the release time on the Settings tab—this will adjust how smoothly the music is turned back up when there's a gap in the voiceover. If you find settings that you like, make sure to save it as a preset!

Auto-update Titles with InDesign

You probably didn't think that InDesign would be in this chapter. But co-author of this chapter, Paul Murphy, actually makes a lot of titles, subtitles, and end credits in InDesign. Here's a video he made on Vimeo (vimeo.com/m/80445034) that explains how he updates multiple titles in Premiere Pro using InDesign.

He export EPS or PNG files from InDesign and use these in the Premiere Pro timeline. The result and workflow are very similar to the Spreadsheets to Lower Thirds technique in Photoshop. But, if you know InDesign, this might be an alternative to try.

Ingest with Adobe Prelude

Prelude is an app that lets you ingest, transcode, tag, mark, rough-cut, and back-up your footage (Figure 11-113). It's mostly geared toward bigger operations that have loggers who wade through all the material before it's sent to the editors, but even smaller companies and one-man bands can benefit from its quick-tagging and other features.

Figure 11-113. *Prelude looks a lot like Premiere, and many of the keyboard shortcuts are the same*

So, in Prelude you can review clips from a camera card or a disk and copy them to a hard drive. Maybe you want to transcode to a more edit-friendly codec, and in Prelude this can be done while you're copying the material to the hard drive and simultaneously doing a backup of the material to one or more other places (Figures 11-114 and 11-115).

Figure 11-114. *The Ingest view in Prelude looks a lot like the media browser in Premiere. Footage courtesy of Shutterstock*

Figure 11-115. Prelude can copy, backup, transfer, and ingest files simultaneously

When the clips are imported, you can log comments and other markers and add metadata while you build a rough cut (Figure 11-116).

Figure 11-116. *Add comments, markers, and metadata, and even create a rough cut in Prelude*

The project can then be exported as a Premiere Pro project (Figure 11-117) or as an FCP XML file that can be opened by any NLE that supports that format, like Premiere or FCP7.

Figure 11-117. *You can export a Premiere Pro project file or a Final Cut Pro XML file*

If you don't click *Export*, but instead click **File ➤ Send to Premiere Pro** or choose the same via right-click (Figure 11-118), the rough cut and the media will instantly appear in the Project panel in Premiere. Markers and metadata are of course intact, and you can start refining the cut (Figure 11-119).

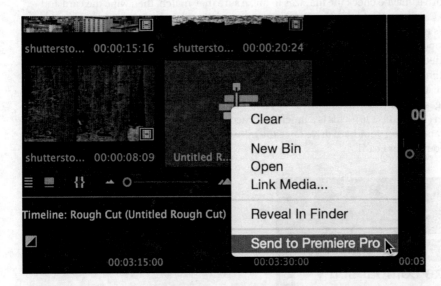

Figure 11-118. *You can also send the ingested material directly to the project that's open in Premiere Pro*

Figure 11-119. *All the metadata, markers, comments, subclips, and even the rough cut carry over to Premiere*

MD5 Comparison

You're on location filming and your camera card is full—what do you do? To free up the card, you copy the card to an external drive, maybe check the file sizes to make sure they match, then wipe the card and continue shooting.

But, guess what? It's not until you open the drive in the edit suite that you discover that half the footage is corrupt and lost for good.

This is not a hypothetical—this actually happened to me on a very large and expensive project. We lost several days of footage filmed overseas, and we didn't realize it until a month later.

Ever since then, I've always used Prelude for transferring footage from camera cards to hard drives. Why? Because in the Ingest window, if you click the *Verify* checkbox, you can choose a verification method called MD5 Comparison (Figure 11-120). This is a much more accurate way of comparing whether the file on the camera card is the same file on your hard drive once the transfer is complete, and will give you peace of mind before you wipe your camera card.

Figure 11-120. *MD5 is a reliable way to copy media from a camera drive*

Adding Voiceover to Rough Cuts

Sometimes directors/producers will want to use Prelude to make quick assemblies before they pass them on to editors for the grunt work. Often times, these rough cuts will also require scratch voiceover tracks. You can easily record VO in Prelude, and it's a very similar process to doing so in Premiere.

With your rough-cut timeline open, choose **Rough Cut ➤ Add Audio Track** and then choose the number of channels (most likely mono if you're just recording voiceover). Right-click your audio track and choose **Voice-Over Record Settings**. Here, you can choose your input device, where the file will be saved, whether you need preroll before the recording begins, and so on (Figure 11-121).

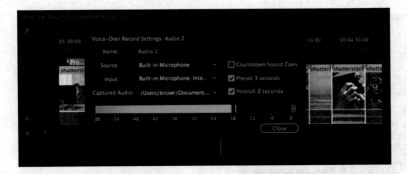

Figure 11-121. *Record a voiceover track directly into Prelude*

Once you're happy with your recording settings, just click the microphone icon on the track to start recording, and press **Spacebar** when you're done.

As you can see, most of the functionality in Prelude is duplicated in Premiere in the latest versions. So, for most users, adding Prelude to the mix will probably feel like overkill. But, if you learn to use the super-fast markers features in Prelude, you will be able to tag your footage a lot faster in Prelude than in Premiere.

Adobe Story Workflow

Story is a professional scripting tool made for screenwriters, writing teams, producers, production managers, and directors, but it's also much more than that. Yes, it will help you while you write your script, but it can also give you lists that show what locations are involved, what actors and extras are active in each scene, what props you need for each scene, a character's bio, and so on. Plus, it integrates well with Premiere, Prelude, and the Media Encoder.

Story comes in two flavors. Adobe Story Free is an online application exclusively for screen writing. Adobe Story Plus can be used both online and offline and adds deep metadata-support and production-scheduling features.

If you are a Creative Cloud subscriber, you already have access to Story Plus and all the features that come with it. You can export your script from Story and connect it to your Prelude or Premiere Pro project, as well as populate the metadata fields with lots of useful info like scene, take, dialog, and so on. With Story, you can start a new script from scratch or import one you've written in Word or another script-writing app.

Figure 11-122 shows some screen grabs from Adobe Story.

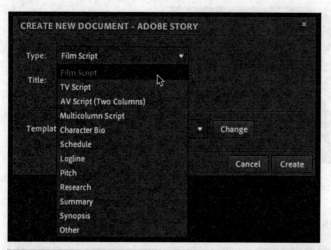

Figure 11-122. *Story is much more than a scripting tool. It can also be a big help when planning your shots. You can export a lot of different reports*

So, what has this got to do with Premiere? Well, for a start, Premiere has its own Story panel: **Window ➤ Story**. This gives you a read-only view of the chosen script (Figure 11-123).

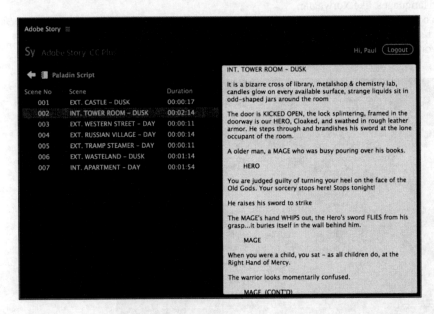

Figure 11-123. *Premiere has a dedicated Story panel where you can read, import, and attach scripts*

If you hit **File ➤ Export As ➤ Adobe Story Interchange Format (.astx)** in Story, you export a script file that can be connected to clips in Premiere.

In a bin or the Project panel in Premiere Pro, input scene numbers for the clips you want to connect. This isn't entirely necessary, but helps you in the process later.

To attach a script to one or more clips, select the clip(s) in the bin and click **File ➤ Adobe Story ➤ Attach Script File**—or drag-n-drop a scene from the Story panel onto one or more files in a bin (Figure 11-124).

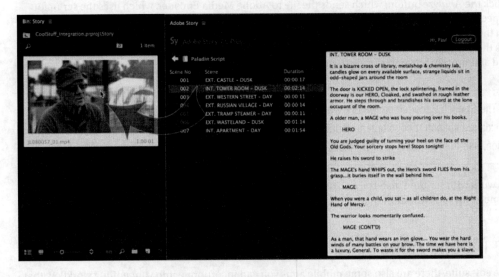

Figure 11-124. *Drag script from the Story panel onto the selected clips*

This populates the metadata field named *Embedded Adobe Story Script* with the spoken words from the script—and this is searchable from within the Metadata panel, but unfortunately not from a bin. This even works with unsupported languages, like Norwegian.

Speech recognition combined with a script will get you very close to 100 percent correct recognition (Figure 11-125). Speech recognition has been removed in CC 2014.2 and newer versions, but clips analyzed in earlier versions still work nicely.

Figure 11-125. *Speech recognition combined with a script will get you very close to 100 percent correct recognition*

If you're lucky, and your production is done in one of the supported languages (English, Italian, German, French, Japanese, Korean, and Spanish) and you have Premiere Pro CC 2014.1 or older, you can also click the *Analyze* button, which sends the file to Adobe Media Encoder, which uses the script for accurate speech recognition.

When the analysis is done, AME writes the spoken words into the Speech Analysis field in the metadata and makes the dialog searchable, even from a bin. You will be able to go straight to the part where that word is delivered and quickly set your in and out points.

■ **Note**   The Speech Recognition feature was removed in the 2014.2 update, but the newer versions will still work with existing speech recognition metadata, so I keep an older version on my system just for this. Analyze in old version, use the metadata in new version.

If you work with scripted material or have transcodes of interviews in documentary-style productions, Story can speed up your workflow quite a bit.

Adobe Mobile Apps

Beyond the edit suite, there are also some mobile apps you can incorporate into your editing workflow that are also part of your Creative Cloud membership.

Adobe Capture

Adobe Capture is actually several apps combined into one. It can create shapes, patterns, and brushes or turn a photo into a vector image. But one of the really interesting features is its ability to create a look based on a photo.

With the app open, choose the Look tab and click the plus symbol. Tap the photo icon to take a photo on the spot, or use one already stored on your phone.

The app will offer a variety of looks based on the photo, and you can also use the slider to adjust the intensity. Then, click Next and save it to your library. The great thing about saving to your library is that this look will now be available to you next time you open Premiere.

Figures 11-126 to 11-129 show the LUT creation workflow in Adobe Capture.

I've found this app especially handy when I've been on location shooting Log footage and needed a reference look for what I saw on the day of the shoot.

Figure 11-126. *Create LUTs with your smartphone!*

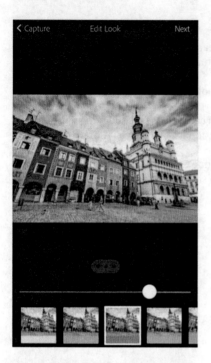

Figure 11-127. *Choose the look that best matches your scene and adjust the intensity*

Figure 11-128. *Save the look to your library*

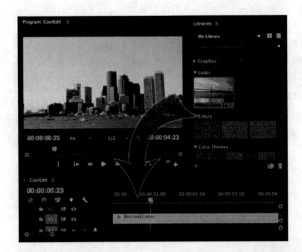

Figure 11-129. *Apply the LUT directly from your Library in Premiere*

Premiere Clip

Premiere Clip is a simple editor for your phone/tablet. You can use it to load footage from your device's library, Creative Cloud account, or even Dropbox, edit it together, and add looks and music (Figure 11-130).

Figure 11-130. *Edit and mix clips together directly on your phone!*

It's definitely not designed for complex edits, but there is something very cool about editing directly on your phone. The tactile experience of dragging in and out points with your finger and tapping the screen when you want to make an edit point makes the whole process highly addictive.

Once you've finished cutting your masterpiece on your phone, you can publish the final video to YouTube, Twitter, and so on, or even send the project to Premiere Pro for further editing tweaks, which also transfers all the settings for speed changes, color effects, and audio fades (Figure 11-131).

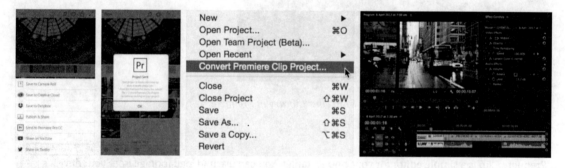

Figure 11-131. *Send your edit to Premiere Pro for further tweaks*

To open your Clip project, choose **File ➤ Convert Premiere Clip Project** (11-131), which takes you to the AdobePremiereClipExport folder inside your Creative Cloud Files folder. Select your Clip project file (it will be an XML) and continue editing.

Other Video Applications

When it comes to transferring edits to other video applications, one of the most reliable methods is exporting an XML file, but there are a few gotchas to keep in mind.

XML Gotchas

If you are exporting just a sequence to XML, select the sequence in either the Project or Timeline panel before you export. Otherwise, if you want to send the entire project, set your focus to the Project panel and make sure nothing is selected.

When working on a Premiere project with media that needs to be scaled up or down, it's important to use Set to Frame Size, not Scale to Frame Size. Scale to Frame Size will resample the footage but leave its scale property at 100 percent. If you import this into another application, the footage will be its original size. Much better to use Set to Frame Size, which will change the scale property (Figure 11-132).

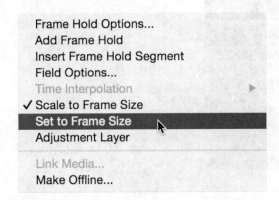

Figure 11-132. *Most other NLEs won't understand Scale to Frame Size—best to use Set to Frame Size*

Similarly, multi-camera and nested sequences are not supported by most other applications; if you need to transfer these items, it's best to flatten them first.

Finally, if you are importing multiple XML files into Premiere from other NLEs and they reference the same media, Premiere might import this media multiples times, which creates duplicates. A workaround for this is to import the XMLs into separate Premiere projects first, then import those into your master project through the media browser.

DaVinci Resolve

You may find that some of your clips are not relinking when you import into Resolve; this sometimes has to do with the way Premiere stores file names and locations. Here's a good tutorial on how to get around this issue by loading the XML in a text editor and using Find/Replace: vimeo.com/188175744.

Final Cut Pro 7

For edits made in Final Cut Pro 7, the process of exporting an XML and importing it in Premiere should be fairly straightforward. The one area that really doesn't translate well is titles. There is a better way to import these, and it involves After Effects.

With After Effects open, choose **File ➤ Import ➤ Pro Import After Effects** and select your Final Cut Pro XML file. This will import all of your edits, as well as your titles, and they should look the same (Figure 11-133).

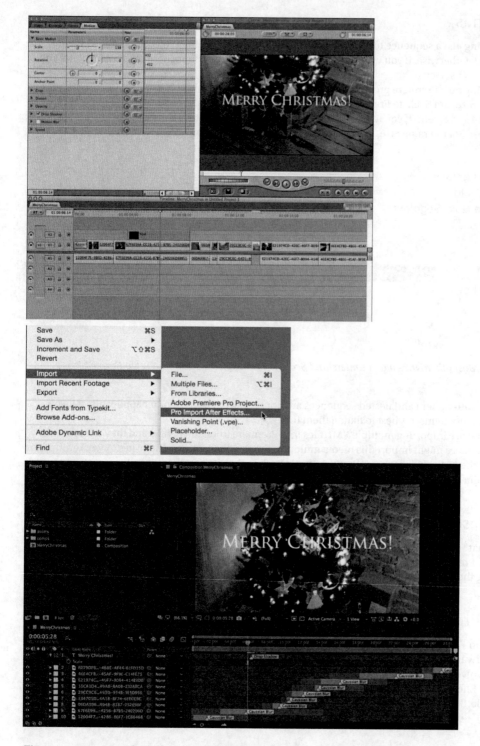

Figure 11-133. *Use After Effect's Pro Import feature to import titles from Final Cut Pro 7*

To get these titles into Premiere, you could turn each of them into motion graphics templates, which will allow you to continue to edit them in Premiere.

If you don't have After Effects, take a look at the following link. Editor Sam Hardy wrote about dealing with FCP7 Titles in Premiere on LinkedIn. The new graphics engine in Premiere makes it a lot faster to change all the wrong-looking text clips: `linkedin.com/pulse/adobe-premiere-cc-171-hot-tip-adapting-fcp7-titles-new-sam-hardy`.

Final Cut Pro X

Since upgrading to Final Cut Pro X, Apple has stopped using their original XML schema to exchange edits, which means you'll need to convert their new format to something Premiere can understand.

XtoCC from Intelligent Assistance is a great application that can do just that. It will convert this new schema to the original FCP XML format, which you can then import into Premiere. You can find out more information here: `intelligentassistance.com/xtocc.html`.

Avid Media Composer

Unlike with Final Cut or Resolve, the most straightforward way to exchange edits between Premiere and Avid Media Composer is using Avid's own AAF format. Going from Media Composer to Premiere is usually a more reliable conversion, including titles and motion effects, as opposed to going from Premiere to Media Composer. Here's a great tutorial that goes through the process in both directions, including the advantages and disadvantages of each: `youtube.com/watch?v=yOmc58oVOOo`.

If you find yourself regularly switching to Premiere in an Avid environment, you may want to look into the MediaCentral I UX Connector for Premiere Pro. This allows Premiere Pro editors to access assets, metadata, and sequences through Avid Interplay using a panel inside Premiere. For more information, read this guide: `resources.avid.com/SupportFiles/attach/Interplay_Central/MediaCentral_PremiereConnector_ReadMe_v291.pdf`.

Export a Sequence List

It's not exactly for another video application, but sometimes, in addition to supplying your edits, you also need to supply a list of all your stringout sequences to a colorist, producer, sound mixer, and so on. For this, you can use a much older exchange format called an EDL.

Start by creating a new Search bin without entering anything in the Search field. Just click the *Create Search Bin* button. Enter *Sequence* as the Media Type. If you've named your stringouts properly, you can also choose to only show sequences with "Stringout" in the Name field (Figure 11-134).

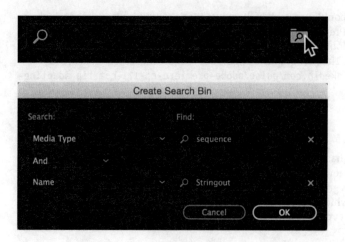

Figure 11-134. *Create a Search bin for all the sequences in your project*

This gives you a bin containing all of your sequences. Now, put all of them into a new sequence. Make sure you don't use the word *Stringout* in its name just yet. You can rename it later if needed. Put everything from your Search bin into the new sequence as nested sequences (Figure 11-135). Make sure the *Nest-or-Not* button is active to achieve this.

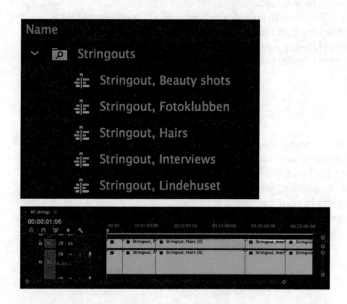

Figure 11-135. *Drag all of your sequences into a new sequence*

Now, select your sequence and choose **File ➤ Export ➤ EDL**. Choose the tracks you want to export and hit *OK* (Figure 11-136).

Figure 11-136. *Export your new sequence as an EDL*

Now, you need to import the .edl file into a word processor or a spreadsheet. I prefer a spreadsheet, so I'll explain how to do this in Microsoft Excel.

In Excel: **File ➤ Open** and choose to show all files types so you can find the .edl file and open it. If you don't have this option, then just change the extension of the file to .txt. Choose *Space* as the column separator. You can also select the different columns and choose not to import all of them. Figure 11-137 shows my list after I've chosen not to import most of the columns, so I have only the sequence name and the length.

```
TITLE: All strings
FCM: NON-DROP FRAME

001  AX        B      C        00:00:00:00 00:01:46:25 00:00:00:00
00:01:46:25
* FROM CLIP NAME: Stringout, Beautyshots

002  AX        B      C        00:00:00:00 00:00:26:30 00:01:46:25
00:02:13:05
* FROM CLIP NAME: Stringout, Fotoklubben

003  AX        B      C        00:00:00:00 00:00:02:25 00:02:13:05
00:02:15:30
* FROM CLIP NAME: Stringout, Hairs

004  AX        B      C        00:00:00:00 00:00:38:44 00:02:15:30
00:02:54:24
* FROM CLIP NAME: Stringout, Interviews

005  AX        B      C        00:00:00:00 00:00:13:40 00:02:54:24
00:03:08:14
* FROM CLIP NAME: Stringout, Lindehuset
```

	A	B	C
1			
2	**My Stringout Sequences**		
3			
4	00:01:46:25		
5	Beautyshots		
6			
7	00:00:26:30		
8	Fotoklubben		
9			
10	00:00:02:25		
11	Hairs		
12			
13	00:00:38:44		
14	Interviews		
15			
16	00:00:13:40		
17	Lindehuset		
18			

Figure 11-137. Open your EDL in Microsoft Excel

The formatting leaves a lot to be desired, of course—but, then again, it's free! If you want to automatically move every other row up one row and to the right, use the method described here by Excel guru Mike Wong: linkedin.com/pulse/how-move-every-other-row-column-excel-mike-wong.

Figure 11-138 shows my list after using this method.

Sequence Name ⬛	Sequence Duration ▾
Beautyshots	00:01:46:25
Fotoklubben	00:00:26:30
Hairs	00:00:02:25
Interviews	00:00:38:44
Lindehuset	00:00:13:40

Figure 11-138. List of sequences, with length column, in Excel

1054

Other Audio Applications

The two main formats for exchanging audio with other programs are OMF and AAF. Let's take a closer look at the differences and gotchas for each of these.

OMF

OMF (Open Media Framework) is the older of the two formats and so has more limitations.

Gain adjustments on clips will overwrite the keyframes in an OMF. Also, if your combined gain/volume results in an adjustment above 12 db, the clip will have its volume turned all the way down in the OMF file. For more information about how gain can affect OMFs, watch co-author of this chapter, Paul Murphy's video here: thepremierepro.com/blog-1/2015/9/2/exporting-omfs-with-audio-gain.

The best way to avoid having gain mess up your OMF is to select all your clips before export and set your gain to 0 db.

It's also good practice to not mix mono and stereo files on the same track in your project, as this creates a new audio track for each and can result in a lot of unnecessary tracks in your OMF (Figure 11-139).

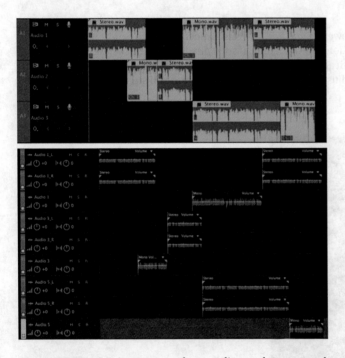

***Figure 11-139.** Mixing mono and stereo clips on the same track can result in a mess of unnecessary tracks in your exported OMF*

It's especially important to be aware that OMF files can't exceed 2 GB (did I mention it's an old format?). This means if you need to export an embedded file (like a zip file, with all the media and edits bundled together into one file), you may have to break up your timeline into chunks and export each one individually. Otherwise, exporting the audio separately will help you avoid this limitation (Figure 11-140). It's always best to ask your post house what their preference is in this case.

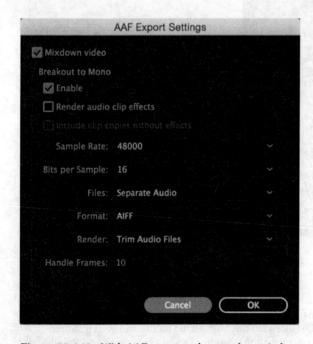

Figure 11-140. *Exporting your OMF with separate audio will help you avoid the 2 GB limitation of the file size*

AAF

AAF (Advanced Authoring Format) is a newer format and, as you'd expect, is able to export more information than OMF is. AAF has the option to also include a video mixdown of your sequence as a reference (Figure 11-141). This is automatically linked when the file is opened in Pro Tools. It's also a good idea, as with OMFs, to remove any gain adjustments and avoid mixing mono and stereo clips on the same track.

Figure 11-141. *With AAF, you can also supply a mixdown of your video tracks*

One of the great things about the AAF export in Premiere is that if you've already exported an AAF with separate files, and you just need to update the edit, by your exporting to the same location as before it won't create all those audio files again.

Sound editor Jeff Hinton wrote a good article on blog.frame.io with the headline "How to Keep Your Sound Editor Happy (According to a Sound Editor)." It can't hurt to read it before you export an AAF for your sound editor: blog.frame.io/2017/04/10/how-to-keep-your-sound-editor-happy/.

Summary

That concludes this chapter on integration. I hope that by now you have an understanding of how the different apps in the Creative Cloud can help you create pretty advanced stuff with ease. If you're a Creative Cloud subscriber, I urge you to explore the available apps and discover new ways to work faster.

As you've clearly seen, Premiere really is a HUB in the Adobe workflow.

CHAPTER 12

Export

By Jarle Leirpoll

Exporting is probably where most people get in trouble. They manage to import their sources, edit the sequences, and fine-tune their video and audio. Everything looks great. Then, at export time, they mess up a setting or two, and their finished film looks bad, or the export takes forever to finish. Let's make sure that *your* films have great quality, and that your exports are quick.

Don't forget to save custom export presets for the kinds of exports you do often. There is absolutely no point in wading through settings every time with the added possibility that you mess up some setting when you're stressed and in a hurry. Always make presets and give them meaningful names. That way, you can start your exports faster, and you always get the best quality.

Note that if you have a capture card or a plug-in that has export features, you may have some additional dialog boxes that are not mentioned here.

What Processor Does What?

The programmers on the Premiere Pro team have cleverly spread the computation load between the CPU (Central Processing Unit) and the GPU (Graphics Processing Unit, aka video card, display card, graphics card, display adapter, or graphics adapter). This makes Premiere do several things at the same time, and generally speeds up your editing—and the export. But when we export, which processor does what part, exactly?

CPU Does the Encoding

Exporting has two phases: rendering the image frames and encoding the images into the output format. Note that the encoding itself always happens on the CPU, so if you're exporting a sequence to the same size and frame rate, with no color grading or other effects, you will not see a huge difference by adding GPU power.

More CPU cores will give you faster exports if they have enough RAM to play with—at least 2 GB RAM per core—and virtual cores do count here. So, a six-core CPU with hyper-threading would perform best with 24 GB RAM or more.

■ **Note**   That isn't to say that the GPU doesn't speed up your exports. Anything that the GPU takes care of during playback, it will also do during export. The difference is that Premiere can use multiple GPUs during exports and renders, but during playback it'll use only one. The GPU offloads processing for things like GPU-accelerated effects, de-Bayering, scaling, and so on, letting the CPUs focus on the encoding.

© Jarle Leirpoll 2017
J. Leirpoll et al., *The Cool Stuff in Premiere Pro*, DOI 10.1007/978-1-4842-2890-6_12

One GPU = Fast Exports. Two GPUS = Even Faster

So, if you add effects, color grading, scaling, or frame-rate conversions (don't we always?) or use a RAW format that needs de-Bayering, then a good GPU will deliver frames to the CPU many times faster than the CPU itself could manage, and your exports will be faster. Adding a second GPU will increase export performance even more.

Premiere can use two GPUs on export (but not more than that). If your power supply has the juice to drive two GPUs, you should see a noticeable boost by adding a second GPU. Don't connect any monitors to the second GPU; just let it do its thing.

There are some caveats to a dual-GPU setup: the cards should ideally be of the same kind and use the exact same driver. If they're not the same, the primary screen with the Premiere Pro monitors should be on the fastest card.

Having a good GPU or two, plus as many processor cores and as much RAM as you can afford, will speed up your renders. And, of course, the drives must be fast enough to deliver the frames to the GPU and CPU when they need them.

To Sum Up What Happens on Which Processor During Export

■ **Note** The encoding always happens on the CPU. The GPU does de-Bayering, effects, scaling, and other image-altering stuff.

Encoding several versions of a file at once (CineForm for Archive, H.264 for YouTube, and so on) will be faster than doing them one by one, since the frames to encode will already exist in RAM.

The Adobe forums have an FAQ article on how to speed up your exports, with lots of info on this topic: forums.adobe.com/message/8617455.

Preflight Checklist

Before you export your movie, make sure you do your preflight check so you don't have to export again, and again, and again. After that, we'll get to the actual export.

The Basics

First, the very basics: check that your frame size, aspect ratio, field choices, and frame rate are what they need to be. If you don't know what they should be, you need to do some research first. It depends on where and how your film will be watched. Local playback? Broadcast? Cinema? Web?

Close Gaps

You don't want to have black frames between your clips just because you failed to discover them during editing. Spotting them in a long timeline can be hard. Watching the whole thing to spot gaps takes a long time, since it needs to be done in real time—and there's always the chance that you're not watching the monitor exactly at that time because you're taking a note or just blinking at the wrong time. So, let's make Premiere do this for us.

First, zoom your timeline all the way in so you can see individual frames. Also, make sure all your tracks are targeted and that your playhead is at the beginning of the sequence. Then, click **Sequence ➤ Go to Gap ➤ Next in Track**. No, actually, this is a situation where you really need to use a shortcut! There is none by default, so make sure you create one, or you'll wear out your mouse buttons. Every time you hit the shortcut, the playhead moves to the next gap in any targeted track. Yes, the targeted/highlighted tracks only (Figure 12-1).

Figure 12-1. *It's hard to see short gaps when the timeline is zoomed out. When zoomed in a lot, however, the gaps can easily be seen*

Depending on your edit, you'll need to ripple delete gaps or move in and out points of adjacent clips.

I find the *Next Gap in Track* command much more useful than the *Next Gap in Sequence* command. Very seldom do I have a gap in all tracks at the same frame. My timelines are multi-track and often complex. I sometimes use adjustment layers that cover the whole sequence, so there will be no gap in the sequence, but there could still be gaps in a track. For a music video, the music track will be a continuous file without gaps, while we could still have lots of gaps in the video tracks. So, I stick to *Next Gap in Track*.

Remove Through Edits

You may also want to remove all "invisible cuts." These are cuts which are just splitting the clip, but don't add or remove any frames. Hit the keyboard shortcut for Add Edit, or use the Razor tool to cut it in half, and you have created an invisible cut, aka through edit. To do so quickly and easily, create a keyboard shortcut for *Join All Through Edits*. But be aware that any changes you've done in segments other than the first one will be lost. The *Show Through Edits* preference in the timeline isn't on by default, so make sure you turn it on so you can see where they are. It may be safer to manually select and delete through edits individually or in groups.

Check for Duplicate Frames

You may want to check your timeline for duplicate use of frames before export. In the wrench menu, you'll find *Show Duplicate Frame Markers* (Figure 12-2). Activate it, and you get colored stripes on clips that are used more than once. The stripes are conveniently color coded, so it's easy to find out where the duplicates are. Keyboard shortcuts for *Go to Next/Previous Marker* will also respect the dupe frame markers, so they're easy to find this way, too.

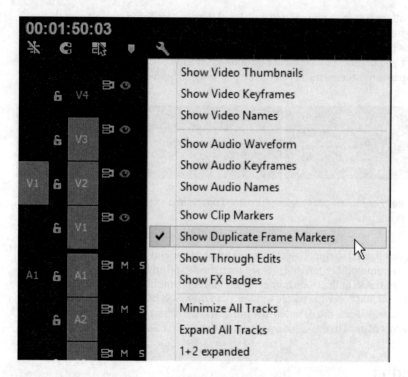

Figure 12-2. *Show Duplicate Frames menu*

Take a look at both instances with the same color and decide which clip to change, move, slip, or delete (Figure 12-3).

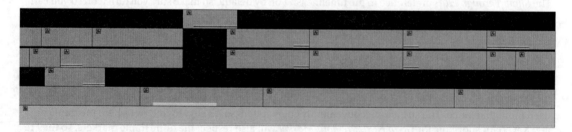

Figure 12-3. *Color coding makes it easy to see where the frames in a clip are duplicated*

Hide Banner on Warp Stabilizer

The warp stabilizer needs to re-analyze your footage if you trim a clip so non-analyzed frames are included. This will cause a banner to show (Figure 12-4). If you forget to re-analyze, the banner will show on your exported video file!

Figure 12-4. *Warp stabilizer warning banner*

Open the Advanced twirly in the warp stabilizer effect and check the *Hide Warning Banner* option to avoid this problem.

Make Sure You Don't Export Media Offline

If you export a sequence with missing media files, the dreaded Media Offline graphic will show in the exported file. When you try to export such a sequence from Premiere, you'll get a warning, so you get a chance to find the missing media and relink it (Figure 12-5).

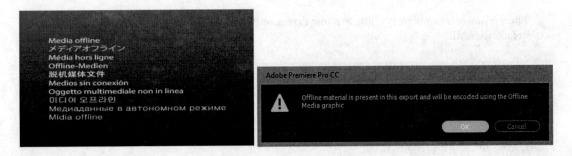

Figure 12-5. *Media iffline graphic and media offline warning*

But, what if you use Adobe Media Encoder to import an existing Premiere Pro project with missing media, and don't get this warning? AME has a preference where you can tell it to never encode sequences with missing media (Figure 12-6).

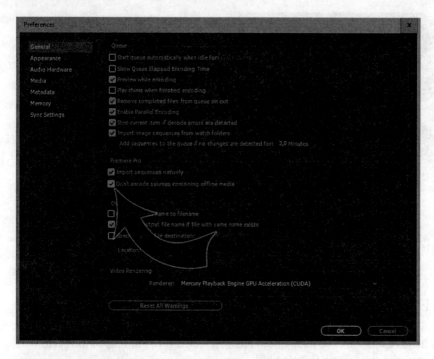

Figure 12-6. *Media offline AME Don't encode option*

Show errors or a complete log (**File ➤ Show Errors** or **File ➤ Show Log**) if you want to see why an export failed in AME.

Optimize Stills May Cause Funky Frame Rates

Beware of the *Optimize Stills* setting in QuickTime export! This setting permits the QuickTime exporter to treat frames that don't change over a period—like stills, black video, titles, and so on—as long-duration frames, and this gives the final export a funky frame rate. Instead of 25 fps you get strange numbers like 22.51, 23.63, or 13.08 fps (Figure 12-7).

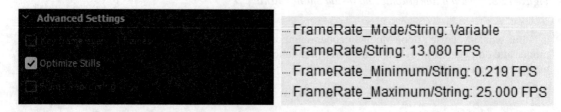

Figure 12-7. *Optimize Stills export setting, and the resulting video analyzed in Media Info*

■ **Note** *Optimize Stills* causes a variable frame rate. Most software, including Premiere, does not interpret the files correctly. Still images will show as short flashes, audio gets out of sync, and the duration is wrong. A file like this will only play back correctly in certain players, and will be rejected by quality control at broadcasters. Avoid *Optimize Stills* if you don't like trouble.

This test timeline has two still images that are not animated. To save bits, *Optimize Stills* makes the still images just one or two frames long, and at playback, these frames are supposed to be repeated for the duration of the still image. But Premiere and some other software do not understand this, so the result is that still images are shown in just a short flash.

My test sequence in Figure 12-8 was 19 seconds long. MediaInfo reads the length of the exported QuickTime file correctly, and both VLC Player and PotPlayer play the file correctly. But, when I import it back to Premiere, it's less than ten seconds long, which is just a few frames longer than the duration of the video clips. The duration of the stills is almost completely gone. After the first two-frame flash of a still image, the audio is also completely out of sync.

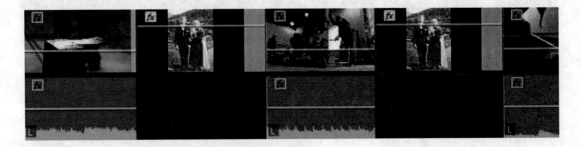

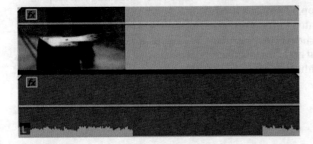

Figure 12-8. *Sequence before export, and resulting video file imported back into Premiere. Optimize Stills made it shorter*

Letterboxing

You may want to export your film with letterboxing, but for most uses I don't recommend it. Why waste bandwidth and disk space on black borders? You'll get a better result if you just export the film in the size you want it to be. If you've edited in a sequence with the right dimensions, you can just make sure the frame size matches the sequence, and you're good (Figure 12-9).

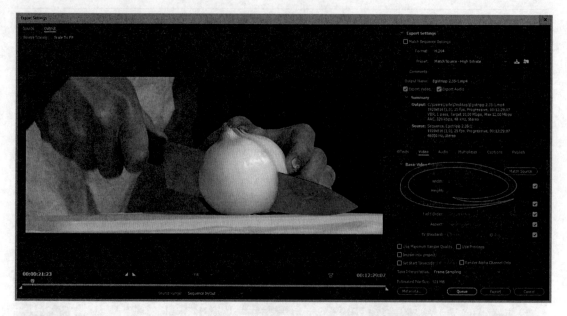

Figure 12-9. *When your edit sequence matches your output, just match the source size. Footage from "Egotripp" by Kjetil Fredriksen and Jan Olav Nordskog*

If you've edited in a standard sequence, say 1920 × 1080, with black borders on the top and bottom, and want to output a cropped version, you need to set your crop settings correctly (Figure 12-10).

The most common aspect ratios are 1.85:1 = 1920 × 1038 and 2.35:1 = 1920 × 817. Some codecs do not accept uneven pixel sizes, so let's round that 2.35:1 size off to 1920 × 816 to be safe—meaning you crop off 132 px at both the top and bottom. For 1.85:1, crop off 21 px on each.

Note that the video height is set to 816 to match the cropped area (Figure 12-10 again). Also note that you get an overlay in the Source panel when you hover over the image, telling you exactly how large your cropped area is. If the video height of your output matches this size, you'll get no black borders. If you do this kind of export regularly, save an export preset with these settings.

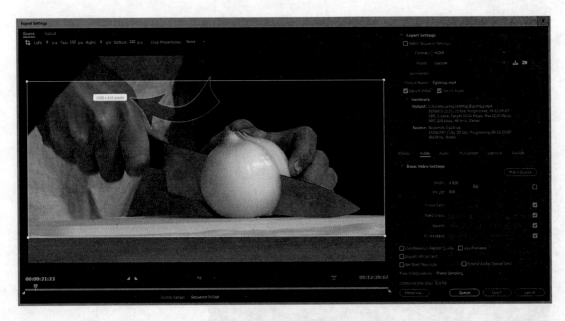

Figure 12-10. *Set your video export height to the height shown in the pop-up in the Source Cropping view*

Custom Start TC

By default, your exported file will get the same timecode as your sequence. So, to make your exported file start with 10:01:00:00, set your sequence start time to the same. You'll find the *Start Time* choice in the Timeline panel menu (Figure 12-11).

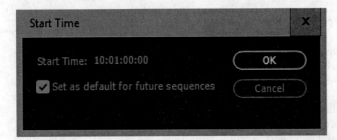

Figure 12-11. *Set your Sequence Start Time to what you want it to be in your exported file*

Many video formats will give you the option to override the sequence timecode. Look for *Set Start Timecode* in the lower part of the export dialog (Figure 12-12). By default, it's set to zero.

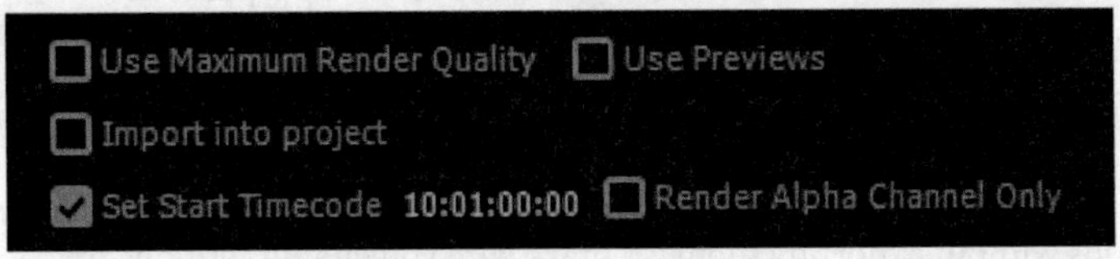

Figure 12-12. *If you don't want to change the sequence start time, change the Start Timecode in the Export Settings dialog*

Reduce Noise and Grain

Noise and grain are the enemies of every codec. Both noise and grain are random, and randomness cannot be compressed, because there is no pattern that can be predicted or recognized. So, noisy video needs higher bit rates to get good quality and will cause inferior quality at a given bit rate compared to video without noise.

Thus, if you export to low bit rates it's a good idea to remove noise and grain. Ideally, use the *remove grain* effect in After Effects on noisy or grainy material before export, but it's a very slow process, so budget some extra time for denoising.

Time Tuner

Found under Effects in the Export Settings, the Time Tuner lets you change the duration of the exported film by up to 10 percent. A dramatic speed change like that would be very noticeable, but I have done some testing with around a 3-percent reduction in duration where I cannot for the life of me see or hear that anything has been done (Figure 12-13).

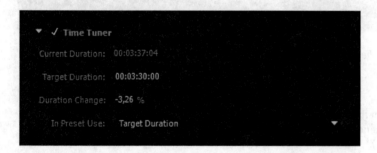

Figure 12-13. *Time Tuner settings*

It's a very clever algorithm that takes the amount of movement and the cutting rhythm into account. On some material, it's impossible to see that it's been changed. On other material, it will be noticeable. Music is very sensitive to speed changes, so a piece with music from start to finish would not be a good candidate for time tuning.

Time Tuner looks for frames with very little motion, black frames, pauses in the action, and so on and removes them. Generally, it removes frames at a cut. These automated edits can reduce the length of the show without a perceptible change if you don't reduce it too much. Time Tuner can also extend the length of a show using morphing tech found in the Morph Cut video transition to create additional frames.

Multi-Channel Audio Output

Read everything about multi-channel and 5.1 audio export for intermediate and archive purposes in chapter 3 on audio in Premiere.

Make Sure You Export Captions If You Have Them

There's not much use in creating captions without exporting them, so make sure you enable captions on export and choose the right format (Figure 12-14). I recommend that you make an Export preset with the correct settings so as to avoid errors in future exports.

Figure 12-14. *If you don't have captions in your sequence, the choice will be grayed out in the Export settings*

If You Export HDR, Check the SDR Conform Settings

When you export High Dynamic Range video, HDR, you will often need to export a Standard Dynamic Range, SDR, file, too. Make sure the *SDR Conform* checkbox in the Export settings is selected when you export HDR, and unchecked when you export SDR (Figure 12-15). Again, I recommend that you build presets that have the correct settings.

Figure 12-15. *SDR Conform settings*

Export VR—Equirectangular Video

If your video is VR, remember to add a metadata flag in the Export settings to ensure your viewers get the full panoramic experience on supported sites like YouTube and Facebook (Figure 12-16). Read more about VR export in Premiere Help: helpx.adobe.com/premiere-pro/using/VRSupport.html#PublishingyourVRVideo.

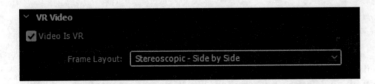

Figure 12-16. *VR Export settings*

Decide What Metadata to Export

You can choose what XMP metadata, if any, to include in the output file (when the format allows it) or in a sidecar XMP file. This is most useful when you use your own metadata export presets in cases where you've already decided what kind of metadata to keep. Read more about custom metadata export presets in chapter 10 on customizing Premiere.

The Metadata Display settings will contain all the ticked properties in the list on the left, so choose only the ones you want or need to see (Figure 12-17). Most of the time, source metadata can safely be included, but not if you've added some metadata that doesn't look good in public.

Figure 12-17. Create metadata export templates to make sure you don't accidentally export secret or unnecessary metadata

I highly recommend that you make presets for this so you don't have to worry about accidentally sending out all those metadata fields with non-flattering descriptions like "Ugly woman eats fish" and "Idiot falls off his ridiculously expensive bicycle."

To remove all source metadata for security purposes or privacy concerns, simply choose *None* under Export Options (Figure 12-18), and then no added XMP metadata will be exported. Basic XMP metadata about the exported file, such as export settings and start timecode, is always exported, even when *None* is chosen. Copyright info and other extra metadata about the exported file (not the source files) can still be added.

Figure 12-18. Sometimes, removing all source metadata is the quickest and easiest choice

Use Preview Files for Export—or Not?

When you export from a Premiere timeline, AME will, by default, use the original source media files, add all the effects, and encode this directly to your export format. That way, you get the best quality possible—and it takes a while.

If you work in software mode and you have rendered previews of your effects in the timeline, you will potentially save some time by using the previews at export (Figure 12-19). While this can vastly speed up your export, you will compress the material twice, and that will affect quality. Some editing modes (XDCAM-EX, RED R3D, HDV, ARRI, AVCHD, and SLR) use MPEG-2, I-frame only, at 23 mbps for their previews by default—not what you'd call great quality. **Never ever use that for anything if you remotely care about how your film looks!**

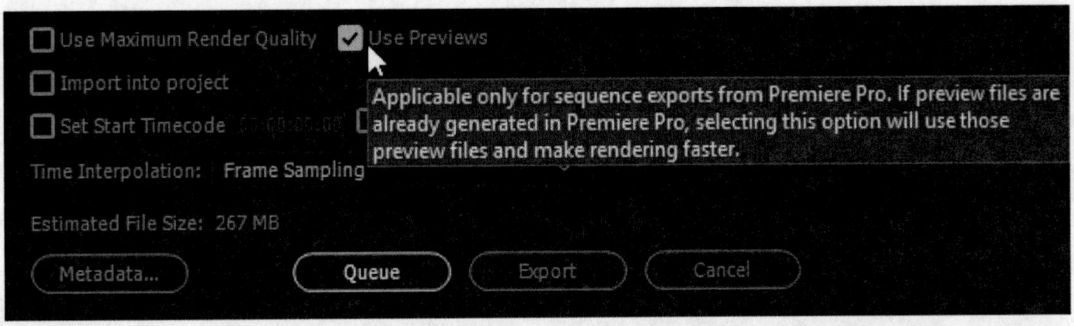

Figure 12-19. Only choose to use previews at export if you have set your sequence video previews to render to a good intermediate codec

So, unless you're using a good format for the render files, you will never get max quality this way. If your sequence uses DNxHD, ProRes, Go-Pro CineForm, or other lightly compressed formats for previews, it absolutely does make sense to use the preview renders.

Luckily, with a GPU-enabled system and by using GPU-accelerated effects, you're most likely not rendering any previews anyway, so on a good system this is less of an issue. And for professional editing, you should have a good system.

■ **Note** There are some situations where you'll want to render your timelines even if you don't have to. We'll come back to this when we talk about smart rendering.

Legalization

If you're exporting to YouTube, you'll probably not care about this, but when we export to broadcasters, cinema, or streaming channels like Netflix, we need to make sure our video levels are "legal." But what is broadcast legal? That depends on the broadcaster!

Broadcast-Safe Video Levels

There are many standards, so you'll need to find out what levels that particular broadcaster will accept. Exporting the file is the easy part. Getting a hold of the tech specs often means extensive phone time with the "techies."

Most editors that I know who work in broadcasting have no idea what their broadcaster's rules for broadcast safe are! The tech people have put a little box in the main control room, clipping or compressing overbrights and oversaturated colors, while most editors are unaware that it's even there. So, editors working on news, sports, and other formats don't even think about legal levels, and they don't have to.

Documentaries, drama, and other programs will be treated by a colorist before going to air, so even on those shows, editors don't need to know. But the editors, or at least the colorists, in external production companies need to know.

Legalization Is a Waste of Useful Gamut

This may sound strange, but in most countries there is actually no reason why the broadcasters should still require "legal" video levels in digital video!

■ **Note**   The restrictions were designed for analog equipment and analog transmission (VHF/UHF) of standard definition composite NTSC and PAL. Since you're delivering a digital file, and levels can never get above 255 (8-bit) or 1023 (10-bit) anyway, there is no reason for the levels to be restricted.

There is a movement to stop this nonsense. Charles Poynton is a Fellow of the Society of Motion Picture and Television Engineers (SMPTE) committee—the people who create the standards. He argues that "Legalizers Should Be Outlawed" and that we should use the current footroom and headroom regions to get better image quality through a wider color gamut and higher dynamic range:

> *Colorists are faced with having to attenuate or clip their specular highlights for no good reason other than to avoid rejection of their finished programs.*

But since broadcasters still require you to pass their evaluation, you'll have to comply, or your film will not get accepted. It's a strange world.

Motion Graphics Can Cause Illegal Levels

When using blend modes and glows in a 32-bit color space, we'll often create levels that are totally out of bounds. You can add color correction to an adjustment layer to lower the levels and saturation.

Beware of the Sharpen Effect

Sharpen works by making high levels higher and low levels lower wherever there are edges in the image. This causes both high and low spikes that go far into illegal ground (Figure 12-20). The same goes for the unsharp mask effect.

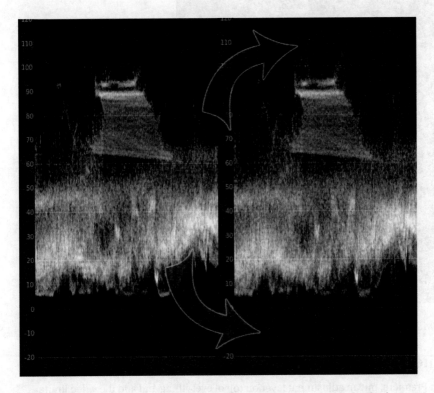

Figure 12-20. *To the left is before sharpening, and there are very few levels above 100 and below 0. After sharpening, there are both high- and low-level spikes*

Strategies to Make the Program Broadcast Safe

Mainly, making a program broadcast safe means getting rid of overbrights and oversaturated colors. The combination of the two—oversaturated highlights—is the main offender. You can use a plug-in that automates the process, but it *will* clip or compress your levels.

By using the manual approach, you can fine-tune everything a bit better using secondary color correction and finer adjustments. Then, you can add a legalizer like *video limiter* on an adjustment layer on top for added security—or just add it in Export settings when you export the finished video.

Video Limiter in Export Settings

The easiest method with which to make your video broadcast safe is to add it in the Export Settings dialog (Figure 12-21). It will be used on the entire video during export, and it's applied after all the other export effects. It's not 100 percent foolproof, but most broadcasters will accept files exported this way.

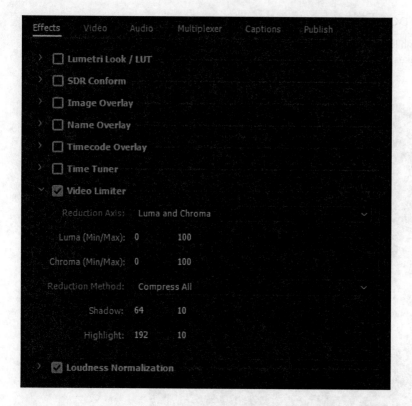

Figure 12-21. *Video Limiter added in Export Settings, with very conservative settings*

The Video Limiter in the Timeline

To ensure legal levels in Premiere, put an adjustment layer on top of everything and add the video limiter effect. Get the rules for legal levels from the broadcaster in question, and input those parameters in the video limiter effect and make a preset for later use. In Europe, you can guess it's the EBU Tech Recommendation R103-2000, but to be absolutely sure, you'll have to ask.

If you've done your color grading carefully, adding the video limiter or other legalizer plug-in shouldn't do too much to your image. So, using these as a security measure after the grading is done should be a pretty safe workflow. Always check your film carefully anyway.

Brute-Force Methods for Broadcast Safe

Some editors report that quality control at some broadcasters rejects their exported files, even with the video limiter set correctly. Although most broadcasters will allow some stray levels between -5 percent and 105 percent, some are very conservative and want everything to be fully within 0-100.

The video limiter doesn't offer a failsafe setting for this, so we need a brick wall limiter. Color mattes to the rescue! Read on.

Use Color Mattes as a Video Limiter

Editor & Colorist Julien Chichignoud describes this clever method on his blog. Basically, he's adding two clips above everything else in the timeline—a *black color matte* with Blend Mode set to *Lighten* and a *white color matte* set to *Darken*. This will clip anything above 100 and below 0. Figure 12-22 shows a comparison of my timeline before and after using this method. See his blog here: `julien.chichignoud.com/blog/quick-tip-simple-video-limiter-in-adobe-premiere/`.

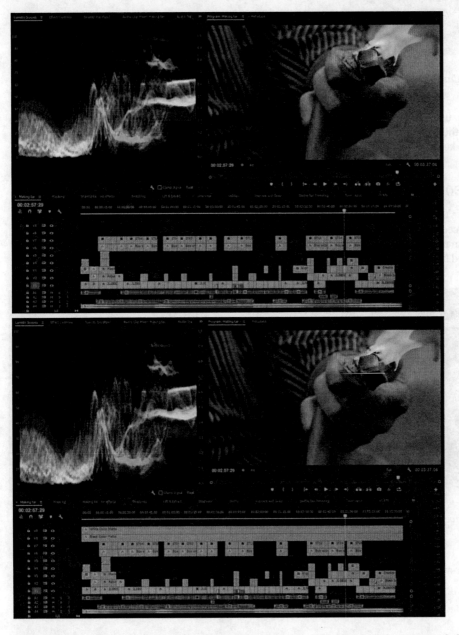

Figure 12-22. *Before and after adding the color matte layers with blend modes. No trace below 0 or above 100 after adding the color mattes*

A big benefit of this approach is that is cuts *everything* above 0 and 100, and I also like that you can clearly see how the clipping looks before you export. You can combine this method with the video limiter—just add an adjustment layer with the video limiter effect on it below the two color matte layers (Figure 12-23).

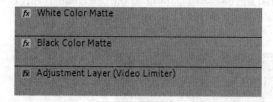

Figure 12-23. *Adjustment layers with color mattes and video limiter*

If you want to use this method on a regular basis, I recommend that you create a template project where you already have these color matte clips in a bin. It would also help speed things up if you make effects presets for the darken and lighten blend modes.

How the Video Limiter Works

Here's a clip where the editor has increased contrast and saturation to give the image more punch. Doing that, they introduced levels below 0 and above 100, plus some oversaturated colors. We can easily see this in both the waveform monitor (Figure 12-24) and the vector scope (Figure 12-25). The spike that goes upward straight toward red in the vector scope is the little girl's red jacket.

Figure 12-24. *Waveform scope showing levels beyond broadcast safe*

Figure 12-25. *Vector scope showing levels beyond broadcast safe*

Putting an adjustment layer above the other layers, I added the video limiter effect and used these settings to keep levels within our margins. Since the broadcasters have never agreed on one single standard, we have to set our own numbers for max level and so forth. Limiter is a bit of a misnomer, by the way, since it can also do different sorts of compression with a limitation on top. Figure 12-26 shows the video limiter with settings that should be pretty safe.

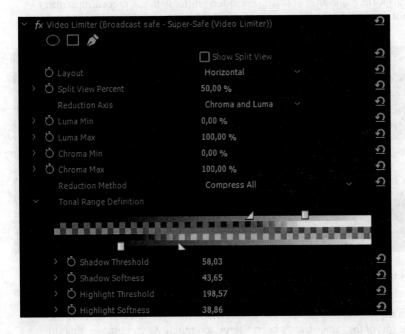

Figure 12-26. *These settings in the video limiter effect should leave absolutely safe levels, even when sending to the most conservative broadcasters*

Figure 12-27 shows the image and vector scope after applying the video limiter with the preceding settings. Notice the red spike is shorter and almost completely inside the legal boundaries, and the jacket is noticeably less saturated.

Figure 12-27. *Vector scope after applying the video limiter*

Figure 12-28 shows the waveform scope after applying the video limiter with the preceding settings. Notice that the luma trace is not exceeding 0 and 100.

Figure 12-28. *Waveform scope after applying the video limiter with the preceding settings*

Compare the red jacket on the girl before and after the video limiter, and you'll see how the limiter affects the image. However, the rest of the image hasn't been altered too much. As you can see, this still leaves some short spikes above and below legal levels, but it should be OK to send this to most broadcasters.

Never just throw the video limiter onto your film unless you're in a pinch. Grade your film while keeping an eye on the levels, then use the effect more as a security net than as an automatic, fix-it-all solution.

Some editors prefer to work with the adjustment layer with the video limiter while grading. They'll grade on clips or adjustment layers below this layer, but want to see how the final image looks. I sometimes do that, too, but I tend to work with the layer switched off, temporarily switching it on when I'm in doubt.

When the whole film is graded, I'll turn the layer on and play through everything to see if I can spot any strange artifacts or harsh clipping. I show the scopes in the program monitor when doing this because that gives me real-time scopes during playback while watching full-screen video on the second monitor.

Manual Methods for Broadcast Safe

Using the scopes, you can spot problem areas and adjust only those areas using a combination of primary and secondary color correction in the Lumetri Color panel. Make sure you make the scopes big on your screen so you can see finer details. So, what is considered a legal signal? Since the broadcasters all have their own rules, the best thing is to get the specs from each broadcaster.

If you don't know what your broadcaster will approve, you'd better stick to the strictest rules. Keeping luminance levels between 0 and 100 IRE (0.3 and 1.0 V) should be a safe bet. In the waveform scope, that means your luminance levels should stay between the purple lines indicated in the illustration in Figure 12-29. That's all most colorists will check.

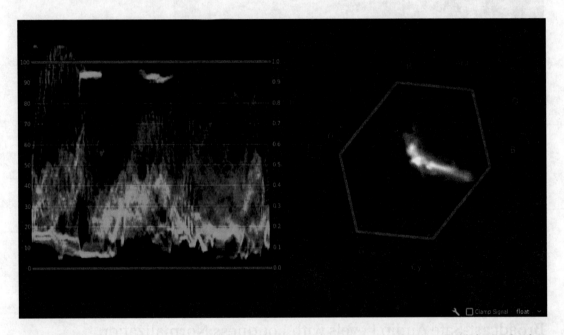

Figure 12-29. *The purple lines indicate conservative boundaries for broadcast-safe luma and chroma levels*

If you've done your color grading carefully, adding the video limiter or other legalizer plug-in shouldn't do too much to your image. Using these as a security measure after the grading is done should be a pretty safe workflow. Always check your film carefully anyway.

Now, some books and tutorials advocate that saturation should stay within the purple boundaries indicated in the vector scope. You're supposed to reduce the saturation of the offending colors until the trace falls within this line. However, I've found no mention of this rule in any delivery specs that I've read from any broadcaster.

The easiest way to spot the highest level is to watch the histogram (Figure 12-30). Use your favorite color-correction tool to adjust the levels and saturation until no numbers go above 100 or below 0.

Figure 12-30. *The histogram will show the max and min levels in actual numbers*

Forget Set-up

You will not find Set-up in the Lumetri scopes. Set-up is an all-American thing used for *analog* NTSC video; it raises the black level from 0 to 7.5 IRE. NTSC in Japan does not use Set-up, and neither does PAL. No Set-up should ever be added in digital video, ever. Since Set-up is a purely analog thing, and we are dealing exclusively with digital video inside of Premiere, we can forget about it.

If you go out to analog, let your output device take care of Set-up if needed. Always use 0 percent as your black point in Premiere.

Broadcast-Safe Audio Levels with Loudness Normalization

The same goes for audio. Your levels need to be "legal" if you send your film to a broadcaster or to digital cinema. Unlike for video, there are agreed-upon standards for audio. A limiter might help take the illegal peaks off, but to get your film accepted, you also need it to meet the loudness standards.

Use the *loudness normalization* effect in the Export Settings dialog to process the tracks you want to meet the standards (Figure 12-31). It's important to define the correct types of channels for the loudness normalization. Running normalization as two mono channels on a stereo pair will not give the correct loudness measurement. This is even more important when you want to normalize a 5.1 stream. Running this as mono would cause a very wrong measurement.

If you do this often, I recommend that you save the proper loudness normalization effect settings in an export preset. Read more about legal audio levels in chapter 3 on audio editing.

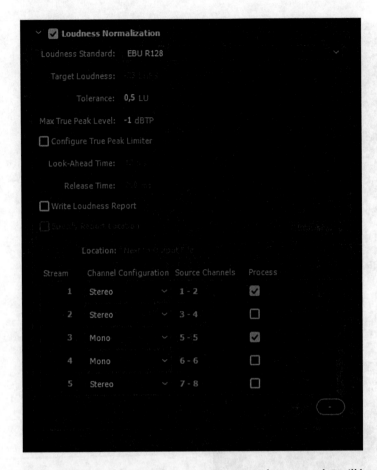

Figure 12-31. *In this example, stereo pair 1+2 and mono track 5 will be normalized*

European DPP Delivery Standards

Many European broadcasters base their delivery specs on the standards from Digital Production Partnership. You can find them here: digitalproductionpartnership.co.uk/what-we-do/technical-specifications/. These are again based on *EBU Rec103*:

RGB components must be between -5 percent and 105 percent (-35 and 735mV) and luminance (Y) must be between -1 percent and 103 percent (-7mV and 721mV). Slight transient overshoots and undershoots may be filtered out before measuring, and an error will only be registered where the out-of-gamut signals total at least 1 percent of picture area.

AS-10 Compliant Delivery

AS-10 is a broadcast format specification that uses shims to define the available export options. There are specific shims for CNN and NRK, and a more general shim named HIGH_HD_2014 (CANAL) (Figure 12-32).

More information about these shims and AS-10 in general can be found in this PDF: amwa.tv/downloads/specifications/AS-10_MXF_for_Production-V1.1.pdf.

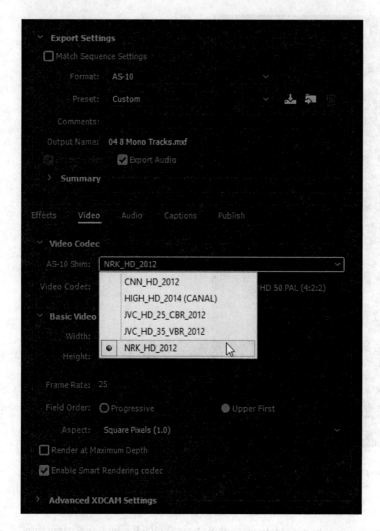

Figure 12-32. *AS-10 NRK Shim*

AS-11 Compliant Delivery

UK broadcasters are moving to a new format of file delivery called AS-11 in an MXF wrapper. Your AS-11 workflow starts in Premiere Pro, where you can add all required metadata and add markers for segmentation. To export an AS-11 DPP version 1.1 compliant file, simply choose *AS-11* as the format and then choose *SD* or *HD*.

This will choose the right video codec—meaning AVC-Intra Class100 1080 for HD and IMX 50 PAL (MPEG-2) for SD. It also chooses the right AS-11 Shim (Figure 12-33).

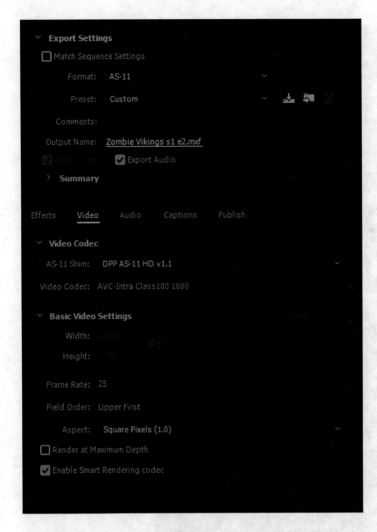

Figure 12-33. *AS-11 export settings*

To fully comply with the AS-11 standard, you also need to submit all the required metadata in the correct way. You can input the metadata in the export dialog in Premiere (Figure 12-34), but to check that it follows the standard, go to the Digital Production Partnership (DPP) download site at digitalproductionpartnership.co.uk/downloads/ and download and install the DPP Metadata application (Figure 12-35). This app validates both the MXF file and the metadata and gives you a very visible red alert when something's missing.

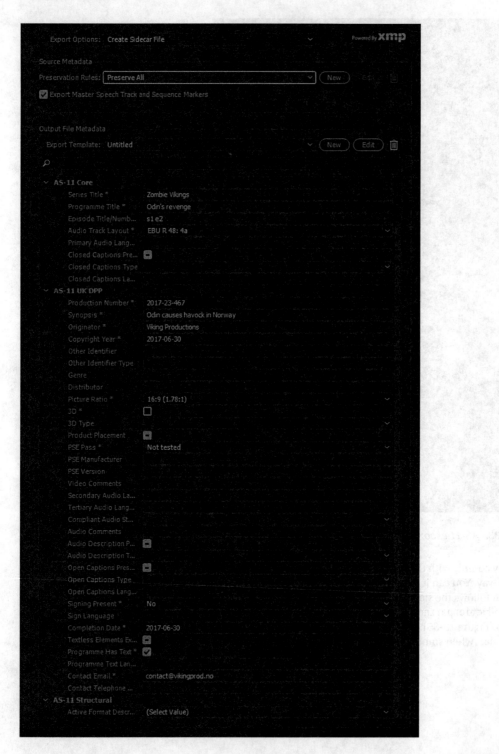

Figure 12-34. *Export to the AS-11 format if that's required from your broadcaster. Remember to also include the required metadata fields*

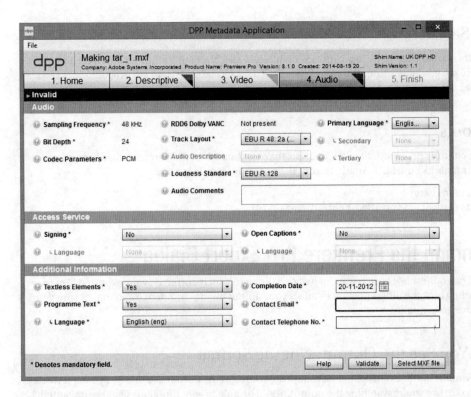

Figure 12-35. *The DPP Metadata app validates your output and alerts you quite visually when something's wrong or missing*

To learn how to create custom metadata schemas so you don't have to put in all the metadata by hand every time, read chapter 10 on customizing Premiere.

Read the complete specification of AS-11 here: amwa.tv/downloads/specifications/Technical_Overview_of_AS-11_Specifications.pdf.

IRT Profile Support for German Broadcasters

IRT (Institut für Rundfunktechnik) publishes the technical guidelines and specifications of Germany's public broadcasters. Premiere Pro and AME have six MXF Profiles as specified by ARD, ZDF, ORF, and ARTE (Figure 12-36).

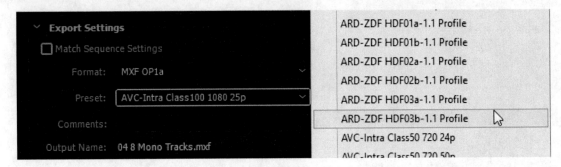

Figure 12-36. *IRT export presets*

Broadcast-Safe Titles

It's not just your levels that need to be legal; most broadcasters also have strict rules for crediting and lots of other stuff. Here are guidelines from BBC and PBS: `bbc.co.uk/commissioning/tv/production/credit-guidelines.shtml` `pbs.org/producing/red-book/`.

Analyzer Tools

If you need more control and a more detailed analysis than the built-in tools Premiere can offer, you can purchase analyzer tools like the MXF Analyzer from IRT or Cerify from Tektronix:

```
mxf.irt.de/tools/analyzer/
tek.com/file-based-qc/cerify-video-content-analysis
```

Understanding the Premiere Pro Export Dialog

The Export panel has quite a few options, and if just one of them is set incorrectly, your exported film may suffer. Understanding how the different choices affect your output builds confidence and makes sure your exports always have great quality.

Make Sure You See the Output, Not the Source

The main video window in the Export panel can show the source or the output. No one but yourself will see your source, so make sure you're watching the output. You'll be able to spot problems like the unwanted introduction of pillar boxes or letterboxes, interlacing issues, and so on.

In Figure 12-37, the output shows letterboxing will occur, while the source just shows a full-frame image.

Figure 12-37. *Watch the output, not the source, if you want to see how the exported file will look*

The Source view is also where you find crop settings, in case you need to change the aspect ratio of your video (Figure 12-38).

Figure 12-38. *If you need to crop the image, look at the source and adjust your crop settings as needed*

Proxies Are Not Used on Export

Premiere will always export in full res, even if proxies are enabled. The only exception is if full-res files are offline and proxies are online, in which case there will be a warning, and proxies will be used for export.

Even if you enable proxies, preview renders in your sequence will also always be full res. This means it's OK to use previews on export in proxy workflows.

Render at Maximum Bit Depth

If you have a GPU-accelerated system and only use GPU-accelerated effects, move on. There's nothing for you here. If you have a software-only system or use non-accelerated effects, you need to know this, so read on.

Hovering over the *Render at Maximum Bit Depth* text gives you an explanation in a tool tip (Figure 12-39).

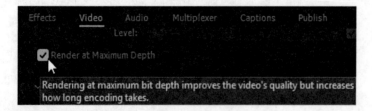

Figure 12-39. *This switch only affects software rendering, but you may be rendering in software mode even if you thought you weren't!*

OK, that tool tip wasn't very helpful. Better quality in what way? What this means is that all the calculations (effects, color corrections, blending modes, compositing, blurs, etc.) will be done in 32-bit-per-channel color. **If you're using GPU acceleration, and all effects are GPU accelerated, the switch does absolutely nothing!** GPU-accelerated mode is always 32-bit.

But you may not be rendering in GPU mode even though you think you are! Even on a GPU-enabled system, **if you use a non-accelerated effect, rendering falls back to software mode**. So, to actually render everything in 32-bit, you'll need to turn *Render at Maximum Bit Depth* on in the Export dialog.

Back to software mode; **this setting in the Export dialog overrides the one in your sequence**. Don't export in Max Bit Depth if you've not composited with Max Bit Depth in the sequence. You might get ugly surprises. Your color correction and your blending modes can look very different from what you saw in 8-bit. Make sure this switch in the Export dialog matches the same setting in your sequence.

The left image in Figure 12-40 shows the output after rendering in software mode with Max Bit Depth switched off, resulting in 8-bit rendering and clipping. The image on the right shows the output with the Max Bit Depth switch on. I think you'll like the sky and clouds in the right one better.

Figure 12-40. *Left: Rendered in software mode with the Max Bit Depth switch off. Right: Rendered in software mode with the Max Bit Depth switch on*

Why did clipping occur? I adjusted Input White in the levels effect until the dark areas looked good. Then, I added another adjustment to make a nice roll-off in the sky and clouds.

The left image in Figure 12-41 shows output when Max Bit Depth was set in the sequence, but not in the Export dialog, again causing 8-bit rendering and clipping. On the right, Max Bit Depth was set in the Export dialog, resulting in 32-bit rendering and no clipping.

Figure 12-41. *Left: Max Bit Depth was set in the sequence, but not in the Export dialog, causing 8-bit rendering and clipping. Right: Max Bit Depth was set in the Export dialog, resulting in 32-bit rendering and no clipping*

There's even a gotcha while editing in software mode in a sequence with Max Bit Depth on—**the monitors show 8-bit colors while playing back the timeline until you render a preview**. So, you may never have seen what you're about to export. Be aware! What you'll see in the exported file is the same thing you'd see in a sequence with Max Bit Depth on *after the timeline has been preview rendered*.

Because of all this potential for total confusion, my advice is to avoid *Render at Maximum Bit Depth* in your sequences and at export if you're on a software-only system—unless you're into self-punishment. It's taxing the system heavy anyway. Get a decent GPU, and life is good—unless you use non-accelerated effects.

Steve on Maximum Bit Depth

These examples from Senior Engineering Manager for Premiere Pro, Steve Hoeg, should help you understand a bit more about 8-bit, 10-bit, and 32-bit rendering.

1. A DV file with a blur and a color corrector exported to DV without the Max Bit Depth flag. We will import the 8-bit DV file, apply the blur to get an 8-bit frame, apply the color corrector to the 8-bit frame to get another 8-bit frame, then write DV at 8-bit.

2. A DV file with a blur and a color corrector exported to DV with the Max Bit Depth flag. We will import the 8-bit DV file, apply the blur to get a 32-bit frame, apply the color corrector to the 32-bit frame to get another 32-bit frame, then write DV at 8-bit. The color corrector working on the 32-bit blurred frame will be higher quality than in the previous example.

3. A DV file with a blur and a color corrector exported to DPX with the Max Bit Depth flag. We will import the 8-bit DV file, apply the blur to get a 32-bit frame, apply the color corrector to the 32-bit frame to get another 32-bit frame, then write DPX at 10-bit. This will be still higher quality because the final output format supports greater precision.

4. A DPX file with a blur and a color corrector exported to DPX without the Max Bit Depth flag. We will clamp 10-bit DPX file to 8-bits, apply the blur to get an 8-bit frame, apply the color corrector to the 8-bit frame to get another 8-bit frame, then write 10-bit DPX from 8-bit data.

5. A DPX file with a blur and a color corrector exported to DPX with the Max Bit Depth flag. We will import the 10-bit DPX file, apply the blur to get a 32-bit frame, apply the color corrector to the 32-bit frame to get another 32-bit frame, then write DPX at 10-bit. This will retain full precision through the whole pipeline.

6. A title with a gradient and a blur on an 8-bit monitor. This will display in 8-bit and may show banding.

7. A title with a gradient and a blur on a 10-bit monitor (with hardware acceleration enabled). This will render the blur in 32-bit, then display at 10-bit. The gradient should be smooth.

I'll add to this that when we're in GPU-accelerated mode, all formats will be imported at their native bit depth, all calculations will be done in 32-bit, and the export will be written to the format's native bit depth. So, in GPU mode we don't have to think about this.

What Is Maximum Render Quality?

This setting too only applies to software rendering, so **when in GPU-accelerated mode with only GPU-accelerated effects, it does absolutely nothing**. GPU mode uses an even better algorithm for scaling and will override this setting. So, the same applies here as for the Max Bit Depth explanation: if you have a GPU-accelerated system and only use GPU-accelerated effects, move on.

Maximum Render Quality (MRQ) is mainly about scaling. It uses a different algorithm (bicubic standard) than what's normal for CPU mode (Gaussian) for scaling, and will give sharper details if you're scaling clips in any way—in the timeline or at export (Figure 12-42). It also includes a better de-interlacer—and it makes your export times many times longer and eats your RAM!

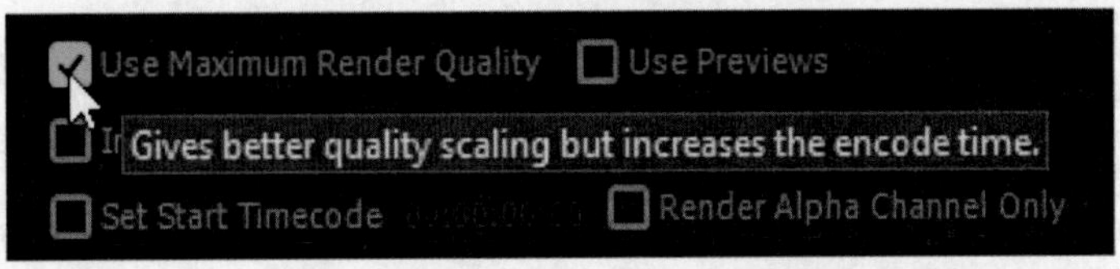

Figure 12-42. Max Render Quality switch in Export settings

As explained earlier, you may be rendering in software mode even if you don't think you are. If you've used a non-accelerated effect, you're at least partly rendering those frames in software mode, and this setting can give sharper details after scaling. However, sharper isn't always better. Noise and compression artifacts will get more visible, and you can get strange jitter and aliasing.

Just like with the Max Bit Depth setting, this setting also overrides the one you've set in your sequence. Be aware that the warp stabilizer involves some scaling and is affected by MRQ!

Steve on Maximum Render Quality

Another example from Senior Engineering Manager Steve Hoeg may help you understand this better. In Steve's words:

> *The MRQ setting doesn't make any difference for scaling or compositing done on the GPU, but it does for anything rendered in software as part of a GPU render. As an example, consider on the bottom layer a clip with scale to frame size, followed by an unaccelerated twirl, then an accelerated three-way. On the upper layer, another clip with scale to frame size and RGB curves. This will be rendered as follows:*

1. Scale to frame size will be rendered on the CPU, respecting the MRQ setting.

2. Twirl will be rendered on the CPU.

3. The frame will be uploaded to the GPU.

4. Three-way will be applied on the GPU.

5. The second clip with be uploaded to the GPU.

6. Scale to frame size will be rendered on the GPU, which is always MRQ.

7. RGB curves will be rendered on the GPU.

8. The clips will be composited together on the GPU.

Again, in full GPU-accelerated mode (no non-accelerated effects), all formats will be scaled on the GPU, and the setting does nothing. Max Render Quality (MRQ) only applies when scaling in software mode. It gives sharper scaling and increases export time dramatically.

Composite in Linear Color

This is not a setting you'll find in the Export dialog—so why am I including it here? Well, Maximum Render Quality does more than just sharpen scaling. Just like in your sequence, it also has an effect on the *Composite in Linear Color* feature. So, clicking this switch will also affect how your compositing, cross-dissolves, and color grading look!

Figures 12-43 and 12-44 show a few screenshots of the different rendering results in both software and GPU mode, with and without MRQ and linear color. Note the different looks of the one with MRQ and linear mode before and after rendering (Figure 12-43). Software mode and Max Bit Depth can give you some unpleasant surprises at export time. Get yourself a decent GPU to avoid all this.

Figure 12-43. *Left: Software mode, Max Bit Depth, Max Render Quality, Normal blending mode, Composite in Linear Color, before rendering timeline. Right: Software mode, Max Bit Depth, Max Render Quality, Normal blending mode, Composite in Linear Color, after rendering timeline. Should be very similar to GPU mode*

Figure 12-44. *Left: GPU mode, Max Bit Depth, Max Render Quality, linear Color, Normal blending mode. Right: GPU mode, Max Bit Depth, Max Render Quality, linear Color, Lighten blending mode*

Before rendering previews, I couldn't tell the one in Lighten blending mode from the one in Normal blending mode. After rendering, there was a huge difference. Before rendering, the software-only version with Normal blending mode actually looks much more like GPU mode with Lighten blending mode than the one with the actual Normal mode.

In GPU mode, on the other hand, what you see is what you get. No surprises.

The test was done by putting a Photoshop PSD file with an outer glow layer style on top of a background that's just a Premiere Pro legacy title with a four-color gradient fill.

Summarizing Max Quality and Bit Depth

I know this is quite a bit of info to digest. Here's an attempt to summarize it all:

1. Software mode + Maximum Render Quality uses a better scaling algorithm than without Maximum Render Quality, but not identical to the GPU scaling.

2. GPU mode always uses 32-bit processing and a superior scaling algorithm.

3. Rendering on export falls back to software mode when a non-accelerated effect is used, but only for the calculations after the non-accelerated effect.

4. Setting either the Maximum Render Quality or Maximum Bit Depth option to ON in the Export window will always result in those settings' being applied, regardless of sequence settings.

5. Setting either the Maximum Render Quality or Maximum Bit Depth option to OFF in the Export window will always result in those settings' *not* being applied, regardless of sequence settings.

6. Composite in Linear Color can be overridden in both GPU and software mode in the sequence settings, but when you export without Maximum Render Quality, clips will not be composited in linear color.

If you're a highly technical person and want to know exactly what scaling algorithms are used, Software MRQ uses a variable-sized bicubic, while GPU uses a Lanczos2 low-pass filtered with a bicubic.

Frame Blending

The tool tip in Figure 12-45 tells you pretty clearly that this is only applicable when you're exporting to a frame rate that doesn't match your sequence, although it's not true if you choose *Frame Sampling*, which is the default. It's only true when you choose *Frame Blending* or *Optical Flow*.

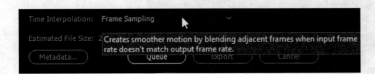

Figure 12-45. Frame blending can help when your source material doesn't match the frame rate of your sequence, but the quality will vary

Say you've edited a 24p sequence and want to export it to 50p. Without frame blending, you'll get whole frames only, some frames will be shown twice, other frames will be shown three times, and the motion will not be smooth. Blending the frames can help smooth out the motion, but you stand the chance of getting artifacts, like partly transparent duplicates of moving objects, in some frames.

The same thing happens if you export 25p as 24p. Without frame blending (when Time Interpolation is set to *Frame Sampling*), you'll simply skip whole frames. Once again, frame blending can help a little. To get a much better 24p export from a 25p film, see the section on DCP export that follows. Unfortunately, choosing *Frame Blending* does not update the output preview to show how it will look (Figure 12-46), so you'll have to export a short sample and play it back if you want to see the effect it has on your export (Figure 12-47).

Figure 12-46. *24 fps from 25 fps preview. Even with Frame Blending on, the export preview doesn't show it*

Figure 12-47. *24 fps from 25 fps result. This is how the actual export looks. Notice the blurry text due to Frame Blending*

Little known fact: In software mode, setting Maximum Render Quality makes Premiere use linear color when frame blending.

When you choose Optical Flow here, you'll get the same pros and cons as in the timeline. Some footage (mainly that with little motion blur and definite edges) will look gorgeous, and some (mainly that with blur or motion blur, or lots of details) will look extremely bad!

Make sure you always check your exported file when you choose Optical Flow here! Keep in mind that Optical Flow will make the export very slow!

Effects Settings

In the Effects panel, you can add timecode, clip name, logos, and other stuff to the exported clips. You can also make sure the exported file conforms to broadcast audio and video standards, or maybe change the duration by a few percent. The choices are pretty much self-explanatory (Figure 12-48). Read more about these choices in the "Custom Export Presets" section in chapter 10 on customizing Premiere.

Figure 12-48. Export Effects choices

The export in Figure 12-49 has a logo overlay, timecode overlay, clip name overlay, and a sepia Lumetri LUT. All of these were added at export, not in the timeline.

Figure 12-49. Result of export with some effects

1095

Publish Settings

This is great for us lazy people! If you trust that Premiere—or Adobe Media Encoder—will not crash or otherwise act up during export, you can let the software log into your FTP server or Facebook, Vimeo, Twitter, YouTube, Creative Cloud, or Behance account and upload the file when it's finished encoding (Figure 12-50). I've used it to get review copies out to customers on FTP servers while I was sleeping.

| Effects | Video | Audio | Multiplexer | Captions | Publish |

> ☐ **Adobe Creative Cloud**

> ☐ **Behance**

> ☐ **Facebook**

> ☐ **FTP**

> ☐ **Twitter**

> ☐ **Vimeo**

> ☐ **YouTube**

Figure 12-50. *Publish settings*

Start the export when you go to bed, and wake up to comments from your clients in your inbox. Nice! Note that when you auto-publish to your Creative Cloud folder, your file will be synced to both your local folder and the cloud.

Dear Adobe: There Is No PAL or NTSC in HD

This is something that has been bothering me for a long time. Even in the HD presets, you'll find PAL and NTSC under TV Standard. Those are very specific formats, exclusively relevant to SD, with very restricted rules for frame rates, frame sizes, interlacing settings, and so on.

There is no such thing as a PAL HD clip, nor does an NTSC HD clip exist. I do get it—they are just convenient shorthand, and the names indicate that the frame rates are compatible with PAL or NTSC. But really, it's just plain incorrect to use those terms here (Figure 12-51).

Figure 12-51. *No PAL or NTSC in an HD video file*

It's even possible to export files with the wrong tag, such as a progressive H.264 720p50 file tagged as NTSC! This makes absolutely no sense whatsoever. Let's remove TV Standard from the Export dialog in the future, or at least rename the settings to something vaguely correct.

Conforming 25p to 24p in Premiere

If you've edited your film in 25p or 50p, and your export is a 24fps DCP, you have a few options. Let's do the easiest one first—knowing that it's also the one with the most artifacts.

Nest your existing sequence in a 24p sequence—and you might as well make it 1998 × 1080, 2048 × 858, or 2048 × 1080, depending on your final DCP file being flat, scope, or full raster. That way, you can see exactly what you're about to export.

This will do the standard frame-rate conversion by simply removing frames, and the result is that you get perfect frames, but you don't get perfectly smooth movement (as seen in the first image in Figure 12-52). Frame blending can help a little, but your credits will be blurry (as seen in the second image in Figure 12-52), and movement will still not be perfectly smooth. Proper conforming looks better than this.

Figure 12-52. *Frame blending causes blurry motion. Smoother, but not very sharp*

25p or 50p in a 24p sequence will always give stuttering movement. But if we change the speed to 96 percent, the clip will get about 4 percent longer, and each frame will be shown exactly once, with smooth movement as a result! So, go ahead and change the speed of your nested sequence to 96 percent.

A Better Conversion, with Less Artifacts

A better way to do this—if a change in speed/duration is OK—would be to export the film first to an intermediate codec, then import the file and interpret it to 24p by clicking **Modify ➤ Interpret Footage ➤ Frame Rate** and entering a frame rate of 24 fps.

Note the new length of your film in a 24p timeline—you'll need it later. My length was 3:45:21.

OK, so the video now looks good, but the audio will sound horribly bad, so mute the audio tracks. We'll use Audition for good-quality stretching. Go back to the original 25p sequence and export your audio to a 96 kHz 32-bit WAV file. You want the best possible quality for stretching and pitch shifting.

Import it into Audition and click **Effects ➤ Time and Pitch ➤ Stretch and Pitch (Process)**. I chose the *Audition Algorithm at High Precision*, and I chose *Constant Vowels* in the Advanced section.

Enter your new duration this way: **3:45.875**. Yep, a colon as a divider first, and then a full stop for the next (Figure 12-53).

Figure 12-53. Stretching the audio in Audition gives you a much better result than doing it in Premiere

---

■ **Note**   The decimals you enter in the New Duration field in Audition will not be the same as what you see in your Premiere timeline. Audition operates with milliseconds, while Premiere does frames. Do the math before you enter the new duration. In my case, it was 21 frames, and my calculator app gave me this result: 21 / 24 = 0.875. So instead of 3:45.**21**, I entered 3:45.**875** for New Duration. Get it?

Now, export the processed file as a 48 kHz 32-bit WAV file from Audition, import it into Premiere, and put it in the 24p timeline. It should match the length of your stretched video, and after you've panned the audio (if necessary) you can export your DCP. See Figure 12-54.

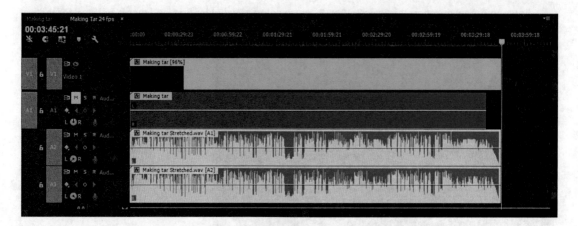

Figure 12-54. *Mute the original sound tracks and use only the stretched audio from Audition*

The pitch shift will be good, but not perfect. A trained ear may hear that the audio is processed, and people with absolute pitch (aka perfect pitch) will probably notice some artifacts in the music. If you ask me, stretching the audio and getting perfect movement and high-quality video is much better than keeping the audio and getting stutter and blurry video.

Conforming 23.976p to 24p in Premiere

You can conform 23.976p to true 24p the same way as we conformed the 25p film, but you will be stretching the audio by about 100.1 percent.

Convert a 23.98 fps Master to 60i

To convert 23.98p masters to 60i (which is really 59.94i) to deliver for North American broadcast, just export the sequence or your master as 60i. Premiere will add 2:3 pulldown automatically.

Convert a 23.98 fps Master to 50i

Say you have a 23.98 master file or sequence for which your client has requested that you make deliverables for a broadcast in Europe. Since the numbers do not add up in this type of conversion, you have a few different options. Which one you choose depends on whether you need to preserve the exact original duration or not.

If you're allowed to change the duration, you can interpret the master as 25 fps and apply a speed change to the audio in Audition like we did for the 25-to-24-fps conversion. The result is a perfect frame-for-frame copy that runs 4 percent faster. Then, export this as 50i.

If you're not allowed to change speed/duration, you'll have to create some new frames in one way or another. The easiest method would be to just export a new file from the master at 50i. For some material, it would look OK, because you're essentially creating a pulldown pattern of 2:2:2:2:2:2:2:2:2:2:2:3, and that extra field every half second may not look terrible. But if there are very smooth pans or rolling or crawling text, you'll notice.

For a better result, you can run the conversion through something like Teranex: `blackmagicdesign.com/products/teranex`.

Queue or Direct Export?

If you click the *Export* button, Premiere will take care of the export, but you will not be able to use Premiere until the export is done. It's nice to have the option of doing quick direct exports of short pieces, and it's useful if the Queue option fails. But, normally, we use the queue (Figure 12-55).

Figure 12-55. *Queue or export?*

When you send a sequence to the AME queue, a copy of the project is made on disk, and this is the file that AME references. This frees Premiere for other tasks, so you can continue editing your great show. AME actually loads a copy of the project into memory. This is a good thing; if you could change the project mid-export, then bad things would happen.

By default, AME has a lower priority than Premiere, so if you play back the timeline or scrub media in Premiere, AME will slow down until it gets more resources. This can be changed in your Playback preferences.

Adobe Media Encoder Features

As an editor, you probably run the Adobe Media Encoder from Premiere most of the time. But the Media Encoder has some great features you will only find when you use it on its own.

Stitch Files

AME has a drop-zone where you can drag files from its media browser to stitch them together as one file (Figure 12-56). This is handy if you receive spanned camera clips that are removed from their folders, in which case you don't have the metadata. You can quickly stitch that long interview into one file. If the format is supported for smart rendering, you can do this without quality loss.

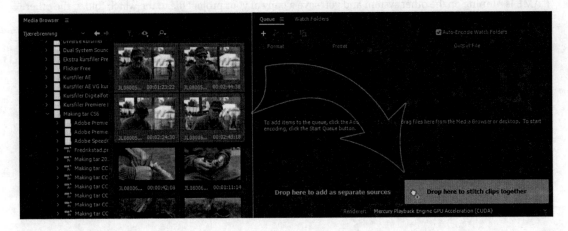

Figure 12-56. *AME stitching*

Watch Folders

The watch folder feature in AME can be a huge timesaver. If you need to export different versions of your film, the watch folder can take care of this for you. You just export your master file—like a high-quality DNxHR file—to the watch folder, and AME creates all the extra copies you need (Figure 12-57).

Figure 12-57. *AME watch folder*

To create a watch folder, click the + icon and drag one or more presets from the presets browser. Here, I've told AME to make a YouTube version and a version with burnt-in TC, which I'll send to the company that transcribes the text to captions. If your presets contain publishing info on uploading to YouTube and to an FTP server, AME does most of the job for you. Just remember to send an email to the transcription service.

Oh, and make sure you enable the *Auto-Encode Watch Folders* switch in the Queue panel. Also, AME needs to be running for watch folders to work.

Render the Export on a Separate System

AME watch folders will also export sequences from Premiere Pro (and After Effects) project files. Click **File ➤ Save a Copy** and save the copy in your AME watch folder. AME will kick out the files and formats specified by the watch folder.

This can be used for "remote rendering" of your exports to ease the load on your editing system. Create a watch folder on a separate system and make sure both systems have access to the folder and the media files. Shared storage is normal in facilities with multiple systems anyway, so you're probably all set for this. If AME is running on the other system and you save a copy of your project file to the watch folder, the other system will start exporting.

■ **Note**   AME's watch folders will pick up only the sequences (or comps, if you're doing this from After Effects) that are at the top level of the project. Sequences in bins will not be exported. Make sure that the sequences you want AME to export, and only those sequences, are at the top level of the project.

The paths to the project file and the footage must be the same on both systems, and they need to have the same fonts and plug-ins. It's also a good idea to set them both to use the same GPU acceleration—like CUDA or OpenCL.

If your other system doesn't have access to the media files, you can use the Project Manager to put the project and media files in a folder that the system has access to. This will take a lot longer than just saving a copy of the project file of course.

Copy Your AME Presets

To move your AME export presets to other systems or to do backups, use the two icons in the Preset Browser panel to export and import presets (Figure 12-58).

Figure 12-58. *Click this button to export a preset and the other one to import presets*

Note that different operating systems require separate EPR files. When you update AME, it's sometimes a good idea to rebuild the presets. New menu options don't always translate, and a fresh one will solve this.

Some Noteworthy AME Preferences

Like Premiere, AME has preferences that you can adjust to your needs (Figure 12-59). I think it's a good idea to make AME start the export queue automatically after a few minutes if I forget to click the *Play* button to start the queue.

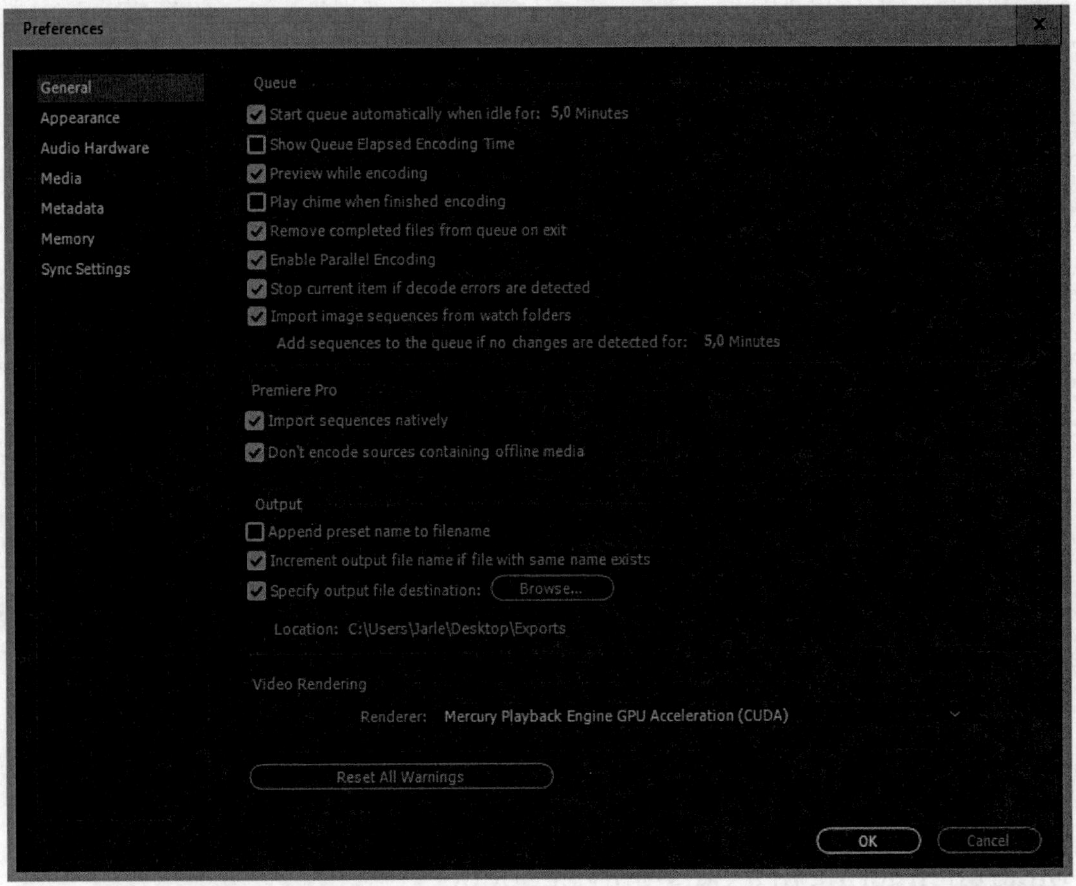

Figure 12-59. *AME preferences*

To avoid clutter in my queue, I also make sure that AME deletes the queue on exit, so I start with a clean slate every time. If the export format supports it, parallel encoding will be faster, so I leave it on. To avoid surprises in the export, I leave the *Stop current item if decode errors are detected* option checked.

There are two Premiere Pro–specific choices in the AME preferences (Figure 12-60). *Import sequences natively* will make AME import the project, and not use Premiere for the export. Premiere doesn't even need to be installed on the system. Turning this off will make AME always use Dynamic Link for the export and start a headless full version of Premiere in the background.

Figure 12-60. *AME Premiere preferences*

Using Dynamic Link is known to solve some export problems, so if you have any problems, try switching this option off.

The *Don't encode sources containing offline media* choice should be self-explanatory. It's another safety net that I like to leave on. It only works when *Import Sequences Natively* is selected. Note that none of these will affect sequences already in the queue. It's only for future exports.

Notification on Smartphone When Render Is Done

Here's a little tip from Italian video editing professor Giacomo Fabbrocino for receiving a notification on your smartphone when AME has finished a job. Set a single-frame render task at the end of your render queue and tell AME to output that in your Dropbox folder.

Install the Dropbox app on your phone, and you will be alerted when the render queue is over. Clever!

Smart Rendering

When you export to supported formats, the *Enable Smart Rendering Codec* choice will be shown. Smart rendering is a very good thing! It enables fast and high-quality exports. It means we're exporting to the same format as our source, and the *zeros and ones describing each frame are not touched—the bits are just passed over to the exported file.* No re-encoding or transcoding! Think of it as more of a copy/paste operation than re-encoding.

This means absolutely no generation loss, and getting the best quality you can get with the codec you're using. Smart rendering is also much faster than encoding the material to a new format, so generally it will give both the fastest and the best exports. It kicks in whenever possible.

There is no way to tell if Premiere is doing smart rendering or not, but if you choose the right settings, there's a good chance you'll understand when and why it happens. Well, if you look around in the console, you'll find a way to tell.

Smart Rendering in a Cuts-only Sequence

Cuts are easy, especially with intra-frame codecs. Each frame is compressed on its own, with no relationship to frames before or after. So, if you cut away some frames—as we do when setting in and out points—only the bits and bytes for the remaining frames will be kept. With I-frame-only formats and cuts only, every frame will be smart rendered.

Smart Rendering Long-GOP

If you're editing Long-GOP material, such as XDCAM, then only whole GOPs will be smart rendered. Where you have cuts that don't fall on I-frames, a new GOP will be created between the I-frames at each side. So, just a few frames before and after the cut will be re-encoded, as opposed to whole clips.

Smart Rendering in a Sequence with Transitions and Effects

OK, so when we do straight cuts, smart rendering will kick in when the criteria (discussed soon) are met. Scaling, moving, or cropping a clip or adding effects and transitions means the pixels have been altered, and those frames cannot be smart rendered. Premiere will encode the frames to the output format as normal.

Smart Rendering with Preview Renders

So, does that mean we cannot benefit from smart rendering when we use color correction, effects, and transitions, or otherwise alter our pixels? Not really. If you have *Use Previews* checked in the Export dialog, Premiere (or AME) will use the preview files as the source to render to the final output.

So, if the timeline is already rendered for preview, and the preview format matches the output format, then smart rendering will kick in. A lot of editors are used to working this way, and will render previews when getting coffee, when talking on the phone, or when speaking with the director. After each short break, all effects in the timeline will be fully rendered.

Criteria for Effective Smart Rendering

Here's a short checklist for smart rendering. When all these criteria are met, smart rendering will happen.

1. You must output to one of the supported codecs.

2. Your source material must match exactly the format used for output in order to smart render untouched material.

3. Your sequence preview renders must be the same format as your output in order to smart render parts of the timeline with format mismatches, effects, and transitions.

4. *Enable Smart Rendering Codec* must be checked on Export, except for the DV flavors.

So, if you're importing ProRes 422 HQ, rendering previews in ProRes 422 HQ, and exporting ProRes 422 HQ, your exports will be fast and look great. The same goes for any flavor of DNxHD and other supported formats, of course. All settings for the codec must match, including frame size, frame rate, interlacing or progressive, VBR or CBR (for long-GOP), and so on. Everything!

For a typical news cut, most of the timeline will smart render. For documentaries and more complex edits with effects and transitions, previewed areas of the timeline will smart render.

Supported Codecs and Formats for Smart Rendering

The following formats and codecs are supported for smart rendering in Premiere CC, according to Adobe Premiere Pro Help at helpx.adobe.com/premiere-pro/using/smart-rendering.html.

- DV Formats

    - DV

    - DVCPRO

    - DVCPRO HD

- MXF OP1a

    - XDCAM HD (Format ➤ MXF OP1a & Format ➤ AS-10)

    - XDCAM EX (Format ➤ MXF OP1a)

    - AVC-Intra in MXF (Format ➤ MXF OP1a & Format ➤ AS-11)

    - XAVC-Intra in MXF (Format ➤ MXF OP1a)

    - DNxHD & DNxHR in MXF (Format ➤ DNxHR/DNxHD MXF OP1a)

    - MXF OP-Atom AVC Intra to MXF OP1a AVC-Intra

    - QT XDCAM to MXF OP1a XDCAM

    - DNxHD MXF OP-Atom to DNxHD MXF OP1a

    - MXF OP1a to DNxHD MXF OP1a

    - QT AVC-Intra to MXF OP1a AVC-Intra

- QuickTime

    - GoPro CineForm

    - NONE: Uncompressed RBG 8-bit

    - Animation

    - DNxHD/DNxHR

    - MXF OP1a AVC-Intra to QT AVC-Intra

- ProRes (QuickTime—Mac only)

    - ProRes 422

    - ProRes 422 (HQ)

    - ProRes 422 (LT)

    - ProRes 422 (Proxy)

    - ProRes 4444

- JPEG 2000 in MXF (only works when using the 12-bit PQ space)

■ **Note**   Most flavors of XDCAM HD, AVC-U, and XAVC can be smart rendered, but you can't use these formats for preview render files. Smart rendering with these formats will only kick in for source footage with no effects applied.

QuickTime Rewrap Preset

When you choose QuickTime as the format, one of the presets is Match Source (Rewrap). This is in addition to the standard Match Sequence Settings feature. If the source format and your sequence contain one of the supported codecs (found in the tool tip when you hover over the preset; see Figure 12-61) the pixels will not be altered, just wrapped in a QuickTime container.

Figure 12-61. *QuickTime rewrap*

Even if your sequence has non-MOV sources like DV AVI, you can sometimes use this preset to rewrap the video in a MOV file with the same codec. It will be super-fast and have no quality loss. If you try this with a non-supported format, you will immediately get an error message telling you the format is not supported.

Export to Intermediate and Archive File Formats

High-quality video and audio codecs suitable for archives or for interchange between workgroups are often called intermediate or mezzanine codecs. Only a few codecs are suitable for this.

Saving to a lossless format sounds like a good idea, and it kind of is, but the files can get ginormous. If you're just putting it on a drive on the shelf or on a big and fast local RAID, that may be OK. However, if you're sending it to others via a network or otherwise, uncompressed is not practically workable. Apart from the huge file sizes, you will also greatly reduce the number of places and/or programs that can play your film master.

A very common compromise is to render to a visually lossless codec, like the highest bit rate ProRes or DNxHD flavors. What does "visually lossless" mean? It means that some people in a committee decided (after some brief research) that viewers could see no difference between an uncompressed file and the file using the codec in question. But even visually lossless codecs can cause trouble for VFX work, like green-screen keying, further downstream, so beware.

Files from mathematically lossless codecs, on the other hand, are exactly the same quality as uncompressed, just smaller. They are mostly still too big for most interchange purposes, though.

Most intermediate formats are intra-frame, so each frame is compressed separately. This makes them easily scrubbable, suitable for smart rendering, and generally easy to edit, manage, and use.

Widely Used Visually Lossless Codecs

Popular intermediate codecs are Avid's DNxHD (en.wikipedia.org/wiki/DNxHD_codec) and Apple's ProRes (en.wikipedia.org/wiki/Apple_ProRes). Both are easy-to-edit intra-frame codecs based on JPG-like DCT compression of each individual frame. DNxHD is truly cross-platform, but ProRes is not, since writing to ProRes on Windows is not something Apple wants us to do. Some third-party solutions exist, but they're not perfect, and using some of them might even be a violation of the law in some countries.

The quality at equal bit rates is close to identical on the two, with ProRes being just a hair better than DNxHD. DNxHD is a more constrained format than ProRes. While ProRes is somewhat resolution flexible, supporting even SD, 2K, 4K, and 5K up to 12-bit with alpha channels, DNxHD supports only 1920 × 1080 and 1280 × 720 pixels in 8-bit or 10-bit in Premiere. DNxHR supports 2K, 4K, and UHD.

DNxHD and DNxHR

This is Avid's Digital Non-linear eXtensible High Definition file format. For higher-than-HD resolutions, we have DNxHR—Digital Nonlinear eXtensible High Resolution.

DNX is always 4:2:2 or 4:4:4 and always square pixels, and it can be 8-bit or 10-bit. An X at the end of the preset name indicates 10-bit, and without the X it's 8-bit. DNX can be wrapped in either MXF or QuickTime containers. Table 12-1 shows the available flavors.

Table 12-1. *DNX Flavors*

444	*4:4:4 color space, for high-quality color correction and finishing*
HQX	*High-quality extended, for color correction and mastering*
HQ	*High quality, smaller bandwidth for editorial*
SQ	*Standard quality, for editorial*
LB	*Low bandwidth, for remote workflows and saving storage*

To use alpha channels in DNX in Adobe applications, use uncompressed alpha channels, not compressed alpha channels (Figure 12-62).

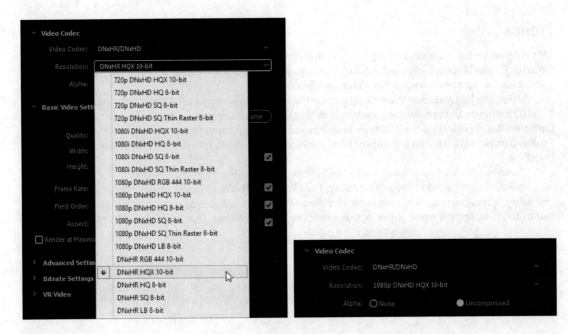

Figure 12-62. DNX export settings and DNX uncompressed alpha

Using it for smart rendering isn't always as straightforward as you'd wish. If you create a new sequence from a DNX HQX 1080p 25 clip, Premiere will create a sequence with DNX 1080p 25 editing mode. Great—but if you examine the sequence settings you'll find that it uses DNX SQ 1080p 25 for the preview renders.

We'll have to guess that it does so to keep the size of the preview renders down. But that format is also 8-bit, and our HQX format was 10-bit. Hitting *Match Sequence Settings* in the export dialog would seem like a logical thing to do, but that will match the Preview render format. The result is an 8-bit output that's both slower and of less quality than your source file. If you create a sequence from a high-quality DNxHD clip, make sure you change the previews to match it (Figure 12-63).

Figure 12-63. DNxHQ default preview and DNxHQ custom preview. You will not get smart rendering with the default

A much safer approach is to create your sequences manually, choosing the preferred quality in the New Sequence dialog. Better yet, create your own presets in which these settings are always correct, and get the added benefit of preconfigured audio routing.

More on DNxHD can be found in on Avid's web pages: `avid.com/en/products/avid-dnxhr-and-dnxhd`.

ProRes

This is Apple's editing codec, and the compression is very similar to that of DNxHD, using DCT. Just like DNxHD, ProRes is always 4:2:2 or 4:4:4, but it does support non-square pixels, which is not necessarily a good thing, but can be convenient in some workflows.

ProRes can be used as an intermediate codec on a MacOS system in pretty much the same way as DNxHD can be on both platforms—making sure that the source, sequence, and output use the same ProRes flavor. ProRes encoding on the Windows platform is more complicated. Windows systems can read most ProRes flavors, and Premiere will import and play ProRes natively on Windows, without QuickTime's being installed.

However, Windows systems cannot write ProRes without some third-party mojo.

ProRes is a very good intermediate codec. I just wish Apple would make it cross-platform by default. But since they're making money when people buy their Macs, that's not very likely to happen. More on ProRes can be found in Apple's white paper: `apple.com/final-cut-pro/docs/Apple_ProRes_White_Paper.pdf`.

GoPro CineForm

GoPro CineForm (Figure 12-64) is a fantastic codec! It's wavelet based, like JPEG 2000 used in digital cinema, has support for alpha channels, can be 10- or 12-bit, and has near lossless quality. It withstands reiterative compressions very well, so it's perfect as an intermediate and/or archive codec.

Figure 12-64. *CineForm logo*

CineForm is standardized by SMPTE (Society of Motion Picture and Television Engineers) as the VC-5 Standard. You can export CineForm video with frame sizes up to 8K from Premiere.

■ **Note**　There are some constraints regarding frame size—the frame width *must* be divisible by 16. If you enter other values, they are automatically rounded to a valid value. Check carefully before export. All the standard video frame sizes are divisible by 16, though, so this is not a big problem.

You may need to download the CineForm decoder from `CineForm.com/gopro-CineForm-decoder` to be able to play the files in some players, like Windows Media Player and QuickTime Player. Of course, it will play back beautifully in Premiere.

To export a GoPro CineForm file from Premiere, choose QuickTime as the format and then choose one of the available GoPro CineForm presets (Figure 12-65). Drag the Quality slider if you want higher or lower quality.

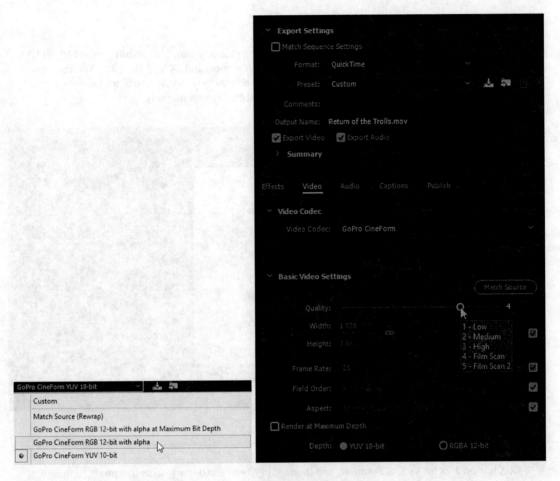

Figure 12-65. *Settings for the GoPro CineForm presets in QuickTime*

When you export GoPro CineForm, you can specify multi-channel audio as stereo or mono pairs, as you can with many other formats in QuickTime. See Figure 12-66.

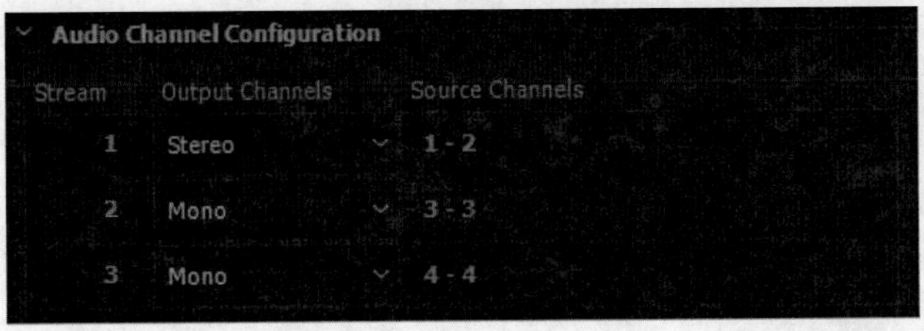

Figure 12-66. *The Audio Channel Configuration settings available in the QuickTime format*

Uncompressed DPX

You can export image sequences with very high quality using industry-standard uncompressed 10-bit DPX files. DPX export in Premiere supports full HD at several frame rates, and 2K and 4K at 24p. You can choose presets for Full Range, Over Range, Standard, and Video, or manually set white and black points, gamma, and so on (Figure 12-67). There is no audio, so that has to be exported separately.

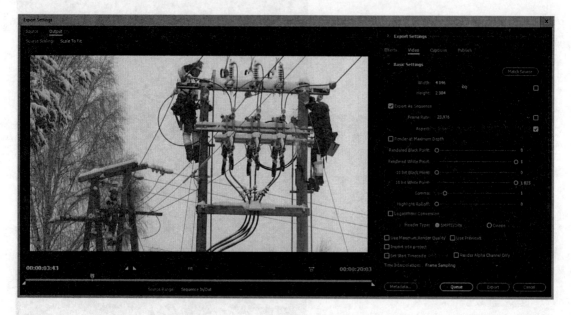

Figure 12-67. *DPX Export settings*

DPX is used a lot for VFX, 3D renders, and interchange between departments in a production line.

Visually Lossless MPEG-2

You can create high-quality MPEG-2 files by forcing it to I-frame-only and setting a high bit rate. Start with the *Match Source – High Bitrate* setting and work from there.

Before you choose any video- or audio-related settings, go to the Multiplexer tab and set it to *None*. Then, set Audio to *PCM*. You'll be restricted to *Stereo – no multichannel output*. Set the Profile to *High*, choose *CBR*, drag Bitrate all the way up *100 Mbps*, and set both M- and N-frames to *1* (Figure 12-68).

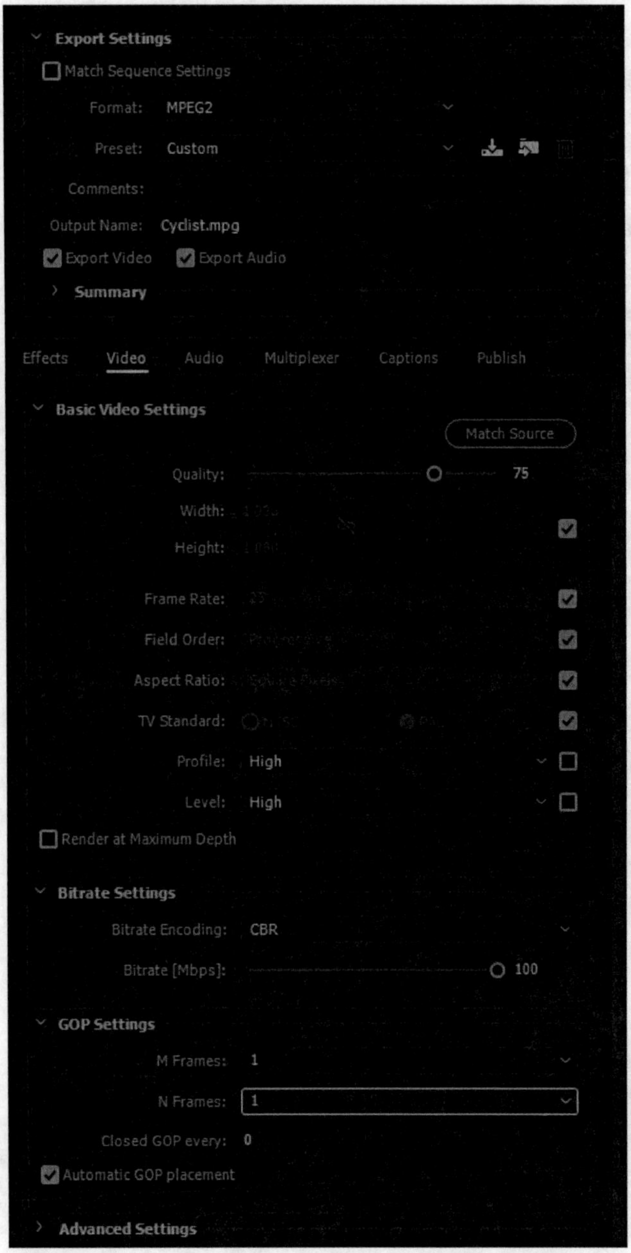

Figure 12-68. *High-quality MPEG-2 export*

This will result in an uncompressed stereo WAV file and an .M2V file.

High-quality MPEG-2 is a good alternative, since it can be played on pretty much any system. In case you are wondering, M Frames is the number of bi-directional frames between consecutive I frames and predicted frames. N Frames is the number of frames between I frames. This value must be a multiple of the M frames value.

1113

AVC Intra and XAVC

AVC Intra and XAVC are also good formats for archive or intermediate files. To export AVC Intra, choose MXF OP1a as the format, and you get presets for AVC Intra Class 50 and 100 for 720p and 1080p. This may lead you to think that you can't export Class 200—but you can. There's just no preset for it.

Dive into the Video tab, and you can choose AVC Intra Class 200. Read more about AVC Intra/Ultra from Panasonic: panasonic.com/business-solutions/avc-ultra.asp.

To export XAVC, choose one of the available flavors in the list (Figure 12-69). More info on XAVC from Sony can be found here: sony.co.uk/pro/article/broadcast-products-xavc-faqs.

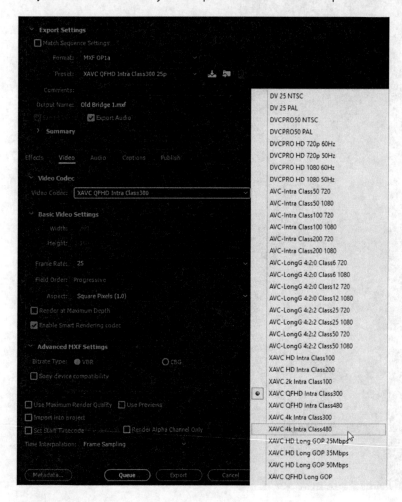

Figure 12-69. *XAVC export*

Grass Valley HQX Codec

Less known than some of the other formats, Grass Valley HQ and HQX are great high-quality codecs. Create an account with Grass Valley, and you get access to download the Grass Valley Codec Pack: grassvalley. com/products/hqx_codec. The codec is free, cross-platform, and supports a wide array of frame rates, frame sizes, and bit rates. It's a 10-bit codec, and it can also store an alpha channel, making it suitable for interchange in motion graphics and compositing workflows.

So, it's very flexible, and very good. In Premiere, you can export Grass Valley HQ and HQX in a MOV or AVI wrapper, so they will appear under these format choices in the export dialog. The codec can also be stored in an MXF wrapper, but I have not found a way to do so in Premiere. See Figure 12-70.

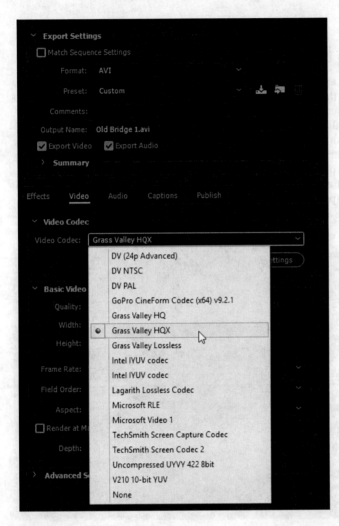

Figure 12-70. Grass Valley HQX export

As with any other codec you install yourself, you need to create export presets yourself for these.

IMF Delivery

IMF (Interoperable Mastering Format) is mostly used for the delivery of a high-quality FINAL master with all the audio and video components, version components, and technical metadata. Netflix and other distributors often require the master in IMF format for 4K features and series.

IMF is a bundle of files. Video and audio are in individual MXF track files, and so is dynamic metadata. A composition playlist (CPL) combines and synchronizes track files. There's an output profile list (OPL) that includes transcode profiling and packages. To keep track of it all, there's a packing list.

Premiere Pro cannot export the IMF format, but you can export the video as JPEG 2000 or some other near-lossless format and use third-party tools to create the IMF package.

If you're delivering to Netflix, make sure you read the requirements on the Netflix Partner help center: backlothelp.netflix.com/hc/en-us.

Digital Cinema Package Export

When featuring your movie at film festivals and at local cinema screenings, DCP export is the way to go. You will export in 24p or 25p when you use the bundled version of Wraptor DCP. The limitations are: 2K (full, scope, or flat), 24 or 25 fps, 48 kHz stereo or 5.1 24-bit audio, and a 250 Mb/s DCI data-rate limit. The exporter assumes Rec.709 video and will automatically apply XYZ and DCP gamma.

Enable frame blending if you feel that the frame-rate conversion from 29.97, 23.976, or other frame rates causes stuttery movement. The problem will be most visible in steady pans and tilts, as well as in your rolling credits. There's not much you can do to the pans and tilts, but you can choose to nest your sequence into a 24p or 25p sequence and add your rolling there instead of doing it in the original sequence. A better solution is to manually conform the film to 24 or 25 fps as explained earlier.

Figures 12-71 to 12-73 show full, scope, and flat video dimensions.

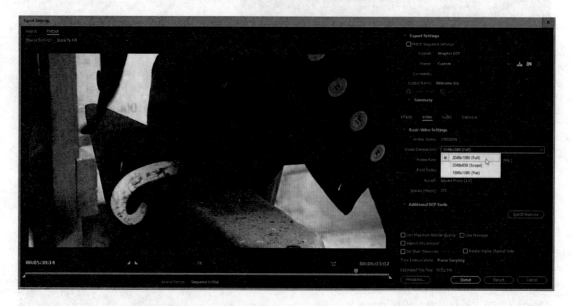

Figure 12-71. *At "full," the image will be cropped a little bit at top and bottom*

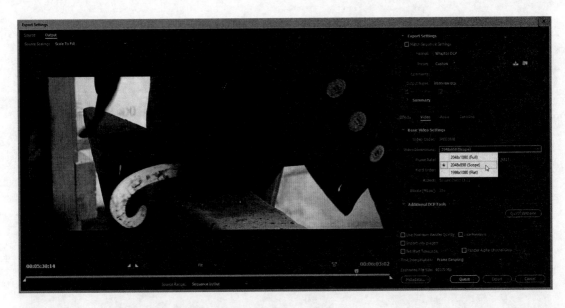

Figure 12-72. *Choosing "scope" causes more vertical cropping*

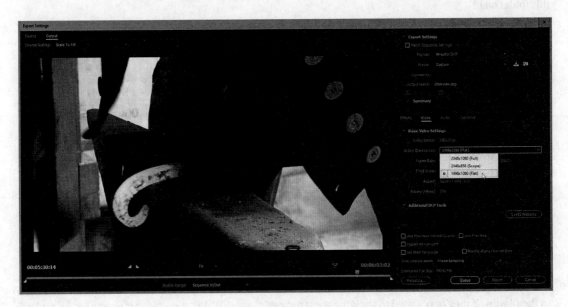

Figure 12-73. *Choosing "flat" causes very little vertical cropping on standard 16 × 9 footage*

No matter what flavor of DCP you export, you'll end up with a folder with the name of the sequence followed by .dcp (Figure 12-74).

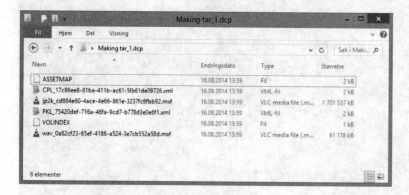

Figure 12-74. DCP folder. This whole folder is what you are creating when you export a DCP. It contains video, audio, and some metadata files

When you deliver the film to a cinema or a festival, make sure to transfer this to a hard drive with only this folder on it!

■ **Note**   To actually set the content kind in metadata, add a line in the cpl.xml file:

`<ContentKind>trailer</ContentKind>`

You can choose feature, trailer, test, teaser, promo, rating, advertisement, short, transition, public service announcement, or policy.

There are, of course, other DCPs' creation tools. Some involve exporting 10-bit TIF or DPX image sequences that can then be converted into JPEG 2000 by third-party software, and others can convert directly to JPEG 2000: en.wikipedia.org/wiki/Digital_Cinema_Package%23DCP_and_KDM_creation_tools.

Some DCP-creation tools add some metadata to the name of the file, so a title would be Making_Tar_24p_2K_F_5.1. If the cinema technician is used to seeing this in the file name, and it's not there, he or she may not know where else to find the info. Adding this to the title certainly will not hurt. Making_Tar_24p_2K_F_no_no_20.dcp means a 24 fps 2K flat file with Norwegian language and Norwegian subtitles with 2.0 audio. You get the idea.

I've been told by one cinema technician (that's you, Jon Andreas Sanne) that tagging your movie as a *short film*, not a feature, can freak out some cinema tech people, because the film entry will get another color in the playlist. If they're not used to showing short movies, they will think something is wrong with your DCP. It's even possible that they have a filter in the playlist view that shows only commercials and features, and your short movie will simply not appear in the list of available films. It's a jungle out there.

If you need 4K, 3D, HFR, or frame rates other than 24 and 25, you can buy the full Pro version of Wraptor DCP—or even rent it for 30 days for a very reasonable price! The Pro version adds 4K, HD, and UHD advertising formats, all the other frame rates, 7.1 audio, increased data rate, and faster encodes.

Need more info? Just click the *QuVIS* button in the DCP Export panel, and it'll take you to quvis.com/dcp-tools/, where you can read more about Wraptor DCP for Premiere.

DCP Subtitling Tools

The bundled version of Wraptor doesn't support subtitles, but there is a way around this limitation. Croatian video editor Bruno Režek told me on LinkedIn that he uses Michael Cinquin's online DCP subtitling tools (`michaelcinquin.com/tools/DCP/DCP_subtitling`) and DCP versioning to make DCP subtitles (Figure 12-75). You upload the subtitles in FCP or SRT format and get a standardized XML subtitle for DCP. Then, you upload the CPL and Assetmap files from your DCP export folder accompanied by a font.

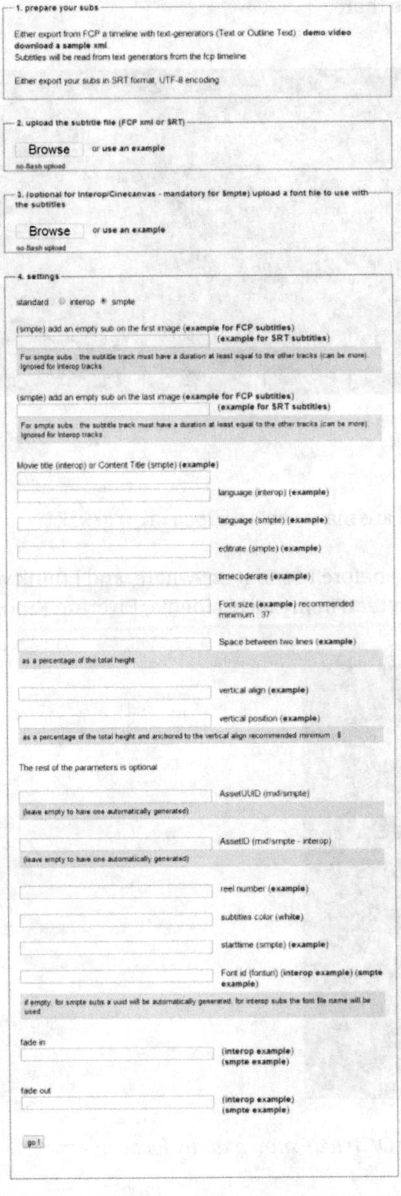

Figure 12-75. The online DCP subtitling tools make it easy to add subtitles to your DCP

1119

When you get your modified files back from Michael's site, you simply replace the corresponding files in your DCP folder, and you have a working, subtitled DCP. What a great resource!

Checking Your DCP

I use DCP Player Free to view my DCP exports (`.digitall.net.au/dcpplayerfree/`). It converts the color space so the film looks good on your computer screen. Figure 12-76 shows both an embedded and a full-screen view. In the free version, the logo overlay will always be there.

Figure 12-76. *DCP Player Free and DCP Player Free full screen*

Of course, you can use any other DCP player you want. There are many: `en.wikipedia.org/wiki/Digital_Cinema_Package%23Software_DCP_players`.

I do like to visit a theater to watch the film in an actual cinema before I send it anywhere, and I think you should, too. Figure 12-77 shows my *Making Tar* movie on the big screen in my local cinema, Elverum Kino.

Figure 12-77. *DCP in Cinema. This is what it looked like when my DCP was shown at my local cinema*

JPEG 2000 MXF OP1a Export

If you just want to export the video and audio from Premiere and use third-party software to create the DCP, then you can export JPEG 2000 MXF OP1a. Simply select the JPEG2000 MXF OP1a format and adjust your settings as desired (Figure 12-78).

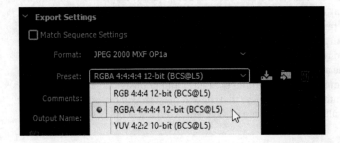

Figure 12-78. JPEG 2000 export

DCP Export Is Partly Broken in CC2017

The makers of the Wraptor DCP exporter (quvis.com) have announced that the makers of GDC players, digital cinema players for theaters, released a software update in 2016 that broke compatibility with several DCP tool providers, including QuVIS. The issue involved the locations in which image-size information can "correctly" be placed in the MXF and XML files.

QuVIS has made an update for its stand-alone Wraptor DCP software that's been approved for US DCP distribution in 2017. It's unclear when this update will be included in the Premiere exporter.

Golden Rules for Good Compression

These days, we don't just export a master file of the finished movie. Rough cuts, teasers, and client review versions—and of course the finished movie—are exported to the web and watched on iPads and smartphones. We need to compress our video, heavily. We throw away pixel information hoping that we will not miss it in order to get file size down.

■ **Note** Contrary to what some people seem to believe, file size isn't hard to figure out or to influence. **The only thing that dictates the resulting file size is the bit rate**—the number of zeros and ones per second. **Bit rate × Seconds = File Size**.

Frame size, frame rate, and image complexity do *not* change the number of zeros and ones, but they significantly affect how good the image looks. So, compression is about what quality we can squeeze out at any given file size or bit rate, unless we can increase bit rate and file size however much we want.

H.264, also known as AVC (Advanced Video Coding), is a codec used everywhere from smartphones to Blu-ray and even for high-end editing. H.264 is also a perfectly good intermediate format if you use the higher-end specs. It can do intra-frame, deep color, and high bit rates, but where we're most likely to see H.264 is probably on the web. It's also very good for local playback on a laptop, tablet, or smartphone.

Few Touches

To get great-quality exports, we want to touch the pixels as few times as possible. Even a conversion to lossless can be destructive if the color space or bit depth is changed. Premiere was built with this in mind, and will read the original source file and do all the calculations for color correction, transitions, blend modes, and so forth with 32-bits-per-channel floating-point accuracy, as well as deliver a full-quality frame to the encoder.

So, the original recording from your camera will only be compressed once, and that's on output. When smart rendering, it will not even touch the pixels, and the source and the output will be identical. This ensures you get the best possible quality output. So, let Premiere do its thing and don't mess with the quality by transcoding unless you have a very good reason.

Cascaded codecs is a problem. Imagine a book written in English, translated into Norwegian, then to Chinese, and back again to English. Then, imagine a book written in English and published in English, or a book written in Norwegian and translated into English. It's clear that the text most true to the original is the text that has been translated just once, or not at all. The same is true with video. Avoid transcoding when possible.

How Low Can You Go?

We generally want our files to be as small as possible without losing quality. However, if we keep on lowering the data rate, the quality at some point becomes unacceptable. There is no exact bit rate at which HD video gets too bad. The quality you get at a certain bit rate will depend on the codec, frame rate, frame size, and how much movement and detail you have in your film.

If you're in doubt, just export a short segment of your film and play the exported file back. If it looks good, it's OK. If not, export again with better quality settings.

A Quarter of the Frame Size Can Be Better

Generally, it's better to reduce the size of the video frame than it is to keep it at full res when you reach the lowest bit rates. You would get much better quality if you were to output a 500 kbps 960 × 540 file and view it at double size than you would if you were to export a full-res 1920 × 1080 file. Remember: half the height and half the width means ¼ of the amount of pixels.

Also, half the frame rate will cut the required bit rate, but not in half, as you might expect if you're outputting to a long-GOP format like H.264. Since the changes between frames will get bigger, the codec needs more bits to describe them.

VBR Beats CBR, Especially at Low Bit Rates

For heavy compression, encoding every frame using the same number of bits isn't necessarily smart. But that's what Constant Bit Rate encoding does. CBR will result in complex images' having more artifacts than simpler images, but if the bit rate is high enough, this will not be a big problem.

Variable Bit Rate means that the codec uses more bits to describe a difficult-to-encode part of the film (high detail, quick changes, fast motion) and fewer bits to describe easy-to-encode parts (low detail, small changes, low motion). That's a good thing, but it takes a lot longer to encode at VBR two-pass, so you might want to use CBR when you're in a hurry. One-pass VBR is an OK compromise.

At high bit rates, you probably won't spot any difference between CBR and VBR, but at low bit rates it makes a big difference. How much will depend on the footage.

Ban Non-Square Pixels and Interlacing

Using non-square pixels is stupid, but quite a few video formats actually do use them. Make sure you always use square pixels when creating your H.264 file. Interlacing is also a bad, bad thing.

Fortunately, the H.264 presets in Premiere are square pixels and progressive. Don't mess with those settings, and you're fine.

Audio Matters—A Lot

Give audio the bandwidth it needs to sound good. We tolerate video artifacts much better than we do audio artifacts. Make sure you create or use presets with good audio quality.

H.264 for the Rest of Us

Why is H.264 so important? Because it's a format that's literally everywhere and that can be played by a huge number of different devices. It's read by Android, iOS, MacOS, Windows, smart TVs, DSLRs, cable TV, TV over the air, YouTube, Netflix, Blu-ray, and more. It's all over the place!

Computer scientist Kush Amerasinghe from Adobe wrote a great intro to the H.264 codec with the title *H.264 for the Rest of Us*. You can download both the English and the Spanish versions as PDF files from adobe.com/devnet/flashmediaserver/articles/h264_primer.html.

H.264 for Local Playback

If you need to store a video file on a USB stick, upload it for someone to review, or have it on a laptop for playback on a projector, then H.264 with AAC audio in an MP4 wrapper is your best bet. A MOV wrapper is not recommended, since it's 32-bit on Windows and is not supported on all Android devices. Roughly 90 percent of the corporate world is on Windows.

If you want to store it on a USB stick, you need some info before you make your choices. FAT32 is the most common formatting for USB sticks, because almost any device can read it. But it has a file size limit of 2 GB. If your video file is larger, you could format it as exFAT, which supports file sizes up to several petabytes (that's over a million terabytes!). exFAT is supported by most modern devices, but support is not as widespread as for FAT32.

NTFS and HFS+ are not recommended since they're not supported on many devices.

Because of this, if your film is long, you have to decide if it's best to have good quality (larger file) and thus limit the number of compatible playback devices with exFAT. If the film is short, you can offer two versions—one with a high resolution and bit rate and one with a lower resolution (720p) and lower bit rate (6 mbps) at a lower level to make sure that it plays fluently on almost any machine.

Did I say level? Yes, you also need to decide on a profile and a level for the encoding—and this is where it gets complicated. Take a deep breath.

H.264 Profiles

The profile is what defines how complex the encoding is. A profile sets rules for how the encoding is achieved. The higher the profile, the more advanced the encoding will be, and the more processing power and memory it demands from the playback device.

So, the lowest profiles can be viewed even on older cell phones, while the highest profiles can be hard to play back even on a modern PC/Mac. Encoding for early models of iPhone would need to be Baseline profile, while for local playback on a recent PC we can use the High profile. Premiere can create files with Baseline, Main, or High profiles (Figure 12-79).

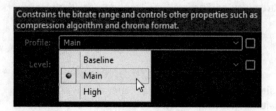

Figure 12-79. *Your choice of profile is dictated by what kind of devices you want the video to be played on*

All these profiles have 4:2:0 color sampling. Find more on profiles on Wikipedia: en.wikipedia.org/wiki/H.264/MPEG-4_AVC#Profiles.

H.264 Levels

The levels put constraints on what numbers we can set the different parameters to (Figure 12-80). Levels limit the frame size and frame rate we're allowed to set. So, while profiles set the complexity and processing power demands, levels set restrictions on max resolution and bandwidth—among other things.

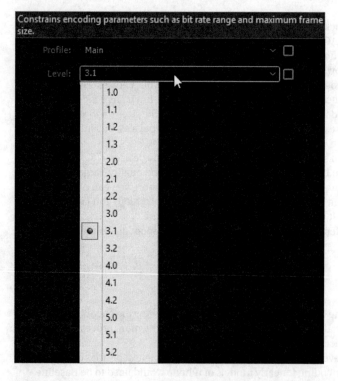

Figure 12-80. *The levels introduce limitations on frame rate, frame size, and bandwidth*

Note that if you change the level, even with *Match Source* checked, your frame size and frame rate may be changed as well to comply with the restrictions in the chosen level (Figure 12-81). Make sure you check thoroughly before you export the video. Using custom presets is a good way to avoid problems like this.

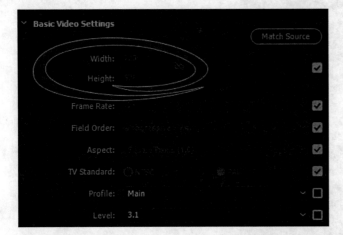

Figure 12-81. *Changing the level may change the frame size*

High profile at Level 4.2 should be more than good enough for HD and 2K exports if you increase the bit rate to 20 or more. Read everything about levels on Wikipedia: en.wikipedia.org/wiki/H.264/MPEG-4_AVC#Levels.

4K H.264

You can easily output 4K 16 × 9, 4K2K or UHD size H.264 video from Premiere. If you export from a sequence that has the correct frame size and frame rate, start by choosing *Match Source, High Bitrate*. This sets the right level, but I'd change the profile from Main to High. For local playback, I suggest a target bit rate of 20 mbps or more for 4K. My preset has 40 mbps (Figure 12-82).

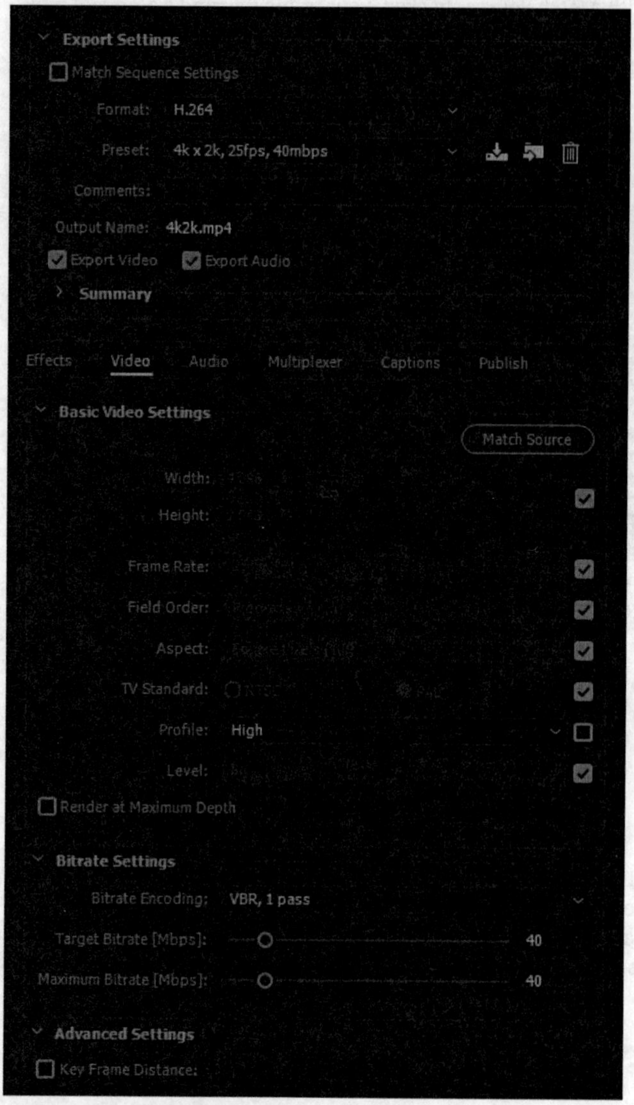

Figure 12-82. *4K H.264 export*

For web distribution, go as low as you can without too much image degradation. Do a few short tests before you decide on the bit rate.

AME enforce standards with some vigor, so you can't export 4K by 4K, since it's not part of the standard. There are third-party apps that can do this, but you can be sure that a lot of devices can't play it.

Dolby Digital 5.1 and 7.1 Audio Export

For formats that support Dolby Digital Plus—like H.264 and H.265—you can output up to 7.1 surround audio (Figure 12-83). Other formats support up to 5.1, like Windows Media, WebM, Waveform Audio, and more.

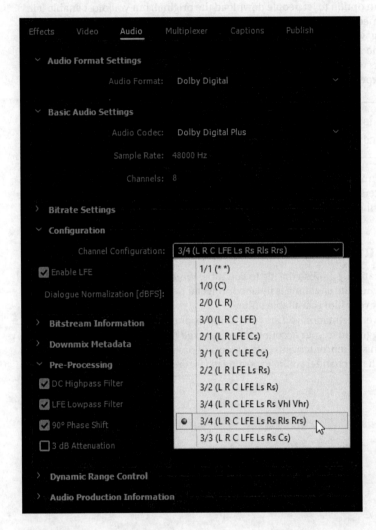

Figure 12-83. *Dolby Digital 7.1 export*

Some formats support up to 32 mono channels, so you can definitely export 7.1 to those, but they will not be tagged as 5.1 or 7.1—they will just be separate tracks that the user will need to route correctly.

Export to Vimeo, YouTube, etc.

The file you upload is not what people see when they're watching YouTube or Vimeo! The uploaded file will always be re-encoded to optimize playback and stability at different resolutions. They'll never see the file you uploaded. Well, Vimeo has an option to let people download the original, but you must enable it in Vimeo, and the file will not be streamed, but rather will be saved locally.

Since we know that re-encoding will happen, we want to export at pretty high quality so the hardware encoder on Vimeo or YouTube can do a good job.

The YouTube and Vimeo presets were greatly improved in two Premiere Pro CC 2014 releases, and now result in good quality. That's to be expected, since the bit rate was more than tripled (!) from 5 to 16 mbps.

■ **Note**   The H.264 files you export for use on YouTube will also be very good for local playback on a Mac or PC, from a USB stick in your TV set, and on tablets.

If you want even better quality on YouTube, Vimeo, and so forth, upload a ProRes file, DNxHD, or any of the mezzanine formats used for masters and intermediate files. Just make sure the destination site supports the format. A short test before uploading the actual file would be smart, as transferring large files will take a while.

Auto-publish to FTP, Vimeo, YouTube, and Social Media

The Publish tab allows you to automatically publish the file to YouTube, Vimeo, Creative Cloud, Facebook, Twitter, Behance, or an FTP server when the encoding is finished. You can basically just start the export and leave the computer, and a while later your film is available online.

You need an account for whatever destination you are publishing to, and you need to let the Adobe Media Encoder get access to it by logging in to your account. If you're asked to allow AME to access your account, you need to confirm this. Then, enter your user name and password. The settings are very straightforward if you're familiar with the channel you're exporting to (Figure 12-84).

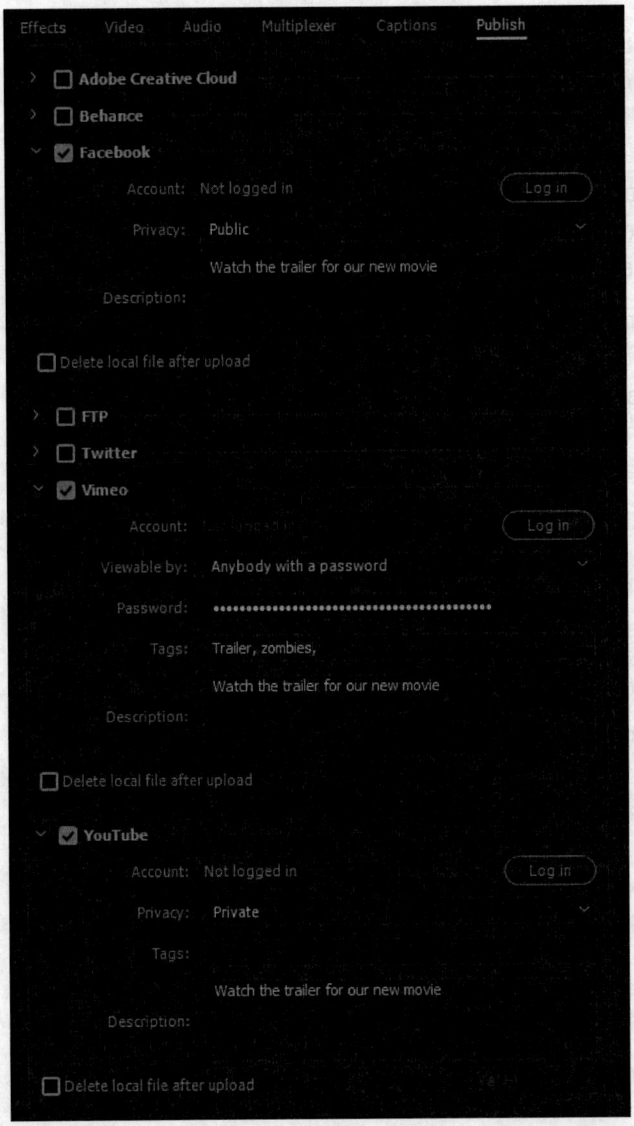

Figure 12-84. *The auto-publish settings can be saved as part of a preset. Privacy settings are supported, of course*

A Google Video Hacker's Tips on Encoding for YouTube

Colleen Henry, Video Hacker at Google Video Infrastructure, has some suggestions to help you get the best video quality on YouTube. Since Google owns YouTube, we should listen to her.

It's important to think of the files you upload to YouTube as golden masters, as they will be used as source material to generate video streams for years to come. Simply put, the better the quality of the file you upload to YouTube today, the better quality the viewer's experience will be throughout your video's life on YouTube.

As displays increase in size, compression techniques become more efficient, playback devices become more sophisticated, and internet connections improve, so will the quality YouTube will be able to provide to the viewers of your videos. This means, while you may reach a limit on perceived benefits from higher bitrates or more efficient encoding if you were to test it today, that does not mean you should stop there. You will see a huge benefit over the lifetime of your video being available on YouTube, as internet speeds, hardware, and software evolve. Upload the best quality video that you can create and squeeze through your internet connection!

The following are bonus tips:

- Many encoders can spend more CPU time to create a much more efficient file. If you have a powerful computer, but a slow internet connection, look into using more complex and efficient encoding to save upload time.

- You can noticeably improve the quality of your video on YouTube by using a sophisticated, scene aware, denoising filter prior to uploading.

- Keyframe interval doesn't really matter much at this moment in time, but please keep it under 5 for VOD.

- The sample rate of your audio should match your source's sample rate in which it was produced.

- If you make sure to use a streaming format, like an mkv, .mp4 or a .mov, with the metadata at the front of the container we will begin processing your video WHILE you are uploading it, drastically reducing overall turnaround time. This will make things MUCH faster, with no negative side effect. You can add the metadata atom to the front of your file with something qtfaststart, or select it when you are creating the file in Squeeze, Episode, etc.

- It is ideal to use constant quality encoding. This will let you create a high quality variable bitrate file, at the speed of a single pass. It will maintain a consistent target quality throughout the file, rather than trying to allocate bits to hit an arbitrary bitrate, which can easily under-shoot or over-shoot, and with two pass, take extra long to create.

- You can put uncompressed PCM audio in an .mov or .mkv container and deliver it to us if you like. However, make sure not to create multiple discrete mono streams when you do it.

Source: streamingmedia.com/Articles/Editorial/Featured-Articles/Encoding-for-YouTube-How-to-Get-the-Best-Results-83876.aspx, *which is an old article with some outdated info about Premiere, but the update from Google is good.*

HDR Export for YouTube

If you have HDR footage and an HDR-capable system, including an HDR monitor, you can deliver H.265 HDR video to YouTube (Figure 12-85). In addition to the video, the file needs correct metadata. According to Google, the only software that exports standards-compliant HDR metadata is DaVinci Resolve (January 2017).

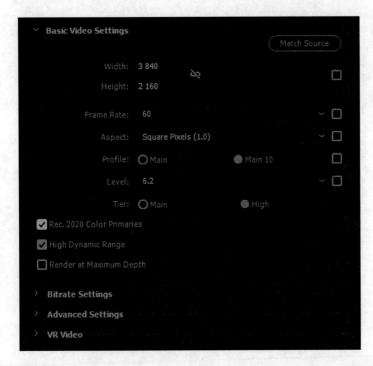

Figure 12-85. *To export H.265 HDR files, you must use the Main 10 Profile and check the Rec.2020 Color Primaries checkbox*

For files exported from Premiere with missing metadata, you'll need to add the metadata manually. Google recommends the YouTube HDR Metadata tool, found at `github.com/youtubehdr/hdr_metadata`.

To avoid trouble, read the recommendations from YouTube before you upload your HDR movie: `support.google.com/youtube/answer/7126552`. See Figure 12-86.

HDR video requirements

Once you upload a video, YouTube supports all resolutions and will auto-convert HDR video to SDR videos when necessary.

Upload requirements ∧

Resolution	720p, 1080p, 1440p, 2160p *For best results, use UHD rather than DCI widths (e.g. 3840x1600 instead of 4096x1716).*
Frame rate	23.976, 24, 25, 29.97, 30, 48, 50, 59.94, 60
Color primaries	Rec. 2020 or Rec. 709
EOTF	HLG (BT.2100)* or PQ (SMPTE ST 2084)
Video bitrate	For H.264 encoded, use the recommended upload encoding setting.
Audio	Same as the recommended upload encoding setting

* HLG playback currently has limited playback support.

HDR video file encoding ∧

Container	Encoding
MOV	H.264 10 bit
	ProRes 422
	ProRes 4444
	DNxHR HQX
MP4	H.264 10 bit,
	DNxHR HQX
MKV	H.264 10 bit
	VP9 profile 2
	ProRes 422
	ProRes 4444
	DNxHR HQX

HDR metadata ∧

In order to be processed, HDR videos must be tagged with the correct transfer function (PQ or HLG), color primaries (Rec. 2020 or Rec. 709), and matrix (Rec. 2020 or Rec. 709).

HDR videos using PQ signaling should also contain information about the display it was mastered on (SMPTE ST 2086 mastering metadata) and about the brightness of the content (CEA 861-3 MaxFALL and MaxCLL). If it's missing, we assume the content was mastered on a Sony BVM-X300 display.

Currently, MKV is the only container format to support SMPTE ST 2086 and CEA 861-3 metadata.

Figure 12-86. *YouTube HDR requirements*

HDR support in Premiere feels a bit limited now, but it will definitely get better. If you're new to HDR, you must read up. Good sources for info are the white papers directly from the sources. You can find the white paper on Dolby Vision here: dolby.com/us/en/technologies/dolby-vision/dolby-vision-white-paper.pdf.

Beyond 4K Export

The max size you can export depends on the format and the codec. The CineForm codec supports 8K video with 4K height. So do the H.265 format, the WebM format (install free plug-in), OpenEXR, and the Grass Valley HQX codec in QuickTime wrapper (install free codec). DPX supports up to 16K with a max height of 8K!

Several formats support the standard 4K sizes, like H.264 and the JPEG 2000 MXP format, and of course the ones just mentioned—plus many more.

Set Thumbnail, aka Poster Frame

AME cannot set the poster frame/thumbnail that the video file gets when it's on your computer. It's Finder on MacOS and Explorer on Windows that randomly pick a frame about three seconds in and use that as the poster frame (Figure 12-87). This random choice may or may not be a good one, and you have no control over which one is shown.

Figure 12-87. *Use iTunes to change the poster frame that computers display for the video file*

You can use iTunes to change the thumbnail. This is the only reason I still have iTunes on my computer. Export a still frame from the video—or create one from scratch in Photoshop. Then, import and select the video in iTunes, right-click, and choose *Get Info*. Change the image/artwork from there (Figure 12-88). You can drag an image from the desktop or a folder right into the UI.

Figure 12-88. *iTunes' Get Info panel*

Some people also recommend the Media Monkey software for this, but I've never tried it: mediamonkey. com/information/free/.

Gamma Shift Problems

A very common question is *"Why does my H.264 video have less color and a different gamma after export"*? And the answer is very often *"Because you watch it in QuickTime Player."* QuickTime Player is probably the worst way to watch your H.264 MP4 videos if you want accurate colors, especially on a Windows system. The free VLC Player is a lot more accurate, and so is the free PotPlayer. And—surprisingly—among the most accurate ones is the built-in one in Windows 10.

Different video players have variations between full and limited dynamic range. They can use 0-255, 16-235, or 16-255 and add different gamma/contrast/hue interpretations. Then, you can play back video from different places on the net (Vimeo, Facebook, YouTube, etc.) in different browsers on different OSes. It's a huge mess!

Figure 12-89 shows how different an H.264 video in MP4 wrapper (exported using the YouTube preset) looks when played back on my system. Each player is shown both with the default video settings in the Nvidia driver (which means the player sets the dynamic range) and with Dynamic Range set to *Full*.

Figure 12-89. *From top left: Premiere Pro, built-in Windows 10 player, VLC player, Vimeo played in Edge browser, Vimeo played in Chrome browser, QuickTime player, PotPlayer, Edge browser, Chrome browser*

There are some additional settings that can affect the video levels on your system as well. Your GPU driver settings can especially throw things off. Figure 12-90 shows the Video Color settings in the driver for my Nvidia card.

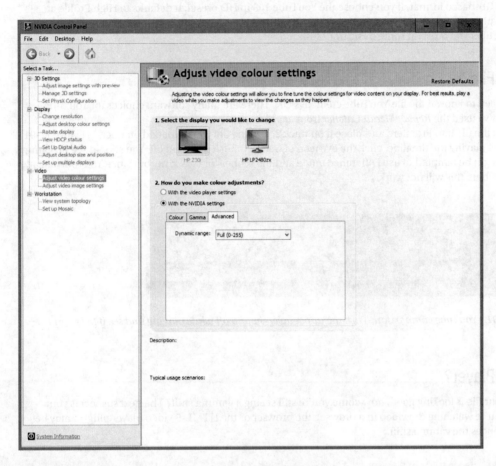

Figure 12-90. *Changing your Video Color settings to Full (0-255) in the Nvidia Driver Dynamic Range settings fixes the gamma issue in most players*

Switching this from Limited (16-235) to Full (0-255) makes the gamma shift in most players go away or be less dramatic. The default is to let the video player decide this, and we have little control over what the player does. This setting makes sure all video players behave the same.

There's a big problem with this method. It only works on *your* system. You have no control over which player your viewers will use or what GPU driver settings they have. Most people don't even know how to change them.

As if all these problems aren't enough, monitor profiling (often wrongly called monitor calibration) can also make your video look completely different in different software. Software that supports color management will take the profiles and color spaces into account, while software without such support will ignore them. True monitor calibration will not cause any trouble.

Fix for Gamma Shifts on YouTube

If you export a YUV-based format, the YouTube engine shouldn't touch gamma at all. It may do so if you export an RGB-based format. If you choose the YouTube 1080p HD preset, it defaults to High Profile at Level 4.2, which means it's YUV, so you should be fine. If you experience gamma shifts after uploading the clip to YouTube, you must do some basic troubleshooting.

Is It the File?

First, you need to know if the file YouTube created is OK. There are many software choices for YouTube download. I've used the *Replay Media Catcher* from `applian.com`.

Import the file into Premiere and place it on track 2, and the file you uploaded on track 1 (Figure 12-91). While you're playing the timeline, click the eye icon of track 2 to turn it on and off. You should see no gamma shift. You might be tempted to use Difference mode and the scopes for checking, but since YouTube usually adds a bit of blur, this will not work.

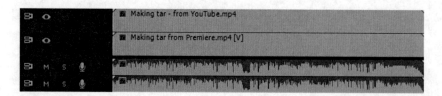

Figure 12-91. *YouTube comparison. Turn the upper layer on and off while playing and see if the gamma changes*

Is It the Player?

OK, so if your file is looking good, how come you're still seeing a gamma shift? The next suspect is your player. If you're watching the video in a browser, the browser or the HTML-5 video player plug-in may be what introduces the gamma shift.

Something Else?

If the player doesn't seem to do anything suspicious, it could be your display, some color profile left from monitor calibration, or some settings in the GPU driver. See the previous section, on "Gamma Shift Problems".

Why Game Videos Look Worse Than Real-life Footage

If you do screen recording of games and upload the edited files to YouTube, you will be a bit disappointed. Gaming videos have lots of sharp details, no motion blur, and often high frame rates. These are hard things to compress.

Because the game video has more details, it would need a higher bit rate to get the same visual quality, but it doesn't get it. To limit bandwidth, YouTube will lower the bit rate, and this makes the artifacts from the YouTube recompression really stand out.

So, the degradation is more noticeable because you start with something that's got more details than real-life video, and you end up with something with more blur, blockiness, and smear. It literally starts out with better quality and ends up worse.

More Control over the H.264 Export with x264

If the built-in H.264 export doesn't give you all the options and control you want, you can buy the x264 PRO Encoder plug-in from x264pro.com. It reveals a lot more options than the built-in one from Main Concept (Figure 12-92).

Figure 12-92. x264 export settings

Some examples of what x264 can do: you can set the Color Space to Rec.709 or Rec.601 and the Entropy Coding to CAVLC or CABAC (out of the box, Premiere and AME do CABAC only), and make custom GOP encoding settings.

Some users claim that files encoded with x264 have fewer gamma problems than the ones from the default H.264 exporter in Premiere and AME. Read about CAVLC here: en.wikipedia.org/wiki/Context-adaptive_variable-length_coding. Read about CABAC here: en.wikipedia.org/wiki/Context-adaptive_binary_arithmetic_coding.

Alternatives to H.264

H.264 has some potential issues with licensing, so we don't really know if it's going to be free for video enthusiasts and professionals to watch and encode H.264-encoded files forever. For this reason, free and open formats like WebM and Ogg Theora have been developed as alternatives to H.264.

Also, the maximum resolution for H.264 (at level 5.2) is 4096 × 2304 pixels, so it's just enough for 4K. For bigger frames, a new codec is needed, and even at 4K the H.264 bit rate gets pretty high.

H.265—HEVC

The H.265 High Efficiency Video Coding (en.wikipedia.org/wiki/High_Efficiency_Video_Coding) is a successor to H.264 as we move into 4K streaming and beyond. It promises about half the data rates at "the same subjective image quality," whatever that means. It's more complex, and consequently more demanding, to play back and to encode. H.265 has a max resolution of 8192 × 4320 pixels, so it supports 8K. You can export frame rates up to 300 fps.

Just like its predecessor, H.265 has various profiles and levels for different uses. Premiere can export Main (8-bit) and Main 10 (8-bit or 10-bit) profiles at up to level 6.2 (Figure 12-93). As with H.264, a level is a set of constraints for a bit stream. The H.265 format complicates things by adding tiers to the levels, named Main and High, which are guaranteed be confused with the Main profile.

H.265 may be riddled with some of the same licensing issues that H.264 has seen.

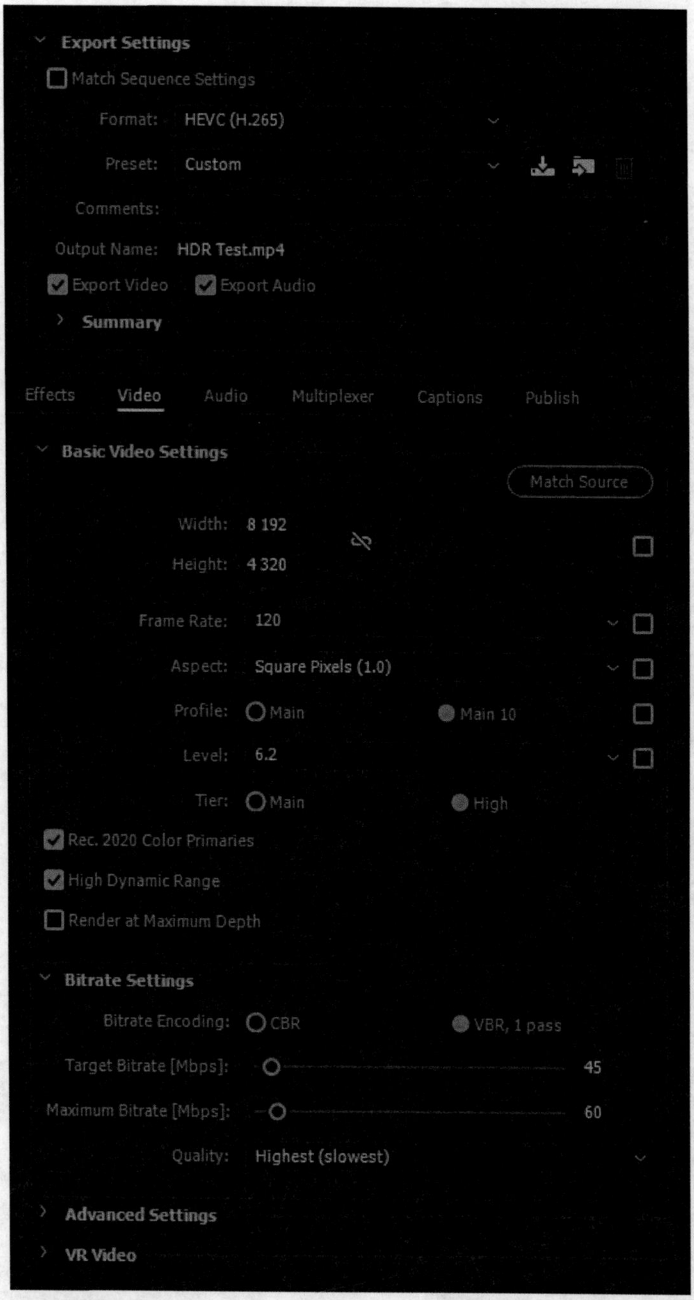

Figure 12-93. *H.265 export*

WebM, aka VP9

WebM is an open, royalty-free media-file format designed for the web, developed by Google, and supported by the Alliance for Open Media (aomedia.org). It's got fewer codec profiles and sub-options, so is easier to use. With VP9 compression, WebM is a competitor to H.265, claiming the same quality as H.264 at half the data rate. With VP8 compression, it's a competitor to H.264. YouTube uses WebM in their HTML5 player. Read more about WebM on their official web site: webmproject.org/.

Premiere doesn't export WebM out of the box, but you can download Brendan Bolles' Open Movie Plug-In for Premiere to open and export WebM in Premiere and AME (Figure 12-94): fnordware.com/WebM/.

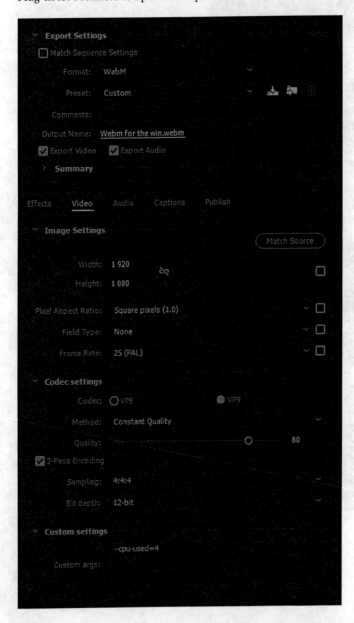

Figure 12-94. *With the Open Movie plug-in, you can export WebM from Premiere*

Compared to other exports, this is *very* slow, partly because it doesn't use all the processor power available when analyzing the video, and partly because it's so complex. Encoding VP9 with Encoding Quality set to *Best*, it takes more than 12 hours just to export even a 30-second spot—but the quality is fantastic. At lower quality settings, it's faster, but don't expect real-time encoding.

Make sure you read the manual to get the most out of the plug-in: github.com/fnordware/AdobeWebM/ tree/master/src/premiere/doc.

Animated GIFs

Well, they are not exactly an alternative for H.264 in all cases, but animated GIFs are very popular in social media because they're lightweight and play just about anywhere.

To create an animated GIF, create a short clip in a sequence that matches the footage. Set the playback to *loop* so you can see how the GIF will look when it loops.

Make a new sequence at the desired resolution, say 400 × 400 px. Then, nest the sequence containing the clip into this non-standard sequence and scale and reposition it so the main action is within the frame.

Export your social media masterpiece by choosing *Animated GIF* in the Export Settings. If smooth movement in your GIF isn't critical, I recommend that you lower the frame rate to around 10 fps to save even more bandwidth.

Still-Image Export

Premiere can export a still from the source monitor or the program monitor, and from the timeline. With one of the monitors, or the timeline, active, hit the shortcut for Export Still Frame, or click the little camera icon in the transport controls.

You get to choose between eight formats on Windows and six on MacOS (no BMP or GIF), but you have no further control over quality settings or other parameters (Figure 12-95). Luckily, JPG exports will always be saved with a high-quality setting.

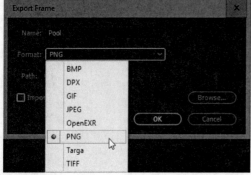

Figure 12-95. *Export still frame*

If you need to export a still image with an alpha channel, make sure you choose a format that supports alpha. Figure 12-96 shows a PNG file with alpha.

Figure 12-96. *Make sure you choose a format that support alpha channels if you need transparency*

Beware of Non-Square Pixels

Premiere always exports stills in the same frame size as your sequence. If you're editing in a non-square pixel-format sequence, you'll need to convert the exported file to square pixels in Photoshop or another image editing app. As a quick workaround, you can nest the sequence into another one with square pixels and export from there. See Figure 12-97.

You can export still images from the timeline, from the source monitor, and from the program monitor.

Figure 12-97. *Beware of picture aspect ratio problems if your sequence has non-square pixels. This image got squished*

My preferred choice is to create a Photoshop droplet (Figure 12-98) on which I can throw the exported frame in order to auto-convert it to square pixels and my chosen format and quality. Read about Photoshop actions and droplets in chapter 11 on integration with other software.

Figure 12-98. *PS droplet icon*

Forget about DPI

In the printing business, DPI (dots per inch) makes a lot of sense; the higher the DPI, the better quality print you get, until your raster or ink-drop size limits the resolution. However, there is no DPI in digital video. We only have pixels. Those pixels can be displayed on everything from smartphones to 60-inch screens and larger, and the DPI will vary wildly.

■ **Note**   If your HD monitor is 7.34 inches, your DPI is 300. In 4K, your screen can be a whopping 15.7 inches if you want to maintain 300 DPI resolution.

According to printshop logic, a smartphone HD display would be much better than a nice 50-inch display because the same number of pixels would be gathered on a smaller surface.

The video standard sets the frame size, so a still exported from a Full HD 1080p timeline will be 1920 × 1080 pixels—always. What DPI settings it gets is pretty much irrelevant, but it will probably be 96. We shouldn't care, and neither should print people—but they sometimes do.

I once shot some DV footage of a crime scene before the rest of the press arrived and was kept at a distance by the police. When it was aired on the news, a local newspaper wanted to use a still image. So, I sent them a 720 × 576 pixel JPG, because that's the size of PAL DV. They called me back and told me they needed an image with a higher DPI. I opened it in Photoshop and changed the DPI to 300 without changing the pixels. It's all metadata, actually.

They were happy with this image, which had the exact same pixels, and blew it up over half of the front page! This effectively lowered the DPI to around 45—and no, it didn't look very sharp. . . The person who did this clearly had no idea.

Export to Tape

You can export a sequence or clip to videotape in a supported VTR. I will not cover export to DV and HDV via FireWire, because I think you should not export to those formats in this day and age.

But, you may be in a production environment where high-end tape formats are still a valid way to distribute your shows. In that case, you'll need a third-party I/O card with SDI out. This card will then have drivers that you need to keep up to date, and its own preferences and settings.

Generally, you'll have to enable Mercury Transmit by choosing your I/O device in the **Preferences ➤ Playback** settings. If you have red, unrendered areas in the timeline, you need to render those first, or you risk dropping frames.

The web pages for your I/O device should provide the info you need. The most common are Matrox, AJA, and Blackmagic Design: matrox.com/en/, aja.com/, blackmagicdesign.com/.

Making Dailies

Need to push out dailies from REDRAW, ArriRAW, Cinema DNG, F65, or other recordings? Here's a way to output one file with all the footage in one sequence.

Do a quick rough cut or just throw everything in a sequence, add LUT to adjustment layer, add clip name effect and timecode effect on same adjustment layer, and set them to take timecode and clip name from Video 1. Making dailies can be automated by building an effects preset that has all these settings applied.

You can do pretty much the same thing by adding the same effects/overlays in the Export panel (Figure 12-99). Either way will do. If you need separate video files for each source file, Adobe Media Encoder is a better choice.

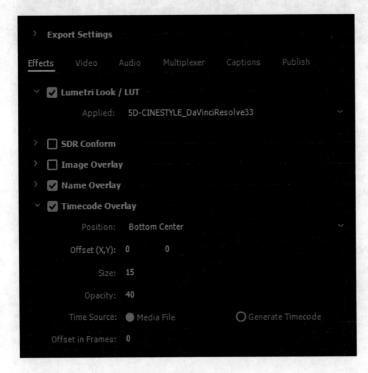

Figure 12-99. Dailies with TC, LUT, and name overlay

Export good- and medium-quality H.264, ProRes, and other files via AME Queue and set it to auto-FTP when finished. Of course, you should make a preset for this procedure, so you just add an adjustment layer, throw on your Dailies Effect preset, and export.

If you need to export dailies as separate clips, select all clips in your bin, right-click, and choose *Export Media*. Add LUT, timecode overlay, and name overlay and set it to export via AME Queue and auto-FTP (Figure 12-100). This should also be saved as a preset, named *Dailies Separate Files*.

Figure 12-100. *Dailies Export Preset 1080*

Shiny Disc Export

Although the demand for DVDs and Blu-rays is rapidly diminishing, some customers still want a shiny disc to put in the drawer. So, we need to make some. If you're creating a DVD, I recommend that you nest your HD sequences into an SD sequence, right-click the nested sequence, and choose *Set to Frame Size*. This will give you a good preview of how the resulting video will look.

If you're going out to Blu-ray, you can follow pretty much the same steps that follow, but choose MPEG2 Blu-ray instead of MPEG2-DVD.

The latest version of Encore is CS6, and you have access to it if you're subscribing to Creative Cloud. This document describes how to download it: helpx.adobe.com/encore/kb/encore-cs6-installed-cc.html.

Before you start building your DVD, make sure you gather all the assets into one folder so it's easy to find everything later (Figure 12-101).

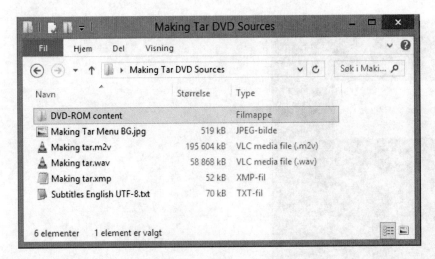

Figure 12-101. *Collect all the assets before you start building your DVD or Blu-ray project*

Add Chapter Markers

Scrub your timeline, and wherever you want a chapter marker on your DVD, hit **M** to create a marker. Turn every marker into a chapter marker and give them a name. This is important! If you don't give them names, they will not import to Encore. By default, chapter markers in Premiere are red. The markers in Figure 12-102 have names and will carry over as chapter markers in Encore.

You know you have a chapter marker when it's got a red icon and the name appears when you hover your cursor over it. You can also see it clearly in the Markers panel.

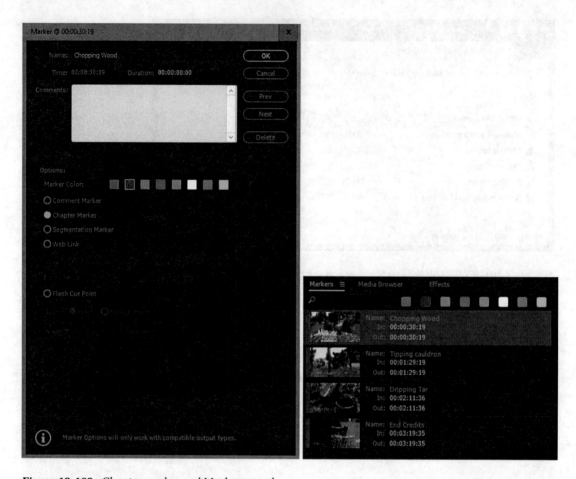

Figure 12-102. *Chapter marker and Markers panel*

Export to DVD Formats

In the Export dialog, choose *MPEG2-DVD* and *Widescreen 16:9*. If you want to get rid of the black pillar boxes, choose *Scale To Fill* in the Source Scaling drop-down menu in the Output tab above the preview image (Figure 12-103).

Figure 12-103. *Choose MPEG-2 for DVD as your format. Metadata like chapter markers are stored in an XMP XML sidecar file*

The pillar boxes will not show when played on a DVD player connected to a TV, but may show when the DVD is played on a PC or Mac. Older versions of Premiere used to stretch the image horizontally to fit. If you absolutely want the image to fit perfectly like it used to—and destroy your aspect ratio—you can. Just choose *Stretch To Fill* instead of *Scale To Fill*.

I generally choose *PCM Audio*, but you can also export Dolby Digital. Set Multiplexer to *None*. I've found that exporting as progressive increases the quality, especially on software DVD players. I've also increased the bit rates from the preset—but don't go much above 7.5 for the maximum bit rate.

Now, export. This results in three files: M2V video, WAV audio, and an XMP file. The XMP file has the chapter markers, so *do not delete it!*

■ **Note**   Markers may not be frame accurate in Encore since they can only be placed on I-frames in the MPEG GOP. If you want frame-accurate markers, you could try this: change the Bitrate Encoding to 2-pass. Theoretically, this will analyze the edit and place I-frames at your cut points. So, if you place the markers on cut points, you should increase your chances of getting frame-accurate markers.

The marker metadata in Premiere has changed since Encore went out of development, so you need to import your exported .m2v and .wav files as a timeline, and not as an asset. If you import them as a timeline, the Premiere markers will be preserved, all the way through to the shiny disc.

Get Free PDF on Shiny Disc Export

The 2014 version of this book had a section on creating DVDs in Adobe Encore (Figure 12-104). You can download this section for free from PremierePro.net. Note that the overlapping info has been updated in the 2017 version (the one you're reading now): premierepro.net/dvd-authoring/shinydisc/.

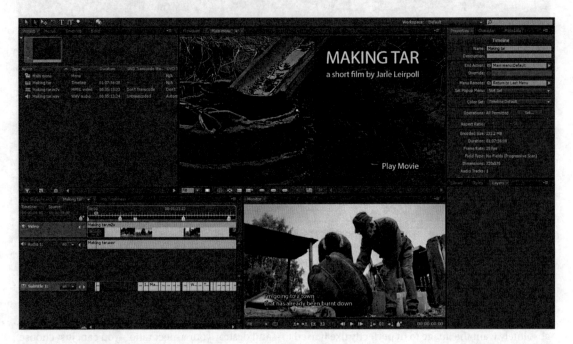

Figure 12-104. Encore workspace

Online DVD Info and Tools

Jim Taylor's book "DVD Demystified" on the DVD format was the bible on DVD when it was published. It has a web site with lots of technical info for the nerds: dvddemystified.com/dvdfaq.html.

If you're on the other side of the fence and don't want to worry about formats and technical stuff, you can use MediaZilla, which can output your videos in lots of ways, including DVD and Blu-ray: mediazilla.com/.

Common Causes for Export Failure

There are so many things that can go wrong during an export that I can't even begin to cover them all here. However, there are a few issues that seem to pop up more often than others, so here we go.

Wrong Frame Rate

A 25 fps sequence exported to 29.97—or the other way around—will not show smooth movement. Make sure you match the sequence fame rate or do a proper conversion.

Pillar Boxes and Letterboxes

When the frame size of the exported file doesn't match the sequence, you'll get black borders somewhere. Make sure your sequence and your export settings match. Also, make sure you're watching the output, not the source, in the Export dialog. This way, you'll spot the problem before you start the export.

Error Compiling Movie

This message, followed by "Unknown Error," doesn't really help. What went wrong? In the newest versions of Premiere, we get additional info. The error now gives some more diagnostic info, such as the timecode in the sequence where something went wrong. This can be very useful when tracking down the cause of failure. The following section discusses a few of the possible problems.

Unsupported Characters in File Names

Avoid forward and backward slashes (/ and \) and other special characters in your file names, as some operating systems may struggle with them. Letters, numbers, and underscores take you a long way, so you should be OK without the special characters.

Network Disk Write Permissions

If you are exporting to a network disk and there is a problem with write permissions, the export will fail. Try exporting to a local drive, and manually copy the file to the network drive. If that solves the problem, you need to talk to the network admin and get the permissions you need so you avoid this in the future.

Corrupt Media Files in Sequence

If the encode fails at the same point in the timeline every time, it could be that one or more media files are corrupted. Make a duplicate sequence and delete the second half. If the export works now, the corrupt media is in the first half. If not, it's in the remaining half. Keep on making copies and halving the remaining parts of the timeline until you find out what media file is causing the trouble. Quite often, it is a JPG file or an MP3 file—but it could also be any video file or an effect like the morph cut.

When you find a corrupted file or the offending effect, you have two choices: remove it from the film or try repairing it by converting the file to another format using third-party software and then replace it in the timeline.

Wrong Disk Formatting

Failing at the same point can also have another reason: some disks, and many USB thumb drives, are formatted as FAT32, not as NTFS, exFAT, or HFS+. Since the FAT32 file system only supports file sizes up to 4 GB, exporting a long movie with good settings will fail. Make sure your drives can handle large video files, and use a modern file system.

Big Images and Layered Photoshop Files

Using many large images or layered Photoshop files can put a lot of stress on encoding. If you don't need separate layers, it's best to flatten and maybe even resize these images prior to encoding.

Big Multi-camera Edits That Aren't Flattened

If your multi-camera edit still has nested multi-camera source sequences in it—especially if they have lots of cameras with lots of audio tracks—this will slow down the export. Flatten before export to avoid slow exports.

Adobe Help on Fixing Error Compiling Movie

The online Help has a special URL for info on "Error Compiling Movie" errors: helpx.adobe.com/premiere-pro/kb/error-compiling-movie-rendering-or.html.

Handbrake

If you need to convert a video file to make it work correctly on export, Handbrake is a good alternative: handbrake.fr/.

Don't Import Sequences Natively

If you're exporting via AME and it fails, try to switch off the preference for *Import sequences natively*, and then try to export again (Figure 12-105).

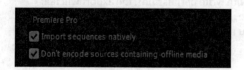

Figure 12-105. *Premiere preferences in AME*

Use and Share Your Export Presets

One way to avoid export problems is to make your own export presets instead of wading through settings each time. This eliminates human error in stressed situations. If you're on a team, you should all use the same presets to get consistent quality across the workgroup. When you've created an export preset in the Export dialog window, you can share it by **Alt-clicking** the *Save Preset* button. This throws up an Export Preset dialog, and you can decide where to save it.

Tweeted by @LuisSilvaTV

Commandment #4: Thou shall not name thy exports "final" "final_v2" "finalv3_temp" "final_v4_kindofapproved_notreally"

Summary

Premiere and AME can export to almost any format you want, but to get the best quality output, you need to know a few things about different codecs and formats. You also need a thorough knowledge of the technical choices in the sequence settings and export settings. All this is provided in this chapter, and you should now have a solid foundation to build on.

I don't expect you to remember every little detail about every format and codec, but if you have a general idea of their different uses, you will make better choices while editing and when you do the export.

APPENDIX A

Troubleshooting

By Jarle Leirpoll and Andy Edwards

When it comes to troubleshooting, it helps to think of software as what it really is: a collection of files that live on your SSD or HDD drive. So, when something goes terribly wrong, it's probably because one or more of these files are damaged or, as an IT engineer would say, corrupted–or just a setting that's been changed.

In this appendix, you'll get a good overview of the different files that Premiere needs and the settings that are most likely to cause trouble.

It Might Not Be a Premiere Pro Problem

When you experience crashes, playback problems, instability, export issues, and so on in Premiere, it's super frustrating. And it's easy to blame Premiere. After all, all the other software on your system is working fine, right?

But the real problem may be settings in other software, permissions issues, firewall settings, third-party plug-ins, and even hardware related.

Adobe System Requirements

Adobe has a web page dedicated to system requirements and recommendations for Adobe Premiere. Make sure your hardware meets the requirements, and then some. The minimum specs are not enough for high-end professional work. Go to the following:

helpx.adobe.com/premiere-pro/system-requirements.html

MediaInfo & MediaInfo Diff Apps

Two applications I always have installed on my edit system are MediaInfo and MediaInfo Diff. Have you ever wanted to dig into a video file and find all the specs about that file? Well, these two apps can help you answer those questions. Just open a file in MediaInfo and up pops all pertinent info on the file. See Figure A-1.

J. Leirpoll et al., *The Cool Stuff in Premiere Pro*, DOI 10.1007/978-1-4842-2890-6

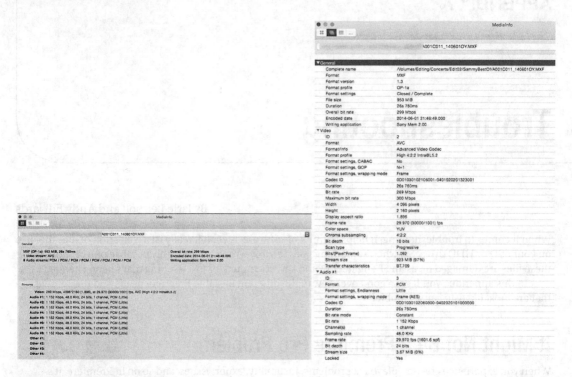

Figure A-1. *MediaInfo*

To use MediaInfo Diff, you import two files you want to compare. The program highlights in yellow everything it sees that is different between the files (Figure A-2). This is very helpful when checking codecs used, audio channels, frame size issues, and so forth. MediaInfo Diff is MacOS only.

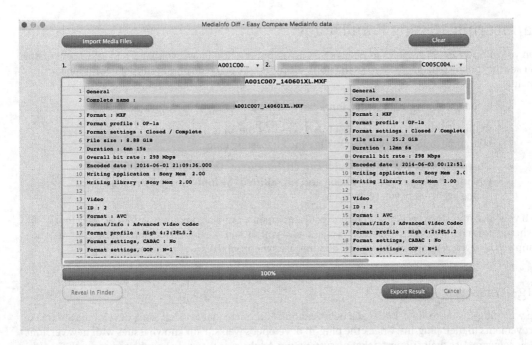

Figure A-2. *MediaInfo Diff*

It is available in the App Store or at mediaarea.net/en/MediaInfo and sourceforge.net/projects/mediainfo/.

Creative Cloud Firewall Access Points

Some of you might be working in a broadcast or corporate environment with an IT department that has a firewall to protect your network. If you are having problems with your Creative Cloud desktop application's communication with Adobe servers, you can check this page for specific sites you can whitelist in your Firewall rules: adobe.com/devnet/creativesuite/enterprisedeployment.html.

Firewall whitelist-specific document can be found here: helpx.adobe.com/content/dam/help/attachments/Creative_Cloud_for_enterprise_Service_Endpoints.pdf.

Creative Cloud Cleaner Tool

If you are having multiple issues with your Adobe applications, it might be a good idea to start fresh. Adobe has a tool you can download to remove all parts of your Creative Cloud applications that might have become corrupt. You can read about how to use this tool at the following Adobe web page: helpx.adobe.com/creative-cloud/kb/cc-cleaner-tool-installation-problems.html.

Trouble Syncing Your Settings

If you have trouble syncing your settings, there's something wrong with your Creative Cloud installation. If uninstalling all Creative Cloud applications, running the Creative Cloud Cleaner Tool, and reinstalling everything doesn't solve it, contact Adobe Support to get help fixing this: helpx.adobe.com/contact.html?step=CCSN.

Reappearing Missing Font Dialog

When you import motion graphics templates that use a font you don't have, you'll get a Missing Font dialog. If you see that dialog repeatedly for the same font, prompting you to sync missing Typekit fonts, check the following:

- Is the CC app running so that fonts can be synced?

- In the CC app, check under Assets ➤ Fonts that the fonts have been synced. This can take some time, as it also checks the sync for existing fonts.

- Quit the project and/or app and relaunch. Important: **Don't save the project after you may have ignored the dialog and substituted the font.** This will bring up the dialog again when you relaunch it!

If you have done the preceding steps correctly and open a project containing a graphic with that font, you should not see the Missing Fonts dialog again, and you should see the correct font in the graphic. The CC app will also give you a notification that all fonts are synchronized.

Plug-in Issues

Keep your plug-ins up-to-date. With each new version of Premiere that gets released, developers also make improvements to their plug-ins. Check the plug-in developer's web site for known issues with new versions of their software. Use their support ticketing system, not Adobe's, as they may have already seen the problem you are experiencing.

Using Illegal Characters Can Cause Issues

Illegal characters should not be used in file names, especially if you're working on shared network storage.

Try to use only a through z (upper- or lowercase) and zero through nine (0-9).

Some people also advise not to use the following characters inside of Premiere Pro. It never hurts to be careful. The following reserved characters are *NEVER* to be used:

< > : " / \ | ? *

Here are other helpful rules:

- Never use two consecutive dots (periods).

- Do not begin or end with a space when naming your folder or files.

- Do not use any of these common illegal characters/symbols:

  - # pound

  - < left angle bracket

  - $ dollar sign

  - + plus sign

  - % percent

  - > right angle bracket

  - ! exclamation point

  - ` backtick

- **&** ampersand
- ***** asterisk
- **'** single quotes
- **|** pipe
- **{** left bracket
- **?** question mark
- **"** double quotes
- **=** equal sign
- **}** right bracket
- **/** forward slash
- **:** colon
- **** backslash
- blank spaces
- **@** at sign

GPU Trouble on Mac Systems

If you own a Mac manufactured during one of the following periods, you *will* have lots of strange problems in Premiere: crashes, instability, playback problems, export problems, and so on. They will not go away until you have the GPU changed. Apple will do this for free.

Here is an article on faulty GPUs on MacBook Pros manufactured 2011-2013: macworld.co.uk/news/mac/widespread-2011-macbook-pro-failures-petition-lawsuit-repair-programme-3497935/.

Here is an article on faulty GPUs on MacPros manufactured in 2013: macrumors.com/2016/02/06/late-2013-mac-pro-video-issues-repair-program/.

Here is an article on faulty GPUs on MacPros manufactured in 2015: 9to5mac.com/2016/02/06/apple-mac-pro-repair-program-graphics-video/.

The team that edited *Deadpool* in Premiere and After Effects on six MacPro systems burned ten MacPros due to faulty GPUs(!), even though they had fans blowing air on the systems.

If you experience crashes in Premiere on a Mac, reading these articles may help:

/blogs.adobe.com/kevinmonahan/2014/09/10/premiere-pro-cc-freezing-on-startup-or-crashing-while-working-mac-os-x-10-9-and-later/

computerworld.com/article/3042583/apple-mac/how-to-use-apple-diagnostics-to-identify-mac-hardware-problems.html

Mac App Nap Settings

App Nap is an energy feature built into the Mac OS. It monitors applications to help reduce the power usage of your computer. For laptops, this is an efficient way to save battery life, but not so much for a tower or desktop Mac plugged into constant power. If you have multiple applications open—for example, Adobe Premiere, Adobe Media Encoder, and a web browser—App Nap will keep track of inactive applications and make them go into a paused state. If you are encoding with AME in the background and editing in Premiere at the same time, enabling the App Nap setting can lead to unwanted results. AME could go to sleep and not finish encoding if this setting is not turned off.

Depending on your OS version, you can take charge of these settings and prevent App Nap from interfering with your Adobe applications.

▓ **Note**   At the time of writing this tip, most CC2017 versions of the Adobe video and audio apps have been removing App Nap settings from the application info window, so check your version of software and see if it still applies.

Apple Deep Dive into App Nap

Here's some info on App Nap directly from the source.

developer.apple.com/library/content/documentation/Performance/Conceptual/power_efficiency_
guidelines_osx/AppNap.html

Turn It Off

Go to your *Applications* folder and get info on each of the Adobe video and audio applications' icons (Figure A-3). Check the box for *Prevent App Nap*. The latest versions of Premiere Pro and Adobe Media Encoder will turn off App Nap automatically, so you shouldn't have to do it manually.

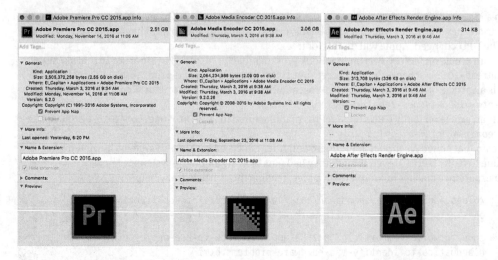

Figure A-3. *After Effects' App Nap setting can be found under the Render Engine icon, not the application's*

System Preferences Energy Pane

Additionally, you can turn App Nap off in the Energy Saver settings of System Preferences. Uncheck the box called *Enable Power Nap* (Figure A-4).

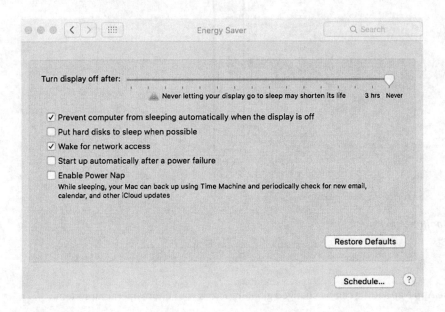

Figure A-4. *System preferences for App Nap*

Activity Monitor

If you launch the Activity Monitor, click on the Energy tab to see a list of all your system details that have App Nap enabled or disabled. See Figure A-5.

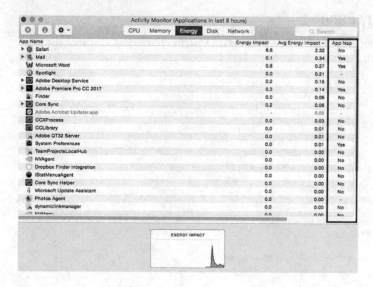

Figure A-5. Activity Monitor–App Nap

Terminal Option

For advanced users, the App Nap setting can be changed globally across your entire operating system.

■ **Warning**　Please be careful when using the terminal, as you can cause serious harm to your computer if you do not apply the proper instructions.

You can find the terminal commands required on this web site: osxdaily.com/2014/05/13/disable-app-nap-mac-os-x/.

General Premiere Pro Troubleshooting Tips

Of course, your problems may also be caused by Premiere Pro. Let's say you've ruled out the hardware, plug-ins, and network issues as the root of your problem. Then, chances are it's a problem within Premiere.

■ **Note**　Files on computers can get corrupted, and Premiere Pro uses and creates a lot of files: media cache files, workspace files, effects presets files, preferences files, keyboard shortcuts files, export presets files, and so on. If they get corrupted, something will break.

Then there's the actual Premiere Pro project file (.prproj), which can also get corrupted. Since it's got an XML-like file structure, an error in one part doesn't mean that the whole project stops working, but your sequences can get corrupted—or your bins, or the project's workspace, and so on. Your trouble will not go away until it's fixed.

Things to Try When Premiere Pro Is Acting Up

The following list was compiled over a long time using info from many user forums, Facebook groups, emails with Adobe engineers, and personal experience.

Quit Premiere, Reboot Computer, Launch Premiere Again

Please don't laugh. This has solved many issues for many editors. Sign out of Creative Cloud and sign in again. If that doesn't help, sign out, reboot the system, and sign in again. This can solve codec licensing problems, sync settings problems, and so forth. See here: `helpx.adobe.com/creative-cloud/help/sign-in-out-activate-apps.html`.

Update Your GPU Drivers

GPUs are responsible for drawing the user interface (UI), for de-Bayering some RAW formats, for effects and transforms, and for displaying the video. They are crucial to a Premiere Pro editing system. Premiere is only tested with a handful of the latest drivers. If your drivers are old, you will most likely get into trouble. Keep the GPU drivers up-to-date to avoid trouble, but don't go for beta versions–use only the solid ones.

If you have a CUDA GPU, ensure that the Mercury Playback Engine is set to CUDA, not OpenCL.

If you have an AMD GPU, make sure CUDA drivers are not installed. CUDA is an Nvidia thing. It should be safe with the newest versions of CUDA drivers and Premiere, but why gamble on that? See here:

> `blogs.adobe.com/kevinmonahan/2014/03/19/avoid-installing-nvidia-cuda-drivers-on-computers-with-amd-gpus/`
>
> Nvidia drivers: `nvidia.com/Download/index.aspx`
>
> AMD drivers: `support.amd.com/en-us/download`
>
> Intel drivers: `intel.com/content/www/us/en/support/detect.html`

Delete the Media Cache Files

These are known to be corrupted very easily, and forcing Premiere to rebuild them can solve many strange problems. See the later, separate section on Media Cache files for details on how to do this.

Import Bad Project into a Fresh One

This can sometimes "heal" the project file XML and make a corrupted project work again.

Use After Effects to Clean the Project File

Even if Premiere can't open the project, After Effects may be able to. In After Effects, click **File ➤ Import ➤ Adobe Premiere Pro Project**. Some effects and lots of other things will be gone, but your basic editing decisions should be intact. Then, click **File ➤ Export ➤ Adobe Premiere Pro Project**. Open the new project in Premiere and see what's missing.

Fixing a "This Project Could Not Be loaded" Error

If you have used elements from a Creative Cloud library in your project, you may get this message: *"This project could not be loaded. It may be damaged or contain outdated elements."* Opening an auto-saved file will probably not work either.

A user reported that he could make Premiere open the project again after renaming the *Creative Cloud Libraries* folder, located under **/Users/<username>/Library/Application Support/Adobe**. The corresponding folder on Windows would be found at **\Users\<username>\AppData\Roaming\Adobe**.

That nuked all his libraries, of course, so do this at your own risk! It's a good idea to make backups of your libraries. The Libraries panel menu has an option to export libraries.

Pro Maintenance Tools

I haven't used this myself, but Digital Rebellion offers the (MacOS only) *Pro Maintenance Tools* that can repair corrupted project files: digitalrebellion.com/promaintenance/.

XML:Wrench

This is not for the faint of heart, so proceed with care. Premiere Pro uses an XML-based project file. The .prproj file is actually a zipped XML file. So, if you un-zip it with software like 7ZIP (7-zip.org/), you can open it in XML:Wrench and see if the XML is properly formatted. If it finds errors, you can fix them manually and save again, then zip it again and save as a .prproj file.

If you're on MacOS, try the online version of XML:Wrench: xmlwrench.com/.

Trash Your Preferences

A corrupted preferences file can cause a lot of different problems. Corrupted preferences files are such a big problem on MacOS that resetting preferences is the go-to solution for problem solving. On Windows, it happens very seldom, but it's not unheard of. Press and hold **Alt** (Option) while the application is starting. You can release the key when the splash screen appears. To trash preferences and plug-in cache at the same time, hold down **Shift+Alt** (Windows) or **Shift+Option** (MacOS) while the application is starting.

Check the Permissions (MacOS Only)

Make sure Premiere can write to its own folders. MacOS is known to mess with permissions for the Adobe folders in Preferences, Applications Support, and Documents—especially when you install security updates. You can reset them manually, do a repair permissions routine in MacOS, or reinstall Premiere Pro. See here:
macworld.com/article/1052220/software-utilities/repairpermissions.html blogs.adobe.com/kevinmonahan/2014/09/10/premiere-pro-cc-freezing-on-startup-or-crashing-while-working-mac-os-x-10-9-and-later/

Delete Your Preview Files

They're usually located in a subfolder in the same folder as your project file.

Remove Plug-ins

Third-party plug-ins may cause lots of strange behavior in Premiere if they're badly written, or if you've neglected to update them. You can use the uninstaller from the plug-in manufacturer, the Remove Applications feature in your OS, or remove them manually. See here: `forums.adobe.com/thread/1333832?tstart=0`.

Change the Preview Codec

Change it to one that matches your footage in **Sequence ➤ Sequence Settings ➤ Video Previews**.

Disconnect Third-Party Hardware

To make sure the problem is in Premiere, not with third-party hardware or drivers, disconnect the hardware. If playback is smooth in Premiere, but drops frames when you connect your I/O card, then the problem is likely to be with the drivers for the hardware.

Disable App Nap (MacOS Only)

On MacOs, disable App Nap for Premiere and Adobe Media Encoder. This should not be required on newer versions; they should do it automatically. See the section on Mac App Nap Settings above for details.

Create a New User

If everything still fails, create a new user on the system to make sure your user or your settings are not the problem.

Rename the Adobe Folders

I've seen reports that people can make their system run smoothly again after trouble when they rename or move the same folders I mentioned earlier under "Check Your Permissions." I suspect that this is because Premiere will create new folders where the permissions are set correctly, so repairing permissions for them may be just as effective and not as invasive.

Playback Problems

This covers everything from choppy or faulty playback to no playback at all. You may be surprised by some of the reasons for playback trouble. A few of them seem to be completely unrelated to playback—but they're not.

Check Your Audio Hardware Preferences

Premiere will not play back the timeline at all? It may be because the default output device that's set in your audio hardware preferences (**Preferences ➤ Audio Hardware**) is no longer available (Figure A-6). This happens if you have external audio cards that get disconnected or if the list of output devices changes for other reasons.

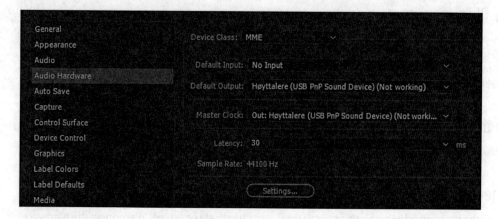

Figure A-6. Audio hardware preferences

When this happens, you may or may not get a message saying "No valid audio output channels for playback found. Please check the audio hardware preferences." Check them even if you don't get this message. Change to an available output device, and everything works again.

Audio Hardware Settings May Cause Stuttering Playback

If you experience stuttering playback of some video formats, and high CPU loads, try changing your Device Class (if available) and Latency (I/O Buffer Size) settings.

Codec Licensing Issue

If you can't play the timeline or some video files in the Source Monitor, it can be because of a missing codec. Most likely, the Creative Cloud app no longer thinks you're logged in and can't know if you have legal access to the codec in question. Sign out of Creative Cloud and sign in again. If that doesn't help, sign out, reboot the system, and sign in again.

■ **Note** A quick way to get the CC app working straight again when it's misbehaving is to force reload it. With the CC app in focus, hit **Ctrl+Alt+Shift+R (Cmd+Opt+Shift+R)** to force restart it. This will often fix a lot of stuff, including syncing problems, licensing problems, and so forth.

AJA

If playback is smooth in Premiere when the AJA card is disconnected, but fails in some way when you output through your AJA card, your first stop should be AJA's web pages. Also, make sure you have the latest drivers. They have web pages dedicated to PC and MAC system configurations that are helpful in configuring your editing system to work efficiently with Adobe Premiere:

    aja.com/support/kona-system-configuration

    aja.com/support/kona-pc-graphics-system-configuration

    aja.com/support/kona-pc-system-configuration

BlackMagic

As with AJA, if playback is smooth in Premiere when the BlackMagic card is disconnected, but fails in some way when you output through your card, your first stop should be BlackMagic's web pages. Also, make sure you have the latest drivers:

```
blackmagicdesign.com/support
```

■ **Note**   Also note that third-party hardware like this often is made for broadcast and only supports broadcast resolutions and frame rates. This means they don't support playback of non-standard frame sizes and frame rates. Newer drivers may have a choice to "scale unsupported frame sizes."

New Item / New Sequence Issues

Pay attention to your sequence settings when you grab a piece of media to create your sequence through the *New Item* icon in the Project panel. Not having your sequences set up correctly can lead to playback and rendering problems. In the following example, I will drag a ProRes 422 video clip called CAM 1 to the *New Item* icon. See Figure A-7. Look at what happens with the codecs in Figure A-8!

Figure A-7. *Project panel: drag clip to New Item icon*

Figure A-8. *New Sequence dialog: strange codec choice*

Why does Premiere create an AVC-Intra editing mode with a Preview file format codec in AVC-Intra? Why doesn't it create a ProRes Sequence editing mode and ProRes Preview file format? It just takes the first preset (in alphabetical order) that matches the frame size, frame rate, and so on.

Look at the sequences in Figure A-9. The AVC-Intra sequence was created by the *New Item* option. The ProRes 422 sequence was a custom-created sequence that was saved in the new sequence menu.

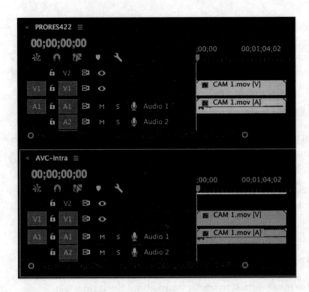

Figure A-9. *Proper sequence setup*

If you plan on relying on your video previews to make fast exports of your sequences, check that your codecs match. Why would you use a codec not matching your source media and have to recreate your preview files with the right codec? Additionally, why would you start out your sequence not matching your media source codec? Playback quality's not matching your codec can slow down your editing.

Adobe Explains the Render Bar Colors in This Blog Post

There is some confusion among editors, where they don't seem to know what the colors on the render bar mean, especially if they come from other NLEs. Here's some accurate info directly from Adobe.

blogs.adobe.com/creativecloud/red-yellow-and-green-render-bars/

- **green**: This segment of the sequence has a rendered preview file associated with it. Playback will play using the rendered preview file. Playback at full quality is certain to be in real time.

- **yellow**: This segment of the sequence does not have a rendered preview file associated with it. Playback will play by rendering each frame just before the CTI reaches it. Playback at full quality will probably be in real time (but it might not be).

- **red**: This segment of the sequence does not have a rendered preview file associated with it. Playback will play by rendering each frame just before the CTI reaches it. Playback at full quality will probably not be in real time (but it might be).

- **none**: This segment of the sequence does not have a rendered preview file associated with it, but the codec of the source media is simple enough that it can essentially be treated as its own preview file. Playback will play directly from the original source media file. Playback at full quality is certain to be in real time. This only occurs for a few codecs (including DV and DVCPRO).

- Note the uses of the word *probably*. The colors aren't a promise. They're a guess based on some rather simple criteria. If you have a fast computer, then a lot of things marked with red may play back in real time; if you have a slow computer, then some things marked with yellow may need to be rendered to preview files before the segment can be played in real time.

To avoid codec issues with your sequences, take the time to create your own custom sequences that match your source footage. When you have created the correct settings that all match up, you should not get a yellow render bar.

Additional Info on the Yellow Render Bar

From the same blog post previously listed, there are more details to understand about the render bar.

- **Mercury Playback Engine GPU Acceleration**

  - yellow: The source media's codec is computationally difficult (such as AVCHD). As mentioned earlier, only very few simple codecs don't get a yellow bar; these include DV and DVCPRO.

  - yellow: The settings of the clip (e.g., pixel aspect ratio, frame rate, field settings) don't match the settings for the sequence.

  - yellow: A CUDA-accelerated video effect or transition has been applied to the clip. (A CUDA-accelerated video transition only causes a yellow bar over the duration of the transition.)

- **Mercury Playback Engine Software Only**

  - yellow: The source media's codec is computationally difficult (such as AVCHD). As mentioned previously, only very few simple codecs don't get a yellow bar; these include DV and DVCPRO.

If you rely on dragging your media to the *New Item* icon, don't think that Premiere actually got it right the first time when you see a yellow bar. Create a custom sequence that you know matches your source media to prevent issues with your media.

2013 Mac Pro Thunderbolt Configurations

Apple has a support document that explains how to configure your Thunderbolt ports on the 2013 Mac Pro. Setting up your third-party equipment the wrong way can saturate the Thunderbolt bus and lead to playback issues in Premiere:

support.apple.com/en-us/HT202801

No Audio on Imported Clips

This can be caused by a lot different problems. Try the steps in this link:
pavtube.com/import-video-to-premiere-no-audio.html

Media Cache Issues

Premiere uses some Accelerator files to make your timeline scrubbing smoother and to in general make the software snappier. They greatly improve performance for previews because the video and audio items do not need to be reprocessed for each preview.

A database retains links to each of the cached media files. This media cache database is shared with Adobe Media Encoder, After Effects, Premiere Pro, and Audition, so each of these applications can read from and write to the same set of cached media files. If you change the location of the database from within any of these applications, the location is updated for the other applications, too. Each application can use its own cache folder, but the same database keeps track of them.

The so-called media cache files are known to cause different types of problems, and you'll often see that people recommend that you delete media cache files if Premiere behaves badly. And it's sound advice.

■ **Note** If you experience weirdness where importing a file that plays fine in other players produces a clip with no audio or no video, try deleting all media cache files.

There Are Two Folders with Media Cache Files

1. The one you set in media preferences

2. The *Common* folder, which is a hidden folder. You need to show hidden files to access this.

Where Are the Media Cache Folders Located?

Common folder on Windows: **\Users\<username>\AppData\Roaming\Adobe\Common\Media Cache Files**
Common folder on MacOS: **/Users/<username>/Library/Application Support/Adobe/Common/Media Cache Files**

The reason for the seemingly strange *Media Cache* folder placement is that this is the only folder on the system that Premiere can write to if the user is not an admin.

But, most likely, you've moved the media cache files to a custom folder on your system. You can see the folder path in the Media Preferences: **Preferences ➤ Media Cache**. See Figure A-10.

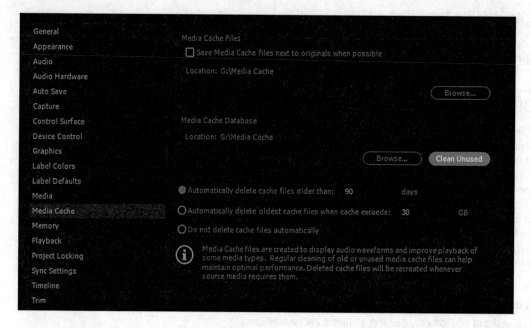

Figure A-10. *Media cache preferences*

There's a Difference Between "Cleaning" and "Deleting" Media Cache

Most of the time, cleaning the media cache will not help fix your issues. You might retrieve some free space on your disk, but your problems will probably not disappear.

■ **Note**   The Clean Unused option in **Preferences ➤ Media Cache** only deletes cache files associated with media files that are no longer available because they were moved or deleted. To delete *all* media cache files, do it manually from Finder or Windows Explorer.

So, cleaning does not always solve corrupt cache issues, while deleting them manually will delete even the files that your current project uses.

Close all Adobe video apps, go to the *Common* folder, and delete the *Media Cache* folder, *Media Cache Files* folder, and *PTX* folder (if you use OpenCL GPU acceleration). Then, go to the *Media Cache* folder you've set in **Preferences ➤ Media Cache** and delete everything. Empty your trash and, for safety, reboot your computer to start fresh.

Deleting cache files will require your project to rebuild the entire cache structure for playback and could take a long time depending on the size of your project.

Accelerator File Glossary from Adobe

Premiere creates many different accelerator files, and it can be challenging to understand what they all do—and where they are located. Table A-1 from Adobe should help.

Table A-1. *List of Accelerator Files and What They Do*

Type	Extension	Description	System Specific?	Default Location
Media accelerator database	.mcdb	Contains list of what accelerators exist for a given file and basic information about them		Media Cache folder
Metadata database cache	.prmdc	Stores metadata for rapid find in the project panel		Media Cache folder
Conformed audio	.cfa	Uncompressed audio data to facilitate random access for compressed sources		Media Cache files
Peak files	.pek	Data for drawing waveforms		Media Cache files
Importer state	.ims	Cache of file properties used to skip rereading the file during project load	yes	Media Cache files
MXF associations	.mxfassoc	Listing of audio files related to an MXF essence		Media Cache files
MPEG index	.mpgindex	File offsets for MPEG2 files		
MainConcept index	.mcaudioindex	File offsets for anything handled by MainConcept		
MainConcept index	.mcvideoindex	File offsets for anything handled by MainConcept		
QT MPEG video type	.vidType	Used to skip parsing unsupported files multiple times		
	.bin	OpenCL (unlike CUDA, and prior to SPIR) requires that our kernels be compiled for the GPU at runtime. This can take quite a while, so we cache the result to disk to improve performance in future releases. BIN files are the ones generated by the RED GPU SDK.	yes	PTX
	.ocl	OpenCL (unlike CUDA, and prior to SPIR) requires that our kernels be compiled for the GPU at runtime. This can take quite a while, so we cache the result to disk to improve performance in future releases. OCL files are the ones we generate ourselves for what we ship.	yes	PTX
Decoded closed captions	.ccxml	Demux'd and decoded captioning data to skip the "Scanning for Closed Captions" step each time the file is imported		

Why Are Media Cache Files Spread in Different Locations?

A lot of broadcasters want this in order to get more control. But, of course, it also complicates things when you're asked to delete the media cache files.

What Are .ims Files?

IMS is short for "importer state." *.ims files = Cache of file properties used to skip rereading the file during project load. This makes projects with Long-GOP media load a lot faster, as it's not re-analyzed by Premiere.

.ims files are system specific and will always generate to the system drive. They cannot be stored on a server or external drive. IMS files would need to be recreated on every system that touches the project.

Deep Dive into Premiere's Media Cache

Jason Cox has shared some good info about media cache files in Premiere on Screenlight.tv:
screenlight.tv/blog/the-definitive-guide-to-adobe-premiere-pros-media-cache/

Workspace Issues

Workspaces can get corrupted. They're just files, remember? When Adobe adds new features, new panels, and new functionality, the old workspaces are supposed to work in new versions—but sometimes they don't.

Prior to Upgrading Premiere, Remove Old Workspaces

The list of workspaces can get pretty long if you're a heavy user of custom workspaces. Figure A-11 shows a pretty short list compared to other systems I've seen.

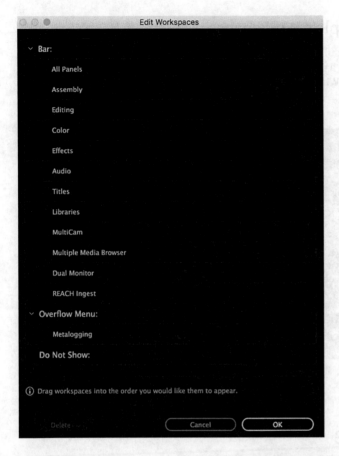

Figure A-11. Remove custom workspaces before upgrading, and rebuild new ones

With the major rebuild under the hood of Premiere over the past few versions, it's a good practice to not bring along old presets, workspaces, and settings when you upgrade. You can locate your old workspaces here:

Win: **C:\Users\<username>\Documents\Adobe\PremierePro\11.0\Profile-<username>\Layouts** (and **\ArchivedLayouts**)

Mac: **/Users/<username>/Documents/Adobe/PremierePro/11.0/Profile-<username>/Layouts** (and **\ArchivedLayouts**)

Within the *Layouts* folder are all the XML files that Premiere uses to set up your workspaces. With Premiere closed, delete them, empty your trash, and restart Premiere to reset the workspaces to the default configuration.

If you've synced settings to Creative Cloud, you will also have copies in **\Profile-CreativeCloud-\Layouts** and **\ArchivedLayouts**.

Losing Your Monitor Image with Dual Monitors

Strangely, losing the image on one monitor may be caused by a faulty workspace. Check your workspace layout and make sure none of the panels are slightly creeping into the other monitor. It could even be a few pixels' worth of panel that you might not catch, and that's enough to lose the whole image.

Avoid Inheriting Other People's Workspaces

Do you share projects with other editors, and every time you swap a project you inherit their workspace? If you experience trouble after opening such a project, the workspace in it may be corrupted. To prevent this from happening if you don't want it, go to **Window ➤ Workspaces** and uncheck *Import Workspace from Project*. See Figure A-12, where it's checked.

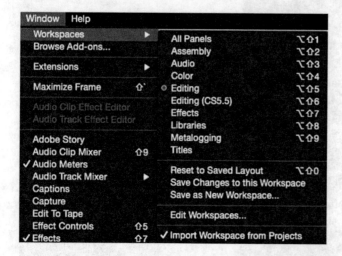

Figure A-12. *Workspaces menu choices*

Export Failure Problems

This is the kind of trouble I hate the most when editing. It's close to deadline, you've finally got everything looking and sounding good, the story works well, the producer is happy, and when you try to export, you get the dreaded error message:

```
Error compiling movie - Unknown Error
```

That message doesn't really help. At least, since version 2015.3, Premiere gives us better feedback, giving you more information about the cause of the error and its approximate location in the sequence/asset. See Figure A-13.

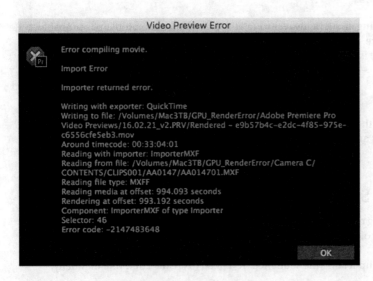

Figure A-13. *Error compiling movie*

You just need to hover over the error exclamation point or look inside the export log. This should help you isolate the cause more easily. In Adobe Media Encoder, go to **File ➤ Show Errors** to see the log file (Figure A-14).

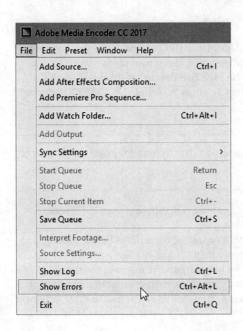

Figure A-14. *The log files are just text files, located in **Documents ➤ Adobe ➤ Adobe Media Encoder ➤ 11.0***

Also, if your crashes are happening about halfway through the export, then the problem is probably about halfway through your sequence. If you're exporting to Adobe Media Encoder, open the preview and watch the encoding until it fails. That is probably the spot in the timeline that needs fixing.

Delete Media Cache

Corrupted media cache files may be the cause of the problems. Follow the steps in the previous section on media cache issues to delete the files and let Premiere Pro rebuild them. This may take a long time on huge projects.

Copy Everything to a New Sequence

Whenever something strange is going on with a sequence, just copy and paste everything into a new sequence. You'd be surprised at how often this solves export issues. Since it's so quick to do, it's usually the first thing I try.

Note that this is different from duplicating the sequence. You need to create a new one manually.

Import Project into a Fresh One

Refresh the project by importing it into a new one, as explained in the earlier troubleshooting section, *but import only the sequence you need to export*. Then try exporting again.

Turn Off GPU Acceleration

When you export a normal project with effects, transforms, and so on, the GPU will be working constantly. If the GPU or the GPU drivers have problems, this is most likely when you will discover them.

First, make sure your GPU is not on the list of faulty GPUs on Mac. See the earlier troubleshooting section. If it is, switch to Software Only renderer in **File ➤ Project Settings ➤ General ➤ Video Rendering and Playback**. Then, try to export again.

■ **Note**   Switching the project to Software Only will often fix the export directly from Premiere, but the export will also take longer.

And, as you've seen in the chapter on color grading, the image may look different than it did with the GPU renderer.

If you have over-heating issues in your GPU, rebooting before exporting sometimes helps. Installing a fan control app and cranking it up to the highest setting sometimes helps. If not, use Software Only.

You could also be running out of GPU RAM, especially if you have large still images in the timeline. See the section on problematic media later in this appendix. And if you have high-res external monitor(s) attached, these will also use GPU RAM, so disconnecting them may free up just enough GPU RAM to be able to export.

Remove Effects

Did you use the Loudness Radar to check your audio levels? Make sure to close the Loudness Radar panel before proceeding with your final exports.

Warp Stabilizer and Morph Cut have been reported to sometimes create issues at export. Remove them, or render previews and use the previews on export.

Also remove any third-party plug-ins used in the timeline. If you depend on them, you may need to update them to get a stable system.

Disable Power Saving on Drives

If you have lengthy exports to make, use a system setting or a utility software that keeps the drives and system from going into power-saver mode. There is software for both Mac OS and Windows that does this named Caffeine, but they are not the same.

MacOS: lightheadsw.com/caffeine/
Windows: zhornsoftware.co.uk/caffeine/

Don't Use Punctuation Marks in File Names

Check if your file names contain punctuation marks. If your output file names contain punctuation marks like periods (".") or if they get carried over from the names of sequences, this can cause export errors. Avoid using this format, and use the underscore ("_") format if required.

Corrupted or Problematic Media Files

Of course, if the problems are not the result of media cache files, misbehaving effects, or GPU problems, the problem may lie in the source media files themselves. I'd say that most of the time failed export is the result of a corrupted file; probably an MP3 or JPG file, but it could also be a video clip. It could also be some specific combo of codecs/effects/plug-ins that Premiere doesn't like.

When this is the case, you must find out what files are causing the problem and then deal with them. To find out which files this may be, try exporting short sections of the timeline.

Export Shorter Sections

If exporting the full timeline fails, try exporting shorter parts of it. Let's look at a quick way to find the offending files.

Export just the first half of the timeline. Did it fail? If no, export just the second half. Did it fail? If yes, export just the first half of the second half. Did it fail? If no, export just the second half of the second half. And so on.

This way, you can isolate the area where you encounter an export error. That's the area where your problematic media file is. Watch for MP3 and JPG files that may be corrupted in the approximate area of the timeline where it crashes. If they came from the Internet, I'd be especially suspicious.

A similar strategy is to mark an I/O range around an area you think may be problematic and use **Sequence ➤ Render In to Out**. You can see the render bar turn green and remain yellow/red where the render fails. That's probably the same spot for export issues.

Do all the clips used during that work area look and sound okay in the Source Monitor?

Another possibility is to turn off layers in a complex timeline to see which layer has the offending file. To narrow down if the issue is caused by your audio or video, try to export with either the audio or video turned off.

Downsize Large Stills

The problem can also be caused by an image that's very big, measured in pixels, so you're running out of GPU RAM (VRAM). There was one that caused serious problems on one of my friends' systems, but exported fine on mine because I had more GPU RAM. The image size is about 10k × 5k, and 3GB GPU RAM was too little, while 8GB was enough. Find it here:

commons.wikimedia.org/wiki/File:Crossing_of_the_Granicus,_G%C3%A9rard_Audran_after_ Charles_Le_Brun,_1672.jpg

If you have just 1GB of GPU RAM, this makes an image from a DSLR a large still. With more GPU RAM, it can handle larger stills. If Chrome, Photoshop, Illustrator, or other GPU-hungry apps were running at the same time, these would compete with Premiere for GPU RAM. Next time you get into GPU RAM starvation mode, try to export with GPU acceleration turned off–Software-only mode. Or, just resize the image in Photoshop and import the lower-res copy.

Why is it not failing when you play back the timeline? It might be because you have not set the playback resolution to full, or that you don't have High Quality Playback enabled, which will save on resources.

Bad Media

Very often when an export fails, there is some "bad" media involved. Very large stills can be a problem, as we've seen. Also, images with CMYK color space instead of RGB can be a problem.

If you set the Video Preview to a good codec that you can use on export (ProRes, DNxHD, or CineForm would work) and then render the whole timeline, usually, if a timeline failed on export, it would fail at the same point in the render of the timeline. Find the time area where the green render bar stops in the timeline, and that is probably where you have bad media.

Delete those clips, import them again, and place them on the timeline again. If that doesn't help, you can delete the media cache files and import again. If Premiere still refuses to export, you may have to convert the file via third-party software, like Handbrake: handbrake.fr/.

Once the timeline is all rendered green, you can then export your timeline like normal, but check *Use Previews*, and your export should work.

Convert MP3 Files to WAV or AIF

MP3 files, especially those you download from various sources on the Internet, may be corrupted or badly formatted. Converting these to uncompressed audio files like AIF or WAV will fix them. You can use Adobe Audition to batch-convert your MP3s if you experience a lot of problems with files from a source you use often.

If Audition will not do it, you can use free software like Switch (nch.com.au/switch/) or online services like FileZigZag (filezigzag.com/ConvertFiles.aspx) or Zamzar (zamzar.com).

Some editors also recommend that you convert 44,100kHz audio clips to 48,000khz, but I have mixed 44.1 and 48 on almost every project and never had any trouble with it, so I doubt that this is a problem. Of course, if you convert a 44,100kHz MP3 to 48,000kHz WAV, you're also getting rid of the MP3 container, which most likely was the problem, not the sample rate.

Permissions Trouble

If your system prevents Premiere from writing files where it needs to write files, something's going to break. As mentioned in the troubleshooting section, MacOS permissions may need to be repaired.

Limited write permissions may also be a problem when you export to network drives. So, if you're trying to export to a network and it fails, try to export to a local drive instead, and then move the file to the network.

On a somewhat related note, if you're exporting to an USB thumb drive, long exports may fail because of the FAT32 formatting, which has a max file size limit of 4GB.

Adobe Media Encoder Issues

If queuing your export from Premiere to Adobe Media Encoder (AME) doesn't work, try opening the project directly in AME.

And if that doesn't work, export a high-quality master from Premiere (ProRes 422, Cineform, etc.) and then import that file into AME.

Offline media cannot be relinked using Adobe Media Encoder, so if your project has offline media, relink it in Premiere Pro before importing it in Adobe Media Encoder. You will be notified before encoding begins if the Premiere Pro sequence contains offline media.

Turn Off Import Sequences Natively in AME

Adobe Media Encoder loads Premiere Pro and Prelude projects natively, which means that the headless version of Premiere Pro is not required, and also the projects are loaded faster. This feature allows AME to be installed on a system that doesn't have Premiere on it.

Adobe recommends that you use this option (which is the default) when you want to import a Premiere Pro sequence comprising Red (.r3d) files that are stored on a Red Rocket card into Adobe Media Encoder. This is because the Red Rocket can be used by only one application at a time.

This is a nice feature, but it's also known to create some problems, like crashing Premiere, failing to export the sequence, and making images and video clips from Dynamic Link clips and motion graphics templates from After Effects go offline in the Premiere Pro project!

This means everything is fine in the project, and you send it to AME and see that there are color bars showing where there should be a logo or some other asset. (This is how AE shows missing media). Not only are the assets missing in the AME export, but when you go back to Premiere, the assets are missing even there!

This seems to be a media cache problem. So, there are two ways to fix it. Either rename the AE project or motion graphics template to force the creation of new media cache files, or shut down Premiere and AME and delete media cache files manually.

But, to avoid the whole problem, you can turn off the *Import Sequences Natively* feature in AME preferences (Figure A-15). And, hopefully, Adobe will find a way to fix this issue.

Figure A-15. *Import Sequences Natively, a preference choice in AME*

Rebuild Adobe Media Encoder Presets

When Premiere makes version changes in the application, you should consider rebuilding your export presets from scratch. This fresh start will guarantee that any old menu settings translate properly when the code under the hood has changed. Just compare some of the new tabs that are now available in the new version of Premiere with those in an older version (Figure A-16).

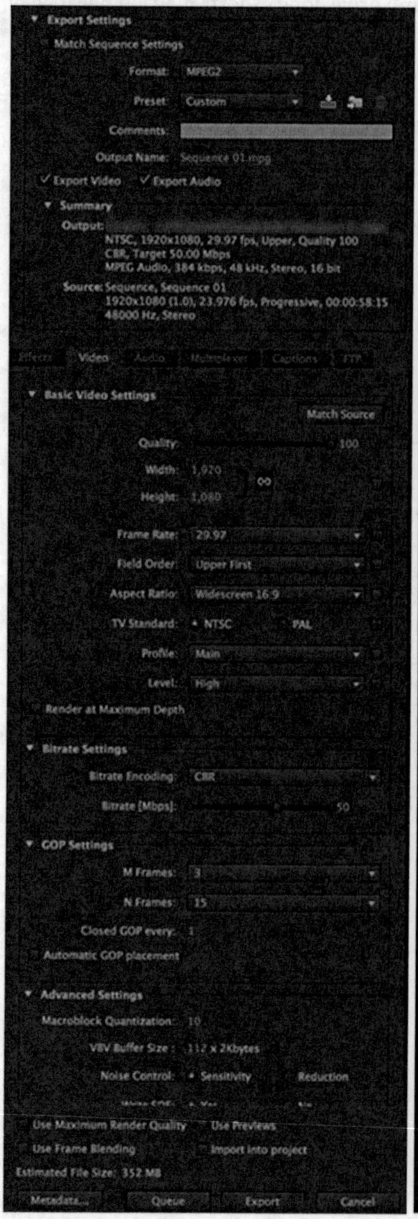

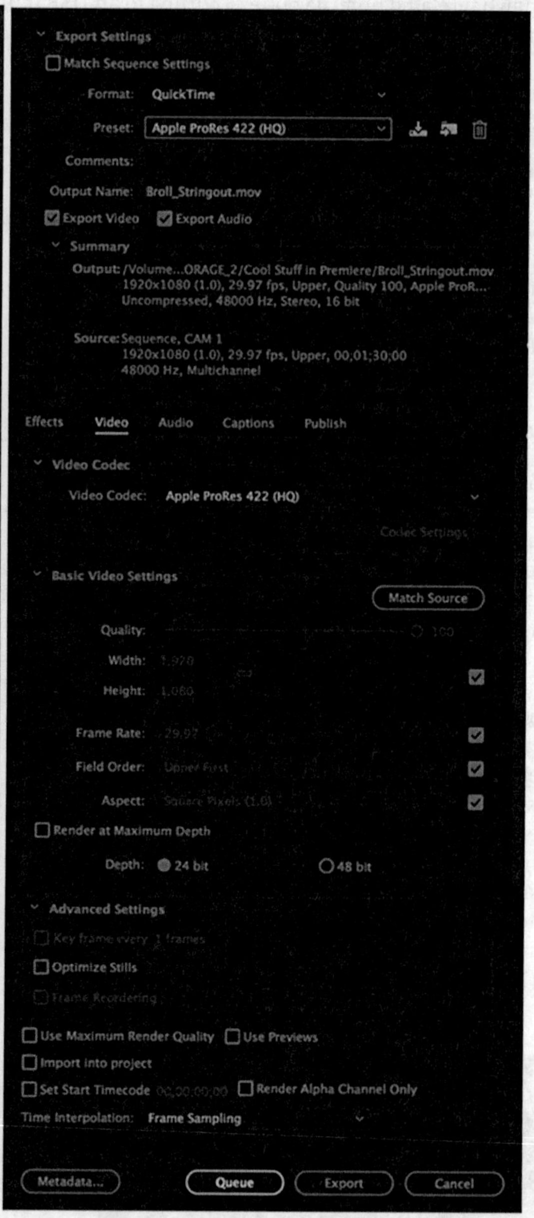

Figure A-16. *It would be almost unreal if new features didn't cause any trouble with existing presets. Rebuild them to ensure full compatibility.*

Try the Other Way

If export via AME (Queue) fails, try Premiere export (Export). If Premiere export fails, try AME.

Adobe Articles on Export Issues

This is a good place to start for you and anyone else getting errors when exporting:

```
helpx.adobe.com/premiere-pro/kb/error-compiling-movie-rendering-or.html
helpx.adobe.com/premiere-pro/kb/error-compiling-movie-warning-or.html
```

Need More Help?

If the info in this appendix doesn't help you solve your problems, try one of these online resources. There are lots of experienced people out there willing to share their knowledge.

Adobe Premiere Pro Forums

This is Adobe's official forum, populated by users, Adobe Community Professionals, and even some Adobe employees:

```
forums.adobe.com/community/premiere/content
```

Facebook Group for Premiere Pro Users

The Moving to Premiere Pro Facebook group is among the best for Premiere Pro users. It's for advanced users, not for beginners, and lots of knowledgeable people are there, including several Adobe employees.

```
facebook.com/groups/premierepro/
```

APPENDIX B

■ ■ ■

MAMs

By Andy Edwards

Media asset management (MAM) is a sub-category of digital asset management (DAM). Where DAM is designed to store many kinds of digital files, particularly text-based files like Word documents, MAM is basically a database of all your media assets that you can archive, retrieve, and search.

Some systems collaborate with an LTO system (LTO = Linear Tape Open, see en.wikipedia.org/wiki/ Linear_Tape-Open). so you can move your assets off to an archive and free up your online storage. Proxy files are made of every asset when ingested into the system with metadata. Users actually see the proxies versus full-resolution media when searching and can update metadata as needed.

Proxy file creation can be tied into a MAM system with the help of a Telestream Vantage system and Lightspeed servers. The Lightspeed server is a rack-mounted server with high-end GPUs that can process massive amounts of files in a short amount of time. Think of it as Adobe Media Encoder on steroids. All the heavy file conversions get pushed into workflows behind the scenes. Once the workflows are run to ingest media with metadata, the Vantage system will crank out the proxies and make them available through the MAM software for all users.

Depending on the size of your MAM deployment, users can access the database of media from multiple locations. Proxy media allows the external streaming of the files so users are not tied to huge file sizes just to view and play back files. With the push to the cloud, many companies, including Adobe, are finding ways to give users greater access to their media. You are not tied to an SAN, NAS, or internal/external storage with your edit system. Laptops with MAM software can easily be used to cut a rough draft of a project and be brought into an edit session and replaced with full-resolution media.

The following are a few companies that create MAM software: Levels Beyond, CatDV, Media Silo, Adobe Bridge (possibly outdated), Vizrt, Strawberry by Flavoursys, AxleVideo, and NeoFinder.

Reach Engine

The MAM I use at work is created by Levels Beyond and is called Reach Engine. It has two main aspects that include web browser functionality: Access, and a Premiere Extensions Panel called *Reach Engine Craft*. There is also a special panel made for Adobe Prelude that can plug into Reach Engine, but that will not be covered in this book. I'm not going to go into all the setup details of the MAM software and hardware required, but instead will give a brief overview of how it is used in our postproduction process.

A MAM is only as good as the metadata detail you put into it. If you don't take the time to develop structured workflows on how you plan on processing your media, then it's just like having tons of hard drive space filled with media you can't find. Take the time to make sure your team of editors, production assistants, producers, and media librarians know how to ingest media properly into the MAM with as much detail as possible. A generic show title might get you the video clip you need, but detailing who, what, where, when, and how into the metadata can pay off when future searching is involved.

© Jarle Leirpoll 2017
J. Leirpoll et al., *The Cool Stuff in Premiere Pro*, DOI 10.1007/978-1-4842-2890-6

Reach Engine Access Browser

Once you log into Access in a web browser like Chrome, you are presented with an interface that can be shown in list view or thumbnail view (Figure B-1). You have a search box into which you enter your query and which will return assets available that meet that specific search term. You can customize your search by category: Music, Image, Video, Video Clips, Documents, Premiere Projects, or Collections. You also can search by date created or date updated.

Figure B-1. *Reach Access list view and thumbnail view*

Once you find the asset you want, you can click on it, and it will take you to a new window (Figure B-2). You can play back the video asset, look at the metadata associated with the file, update the metadata to the asset, add it to a collection, and clip off sub-clips for importing into Premiere.

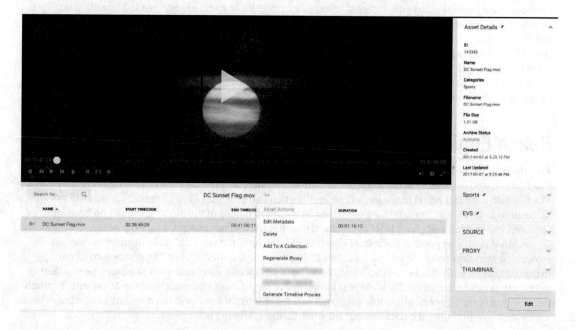

Figure B-2. *Reach asset details*

1186

The asset window has keyboard shortcuts, a lot like your editing software, as seen in Figure B-3.

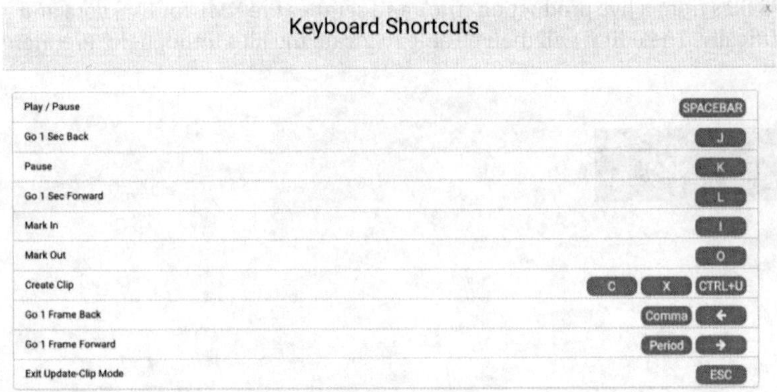

Keyboard Shortcuts	
Play / Pause	SPACEBAR
Go 1 Sec Back	J
Pause	K
Go 1 Sec Forward	L
Mark In	I
Mark Out	O
Create Clip	C X CTRL+U
Go 1 Frame Back	Comma ←
Go 1 Frame Forward	Period →
Exit Update-Clip Mode	ESC

Figure B-3. *Reach Access keyboard shortcuts*

If you select the status menu in the web browser window, all the custom workflows being processed on the servers can be monitored. In Figure B-4, you can see that all the EVS Ingest workflows have completed. This specific workflow ingests EVS files from a live production truck and scrapes the XML for EVS data and fills in the metadata fields automatically. The editor will then be able to locate the files through the Premiere panel with a metadata search.

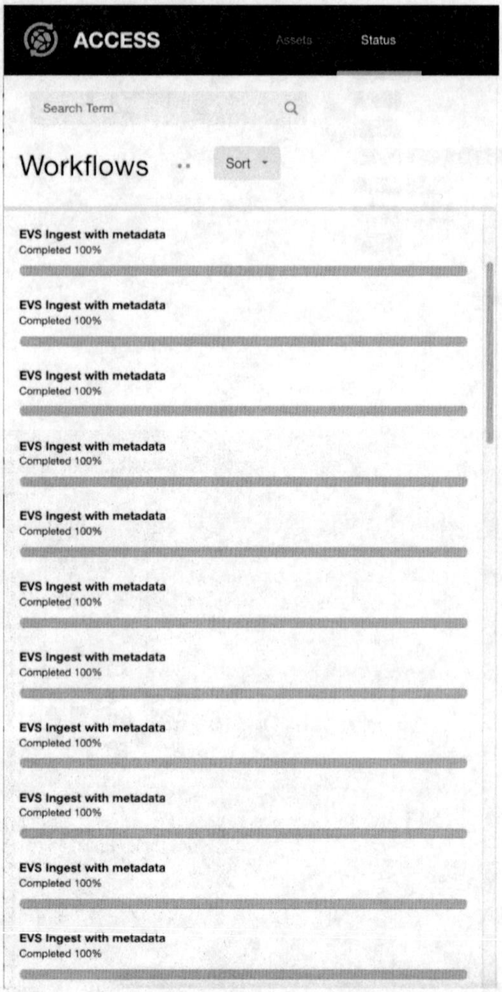

Figure B-4. *EVS workflows*

Reach Engine Craft Premiere Panel

Each Premiere edit system wanting access to Reach Engine will need a panel installed. The developer provides a panel installer that will need to be run and configured to read from your servers where Reach Engine resides. This will be a custom internal address to your company servers. Once installed, any editor can open the panel and log in with their credentials to start using it inside of Premiere (Figure B-5).

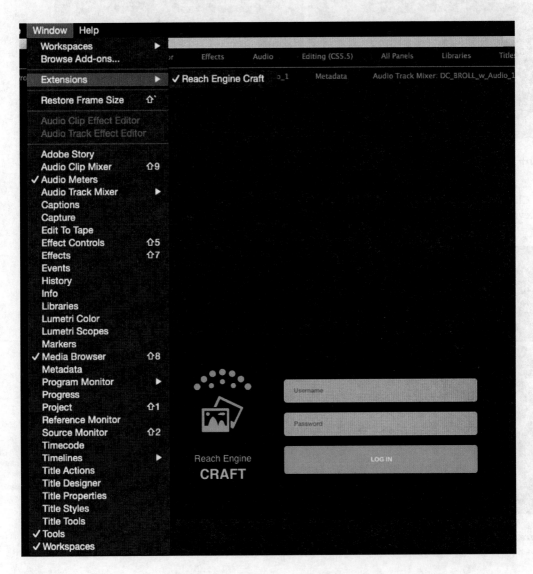

Figure B-5. *The Reach Engine Panel is found in the Window ➤ Extensions menu*

The Premiere Panel can be configured in list view or thumbnail view (Figure B-6).

Figure B-6. *Reach list view and thumbnail view*

Clicking on an asset opens up another window with asset details and a video window to allow the editor to preview the clip (Figure B-7).

Figure B-7. *Reach Panel asset details*

Once an editor is done searching for media to include in the project, they select the group of assets they need and click on the *Open Selected* button. All media is then imported into the Premiere project bin to begin the edit. See Figure B-8.

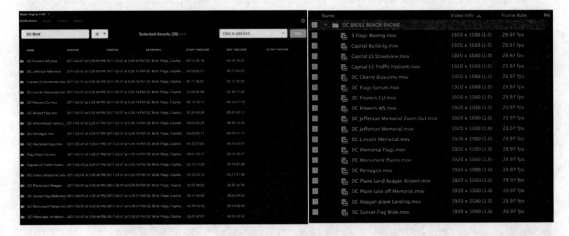

Figure B-8. *Reach Select Media and Reach Media Imported screens*

Premiere Panel/Other Features

In the *Actions* tab of the panel, you can choose a sequence you are working on to be sent to a producer for review (Figure B-9). An H.264 proxy file is generated via Adobe Media Encoder and emailed to the contacts you specify, all from within Premiere. There is no need to export a separate file to upload via FTP or a private YouTube page.

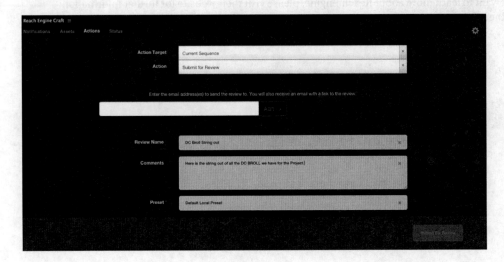

Figure B-9. *Reach Action tab*

Ingest Your Project into Reach Engine

Additionally, in the Actions tab of the panel (Figure B-10) you have the ability to ingest your project or current sequence right into the MAM system. If all your media assets were previously ingested into Reach Engine prior to starting your project, this ability can help with media managing. You can cut down on creating additional media on your SAN/NAS or hard drives when you media manage. Just archive the small Premiere Project file and do not duplicate your media in a media-managed folder.

Figure B-10. *Reach Actions tab*

If you want to learn more about Reach Engine, please visit their website for further information: reachengine.com.

APPENDIX C

■■■

Design Tips and Resources

By Jarle Leirpoll

This appendix is a treasure trove of techniques and resources for the editor who's asked to also do some design. When you're in a hurry, you need to get access to great stuff—fast. The following techniques and resources have helped me on several projects. I hope you find them useful.

Any Clip Can Be an Adjustment Layer

Yes, any clip can be turned into an adjustment layer! Right-click the clip and choose *Adjustment Layer*. Add an effect to it, and the effect only works where the original clip was. In Figure C-1 I've made the Adobe logo an adjustment layer and added some Lumetri color grading to it.

Figure C-1. *Adobe logo made into an adjustment layer*

Save a Graphic Object with Special Characters

Depending on your keyboard layout—which again depends on your language, the computer type, etc., - there are some characters that cannot be easily found on the keyboard—and even though there are some keyboard shortcuts you can use, you can't possibly create, let alone remember, shortcuts for every character.

So, I recommend that you open the Character Map (a part of Windows—just search for it) once and copy all the characters you'll ever need into a Graphic (Figure C-2). Save this as a separate graphics file, and you have easy access to any special character.

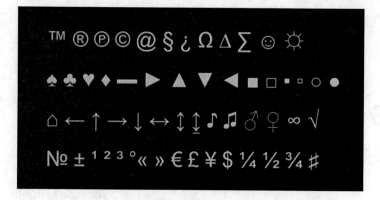

Figure C-2. Copy the most useful special characters into a graphic and save as a motion graphics template

Get Rid of Unwanted Fonts

Tired of wading through lots of fonts when you design your motion graphics? It takes you just a few minutes to get through the *Fonts* folder and delete or move all the fonts you don't like—once, and for all programs.

Windows: Go to **C:** ➤ **Windows** ➤ **Fonts**. There is even a preview of the font in the icon. Move or delete the ones you don't need.

MacOS: Launch *Font Book* (located in /**Applications**/) and remove the ones you don't need.

RTL and Arabic Text

Premiere Pro supports Right-to-left and Arabic text. Eran Stern explains this feature well here: vimeo.com/162751833. You set the preference for RTL text in **Preferences** ➤ **Graphics**.

Grab Colors from Adobe Color

Colors are important, and with Adobe Color (color.adobe.com), finding and creating good color themes is super easy (Figure C-3). Save a screen grab from Adobe Color and import it into your project.

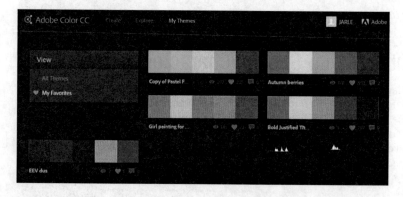

Figure C-3. Use Adobe Color to make sure your colors work nicely together

Keep it in a library or anywhere else you'll find it easily. When you need to grab a color, use the eye dropper tool to steal colors from your color themes! Try out popular themes like Monochromatic, Triad, and Shades.

Use Photoshop to Automate Title Creation

In the section on using Photoshop for video purposes, you'll learn a way to automate the process of making lower thirds. We start with a spreadsheet with all the names, job titles, logos, and so forth and create a Photoshop document that spits out all the lower thirds automatically (Figure C-4). You can also learn this from the free sample chapter at premierepro.net.

Figure C-4. *Photoshop can spit out as many lower thirds as you need from a spreadsheet—automatically! (Photo of Johan Ståhl by Alex&Martin, alexochmartin.se)*

EBU Rules for Safe Areas

Here's a link to the EBU rules for safe areas for 16:9 television production: tech.ebu.ch/publications/r095.

Random Name Generator

This web page generates random names for dummy credits and so forth: random-name-generator.info/.

End Crawl

Found at endcrawl.com/, this is a service for high-end credits and was made by John "Pliny" Eremic, who works at HBO, and Alan Grow. Lots of major films have used it for professional end credits. John blogs about his product and credits in general at endcrawl.com/blog/author/pliny/.

Of special interest is his blog post explaining credit jitter: endcrawl.com/blog/why-are-my-end-titles-jittering/.

Polaroid Frames

If you want a more realistic look, download 17 free high-res Polaroid frames from Fuzzimo (Figure C-5). He also has some sticky-tape textures, vector cassette tapes, and other goodies you should check out: fuzzimo.com/free-hi-res-blank-polaroid-frames/.

Figure C-5. *Polaroid frame from Fuzzimo*

Embossed Labels

Fuzzimos's Embossed Label Generator is also very cool. Type in the text you need, choose a color and a font size, and download the finished label image (Figure C-6): imagegenerator.fuzzimo.com/embossedlabels/.

Figure C-6. *Embossed label from Fuzzimo*

Gun Reticules

Get free Vector (SVG) gun reticules from Wikipedia Commons (Figure C-7): upload.wikimedia.org/ wikipedia/commons/1/10/Reticles_vector.svg. Convert them to AI or PNG format in Adobe Illustrator.

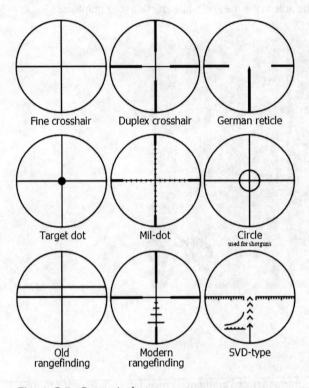

Figure C-7. *Gun reticules*

Use Grids

Paper- and web-based graphic designers use grids a lot. Maybe you should too? Figure C-8 shows the 960 grid system made for web designers by Nathan Smith at 960.gs. If you place a partly transparent grid like this that you can switch on and off on a video track, you'll be able to see the grid while creating your graphics.

Figure C-8. *Grids will help you keep the layout tidy*

Textures

I love textures. Sometimes the clean look of computer-generated gradients is nice, but I often want a more organic look to my graphics. I have a huge (gigantic!) collection of images I've taken of concrete walls, rusty metal, and so on. Figure C-9 shows a tiny bit of my texture collection. Textures combine very well with gradients and blending modes, and they're great for making things rougher, more organic, and grungier.

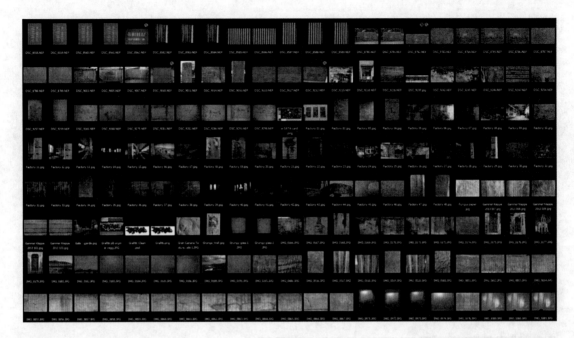

Figure C-9. *Textures*

Computer Gibberish

Using the online Random Code Generator at randomcodegenerator.com, you can output huge amounts of code, and you have lots of control over the type of characters, code length, and so on. You can save the code as CSV, or just copy/paste from the web page. Figures C-10 and C-11 show two code sets I made with different settings.

```
100 unique codes have been generated.
01001101  10001001  00110100  01010010  01000010  11101011  10011100  00011010
10111010  01000001  00010101  10101100  01110000  00101111  11000000  10000110
01011010  01001100  01101101  01001011  01011100  01100011  11011001  01000111
10000010  10010100  10111001  00110000  01110011  10001100  00001000  10001011
01010111  10101000  10000100  00011101  01100101  01111100  00101010  11111001
10110100  01111111  10100111  11100110  11101000  01101000  11101100  01111101
00000000  10111000  00111100  10010000  10110011  10001000  11100000  00011001
11001101  10010010  11111111  10110111  10111111  00001111  01000101  10000101
00000111  10100001  11100011  10010011  00010001  00001100  00011000  11110110
10100100  01001111  00001101  01111011  10010101  10110001  00011100  11010111
01110101  00100100  11011100  00010100  11011010  11000011  01111001  10011001
01011101  00010000  11110101  01110100  11011101  11011000  11010100  01010001
00011011  00101101  11111010  10011111
```

Figure C-10. *Random Code Generator sample 1*

100 unique codes have been generated.							
N5F26A69	T36JNGQE	H8B3QDQP	LUBVBEY7	XKK7EYZV	9WFYV8YZ	FSS2UWNP	N9REDRGP
6Q32XAGL	CFAMPUJP	NRYLEXV8	B4V2Y94R	VE5YDYM6	62H9RKK3	5JHSQSAN	3G68MKGP
BZ9V7UBD	2VRR5HLW	NQ57WQWG	CSCYTE5G	ZGR3Z3K4	UK3SMS29	YWEQYBZE	5FUBWJT5
CFGVQ338	QSYQLKPJ	TUJMYP89	UEKSAYS2	M6RJFPKQ	426CSP7J	5EKVCDLM	X3U9DSSM
95ZN3UGE	8AJFGA6U	HRRNW3TD	FGD93HH3	YZRKG78Q	ENM39638	9Z2KDZNH	TU7WHDLC
FVZV8XYF	V87CFTAL	8HDB2RA6	YJHTNK9Q	U4SSUQ39	AYJ9VSHE	9TAND6PD	F9KFHYZW
6YNW74Z5	35FJKWF5	9VWV69VD	TQYWAXK8	X9TVB92Q	938Q8KTQ	KCEQEQ95	XYGUPFY2
C25SQV6T	LFDFV5GF	BGYXMH55	N9ZSUP8K	PWPFDVHV	CUWY8WNG	WMWKCGAG	FKN8YEB2
KUGMCDQC	6XZAMTQ2	9NRUTD6H	J9RY4UXQ	TP262M69	KT7P5XJ8	9C5CJ9NU	8QHG9U3Z
D56TU4TY	YQW6F3QY	3U3V3KKZ	XHL744NB	9EC4KKXT	6QYLDDWY	6Y8F2JSS	KUJYSTAQ
GGQB4MKN	8TU2D2PF	YBXYQNJP	BG2A7NL3	GLQER3M9	8LR6L47X	BVGBM9KP	WPYGU9NF
V5A8XTRU	G95KGK3E	K8E97ZXD	X6VJSKYN	NY7V7F7L	PVPD68WG	YE2Y8Z5L	SDAWRWG8
YB6CN45C	XDHZEQWD	WF8BR2QT	6GGCPRKZ				

Figure C-11. *Random Code Generator sample 2*

If you're on Windows, download and install—then run—Debugger from Microsoft. I opened a JPG file in Debugger and got the beautiful text seen in Figure C-12. To get readable text from Debugger, go to **Edit ➤ Copy Formatted** and paste the text into Word. Then, edit the text in Word and copy to Premiere. Or, you can save a TXT file from Debugger and copy/paste from there. Add more effects to make it more realistic looking (Figure C-13).

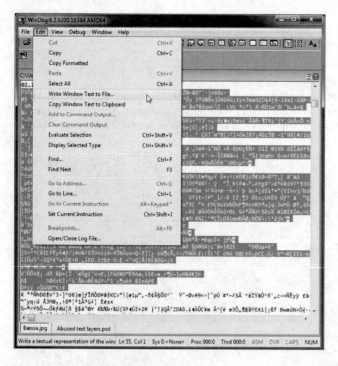

Figure C-12. *Save a text file from Debugger and paste the text into a graphic*

Figure C-13. *Text with Basic 3D effect and a duplicate layer with some blur*

Here's where I downloaded Debugger from: `developer.microsoft.com/en-us/windows/hardware/download-windbg`.

Word Clouds from Wordle

Word clouds are popular, but are very time consuming to create manually. And you don't have to. Use Wordle at `wordle.net` to create your word clouds. You can paste in a bunch of words and customize the colors, the layout, the font, and so on. You can even create a word cloud from a URL. Figure C-14 shows one I made by pointing Wordle to `premierepro.net`.

Figure C-14. *Word cloud*

The page doesn't let you save an image directly, but if you have Acrobat installed you can print to a PDF and export a PNG or JPG file from there. That's what I did, and I got a file of 2200 × 1700 px—enough space for a short zoom in a 1080p timeline.

Royalty Free Video on Vimeo

There is a Royalty Free Community group on Vimeo where people share videos and After Effects project files: `vimeo.com/groups/royaltyfree`.

Free Map Resources

Maps can be very expensive, but there are some free resources out there (Table C-1).

Table C-1. *Free Map Resources*

U.S. Geological Survey	`usgs.gov/pubprod/nationalmap.gov/`
OpenStreetMap	`openstreetmap.org/`
Natural Earth	`naturalearthdata.com/` `naturalearthdata.com/downloads/`
CIA Maps (yes, for real!)	`cia.gov/library/publications/cia-maps-publications/`
QGIS Free Open Source Geographic Information System	`qgis.org/en/site/`

The program manager for Adobe After Effects, Victoria Nece, made a tutorial on some clever map animations on custom maps from QGIS: `victorianece.com/2014/04/adventures-in-map-animation-with-qgis-after-effectsc4d-and-illustrator/`.

There's also an overview of map-related plug-ins: `victorianece.com/2014/04/mapping-plugin-roundup/`.

Free Emojis from EmojiOne

Need emojis for your social media templates? EmojiOne has thousands of them that you can use for free if you give them credit, in PNG sizes up to 128x128 pixels. If you need vector images, emoji fonts or larger PNGs, pay for a premium license.

Figure C-15. *Emoji One emojis*

`emojione.com/`

`emojicopy.com/`

Ransomizer

The Ransomizer web page at `ransomizer.com/` will make cool ransom notes from your text (Figure C-16).

Figure C-16. *Ransomizer*

Project Gutenberg

Project Gutenberg (`gutenberg.org`) offers over 53,000 free e-books—most of them really old. It's great for grabbing text and old images for mockups of news articles and so forth.

Here's one example: *Peeps at Many Lands* is a book on Norway, written in 1911 and describing everything from the Vikings to the "modern" Norway of 1911: `gutenberg.org/files/24676/24676-h/24676-h.htm`. Figures C-17 and C-18 show some images from the book.

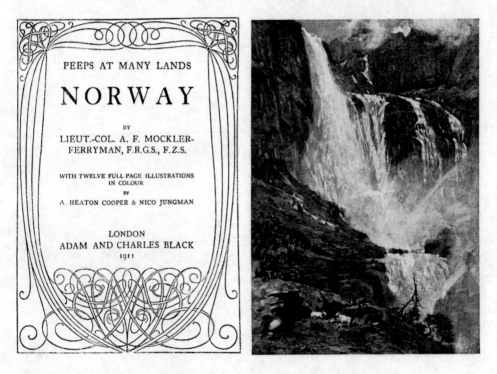

Figure C-17. *A title page and image from old e-book found on Project Gutenberg*

Figure C-18. *Old map from book found on Project Gutenberg*

Afterword

I hope you've learned some techniques and workflows from this book that will help you work faster and with better results in your daily editing.

If you have made templates, effects presets or other customization items that you think others would benefit from using, then please contact me, and I'll share it on premierepro.net, and possibly in a future version of this book. All contributions will be duly credited, of course.

You can reach me at leirpoll@gmail.com, on Facebook (facebook.com/leirpoll), and at premierepro.net.

A book on constantly developing software will soon become obsolete. To extend the life of the book, we'll add info about new features and workflows in future updates of Premiere at premierepro.net/updates/.

Good luck with your further advances in film- and video editing. Have fun!

Elverum, Norway, July 2017
Jarle Leirpoll

Index

Get the eBook for only $5!

Why limit yourself?

With most of our titles available in both PDF and ePUB format, you can access your content wherever and however you wish—on your PC, phone, tablet, or reader.

Since you've purchased this print book, we are happy to offer you the eBook for just $5.

To learn more, go to http://www.apress.com/companion or contact support@apress.com.

Apress®